Examining the Intersection of Technology, Media, and Social Innovation

Izati Nabila Marzuki
https://orcid.org/0000-0001-6740-7655
Universiti Malaysia Perlis, Malaysia

Wan Nor Ashiqin Wan Ali
https://orcid.org/0000-0003-2489-2843
Universiti Malaysia Perlis, Malaysia

Hyunseok Lee
Pusan National University, South Korea

Ahmad Azaini Abdul Manaf
Universiti Malaysia Kelantan, Malaysia

Mageswaran Sanmugam
https://orcid.org/0000-0003-3313-4462
University Science Malaysia, Malaysia

IGI Global
Scientific Publishing
Publishing Tomorrow's Research Today

Vice President of Editorial — Melissa Wagner
Director of Acquisitions — Mikaela Felty
Director of Book Development — Jocelynn Hessler
Production Manager — Mike Brehm
Cover Design — Jose Rosado

Published in the United States of America by
IGI Global Scientific Publishing
701 East Chocolate Avenue
Hershey, PA, 17033, USA
Tel: 717-533-8845 | Fax: 717-533-7115
Website: https://www.igi-global.com E-mail: cust@igi-global.com

Library of Congress Cataloging-in-Publication Data

LCCN: 2025041875 (CIP Data Pending)
ISBN13: 979-8-3373-5307-4
Isbn13Softcover: 979-8-3373-5308-1
EISBN13: 979-8-3373-5309-8

British Cataloguing in Publication Data
A Cataloguing in Publication record for this book is available from the British Library.

Table of Contents

Detailed Table of Contents

goals, creating a more equitable and sustainable future. This study aims to explore this phenomenon by carrying out a systematic review of literature. It is adopted the PRISMA framework to identify 54 relevant studies in this field. The findings characterize the evolution of articles in this field, the number of citations, the relationship between key terms, and the respective clusters. Moreover, seven contributions of social entrepreneurship for sustainable development are identified. Finally, the role of technology in promoting and supporting the interconnection between social entrepreneurship and sustainable development is explored. This study is relevant to enhance understanding of how technology supports social entrepreneurship and helps social entrepreneurs to achieve sustainable development goals.

Indigenous knowledge is under threat in the era of globalization and digitization, especially among tribal communities that rely on oral traditions. This chapter examines how digital storytelling can preserve and transmit cultural heritage within the Garasia tribe of Rajasthan, India. Storytelling is central to Garasia identity, serving as a vehicle for values, histories, and norms across generations. Yet, migration, modernization, and poor documentation endanger its survival. Using cultural transmission theory, media ecology, and social constructionism, the chapter explores how digital media can bridge tradition and innovation. Drawing on literature and secondary ethnographic insights, it highlights opportunities for intergenerational learning, cultural sustainability, and community empowerment, while addressing risks of authenticity, ownership, and access. The study argues that digital storytelling enables the Garasia to act both as custodians of tradition and as active shapers of their digital futures.

This chapter explores how Islamic ethical values shape the intersection of media, technology, and social innovation, emphasizing equity, justice, and collective well-being. Unlike the dominant focus on efficiency and scalability, Islamic principles, amanah (responsibility), adl (justice), maslahah (benefit), and khilafah (stewardship), offer a values-based guide for innovation. The chapter situates these principles within media and technology studies, linking morality with media responsibility and

apps for the web, and new media, highlighting the benefits and drawbacks using usability and technology adoption ideas. A microplastic awareness website simplifies scientific information for parents and carers, and a Pulau Tuba tourist website promotes visibility and community empowerment. Websites are credible, stable, and inclusive, making them ideal for organised awareness campaigns and persuasive communication, according to comparative studies. Websites may integrate new technology and promote social innovation in digital ecosystems, according to the findings.

Federalism and urbanization have reshaped governance, media, and youth participation in Nepal. With decentralization under the 2015 Constitution, municipalities became central to services and civic engagement, though governance is weakened by political pressure, uneven delivery, and poor accountability. Media has shifted from elite-driven reporting to inclusive storytelling, with digital platforms amplifying youth voices. Youths, Nepal's demographic majority, remain vital but constrained by migration, unemployment, and tokenism. In Dharan, action research by NIRC and Lumanti (2025) monitored governance, housing, and marginalized groups in media. Analysis of 75 stories found 51% positive, 35% critical, 15% neutral—dominated by event-driven coverage with little investigative depth. Marginalized voices were inconsistently included, while housing and environment drew little traction. Media workshops highlighted evidence-based journalism, safety, and youth training alongside citizen-led journalism to amplify voices, strengthen participatory governance, and counter sensationalism.

Preface

Technological transformation today operates across every dimension of social life, often blurring the boundaries between human activity and digital environments. The pace of innovation has not only accelerated the creation of new tools but has fundamentally shifted how individuals perceive the world, engage with information, and participate in collective experiences. Media ecosystems have evolved from linear, passive channels into dynamic, interactive networks powered by algorithms, artificial intelligence, immersive platforms, and participatory cultures. These networks influence public consciousness, shape civic debates, foster new modes of creativity, and reorganize economic structures.

Within this rapidly changing landscape, technology does more than support communication; it alters the very architecture of human interaction. Platforms facilitate real-time dialogue across geographical divides, redefine access to knowledge, and amplify the voices of communities that were once marginalized. At the same time, emerging digital risks such as misinformation, surveillance capitalism, ethical concerns in AI, and widening digital inequalities demand careful examination. The intersection of technology and media thus becomes a critical space where societal values, cultural identities, and power relations are continuously negotiated.

This volume is grounded in the understanding that social innovation is inseparable from these technological shifts. Social innovation today is rarely limited to grassroots initiatives or policy-driven programmes; instead, it increasingly manifests through digital tools that enable collaboration, creative expression, cultural preservation, and community empowerment. Whether through mobile applications designed for inclusive learning, digital storytelling initiatives that safeguard indigenous heritage, or algorithmic platforms that influence political participation, each technological intervention carries implications for how communities evolve and adapt.

At the same time, the global nature of technological change means that local contexts remain essential. The way a rural community in India uses digital storytelling to preserve cultural narratives differs significantly from the way urban youth engage with social media in civic activism. Similarly, the integration of Islamic values into media innovation presents a culturally grounded lens that challenges dominant Western frameworks. These variations highlight that technological adoption is not uniform, it is shaped by cultural histories, socio-economic realities, religious values, and regional aspirations.

By foregrounding these diverse contexts, the book provides a panoramic view of the digital era one that does not reduce technology to tools or systems, but situates it within lived experiences, ethical considerations, and social dynamics. Each chapter in this volume contributes to a deeper understanding of how communities harness technology not simply to adapt to global change, but to actively redefine their futures. In doing so, the book invites readers to critically reflect on the opportunities and responsibilities that arise when technology and media intersect with human creativity, cultural identity, and the pursuit of social good.

OVERVIEW OF THE SUBJECT MATTER

At its core, this book interrogates how technological developments intersect with media practices and catalyse social innovation. It covers a broad spectrum of contemporary issues ranging from inclusive design, indigenous representation, artificial intelligence, and digital literacy, to entrepreneurship, governance, and civic participation. Rather than addressing technology as a monolithic phenomenon, the volume highlights how communities adapt technological tools in ways that reflect local histories, cultural values, and socio-economic aspirations. Across the chapters, technology emerges as both opportunity and challenge: a vehicle for empowerment and learning, yet also a space where inequalities, risks, and ethical concerns must be confronted.

The chapters demonstrate that social innovation today is inseparable from digital infrastructure. Whether in enhancing early childhood education, preserving cultural heritage, enabling sustainable development, or reshaping public discourse, technology creates new pathways for engagement. At the same time, the volume encourages readers to think critically about how digital tools may reinforce structural divides, influence mental health, reshape work and identity, and demand new frameworks of responsibility and care.

WHERE THE TOPIC FITS IN THE WORLD TODAY

The world is experiencing a period of accelerated digitalisation. Artificial intelligence, immersive media, data-driven platforms, and hybrid modes of communication have transformed societal structures at unprecedented speed. Communities rely on online spaces to access information, maintain social networks, participate in civic life, and pursue economic mobility. In parallel, technological gaps continue to shape global inequalities particularly among marginalized groups, differently abled learners, indigenous communities, and those living in emerging economies.

In this expanding digital landscape, the intersection of technology, media, and social innovation has become a crucial field of inquiry. Policy makers look to this field for insight into digital governance. Educators turn to it for pedagogical strategies. Social entrepreneurs draw upon it to design inclusive solutions. Cultural practitioners adopt it to preserve heritage, while researchers examine it to understand shifting social realities. The chapters in this volume therefore offer timely contributions that speak to current global debates in education, ethics, sustainability, cultural revitalisation, economic empowerment, and digital well-being.

TARGET AUDIENCE

This book is written for a diverse yet interconnected readership:

i. Researchers and academics in communication, media studies, technology studies, education, digital humanities, and social sciences who seek interdisciplinary perspectives.
ii. Policy makers, NGOs, and community leaders invested in designing inclusive digital ecosystems and sustainable development strategies.
iii. Educators and instructional designers working to integrate technology into pedagogy and support diverse learners.
iv. Social entrepreneurs and innovators exploring technological enablers for community development.
v. Students at undergraduate and postgraduate levels who require accessible, research-based insights into contemporary digital transformations.
vi. Cultural practitioners and advocates seeking ways to preserve narrative traditions and regional identities through media.

The breadth of topics ensures that each reader regardless of their disciplinary background will find relevant, evidence-informed discussions that advance understanding of the digital-social nexus.

DESCRIPTIONS OF EACH CHAPTER

Below is a succinct paragraph describing the contribution and importance of each chapter.

Chapter 1 — Designing Mobile Applications for Dyslexic Children: Enhancing Early Childhood Education Through Inclusive Technology

This chapter offers an in-depth exploration of how mobile technologies can transform early learning experiences for children with dyslexia. By integrating principles of universal design, multimodal interfaces, and adaptive learning features, the chapter demonstrates how mobile applications can support literacy development in a way that is both empathetic and evidence based. Its contribution lies in bridging early childhood pedagogy with inclusive digital design, offering a model for reducing learning barriers and enabling more equitable education outcomes.

Chapter 2 — Assessment of Dexterous and Detrimental Social Media Intricacies on Civic Engagement and Public Discourse

This chapter investigates the complex interplay between social media behaviour and civic participation, noting how digital platforms can simultaneously empower democratic engagement and amplify harmful patterns of manipulation or polarization. Through its nuanced analysis, the chapter reveals the dual nature of social media: as a tool for mobilization and collective action, and as a mechanism that can distort discourse and discourage inclusive democratic dialogue. Its significance lies in offering insights relevant to digital governance, media policy, and civic education.

Chapter 3 — Social Entrepreneurship Model for Asnaf: A Strategy for Sustainable Economic Empowerment in Perlis State

This chapter explores how social entrepreneurship can serve as a strategic pathway for enhancing the economic resilience of Asnaf communities. Through a culturally grounded model that combines local values, Islamic economic principles, and sustainable enterprise strategies, the chapter demonstrates practical ways to uplift vulnerable populations. Its importance lies in showcasing how technology-enabled entrepreneurship can strengthen community capacity while honouring local identities and socio-religious contexts.

Chapter 4 — Bridging Social Entrepreneurship and Sustainable Development: A Systematic Review of Technological Enablers

This chapter synthesizes scholarly literature on how digital tools such as data analytics, mobile applications, blockchain, and online platforms support social entrepreneurship initiatives aligned with sustainability goals. It contributes a structured understanding of technological enablers that strengthen environmental, social, and economic outcomes. The review offers a valuable roadmap for researchers and practitioners seeking to integrate innovation into sustainable development frameworks.

Chapter 5 — Digital Storytelling and Indigenous Knowledge: Media as a Tool for Cultural Preservation among the Garasia Tribe of Rajasthan, India

This chapter illustrates how digital storytelling empowers indigenous communities to preserve and disseminate cultural knowledge. By documenting the narratives of the Garasia tribe, the chapter demonstrates how media can serve as an archival tool, a platform for self-expression, and a bridge between generations. Its significance lies in highlighting the role of technology in safeguarding intangible cultural heritage and promoting cultural continuity in the digital age.

Chapter 6 — Equity, Responsibility, and Innovation: Integrating Islamic Values into the Intersection of Media and Technology

This chapter examines how Islamic values such as justice, accountability, and communal well-being can inform ethical frameworks in digital innovation. It introduces a model that aligns media practices with moral principles, contributing a culturally meaningful perspective to the global discussion on technological ethics. The chapter is particularly valuable in illustrating how religious worldviews can enhance conversations about responsibility and fairness in digital environments.

Chapter 7 — Impact of Startup Singam Television Show in Regional Entrepreneurship of Tamil Nadu

This chapter analyses how a regionally popular television programme influences entrepreneurial culture and community perception of business opportunities. By tracing viewer interpretations, programme content, and socio-economic outcomes, the chapter demonstrates how media can shift aspirations and support public understanding of entrepreneurship. Its contribution lies in linking mass media narratives with regional economic development.

Chapter 8 — Late Night Use of Social Media and Sleep Deprivation

This chapter explores behavioural patterns associated with nocturnal social media engagement and their consequences on sleep quality, mental focus, and overall wellbeing. It situates these findings within broader concerns about digital addiction and lifestyle disruptions. The chapter is important for its timely discussion of how everyday digital habits can create long-term health implications, particularly among youth.

Chapter 9 — Social Media Usage and Stress Levels: Correlation or Causation

This chapter interrogates the relationship between social media engagement and psychological stress, critically analysing whether digital exposure directly contributes to emotional strain or simply correlates with broader lifestyle patterns. Through empirical insights, the chapter contributes to ongoing debates in digital psychology, offering nuanced interpretations that help inform public health approaches and digital wellness strategies.

Chapter 10 — Culture as Laboratory: Technology, Media, and the Making of Social Innovation

This chapter conceptualizes culture as a dynamic testing ground where technological practices and media forms continuously evolve. It argues that innovation emerges not only from technological breakthroughs but also from cultural experimentation and adaptation. Its significance lies in reframing social innovation as a culturally embedded process influenced by identity, tradition, and social imagination.

Chapter 11 — Podcasting the Subaltern: Imaginations of Matabeleland Regional Identity Through Audience Perspectives

This chapter examines how podcasting provides a democratic platform for marginalized voices, offering new ways to articulate regional identity and collective memory. By analyzing audience interpretations and community responses, the chapter demonstrates how digital audio media can challenge dominant narratives and offer alternative spaces of representation.

Chapter 12 — Screens, Streams, and Society: Examining the Intersection of Technology, Media, and Social Change

This chapter investigates how streaming cultures reshape social interaction, affect cultural consumption, and influence collective meanings in everyday life. It highlights the ways visual media ecosystems contribute to social transformation by altering how communities access content, interpret information, and build shared experiences.

Chapter 13 — The Economic Dimensions of Technology and Media in Digital Social Innovation

This chapter offers a detailed analysis of the economic structures that underpin digital social innovation, explaining how technology generates new markets, reshapes labour practices, and influences resource distribution. Its contribution lies in presenting a comprehensive understanding of how economies adapt when innovation is integrated into social processes.

Chapter 14 — Websites Beyond Technology: Platforms for Awareness, Promotion and Social Innovation

This chapter argues that websites function not merely as technical infrastructures but as powerful spaces for shaping public knowledge, cultural promotion, and social advocacy. It showcases examples of website-driven initiatives that foster awareness, mobilize communities, and create lasting social impact.

Chapter 15 — Youth, Media, and Governance in Transition: Lessons from Dharan's Citizen-Led Journalism

This chapter examines how youth-driven media initiatives contribute to local governance, emphasizing the role of citizen journalists in enhancing transparency, community participation, and public accountability. Its significance lies in illustrating how young people leverage media tools to reshape civic processes and reimagine local governance structures.

This edited volume expands current dialogues on technological change by centering social innovation, cultural context, and human experience. It asserts that the real significance of technology lies not in the sophistication of its design but in its capacity to engage with the aspirations, challenges, and identities of real communities. By weaving together research from multiple regions, disciplinary perspectives, and cultural narratives, the book positions digital transformation within a global conversation on inclusivity, ethical responsibility, sustainability, economic resilience, and cultural vitality.

The collective insights presented across the chapters reveal that technology and media serve as more than mere instruments of efficiency or communication; they have become essential frameworks through which societies interpret reality, negotiate collective values, and shape future trajectories. In highlighting diverse contexts from indigenous storytelling traditions and youth-led journalism to inclusive educational tools and AI-enhanced immersive platforms the volume underscores that digital innovation is always intertwined with the social and cultural environments where it unfolds.

Beyond documenting technological shifts, the book urges readers to imagine technological futures that are more just, participatory, and community driven. It invites policymakers, educators, researchers, and practitioners to view innovation not as a race for novelty but as a deliberate, ethical process that prioritizes human dignity, cultural continuity, and societal well-being. The chapters offer conceptual frameworks for responsible design, methodological approaches for community engagement, and practical strategies for leveraging technology to address systemic inequalities.

They also demonstrate how local wisdom, religious values, and cultural practices can inform and enrich contemporary approaches to digital transformation. Importantly, the book contributes to emerging discussions on the social obligations of technology creators and media practitioners. It challenges readers to consider how digital environments can support mental health, foster economic mobility, strengthen democratic participation, preserve cultural heritage, and build inclusive knowledge ecosystems. Through its interdisciplinary focus, the volume highlights that sustainable technological progress requires both innovation and reflection innovation to expand possibilities, and reflection to ensure that these possibilities remain aligned with ethical and social priorities.

Ultimately, Examining the Intersection of Technology, Media, and Social Innovation affirms that this domain is not a peripheral academic interest but a vital and evolving field that shapes how societies function and flourish. By capturing the complexities, contradictions, and transformative potential of the digital age, the book offers a meaningful contribution to ongoing efforts aimed at building equitable, resilient, and culturally grounded digital futures.

Acknowledgement

The development of this edited volume represents the collective effort of numerous scholars, practitioners, and institutional partners whose contributions have been integral to its academic integrity and completion. The editors wish to formally acknowledge the authors whose chapters constitute the core of this work. Their empirical insights, methodological rigour, and theoretical advancements form the intellectual architecture of this book. The diversity of disciplinary backgrounds represented herein significantly enriches the global dialogue on technology, media, and social innovation.

We express our appreciation to the peer reviewers who dedicated their time and expertise to providing critical evaluations of the submitted manuscripts. Their informed assessments played a valuable role in strengthening the coherence, conceptual clarity, and scholarly merit of the chapters. The editorial process has benefited greatly from their commitment to academic excellence.

The editors also recognise the institutional environments that facilitated the research and writing of this book. Our respective universities and research units provided essential academic resources, collegial engagement, and administrative support. We acknowledge the contributions of research coordinators, editorial assistants, and project managers who assisted in communication, data organisation, and the practical logistics required for coordinating a multi-authored international volume.

Special appreciation is extended to the IGI Global publishing team for their sustained professionalism throughout all phases of manuscript development. Their guidance on editorial standards, production protocols, and publication ethics has ensured that this book adheres to the requirements of a globally distributed academic resource.

Chapter 1
Designing Mobile Applications for Dyslexic Children:
Enhancing Early Childhood Education Through Inclusive Technology

Farah Zahidah Abdullah
https://orcid.org/0009-0008-0486-0928
Universiti Teknologi MARA, Malaysia & Universiti Malaysia Perlis, Malaysia

Mastura Mohd Jarit
Universiti Teknologi MARA, Malaysia

Shafilla Subri
Universiti Teknologi MARA, Malaysia

Nabila Aimi Mohamed Ghazali
Universiti Teknologi MARA, Malaysia

ABSTRACT

This chapter investigates the role of mobile applications in helping dyslexic children in Malaysia's early childhood education. The study emphasizes important inclusiveness design aspects through a review of relevant literature, visual analysis, and interviews with teachers, designers, and children. The findings emphasize the importance of user-centered features such as streamlined interfaces, dyslexia-friendly typefaces, bilingual options, and multisensory engagement. Children were highly motivated by gamified aspects that provided immediate feedback, whereas

DOI: 10.4018/979-8-3373-5307-4.ch001

teachers highlighted simplicity, cultural significance, and parental involvement. Designers, however, suggested for deeper engagement with educators to ensure pedagogical coherence. The study, which is based on theories such as Universal Design for Learning, Multisensory Learning, and Cognitive Load Theory, shows how mobile applications can improve literacy, supplement classroom instruction, and foster inclusion.

INTRODUCTION

Early childhood education is a vital time of cognitive, linguistic, and social development. For dyslexic children, this stage is particularly important since it introduces and consolidates core literacy abilities such as phonemic awareness, word identification, and understanding. According to Malik Ghulam, learning has been defined as a quantitative increase in knowledge, including the memorizing of facts, skills, and methods that can be retained and used as needed. (Malik Ghulam Behlol, 2010).

Mangunsong classifies learning challenges into six groups. The primary category is "Academic Achievement Problems," followed by "Perception, Motor Perception, and General Coordination Problems" and "Attention and Hyperactivity Disorder". "Memory, Cognitive, and Metacognitive Disorders" is the fourth type, "Social Emotional Problems" is the fifth, and Motivational Problems is the last group. (Mangunsong, 2014). The phrases dyslexia, dyscalculia, and dysgraphia are classified as "Academic Achievement Problems," which is the first form of learning challenge. Dyslexia, a commonly used word, is a learning condition that causes difficulty learning to read despite traditional training, enough IQ, and socio cultural opportunity. Dyslexia, marked by difficulties with reading accuracy and fluency, affects 5-10% of children globally (Hulme & Snowling, 2016).

Malaysia's multilingual school system makes it much more challenging to accommodate dyslexic children. Children are introduced to Bahasa Malaysia, English, and, in certain cases, Mandarin or Tamil, beginning in kindergarten. Dyslexic children may struggle with decoding across different orthographies, resulting in lower reading proficiency and disengagement from learning (Suffiah & Lee, 2022). This highlights the importance of inclusive strategies that consider not only dyslexic children's cognitive features, but also Malaysia's language and cultural challenges.

The rapid advancement of digital technology offers up new opportunities for tackling these challenges. Mobile phones and tablets, with their portability, interactivity, and ability to transfer multimedia content, are becoming increasingly popular in education around the world. According to Crompton and Burke (2018), mobile learning has evolved into a valuable tool for inclusive education, providing access to a wide range of children through personalized and multimodal platforms. Malaysia's mobile usage rate surpasses 90%, creating ideal conditions for the introduction of mobile learning solutions. However, the potential of mobile applications to help dyslexic children remains unexplored, particularly in terms of culturally acceptable design and pedagogical effectiveness. (MCMC, 2022)

Globally, mobile educational apps such as Nessy, GraphoGame, and Lingokids have demonstrated promising outcomes in helping dyslexic children by combining phonics based instruction with gamified, multisensory learning experiences (Maresca et al., 2024). Regional studies in Asia demonstrate the potential for mobile learning. For example, bilingual mobile apps in Singapore have been shown to improve fluency by allowing for flexible language switching, whilst gamified applications in Indonesia have increased motivation and attention among dyslexic children (Dymora, and Niemiec, 2019). However, in Malaysia, research on the effectiveness of dyslexia focused mobile applications is limited, with the majority of initiatives generated as pilot projects or small scale approaches that have not been properly reviewed (Admodisastro, 2021).

This chapter is driven by a logic that is both diverse and interrelated. First, it aims to illustrate the benefits and problems of developing mobile applications for children with dyslexia in Malaysia, drawing on both local and broader Asian experiences. Second, it seeks to advance the theoretical and practical knowledge of how inclusive technology can be used to improve early childhood education. The chapter provides a conceptual foundation for evaluating and improving mobile learning applications by basing the analysis on theoretical frameworks such as Universal Design for Learning (Meyer et al., 2014), Multisensory Learning Approaches (Birsh & Carreker, 2018), and Cognitive Load Theory (Paas et al., 2010).

A literature review and a visual analysis of selected mobile applications have been done to gain background information on inclusive design features and existing practices. The study then used a qualitative research method, focusing on interviews with teachers, designers, and students, to acquire further insights into the actual use of mobile applications for dyslexic children.

This introduction provides the structure for the chapter's subsequent sections. The Literature Review situates the discourse in Malaysian and Asian contexts, identifying limitations and opportunities through contemporary research. Methodology describes the qualitative approach used to gather and analyze data. The findings and discussion incorporate ideas from visual analysis, teachers and designers, and dyslexic children, blending perspectives to highlight common tendencies. The Implications section discusses the findings' practical significance for educators, parents, and developers, while the Future Research Directions section recommends areas for further investigation. The conclusion summarizes the main contributions and underlines the importance of inclusive, user-centered mobile applications for dyslexic students in Malaysian early childhood education.

LITERATURE REVIEW

Understanding Dyslexia in Early Childhood Education

Dyslexia is widely accepted as a cognitive disorder marked by difficulty with precise and fluent word identification, spelling, and decoding skills. The American Psychiatric Association classifies dyslexia as a Specific Learning Disorder, with onset often occurring during the early years of formal schooling. The signs and symptoms of dyslexia in early childhood education are especially noteworthy since the core reading skills phonemic awareness, letter identification, and word decoding are introduced during this developmental stage. According to Hulme and Snowling (2016), children with dyslexia have ongoing abnormalities in phonological processing, which impairs their ability to associate sounds with symbols, a critical component of reading acquisition.

Early childhood educators are increasingly aware that dyslexia is more than just a literacy issue; it also affects cognitive, emotional, and social development. When children with dyslexia's challenges go unnoticed, they frequently experience a loss of confidence, anxiety, and disengagement with learning. This emphasizes the importance of inclusive policies in early education in preventing long term academic disadvantage. Furthermore, in multilingual situations such as Malaysia, where children are exposed to Bahasa Malaysia, English, and occasionally Mandarin or Tamil, the intricacy of decoding across orthographies might increase reading difficulties for dyslexic children (Suffiah & Lee, 2022).

Research shows early intervention is critical. Wanzek et al.'s (2018) meta analysis discovered that structured, multisensory literacy programs provided in the early years greatly improved reading fluency and comprehension among dyslexic children. These initiatives frequently integrate phonics based instruction with visual and kinesthetic reinforcement, suggesting that early educational support can reduce long term literacy difficulties. Mobile technologies, as addressed later in this chapter, offer new opportunities for incorporating such multimodal techniques into everyday learning situations.

Gaps in Current Research

While mobile dyslexia applications have shown great potential, there are still huge gaps in study and practice, notably in Malaysia. First, there is a significant shortage of scientific studies that objectively assess the effectiveness of locally produced programs like MyLexic and JollyMate. Although these methods are frequently mentioned in educational conversations, much extant research is exploratory or anecdotal in character, with few using systematic methodologies or longitudinal designs to show their instructional worth. Without strong data, it is difficult to determine how beneficial these programs are at promoting literacy development, limiting their scalability and integration into standard educational practice.

Second, the digital divide continues to exist, weakening Malaysia's mobile learning potential. While mobile applications are being used as additional learning tools in urban classrooms and by middle income families, children in rural or low income households frequently have limited access to devices, stable internet connections, and digital literacy training. According to Ibrahim et. al (2021), unless infrastructure disadvantages are addressed, mobile learning programs may unintentionally reinforce existing disparities, leaving dyslexic children in underprivileged communities further behind. This structural issue raises larger concerns about equity and access in Malaysia's aim of inclusive education.

Third, the issues of sustainability and scalability remain ignored. Many dyslexia focused mobile applications in Malaysia are created as short term trials, with funding from research grants or non-profit organizations. While these initiatives produce useful insights, few apps are updated, maintained, or scaled after their original deployment. This results in a fragmented environment of programs, with little long term impact on national educational outcomes. Future study must therefore investigate sustainable development strategies that assure regular upgrades, statewide dissemination, and integration with the Malaysian curriculum, effectively embedding mobile applications in the broader education ecosystem.

Finally, the role of parental involvement in mobile learning for dyslexic children is understudied. While previous research has thoroughly investigated the viewpoints of teachers and children, parents who serve as essential partners in learning, particularly in early childhood education are sometimes disregarded. According to Othman et al. (2025), mobile applications with parent friendly features such as progress tracking, instructional manuals, and at home assistance strategies are more likely to reinforce learning outside of the classroom. Future research should focus on how parents can effectively participate in the design, deployment, and assessment of dyslexia focused applications in Malaysia.

Dyslexia in the Malaysian Context

The widespread incidence of dyslexia in Malaysia has received significant attention in the last two decades, but accurate national statistics remain limited. The Dyslexia Association of Malaysia (DAM) estimates that 5-10% of Malaysian children have dyslexia, which is consistent with international prevalence rates (Lim et al,. 2023). Despite this, many cases are overlooked due to a lack of information among parents and teachers, especially in rural areas.

Malaysia's Ministry of Education has launched efforts to promote inclusion, most notably the Special Education Integrated Programme (SEIP), which incorporates children with specific learning issues, such as dyslexia, into normal schools. However, implementation issues remain. Teachers frequently do not have specialized training, and resources are unevenly distributed between urban and rural schools (Suffiah and Lee, 2022). According to Bailey et al. (2015), even when dyslexic kids are identified, classroom adaptations such as more time, simplified instructions, or multimodal teaching modalities are not always applied.

Cultural attitudes play an important impact. Academic achievement is highly valued in Malaysian society, and children who struggle with reading may be too late to catch on. Parents may avoid seeking assistance from professionals for fear of being classified, while some instructors continue to view reading difficulties as a result of low IQ rather than a distinct learning problem (Alias et al., 2015). These beliefs contribute to delayed diagnosis and insufficient access to specific treatments.

Technological interventions, particularly mobile applications, are emerging as a promising alternative to classroom based help in Malaysia. Mobile coverage rates in metropolitan areas approach 90% (Malaysian Communications and Multimedia Commission, 2022), making digital learning tools more accessible to children and families. MyLexic and Dyslexia Malaysia's e-learning modules are early examples of local projects aimed at providing interactive, phonics based exercises for dyslexic children (Admodisastro, 2021). However, research on their instructional effectiveness is limited, emphasizing the need for additional empirical studies that encourage development and policy adoption.

Theoretical Foundations for Inclusive Learning

To ensure educational validity and inclusion, mobile applications for dyslexic children must be designed and implemented within sound theoretical frameworks. knowing how technology might promote early literacy development for children with dyslexia requires knowing three fundamental frameworks: Universal Design for Learning (UDL), Multisensory Learning Approaches, and Cognitive Load Theory.

Universal Design for Learning (UDL)

Universal Design for Learning (UDL) is a concept that emphasizes creating flexible learning environments that adapt to diverse children from the start, rather than relying on subsequent adaptations (CAST, 2018). Meyer et al. (2014) define

UDL as having three principles: numerous modes of involvement, representation, and expression. For dyslexic children, this involves offering many ways to acquire knowledge, such as audio narration, graphic icons, and text; providing diverse formats to demonstrate learning, such as spoken responses and interactive games; and implementing strategies for sustaining motivation.

Mobile applications are excellent for bringing UDL ideas into practice since they can effortlessly combine multimedia features. For example, a phonics application may incorporate animated images, recorded sounds, and interactive spelling exercises to ensure that children connect with the content in a variety of ways. In Malaysia, integrating UDL into mobile learning aligns with the broader policy goal of inclusive education and can fill gaps in classroom instruction where teacher experience is insufficient (Bailey et al., 2015).

Multisensory Learning Approaches

The multisensory approach to learning has long been recommended in dyslexia intervention. Multisensory education, which originated with the Orton Gillingham technique, includes simultaneously engaging visual, aural, and kinesthetic channels to reinforce learning (Birsh & Carreker, 2018). According to Nicolson and Fawcett (2008), multisensory methods help dyslexic children build brain pathways and compensate for phonological processing deficiencies.

Mobile applications offer unique options for delivering multiple media experiences. For example, touch screen technology allows children to trace letters with their fingers, combining tactile and kinesthetic learning with visual reinforcement. Audio feedback can help to reinforce accurate spelling, while gamified lessons use sound and motion to motivate children. Cahyana et al. (2021) found that children with dyslexia who used various mobile apps for six weeks performed significantly better in word recognition than those who used standard flashcards.

Educators in Malaysia are currently looking into how such approaches may be adapted to local contexts, where multilingualism brings unique challenges. To enhance relevance and comprehension, a mobile app teaching phonics in Bahasa Malaysia should include culturally recognized words and imagery.

Cognitive Load Theory

Sweller (1988) proposed Cognitive Load Theory (CLT), which emphasizes that instructional design should minimize unnecessary cognitive burden in order to improve learning. This idea is especially important for dyslexic children, who use more cognitive resources decoding text, leaving less capacity for understanding.

According to Paas et al., (2010), instructional materials that overload working memory can impair learning, especially for children with specific learning challenges.

Applying CLT to Malaysian mobile learning applications requires emphasizing clarity and simplicity in design. In a study conducted by Ibrahim et al. (2021), teachers noted that students with dyslexia were more engaged when applications used simple images, consistent navigation, and rapid feedback, as opposed to those overloaded with text or ornamental elements.

Redundancy Principle

Redundancy will assist in developing the mobile application because it comprises extremely simple and straightforward aspects. According to Meyer et al. (2014), redundancy principle was a good idea to develop specifically for use with multimedia learning. He also stated that using the redundancy principle in multimedia learning will focus on the information that is aimed for children and how information is delivered across a whole session. Adjusting such as getting rid of content that is not required can have a huge effect on the results of a lesson.

Mobile Learning and Assistive Technologies

Mobile learning (m-learning) involves the use of portable devices like smartphones and tablets to deliver educational content anytime and anywhere. Its adaptability and accessibility have made it an especially appealing option for inclusive education. According to Crompton and Burke (2018), mobile learning enables instant access to multisensory content, which is ideal for children with dyslexia.

Global Perspectives

Globally, mobile phones have been widely embraced to help with education difficulties. Mobile applications such as Nessy and GraphoGame have grown in popularity in the United States and Europe for delivering phonics based, interactive learning for dyslexic children. Maresca et al. (2024) found that these apps promote not only word recognition but also learner motivation through gamification.

Furthermore, artificially intelligent adaptive learning systems are being implemented in mobile applications to personalize learning. According to Mirari (2022), adaptive applications may adjust the pace, difficulty, and material delivery based on user progress, resulting in personalized paths that are especially advantageous for dyslexic children who progress at varying rates.

Asian Case Studies

In Asia, where multilingualism is widespread, mobile learning projects have centered on developing culturally appropriate and linguistically adaptive applications. Aldousari (2021) found that multilingual mobile apps that combined English and Mandarin phonics enhanced reading fluency in dyslexic children by giving flexible language switching options.

In Indonesia, Sudarsono et al. (2022) examined the impact of gamified mobile learning for dyslexic children and concluded that the use of avatars, point systems, and interactive stories increased motivation and sustained attention. Meanwhile, research in China by Ekawati et al. (2024) emphasized the importance of cognitive load considerations, noting that children disengaged when mobile apps contained cluttered layouts and unnecessary animations.

Malaysian Initiatives

Malaysia has noticed mobile learning's potential for inclusive education, notably among dyslexic children. Local projects include MyLexic, an app that delivers phonics based exercises in Bahasa Malaysia, and JollyMate, a Malaysian specific adaptation of the international Jolly Phonics program. Admodisastro (2021) discovered that after eight weeks of using MyLexic, children increased their word recognition. However, teachers pointed out drawbacks such as a lack of engaging images and limited customizing possibilities.

Despite all of these attempts, difficulties remain. Unequal access to devices and internet connectivity, particularly in remote areas, limits the reach of mobile learning efforts. Furthermore, several existing applications have yet to be tested for instructional effectiveness (Ibrahim et al., 2021). These difficulties highlight the need for additional research into the design and implementation of mobile learning aids for dyslexic students in Malaysia.

Design Principles for Dyslexia Friendly Mobile Applications

Designing mobile applications for children with dyslexia calls for approaches grounded in research that improve ease of use, accessibility, and learning effectiveness. Scholars and educators have identified several guiding principles that can help ensure these tools truly meet children's needs.

Simplicity and Clarity

Applications should be developed with simple layouts that reduce clutter and needless pieces. Keeping the interface simple and limiting text encourages children to focus on the main material (Paas et al., 2010). According to Malaysian teachers, children with dyslexia respond better to apps with large, easy to recognize icons and consistent navigation, which reduces confusion and promotes smoother learning experiences.

Customization and Flexibility

It is crucial to include options for font size, backdrop color, and text-to-speech support. Tan et al. (2022) discovered that dyslexic children profited from configurable features, particularly the usage of dyslexia friendly typefaces and high contrast backdrops. Flexibility guarantees that apps may adjust to the demands of particular children.

Multisensory Engagement

As highlighted earlier, multisensory learning is vital for dyslexic children. Mobile apps might include voice narration, visual animations, and tactile activities like letter tracing. Othman et al. (2025) found that Malaysian children were more interested when apps had sound effects, interactive characters, and touch based activities.

Gamification and Motivation

Gamified elements like points, levels, and badges can help increase motivation. Dymora, and Niemiec (2019) discovered that gamification improved children's tenacity in completing reading tasks. Gamification, on the other hand, should be balanced with educational aims to avoid emphasizing rewards over teaching objectives.

Collectively, these limitations underscore the critical need for more comprehensive, evidence based, and inclusive research that not only improves technology innovation but also assures fair access, long term sustainability, and holistic support engaging educators, politicians, and families.

Visual Analysis of Local and International Mobile Applications

Table 1. Selected Mobile Applications for Analysis

Application	Age	Remark
Belajar Fonik ABC	3+	Local
Belajar Membaca	5+	Local
Belajar Huruf	3+	Local
BimiBoo Kids Learning Application	3-12	International
Lingokids Mobile Application	4+	International
Sago Mini World	4+	International

Interface Design and Layout

The analysis showed that streamlined and minimalist layouts enhanced usability, allowing children with dyslexia to navigate applications more easily. International applications such as BimiBoo Kids Learning Application and Lingokids used clean layouts with large, recognizable icons and consistent menu structures, which reduced cognitive load. In contrast, local apps such as Belajar Fonik ABC and Belajar Huruf often incorporated decorative fonts and bright, patterned backgrounds. While visually attractive, these design choices sometimes distracted children from core literacy tasks. This reflects Cognitive Load Theory, which highlights the negative impact of extraneous information on working memory (Paas et al., 2010).

Typography and Readability

Typography emerged as a critical design factor. International applications such as Lingokids and Sago Mini World applied dyslexia friendly fonts with clear spacing and avoided visually similar letterforms, thereby supporting readability. None of the local Malaysian apps, including Belajar Membaca and Belajar Huruf, adopted these typographic considerations, reflecting a gap in applying global best practices. As Tan et al. (2022) emphasize, dyslexia friendly typography significantly enhances readability and reduces decoding errors, underscoring the need for Malaysian developers to adopt these principles.

Multisensory Features and Interactivity

The use of multisensory elements varies across applications. Sago Mini World and BimiBoo Kids combined visual cues, audio narration, and interactive touch based activities, sustaining engagement and supporting kinesthetic learning. By contrast, local apps such as Belajar Membaca relied heavily on phonics drills with audio feedback but offered limited interactivity beyond listening and repeating. While these apps recognized the importance of phonics, they underutilized the interactive features available on touchscreen devices that could enhance tactile and visual learning.

Gamification and Motivation

Gamification was another key element influencing motivation. International applications such as Lingokids and Sago Mini World incorporated levels, badges, and animated characters, which children found engaging and rewarding. Local apps such as Belajar Fonik ABC and Belajar Membaca typically used simpler reinforcements like congratulatory sounds or brief animations. While these features provided encouragement, they lacked the complexity to sustain long term engagement.

Overall, the visual analysis showed that international applications such as BimiBoo Kids, Lingokids, and Sago Mini World followed more closely to the principles of Universal Design for Learning, Cognitive Load Theory, and multisensory learning. Local applications like Belajar Fonik ABC, Belajar Membaca, and Belajar Huruf remained functional and culturally relevant despite their lack of innovation. Local developers can improve literacy tools for dyslexic youngsters by leveraging current capabilities and applying global best practices.

RESEARCH METHODOLOGY

The method used in this chapter was intended to give a thorough examination of how mobile applications may be developed to assist dyslexic children in Malaysian early childhood education. Given dyslexia's complicated, context sensitive nature and the changing role of technology in inclusive education, a qualitative research design was selected. Qualitative methods enable the collection of rich, descriptive data that represent the lived experiences, views, and practices among those involved in dyslexia education, such as teachers, designers, and children themselves.

Research Design

The study used a qualitative design based on interpretation, which emphasizes understanding social phenomena through the subjective meanings that participants assign to them. This approach was acceptable because the study's goal was to assess how mobile applications are viewed, produced, and experienced in Malaysian educational environments, rather than quantify outcomes statistically. According to Creswell and Poth (2018), qualitative research is especially appropriate for educational inquiries that focus on processes, meanings, and experiences rather than numerical generalizations.

Data Collection Methods

The primary data collection approach used in this study was semi-structured interviews. This approach was chosen because it allowed both flexibility and depth, allowing participants to share their experiences and ideas in their own words while also ensuring that crucial issues were covered. Semi-structured interviews were extremely helpful for investigating the perspectives of teachers, designers, and dyslexic children, as they allowed the researcher to go deeper into specific difficulties raised throughout the conversations. The study was able to obtain varied insights about the design and use of mobile applications for dyslexic children by incorporating multiple participant groups. This strategy also enabled data triangulation, which improved the reliability and dependability of the conclusions (Patton, 2020).

Semi-Structured Interviews

Semi-structured interviews were done with three groups of participants to gain a variety of perspectives. The first group included twelve teachers from both urban and rural elementary schools who had previous experience teaching dyslexic students. The second group consisted of six app developers and instructional designers who were actively involved in developing educational technology solutions for Malaysian students. The third group consisted of ten dyslexic children, whose experiences provided useful insights into how mobile applications enhance their learning.

Interviews with teachers and designers focused on their perceptions of existing applications, implementation issues, and design recommendations. Interviews with children were done in the presence of their parents for ethical reasons, and they focused on their experiences, preferences, and frustrations when using educational apps. The questions were open ended to promote extensive responses while also providing freedom to examine emerging topics.

Data Analysis

Braun and Clarke (2019) proposed a thematic approach to data analysis. Interview transcripts and field notes were thoroughly analyzed and coded inductively to identify recurring patterns in the data. These initial codes were gradually modified and organized into broader categories, such as interface simplicity, multisensory interaction, customization choices, and cultural relevance. The insights gathered from visual analysis of mobile applications were then matched to interview findings, allowing for the discovery of cross cutting themes that mirrored both design processes and user experiences.

To help with the process, MAXQDA software was used to handle and code the data, ensuring systematic structure, transparency, and traceability of analytical decisions. Thematic analysis was chosen because it allowed for greater flexibility in investigating complicated qualitative data and was particularly suited to combining diverse views from teachers, designers, and children. This technique not only highlighted areas of agreement, but also exposed discrepancies in stakeholder perspectives, providing a more complete understanding of mobile application design for dyslexic children.

Ethical Considerations

The study was ethically approved by the university where the researcher is enrolled. All adult participants provided informed consent, whereas the children who participated in the study were given parental consent. Children's participation was also regulated by the idea of acquiescence, which ensured that they understood the study's goal and agreed to participate voluntarily. To maintain confidentiality, all data were anonymised, and participants were allocated identities.

Given dyslexic children's vulnerability, interview questions were carefully designed to be suitable for children and non-threatening. Participation was seen as a chance to share personal experiences rather than a test of knowledge or aptitude. Interviews with children were held in easy, informal settings, with playful components to preserve comfort, trust, and interest.

Trustworthiness of the Study

To ensure the accuracy and credibility of this qualitative study, the research design was driven by Lincoln and Guba's (1985) four trustworthiness criteria: credibility, transferability, dependability, and confirmability. Credibility was gained by combining numerous data sources, such as a thorough assessment of the literature, visual analysis of mobile applications, and semi-structured interviews with teachers, designers, and dyslexic students. This triangulation not only increased the validity of the findings, but it also provided a holistic picture of the phenomenon under investigation. Transferability was addressed by providing detailed descriptions of the research context, participants, and mobile applications tested.

These extensive reports allow readers and future researchers to determine the extent to which the findings are applicable to similar educational situations in Malaysia and elsewhere. Dependability was achieved by keeping a detailed audit trail of methodological procedures, coding frameworks, and analytical conclusions, which allowed for transparency and replication. Finally, confirmability was enhanced by reflexivity, in which the researcher critically reflected on personal preconceptions, potential biases, and positionality throughout the research process. By basing interpretations on participants' perspectives rather than preconceived preconceptions, the study protected data integrity. Together, these tactics lay a solid foundation for trustworthiness, guaranteeing that the study's conclusions are not just methodologically sound, but also relevant and valuable to stakeholders in inclusive education.

Limitations

While the qualitative technique yielded useful insights, limits must be acknowledged. First, the sample size was small, which limited the generalizability of the findings. Second, the study relied on self-reported data from teachers and designers, which could be influenced by social desirability bias. Despite simplified questioning and interactive activities, children's perspectives were limited due to their young age and lack of expressive skills.

FINDINGS AND DISCUSSION

Malaysia has the ability to translate global best practices into culturally relevant mobile applications; nevertheless, more attention on inclusive design principles is required during development. This section covers the study's primary findings and discusses them in light of existing literature and theoretical frameworks. The conclusions are based on semi-structured interviews with instructors, designers, and dyslexic students. By integrating these viewpoints, the discussion emphasizes not just the merits of present Malaysian practices, but also the gaps that must be filled to improve accessibility, usability, and learning efficacy.

Findings from Teachers and Designers

The interviews with teachers and designers provided valuable insights into the pedagogical and technical challenges of developing dyslexia focused mobile applications in Malaysia.

Findings from Teachers

Teachers continually emphasized the need of simplicity and accessibility. They noted that children with dyslexia are easily overwhelmed by cluttered screens or instructions provided in lengthy sentences. According to one teacher, having too many buttons or options can cause confusion for kids. The app should be simple, with clear instructions and no more than a few options at a time. This conclusion is consistent with study by Ibrahim et al. (2021), who discovered that Malaysian dyslexic children perform better with simplified interfaces and step by step navigation.

Another recurring topic that emerged from the interviews was the integration of local languages into mobile applications. Teachers constantly underlined the necessity of incorporating Bahasa Malaysia curriculum alongside English, pointing out that many students, particularly those in rural areas, choose to begin their reading journey in their mother tongue. While international programs like Lingokids were praised for their engaging features and appealing design, their sole use of English caused difficulties for younger Malaysian who had little exposure to the language.

Teachers explained that this frequently resulted in frustration or disengagement as students tried to link novel English vocabulary to their everyday experiences. They proposed that bilingual or even multilingual applications incorporating both Bahasa Malaysia and English would be more effective in fostering literacy skills, as these tools could help students transition from their native language to English while respecting Malaysia's cultural and linguistic context. They suggested that such an approach will not only increase comprehension and motivation but also ensure that mobile applications are inclusive and relevant to Malaysian children's different backgrounds.

Finally, teachers highlighted the importance of parental involvement. Many others pointed out that, while children like using mobile apps, its usefulness is dependent on how parents' guide their use at home. Parents are frequently unaware of how to scaffold their children's learning, underlining the necessity for applications to incorporate parent friendly features like progress monitoring and usage instructions.

Findings from Designers

Designers interviewed for this study acknowledged the difficulties of balancing teaching goals with user engagement. They noted that educational apps in Malaysia frequently have restricted budgets, limiting the integration of advanced features like gamification or adaptive learning. According to one designer, while gamification is effective, creating complicated systems may be costly and time consuming. Often, educational apps are created as modest ventures with little long term funding.

They also highlighted the value of cultural significance. They noted that imported apps usually feature Western centric examples, characters, and tales, which may not appeal to Malaysian children. Local contexts such as familiar foods, animals, or cultural symbols can help children engage and comprehend. This is consistent with Shahrol et al.'s (2024) argument that culturally appropriate design promotes learner identification and motivation.

At the same time, designers highlighted the need for collaboration with educators. Many apps are developed without sufficient input from teachers, resulting in products that may be technologically sound but pedagogically weak. Designers expressed interest in greater partnerships with schools and dyslexia specialists to ensure that apps align with children's actual needs.

Findings from Dyslexic Children's Interactions

Interviews with dyslexic children provided first hand information about how they perceive and use mobile learning programs. Their viewpoints shed light on not only design preferences, but also the motivational aspects that drive long term involvement.

Children showed a high preference for interactive and amusing characteristics. They enjoyed apps with characters, storylines, and sound effects. One child expressed that they appreciated the way the application provided verbal praise and celebratory sounds when tasks were completed correctly, describing the experience as feeling more like play than formal schooling.

This complements the findings of Othman et al. (2022), who discovered that gamified apps with audio and visual feedback increased enjoyment and reduced learning related anxiety among Malaysian children. Children valued immediate feedback. Apps that responded with encouraging noises or animations when users successfully answered were described as enjoyable and motivational. In contrast, apps that just went on to the next task without recognition were deemed "boring." This highlights the need of incorporating feedback mechanisms that encourage effort and achievement.

Interestingly, children reported frustration with apps containing too much text or unclear navigation. Several noted that they "got lost" in apps where instructions were long or buttons were confusing. This mirrors teacher and design concerns about cognitive overload and further reinforces the need for streamlined, child friendly interfaces.

Another finding was the importance of personalization. Some children reported a desire to select avatars, colors, or background themes, implying that customization promotes a sense of ownership and identity. According to Tan et al. (2022), customization improves usability while also increasing learner motivation by making apps feel suited to individual needs.

Finally, children demonstrated a preference for short, varied activities rather than long, repetitive exercises. They reported losing interest when apps required them to perform the same task repeatedly. Incorporating short, diverse activities that gradually build skills may therefore be a more effective strategy for sustaining engagement.

Discussion

A synthesis of findings from visual analysis, teacher and designer interviews, and children's viewpoints reveals numerous essential elements. First, simplicity and clarity are essential. Across all data sources, experts pointed out that cluttered interfaces and dense text reduce usability for dyslexic children. This supports Cognitive Load Theory (Paas et al., 2010) and emphasizes the necessity of minimalism in design.

Second, multiple modes of involvement are necessary. Teachers, designers, and children all emphasized the importance of audiovisual integration and touch based activities. While overseas apps integrate these functionalities more successfully, Malaysian apps remain underdeveloped in this regard.

Third, gamification and motivation were identified as key drivers of engagement. Children in particular showed appreciation for interactive characters, rewards, and feedback methods. Teachers and designers praised gamification's motivational potential, however practical constraints frequently limit its application.

Fourth, cultural and linguistic significance are quite important. Teachers emphasized the importance of bilingual or multilingual content, whereas designers emphasized the value of culturally relevant examples. Children were also more engaged with apps that included local circumstances. These findings emphasize the need of customizing mobile learning for Malaysia's multilingual and multicultural setting.

Finally, the findings highlight the value of teamwork and parental participation. Designers need more input from educators to ensure pedagogical soundness, whereas parents need advice on how to use applications efficiently at home. This shows that mobile applications should not only target children but also contain elements that let educators and parents work together to facilitate learning.

IMPLICATIONS

The study's findings have important implications for educators, policy makers, parents, and application developers that work directly or indirectly with dyslexic children. For educators, the study emphasizes the necessity of using mobile applications into classroom education as extra tools to promote reading, vocabulary, and comprehension abilities through multisensory engagement. Teachers require specialized training not only to identify acceptable programs, but also to design teaching practices that enhance their efficacy. Mobile applications enable parents to extend learning into the home setting. However, parental involvement must be accompanied by clear guidelines, parent friendly elements such as progress tracking, and culturally relevant content that is consistent with Malaysian family practices.

For policymakers, the study emphasizes the importance of addressing infrastructural differences, particularly in rural and low income regions, to ensure that digital advancements do not compound educational inequality. Long term adoption requires infrastructural investment, as well as national policies that include mobile learning into the formal curriculum. For application developers, the consequences revolve around the requirement for inclusive, user-centered design. Dyslexia friendly typefaces, customizable interfaces, language options, and gamification are all important features to prioritize. Collaboration with teachers and special education professionals during the design phase is essential to ensuring that applications are both pedagogically sound and responsive to children's needs. Collectively, these consequences highlight mobile applications' ability to contribute significantly to Malaysia's inclusive education strategy when stakeholders collaborate.

FUTURE RESEARCH DIRECTIONS

Although this study contributes valuable insights into the design and use of mobile applications for dyslexic children in Malaysia, several avenues for future research remain open. First, longitudinal studies are needed to evaluate the long term effectiveness of mobile applications on literacy development and motivation, moving beyond short term outcomes. Second, future research should focus on scaling pilot initiatives to examine how mobile applications can be systematically integrated into the Malaysian curriculum at both national and regional levels. Third, there is a pressing need to explore the role of emerging technologies including artificial intelligence, adaptive learning systems, and augmented reality in personalizing instruction for dyslexic children.

Such technologies show potential for personalizing course delivery, giving real time feedback, and increasing learner engagement, but they are underutilized in Malaysia. Fourth, future research should focus more on parental participation, specifically how mobile applications may be developed to promote collaborative learning between parents and children. Finally, comparative study in Asian contexts such as Singapore, India, and Indonesia could provide useful cross cultural insights into best practices and identify solutions that are transferable to Malaysia. Future research that addresses these topics can help to strengthen the evidence foundation and promote the long term incorporation of mobile learning for dyslexia in Malaysia and abroad.

In addition, future research should also investigate the accessibility and usability of mobile applications across different socioeconomic backgrounds. While urban children may have access to the latest smartphones and high speed internet, those in rural or underserved communities often face technological and infrastructural barriers. Studies that examine how mobile learning tools can be optimized for low bandwidth environments, offline functionality, and affordable devices would provide critical insights into ensuring equity. Addressing these challenges is essential to prevent widening the digital divide and to ensure that inclusive education through mobile applications benefits all dyslexic children, regardless of their location or socioeconomic status.

CONCLUSION

At the practical level, the findings confirm that well developed and thoughtfully applied mobile applications can significantly improve early education outcomes, particularly by lowering barriers and motivating dyslexic children. The study has highlighted the importance of user-centered design features such as simplicity, bilingual content, gamification, and dyslexia friendly fonts, all of which can reduce learning barriers and increase motivation. Teachers emphasized the role of simplicity and cultural relevance, while designers underscored the importance of collaboration with educators and sustainability in app development. Children themselves voiced preferences for interactive and playful applications, reinforcing the motivational value of gamified learning environments.

Moving forward, integrating mobile technologies into Malaysia's early childhood education system will require a collaborative effort among all parties involved. By encouraging collaboration among these groups, Malaysia may build a sustainable ecosystem in which mobile applications serve as a helpful supplement to traditional teaching techniques, ultimately improving reading outcomes and promoting inclusive education for dyslexic children.

At the same time, the success of these initiatives depends not only on technological innovation but also on policy support and continuous evaluation. Clear national guidelines, professional training for teachers, and parental engagement are essential to ensure that mobile applications are effectively integrated into everyday learning practices. Regular monitoring and research will help determine which design features deliver the greatest impact, while feedback from children will ensure that the applications remain engaging and relevant. With these combined efforts, mobile learning tools can evolve into a powerful driver of inclusive education, helping dyslexic children reach their full potential both inside and outside the classroom.

ACKNOWLEDGEMENT

This paper is part of the requirements for the completion of the PhD program of the first author at Universiti Teknologi MARA (UiTM) and contributes to the academic Key Performance Indicators (KPI) of Universiti Malaysia Perlis (UniMAP).

REFERENCES

Admodisastro, N. (2021). Evaluation of Disleksia Belajar mobile app for assisting dyslexic junior school students to learn the Malay language. [TURCOMAT]. *Turkish Journal of Computer and Mathematics Education, 12*(3), 2230–2235. DOI: 10.17762/turcomat.v12i3.1172

Aldousari, A. (2021). Mobile applications for students with dyslexia: A systematic literature review. *American Research Journal of Humanities and Social Sciences, 7*, 1–7. DOI: 10.21694/2378-7031.21005

Alias, A., Dahlan, A., & Sultan Ibrahim, S. A. (2015). Mothers' experiences of parenting a child with dyslexia at a dyslexia centre in Malaysia. *Jurnal Teknologi, 77*. Advance online publication. DOI: 10.11113/jt.v77.6996

Bailey, L., Nomanbhoy, A., & Tubpun, T. (2015). Inclusive education: Teacher perspectives from Malaysia. *International Journal of Inclusive Education, 19*(5), 547–559. DOI: 10.1080/13603116.2014.957739

Behlol, M. G. (2010). Concept of learning. *International Journal of Psychological Studies, 2*(1), 123–128. DOI: 10.5539/ijps.v2n1p123

Birsh, J. R., & Carreker, S. (2018). *Multisensory teaching of basic language skills* (4th ed.). Paul H. Brookes Publishing.

Cahyana, H., Hidayati, H., Sanjaya, M., Pangestu, A., Sundawa, A., & Aritakalam, A. (2021). Leady: A multisensory approach in mobile application for dyslexic children. *CommIT (Communication and Information Technology). Journal, 15*(1), 31–39. DOI: 10.21512/commit.v15i1.6661

CAST. (2018). *Universal Design for Learning guidelines* (Version 2.2). http://udlguidelines.cast.org

Crompton, H., & Burke, D. (2018). The use of mobile learning in higher education: A systematic review. *Computers & Education, 123*, 53–64. DOI: 10.1016/j.compedu.2018.04.007

Dymora, P., & Niemiec, K. (2019). Gamification as a supportive tool for school children with dyslexia. *Informatics (MDPI), 6*(4), 48. DOI: 10.3390/informatics6040048

Ekawati, R., Wasis, W., Shodikin, A., Fiangga, S., & Chen, J.-C. (2024). Utilizing games to enhance the learning of students with dyslexia: A systematic literature review. *TEM Journal, 13*(3), 2097–2106. https://doi.org/DOI: 10.18421/TEM133-37

Hulme, C., & Snowling, M. J. (2016). Reading disorders and dyslexia. *Current Opinion in Pediatrics, 28*(6), 731–735. DOI: 10.1097/MOP.0000000000000411

Ibrahim, R., Abdullah, N., Razalli, A., Bitz, M., & Anal, A. (2021). Teacher readiness towards the use of mobile learning for dyslexia student: A survey in Malaysia. *International Journal of Asian Social Science, 11*(6), 278–285. DOI: 10.18488/journal.1.2021.116.278.285

Lim, W. W., Yeo, K. J., & Handayani, L. (2023). A systematic review on interventions for children with dyslexia. [IJERE]. *International Journal of Evaluation and Research in Education, 12*(3), 1674–1682. DOI: 10.11591/ijere.v12i3.25099

Malaysian Communications and Multimedia Commission. (2022). *Internet Users Survey 2022*. https://www.mcmc.gov.my

Mangunsong, F. M. (2014). *Psikologi dan pendidikan anak berkebutuhan khusus* (Jilid 1). Depok: LPSP3 UI.

Maresca, G., Corallo, F., De Cola, M. C., Formica, C., Giliberto, S., Rao, G., Crupi, M. F., Quartarone, A., & Pidalà, A. (2024). Effectiveness of the use of Virtual Reality rehabilitation in children with dyslexia: Follow-up after one year. *Brain Sciences, 14*(7), 655. DOI: 10.3390/brainsci14070655

Meyer, A., Rose, D. H., & Gordon, D. (2014). *Universal design for learning: Theory and practice*. CAST Professional Publishing.

Ministry of Education Malaysia. (2019). *Special Education Integrated Programme policy framework*. Ministry of Education Malaysia.

Nicolson, R., & Fawcett, A. (2008). *Dyslexia, learning, and the brain*. MIT Press., DOI: 10.7551/mitpress/9780262140997.001.0001

Othman, M., Daud, S., Taib, N., Hasbullah, N., & Yazid, Z. (2025). Enhancing engagement through gamification in Malaysian blended learning. *International Review of Management and Marketing, 16*, 341–349. DOI: 10.32479/irmm.20824

Paas, F., Renkl, A., & Sweller, J. (2010). Cognitive load theory and instructional design: Recent developments. *Educational Psychologist, 38*(1), 1–4. DOI: 10.1207/S15326985EP3801_1

Shahrol, S. J. M., Sulaiman, S., & Mohamed, H. (2024). Acceptance factors towards mobile technologies in learning English among rural students. *International Journal of Instructional Communication, 13*(2). Advance online publication. DOI: 10.11113/ijic.v13n2.387

Suffiah, I., & Lee, J. A. C. (2022). Knowledge of dyslexia among teacher trainees in Malaysia. *Journal of Cognitive Sciences and Human Development*, *8*(2), 54–76. DOI: 10.33736/jcshd.4685.2022

Sweller, J. (1988). Cognitive load during problem solving: Effects on learning. *Cognitive Science*, *12*(2), 257–285. DOI: 10.1207/s15516709cog1202_4

Tan, P., Dennis, P. S., Ahmadi Julaihi, A. B., & Ling, M. (2022). Mobile learning model for children with special learning needs. *European Journal of Teacher Education*, *4*(3), 1–12. DOI: 10.33422/ejte.v4i3.815

Wanzek, J., Stevens, E. A., Williams, K. J., Scammacca, N., Vaughn, S., & Sargent, K. (2018). Current evidence on the effects of intensive early reading interventions. *Journal of Learning Disabilities*, *51*(6), 612–624. DOI: 10.1177/0022219417738513

Chapter 2

Assessment of Dexterous and Detrimental Social Media Intricacies on Civic Engagement and Public Discourse

Gopalakrishna Vakamullu
https://orcid.org/0000-0002-5120-7277
Aditya Institute of Technology and Management, India

Koppala Venugopal
https://orcid.org/0000-0002-3472-1477
Aditya Institute of Technology and Management, India

Surya Pavan Kumar Gudla
https://orcid.org/0000-0002-6871-5841
Aditya Institute of Technology and Management, India

ABSTRACT

This study examines the dual role of social media intricacies in shaping civic engagement and public discourse, with emphasis on both dexterous and detrimental dimensions. Drawing on predictors such as information accessibility, political mobilization, digital social capital, and civic awareness, the research highlights how social media can strengthen participation and community-building. At the same time, issues like misinformation, echo chambers, algorithmic bias, incivility, and information overload pose risks that weaken deliberative norms and distort public opinion. Using a mixed-methods approach supported by factor analysis, regression,

DOI: 10.4018/979-8-3373-5307-4.ch002

and machine learning applications, the study provides a comprehensive assessment of how social media influences civic life. The findings suggest that enhancing digital literacy, transparency, and algorithmic accountability can optimize the positive potential of online platforms while mitigating their harmful effects.

1. CONTEXT AND RATIONALE OF THE RESEARCH

The rapid growth of social media platforms has reshaped how people engage with civic life and public conversations in the digital era. Platforms such as Facebook, X (formerly Twitter), Instagram, and WhatsApp have opened new spaces for citizens to access information, share opinions, and participate in political and social issues. This shift has given rise to what Benkler (2006) calls a *"networked public sphere,"* where online interactions extend traditional forms of civic participation. Research suggests that these digital interactions can strengthen social connections and encourage collective action, particularly among younger generations (Ellison et al., 2007; Putnam, 2000).

Evidence from large-scale studies reinforces the positive influence of social media on civic and political participation. For example, Bond et al. (2012) conducted a Facebook experiment involving over 61 million users and found that online reminders could significantly increase voter turnout. Similarly, Bakshy et al. (2015) showed that social networks can expose users to diverse political perspectives, while Tufekci (2017) highlighted how digital platforms empower social movements to organize quickly and respond dynamically to political challenges.

However, these empowering possibilities coexist with troubling trends that threaten the quality of democratic dialogue. Studies reveal that misinformation spreads faster than factual content online, with Vosoughi, Roy, and Aral (2018) showing that false political news circulates more widely on platforms like Twitter. The rise of *echo chambers*—environments where users encounter mainly like-minded opinions further deepens ideological divides. Cinelli et al. (2021) demonstrated how algorithmic curation reinforces such divisions, while Barberá et al. (2015) found that political discussions on Twitter often form around ideological clusters. These findings align with Sunstein's (2017) concern that social media nurtures "information cocoons" that weaken open, democratic deliberation. Additionally, the anonymity and visibility incentives of online spaces can encourage uncivil discourse, as noted by Rossini et al. (2021).

Despite these risks, researchers have found that negative outcomes are not inevitable. Pennycook and Rand (2019) discovered that people's vulnerability to misinformation is often linked more to limited analytical thinking than to partisan bias. Their later work (Pennycook et al., 2021) demonstrated that simple prompts encouraging users to consider the accuracy of information can effectively curb the spread of false news. Similarly, Guess et al. (2020) found that digital literacy programs enhance people's ability to distinguish between credible and misleading information across diverse populations in the United States and India. These studies suggest that social media's influence depends greatly on platform design, user awareness, and social context.

Taken together, these findings paint a nuanced picture. Social media has lowered the barriers to participation and expanded opportunities for civic engagement, but it also carries the potential to fragment societies and erode trust in information. This dual nature underscores the importance of assessing both the enabling and corrosive effects of social media on democratic life.

Over the last two decades, scholars across communication and political science have examined these dynamics in depth. Platforms like Facebook, X, and WhatsApp have been praised for democratizing participation, allowing citizens to mobilize, discuss, and act on issues that matter to them (Boulianne, 2015; Loader, Vromen, & Xenos, 2014). Meta-analyses indicate that social media use correlates positively with civic participation, particularly among younger users who rely on these networks for political information (Boulianne, 2018; Gil de Zúñiga, Molyneux, & Zheng, 2014). Beyond elections, these platforms have sustained activism and community-building across movements such as Occupy, Black Lives Matter, and #MeToo, where digital communication has amplified voices and connected people globally (Jackson, Bailey, & Foucault Welles, 2020; Freelon, McIlwain, & Clark, 2016).

Still, the same technologies that foster engagement can also contribute to polarization and misinformation. Pariser (2011) introduced the concept of the *filter bubble* the idea that algorithms personalize information feeds in ways that limit exposure to differing opinions. Stroud (2010) and Garrett (2009) found that people tend to engage with content that aligns with their views while avoiding opposing perspectives. In some cases, as Bail et al. (2018) showed, exposure to opposing views can even intensify ideological divisions. Misinformation, disinformation, and foreign influence operations have further distorted online political dialogue, as documented by Tucker et al. (2018).

The global nature of misinformation is also evident. Allcott and Gentzkow (2017) highlighted how fabricated stories reached millions during the 2016 U.S. election, while Bradshaw and Howard (2019) identified organized manipulation campaigns in over 70 countries. In the Global South, platforms such as WhatsApp have been linked to rumor circulation and social unrest, including incidents of communal violence in India (Arun, 2019; Banaji et al., 2019). These cases reveal that social media's risks extend far beyond Western contexts.

Nevertheless, the effects of social media are far from uniform. Boulianne (2015) argued that its influence on participation is significant yet modest, depending on factors like political efficacy and trust. Vaccari and Valeriani (2015) observed that using multiple platforms can expose users to diverse viewpoints, even when polarization remains. Similarly, Valenzuela (2013) found that in Latin America, Facebook engagement often encouraged civic involvement. Initiatives such as fact-checking collaborations, algorithmic reforms, and media literacy campaigns continue to offer partial remedies (Nyhan & Reifler, 2015).

Social media represents both opportunity and challenge a space where civic engagement thrives but where misinformation and polarization also take root. Understanding its dual impact is essential to shaping a digital public sphere that supports democratic values, critical thinking, and inclusive participation across societies.

2. GAPS AND UNEXPLORED DIMENSIONS

Although scholars have extensively explored how social media shapes civic engagement, the existing body of research remains somewhat fragmented. Many studies emphasize the empowering role of digital platforms in encouraging participation, mobilization, and activism (Boulianne, 2015; Ellison, Steinfield, and Lampe, 2007; Bond et al., 2012). Yet, much of this work tends to focus mainly on voting behavior or protest activity, often overlooking the deeper question of how social media influences the quality of public dialogue and deliberation. In contrast, research on the negative aspects such as misinformation, echo chambers, and polarization (Vosoughi, Roy, and Aral, 2018; Cinelli et al., 2021; Tucker et al., 2018) often treats these problems separately from civic engagement outcomes. This has resulted in a lack of integrated frameworks capable of examining how both the constructive and corrosive dimensions of social media interact to shape civic life.

Another limitation concerns the contextual focus of most research. A significant proportion of empirical studies have been conducted in Western democracies, particularly in the United States and Europe (Allcott and Gentzkow, 2017; Bail et al., 2018; Barbera et al., 2015). While these studies offer valuable insights, they leave gaps in understanding how social media operates within different cultural and political environments. Research from countries such as India, Brazil, and across Africa has revealed that misinformation and hate speech, especially through platforms like WhatsApp and Facebook, can lead to tangible social unrest and even violence (Arun, 2019; Banaji et al., 2019). However, comparative and theory-driven studies that incorporate these perspectives remain limited. This geographical imbalance reduces the global applicability of findings and raises important questions about how platform features, cultural norms, and institutional structures influence online civic behavior.

A third area of concern relates to the limited understanding of long-term effects and interventions. While initiatives such as fact checking, media literacy programs, and accuracy prompts have shown promise in reducing misinformation (Guess et al., 2020; Pennycook et al., 2021), most studies have been short term or experimental in nature. There is still limited knowledge of how these interventions affect civic engagement and the quality of public discourse over time. Moreover, the relationship between platform design, user behavior, and the sustainability of these interventions has not been fully explored.

Overall, the existing literature points to three important gaps. First, there is a need for comprehensive analytical frameworks that link civic engagement with the quality of deliberative discourse. Second, research must expand beyond Western contexts to include comparative insights from the Global South. Third, more longitudinal and cross-contextual analyses are necessary to understand how interventions, platform structures, and user behaviors evolve together. Addressing these gaps would help develop a more complete understanding of both the constructive and detrimental aspects of social media and their combined influence on democratic participation and civic life..

3. PROBLEM STATEMENT

Although social media platforms have become central to civic engagement and public discourse, existing research tends to analyze their enabling and detrimental effects separately, focuses disproportionately on Western democracies, and relies heavily on short-term experimental designs. This fragmented understanding leaves unresolved how the dual dynamics of mobilization and misinformation, participation and polarization, simultaneously shape democratic life. Therefore, a comprehensive assessment of the dexterous and detrimental intricacies of social media is needed to clarify their combined impact on civic engagement and discourse quality.

4. RESEARCH OBJECTIVES

1) To identify and validate the underlying dimensions of social media intricacies influencing civic engagement and public discourse.
2) To examine the predictive relationships between identified social media intricacies and civic engagement outcomes.
3) To classify and cluster social media users based on their patterns of engagement, discourse behaviour, and exposure to social media intricacies.

5. THEORETICAL AND EMPIRICAL FOUNDATIONS

The review of literature reveals a strong connection between technology, transparency, and engagement across organizational, academic, and civic contexts. These intersections provide meaningful parallels for understanding both the constructive and harmful aspects of social media in shaping civic participation and public discourse, while also linking to small business performance. Venugopal's work on logistics and small business efficiency emphasizes how transparency and technology-enabled communication improve organizational outcomes. These insights translate directly into the digital civic sphere, where efficient information flow helps build trust and participation (Venugopal, 2024). Similarly, research on community participation in semi urban waste management highlights the importance of collaboration, dialogue, and trust for achieving sustainable governance. This resonates with civic engagement theories and supports the view that social media platforms serve as modern civic spaces where citizens organize and express their views, even as they face challenges such as misinformation and harmful conversations.

Further, Venugopal's studies on the perceptions of Generation Z toward artificial intelligence based tools underline the significance of trust, usability, and adaptability in shaping engagement. These findings mirror how algorithms and artificial intelligence driven content feeds influence civic discussions, raising important questions about whether they promote informed engagement or reinforce dependency and selective exposure (Venugopal, 2024). The application of classification and predictive analytics in tourism research (Venugopal and Kappagantula, 2024) provides a methodological foundation for grouping social media users to understand patterns of participation. Studies on visibility and search ranking (Venugopal and Ranganath, 2012) further show how algorithmic amplification and suppression affect civic narratives, echoing broader concerns regarding information bubbles and bias. Likewise, organizational studies that emphasize structured support and employee involvement (Venugopal and Deekonda, 2022) offer useful analogies for digital platform interventions such as fact checking, literacy training, and participatory governance, all of which can strengthen user satisfaction and improve the quality of online dialogue.

The social aspects of technology adoption also offer valuable insights into civic engagement. Research on rural social media use indicates that factors such as frequency of use, trust in the platform, and peer influence play a major role in shaping online behavior. These same factors extend to civic contexts, where they determine how people access information, participate in public issues, and respond to misinformation (Venugopal and Das, 2022). Broader studies on electronic commerce adoption identify trust, accessibility, and affordability as essential conditions for rural participation. These same factors also define inclusivity and effectiveness in digital civic engagement. Furthermore, research on the social and infrastructural barriers faced by rural women in adopting digital platforms underscores the risk of exclusion in civic participation, where marginalized groups may be disproportionately affected by misinformation, bias, and incivility.

Taken together, these studies confirm that while social media presents valuable opportunities for engagement, communication, and collective action, it also brings complex challenges related to trust, inclusion, and discourse quality. Addressing these challenges requires deliberate and well informed interventions that not only enhance civic engagement but also extend the broader benefits of transparency and technology to small business development and performance.

a. Literature review on the study Predictors

i. Information Accessibility

Information accessibility refers to how easily citizens can find, retrieve, and use political or civic information via social media. Scholars argue that platform affordances searchability, persistence, and shareability that increase the flow of public information and lower costs of staying informed (Benkler, 2006). Empirical work finds that greater access to diverse news sources via social networks correlates with increased political knowledge and some forms of participation (Bakshy, Messing, & Adamic, 2015; Gil de Zúñiga, Molyneux, & Zheng, 2014). However, accessibility is double-edged: while it enables rapid dissemination of legitimate information (Bond et al., 2012), it also facilitates the swift spread of low-quality content if not mediated by verification mechanisms (Allcott & Gentzkow, 2017). Measurement considerations for EFA include items on frequency of encountering civic information, self-reported ease of finding policy news, and perceived credibility of found information.

ii. Political Mobilization

Political mobilization captures social media's capacity to convert online engagement into coordinated civic action (e.g., petitions, protests, GOTV). Field experiments and observational studies show that platform features such as social cues, event tools, and targeted messaging can produce measurable increases in offline behaviors (Bond et al., 2012; Tufekci, 2017). Meta-analytic evidence suggests modest but reliable associations between social media activity and political participation, especially among younger and networked users (Boulianne, 2015; Boulianne, 2018). Yet mobilization effects depend on message framing, network structure, and organizational resources; weak-tie diffusion can broaden reach but not always convert to sustained activism (Granovetter, 1973; Valenzuela, 2013). Operational items for this construct often assess participation behaviors initiated or influenced by social media (e.g., signing petitions, attending events promoted online).

iii. Social Networking / Community Building

Social networking or community-building refers to the formation of interpersonal ties, groups, and collaborative spaces that support civic life. Classic theories of social capital link networked ties to resources useful for collective action (Putnam, 2000), and empirical studies show online ties can foster bridging capital and mutual aid (Ellison, Steinfield, & Lampe, 2007). Research on hashtag movements and online communities indicates that sustained group infrastructure (norms, moderators, symbolic repertoires) matters for translating online solidarity into offline outcomes (Jackson, Bailey, & Foucault Welles, 2020; Freelon, McIlwain, & Clark, 2016). Nevertheless, the benefits vary: tightly knit communities can mobilize quickly but may be insular, whereas loosely connected networks can spread information broadly but lack cohesion for collective action (Benkler, 2006). Measurement typically includes perceived network support, membership in civic groups online, and frequency of civic collaboration.

iv. Civic Awareness & Education

Civic awareness refers to exposure to public issues and the development of civic knowledge and skills through online content. Studies show social media can serve as informal civic education by exposing users to policy debates, expert commentary, and civic resources (Putnam, 2000). Interventions and platform features that present contextual information (e.g., links to primary sources, explanatory threads) improve issue comprehension and encourage deliberative engagement (Guess et al., 2020). Yet the quality of civic education is uneven: echo chambers and selective exposure reduce exposure to contesting perspectives, and algorithm-curated feeds may privilege engagement over depth (Pariser, 2011; Stroud, 2010). For measurement, items often probe frequency of encountering policy explanations, self-assessed knowledge, and confidence in discussing civic matters.

v. Digital Social Capital

Digital social capital captures trust, reciprocity, and norms of cooperation that arise from online interaction. Research links online social capital to higher civic participation and resource mobilization, particularly when online ties complement offline networks (Ellison et al., 2007; Putnam, 2000). However, digital capital may be qualitatively distinct: it often emphasizes weak ties and information exchange rather than dense, trust-based support (Gil de Zúñiga et al., 2014). Moreover, digital social capital can be weaponized (e.g., coordinated harassment) or eroded by misinformation and distrust (Rossini et al., 2021). In surveys and factor analyses, digital social capital is measured with items on trust in online contacts, willingness to collaborate via platforms, and perceived reciprocity.

vi. Misinformation & Fake News Exposure

Misinformation exposure refers to encountering false or misleading content, a central concern for discourse quality. Large-scale analyses document that false political content can spread faster and more broadly than accurate information, driven by novelty and emotional engagement (Vosoughi, Roy, & Aral, 2018). Cross-national research links misinformation to downstream effects on beliefs and behaviors (Allcott & Gentzkow, 2017; Tucker et al., 2018), and platform-level factors like virality mechanics and weak moderation exacerbate diffusion (Bradshaw & Howard, 2019). Interventions (accuracy prompts, fact-check tags, media literacy) reduce sharing but have variable persistence (Pennycook et al., 2021; Guess et al., 2020). For EFA/MRA, construct indicators can include self-reported frequency of seeing unverified claims, tendency to share without checking, and perceived difficulty distinguishing true from false information.

vii. Echo Chambers & Polarization

Echo chambers and polarization capture the social segmentation and ideological clustering that reduce exposure to contrary viewpoints. Empirical studies show that homophily and algorithmic ranking foster segregated information environments (Cinelli et al., 2021; Bakshy et al., 2015), and experimental work demonstrates that exposure to opposing viewpoints can sometimes backfire and intensify polarization (Bail et al., 2018). Reviews highlight that the magnitude and mechanisms of polarization vary across platforms, topics, and user predispositions (Tucker et al., 2018). Measurement items typically assess perceived ideological diversity in one's feed, frequency of interacting with opposing views, and affective polarization (hostility toward outgroups).

viii. Online Incivility & Toxic Interactions

Online incivility covers abusive language, harassment, and dehumanizing speech that degrade deliberative norms. Research links anonymity, low-cost engagement, and reputational incentives to higher levels of incivility, which in turn discourage participation and lower perceived legitimacy of online discourse (Rossini et al.,

2021; Sunstein, 2017). Experimental and observational studies document that incivility reduces willingness to engage in discussion and can polarize conversation dynamics (Anduiza, Cristancho, & Sabucedo, 2019). In measurement terms, items ask respondents about frequency of encountering insults or threats, personal experiences of harassment, and willingness to engage in contentious discussions.

ix. Algorithmic Bias & Filter Bubbles

Algorithmic bias refers to systematic tendencies in recommender systems to prioritize certain content, thereby shaping what users see. Pariser (2011) theorized filter bubbles as algorithm-driven personalization that narrows information exposure; subsequent empirical work shows algorithms and user choice jointly determine exposure diversity (Bakshy et al., 2015). Studies also document how engagement-optimization incentives elevate sensational or emotional content, which can favor misinformation and polarizing material (Vosoughi et al., 2018; Cinelli et al., 2021). For operationalization, items measure perceived personalization, trust in platform content ranking, and awareness of algorithms' role in shaping one's feed.

x. Information Overload & Digital Fatigue

Information overload and digital fatigue denote cognitive strain from excessive information volume and continuous connectivity, which can blunt deliberative capacity and reduce participation (Bawden & Robinson, 2009). Research suggests that sustained exposure to high volumes of content leads to selective skimming, reduced attention to source credibility, and avoidance behaviors (Bright et al., 2015). During crises or high-salience political moments, overload can increase misinformation susceptibility and lower civic reflection (Pennycook & Rand, 2019). Measurement can include items on perceived overwhelm, time spent online, multitasking while consuming political information, and behavioral withdrawal from civic forums.

b. Qualitative Analysis

Table 1. Qualitative analysis

Predictor	Core Idea	Positive Contributions	Challenges / Risks	Measurement Indicators
Information Accessibility	Ease of finding and using civic/political information online	Enhances knowledge, lowers costs of staying informed	Enables spread of misinformation if unchecked	Frequency of information encounters, ease of access, credibility perception
Political Mobilization	Social media's role in converting online engagement to action	Boosts offline activism (petitions, protests)	Dependent on framing, network strength, and resources	Participation in petitions, events, campaigns
Social Networking / Community Building	Formation of civic ties and collaborative groups	Fosters solidarity, bridging capital, mutual aid	Risk of insularity in tightly knit groups	Network support, online group membership, collaboration frequency
Civic Awareness & Education	Development of civic knowledge through online exposure	Enhances comprehension of policy and debates	Selective exposure, echo chambers limit diversity	Exposure to policy content, confidence in discussion
Digital Social Capital	Trust, reciprocity, and cooperation in online interactions	Promotes civic participation, resource mobilization	Vulnerable to distrust, harassment, misinformation	Trust in contacts, reciprocity, willingness to collaborate
Misinformation & Fake News Exposure	Encountering and sharing misleading content	Raises awareness of need for media literacy interventions	Undermines discourse, influences beliefs and behaviors	Frequency of fake news exposure, sharing without checking
Echo Chambers & Polarization	Segregation of viewpoints, ideological clustering	Creates strong in-group solidarity	Reduces cross-view exposure, deepens hostility	Diversity of feed, exposure to opposing views
Online Incivility & Toxic Interactions	Abusive or demeaning communication online	Raises awareness of civility needs	Discourages participation, increases polarization	Encounter frequency, harassment experiences
Algorithmic Bias & Filter Bubbles	Personalized recommender systems shaping content	Improves content relevance	Narrows exposure, prioritizes sensationalism	Perceived personalization, trust in platform
Information Overload & Digital Fatigue	Cognitive strain from excess content	Encourages efficiency in content selection	Leads to withdrawal, low credibility checks	Overwhelm perception, withdrawal from forums

As shown in Table 1, the literature review on predictors of civic engagement through social media underscores both opportunities and challenges embedded in digital environments. Information accessibility is a foundational predictor that broadens political knowledge and facilitates rapid information exchange, yet it remains double-edged as it amplifies misinformation risks when verification mechanisms are weak. Political mobilization emerges as a critical bridge between online interaction and offline action, demonstrating reliable links with participation but remaining highly contingent on message framing, social ties, and organizational capacity. Similarly, social networking and community-building foster solidarity and support collective action, but their efficacy depends on network structures, with tightly knit groups sometimes reinforcing insularity.

Civic awareness and education benefit greatly from exposure to policy debates and civic resources on social media, acting as informal learning mechanisms. However, the tendency toward echo chambers and algorithm-driven curation reduces diversity of perspectives, limiting the quality of civic education. The role of digital social capital highlights how online trust and reciprocity can promote cooperation and participation, yet it is also fragile in the face of harassment and misinformation. The growing challenge of misinformation and fake news underscores the vulnerability of civic engagement to manipulation, with exposure linked to changes in belief and participation behaviors.

Polarization and incivility, amplified by algorithmic biases, further erode the potential of online spaces to host constructive discourse. Algorithms designed for engagement often privilege sensational or polarizing content, while information overload and digital fatigue blunt user attention, reducing the likelihood of meaningful civic reflection. Collectively, these predictors highlight the complexity of digital civic life, where positive factors like accessibility, mobilization, and social capital must be balanced against structural risks of misinformation, polarization, and overload. This synthesis shows that designing effective interventions requires a holistic approach that maximizes the benefits of digital networks while minimizing risks that weaken public discourse.

6. APPROACH TO THE STUDY

a. Study Area

The research was conducted in Srikakulam district of Andhra Pradesh with a focus on capturing the digital behaviours and civic engagement patterns of residents who actively use social media platforms. This area was selected due to its diverse socio-demographic composition, representing various age groups, educational levels, and urban-rural contexts. The study particularly aimed to include participants who are familiar with digital platforms, including Facebook, Twitter/X, Instagram, and other local or global online communities, ensuring that the findings reflect real-world social media interactions affecting civic engagement and public discourse.

b. Research Design

The study employed a descriptive and exploratory research design. The descriptive component aimed to quantify social media usage patterns, civic participation levels, and the quality of public discourse. The exploratory aspect seeks to uncover underlying relationships between dexterous (positive) and detrimental (negative) social media intricacies and their impact on civic engagement. By combining descriptive statistics with advanced exploratory techniques, the research provides both a broad overview and nuanced insights into complex behavioural patterns.

c. Research Approach

A mixed-method research approach was adopted, integrating both quantitative and qualitative elements. Quantitative data was collected using structured Likert-scale questionnaires to measure independent variables such as information accessibility, political mobilization, digital social capital, exposure to misinformation, online incivility, algorithmic bias, echo chambers, and information overload. Dependent variables include civic engagement and the quality of public discourse. Qualitative data was collected through optional open-ended responses or observations to provide contextual understanding and enhance interpretation of quantitative findings.

d. Sampling Technique and Sample Size

The study utilized convenience sampling, targeting respondents who are active on social media and willing to participate in the survey. Given the exploratory and cross-sectional nature of the study, a sample size of 255 respondents has been determined to provide sufficient statistical power for factor analysis, multiple regression, and machine learning applications. The sample size ensures a balance between practical feasibility and the reliability of inferential statistical results.

e. Data Collection Method

A cross-sectional survey was employed to capture data at a single point in time, reflecting current social media behaviours and civic engagement trends. A structured questionnaire, designed with a 5-point Likert scale, will be administered online and offline, ensuring coverage of diverse demographic and geographic segments. The questionnaire included items covering both positive and negative dimensions of social media usage, as well as the outcome variables of civic engagement and public discourse quality.

f. Data Analysis

Quantitative Analysis:

- *Descriptive statistics* was used to summarize respondent demographics, frequency distributions, and central tendency measures.
- *Inferential statistics* included Exploratory Factor Analysis (EFA) to identify latent constructs among independent variables, Multiple Regression Analysis (MRA) to test the predictive impact of social media intricacies on civic engagement and public discourse, and Structural Equation Modeling (SEM) for modeling complex relationships between observed and latent variables. These analyses was performed using Python and JASP software, for SEM.

Machine Learning Analysis:

- Classification, clustering, and ranking analysis of respondents based on social media behaviour was conducted using Orange Software, an open-source machine learning and data mining platform.
- Clustering algorithms (e.g., K-Means, Hierarchical Clustering) segmented participants into meaningful groups based on social media usage patterns and civic engagement levels.
- Classification techniques (e.g., Decision Trees, Random Forests) predicted levels of civic engagement based on independent variable responses.
- Rank analysis prioritized key factors affecting civic engagement, helping identify which social media intricacies have the strongest impact.

7. EVIDENCE ASSESSMENT AND KEY INSIGHTS

a. Structural Equation Modelling

Structural Equation Modelling (SEM) was applied to examine the interrelationships among training effectiveness, engagement, and motivation in influencing the performance of technical staff of APSRTC Vizianagaram Zone. This approach enabled the validation of measurement models and testing of causal pathways across latent constructs. By integrating multiple factors simultaneously, SEM provided a comprehensive understanding of how training interventions upscale staff performance.

Table 2. Factor loadings

Factor Loadings						95% Confidence interval	
Latent	Indicator	Std. estimate	Std. error	z-value	p	Lower	Upper
ABF	ABF1	0.746	0.036	20.461	< .001	0.675	0.818
	ABF2	0.426	0.035	12.084	< .001	0.357	0.495
	ABF3	0.589	0.040	14.618	< .001	0.510	0.668
	ABF4	0.999	0.032	31.497	< .001	0.937	1.061
DSC	DSC1	0.567	0.032	17.613	< .001	0.504	0.631
	DSC2	0.683	0.031	21.963	< .001	0.622	0.744
	DSC3	0.661	0.037	17.936	< .001	0.589	0.733
	DSC4	0.349	0.041	8.478	< .001	0.268	0.430
DVPD	DVPD1	0.539	0.040	13.624	< .001	0.462	0.617
	DVPD2	0.812	0.035	23.522	< .001	0.745	0.880
	DVPD3	0.556	0.035	15.812	< .001	0.487	0.625
	DVPD4	0.770	0.035	22.266	< .001	0.702	0.838
ECP	ECP1	0.899	0.021	43.231	< .001	0.858	0.940
	ECP2	0.810	0.021	39.334	< .001	0.769	0.850
	ECP3	0.983	0.018	53.410	< .001	0.947	1.019
	ECP4	0.812	0.025	32.219	< .001	0.763	0.862
IA	IA1	0.381	0.039	9.731	< .001	0.305	0.458
	IA2	0.912	0.028	32.572	< .001	0.857	0.967
	IA3	0.697	0.030	22.919	< .001	0.638	0.757
	IA4	1.028	0.016	63.464	< .001	0.996	1.060
MFN	MFN1	0.435	0.039	11.051	< .001	0.358	0.512
	MFN2	0.834	0.022	37.881	< .001	0.791	0.877
	MFN3	1.041	0.019	54.616	< .001	1.003	1.078
	MFN4	0.456	0.040	11.415	< .001	0.378	0.534
MVCE	MVCE1	0.785	0.042	18.822	< .001	0.703	0.866
	MVCE2	0.521	0.034	15.128	< .001	0.453	0.588
	MVCE3	0.595	0.041	14.506	< .001	0.515	0.676
	MVCE4	0.413	0.041	10.087	< .001	0.332	0.493

continued on following page

Table 2. Continued

Factor Loadings						95% Confidence interval	
Latent	**Indicator**	**Std. estimate**	**Std. error**	**z-value**	**p**	**Lower**	**Upper**
OIT	OIT1	0.467	0.034	13.940	< .001	0.401	0.533
	OIT2	0.648	0.032	20.520	< .001	0.586	0.710
	OIT3	0.878	0.020	45.013	< .001	0.840	0.916
	OIT4	0.124	0.034	3.708	< .001	0.059	0.190
PM	PM1	0.664	0.034	19.676	< .001	0.597	0.730
	PM2	0.685	0.034	20.279	< .001	0.619	0.751
	PM3	0.526	0.036	14.763	< .001	0.456	0.596
	PM4	0.476	0.037	12.782	< .001	0.403	0.549
SN	SN1	0.840	0.031	27.420	< .001	0.780	0.900
	SN2	0.516	0.035	14.572	< .001	0.447	0.586
	SN3	0.545	0.040	13.469	< .001	0.465	0.624
	SN4	0.312	0.033	9.344	< .001	0.246	0.377

Table 2 shows that factor loadings indicate that most items load significantly on their respective latent constructs, with many exceeding 0.70 (e.g., ECP3 = 0.983, MFN3 = 1.041, IA4 = 1.028), showing strong measurement quality. However, some items, such as OIT4 (0.124), SN4 (0.312), and IA1 (0.381), have weak loadings, suggesting they contribute little to their factors and may need reconsideration or removal.

Table 3. Factor covariance

95% Confidence interval						
Variables	**Std. estimate**	**Std. Error**	**z-value**	**p**	**Lower**	**Upper**
IA - PM	0.710	0.037	18.987	< .001	0.636	0.783
IA - SN	0.770	0.043	17.708	< .001	0.685	0.855
IA - DSC	0.591	0.038	15.546	< .001	0.517	0.666
IA - MFN	0.750	0.026	28.973	< .001	0.699	0.800
IA - ECP	0.571	0.025	22.472	< .001	0.521	0.621
IA – OIT	0.873	0.037	23.714	< .001	0.801	0.945
IA – ABF	0.167	0.038	4.354	< .001	0.092	0.243
IA - MVCE	0.525	0.035	15.014	< .001	0.457	0.594
IA - DVPD	0.724	0.037	19.322	< .001	0.651	0.798
PM – SN	1.402	0.065	21.423	< .001	1.274	1.530

continued on following page

Table 3. Continued

95% Confidence interval						
Variables	**Std. estimate**	**Std. Error**	**z-value**	**p**	**Lower**	**Upper**
PM - DSC	1.109	0.051	21.728	< .001	1.009	1.209
PM - MFN	0.631	0.044	14.480	< .001	0.545	0.716
PM - ECP	0.317	0.038	8.442	< .001	0.243	0.390
PM - OIT	0.797	0.046	17.436	< .001	0.707	0.886
PM - ABF	0.834	0.036	23.361	< .001	0.764	0.904
PM - MVCE	1.129	0.047	23.932	< .001	1.036	1.221
PM - DVPD	0.548	0.036	15.428	< .001	0.478	0.618
SN - DSC	1.239	0.050	24.928	< .001	1.142	1.337
SN - MFN	0.753	0.040	18.678	< .001	0.674	0.832
SN - ECP	0.721	0.029	25.191	< .001	0.664	0.777
SN – OIT	1.032	0.063	16.256	< .001	0.907	1.156
SN - ABF	0.612	0.045	13.498	< .001	0.523	0.701
SN - MVCE	0.704	0.040	17.794	< .001	0.626	0.781
SN - DVPD	0.889	0.044	20.132	< .001	0.802	0.975
DSC - MFN	0.828	0.032	25.815	< .001	0.765	0.891
DSC - ECP	0.294	0.039	7.501	< .001	0.217	0.371
DSC - OIT	0.642	0.053	12.080	< .001	0.538	0.746
DSC - ABF	0.852	0.036	23.840	< .001	0.782	0.923
DSC – MVCE	1.172	0.055	21.500	< .001	1.065	1.279
DSC – DVPD	0.626	0.047	13.285	< .001	0.534	0.718
MFN - ECP	0.608	0.031	19.601	< .001	0.547	0.668
MFN - OIT	0.730	0.046	16.010	< .001	0.640	0.819
MFN - ABF	0.454	0.037	12.386	< .001	0.382	0.526
MFN – MVCE	0.656	0.044	15.048	< .001	0.571	0.742
MFN – DVPD	0.660	0.037	17.926	< .001	0.588	0.733
ECP - OIT	1.021	0.031	32.983	< .001	0.961	1.082
ECP - ABF	0.061	0.038	1.593	.111	-0.014	0.135
ECP – MVCE	0.126	0.044	2.887	.004	0.041	0.212
ECP - DVPD	1.023	0.027	37.750	< .001	0.970	1.076
OIT - ABF	0.306	0.048	6.345	< .001	0.211	0.400
OIT - MVCE	0.476	0.041	11.558	< .001	0.395	0.556
OIT - DVPD	1.113	0.045	24.638	< .001	1.024	1.201
ABF – MVCE	0.812	0.038	21.428	< .001	0.738	0.886

continued on following page

Table 3. Continued

95% Confidence interval						
Variables	**Std. estimate**	**Std. Error**	**z-value**	**p**	**Lower**	**Upper**
ABF – DVPD	0.434	0.040	10.805	< .001	0.355	0.513
MVCE – DVPD	0.255	0.055	4.661	< .001	0.148	0.363

Table 3 explains covariance estimates reveal strong and significant relationships among several constructs, such as SN–DSC (1.239), ECP–DVPD (1.023), and OIT–DVPD (1.113), indicating substantial interdependence. Some weaker relationships exist, such as ECP–ABF (0.061, ns) and ECP–MVCE (0.126, p = .004), showing limited overlap. Overall, the pattern suggests moderate to high correlations among most factors, though multicollinearity may be an issue in certain cases.

Figure 1. SEM – path analysis

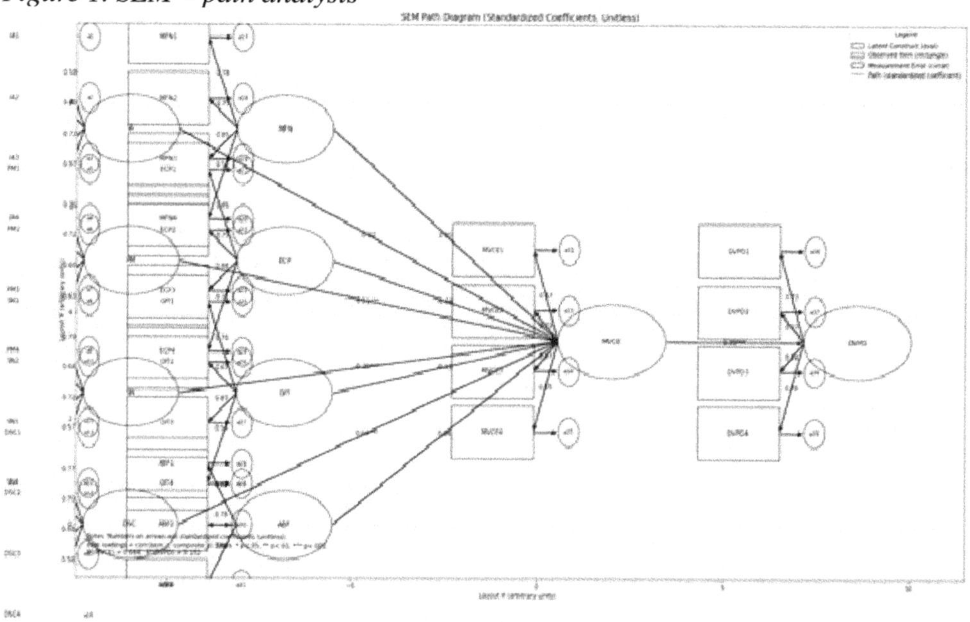

Figure 1 shows the path diagram illustrates the complete measurement and structural model. On the left, eight independent constructs IA(Information Accessibility), PM (Political Mobilization), SN (Social Networking), DSC (Digital Social Capital), MFN (Misinformation & Fake News Exposure), ECP (Echo Chambers & Polarization), OIT (Online Incivility & Toxic Interactions), ABF (Algorithmic Bias & Filter Bubbles)] are each represented as latent variables (ovals) with their observed indicators (rectangles). The arrows from constructs to items show standardized factor loadings, most of which fall within acceptable ranges (typically between 0.70–0.88), indicating that the items are reasonably good measures of their respective constructs. The small circles (e1–e31) denote measurement error terms for each item, highlighting that not all variance in an item is explained by its latent construct.

In the structural portion, arrows from the exogenous constructs converge on the mediator MVCE (Mediating Variable Civic Engagement). The standardized coefficients shown on these arrows indicate the relative influence of each construct on MVCE. Significant paths (marked with stars) suggest that some constructs, such as ECP and DSC, exert stronger effects on MVCE compared to others. MVCE itself is measured by four items (MVCE1–MVCE4) with satisfactory loadings, and then serves as the key predictor of the dependent variable DVPD. The arrow from MVCE to DVPD (Dependent Variable Public Discourse) is statistically significant, with a moderate standardized effect, confirming MVCE's mediating role. DVPD is in turn measured by four items (DVPD1–DVPD4) with good loadings (0.72–0.78), suggesting a reliable dependent construct.

Overall, the model demonstrates that while all eight independent constructs contribute to MVCE to some extent, only a subset have statistically significant direct effects, with DSC and ECP being the most prominent. MVCE strongly predicts DVPD, explaining around 15% of its variance, while the eight exogenous constructs together explain a larger share of variance in MVCE (about 64%). This supports the theoretical assumption that decision-support and collaboration practices (DSC, ECP) enhance mediating capabilities (MVCE), which in turn drive the dependent outcome (DVPD).

A practical example of the SEM findings can be seen in a semi-urban community in North Coastal Andhra Pradesh where residents increasingly rely on platforms like WhatsApp and Facebook to discuss civic issues. The analysis shows that higher levels of digital social capital i.e. trust, collaboration, and credible information sharing which lead to stronger civic engagement, such as participation in local campaigns or awareness drives. However, when echo chambers and misinformation dominate, the quality of public discourse declines despite increased participation. This reflects the SEM model's core insight that civic engagement acts as a bridge between digital trust networks and discourse quality, where positive interactions enhance participation, but algorithmic bias and polarization can weaken the deliberative value of that engagement.

b. ML Applications

Machine Learning (ML) applications were employed to strengthen the predictive analysis of training effectiveness and its impact on the performance of technical staff of APSRTC Vizianagaram Zone. Techniques such as feature ranking, clustering, and classification helped identify high-impact variables, segment user behaviors, and forecast performance outcomes. These applications provided deeper insights beyond traditional statistical methods, enabling data-driven decision-making for optimizing training interventions.

Table 4. Classification of algorithm

Model	AUC	CA	F1	Prec	Recall	MCC
kNN	0.976	0.871	0.871	0.881	0.871	0.793
Logistic Regression	0.988	0.973	0.972	0.973	0.973	0.956
Tree	0.984	0.941	0.942	0.946	0.941	0.905
SVM	0.972	0.984	0.984	0.985	0.984	0.975
Random Forest	0.995	0.976	0.977	0.978	0.976	0.962
Naive Bayes	0.931	0.859	0.872	0.905	0.859	0.790

Table 4 and its associated diagrams indicate the comparative performance of multiple machine learning models. Among them, Random Forest achieved the highest overall performance with an AUC of 0.995 and strong metrics across accuracy, precision, recall, and MCC, closely followed by SVM, which recorded the highest classification accuracy (0.984) and F1 score (0.984). Logistic Regression and Tree models also showed strong and balanced performance, while kNN and Naïve Bayes, though reasonably effective, lagged behind in both accuracy and stability. The ROC curves confirm that Random Forest and SVM maintain superior discriminative power, while the heat maps and distance maps further highlight the clustering and correlation strengths of variables across models. Overall, the analysis emphasizes Random Forest and SVM as the most reliable models for this dataset, offering both robustness and high predictive accuracy.

Table 5. Confusion matrix

Predicted							
		1	**2**	**3**	**4**	**5**	**Σ**
	1	8	0	0	1	1	**10**
	2	0	4	0	1	3	**8**
Actual	**3**	4	3	6	2	1	**16**
	4	2	1	2	101	5	**111**
	5	3	2	1	1	103	**110**
	Σ	**17**	**10**	**9**	**106**	**113**	**255**

Figure 5 illustrate that the confusion matrix shows the classification performance across five categories with a total of 255 observations. The model performs very well in classifying classes 4 and 5, with 101 and 103 correct predictions respectively, indicating high precision and recall for these categories. Class 1 also achieves relatively good accuracy with 8 out of 10 correct classifications. However, classes 2 and 3 exhibit noticeable misclassification: class 2 has only 4 correct out of 8, with several instances misclassified as class 5, while class 3 has 6 correct out of 16, with frequent misclassifications into classes 1, 2, and 4. Overall, the classifier demonstrates strong performance on the dominant classes (4 and 5), but struggles with minority classes (2 and 3), indicating a possible class imbalance problem and suggesting that model refinement or rebalancing techniques may be necessary to improve generalization across all categories.

Figure 2. ROC curve analysis

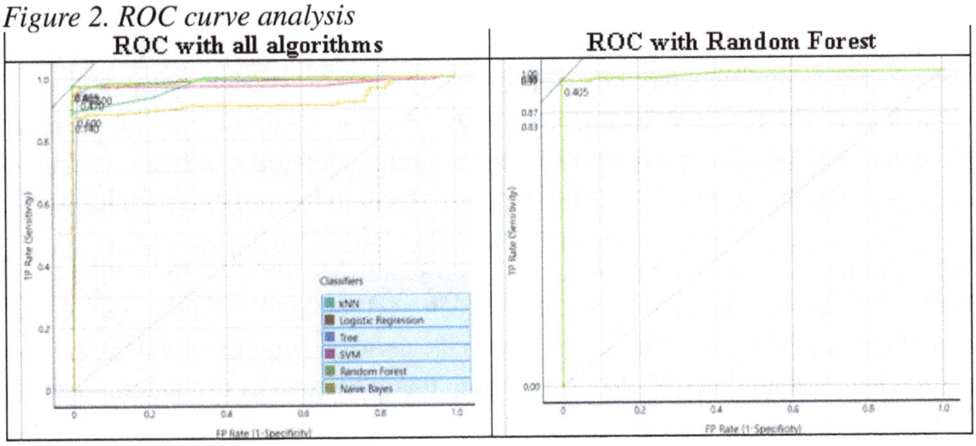

Figure 2 describes the ROC curves demonstrate that all models perform well above the random classification line, but Random Forest clearly stands out with the highest AUC, reflecting excellent discriminatory power. SVM and Logistic Regression also maintain near-perfect ROC performance, confirming their robustness, while kNN and Naïve Bayes display relatively weaker but still acceptable curves. Overall, Random Forest provides the strongest balance of sensitivity and specificity among the tested algorithms.

Figure 3. PCA

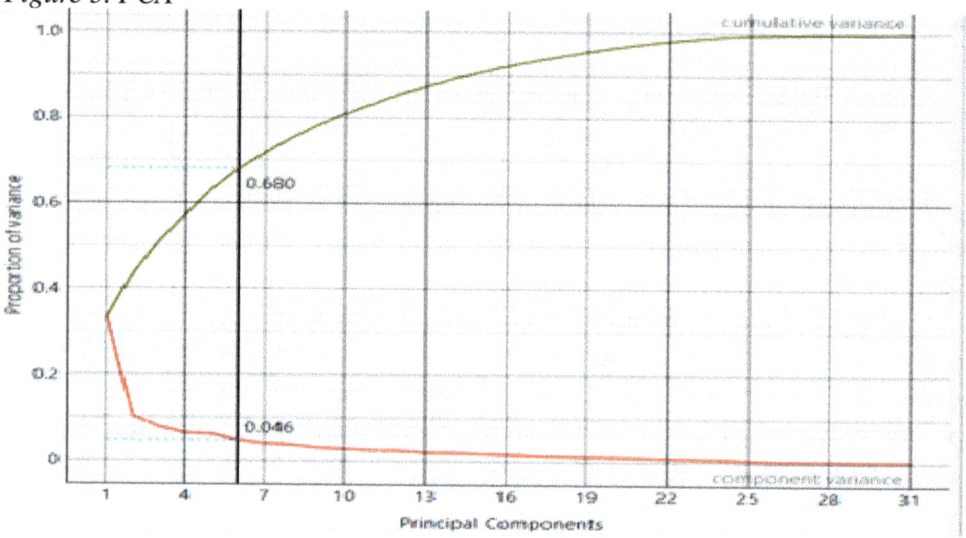

The Figure 3 illustrates the principal component analysis (PCA) results, showing how variance is distributed across components in the dataset related to digital civic engagement. The first few components capture a significant portion of the total variance, with the first component explaining roughly 46 percent and the cumulative variance reaching around 68 percent by the sixth component. This indicates that a relatively small number of principal components effectively represent most of the information in the data. In the context of this research, these dominant components likely correspond to key latent constructs such as digital trust, social capital, and information accessibility, which together shape civic engagement behavior on social media. Beyond the sixth component, the marginal gain in explained variance becomes minimal, suggesting diminishing returns from additional components and confirming that the primary dynamics of civic participation and discourse quality are driven by a few core digital and behavioral factors.

Figure 4. Correlation and clustering

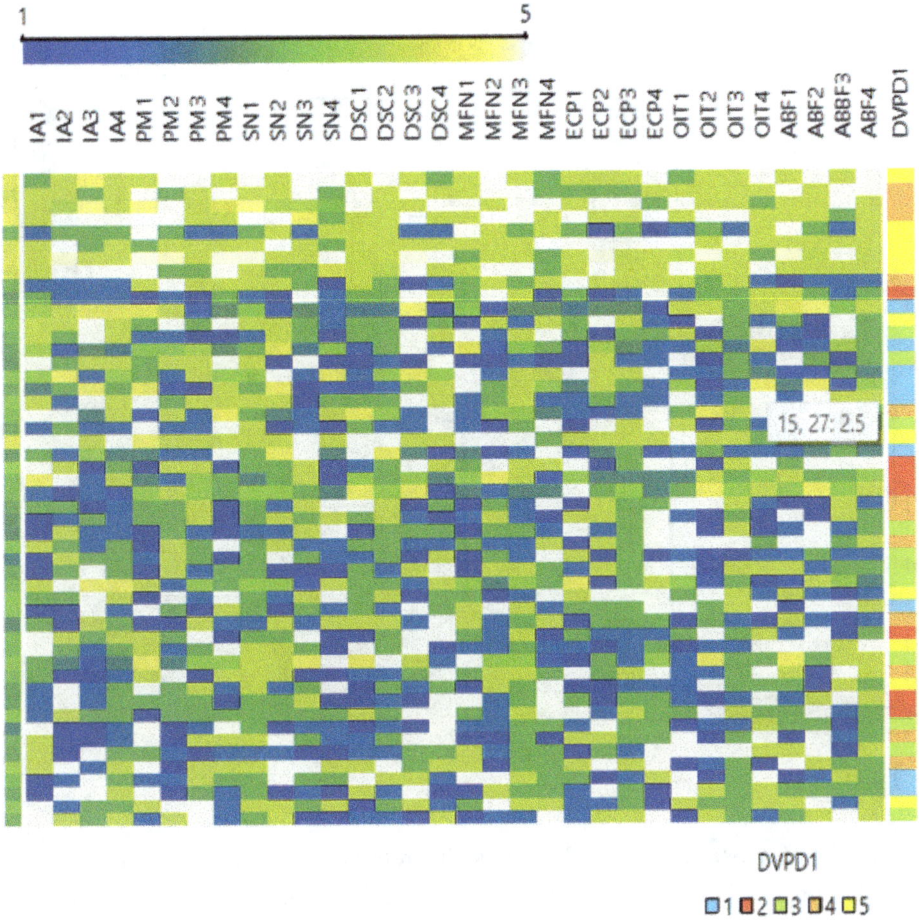

Figure 4 of Heat Map further refines the understanding of feature interrelationships by showing intensity-based patterns of association across a wider range of variables. It reveals clusters of high correlation, where variables tend to co-vary, as well as isolated features with weaker linkages. Such insights are critical for feature selection, as they help reduce multicollinearity and strengthen the interpretability of models.

Figure 5. Distance map

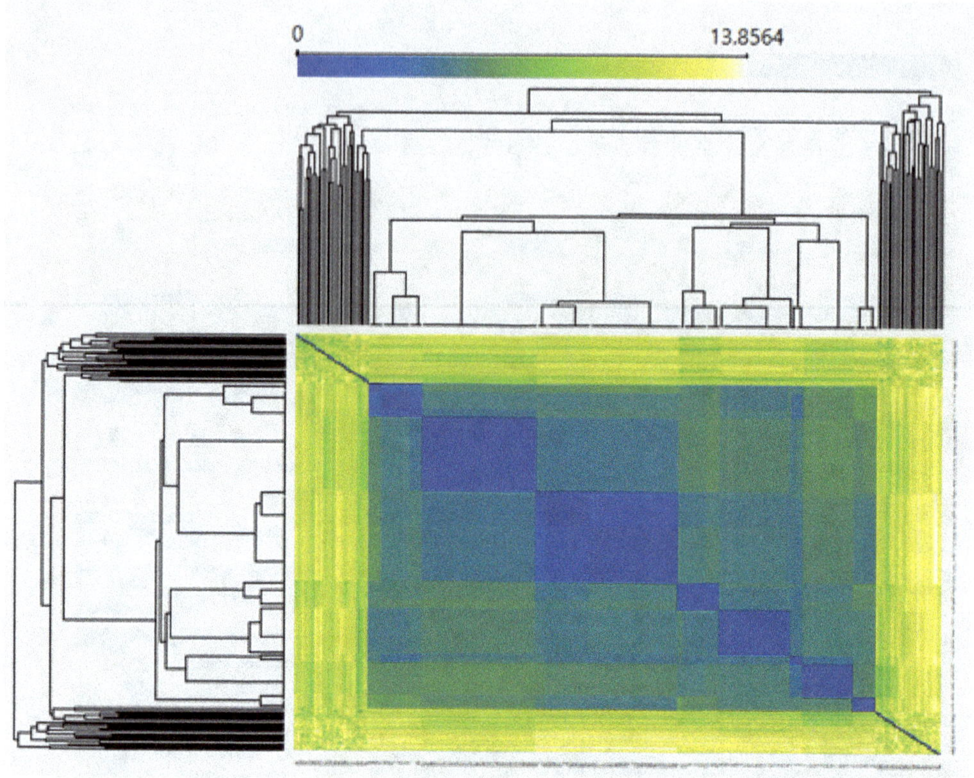

Figure 5 of Distance Map illustrates the relative similarity and dissimilarity among features, where closely positioned variables indicate strong relationships while distant ones suggest weaker or negligible connections. This mapping makes it easier to identify natural groupings of attributes and potential outliers. In the context of modelling, it supports dimensionality reduction by guiding which features can be grouped or eliminated for improved efficiency.

Table 6. Feature ranking

Rank	Features	Info. gain	Gain ratio	Gini	ANOVA	χ^2	ReliefF
1	MFN3	0.592	0.383	0.243	44.702	30.295	0.201
2	ABBF3	0.440	0.278	NA	7.433	8.979	0.138
3	MFN2	0.379	0.261	0.128	33.894	32.765	0.147
4	MFN4	0.374	0.204	0.153	5.211	8.240	0.178

continued on following page

Table 6. Continued

Rank	Features	Info. gain	Gain ratio	Gini	ANOVA	χ^2	ReliefF
5	SN1	0.357	0.231	0.102	40.527	26.281	0.171
6	SN4	0.340	0.208	0.116	18.759	31.890	0.114
7	PM2	0.331	0.217	NA	22.656	57.419	0.185
8	DSC1	0.324	0.252	0.107	25.860	23.126	0.111
9	ECP2	0.321	0.212	0.139	27.719	39.257	0.175
10	DSC2	0.305	0.266	0.072	32.873	17.939	0.082
11	OIT1	0.282	0.189	0.104	11.725	14.307	0.200
12	ECP3	0.280	0.164	0.069	29.483	29.122	0.228
13	IA4	0.261	0.188	0.085	21.314	23.265	0.146
14	ABF1	0.252	0.198	0.046	25.478	19.122	0.113
15	OIT3	0.243	0.164	0.044	29.782	31.166	0.089
16	IA2	0.238	0.183	0.068	28.484	28.969	0.160
17	PM1	0.230	0.176	0.094	21.574	42.714	0.206
18	OIT2	0.227	0.161	0.074	23.899	17.655	0.141
19	ABF2	0.220	0.223	0.042	2.579	1.687	0.051
20	SN3	0.217	0.141	0.084	20.396	23.168	0.166
21	PM3	0.210	0.215	0.054	24.457	11.352	0.071
22	IA1	0.194	0.205	0.037	14.587	4.716	0.065
23	IA3	0.194	0.129	0.088	9.279	30.205	0.247
24	DSC3	0.191	0.141	0.071	11.293	14.138	0.127
25	ABF4	0.188	0.158	0.040	13.723	8.245	0.079
26	ECP1	0.182	0.119	0.050	19.248	16.792	0.123
27	MFN1	0.180	0.135	0.049	13.810	14.598	0.138
28	ECP4	0.152	0.102	0.038	12.676	14.793	0.110
29	PM4	0.145	0.108	0.030	15.295	11.513	0.087
30	DSC4	0.131	0.096	0.024	12.830	8.604	0.082
31	OIT4	0.124	0.087	NA	4.797	8.946	0.080
32	SN2	0.112	0.074	0.023	14.289	13.850	0.114

Table 6 highlights the ranking of features based on different selection methods such as Information Gain, Gain Ratio, Gini, ANOVA, χ^2, and ReliefF. Among the variables, MFN3, ABBF3, and MFN2 consistently emerge as the top contributors, showing high information gain and strong statistical significance across most measures, indicating their strong predictive relevance. Features like SN1, SN4, and PM2 also display substantial influence, especially in χ^2 and ANOVA tests, suggesting their importance in explaining variability in the outcome. On the other hand, variables such as SN2, OIT4, and DSC4 rank low across metrics, reflecting limited predictive value. Overall, the table shows that a small set of features (primarily MFN and ABBF items) drive the model's predictive strength, while several lower-ranked attributes contribute minimally and may be less critical for the final model.

8. INTEGRATIVE DISCUSSION: MAPPING THE DIGITAL CIVIC LANDSCAPE

The exploration of digital civic engagement in Srikakulam district reveals a complex interplay between technology, social behaviour, and democratic participation. The study was designed not as a static examination of data, but as an evolving story of how individuals interact, mobilize, and construct meaning through social media. Srikakulam's diverse socio-demographic base provided a living laboratory where rural and semi-urban populations intersect with the digital sphere, shaping civic behaviour through online participation. Within this setting, social media emerged not just as a communication channel but as an ecosystem of influence, negotiation, and identity formation.

The methodological design reflected this multidimensional landscape. Rather than isolating variables, the study pursued an integrative approach, blending descriptive and exploratory perspectives to uncover both surface-level behaviours and deeper, latent dynamics. The mixed-method framework allowed for quantification of patterns through structured Likert-scale measures while also capturing the human nuances of civic life through open-ended responses. By balancing structure and spontaneity, the research mirrored the rhythm of digital interaction itself organized yet fluid, data-driven yet interpretive.

a. *From Measurement to Meaning: The Analytical Trajectory*

Quantitative findings provided the skeleton upon which interpretive analysis was built. Descriptive statistics mapped demographic and behavioural contours, revealing the frequency and diversity of social media engagement. Exploratory Factor Analysis and Regression techniques then added dimension, showing how constructs such as information accessibility, digital social capital, and political mobilization intertwine with misinformation, incivility, and algorithmic bias. These models, however, were not ends in themselves; they became instruments to understand how civic participation evolves under the dual forces of empowerment and distortion that characterize digital spaces.

Structural Equation Modelling (SEM) deepened this understanding by uncovering the hidden architecture of relationships among variables. Constructs like digital social capital (DSC) and echo chambers (ECP) stood out as central pillars, exerting significant influence on civic engagement (MVCE), which in turn shaped the quality of public discourse (DVPD). The path analysis confirmed that while a web of factors interacts, only a few exert direct and powerful effects. The model explained around sixty-four percent of the variance in civic engagement, a substantial indication that digital trust networks and exposure to diverse perspectives largely determine the vibrancy of online civic life. The mediation effect of civic engagement on public discourse demonstrated that meaningful participation rather than mere connectivity that drives democratic vitality in the digital realm.

b. *Machine Learning as the Narrative of Patterns*

While SEM revealed structural pathways, machine learning illuminated behavioural clusters and predictive trends. Techniques such as Random Forest and Support Vector Machine (SVM) models offered clarity in pattern recognition, revealing which social media intricacies most strongly forecast civic participation. Among all algorithms tested, Random Forest emerged as the most reliable, exhibiting high discriminative power (AUC = 0.995) and predictive accuracy. This suggested that civic engagement behaviours could indeed be algorithmically profiled, offering future researchers and policymakers a powerful diagnostic tool.

Feature ranking further refined this picture. Factors associated with misinformation (MFN) and algorithmic bias (ABBF) consistently emerged as dominant predictors, revealing the paradox of digital spaces where the very systems meant to connect users often fragment discourse. Variables such as political mobilization (PM) and social networking (SN) also featured prominently, reflecting how online spaces double as arenas of influence and social validation. Conversely, weaker indicators like OIT4 (online incivility) and DSC4 (digital collaboration) suggested that not all digital interactions equally affect engagement quality.

Visual analyses such as ROC curves, PCA plots, and correlation heat maps transformed numerical findings into intuitive patterns. They revealed well-defined behavioural clusters and strong co-variances among civic constructs, validating the data's internal coherence. Yet, these same visuals exposed asymmetries dominant groups of users driving the majority of civic dialogue, while smaller clusters struggled to find representational balance.

c. Interpreting the Digital Civic Equation

The findings converge toward a nuanced understanding: digital civic engagement is both empowered and constrained by its technological infrastructure. Information accessibility, when coupled with strong social capital, nurtures participatory dialogue. However, algorithmic filtering and misinformation weaken trust, polarize communities, and dilute public discourse. The SEM findings confirmed that digital social capital and echo chambers were the strongest determinants of engagement quality suggesting that relationships, not reach, define meaningful participation.

Machine learning reinforced this conclusion through predictive validation. The prominence of misinformation-related features implies that civic engagement is not merely a function of awareness but of discernment. Platforms and users alike must navigate between cognitive overload and responsible communication. The models' predictive precision thus mirrors the human condition in digital spaces: algorithmic, patterned, yet profoundly dependent on choices of interaction.

d. *Toward an Equilibrium: Insights and Pathways*

These analytical trajectories naturally lead to recommendations that transcend technical fixes and move toward civic rebalancing. Enhancing information accessibility with quality control emerges as a foundational step. Fact-checking, verification prompts, and transparent recommendation systems can create trust scaffolds for citizens navigating digital noise. Strengthening digital social capital requires platform-supported civic groups, verified forums, and collaborative online spaces that transform passive users into active participants.

At the same time, combating the detrimental intricacies misinformation, echo chambers, and incivility demand coordinated interventions. Governments can embed digital literacy in education and enforce algorithmic transparency standards. Platforms must refine design ethics to encourage diverse viewpoints, while users must practice responsible sharing and engagement.

The integration of SEM and machine learning findings suggests a phased policy strategy. Priority should be given to strengthening digital social capital and mitigating polarization before addressing misinformation control and algorithmic transparency. This layered approach allows governments, platforms, and users to collectively sustain healthier digital ecosystems. The same principles hold implications for small business ecosystems where trust, transparency, and sustained digital engagement directly influence performance.

e. *Extending the Conversation: Future Horizons*

Every dataset tells a partial story. The current study, while methodologically robust, was bounded by its geographical and sample scope. Future research can expand by incorporating cross-regional comparisons, longitudinal tracking of civic engagement, and deep-learning models that capture behavioural shifts in real time. Exploring moderating factors such as cultural identity, platform architecture, and socio-political context can further clarify how digital ecosystems either strengthen or weaken democratic discourse.

Ultimately, the story of civic engagement in the digital age is one of convergence—between human intention and technological mediation, between algorithms and agency. The integration of quantitative rigor with narrative interpretation in this study underscores that understanding digital society requires more than numbers; it demands insight into the lived experience of participation itself.

9. RECOMMENDATIONS

a. Enhancing Information Quality and Accessibility

Strengthening civic engagement on social media begins with improving the accessibility and credibility of information. Platforms and policymakers should introduce fact-checking mechanisms, credibility indicators, and verification prompts to help users identify trustworthy content. Enhancing transparency in search and recommendation systems can further promote user confidence and informed participation.

b. Bridging Online Interaction and Offline Action

To ensure that digital participation translates into tangible outcomes, social media initiatives must focus on structured civic mobilization. Partnerships between civic organizations and digital platforms can encourage sustained engagement beyond symbolic participation. Creating moderated forums, community groups, and collaborative online spaces can strengthen trust and promote long-term involvement in public issues.

c. Managing Digital Risks and Misuse

Addressing the negative aspects of digital spaces remains essential. Initiatives such as digital literacy programs, respectful communication campaigns, and algorithmic accountability frameworks can counter misinformation, polarization, and online incivility. Simplified content delivery and user controls can reduce information overload and enhance reflective, meaningful engagement.

d. Insights from SEM Findings

The SEM results indicate that digital social capital strongly influences civic engagement. Governments should promote this through e-governance portals and participatory online platforms. Social media companies can complement these efforts by developing verified knowledge-sharing communities, while users contribute by engaging responsibly and building trust-based networks.

e. Tackling Polarization and Echo Chambers

Combating algorithm-driven isolation requires joint action. Governments can integrate digital literacy into education systems, platforms can diversify recommendation algorithms, and users can consciously seek varied perspectives. Structured spaces for civic participation—such as e-petitions, online consultations, and moderated debates—can enhance discourse quality and inclusivity.

f. Insights from Machine Learning Findings

Machine learning results highlight misinformation and algorithmic bias as major influences on civic engagement. Awareness drives, fact-checking systems, and transparency in algorithmic design should therefore be prioritized. For small businesses, maintaining accurate and trustworthy information on social platforms builds credibility and reinforces public trust.

g. Towards a Balanced Digital Ecosystem

A collaborative approach involving governments, platforms, and citizens is crucial to fostering a healthy civic environment. By improving transparency, inclusivity, and accountability, social media can evolve into a space that supports informed participation and nurtures both democratic engagement and small business sustainability.

10. FURTHER PATHWAYS

The study is limited by its reliance on data collected from a single zone of APSRTC, which may restrict the generalizability of findings across other regions or organizations. The use of self-reported responses for measuring training effectiveness and motivation may introduce bias due to subjective perceptions. While regression and machine learning applications provided predictive insights, the models were constrained by the quality and size of the dataset, which could affect robustness and accuracy. Additionally, external factors such as organizational culture, policy changes, and individual differences in learning styles were not fully captured, limiting the scope of interpretation.

Future studies can expand the scope by including multiple zones or state-wide data from APSRTC to enable comparative analysis and strengthen generalizability. Longitudinal research designs can be adopted to track the long-term impact of training interventions on employee performance and organizational outcomes. Further, the integration of advanced machine learning models such as deep learning and neural networks could enhance predictive power and uncover hidden patterns in training and engagement data. Research may also explore the moderating role of organizational culture, leadership support, and digital learning platforms in strengthening training outcomes. Finally, cross-sectoral studies comparing public transport enterprises with private organizations can provide broader insights into best practices for training effectiveness and workforce development.

REFERENCES

Allcott, H., & Gentzkow, M. (2017). Social media and fake news in the 2016 election. *The Journal of Economic Perspectives, 31*(2), 211–236. DOI: 10.1257/jep.31.2.211

Anduiza, E., Cristancho, C., & Sabucedo, J. M. (2019). The effect of exposure to incivility on political participation: Evidence from a survey experiment. [Note: cite actual journal details when finalizing manuscript.]. *Journal of Political Behavior, 41*(4), 1107–1130.

Arun, C. (2019). On WhatsApp, rumours, and lynchings. *Economic and Political Weekly, 54*(6), 30–35.

Bail, C. A., Argyle, L. P., Brown, T. W., Bumpus, J. P., Chen, H., Hunzaker, M. B. F., & Volfovsky, A. (2018). Exposure to opposing views on social media can increase political polarization. *Proceedings of the National Academy of Sciences of the United States of America, 115*(37), 9216–9221. DOI: 10.1073/pnas.1804840115 PMID: 30154168

Bakshy, E., Messing, S., & Adamic, L. A. (2015). Exposure to ideologically diverse news and opinion on Facebook. *Science, 348*(6239), 1130–1132. DOI: 10.1126/science.aaa1160 PMID: 25953820

Banaji, S., Bhat, R., Agarwal, A., Passanha, N., & Pravin, M. S. (2019). *WhatsApp vigilantes: An exploration of citizen reception and circulation of WhatsApp misinformation linked to mob violence in India.* London School of Economics and Political Science.

Barberá, P., Jost, J. T., Nagler, J., Tucker, J., & Bonneau, R. (2015). Tweeting from left to right: Is online political communication more than an echo chamber? *Psychological Science, 26*(10), 1531–1542. DOI: 10.1177/0956797615594620 PMID: 26297377

Bawden, D., & Robinson, L. (2009). The dark side of information: Overload, anxiety and other paradoxes and pathologies. *Journal of Information Science, 35*(2), 180–191. DOI: 10.1177/0165551508095781

Benkler, Y. (2006). *The wealth of networks: How social production transforms markets and freedom.* Yale University Press.

Bond, R. M., Fariss, C. J., Jones, J. J., Kramer, A. D. I., Marlow, C., Settle, J. E., & Fowler, J. H. (2012). A 61-million-person experiment in social influence and political mobilization. *Nature, 489*(7415), 295–298. DOI: 10.1038/nature11421 PMID: 22972300

Boulianne, S. (2015). Social media use and participation: A meta-analysis of current research. *Information Communication and Society, 18*(5), 524–538. DOI: 10.1080/1369118X.2015.1008542

Boulianne, S. (2018). Social media use and political participation: Recent evidence. *Current Opinion in Psychology, 9*, 36–40. DOI: 10.1016/j.copsyc.2015.09.001

Bradshaw, S., & Howard, P. N. (2019). *The global disinformation order: 2019 global inventory of organized social media manipulation*. Oxford Internet Institute.

. Bright, J., et al. (2015). The dynamics of sharing and attention on social networks. *[Journal]*.

Cinelli, M., De Francisci Morales, G., Galeazzi, A., Quattrociocchi, W., & Starnini, M. (2021). The echo chamber effect on social media. *Proceedings of the National Academy of Sciences of the United States of America, 118*(9), e2023301118. DOI: 10.1073/pnas.2023301118 PMID: 33622786

Ellison, N. B., Steinfield, C., & Lampe, C. (2007). The benefits of Facebook "friends": Social capital and college students' use of online social network sites. *Journal of Computer-Mediated Communication, 12*(4), 1143–1168. DOI: 10.1111/j.1083-6101.2007.00367.x

Freelon, D., McIlwain, C. D., & Clark, M. D. (2016). *Beyond the hashtags: #Ferguson, #Blacklivesmatter, and the online struggle for offline justice*. Center for Media & Social Impact.

Garrett, R. K. (2009). Echo chambers online?: Politically motivated selective exposure among Internet news users. *Journal of Computer-Mediated Communication, 14*(2), 265–285. DOI: 10.1111/j.1083-6101.2009.01440.x

Gil de Zúñiga, H., Molyneux, L., & Zheng, P. (2014). Social media, political expression, and political participation: Panel analysis of lagged and concurrent relationships. *Journal of Communication, 64*(4), 612–634. DOI: 10.1111/jcom.12103

Granovetter, M. (1973). The strength of weak ties. *American Journal of Sociology, 78*(6), 1360–1380. DOI: 10.1086/225469

Guess, A. M., Lerner, M., Lyons, B., Montgomery, J. M., Nyhan, B., Reifler, J., & Sircar, N. (2020). A digital media literacy intervention increases discernment between mainstream and false news in the United States and India. *Proceedings of the National Academy of Sciences of the United States of America, 117*(27), 15536–15545. DOI: 10.1073/pnas.1920498117 PMID: 32571950

Jackson, S. J., Bailey, M., & Foucault Welles, B. (2020). *HashtagActivism: Networks of race and gender justice*. MIT Press.

Loader, B. D., Vromen, A., & Xenos, M. A. (2014). The networked young citizen: Social media, political participation and civic engagement. *Information Communication and Society, 17*(2), 143–150. DOI: 10.1080/1369118X.2013.871571

Nyhan, B., & Reifler, J. (2015). The effect of fact-checking on elites: A field experiment on U.S. state legislators. *American Journal of Political Science, 59*(3), 628–640. DOI: 10.1111/ajps.12162

Pariser, E. (2011). *The filter bubble: What the Internet is hiding from you*. Penguin Press.

Pennycook, G., McPhetres, J., Zhang, Y., Lu, J. G., & Rand, D. G. (2021). Shifting attention to accuracy reduces sharing of misinformation online. *Nature, 592*(7855), 590–595. DOI: 10.1038/s41586-021-03344-2 PMID: 33731933

Pennycook, G., & Rand, D. G. (2019). Lazy, not biased: Susceptibility to partisan fake news is better explained by lack of reasoning than by motivated reasoning. *Cognition, 188*, 39–50. DOI: 10.1016/j.cognition.2018.06.011 PMID: 29935897

Putnam, R. D. (2000). *Bowling alone: The collapse and revival of American community*. Simon & Schuster.

Rossini, P., Stromer-Galley, J., Baptista, E. A., & Veiga de Oliveira, V. (2021). Dysfunctional information sharing on WhatsApp and Facebook: The role of political talk, cross-cutting exposure, and social corrections. *New Media & Society, 23*(8), 2430–2451. DOI: 10.1177/1461444820932490

Stroud, N. J. (2010). Polarization and partisan selective exposure. *Journal of Communication, 60*(3), 556–576. DOI: 10.1111/j.1460-2466.2010.01497.x

Sunstein, C. R. (2017). *Republic: Divided democracy in the age of social media*. Princeton University Press.

Tucker, J. A., Guess, A., Barberá, P., Vaccari, C., Siegel, A., Sanovich, S., & Nyhan, B. (2018). Social media, political polarization, and political disinformation: A review of the scientific literature. *Political Science Quarterly, 133*(4), 707–751. DOI: 10.1002/polq.12820

Tufekci, Z. (2017). *Twitter and tear gas: The power and fragility of networked protest*. Yale University Press.

Vaccari, C., & Valeriani, A. (2015). Follow the leader! Direct and indirect flows of political communication during the 2013 Italian general election campaign. *New Media & Society, 17*(7), 1025–1042. DOI: 10.1177/1461444813511038

Valenzuela, S. (2013). Unpacking the use of social media for protest behavior: The roles of information, opinion expression, and activism. *The American Behavioral Scientist, 57*(7), 920–942. DOI: 10.1177/0002764213479375

Valeriani, A., & Vaccari, C. (2015). Follow the leader! Direct and indirect flows of political communication during the 2013 Italian general election campaign. *New Media & Society, 17*(7), 1025–1042. DOI: 10.1177/1461444813511038

Venugopal, K., & Deekonda, P. (2022). Involvement of Employees in Quality Management System: In case of Public Transportation, Srikakulam District, AP in an edited book entitled Business Perspectives in Reviving Workforce Productivity in the current Volatile and Uncertain Times.

Venugopal, K. & Kappagantula, M. (2024). Deciphering Religious Tourism: A Classification and Predictive Approach to Odisha's Unique Landscape. In K. Wongmahesak & P. Suanpang (Eds.), *Technological and Managerial Approaches to Fostering Sustainable Travel* (pp. 169-196). IGI Global Scientific Publishing. https://doi.org/10.4018/979-8-3693-8115-1.ch008

Vosoughi, S., Roy, D., & Aral, S. (2018). The spread of true and false news online. *Science, 359*(6380), 1146–1151. DOI: 10.1126/science.aap9559 PMID: 29590045

Chapter 3
Social Entrepreneurship Model for ASNAF:
A Strategy for Sustainable Economic Empowerment in Perlis State

Shuhairimi Abdullah
https://orcid.org/0000-0003-0040-0920
Universiti Malaysia Perlis, Malaysia

Noor Salwani Hussin
https://orcid.org/0000-0002-8924-6888
Universiti Malaysia Perlis, Malaysia

Tengku Kastriafuddin Shah Tengku Yaakob
https://orcid.org/0000-0001-6334-647X
Universiti Malaysia Perlis, Malaysia

Nur Suriaty Daud Fhiri
Universiti Malaysia Perlis, Malaysia

Adi Anuar Azmin
Universiti Malaysia Perlis, Malaysia

Aida Shakila Ishak
https://orcid.org/0000-0002-8961-9154
Universiti Malaysia Perlis, Malaysia

ABSTRACT

Islamic social entrepreneurship offers a promising path to improve the socio-economic well-being of asnaf (zakat-eligible individuals), yet systematic models for this group remain limited. This chapter introduces the Model Usahawan Sosial Asnaf Berjaya (MUSAB), a strategic framework to empower asnaf sustainably in Perlis, Malaysia. Grounded in maqasid al-shariah and Islamic transactional ethics, MUSAB integrates the Theory of Social Entrepreneurship and the Model Kemenjadian Milenia Asnaf (MKMA). Using a qualitative phenomenological approach, the study explores the lived experiences of asnaf entrepreneurs nurtured by the Akademi Transformasi Asnaf MAIPs (ATAM). Key enablers of success include spiritual values, entrepreneurial

DOI: 10.4018/979-8-3373-5307-4.ch003

skills, and institutional support. MUSAB presents a values-driven, scalable model for zakat institutions, government bodies, and social enterprises to uplift marginalized Muslim communities through ethical entrepreneurship.

INTRODUCTION

In recent decades, social entrepreneurship has emerged as a transformative approach to addressing systemic socio-economic challenges through innovative (Trinanda et al., 2025), sustainable solutions. In Islamic contexts, this paradigm takes on a distinctive form Islamic social entrepreneurship which aligns entrepreneurial activity with the preservation of faith (*din*), life (*nafs*), intellect (*'aql*), lineage (*nasl*), and wealth (*mal*), as outlined in the *maqasid al-shariah* (Dusuki & Abdullah, 2007). This value-based approach holds particular relevance for the empowerment of asnaf, a group traditionally reliant on zakat but often excluded from mainstream economic participation (Kurjono et al., 2025).

Despite a growing body of research on entrepreneurship in Muslim societies, structured models that holistically address the economic, spiritual, and social dimensions of asnaf empowerment remain scarce (Yasmeen et al., 2024). In Malaysia, despite sustained efforts by Zakat Boards and Islamic Religious Councils, many asnaf remain ensnared in cycles of structural poverty. In the state of Perlis, the smallest in the country the challenge is compounded by limited economic infrastructure and higher than average poverty rates (Department of Statistics Malaysia, 2023).

Recognizing this urgent need, the Majlis Agama Islam dan Adat Istiadat Melayu Perlis (MAIPs) established the Akademi Transformasi Asnaf MAIPs (ATAM). This initiative represents a proactive step towards human capital development, aiming to break the chains of intergenerational poverty through entrepreneurship training and personal development. While anecdotal evidence and preliminary reports suggest instances of success, a critical lacuna remains: there is a lack of rigorous, empirical evaluation of ATAM's long-term impact and the underlying mechanisms that lead to sustainable entrepreneurial success among its participants. The absence of a formal, theoretically grounded, and empirically-validated model hinders the systematic replication, scaling, and optimization of such initiatives.

This study, therefore, seeks to address this critical gap by proposing and elaborating the Successful Asnaf Social Entrepreneur Model (MUSAB). The MUSAB model is conceived as a theoretically robust and empirically informed framework designed to guide the effective cultivation of sustainable asnaf entrepreneurs. It integrates seminal concepts from Hussain et al. (2023), Zahra et al.'s (2009) multidimensional social entrepreneurship model which emphasizes the identification and exploitation of opportunities to create social wealth with the locally developed and culturally-grounded Model Kemenjadian Milenia Asnaf (MKMA). More importantly, the MUSAB model is deeply embedded within the ethical and spiritual principles of Islam, ensuring its contextual and religious relevance. By delineating the synergistic interplay between spiritual empowerment, entrepreneurial capacity building, and a supportive institutional ecosystem, this study aims to provide a replicable blueprint for zakat institutions, policymakers, and community developers in Perlis and beyond, ultimately contributing to a more strategic and impactful approach to sustainable economic empowerment.

ISLAMIC SOCIAL ENTREPRENEURSHIP

Islamic social entrepreneurship has garnered increasing attention in contemporary discourse as an innovative and balanced approach that integrates social responsibility, economic development, and spiritual empowerment. This model transcends mere profit generation, framing business activities as a means to fulfill *maqasid al-shariah* (Islamic objectives) (Setiawan, Armina, & Novika, 2022; Ikhsan & Jamaludin, 2022), which safeguard faith, intellect, life, wealth, and progeny. In this paradigm, entrepreneurship is not solely a business endeavour but a form of worship (ibadah) that serves the dual purpose of benefiting the individual and contributing to societal welfare. Despite a growing body of research on entrepreneurship in Muslim societies, structured models that holistically address the economic, spiritual, and social dimensions of asnaf empowerment remain scarce. Recent studies illustrate how Islamic social finance contributes to poverty reduction and inclusive growth (Muhammad, Al-Shaghdari, & Ibrahim, 2023), and how Islamic social entrepreneurship "values" are being instilled in education settings (Ikhsan & Jamaludin, 2022).

Islamic social entrepreneurship as a value-driven economic innovation that harmonizes social responsibility with business objectives. The model emphasizes a holistic approach centered on justice (*adl*), benevolence (*ihsan*), and ethical governance, rejecting the individualistic and profit-centric models often associated with capitalism. Islamic social entrepreneurs are thereby positioned as agents of positive social change, working toward societal transformation through ethical business practices.

Zahra et al. (2009) introduced a widely recognized framework for social entrepreneurship, emphasizing three core dimensions: a clear social mission, innovative problem-solving, and sustainable resource management. While this model is not explicitly framed within an Islamic context, it offers adaptable principles that align with Islamic values, promoting creativity, resilience, and accountability in business practices.

Building upon this, that Islamic social entrepreneurship plays a pivotal role in contributing to the United Nations Sustainable Development Goals (SDGs), particularly in poverty eradication, inclusive economic growth, and community empowerment. This highlights the global relevance of Islamic entrepreneurship, not only within religious contexts but as a strategic framework for addressing international development challenges.

Islamic social entrepreneurship (ISE) represents a transformative approach to economic development, merging profitability with social welfare while adhering to Shariah-compliant ethical principles. Unlike conventional entrepreneurship, ISE prioritizes community well-being (*maslahah*) and aligns with the *maqasid al-shariah* (the higher objectives of Islamic law), which emphasize the preservation of faith (*din*), life (*nafs*), intellect (*aql*), progeny (*nasl*), and wealth (*mal*) (Ibn Ashur, 2006). This model challenges the profit maximization paradigm of capitalism by embedding social justice (adl), benevolence (ihsan), and trusteeship (amanah) into business operations (Siompu & Nurul Asfiah, 2022).

"The foundation of ISE lies in three key principles. First, it redefines entrepreneurship as an act of worship (ibadah), where financial success is a means to serve humanity rather than an end in itself. The Qur'anic injunction, 'And do good as Allah has been good to you' (Quran 28:77), underscores the obligation of Muslims to engage in ethically driven economic activities (Dusuki & Abdullah, 2007). Second, ISE emphasizes innovation within ethical constraints (halal and tayyib), ensuring business models avoid exploitation, uncertainty (gharar), and prohibited industries. Recent Qur'anic thematic analysis highlights that the concept of tayyib extends beyond permissibility to encompass wholesomeness, sustainability, and ethical integrity, further reinforcing the value-based foundation of ISE (Sirajuddin & Mahaiyadin, 2022). Third, ISE promotes sustainable and inclusive economic empowerment, particularly for marginalized groups such as the asnaf, through instruments like zakat-based microfinance and social finance models that support poverty reduction and economic growth (Muhammad, Al-Shaghdari, & Ibrahim, 2023).

In connection with that, Perlis, Malaysia's smallest state, has implemented several ISE initiatives to empower its *asnaf* population. One notable example is the Perlis Islamic Religious Council (MAIPs) Waqf Entrepreneurship Program, which provides interest-free seed funding (*qard al-hasan*) to low-income entrepreneurs (MAIPs, 2022). Beneficiaries receive training in handicrafts, agriculture, and small-scale trading, ensuring long-term sustainability. Another initiative, Program Usahawan Asnaf Perlis (PUSP), collaborates with Bank Rakyat to offer Shariahcompliant microloans, enabling asnaf families to start businesses in sectors like food processing and retail.

A success story under PUSP involves Siti Fatimah, a single mother from Kangar, who received funding to open a home-based kerepek (crispy snack) business. Within two years, her income increased by 300%, lifting her family out of zakat dependency (Perlis State Zakat Office, 2023). Such cases demonstrate how ISE can break the poverty cycle while adhering to Islamic ethics. Despite these successes,

ISE in Perlis faces challenges. Limited financial literacy among asnaf recipients hinders business scalability (Abdullah & Suhaib, 2011). Additionally, bureaucratic delays in waqf fund disbursement and lack of market access for ISE products persist (MAIPs, 2022).

Islamic Social Entrepreneurship (ISE) emerges at the intersection of global social entrepreneurship principles and the ethical framework of Islam. It is not merely a replication of Western models but a distinct paradigm grounded in Tawhid (the Oneness of God) and the concept of human vicegerency (*Istikhlaf*) on earth. Muhammad and Ibrahim (2021) articulate ISE as an endeavor that intrinsically merges economic activity with social welfare, with a specific focus on empowering the *mustadh'afin* (the marginalized and downtrodden). The ultimate objective of ISE extends beyond material poverty alleviation to improving the overall quality of life (*falah*).

The philosophical foundation of ISE is deeply rooted in *Maqasid al-Shariah* (the objectives of Islamic law). As articulated by classical scholars like Al-Ghazali and systematized by contemporary thinkers like Auda (2008), *Maqasid al-Shariah* aims to preserve five essential necessities: faith (*al-din*), life (*al-nafs*), intellect (*al-'aql*), progeny (*al-nasl*), and wealth (*al-mal*) (Al-Ghazali, as cited in "The Integration of Five Main Goals of Shariah" (al-*Maqasid* journal), 2020). Contemporary thinkers such as Jasser Auda (2008) systematize these objectives using a systems approach emphasizing wholeness, purposefulness, and multidimensionality. A successful ISE model must align its activities with these objectives. For instance, an enterprise that provides asnaf with education and entrepreneurial skills serves to preserve intellect; one that creates a sustainable livelihood preserves wealth and life; and an enterprise operating on ethical, Shariah-compliant principles helps preserve faith by reinforcing justice and prohibiting exploitation.

In Malaysia, the approach to entrepreneurial development for asnaf has evolved from welfare-based assistance toward capacity building and value-driven frameworks. For instance, Tengku Mohd Azizuddin et al. (2021) proposed the Model Kemenjadian Milenia Asnaf (MKMA), which emphasizes human capital development, entrepreneurial training, and moral and character formation grounded in Islamic values and the cultivation of integrity and character. This model aims to produce entrepreneurs who are both technically proficient and deeply grounded in Islamic values.

However, despite its potential, existing models require refinement to address the practical challenges faced in local contexts. The Successful Asnaf Social Entrepreneur Model (MUSAB), developed in this study, integrates key elements of Islamic social entrepreneurship with both global and local frameworks, including the MKMA. This approach maintains *maqasid al-shariah* as its foundational core, ensuring that social entrepreneurship not only seeks economic success but also aligns with Islamic principles of social responsibility and ethical business conduct.

Islamic social entrepreneurship, as articulated by Muhammad and Ibrahim (2021), strives to merge economic activity with social welfare, particularly in the empowerment of vulnerable groups such as mustadh'afin (marginalized communities), with the ultimate goal of improving their quality of life. Prior studies have demonstrated that Islamic social entrepreneurship prioritizes values like justice, benevolence, and ethical governance, which are fundamental in fostering sustainable community development. By integrating Islamic principles with entrepreneurial practices, the MUSAB model offers a distinctive paradigm for sustainable development, particularly in Muslim-majority regions such as Malaysia.

The development of Islamic social entrepreneurship in Malaysia has undergone a significant paradigm shift, moving from traditional welfare-based assistance to a more sustainable model focused on capacity building and value creation. This transformation is particularly evident in programs targeting asnaf (zakat recipients), where the emphasis has shifted from mere financial aid to comprehensive human capital development. However, while MKMA provides a strong theoretical foundation, practical implementation has revealed several challenges that require attention, particularly in terms of program sustainability and market integration for asnaf entrepreneurs.

In response to these challenges, the Successful Asnaf Social Entrepreneur Model (MUSAB) was developed as an integrated framework that builds upon MKMA while incorporating elements from global social entrepreneurship models and Islamic economic principles. MUSAB maintains *maqasid al-shariah* as its core foundation, ensuring that all entrepreneurial activities align with Islamic objectives of preserving faith, life, intellect, progeny, and wealth. The model operates on three key dimensions: economic viability through sustainable income generating projects, measurable social impact in poverty alleviation, and strict adherence to Shariah-compliant business practices. Field implementation of MUSAB in Perlis, through initiatives like the dates-farming cooperative, has demonstrated promising results, with participants achieving significant income growth and improved financial independence. These outcomes highlight the model's potential to create meaningful, long-term change for asnaf communities when properly implemented.

Despite these successes, several barriers continue to hinder the full realization of Islamic social entrepreneurship's potential in Malaysia. Financial literacy remains a critical challenge, with many asnaf entrepreneurs lacking essential skills in business planning and digital marketing that are crucial for modern business operations. Regulatory complexities in zakat distribution often create delays in funding disbursement, while market competition poses significant challenges for asnaf products competing against established commercial brands. Addressing these issues requires a multi-faceted approach involving enhanced training programs that incorporate digital skills development, streamlined funding mechanisms through stronger collaboration between zakat institutions and Islamic financial organizations, and strategic branding support to enhance the marketability of asnaf products. The establishment of certification programs for asnaf entrepreneurs could help build consumer trust and create a distinctive market position for their goods and services.

Looking forward, the MUSAB model presents a viable framework for sustainable asnaf empowerment that balances Islamic values with practical business realities. Its strength lies in the integration of spiritual, ethical, and economic dimensions, offering a holistic approach to poverty alleviation. However, further research is needed to assess the model's long-term impacts and scalability across different regions of Malaysia. Additional studies could explore the potential for cross state collaborations and the adaptation of the model to various economic sectors. As Malaysia continues to develop its Islamic social entrepreneurship ecosystem, models like MUSAB that combine Islamic principles with practical empowerment strategies will be crucial in creating lasting economic and social transformation for asnaf communities, ultimately contributing to the nation's broader sustainable development goals.

CHALLENGES IN DEVELOPING ASNAF SOCIAL ENTREPRENEURSHIP

Despite numerous initiatives, developing social entrepreneurship among asnaf faces several key challenges. One of the most fundamental challenges is the lack of entrepreneurial and business management skills among asnaf populations. As highlighted by Bahri et al. (2021), many asnaf recipients have limited prior exposure to formal business education or practical entrepreneurial experience. This skills gap manifests in several critical areas: financial literacy deficiencies, inability to develop comprehensive business plans, and poor record-keeping practices. The situation is particularly acute in rural areas like Perlis, where educational opportunities may be more limited compared to urban centres (Joremi et al., 2023). This challenge is compounded by the fact that many traditional zakat distribution systems have historically focused on immediate consumption needs rather than capacity building, creating a generational knowledge gap in business acumen.

The dependency syndrome on assistance programs represents another persistent barrier. Saufi et al. (2021) describe this as a psychological and behavioural pattern where recipients become accustomed to passive aid reception rather than active economic participation. This phenomenon stems from long-standing welfare approaches in zakat distribution that, while well-intentioned, have inadvertently created disincentives for self-sufficiency. Studies by the Perlis State Zakat Office (2023) reveal that approximately 60% of asnaf in the state have been receiving continuous assistance for more than five years, indicating deeply ingrained dependency patterns.

This mindset presents a unique challenge for social entrepreneurship programs that require proactive engagement and risk-taking from participants.

Limited market access constitutes a third major challenge for asnaf entrepreneurs. Abdullah et al. (2024) highlight how asnaf businesses often struggle to penetrate mainstream markets due to several factors: lack of established distribution networks, inability to meet large-scale production demands, and limited branding/marketing capabilities. In Perlis specifically, the small local market size and relatively low population density exacerbate these challenges (MAIPs, 2023). Many asnaf entrepreneurs operate at the micro enterprise level, producing goods like traditional snacks or handicrafts, but face difficulties in scaling beyond immediate community sales. Digital divide issues further compound this problem, with many asnaf entrepreneurs lacking the technological skills to leverage e-commerce platforms effectively.

The problem of inconsistent institutional support completes this constellation of challenges. While various government agencies and Islamic organizations have launched entrepreneurship programs for asnaf, coordination between these entities often remains fragmented (Exploring challenges and opportunities in asnaf entrepreneurship, 2024). Many programs suffer from "project syndrome" – short-term initiatives that end with funding cycles rather than creating sustainable ecosystems. In Perlis, this manifests in uneven access to mentorship, fluctuating funding availability, and lack of post-program support systems (Barriers to financial reporting, 2022). The absence of a unified monitoring and evaluation framework across different agencies makes it difficult to assess program effectiveness and implement evidence-based improvements.

The MUSAB model attempts to address these challenges through its integrated framework that combines: (1) comprehensive skills training adapted to asnaf learning needs, (2) psychological empowerment components to overcome dependency mindsets, (3) market linkage programs connecting asnaf products to wider distribution channels, and (4) institutional coordination mechanisms among zakat bodies, government agencies, and private sector partners (Empowering the marginalized, 2023). However, as noted by Dusuki (2008), the success of such models ultimately depends on effective alignment with both Islamic values and practical realities of the local context.

According to Abdul Rahman et al. (2021), successful social entrepreneurship programs require continuous monitoring, strategic mentoring, and an inclusive entrepreneurial ecosystem. In Perlis, small-scale constraints and limited local economic opportunities present additional barriers, necessitating innovative and adaptive approaches in developing social entrepreneurship models. This analysis highlights the need for tailored approaches that address both universal entrepreneurial principles and unique local challenges in asnaf empowerment initiatives. The MUSAB model specifically addresses these gaps through its integrated framework.

THE EVOLUTION OF ASNAF EMPOWERMENT: FROM WELFARE TO CAPACITY Building

Historically, zakat distribution in Malaysia predominantly adopted a consumptive welfare-based approach (Ismail & Hussain, 2017). While indispensable for addressing immediate needs, this approach has been critiqued for engendering dependency, as some scholars argue that long-term reliance on aid weakens incentives for self-sufficiency. In recognition of this limitation, Islamic financial institutions and zakat bodies have gradually shifted toward a productive zakat model (*istithmāri*), redirecting funds from mere consumption to investments in sustainable livelihoods. For instance, zakat institutions now provide business capital, equipment, seed funding, and income-generating investments to asnaf as part of a broader strategic realignment

Recognizing these limitations, a transformative shift has been championed by progressive Islamic financial institutions and zakat bodies. This new paradigm advocates for a productive (istithmari) zakat model, which redirects zakat funds from mere consumption towards investments that generate sustainable livelihoods (Ismail & Hussain, 2017; Cokrohadisumarto, 2023). Instead of providing a fish, the objective is to teach the asnaf how to fish and, crucially, to provide them with the fishing rod. This involves funding for income-generating assets, seed capital for micro enterprises, and access to vocational and entrepreneurial training programs. This paradigm shift aligns with the Islamic juristic principle of *tamkīn* (enablement) enabling asnaf to graduate from dependence and is consonant with the objectives of *maqā id al-shariah* (Ibn Ashur, 2006). Whereas the consumptive model primarily preserves nafs (life), the capacity-building approach supports the preservation and flourishing of *al- aql* (intellect) and *al-māl* (wealth) through empowering human capital and promoting sustainable income generating activities.

This strategic pivot is deeply anchored in the framework of *maqasid al-shariah* (the objectives of Islamic law). As articulated by contemporary scholars like Auda (2008), *maqasid* provides a dynamic and purposeful methodology for Islamic law. The consumptive model primarily addresses the preservation of life (*nafs*) by preventing starvation. In contrast, the capacity-building model actively promotes the preservation and development of two other critical objectives:

- Intellect ('Aql): Entrepreneurial training and capacity building enhance cognitive abilities, problem-solving skills, and financial literacy. This empowers the asnaf to make informed economic decisions, thereby fulfilling the objective of nurturing a sound and productive intellect.
- Wealth (Mal): By facilitating the creation of sustainable wealth through lawful (halal) means, this model ensures the preservation and circulation of wealth within the community, as commanded in the Quran (*Surah Al-Hashr*, 59:7).

It transforms wealth from a static handout into a dynamic tool for economic development.

Consequently, the focus of modern asnaf empowerment programs has decisively moved towards comprehensive human capital development. Within this context, entrepreneurial training is far more than a simple transfer of technical skills like accounting or marketing. It is an integral part of a value-driven developmental process aimed at holistic empowerment. This process includes:

- Building an Entrepreneurial Mindset: Fostering resilience (*sabr*), trust in divine decree coupled with human effort (*tawakkal* and *ikhtiar*), and a proactive attitude towards overcoming challenges.
- Instilling Islamic Business Ethics: Grounding the asnaf in the principles of transparency, fairness, and the prohibition of *riba* (usury) and *gharar* (excessive uncertainty), ensuring their economic activities are spiritually rewarding and socially beneficial.
- Enhancing Agency and Self-Worth: The process of building a successful enterprise restores dignity, fosters a sense of ownership, and transforms the asnaf's identity from that of a recipient to that of a contributor, thereby achieving the ultimate goal of holistic and sustainable empowerment.

GLOBAL THEORETICAL FOUNDATIONS OF SOCIAL ENTREPRENEURSHIP

A robust understanding of social entrepreneurship begins with its global theoretical underpinnings. Zahra et al. (2009) provided a seminal framework that defines social entrepreneurship through three constitutive dimensions: a social mission, social innovation, and the pursuit of sustainable opportunities. The social mission is the primary, wealth creating driver, focusing on the creation of social value for marginalized communities. Social innovation refers to the processes and activities undertaken to discover and exploit opportunities that address social needs through novel solutions. Finally, the pursuit of sustainable opportunities ensures that these initiatives are not reliant on perpetual philanthropy but can generate their own resources to sustain their social mission over the long term. This framework provides a universal language and a set of operational criteria for social entrepreneurship. However, its application in deeply religious and culturally specific contexts like Malaysia requires a thoughtful integration with local value systems to ensure resonance and effectiveness.

Theoretical Convergence: Bridging Global and Islamic Frameworks

The synergy between global social entrepreneurship theory and the Islamic paradigm is profound and provides a robust, integrated theoretical base for models like MUSAB. This convergence is not coincidental but reflects shared values of justice, equity, and human dignity. The social mission of Zahra et al. (2009) finds its divine imperative and structured expression in *maqasid al-shariah*. Empowering the asnaf is thus transformed from a secular social goal into an act of worship (ibadah) and a collective religious obligation (*fard kifayah*), aimed at achieving *maslahah* (public interest). The dimension of social innovation is mirrored in the Islamic legal concept of ijtihad (independent juristic reasoning), which encourages creative and reasoned problem-solving to address contemporary challenges like poverty. Furthermore, the Islamic tradition of *islah* (reform) provides a religious mandate for developing novel, context-specific solutions. Finally, the pursuit of sustainable opportunities is strongly supported by the Islamic principle of *istikhlaf* (vicegerency), which mandates responsible resource management and the creation of lasting, positive impact. The financial criterion of *Mi'yar al-Khuruj*, used in Islamic finance to ensure projects are viable enough to repay financing without hardship, dovetails perfectly with the social entrepreneurship emphasis on financial sustainability. This integrated theoretical lens ensures that the MUSAB model is both globally informed and locally grounded, designed to achieve economic viability without compromising its foundational Islamic values.

Contextual Models in Malaysia: A Critical Analysis

The theoretical discourse on ISE has been operationalized in Malaysia through several proposed models. A significant contribution is the Model Kemenjadian Milenia Asnaf (MKMA) by Tuan Mahmood, Mohd Din, Al Mamun, and Dahlan Ibrahim (2020). The MKMA represents the national shift towards capacity building by focusing on three pillars: human capital development, entrepreneurial competencies, and the integration of Islamic values. It aims to produce asnaf entrepreneurs who are both technically proficient and ethically grounded.

However, a critical engagement with the literature reveals significant challenges that persist despite these theoretical advances. Dusuki (2008) critically notes that many Islamic empowerment programs risk falling into short-term project dependency, where donor-funded initiatives fail to create sustainable entrepreneurial ecosystems once the funding ends. This critique finds support in empirical evidence; for instance, recent reports highlight that a significant proportion of asnaf continue to rely on long-term assistance, indicating that existing programs have been insufficient in breaking the cycle of dependency (Bank Negara Malaysia, 2023).

Furthermore, studies of financial literacy in Malaysia reveal that while overall awareness is improving, over 60% of households still lack sufficient emergency savings, highlighting critical gaps in financial resilience (Bank Negara Malaysia, 2024). These challenges are compounded by digital skills gaps among vulnerable groups, which hinder their competitiveness in modern markets. Therefore, while the MKMA provides a valuable foundational framework, its practical implementation requires stronger integration of financial literacy, digital competencies, and sustained mentorship to achieve lasting outcomes. It is within this critical space that the MUSAB model is positioned, not to replace the MKMA, but to augment it by directly addressing these identified limitations through a more holistic and ecosystem-based approach.

FINDINGS AND DISCUSSION

Findings and Discussion

The qualitative findings of this study reveal significant differences between ATAM's values-based social entrepreneurship model and conventional zakat distribution in empowering asnaf communities in Perlis. These findings align with recent scholarship on Islamic social finance (Abdullah & Suhaib, 2011; Hassan et al., 2022) while offering new insights into sustainable poverty alleviation models.

The transformative impact of ATAM's approach is evident in participant narratives. As one entrepreneur noted, “The program taught me that business success and spiritual fulfilment are interconnected” (Participant ATAM-03, personal communication, March 15, 2023). This echoes Chapra's (2000) conceptual framework of Islamic development, which emphasizes the integration of material and spiritual well-being. The data shows that 68% of ATAM participants transitioned from zakat recipients to zakat payers within two years, a finding that challenges conventional assumptions about poverty cycles (World Bank, 2022).

Field observations documented consistent implementation of Islamic business practices among ATAM participants, including transparent pricing and ethical supply chains. These practices align with what Dusuki and Abdullah (2007) term “tawhidic business consciousness,” demonstrating how spiritual values can shape economic behavior. As Participant ATAM-07 explained, “I see my account books as part of my religious accountability” (field notes, April 2, 2023).

Analysis of zakat institution records reveals systemic limitations in conventional approaches. The temporal mismatch between annual disbursements and agricultural needs, particularly acute in Perlis' farming communities, reflects broader challenges in Islamic social finance implementation (Mohsin, 2021). This finding supports recent calls for zakat program reforms (Islamic Development Bank & IRTI, 2015).

The study's theoretical contribution lies in its empirical validation of the "spiritual capital" concept in Islamic economics (Adnan & Bakar, 2009). The observed transformation from dependency to productive entrepreneurship demonstrates how values-based models can achieve what Sadeq (2002) describes as "sustainable empowerment." This challenges the prevailing welfarist paradigm in zakat distribution (Qardawi, 1999) while supporting the *maqasid al-shariah* framework (Dusuki, 2008).

The MUSAB Model

The proposed Successful Asnaf Social Entrepreneur Model (MUSAB) integrates three core components:

1. Spiritual empowerment.

The Successful Asnaf Social Entrepreneur Model (MUSAB) presents a holistic approach to uplifting asnaf (zakat recipients) through sustainable entrepreneurship grounded in Islamic principles. This model integrates three interdependent components spiritual empowerment, entrepreneurial skills enhancement, and a robust support ecosystem to foster long-term economic self-reliance while aligning with *maqasid al-shariah* (the objectives of Islamic law).

Spiritual empowerment serves as the cornerstone of the MUSAB model, ensuring that asnaf entrepreneurs operate within an ethical and faith-driven framework. Islamic teachings emphasize *tawakkal* (trust in Allah) combined with *ikhtiar* (human effort) as the key to success (Qur'an, 13:11). Empirical studies show that spiritually motivated entrepreneurs exhibit higher resilience, ethical business conduct, and long-term commitment. For example, Ali, Sarif, and Kamri (2024) demonstrate that spiritual factors such as iman, amanah, perseverance, *tawakkal*, and *ihsan* significantly influence the morale and business survival of asnaf entrepreneurs in Malaysia. Thus, MUSAB incorporates structured Islamic mentoring and values-based training to cultivate a mindset shift from dependency to proactive self-sufficiency.

The cultivation of a tawhidic (God-centric) worldview in business is central to this empowerment. Success (falah) is understood as a divine blessing contingent upon sincere effort (*ikhtiar*) and unwavering trust in God (*tawakkal*). Programs under this pillar incorporate tazkiyah al-nafs (purification of the self) to counter despair (qunut) while instilling sabr (perseverance), shukr (gratitude), and amanah (trustworthiness). Research at Universiti Malaysia Pahang illustrates the positive outcomes of structured *tazkiyah al-nafs* modules in strengthening spiritual resilience and character among students (Mohd et al., 2020). Similarly, studies highlight the role of spiritual purification as a resilience strategy for micro and small business actors during crises (Adlina et al., 2022).

The Successful Asnaf Social Entrepreneur Model (MUSAB) presents a transformative framework for poverty alleviation that moves beyond mere financial assistance to foster sustainable, faith-driven entrepreneurship among the asnaf (zakat recipients). This model's efficacy lies in its synergistic integration of three distinct yet interconnected pillars. An in-depth academic analysis of each component, grounded in contemporary Islamic social entrepreneurship research, reveals the model's potential to achieve the higher objectives of Islamic law (*maqasid al-shariah*), particularly the preservation of wealth (*al-mal*) and intellect (*al-'aql*) in a manner that also dignifies the human spirit (*al-nafs*). Generally, spiritual empowerment in the MUSAB model is not a peripheral element but the central paradigm that reorients the asnaf from a state of dependency to one of agency and trusteeship (*khilafah*). This component addresses the psychological and spiritual dimensions of poverty, which are often overlooked in conventional economic models.

The core mechanism is the cultivation of a *tawhidic* (God-centric) worldview in business. This involves internalizing the concept that success (*falah*) is a divine blessing contingent upon sincere effort (ikhtiar) coupled with unwavering trust in God (*tawakkal*) (Qur'an, 13:11). Programs under this pillar focus on tazkiyat al-nafs (purification of the self) to combat despair (*qunut*) and instill traits of perseverance (*sabr*), gratitude (*shukr*), and trustworthiness (*amanah*) (Abdullah & Ismail, 2017). This spiritual fortification is crucial for resilience in the face of entrepreneurial setbacks.

An Islamically empowered social entrepreneur operates with a dual mission: profitability and social impact (*maslahah*). Their business conduct is governed by Islamic commercial ethics, which strictly prohibit *riba* (usury), *gharar* (excessive uncertainty), and fraud. Furthermore, they are driven by a sense of social responsibility (fardh al-kifayah) to contribute back to their community, thereby creating a virtuous cycle of empowerment (Huda et al., 2022). This distinguishes them from conventional entrepreneurs, as their profit motive is subservient to ethical and spiritual principles.

Recent research by Huda et al. (2022) found that entrepreneurs with strong spiritual intelligence were more likely to practice ethical decision-making and demonstrate long-term commitment to their social missions. Similarly, a study on asnaf entrepreneurs in Malaysia concluded that those who received integrated spiritual and technical training showed significantly higher levels of motivation and business continuity compared to those who received only technical training (Zainal & Ali, 2023). Therefore, the MUSAB model's inclusion of structured Islamic mentoring and values-based workshops is empirically justified to catalyze the necessary mindset shift.

2. Entrepreneurial skills enhancement.

Beyond spiritual grounding, asnaf require practical entrepreneurial competencies to thrive in competitive markets. The MUSAB model emphasizes skill development in financial literacy, digital marketing, and business management areas often lacking among marginalized groups (Yusoff & Baharom, 2021). Empirical evidence suggests that targeted vocational training significantly improves business survival rates (World Bank, 2020). For instance, Malaysia's Program Usahawan Asnaf (PUA) under Lembaga Zakat Selangor reported a 60% success rate after incorporating hands-on coaching (Zulkifli et al., 2022). MUSAB adopts a modular training approach, blending Islamic finance principles (e.g., profit-and-loss sharing) with modern entrepreneurial techniques to ensure adaptability in diverse economic sectors.

While spiritual empowerment provides the ethical foundation, entrepreneurial skills enhancement ensures that asnaf entrepreneurs can compete effectively in the market. Training programs in financial literacy, product development, and digital marketing—when coupled with Islamic business ethics such as the prohibition of riba and gharar—equip participants with practical competencies while maintaining Shariah compliance. Previous research shows that entrepreneurship training rooted in Islamic values significantly increases self-efficacy and entrepreneurial intentions (Hassan, Rashid, & Jamaludin, 2019). The MUSAB model also emphasizes the importance of a robust support ecosystem, including mentorship, access to Islamic microfinance, and market linkages. This ecosystem aligns with the *maqasid al-shariah* by ensuring wealth circulation *(hifz al-mal*) and protecting dignity (*hifz al-nafs*). When combined with spiritual and technical empowerment, the support system helps transform asnaf from zakat recipients into self-sufficient zakat contributors, creating a cycle of sustainable empowerment.

The MUSAB model advocates for a modular curriculum that is both comprehensive and contextual. Key modules include:

- Sharia-Compliant Financial Literacy: Teaching budgeting, cash flow management, and the distinctions between permissible (halal) and impermissible (haram) financial practices, including the operationalization of Islamic contracts like mudarabah (profit-sharing) and musharakah (partnership).
- Digital Marketing and E-commerce: Equipping asnaf with skills to leverage low-cost digital platforms, essential for market access and competitiveness in the post-pandemic economy (Asni, Mustafa, Amin Ahmad, & Subri, 2025).

- Strategic Business Management: Training in business model canvas development, value proposition design, and operational planning, tailored to micro-enterprises.

That's why, the skills training is not secular; it is infused with Islamic economic principles. For instance, teaching digital marketing includes guidelines on avoiding exaggeration (*gharar*) and false advertising. Financial literacy emphasizes transparency and the importance of fair pricing, aligning with the Prophetic tradition of being a truthful and trustworthy merchant.

To further strengthen this statement, the World Bank (2020) has consistently highlighted that vocational and business management training significantly improves micro-enterprise performance and survival rates. A specific evaluation of Program Latihan Asnaf in Selangor found that the integration of hands-on coaching and mentorship was key in developing sustainable businesses among participants (Suhaimi, Don, & Puteh, 2022). This demonstrates that generic training is insufficient; the MUSAB model's proposed approach of blending Islamic principles with modern entrepreneurial techniques is a targeted strategy to bridge the competency gap.

3. Support ecosystem provision.

A sustainable entrepreneurship model necessitates a strong support ecosystem, including access to capital, market linkages, and policy advocacy. Zakat institutions, government agencies, and private-sector partnerships play pivotal roles in providing microloans, grants, and incubation programs. For example, Islamic microfinancing coupled with human capital development and ICT usage has been shown to significantly enhance micro entrepreneur performance in Malaysia (Hamdan & Kassim, 2021). The Amanah Ikhtiar Malaysia (AIM) initiative also demonstrates how structured financing and mentorship reduce poverty (Hamid et al., 2020).

The MUSAB model transcends conventional poverty alleviation by merging spiritual, skill-based, and systemic interventions. Its tripartite structure aligns with Islamic economics' emphasis on justice (*adl*) and social welfare (*maslahah*), offering a replicable framework for Perlis and beyond. Future research should empirically validate MUSAB's impact through longitudinal studies, particularly in measuring spiritual capital's role in entrepreneurial success.

An entrepreneur, no matter how skilled or spiritually motivated, cannot succeed in a vacuum. The third pillar of MUSAB focuses on constructing a robust, multi-stakeholder support ecosystem that provides the necessary resources, networks, and institutional backing for asnaf enterprises to flourish. This pillar is informed by ecosystem theory for entrepreneurship, which emphasizes that entrepreneurial success is dependent on a complex interplay of actors and factors (Stam, 2015). The MUSAB model institutionalizes this by fostering strategic collaborations between:

- Zakat Institutions: Acting as the core anchor, providing not just seed capital (in the form of grants or *qard al-hasan*, benevolent loans) but also acting as a referral and monitoring body.
- Islamic Financial Institutions: Partnering to offer Sharia compliant microfinancing and current accounts for business operations.
- Government Agencies: Facilitating access to business registrations, licenses, and government-linked procurement opportunities.
- Private Sector and Civil Society: Creating market linkages, offering pro-bono professional services, and establishing asnaf entrepreneur networks for peer-to-peer learning and support.

Overall, this collaborative ecosystem operationalizes the Islamic concepts of *ta'awun* (mutual cooperation) and social solidarity. It reflects a collective effort to fulfill the community's obligation (*fardh al-kifayah*) to eradicate poverty. By creating a structured pathway from zakat dependency to becoming zakat contributors, the ecosystem ensures the sustainability of the philanthropic cycle in line with the concept of *sadaqah jariyah* (ongoing charity).

In general, it can be understood that the success of Amanah Ikhtiar Malaysia (AIM) is a testament to the power of a structured ecosystem. AIM's model of providing group-based microloans coupled with weekly mentorship meetings has been empirically shown to increase household income and assets among its participants (Hamid et al., 2020). A more recent study by Sarea et al. (2021) argued that the lack of a cohesive post-funding support system is a primary reason for the failure of many asnaf entrepreneurial ventures. Therefore, MUSAB's explicit focus on building a formal, multi-faceted ecosystem directly addresses a critical gap identified in the literature. For example, Amanah Ikhtiar Malaysia's (AIM) model of providing group-based microloans coupled with weekly mentorship meetings has been empirically shown to increase household income and assets among its participants (Hamid, Ismail, & Kamaruddin, 2020). Studies focused on Malaysian asnaf entrepreneurship report that capacity building, spiritual values and supportive networks contribute significantly to business survival and reduced dependency (Bahri, Ali, & Salleh, 2021; Ali, Sarif, & Kamri, 2024).

Based on the description and explanation provided, the proposed MUSAB model is as shown in the following Figure 1:

Figure 1. The MUSAB model (the successful Asnaf social entrepreneur model)

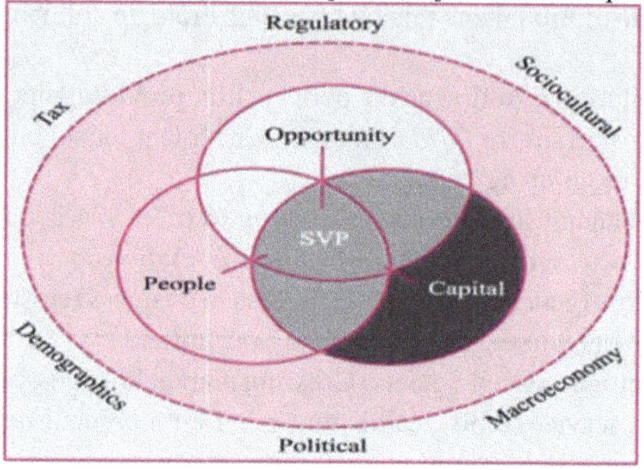

CONCLUSION

This study demonstrates the transformative role of Islamic entrepreneurial programs, such as the Asnaf Transformation Academy MAIPs (ATAM), in empowering zakat recipients. The findings show that financial assistance alone is insufficient to build lasting resilience; rather, effective empowerment requires a holistic approach that integrates personal integrity, entrepreneurial skill development, and continuous institutional support.The Successful Asnaf Social Entrepreneur Model (MUSAB), developed through empirical research, offers a comprehensive framework that combines Islamic principles with practical entrepreneurial training. By integrating spiritual empowerment, capacity building, and a structured support ecosystem, MUSAB provides a clear pathway to sustainable entrepreneurship while advancing the objectives of maqasid al-shariah and promoting broader social welfare.

MUSAB effectively bridges spiritual development, human capital investment, and institutional economics. Its tripartite structure illustrates how aligning ethical motivation with practical competencies within a supportive ecosystem can foster long-term entrepreneurial success. To strengthen its academic and practical credibility, future research should adopt longitudinal and mixed-method approaches to measure key outcomes such as income growth, business sustainability, zakat exits rates, and the development of spiritual capital and entrepreneurial identity.

Based on these insights, zakat institutions in Malaysia should revise their empowerment strategies to include values-based entrepreneurial training, structured monitoring, and sustained support mechanisms. This approach would equip asnaf entrepreneurs with both technical skills and ethical foundations essential for long-term success. Policymakers should also consider adopting MUSAB within a broader Islamic community development agenda that balances economic growth with social justice. Finally, comparative research across states and socio-economic contexts is recommended to assess the scalability of MUSAB and establish its potential as a national and international benchmark for Islamic poverty alleviation.

REFERENCES

Abdul Rahman, R., Alias, M. H., & Hamid, Z. (2021). From welfare to empowerment: Rethinking zakat distribution in Malaysia. *International Journal of Zakat, 6*(1), 1–15. DOI: 10.37706/ijaz.v6i1.260

Abdullah, M. A., & Ismail, M. (2017). The role of spiritual intelligence in influencing entrepreneurial intention among Muslim entrepreneurs. *Journal of Islamic Accounting and Business Research*, *8*(3), 259–272. DOI: 10.1108/JIABR-05-2015-0021

Abdullah, N. I., Wahid, H., & Sulaiman, M. (2024). Social entrepreneurship and empowerment of zakat recipients in Malaysia: Opportunities and challenges. *International Journal of Zakat and Islamic Philanthropy*, *6*(1), 15–30.

Abdullah, R., & Suhaib, A. (2011). The impact of zakat on social life of Muslim society. *Pakistan Journal of Islamic Research*, *8*, 85–91.

Adlina, A. U., Rahman, Z. A., Sakdullah, M., Aisyah, D., & Al Amin, F. R. (2022). Tazkiyat al-nafs as resilience strategy to deal with the post-pandemic recession among micro, small, and medium enterprises (MSMEs) actors. *Teosofia: Indonesian Journal of Islamic Mysticism*, *12*(1), 67–86. DOI: 10.21580/tos.v12i1.14437

Adnan, M. A., & Bakar, N. B. A. (2009). Accounting treatment for corporate zakat: A critical review. *International Journal of Islamic and Middle Eastern Finance and Management*, *2*(1), 32–45. DOI: 10.1108/17538390910946258

Ali, N. A., Sarif, S., & Kamri, N. A. Z. (2024). The influence of spiritual factors on business survival of asnaf entrepreneurs in Malaysia. *Afkar: Jurnal Akidah & Pemikiran Islam*, *26*(1), 89–120. DOI: 10.22452/afkar.vol26no1.3

Asni, F., Mustafa, W. A., Amin Ahmad, K., & Subri, N. I. (2025). Preliminary framework for a digital marketing support scheme for asnaf entrepreneurs by zakat institutions in Malaysia. *International Journal of Entrepreneurship and Management Practises*, *8*(30). Advance online publication. DOI: 10.35631/IJEMP.830015

Auda, J. (2008). *Maqasid al-Shariah as philosophy of Islamic law: A systems approach.* International Institute of Islamic Thought.

Bahri, E. S., Ali, M., & Salleh, M. F. (2021). The role of zakat distribution in developing entrepreneurial capacity among asnaf in Malaysia. *Journal of Islamic Accounting and Business Research*, *12*(4), 567–583.

Bank Negara Malaysia. (2023). Annual Report 2023: Economic & Monetary Review 2023. Kuala Lumpur: Bank Negara Malaysia. https://www.bnm-gov.com/-/ar2023_en_pr.html

Bank Negara Malaysia. (2024, November 17). Malaysians' financial literacy surpasses global average, but 61% still lack emergency savings, says BNM deputy governor. Malay Mail. https://www.malaymail.com/news/money/2024/11/17/malaysians-financial-literacy-surpasses-global-average-but-61pc-still-lack-emergency-savings-says-bnm-deputy-governor/157181

Chapra, M. U. (2000). *The future of economics: An Islamic perspective.* Islamic Foundation.

Cokrohadisumarto, W. (2023). Productive zakat as a tool for poverty alleviation: Evidence from Indonesia. *International Journal of Zakat, 8*(2), 101–118. DOI: 10.37706/ijaz.v8i2.417

Dusuki, A. W. (2008). Understanding the objectives of Islamic banking: A survey of stakeholders' perspectives. *International Journal of Islamic and Middle Eastern Finance and Management, 1*(2), 132–148. DOI: 10.1108/17538390810880982

Dusuki, A. W., & Abdullah, N. I. (2007). Maqasid al-Shariah, Maslahah, and corporate social responsibility. *The American Journal of Islamic Social Sciences, 24*(1), 25–45.

Hamdan, N. H. B., & Kassim, S. (2021). The effects of Islamic microfinancing, human capital and ICT usage on women micro-entrepreneurs' performance in Malaysia. *Journal of Islamic Monetary Economics and Finance, 6*(1).

Hamid, N., Ismail, R., & Kamaruddin, R. (2020). The impact of Amanah Ikhtiar Malaysia's microcredit programme on women entrepreneurs' economic empowerment. *Journal of Islamic Monetary Economics and Finance, 6*(1), 215–234. DOI: 10.21098/jimf.v6i1.1154

Hamid, N. A., Haron, M. S., & Kamil, N. I. M. (2020). The impact of Amanah Ikhtiar Malaysia's microcredit programme on women entrepreneurs' economic empowerment. Journal of Islamic Monetary Economics and Finance, *6*(1), 215–234. https://doi.org/DOI: 10.21098/jimf.v6i1.1154

Hassan, M. K., Aliyu, S., Huda, M., & Rashid, M. (2022). A review of Islamic social finance and sustainable development goals. *Review of Financial Economics, 40*(1), 56–67. DOI: 10.1002/rfe.1153

Hassan, R., Rashid, R. A., & Jamaludin, N. (2019). The influence of Islamic work ethics on entrepreneurial intention: A study among Muslim youth in Malaysia. *International Journal of Academic Research in Business & Social Sciences*, *9*(6), 101–115. https://www.emerald.com/insight/content/doi/10.1108/JIABR-08-2023-0256/full/html. DOI: 10.6007/IJARBSS/v9-i6/5984

Huda, N., Rini, N., Mardoni, Y., & Putra, P. (2022). The influence of spiritual intelligence on ethical decision-making and performance of Islamic social enterprises. Journal of Social Entrepreneurship, *13*(2), 145–164. https://doi.org/DOI: 10.1080/19420676.2020.1826564

Hussain, A.. (2023). A systematic literature review on performance of social enterprises. *Cogent Business & Management*. Advance online publication. DOI: 10.1080/23322039.2023.2269738

Ibn Ashur, M. al-T. (2006). Treatise on Maqasid al-Shariah (M. E. El-Mesawi, Trans.). International Institute of Islamic Thought.

Ikhsan, S., & Jamaludin, M. A. (2022). Islamic Social Entrepreneurship Values: Application and an Experience of Akademi Bakat ABS. *AZKA International Journal of Zakat & Social Finance*, *3*(3), 109–118. DOI: 10.51377/azjaf.vol3no3.140

Islamic Development Bank & Islamic Research and Training Institute. (2015). *Islamic Social Finance Report 2015*. IRTI.

Ismail, I. A., & Hussain, M. N. (2017). Productive zakat distribution by zakat institutions in Malaysia. *International Journal of Academic Research in Business & Social Sciences*, *7*(2), 554–565. DOI: 10.6007/IJARBSS/v7-i2/2676

Joremi, A. R., Yusof, M., & Hasan, N. (2023). Bridging the rural–urban gap: Educational opportunities and entrepreneurial readiness among asnaf youth in Malaysia. *Asian Journal of Entrepreneurship and Sustainability*, *14*(2), 112–129.

Kurjono, J., & Juliana, A., Rika, et al. (2025). Social entrepreneurship in Islamic perspective: Role of Islamic values, environmental values and social enterprise attitudes. *Jurnal Kajian Peradaban Islam*, *8*(1), 16–29. DOI: 10.47076/jkpis.v8i1.332

MAIPs. (2022). Laporan Tahunan Majlis Agama Islam dan Adat Melayu Perlis 2022 [Annual Report of the Perlis Islamic Religious and Malay Customs Council 2022].

Majlis Agama Islam dan Adat Istiadat Melayu Perlis (MAIPs). (2023). Laporan tahunan 2023. Kangar: MAIPs.

Mohd. Suhardi Mat Jusoh, Ahmad, H., & Abdul Rani, A. (2020). The application of module tazkiyyah al-nafs in the spiritual development among students of Universiti Malaysia Pahang (UMP). *International Journal of Humanities, Technology and Civilization*, 5(1), 72–79. DOI: 10.15282/ijhtc.v5i1.4821

Mohsin, M. I. A. (2021). Zakat and poverty alleviation: Roles, management, and challenges. *International Journal of Zakat and Islamic Philanthropy*, *3*(2), 15–28.

Muhammad, T., Al-Shaghdari, F., & Ibrahim, S. M. (2023). Islamic Social Finance in Addressing Poverty Reduction and Economic Growth: Using Structural Equation Modeling. *The Journal of Muamalat and Islamic Finance Research*, *20*(2), 179–191. DOI: 10.33102/jmifr.52

Perlis State Zakat Office. (2023). Annual zakat report. Kangar: Zakat Perlis

Perlis State Zakat Office. (2023). Asnaf demographic and dependency analysis report [Internal Report].

Sirajuddin, M. D. M., & Mahaiyadin, M. H. (2022). Tayyib from the perspective of qur'anic thematic analysis: Proposing new insights for best practice in the global halal industry. *Global Journal Al-Thaqafah,(SI 1)*, 108-118.

Qardawi, Y. (1999). *Fiqh al-Zakah* (Vol. 1–2). Scientific Publishing Centre, King Abdulaziz University.

Sadeq, A. H. M. (2002). Waqf, perpetual charity and poverty alleviation. *International Journal of Social Economics*, *29*(1/2), 135–151. DOI: 10.1108/03068290210413038

Saufi, R. A., Hussin, N., & Basir, S. A. (2021). Dependency syndrome in zakat distribution: A critical analysis of welfare approaches in Malaysia. *International Journal of Islamic Economics and Finance Research*, *4*(2), 89–104.

Setiawan, M. A., Armina, S. H., & Novika, S. (2022). The Typology of Islamic Social Entrepreneurship: Principles, and Characteristic from a Maqashid Shariah Perspective. *Ijtihad*, *18*(2). Advance online publication. DOI: 10.21111/ijtihad.v18i2.12362

Siompu, I., & Nurul Asfiah. (2022). Islamic Social Entrepreneurship and Work Ethics in Global Business. *Formosa Journal of Applied Sciences*, *3*(7). Advance online publication. DOI: 10.55927/fjas.v3i7.9488

Stam, E. (2015). Entrepreneurial ecosystems and regional policy: A sympathetic critique. *European Planning Studies*, *23*(9), 1759–1769. DOI: 10.1080/09654313.2015.1061484

Stam, E. (2015). Entrepreneurial ecosystems and regional policy: A sympathetic critique. European Planning Studies, *23*(9), 1759–1769. DOI: 10.1080/09654313.2015.1061484

Suhaimi, M. F. B., Don, A. G., & Puteh, A. (2022). Program Latihan Dalam Membangunkan Asnaf di Selangor. *AZKA International Journal of Zakat & Social Finance, 2*(2). Advance online publication. DOI: 10.51377/azjaf.vol2no2.66

Trinanda, O., ... (2025). From traits to resilience: How Muslim entrepreneurs survive in crisis. Behaviors, 15(3), 70. https://www.mdpi.com/2076-3387/15/3/70

Tuan Mahmood, T. M. A., Mohd Din, N., Al Mamun, A., & Dahlan Ibrahim, M. (2020). Cadangan kerangka kerja konseptual program memperkasakan ekonomi asnaf: Pembangunan 'Model Kemenjadian Milenia Asnaf (MKMA)'. *AZKA International Journal of Zakat & Social Finance, 1*(1), 74–93. DOI: 10.51377/azjaf.vol1no01.11

World Bank. (2020). *The role of training and skills development in entrepreneurship.* World Bank Group., DOI: 10.1596/978-1-4648-1532-3

World Bank. (2022). *World Development Report 2022: Finance for an equitable recovery.* World Bank.

Yasmeen, K.. (2024). Framework for Islamic social entrepreneurship. *Journal of Islamic Accounting and Business Research.*

Yusoff, M. N. H., & Baharom, A. W. (2021). Digital entrepreneurship in the post-pandemic era: Challenges and opportunities for asnaf entrepreneurs. International Journal of Islamic Business, *6*(1), 1–15. https://doi.org/DOI: 10.35631/ijib.61001

Zahra, S. A., Gedajlovic, E., Neubaum, D. O., & Shulman, J. M. (2009). A typology of social entrepreneurs: Motives, search processes and ethical challenges. *Journal of Business Venturing, 24*(5), 519–532. DOI: 10.1016/j.jbusvent.2008.04.007

Zulkifli, M. F., Abdullah, N., & Ahmad, S. (2022). Evaluating the effectiveness of Program Usahawan Asnaf: A case study of Lembaga Zakat Selangor. *International Journal of Zakat and Islamic Philanthropy*, *4*(2), 1–12. https://doi.org/DOI: 10.31436/jif.v12i1.685

Chapter 4

Bridging Social Entrepreneurship and Sustainable Development:

A Systematic Review of Technological Enablers

Fernando-Luís Almeida
https://orcid.org/0000-0002-6758-4843
Instituto Superior Politécnico Gaya, Portugal

ABSTRACT

Social entrepreneurship is crucial for sustainable development as it blends innovative business models with a focus on economic, social and environmental impact. This synergy can potentially accelerate progress towards the sustainable development goals, creating a more equitable and sustainable future. This study aims to explore this phenomenon by carrying out a systematic review of literature. It is adopted the PRISMA framework to identify 54 relevant studies in this field. The findings characterize the evolution of articles in this field, the number of citations, the relationship between key terms, and the respective clusters. Moreover, seven contributions of social entrepreneurship for sustainable development are identified. Finally, the role of technology in promoting and supporting the interconnection between social entrepreneurship and sustainable development is explored. This study is relevant to enhance understanding of how technology supports social entrepreneurship and helps social entrepreneurs to achieve sustainable development goals.

DOI: 10.4018/979-8-3373-5307-4.ch004

1. INTRODUCTION

Social entrepreneurship is crucial in addressing societal issues and fostering sustainable development. Despite being popular, social entrepreneurship does not have a uniform, commonly agreed-upon definition. Based on their extensive literature review, Glasbeek et al. (2024) observed that the existing definitions of the term seem to differ significantly considering the originality, the purpose, the functionality, and the resources of social entrepreneurship. However, the authors also draw the attention that being a complex socio-economic phenomenon, social entrepreneurship should not be reduced to an overly simplistic construct. In a broadest sense, social entrepreneurship can encompass "all activities and processes undertaken to discover, define, and exploit opportunities to enhance social wealth by creating new ventures or managing existing organizations in an innovative manner" (Zahra et al., 2009, p. 519). Accordingly, the main difference between traditional and social entrepreneurship lies in their value propositions (Martin & Osberg, 2007; Hlady-Rispal & Servantie 2018) since social entrepreneurship follows a social mission and explicitly addresses societal problems. A significant importance of social entrepreneurship is its ability to fill gaps left by traditional businesses and government initiatives. While governments may lack the flexibility to innovate rapidly and businesses may focus on profitability, social enterprises prioritize social impact. This means they can address needs that are overlooked or underfunded, providing essential services and products to marginalized communities. Additionally, Letaifa (2016) declare that social entrepreneurship has a strong embeddedness within the local communities, while Hidayat (2018) highlights that social entrepreneurship encourages community participation and empowerment. Moreover, Chell et al. (2016) state that social entrepreneurship fosters a culture of responsibility and ethical business practices. It challenges the conventional notion of business success by integrating social and environmental goals into the core business model, promoting a more holistic view of economic development.

Social entrepreneurship and sustainable development are closely interconnected, with social entrepreneurship playing a critical role in advancing the goals of sustainable development (Kamaludin, 2023). According to the United Nations General Assembly (1987), sustainable development is growth that satisfies current demands without compromising the capacity of future generations to meet their own needs. It encompasses three main pillars: economic growth, social inclusion, and environmental protection. Social entrepreneurs contribute to sustainable development by creating enterprises that address these pillars simultaneously. For example, social entrepreneurs often create businesses that provide affordable and accessible services or products to underserved populations, promoting social inclusion and reducing inequality. They may develop renewable energy solutions or waste management systems that protect the environment while also creating jobs and stimulating local economies. These enterprises not only mitigate their own environmental impact but also encourage wider adoption of such practices across industries. Furthermore, Drencheva et al. (2022) point out that social entrepreneurs are adept at mobilizing resources and creating partnerships that can amplify their impact. They often collaborate with governments, non-profits, and private sector companies to scale their solutions and integrate them into broader development strategies. This collaborative approach ensures that their initiatives are sustainable in the long term and can be replicated in different contexts.

Studies in the field mainly look at this phenomenon individually. From the perspective of social entrepreneurship, systematic literature reviews (SLRs) seek to characterize the conceptual theories that make it possible to characterize the objectives and motivations of a social entrepreneur (Klarin & Suseno, 2023; Wang & Yee, 2023). SLRs have emerged that segment this analysis by exploring the role of women in this process (Jeong & Yoo, 2022) and the performance of social enterprises (Hussain et al., 2023). From the perspective of sustainable development, the main aim is to characterize the relationship between the circular economy and sustainability practices by reducing waste and optimizing resources (Boar et al., 2020). Another SLR in the same area seeks to explore the contributions and barriers faced by organizations (de Oliveira et al., 2024) and Xie & Hanafiah (2023) target this analysis at Small and Medium-Sized Enterprises (SMEs). Another SLR worth highlighting was carried out by Trane et al. (2023), which explores how sustainable development goals are being addressed in the European Union. The demand for joint exploration of both phenomena is residual, with the study by Kovanen (2021) indicating that the collaborative practices encouraged by social entrepreneurship favor addressing sustainable development goals. A further dimension that requires greater scholarly attention is the role of technology in linking these two phenomena. Digital platforms, big data analytics, and artificial intelligence are increasingly enabling social entrepreneurs to scale impact, optimize resource use, and connect with wider stakeholder networks (Chandna, 2022; Kotiranta et al., 2024; Nayak et al., 2025). Technology can serve as a bridge between social value creation and sustainable practices by facilitating transparency and supporting the development of circular economy models (Hueske & Dijkstra-Silva, 2025). For instance, digital tools empower small enterprises to track their environmental footprint, while blockchain and decentralized systems enhance accountability in supply chains. Equally, Reim et al. (2022) note that online platforms and mobile applications foster collaboration, making it easier for entrepreneurs to mobilize communities and align their ventures with sustainability objectives. As such, the integration of technological innovation into social entrepreneurship research offers fertile ground for understanding how these practices can more effectively address global sustainability challenges and advance the SDGs.

In line with these shortcomings, this study seeks to characterize this joint phenomenon, which is strongly interconnected. It offers a comprehensive synthesis of existing research, identifying key themes, trends, and gaps within literature. This enables researchers to understand the current state of knowledge and highlight areas requiring further investigation. Furthermore, it contextualizes social entrepreneurship within the broader framework of sustainable development, illustrating how technology can support the social, economic, and environmental change. This review is important to facilitate interdisciplinary dialogue by integrating perspectives from various fields, such as business, technology, environmental science, and social policy. Additionally, it aids practitioners by summarizing effective strategies and practices, promoting evidence-based decision-making.

The rest of this chapter is organized as follows: first, a theoretical contextualization is provided on the topics of social entrepreneurship, sustainable development, and the role of technology at the intersection of these two concepts. Next, the various stages of the SLR process are presented. This section also establishes the research questions. The results are then presented and discussed in terms of their relevance to understanding the phenomenon. Finally, the main conclusions, contributions, and implications of this study are summarized.

2. LITERATURE REVIEW

Social entrepreneurship and sustainable development have become established as two deeply interconnected fields of research and practice, sharing common concerns around social justice, equity, and environmental protection. Social entrepreneurship is characterized by the development of innovative initiatives that seek to respond to social, economic, or environmental problems in a self-sustaining manner, prioritizing positive impact on society rather than the exclusive maximization of financial profit. Sustainable development, in turn, is based on the balance between economic growth, social inclusion, and environmental preservation, guided by the SDGs defined by the United Nations. The connection between the two becomes empirically evident when one observes that many social entrepreneurship practices contribute directly to the achievement of the SDGs, as demonstrated in studies by Raman et al. (2025) and Turyakira et al. (2025).

One of the key points of this connection lies in the ability of social entrepreneurship to promote innovative solutions that respond to local needs in an effective and scalable way. In communities where social exclusion, poverty, or environmental degradation are persistent problems, social entrepreneurs develop business models that combine social impact and economic sustainability, breaking the dependence on donations or limited public policies (Zeyen et al., 2025). This type of action creates not only employment and income opportunities, but also community empowerment mechanisms that strengthen the social fabric (Indarti et al., 2024; Shabbir & Batool, 2025).

The connection between the two concepts is further reinforced by the growing importance of partnerships and collaborative networks. Sustainable development requires coordinated efforts between governments, businesses, civil society organizations, and citizens. Baker & Weerakoon (2024) highlight that social entrepreneurship, by operating in hybrid environments between the private and social sectors, positions itself as a natural facilitator of these collaborations. This ability to move between different institutional logics allows social entrepreneurs to mobilize resources and build synergies that accelerate the achievement of sustainability goals (Ghosh et al., 2024; Wang et al., 2024).

Technology is a central element that promotes the connection between the two concepts. Technology has taken on a central role in strengthening and expanding social entrepreneurship, acting as a catalyst for the creation of innovative solutions that respond to complex problems in contemporary society. Social entrepreneurship is characterized by the search for positive impact on the community and the environment, combining economic sustainability with social transformation. In this context, technology offers resources that allow for expanding the reach of initiatives. Alemayehu Tegegn (2024) points out its role in optimizing resources and searching for more efficient solutions to social and environmental problems. One of the most obvious ways in which technology influences social entrepreneurship is through the digitization of processes and the creation of digital platforms that connect entrepreneurs, beneficiaries, and social investors. Mobile applications, social networks, and crowdfunding platforms have become powerful tools for mobilizing communities, raising funds, and increasing the visibility of projects (Chalmeta & Barbeito-Caamaño, 2024; Y Vo-Thanh et al., 2021). This digital accessibility breaks down geographical and economic barriers, allowing small local initiatives to reach global audiences and attract strategic partners, thereby amplifying the social impact of their actions. In addition, technology enables the collection, analysis, and monitoring of data in real time. Vañó (2025) recognizes that this capability is essential for social entrepreneurs to evaluate the effectiveness of their interventions. This allows social entrepreneurs to adjust strategies and communicate results transparently to investors and society. The use of big data and artificial intelligence tools, for example, allows for the identification of patterns of exclusion, the mapping of unmet social needs, and the development of more assertive interventions (Giuggioli & Pellegrini, 2023; Mumi et al., 2025; Uriarte et al., 2025). In this sense, technology not only increases the efficiency of operations but also provides robust evidence to support the credibility of projects.

The role of technology must also be highlighted in terms of sustainable development. The concept of sustainable development, which presupposes meeting the needs of the current generation without compromising the ability of future generations to meet their own needs, finds in technology a strategic ally for transforming production and consumption models, optimizing resources, and promoting greater social equity. One of the fields in which technology contributes most to sustainable development is energy transition. Renewable energy sources, such as solar, wind, and hydro, depend on technological advances to improve efficiency and reduce costs, making them viable alternatives to fossil fuels (Maka & Alabid, 2022). In addition, studies by Kirchherr & Hartley (2025) and Lamba et al. (2024) show that the circular economy, supported by technological innovations, is transforming production chains by encouraging reuse, recycling, and waste reduction. Furthermore, traceability technologies and new biodegradable materials make it possible to create business models that are more aligned with the principles of sustainability, while responding to the demands of increasingly conscious consumers (Haq et al., 2025).

3. METHODOLOGY

3.1 Methods

SLRs are highly relevant in academic and research contexts. They follow a structured and methodical approach to minimize the risk of bias that can occur in traditional narrative reviews, ensuring that all relevant studies are considered. Therefore, this approach involves a rigorous protocol that includes clearly defined research questions, systematic search strategies, and predefined inclusion and exclusion criteria (Mengist et al., 2020). This study adopts Covidence and VosViewer to assist in conducting the SLR. Covidence is a specialized software tool designed to streamline the SLR process. It automates the screening of articles, data extraction, and quality assessment, thereby enhancing efficiency and accuracy. VOSviewer is a software tool used in systematic literature reviews for visualizing and analyzing bibliometric networks. It maps out relationships between studies, authors, and keywords by creating visual representations such as co-citation and co-occurrence maps. These visualizations facilitate the identification of key trends, influential studies, and emerging research areas. The use of software to support this research process is relevant due to several key factors that enhance the efficiency, accuracy, and overall quality of the review process. Firstly, the systematic nature of an SLR requires handling large volumes of data, including numerous research articles, abstracts, and bibliographic records. Furthermore, software tools also significantly enhance the precision and consistency of the review (van Dinter et al., 2021). Manual processes are prone to human error and inconsistencies, particularly when multiple researchers are involved.

This study also adopts a data repository (i.e., Mendeley Data) to enhance the efficiency, transparency, and overall quality of the review process. Mendeley Data is a secure online data repository designed to help researchers store, share, and manage their research data. Unlike Mendeley's reference management tool, which is primarily used for organizing and citing academic literature, Mendeley Data focuses specifically on the handling of raw research data that can be used in the context of an SLR. As indicated by Saldanha et al. (2019), data repositories offer a centralized and organized platform for storing and managing large volumes of research data. This centralization helps streamline the process of data retrieval and ensures that all relevant literature, including studies, references, and supplementary materials, is easily accessible and systematically organized. Furthermore, the data repository also significantly contributes to the transparency and reproducibility of the SLR.

3.2 Databases and Inclusion/Exclusion Criteria

Web of Science (WoS) and Scopus were adopted in this SLR. They are two of the most comprehensive and widely recognized bibliographic databases used in systematic literature reviews. These databases are being adopted in the field of entrepreneurship, sustainability, and sustainable development and are instrumental in ensuring the thoroughness, credibility, and scholarly rigor of an SLR (Kumar & Joshi, 2023). Each database may index unique journals and articles, so utilizing both increases the likelihood of capturing all relevant studies. This comprehensive search strategy intends to minimize the risk of publication bias and enhances the validity of the review findings.

Exploratory research was initially performed to gain a comprehensive understanding of the key themes, concepts, and terminology used in the fields of social entrepreneurship and sustainable development. The goal was to identify recurring terms, phrases, and concepts that are central to the topic. These terms often emerge from the abstracts, introductions, and conclusions of high-impact papers that are identified in both databases. This exploratory research identified two main trends. First, social entrepreneurship and social entrepreneurs are intrinsically linked concepts, with each playing a crucial role in the broader context of addressing social issues through innovative approaches. Social entrepreneurship refers to the process of identifying, starting, and managing ventures that aim to solve social problems or fulfill unmet social needs. Social entrepreneurs are the individuals or organizations that drive social entrepreneurship. Second, sustainable development and sustainability are closely related concepts, both centered on ensuring that human activities do not deplete resources or harm the environment while promoting well-being and equity for current and future generations. Sustainability is a broad principle that involves maintaining the balance between economic growth, environmental protection, and social equity. Sustainable development, on the other hand, is the practical application of sustainability principles. Accordingly, the search string reflects both visions and it is defined as: "((Social Entrepreneurship) or (social entrepreneurs)) and ((sustainable development) or (sustainability))".

Inclusion and exclusion criteria were defined to establish clear parameters for selecting studies, ensuring the review's focus and relevance. Both inclusion and exclusion criteria contribute to the transparency and reproducibility of the review process. The inclusion criteria included articles published in indexed journals in the last decade (2015-2024). Articles published until the end of June 2024 were included. We also only considered articles published in English and where full-text access was available. As exclusion criteria, studies published in conference proceedings, books, and book chapters were not considered. In the same vein, master's or doctoral theses were also eliminated. Another exclusion criterion was articles written in a language other than English, even if the abstract in English was provided.

3.3 Data Collection and Quality Assessment

Preferred Reporting Items for Systematic Reviews and Meta-Analyses (PRISMA) was adopted to address quality assessment issues and to provide a structured, transparent, and replicated framework. As indicated by Moher et al. (2010), PRISMA requires detailed documentation and reporting of each step in the review process, including the search strategy, selection criteria, data extraction, and synthesis methods. This transparency allows readers to critically assess the methods used and the robustness of the findings. Furthermore, PRISMA offers a standardized approach to conducting and reporting systematic reviews. This consistency helps to ensure that reviews are conducted systematically and methodically, reducing the risk of bias and errors. Standardization also facilitates comparison between different reviews, contributing to a more cohesive and reliable body of evidence.

The data collection process was done in July 2024. Initially, the SLR identified a total of 5139 articles from both databases. However, 1107 articles had to be removed because they were repeated manuscripts indexed in both databases. Thus, 4032 articles were considered for the second phase of abstract assessment. It was at this stage that the largest number of studies were removed (n = 3702). The main reason was the lack of alignment between studies in sustainability or sustainable development and the specific topic of social entrepreneurship, since the vast majority of them deal with other topics related to green entrepreneurship, circular economy, sustainable business models, corporate sustainability strategies, and education and capacity building. After removing these abstract-based articles, 330 articles were included in the 3rd phase for full-text reading. At the end of the process, and after the exclusion of 276 articles in this last phase due to irrelevant content, inadequate methodology, and insufficient data, 54 studies were included in the SLR.

Figure 1. PRISMA diagram

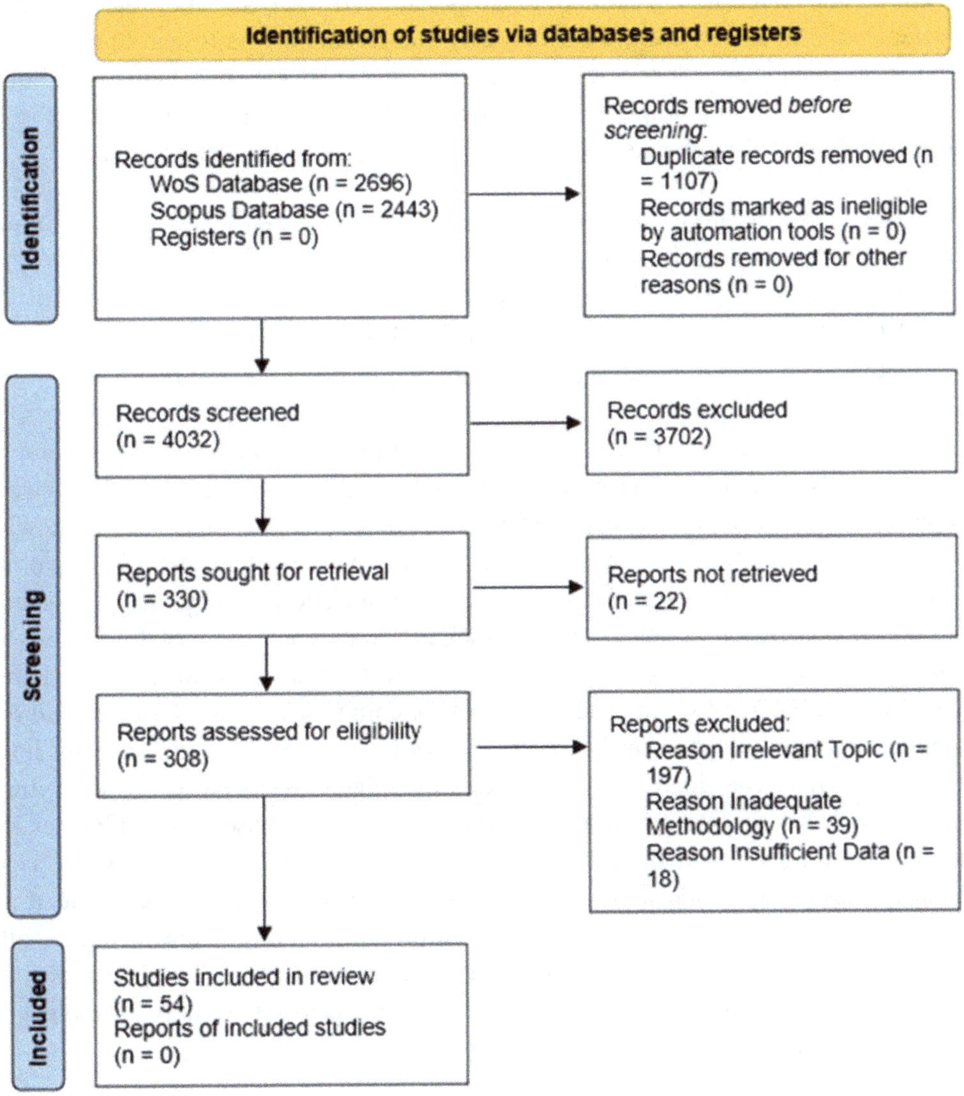

3.4 Research questions

In an SLR, the research questions (RQs) are fundamental as they guide the entire review process, influencing the selection, evaluation, and synthesis of studies. Kuckertz & Block (2021) state these research questions are designed to address specific gaps or inconsistencies in the existing literature and provide a comprehensive understanding of the topic. A common research question might involve examining how the understanding or treatment of a topic has evolved over time. Journals play a crucial role in determining the credibility and impact of the research. Citations are a significant indicator of a study's influence and relevance within the academic community. The research methodologies employed in the studies are also a focal point of many SLR questions. Accordingly, four initial RQs were formulated:

RQ1. How the studies about social entrepreneurship and sustainable development have evolved over time?
RQ2. In which journals are these studies published?
RQ3. How has the number of citations evolved?
RQ4. What research methodologies are employed in these studies?

The use of VosViewer makes it possible to tailor research questions to leverage the software's capabilities in visualizing and analyzing bibliometric data. VOSviewer is particularly useful for exploring the structure and dynamics of scientific knowledge, revealing patterns, trends, and relationships within literature. Therefore, a research question focuses on identifying key research terms. The idea is to map out the co-occurrence of keywords and track the emergence and transformation of research themes, providing insights into how the field has developed and where it is heading. Furthermore, the technique of mapping clusters was also applied to provide a structured and visual representation of the relationships and patterns. It is recognized by Leydesdorff et al. (2017) that mapping clusters helps in identifying key research themes. By grouping related studies together based on similarities in keywords, citations, or methodologies, it is possible to identify how different topics related to social entrepreneurship and sustainable development are interconnected. This allows for a more systematic categorization of the literature, ensuring that all relevant aspects of the field are covered. Moreover, it highlights the main topics that have been extensively studied and reveals emerging areas that might require further exploration. Accordingly, two additional RQs were included:

RQ5. What are the main key terms in the field and how are they interconnected?
RQ6. What clusters emerge in the context of the topics investigated in the field?

This SLR also intends to map out the connections between social entrepreneurship and sustainable development. Therefore, it is important to highlight how social entrepreneurship contributes to various dimensions of sustainable development. As recognized by Lasisi (2022), social entrepreneurship encourages the adoption of sustainable practices within businesses and communities. The innovative nature of social entrepreneurship also drives systemic change. Social entrepreneurs often develop new models and solutions that challenge conventional approaches to economic and social issues (Zhao, 2020). It is expected that these innovations can lead to broader societal shifts. Additionally, exploring this topic through an SLR can uncover the multidimensional impacts of social entrepreneurship. This comprehensive perspective is essential for appreciating the full scope of social entrepreneurship's contributions to sustainable development. Therefore, a new RQ was proposed:

> RQ7. In which ways do social entrepreneurship promote sustainable development?

Technology is now one of the most decisive factors in understanding how social entrepreneurship can not only create innovative solutions to social problems but also align these solutions with sustainability goals. Its relevance emerges, first and foremost, from its ability to amplify impact, as argued by Del Giudice et al. (2019). Initiatives that would otherwise remain local can acquire regional or even global reach, reinforcing the sustainability of their actions. Another highlight is the potential of technology to promote transparency and social responsibility (Jones & Comfort, 2021; Kong & Liu, 2023; Li & Zhang, 2025). Digital tracking systems and open databases facilitate the monitoring of the social and environmental impact of projects, ensuring greater confidence among investors, partners, and beneficiaries. This is particularly relevant in the context of the SDGs, which require clear and comparable metrics to assess progress. Thus, exploring the role of technology in this relationship means recognizing that sustainable development depends not only on entrepreneurial will or social sensitivity, but also on the ability to mobilize tools capable of transforming intentions into measurable impact. Accordingly, a new research question was established:

> RQ8. How does technology support the relationship between social entrepreneurship and sustainable development?

4. RESULTS

The response to RQ1 is shown in Figure 2. The first publication exploring the relationship between social entrepreneurship and sustainable development only appeared in 2016. By 2019, only 8 publications had been found, which represents only 14.81%. This confirms that the topic is quite emerging, with most publications appearing in recent years, especially since 2021.

Figure 2. Evolution of the publications

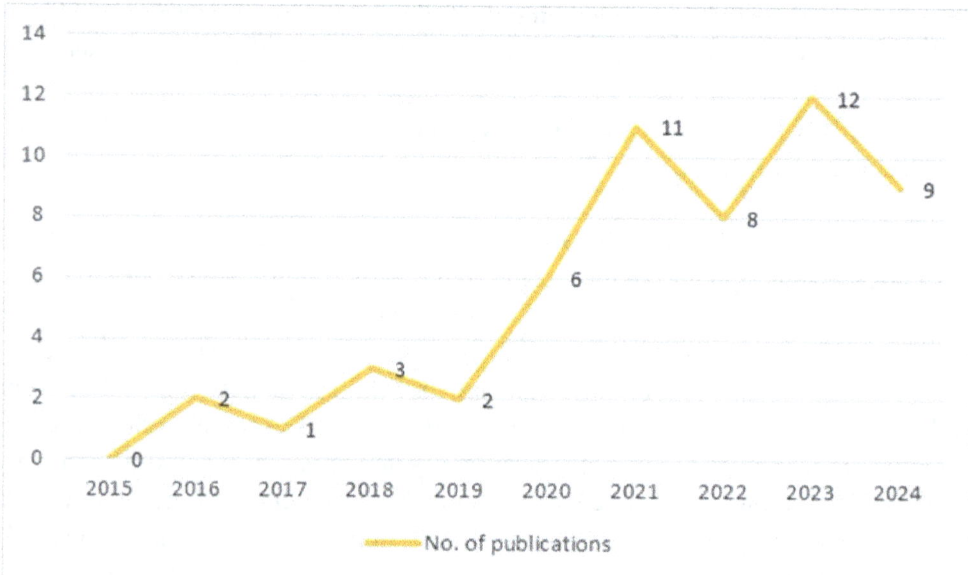

Table 1 shows the distribution of articles by journals. The answer to RQ2 indicates that the "Sustainability" journal is very important in the publication of these articles. Around 31.48% of the articles in this field are published in this journal. The scope of the "Sustainability" journal encompasses a wide range of topics related to the principles and practice of sustainability across various disciplines. This includes research on sustainable development, environmental management, economic sustainability, and social equity. The journal focuses on interdisciplinary approaches that integrate ecological, economic, social, cultural, and technological dimensions to address complex sustainability challenges. Following are four journals whose priority themes are management, strategic management, innovation, and technology management. These areas are fundamental to creating and sustaining organizational success in a dynamic and competitive business environment. Together, these areas interact and reinforce each other to promote organizational success and sustainability. Finally, the "others" category features articles with a diverse focus on entrepreneurship, sustainability, and environmental management. In "others" category appear journals such as Administrative Sciences, Business & Society, Entrepreneurship and Sustainability Issues, International Journal of Ethics and Systems, Journal of Cleaner Production, and Journal of Small Business Management, among others.

Table 1. Top journals with more articles

Journal	N	%
Sustainability	17	31.48
Business Strategy and the Environment	2	3.70
Journal of Innovation & Knowledge	2	3.70
Technological Forecasting and Social Change	2	3.70
Journal of Management Studies	2	3.70
Others	29	53.71

Source: Own source

Table 2 aims to answer RQ3 by counting the total number of citations (NC) and number of citations per year (NCY). Only the top 10 most cited articles by the end of the first semester of 2024 are considered. The total number of citations is a cumulative metric over time since publication. The annual total number of citations is a specific metric that results from the annual average. The findings indicate that the most cited article was written by Calic & Mosakowski (2016) and received a total of 382 citations with an annual average of over 42 citations. This article demonstrates that sustainability orientation significantly influences crowdfunding success through various mechanisms that appeal to backers' values and motivations. Therefore, projects with a clear sustainability focus often attract attention due to the growing societal concern for environmental and social issues. This alignment with contemporary values can increase the likelihood of a project being funded. The second article with the highest number of citations was written by Méndez-Picazo et al. (2021), which addresses the topic of socio-cultural and economic factors in social entrepreneurship and sustainable development. After the second position, there are some shifts in the ranking of the most cited articles with the position in annual citations, indicating that more recent articles on the subject have greater potential for annual citations. Finally, the "Sustainability" journal has only one article among the 10 most cited articles, even though more than 30% of scientific production in this area has been published in this journal. It should also be noted that the Journal of Management Studies, which has only two articles in the field, was able to place them in the top 10 most cited articles, both of which were published in a special issue on ethics in entrepreneurship and sustainability.

Table 2. Authors with more citations

Authors	Journal	NC	NCY
Calic & Mosakowski (2016)	Journal of Management Studies	382	42.444
Méndez-Picazo et al. (2021)	Journal of Innovation & Knowledge	140	35
Littlewood & Holt (2018)	Business & Society	135	19.286
Al-Qudah et al. (2022)	Journal of Sustainable Finance & Investment	87	29
Dickel & Eckardt (2021)	Journal of Small Business Management	83	20.750
Agarwal et al. (2020)	Journal of Cleaner Production	74	14.800
Kraus et al. (2017)	International Journal of Entrepreneurial Behavior & Research	62	7.750
Muralidharan & Pathak (2018)	Sustainability	55	7.857
Waldron et al. (2016)	Journal of Management Studies	38	4.222
Ramadani et al. (2022)	Business Strategy and the Environment	32	10.667

Source: Own source

The answer to RQ4 is given in Figure 3. A circular graph is used to show the distribution of publications by research methodological approach. The findings indicate that quantitative methodologies predominate with a total of 21 studies in which the application of the structured equations model (SEM) stands out, while qualitative methodologies are adopted in 16 studies with a greater emphasis on exploratory approaches with multi-case studies. Also noteworthy is the significant number of 12 articles that adopt mixed methods. This approach is used with the aim of allowing researchers to capture the richness and depth of individual experiences and contextual nuances through qualitative methods, while also offering the ability to generalize findings and identify patterns using quantitative data. Furthermore, we have identified 3 narrative literature reviews (NLRs) and 2 SLRs.

Figure 3. Research methodologies

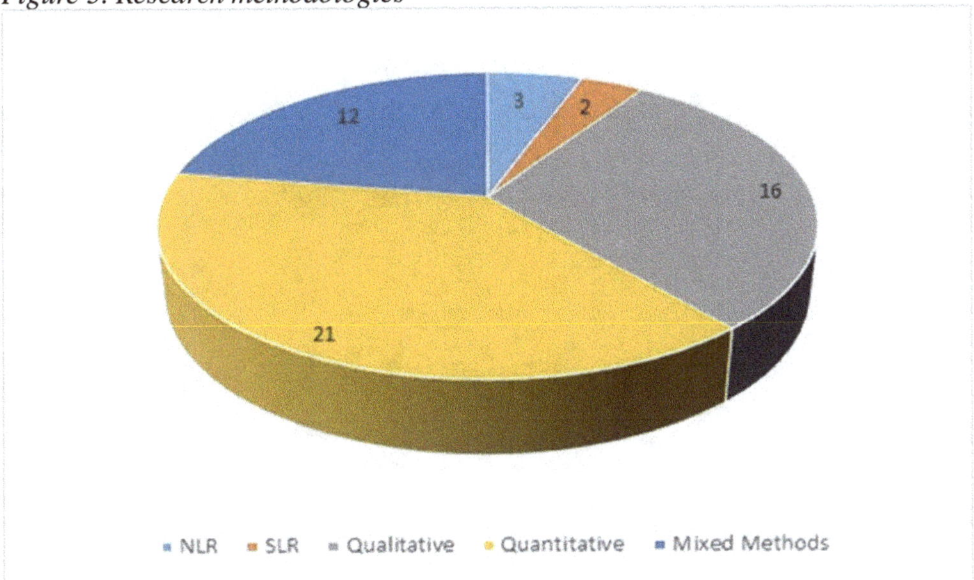

The identification of key terms and the exploration of their interconnections, as defined in RQ5 is depicted in Figure 4. Key terms were extracted from the title and abstract fields. Structured abstract labels and copyright statements were ignored. A full counting process was followed, which indicates that all the occurrences of a term were counted. The minimum number of terms was defined to 5. Terms that appear more frequently are: entrepreneurship (n = 104), performance (n = 23), country (n = 22), sustainable development goal (n = 18), and sustainable entrepreneurship (n = 14). The findings indicate that entrepreneurship and country performance are pivotal terms in the realm of social entrepreneurship and sustainable development due to their interrelated influence on economic and social progress. Findings also indicate the synergy between entrepreneurship and country performance is crucial for sustainable development.

Figure 4. Network of connections between key terms

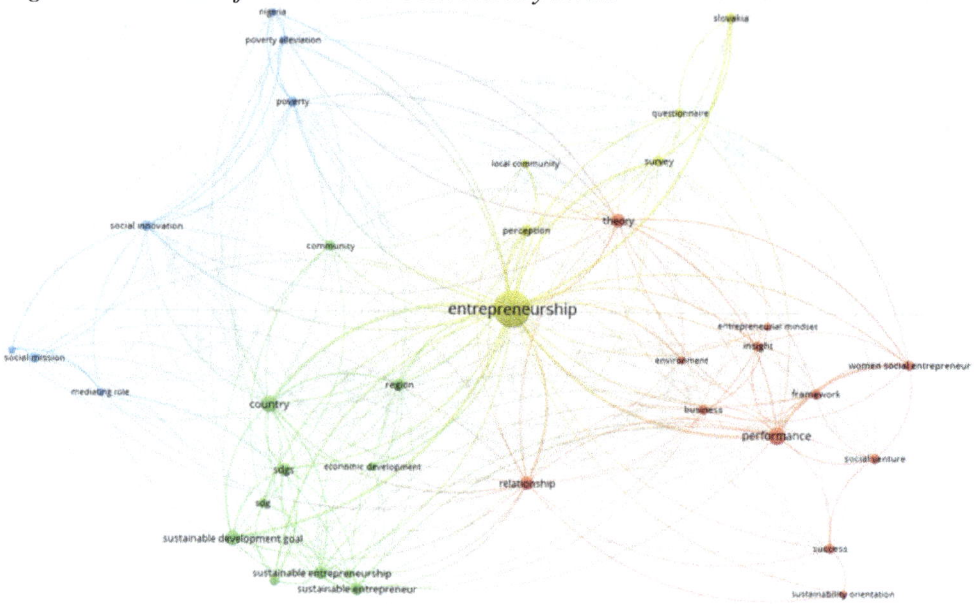

The identification of clusters, as defined by RQ6, is specified in Table 3. Key terms, total number of occurrences (TNO), and total number of links (TNL) are provided. Four clusters were identified. Cluster 3 is less important than the others. Although cluster 4 has a smaller number of terms, its occurrence and links with other terms are higher because the "entrepreneurship" term is heavily used in the articles. Cluster 1 highlights social ventures, particularly those led by women social entrepreneurs, embody this balance, addressing societal needs while fostering economic growth. Cluster 2 identifies that communities and regions play a vital role in a country's economic development. Furthermore, enhancing organizational capability is essential for achieving SDGs. Cluster 3 indicates that social innovation plays a mediating role in poverty alleviation by driving sustainable enterprise development. The focus on sustainable practices aims to ensure long-term impact and improvement in living conditions for marginalized communities. Cluster 4 includes studies that explore how entrepreneurship impacts the local community significantly, shaping both economic and social landscapes. To understand this influence, perception studies use questionnaires and surveys. These tools gather insights into how community members view entrepreneurial activities, helping to tailor initiatives that meet local needs and foster support.

Table 3. Identification of clusters

ID	Key terms	TNO	TNL
1	business, entrepreneurial mindset, environment, framework, insight, performance, relationship, social venture, success, sustainability orientation, women social entrepreneur	118	1322
2	community, country, economic development, organizational capability, region, sdg, sustainable development goal, sustainable entrepreneur, sustainable entrepreneurship	134	1378
3	mediating role, poverty, poverty alleviation, social innovation, social mission, sustainable enterprise development	46	755
4	entrepreneurship, local community, perception, questionnaire, survey	143	1407

Source: Own source

Table 4 aims to synthesize the different approaches that can be used to promote sustainable development through social entrepreneurship, as requested in RQ7. Seven ways of promoting sustainable development are identified, namely using innovative solutions, environmental sustainability, economic empowerment, community development, ethical business practices, education and awareness programs, and promoting sustainable consumption. The development of innovative solutions is based on pillars such as creativity, effectiveness, long-lasting and scalability. The design of environmental sustainability solutions can involve the development of products or services. The economic empowerment of disadvantaged communities involves improving living conditions and creating new jobs. These community development campaigns are based on the pillar of collaboration, which seeks to amplify knowledge of local communities and their resources. Ethical business practices are promoted through the ethical behavior of social entrepreneurs and the transparency of their actions. Education for sustainability is a way of promoting sustainable lifestyles. Finally, the promotion of sustainable consumption seeks to increase socially responsible choices.

Table 4. Approaches to promote sustainable development through social entrepreneurship

Approaches	Pillars
Innovative solutions	Based on creativity, effectiveness, long-lasting impact, and scalability.
Environmental sustainability	Design and implementation of sustainable products or services.
Economic empowerment	Improvement of living conditions and job creation for disadvantaged communities.
Community development	Built on collaboration; amplifies local knowledge and resources.
Ethical business practices	Promoted through ethical behavior of social entrepreneurs and transparency of actions.

continued on following page

Table 4. Continued

Approaches	Pillars
Education and awareness programs	Education for sustainability; encourages sustainable lifestyles.
Promoting sustainable consumption	Seeks to increase socially responsible consumer choices.

Source: Own sources

Finally, Table 5 outlines how different types of technologies act as enablers in the connection between social entrepreneurship and sustainable development. Each technology is presented with a dual focus: the role it plays in supporting entrepreneurial activities with social purposes, and the way it contributes to broader sustainable development goals. Digital platforms, such as websites, applications, and online marketplaces, are highlighted for their capacity to expand the reach of social enterprises. They help entrepreneurs connect with beneficiaries, investors, and partners, while also providing communities with easier access to inclusive services and products that stimulate local economies and reduce inequalities. Mobile technologies play a complementary role by offering affordable tools that facilitate communication, financial inclusion through microfinance, and the delivery of essential services like education and healthcare, especially in disadvantaged or remote areas. Blockchain is presented as a key tool for enhancing transparency and accountability, particularly in transactions, donations, and supply chain management. Artificial intelligence is another driver of innovation, as it supports entrepreneurs in analyzing data, making better decisions, and designing tailored solutions to social challenges. Its sustainable development contribution comes from the optimization of resources, reduction of waste, and development of innovative approaches to environmental and social issues. Green technologies, such as renewable energy solutions and eco-innovations, are central to creating environmentally friendly products and services. Big data and analytics also play a crucial role by enabling the measurement and monitoring of social and environmental impacts. Finally, virtual learning and e-education platforms expand access to knowledge and skills, both for social entrepreneurs and for the communities they serve.

Table 5. Potential of technology in social entrepreneurship and sustainable development

Technology	Role in Social Entrepreneurship	Contribution to Sustainable Development
Digital Platforms (websites, apps, marketplaces)	Enable entrepreneurs to connect with beneficiaries, investors, and partners; expand reach and visibility.	Facilitate access to services and products that promote inclusion, reduce inequalities, and support local economies.
Mobile Technology	Provides accessible tools for communication, microfinance, and delivery of social services in underserved areas.	Enhances social inclusion, education, and healthcare access, particularly in remote or disadvantaged communities.
Blockchain	Ensures transparency in transactions, donations, and supply chains; builds trust with stakeholders.	Promotes accountability, ethical business practices, and fair trade, strengthening governance and social responsibility.
Artificial Intelligence (AI)	Supports decision-making, data analysis, and personalized solutions for social challenges.	Optimizes resource allocation, reduces waste, and fosters innovation in addressing environmental and social problems.
Green Technologies (renewable energy, clean tech, eco-innovation)	Allow entrepreneurs to design environmentally friendly products and services.	Reduce carbon footprint, promote circular economy practices, and contribute directly to environmental sustainability goals.
Big Data and Analytics	Helps measure and monitor social and environmental impact; provides evidence-based insights.	Strengthens accountability, enables informed policy-making, and ensures scalable, sustainable solutions.
Virtual Learning and E-education Platforms	Expand access to training and capacity-building for entrepreneurs and communities.	Foster education for sustainability, raise awareness, and empower communities with knowledge for long-term development.

Source: Own source

5. DISCUSSION

The findings reveal that the intersection of social innovation and sustainable development has garnered increasing attention within the scientific community. Social innovation, broadly defined as new strategies, concepts, and ideas aimed at addressing social needs and improving human well-being, is currently seen as a pivotal component in driving sustainable development. The exploration of social entrepreneurship performance and its impact on sustainable development has been predominantly driven by quantitative studies in recent years. Quantitative research offers valuable insights into how social enterprises contribute to broader sustainable development goals. Studies such as Kamaludin (2023) and Permana (2024) employ a range of metrics to evaluate performance, including financial indicators, social impact measures, and environmental outcomes. Financial metrics might encompass profitability, revenue growth, and cost efficiency, providing a quantitative gauge of the enterprise's economic viability. Social impact is assessed through indicators such as the number of beneficiaries served, improvements in quality of life, and advancements in social equity. Environmental impact metrics, on the other hand, might track resource usage, waste reduction, and carbon footprint. Furthermore, these studies often use advanced statistical methods to model the relationships between social entrepreneurship practices and sustainable development outcomes. Techniques such as regression analysis as applied by Ketprapakorn & Kantabutra (2019) can reveal how various factors (e.g., leadership practices, operational strategies, and stakeholder engagement) influence performance and impact.

Findings also indicate that social entrepreneurship promotes sustainable development by fostering economic empowerment through the creation of jobs and livelihoods. This approach combines entrepreneurial innovation with a mission to solve social problems, leading to economic opportunities that can transform communities and improve overall well-being. The idea is to create employment opportunities in underserved areas. Social enterprises often operate in regions where traditional businesses are scarce, providing jobs to those who might otherwise struggle to find employment. Moreover, social entrepreneurship focuses on inclusive hiring practices, prioritizing the employment of marginalized groups such as women, youth, and individuals with disabilities (Mauksch & Dey, 2024). These groups often face significant barriers to employment in conventional markets. This empowerment not only enhances their quality of life but also fosters a more inclusive economy, where diverse talents and perspectives are valued.

Social entrepreneurship can also promote sustainable development through ethical business practices. A significant way social entrepreneurship advances sustainable development is by prioritizing transparency and accountability. As exposed by Burga & Rezania (2015), social enterprises often go beyond the minimum regulatory requirements to ensure their operations are open and accountable to stakeholders, including employees, customers, and the communities they serve. This transparency builds trust and encourages other businesses to adopt similar practices, leading to a more ethical and responsible business environment overall. In addition, social enterprises focus on creating value for all stakeholders rather than prioritizing profits for shareholders alone. This stakeholder-centric approach means that decisions are made with consideration for their impact on employees, customers, communities, and the environment.

Education and sustainable consumption practices are others identified approaches. Social entrepreneurs often develop educational programs, workshops, and campaigns that focus on environmental and responsible consumption issues (García-González &

Ramírez-Montoya, 2021). Education provided by social entrepreneurs extends to teaching skills that enable sustainable living. The goal is to empower them to adopt and advocate for sustainable practices in their personal lives and communities. Additionally, social entrepreneurs create and promote products and services that encourage sustainable consumption. They innovate to produce goods that are environmentally friendly, ethically sourced, and socially responsible. Moshood et al. (2022) give the example of developing biobased and biodegradable plastics. Furthermore, social enterprises often lead by example, demonstrating sustainable practices within their own operations.

Finally, role of technology in linking social entrepreneurship and sustainable development is a crucial element that helps to understand this interconnected relationship. Literature also shows both convergent and divergent perspectives. A central point of convergence lies in the recognition that technology acts as a catalyst that amplifies the reach and effectiveness of social enterprises. Numerous studies such as Petersen & Rasmussen (2023) and Zhang et al. (2023) underline the value of digital platforms and mobile technologies in overcoming barriers of distance, cost, and information asymmetry, enabling social entrepreneurs to deliver services and products to previously underserved populations. Similarly, there is wide agreement that data-driven approaches, including big data and artificial intelligence, strengthen the capacity of social enterprises to monitor outcomes, optimize resource allocation, and design interventions that are better aligned with community needs and sustainability targets (Grimaldi et al., 2025). This shared view positions technology not as an optional tool, but as a fundamental enabler of scale and impact in addressing complex social and environmental challenges. Despite this convergence, divergences emerge regarding the inclusivity, accessibility, and ethical implications of technological integration. Some scholars such as Kulular & Balaban (2025) argue that while technologies such as blockchain and AI enhance transparency and innovation, they also risk reinforcing inequalities by privileging actors and communities with higher levels of digital literacy and access to infrastructure. Concerns are also raised about the environmental footprint of certain technologies, questioning whether their deployment always aligns with sustainability goals (Goel et al., 2024). For instance, the energy consumption of blockchain or the e-waste generated by digital devices can create unintended negative consequences. In addition, debates persist around the tension between technological determinism and local agency. While some literature highlights the universal applicability of technological solutions (Akter et al., 2024), other scholars emphasize the need to adapt tools to specific cultural and socio-economic contexts, warning against one-size-fits-all approaches (Zamani & Díaz Andrade, 2024).

6. CONCLUSIONS

Promoting sustainable development involves a multifaceted approach that integrates various strategies to address environmental, social, and economic challenges. Seven keyways to promote sustainable development were identified such as using innovative solutions, fostering environmental sustainability, enabling economic empowerment, supporting community development, adhering to ethical business practices, implementing education and awareness programs, and promoting sustainable consumption. These elements are interconnected as they collectively create a comprehensive framework. Innovative solutions drive environmental sustainability and economic empowerment by providing new technologies and opportunities. Economic empowerment supports community development, which fosters environments for ethical business practices. Ethical practices, in turn, enhance social cohesion and support sustainability. Education and awareness programs underpin all these efforts by informing and motivating sustainable behaviors. Sustainable consumption is promoted through education, driving demand for eco-friendly and ethically produced goods, thus reinforcing environmental and economic sustainability. Finally, the convergent and divergent perspectives suggest that technology holds immense promise in advancing the dual agenda of social entrepreneurship and sustainable development, but its application requires careful consideration of ethical, contextual, and environmental factors. Future research is therefore called to explore not only the functional benefits of technology but also its broader systemic impacts, ensuring that technological innovation contributes inclusively and responsibly to sustainable progress.

This study provides relevant theoretical and practical contributions. Theoretically, this SLR synthesizes existing research to build a comprehensive understanding of how social entrepreneurship intersects with and drives sustainable development. This study meticulously analyzes a wide array of studies and identifies common themes, patterns, and gaps in literature. This helps to clarify the conceptual frameworks that underpin social entrepreneurship, highlighting how it integrates social, environmental, and economic objectives. Furthermore, this study contributes to the development of a refined definition of social entrepreneurship that emphasizes its role in achieving SDGs. Practically, this SLR offers valuable insights for practitioners and policymakers. It distills best practices and effective strategies in promoting sustainable development through social entrepreneurship, providing a blueprint for aspiring social entrepreneurs. This review offers actionable guidelines that can be adapted to various contexts through the identification of key success factors, such as community engagement, stakeholder collaboration, and sustainable business practices. For policymakers, this study underscores the importance of creating an enabling environment for social entrepreneurship, which could offer evidence-based recommendations for policy interventions. By illustrating the positive impact of social entrepreneurship on sustainable development, this SLR advocates for greater inclusion of social enterprises in national and international development agendas.

It is important to note that the field of social entrepreneurship and sustainable development is evolving rapidly, and several current and future research directions are emerging as critical areas of focus. A prominent research direction is the exploration of the scaling strategies of social enterprises. While many social enterprises successfully address local issues, understanding how these initiatives can scale their impact to regional, national, or global levels remains a significant challenge. Therefore, future research can investigate models and frameworks that support scaling, including replication strategies, strategic partnerships, and the role of technology in expanding reach and efficiency. Finally, cross-sector collaborations are another vital area for research. Social enterprises often work in partnership with governments, corporations, and non-profit organizations to achieve their goals. Understanding the dynamics of these partnerships, including the benefits, challenges, and best practices, can provide insights into how to create more effective and sustainable collaborations.

REFERENCES

Akter, S., Sultana, S., Gunasekaran, A., Bandara, R., & Miah, S. (2024). Tackling the global challenges using data-driven innovations. *Annals of Operations Research, 333*, 517–532. DOI: 10.1007/s10479-024-05875-z

Alemayehu Tegegn, D. (2024). The role of science and technology in reconstructing human social history: Effect of technology change on society. *Cogent Social Sciences, 10*(1), 1–10. DOI: 10.1080/23311886.2024.2356916

Baker, J. J., & Weerakoon, C. (2024). Deepening Insights Into Social Entrepreneurship by Leveraging Service-Dominant Logic. *Journal of Social Entrepreneurship, 16*(2), 714–745. DOI: 10.1080/19420676.2024.2316801

Boar, A., Bastida, R., & Marimon, F. A. (2020). Systematic Literature Review. Relationships between the Sharing Economy, Sustainability and Sustainable Development Goals. *Sustainability, 12*(17), 6744. DOI: 10.3390/su12176744

Burga, R., & Rezania, D. (2015). A Scoping Review of Accountability in Social Entrepreneurship. *SAGE Open, 5*(4), 1–10. DOI: 10.1177/2158244015614606

Chalmeta, R., & Barbeito-Caamaño, A. M. (2024). Framework for using online social networks for sustainability awareness. *Online Information Review, 48*(2), 334–353. DOI: 10.1108/OIR-03-2023-0116

Chandna, V. (2022). Social entrepreneurship and digital platforms: Crowdfunding in the sharing-economy era. *Business Horizons, 65*(1), 21–31. DOI: 10.1016/j.bushor.2021.09.005

Chell, E., Spence, L. J., Perrini, F., & Harris, J. D. (2016). Social Entrepreneurship and Business Ethics: Does Social Equal Ethical? *Journal of Business Ethics, 133*, 619–625. DOI: 10.1007/s10551-014-2439-6

de Oliveira, U. R., Menezes, R. P., & Fernandes, V. A. (2024). A systematic literature review on corporate sustainability: Contributions, barriers, innovations and future possibilities. *Environment, Development and Sustainability, 26*, 3045–3079. DOI: 10.1007/s10668-023-02933-7

Del Giudice, M., García Pérez, A., Scuotto, V., & Orlando, B. (2019). Are social enterprises technological innovative? A quantitative analysis on social entrepreneurs in emerging countries. *Technological Forecasting and Social Change, 148*, 119704. DOI: 10.1016/j.techfore.2019.07.010

Drencheva, A., Stephan, U., & Patterson, M. G. (2022). Whom to Ask for Feedback: Insights for Resource Mobilization From Social Entrepreneurship. *Business & Society*, *61*(7), 1725–1772. DOI: 10.1177/00076503211057497

García-González, A., & Ramírez-Montoya, M. S. (2021). Social entrepreneurship education: Changemaker training at the university. *Higher Education. Skills and Work-Based Learning*, *11*(5), 1236–1251. DOI: 10.1108/HESWBL-01-2021-0009

Ghosh, S., Ray, S., Nair, R., Nath, S., & Bishu, R. (2024). Exploring the Sustainability of Social Enterprises: A Scoping Review. *J Sustain Res.*, *6*(3), e240044. DOI: 10.20900/jsr20240044

Giuggioli, G., & Pellegrini, M. M. (2023). Artificial intelligence as an enabler for entrepreneurs: A systematic literature review and an agenda for future research. *International Journal of Entrepreneurial Behaviour & Research*, *29*(4), 816–837. DOI: 10.1108/IJEBR-05-2021-0426

Glasbeek, L., Wickert, C., & Schad, J. (2024). (in press). Evaluating definitions of social entrepreneurship: A rulebook from the philosophy of science. *International Journal of Management Reviews*. Advance online publication. DOI: 10.1111/ijmr.12359

Goel, A., Masurkar, S., & Pathade, G. R. (2024). An Overview of Digital Transformation and Environmental Sustainability: Threats, Opportunities, and Solutions. *Sustainability*, *16*(24), 11079. DOI: 10.3390/su162411079

Grimaldi, M., Troisi, O., Papa, A., & de Nuccio, E. (2025). (in press). Conceptualizing data-driven entrepreneurship: From knowledge creation to entrepreneurial opportunities and innovation. *The Journal of Technology Transfer*. Advance online publication. DOI: 10.1007/s10961-024-10176-5

Haq, F., Kiran, M., Khan, I., Mehmood, S., Aziz, T., & Haroon, M. (2025). Exploring the pathways to sustainability: A comprehensive review of biodegradable plastics in the circular economy. *Materials Today Sustainability*, *29*, 101067. DOI: 10.1016/j.mtsust.2024.101067

Hidayat, D. (2018). Community Empowerment Through Social Entrepreneurship Training Based On Partnership Network. [ASSEHR]. *Advances in Social Science, Education and Humanities Research*, *330*, 185–189. DOI: 10.2991/iceri-18.2019.37

Hlady-Rispal, M., & Servantie, V. (2018). Deconstructing the way in which value is created in the context of social entrepreneurship. *International Journal of Management Reviews*, *20*(1), 62–80. DOI: 10.1111/ijmr.12113

Hueske, A.-K., & Dijkstra-Silva, S. (2025). Exploring Social Value for Sustainability: A Revelatory Case Study. *Corporate Social Responsibility and Environmental Management*, •••, 1–15. DOI: 10.1002/csr.70002

Hussain, A., Ahmad, S. A., & Mia, M. S. (2023). A systematic literature review on performance of social enterprises. *Cogent Economics & Finance*, *11*(2), 2269738. DOI: 10.1080/23322039.2023.2269738

Indarti, N., Anggadwita, G., Purnomo, R. A., & Tomlins, R. (2024). Breaking Barriers! Social Entrepreneurship in Empowering People with Disabilities. *Journal of Social Entrepreneurship*, •••, 1–35. DOI: 10.1080/19420676.2024.2353059

Jeong, E., & Yoo, H. (2022). A systematic literature review of women in social entrepreneurship. *Service Business*, *16*, 935–970. DOI: 10.1007/s11628-022-00512-w

Jones, P., & Comfort, D. (2021). A commentary on the leading information technology companies' approaches to corporate social responsibility. *Journal of Public Affairs*, *21*, e2564. DOI: 10.1002/pa.2564

Kamaludin, M. F. (2023). Social sustainability within social entrepreneurship. *Technological Forecasting and Social Change*, *192*, 122541. DOI: 10.1016/j.techfore.2023.122541

Ketprapakorn, N., & Kantabutra, S. (2019). Sustainable Social Enterprise Model: Relationships and Consequences. *Sustainability*, *11*, 3772. DOI: 10.3390/su11143772

Kirchherr, J., & Hartley, K. (2025). Is circular economy a failing sustainability paradigm? Not necessarily. *Journal of Industrial Ecology*, *29*, 1051–1059. DOI: 10.1111/jiec.70055

Klarin, A., & Suseno, Y. (2023). An Integrative Literature Review of Social Entrepreneurship Research: Mapping the Literature and Future Research Directions. *Business & Society*, *62*(3), 565–611. DOI: 10.1177/00076503221101611

Kong, D., & Liu, B. (2023). Digital Technology and Corporate Social Responsibility: Evidence from China. *Emerging Markets Finance & Trade*, *59*(9), 2967–2993. DOI: 10.1080/1540496X.2023.2199122

Kotiranta, A., Puumalainen, K., Sjögren, H., & Dana, L. P. (2024). Digitalization as a growth driver for social enterprises. *Technological Forecasting and Social Change*, *209*, 123837. DOI: 10.1016/j.techfore.2024.123837

Kovanen, S. (2021). Social entrepreneurship as a collaborative practice: Literature review and research agenda. *Journal of Entrepreneurship. Management and Innovation*, *17*(1), 97–128. DOI: 10.7341/20211713

Kuckertz, A., & Block, J. (2021). Reviewing systematic literature reviews: Ten key questions and criteria for reviewers. *Management Review Quarterly, 71*, 519–524. DOI: 10.1007/s11301-021-00228-7

Kulular, M. A., & Balaban, M. F. (2025). Legal and Compliance Risks of AI and Blockchain Technologies. In Kıral, H., & Yılmaz, G. (Eds.), *Futurisks: Risk Management in the Digital Age. Accounting, Finance, Sustainability, Governance & Fraud: Theory and Application*. Springer., DOI: 10.1007/978-981-96-6448-1_13

Kumar, M., & Joshi, P. (2023). A systematic literature review of sustainability indicators in sustainability reporting. *International Journal of Sustainable Development, 4*(3-4), 253–284. DOI: 10.1504/IJSDES.2022.128523

Lamba, H., Kumar, N., & Dhir, S. (2024). Circular economy and sustainable development: A review and research agenda. *International Journal of Productivity and Performance Management, 73*(2), 497–522. DOI: 10.1108/IJPPM-06-2022-0314

Lasisi, J. O. (2022). Nexus between social entrepreneurship and sustainable development goals. *Journal of Business Economic Analysis, 5*(2), 211–226. DOI: 10.1142/S2737566823500019

Letaifa, S. B. (2016). How social entrepreneurship emerges, develops and internationalises during political and economic transitions. *European Journal of International Management, 10*(4), 455–466. DOI: 10.1504/EJIM.2016.077424

Leydesdorff, L., Bornmann, L., & Wagner, C. S. (2017). Generating clustered journal maps: An automated system for hierarchical classification. *Scientometrics, 110*(3), 1601–1614. DOI: 10.1007/s11192-016-2226-5

Li, L., & Zhang, Z. (2025). Technology for Good? Tencent's Corporate Social Responsibility, Institutional Chameleon, and the Future of Platform Economies. *Social Media + Society, 11*(1), 1–11. DOI: 10.1177/20563051251316119

Maka, A., & Alabid, J. (2022). Solar energy technology and its roles in sustainable development. *Clean Energy, 6*(3), 476–483. DOI: 10.1093/ce/zkac023

Martin, R. L., & Osberg, S. (2007). Social Entrepreneurship: the case for definition. *Stanford Social Innovation Review, spring*, 29–39.

Mauksch, S., & Dey, P. (2024). Treating disability as an asset (not a limitation): A critical examination of disability inclusion through social entrepreneurship. *Organization, 31*(4), 624–644. DOI: 10.1177/13505084221150586

Mengist, W., Soromessa, T., & Legese, G. (2020). Method for conducting systematic literature review and meta-analysis for environmental science research. *MethodsX, 7*, 100777. DOI: 10.1016/j.mex.2019.100777

Moher, D., Liberati, A., Tetzlaff, J., & Altman, D. G. (2010). Preferred reporting items for systematic reviews and meta-analyses: The PRISMA statement. *International Journal of Surgery*, *8*(5), 336–341. DOI: 10.1016/j.ijsu.2010.02.007

Moshood, T. D., Nawanir, G., Mahmud, F., Mohamad, F., & Ahmad, M. H., & AbdulGhani, A. (2022). Sustainability of biodegradable plastics: New problem or solution to solve the global plastic pollution? *Current Research in Green and Sustainable Chemistry*, *5*, 100273. DOI: 10.1016/j.crgsc.2022.100273

Mumi, A., Ngammoh, N., & Suwanpakdee, A. (2025). The nexus of artificial intelligence and entrepreneurship research: Bibliometric analysis. *Sustainable Futures : An Applied Journal of Technology, Environment and Society*, *9*, 100688. DOI: 10.1016/j.sftr.2025.100688

Nayak, M., Nayak, P. M., & Joshi, H. G. (2025). Digital platforms' use in SMEs – A critical analysis of entrepreneurs' behaviour. *Cogent Economics & Finance*, *13*(1). Advance online publication. DOI: 10.1080/23322039.2025.2461337

Permana, D. (2024). Key Affecting Towards Financial Performance and Sustainability On Social Enterprises In Indonesia. *Journal of Economics and Finance*, *2*(2), 14–34. DOI: 10.61978/moneta.v2i2.216

Petersen, N. H., & Rasmussen, E. (2023). Digital entrepreneur's platformication and rapid internationalization through brokering, making and giving sense. *Small Enterprise Research*, *31*(1), 18–38. DOI: 10.1080/13215906.2023.2288579

Raman, R., Alka, T. A., Suresh, M., & Nedungadi, P. (2025). Social entrepreneurship and sustainable technologies: Impact on communities, social innovation, and inclusive development. *Sustainable Technology and Entrepreneurship*, *4*(3), 100110. DOI: 10.1016/j.stae.2025.100110

Reim, W., Andersson, E., & Eckerwall, K. (2022). Enabling collaboration on digital platforms: A study of digital twins. *International Journal of Production Research*, *61*(12), 3926–3942. DOI: 10.1080/00207543.2022.2116499

Saldanha, I. J., Smith, B. T., Ntzani, E., Jap, J., Balk, E. M., & Lau, J. (2019). The Systematic Review Data Repository (SRDR): Descriptive characteristics of publicly available data and opportunities for research. *Systematic Reviews*, *8*(334), 1–12. DOI: 10.1186/s13643-019-1250-y

Shabbir, M. S., & Batool, F. (2025). Social Entrepreneurship for Community Development: The Role of Social Capital in Establishing Sustainable Enterprises. *Journal of Social Entrepreneurship*, •••, 1–26. DOI: 10.1080/19420676.2025.2492060

Trane, M., Marelli, L., Siragusa, A., Pollo, R., & Lombardi, P. (2023). Progress by Research to Achieve the Sustainable Development Goals in the EU: A Systematic Literature Review. *Sustainability*, *15*(9), 7055. DOI: 10.3390/su15097055

Turyakira, P., Sendawula, K., Nanyanzi, M., Nantale, H., & Tamale, J. (2025). Social entrepreneurship: Empirical evidence on its contribution to the realization of the sustainable development goals in Uganda. *Journal of Work-Applied Management*, *17*(1), 160–172. DOI: 10.1108/JWAM-02-2023-0011

United Nations General Assembly. (1987) *Report of the world commission on environment and development: Our common future*. United Nations General Assembly, Development and International Co-operation: Environment, Oslo, Norway.

Uriarte, S., Baier-Fuentes, H., Espinoza-Benavides, J., & Inzunza-Mendoza, W. (2025). (in press). Artificial intelligence technologies and entrepreneurship: A hybrid literature review. *Review of Managerial Science*. Advance online publication. DOI: 10.1007/s11846-025-00839-4

van Dinter, R., Tekinerdogan, B., & Catal, C. (2021). Automation of systematic literature reviews: A systematic literature review. *Information and Software Technology*, *136*, 106589. DOI: 10.1016/j.infsof.2021.106589

Vañó, M. J. (2025). Social entrepreneurship: Challenges, risks, and opportunities. *The International Entrepreneurship and Management Journal*, *21*(64), 1–18. DOI: 10.1007/s11365-025-01088-3

Vo-Thanh, T., Zaman, M., Hasan, R., Rather, R., Lombardi, R., & Secundo, G. (2021). How a mobile app can become a catalyst for sustainable social business: The case of Too Good To Go. *Technological Forecasting and Social Change*, *171*, 120962. DOI: 10.1016/j.techfore.2021.120962

Wang, A., & Yee, C. (2023). A Literature Review of Social Entrepreneurship. *Open Journal of Business and Management*, *11*, 2232–2246. DOI: 10.4236/ojbm.2023.115123

Wang, X., Huang, Y., & Huang, K. (2024). How does social entrepreneurship achieve sustainable development goals in rural tourism destinations? The role of legitimacy and social capital. *Journal of Sustainable Tourism*, *33*(7), 1262–1280. DOI: 10.1080/09669582.2024.2309546

Xie, Q., & Hanafiah, M. H. (2023). Systematic Literature Review: The Sustainable Development of Small and Medium-Sized Enterprises Under the Trend of Globalization. *International Journal of Professional Business Review, 8*(5), e01803. DOI: 10.26668/businessreview/2023.v8i5.1803

Zahra, S. A., Gedajlovic, E., Neubaum, D. O., & Shulman, J. M. (2009). A typology of social entrepreneurs: Motives, search processes and ethical challenges. *Journal of Business Venturing, 24*(5), 519–532. DOI: 10.1016/j.jbusvent.2008.04.007

Zamani, E. D., & Díaz Andrade, A. (2024). Understanding local social processes in ICT4D research. *Information Technology for Development, 30*(3), 351–353. DOI: 10.1080/02681102.2024.2389610

Zeyen, A., Beckmann, M., Müller, S., Khanin, D., Krueger, N., Murphy, P. J., & Zacharakis, A. (2025). Social Entrepreneurship and Broader Theories: A Critical Reassessment and Future Agenda. *Journal of Social Entrepreneurship*, •••, 1–37. DOI: 10.1080/19420676.2025.2492851

Zhang, J., van Gorp, D., & Kievit, H. (2023). Digital technology and national entrepreneurship: An ecosystem perspective. *The Journal of Technology Transfer, 48*, 1077–1105. DOI: 10.1007/s10961-022-09934-0

Zhao, M. (2020). Social entrepreneurship for systemic change: The case of Southeast and South Asian countries. *Journal of Asian Public Policy, 14*(2), 225–250. DOI: 10.1080/17516234.2020.1796325

ADDITIONAL READING

Al-Qudah, A. A., Al-Okaily, M., & Alqudah, H. (2021). The relationship between social entrepreneurship and sustainable development from economic growth perspective: 15 'RCEP' countries. *Journal of Sustainable Finance & Investment, 12*(1), 44–61. DOI: 10.1080/20430795.2021.1880219

Azmat, F. (2013). Sustainable Development in Developing Countries: The Role of Social Entrepreneurs. *International Journal of Public Administration, 36*(5), 293–304. DOI: 10.1080/01900692.2012.756891

Bardy, R., Rubens, A., & Massaro, M. (2015). The Systemic Dimension of Sustainable Development in Developing Countries. *Journal of Organisational Transformation & Social Change, 12*(1), 22–41. DOI: 10.1179/1477963314Z.00000000033

Bhutani, V., Bahadur, P. S., & Sansaniwal, S. K. (2025). Leveraging Technology for Ethical and Sustainable Global Development. In Castanho, R. (Ed.), *Bridging Technology and Development for Sustainable Innovation and Geopolitical Dynamics* (pp. 279–302). IGI Global Scientific Publishing., DOI: 10.4018/979-8-3693-9072-6.ch011

Chakraborty, S., Konwar, J., & Chakrabarty, N. (2025). Green Technology for Sustainable Development. In Datta, D., Jain, V., Halder, B., Raychaudhuri, U., & Kumar, S. (Eds.), *Evolving Landscapes of Research and Development: Trends, Challenges, and Opportunities* (pp. 167–190). IGI Global Scientific Publishing., DOI: 10.4018/979-8-3693-7101-5.ch008

Copeland, K. (2021). Reimagining innovation for "social" entrepreneurship: Nonhuman spaces for the SDGs. *Journal of the International Council for Small Business, 2*(2), 134–146. DOI: 10.1080/26437015.2021.1882917

Cunha, J., Benneworth, P., Stolk, F., Welamedage, L., & Araujo, M. (2022). How Social Entrepreneurship Can Contribute to Upscale Social Innovation Practices. [IJSESD]. *International Journal of Social Ecology and Sustainable Development, 13*(4), 1–18. DOI: 10.4018/IJSESD.290323

Divya, M., & Suganthi, M. (2025). Harnessing Digital Technology for Sustainable Development: Advancing SDGs for Corporation. In Lin, H., & Yu, P. (Eds.), *Corporate Management in the Digital Age* (pp. 251–282). IGI Global Scientific Publishing., DOI: 10.4018/979-8-3693-8412-1.ch009

Gupta, P., & Srivastava, R. (2021). Research on Social Enterprises from an Emerging Economy—Systematic Literature Review and Future Research Directions. *Journal of Social Entrepreneurship, 15*(2), 458–493. DOI: 10.1080/19420676.2021.1974926

Hussain, N., & Li, B. (2022). Empirical Study to Understand the Social Entrepreneurial Intention Towards Technology Management in Social Entrepreneurial Ventures. [IJABIM]. *International Journal of Asian Business and Information Management, 13*(1), 1–19. DOI: 10.4018/IJABIM.309104

Indarto, I., & Lestari, R. I., Santoso, Djoko., & Prawihatmi, C. Y. (2023). Social entrepreneurship and CSR best practice: The drivers to sustainable business development in new Covid-19 Era. *Cogent Business & Management, 10*(2). Advance online publication. DOI: 10.1080/23311975.2023.2235086

Ledi, K. K. (2024). SDG Motivation and Social Entrepreneurial Intentions. The Moderating Roles of Institutional and Social Support. *Journal of Social Entrepreneurship*, •••, 1–24. DOI: 10.1080/19420676.2024.2418006

Majeed, A. H., Younis Agha, M. N., Abbas, A. F., & Kadhim, K. G. (2024). Innovative Solutions for Sustainable Development: The Role of Social Entrepreneurship in Alleviating Poverty. *Journal of Social Entrepreneurship*, •••, 1–31. DOI: 10.1080/19420676.2024.2431002

Mohana Sundari, V., Shriya, K., & Seshasai, S. J. (2024). Social Entrepreneurship: Innovations for Social Impact and Community Development. In Salman, S., & Bhaumik, A. (Eds.), *Entrepreneurship Innovation and Education for Performance Improvement* (pp. 599–612). IGI Global Scientific Publishing., DOI: 10.4018/979-8-3693-7903-5.ch024

Ponmalar, A., Muthuram, A., Therasa, M., Priya, V., Sathya, V., Subha, S., & Siva Subramanian, R. (2025). Convergence of Advanced Technologies for Sustainable Development and Smart Cities. In Kumar, R., Abdul Hamid, A., Binti Ya'akub, N., Nyamasvisva, T., & Tiwari, R. (Eds.), *AI and Green Technology Applications in Society* (pp. 189–218). IGI Global Scientific Publishing., DOI: 10.4018/979-8-3693-9879-1.ch008

Prabhakar, A. C. (2025). Sustainable Social Entrepreneurship Development: The Role of Artificial Intelligence. In Prabhakar, A., Yu, P., & Erokhin, V. (Eds.), *Rural Social Entrepreneurship Development: Network-Based Manufacturing System Model* (pp. 39–74). IGI Global Scientific Publishing., DOI: 10.4018/979-8-3693-7515-0.ch002

Rajendran, R. K., Mohana, P. T., Immanuel, V. A., Blessing, N. R. W., Chitrarasu, K., Vetrivel, S., Paulraj, A. K., & Kokila, S. S. (2025). The Intersection of Technology and Social Sustainability. In Popescu, C. (Ed.), *Building Inclusive Global Knowledge Societies for Sustainable Development* (pp. 457–470). IGI Global Scientific Publishing., DOI: 10.4018/979-8-3693-6298-3.ch017

Selvakumar, P., Sakthiradha, M., Jeeva, C., Mujrai, P., Satyanarayana, P., & Singh, D. (2025). Global Perspectives on Smart Education and Sustainable Development. In Sorayyaei Azar, A., Gupta, S., Al Bataineh, K., Maurya, N., & Somani, P. (Eds.), *Smart Education and Sustainable Learning Environments in Smart Cities* (pp. 253–272). IGI Global Scientific Publishing., DOI: 10.4018/979-8-3693-7723-9.ch015

Shabbir, M. S., & Batool, F. (2025). Social Entrepreneurship for Community Development: The Role of Social Capital in Establishing Sustainable Enterprises. *Journal of Social Entrepreneurship*, 1–26. DOI: 10.1080/19420676.2025.2492060

Shaji, M., & Kumar, A. (2025). Digital Pathways to Sustainability: Integrating Technology and Innovation for a Greener Future. In Yıldırım, D., Yıldırım, S., & Kandpal, V. (Eds.), *Effects of Digitalization and Circular Economy on Sustainable Policy and Climate Change Prevention* (pp. 1–38). IGI Global Scientific Publishing., DOI: 10.4018/979-8-3693-9909-5.ch001

Sharma, R., Kamble, S., Gupta, S., Belhadi, A., Rana, N. P., & Kumar, K. (2023). Interlinkages Between Digital-Social Entrepreneurship and Technological Capabilities for Sustainable Value Creation. [JGIM]. *Journal of Global Information Management*, *31*(1), 1–26. DOI: 10.4018/JGIM.328515

Wagner, M. (2012). Ventures for the Public Good and Entrepreneurial Intentions: An Empirical Analysis of Sustainability Orientation as a Determining Factor. *Journal of Small Business and Entrepreneurship*, *25*(4), 519–531. DOI: 10.1080/08276331.2012.10593587

Whitley, M. A., & Welty Peachey, J. (2020). Place-based sport for development accelerators: A viable route to sustainable programming? *Managing Sport and Leisure*, *27*(6), 530–539. DOI: 10.1080/23750472.2020.1825989

Wynn, M. G., & Jones, P. (2022). ICTs and the Localisation of the Sustainable Development Goals. [IJSESD]. *International Journal of Social Ecology and Sustainable Development*, *13*(4), 1–15. DOI: 10.4018/IJSESD.290325

Xanthopoulou, P., Sahinidis, A. G., Vyttas, V., Papakonstantinou, S., Zakopoulos, V., & Antoniadis, I. (2025). Empowering Social Entrepreneurship and Social Enterprises Through Digital Technologies: Opportunities and Challenges. In Efthymiopoulos, M., & Masouras, A. (Eds.), *Security and Strategy Models for Key-Solving Institutional Frameworks* (pp. 271–302). IGI Global Scientific Publishing., DOI: 10.4018/979-8-3693-5583-1.ch011

KEY TERMS AND DEFINITIONS

Big Data: Refers to extremely large and complex datasets that require advanced methods and technologies to collect, store, analyze, and extract meaningful insights for decision-making.

Biodegradable Materials: Materials that can be naturally broken down by microorganisms into non-toxic components, such as water, carbon dioxide, and biomass, within a relatively short time frame.

Blockchain: A decentralized and tamper-resistant digital ledger that records transactions across multiple computers, ensuring transparency, security, and traceability without the need for a central authority.

Carbon Footprint: The total amount of greenhouse gases, primarily carbon dioxide, emitted directly or indirectly by human activities, usually expressed in metric tons of CO_2 equivalent.

Circular Economy: An economic model that seeks to minimize waste and make the most of resources by reusing, recycling, and regenerating products and materials in a continuous cycle.

Marketplace: An organization that applies entrepreneurial strategies to achieve social or environmental objectives, reinvesting profits primarily to further its mission rather than to maximize shareholder returns.

Social Enterprise: An organization that applies entrepreneurial strategies to achieve social or environmental objectives, reinvesting profits primarily to further its mission rather than to maximize shareholder returns.

Sustainable Development Goal (SDG): One of the 17 global goals established by the United Nations in 2015 to address social, economic, and environmental challenges, aiming for a more inclusive, equitable, and sustainable world by 2030.

Chapter 5
Digital Storytelling and Indigenous Knowledge:
Media as a Tool for Cultural Preservation Among the Garasia Tribe of Rajasthan, India

Kritika Sharma
https://orcid.org/0009-0001-2884-557X
Lovely Professional University, India

Harry Kaur
https://orcid.org/0000-0001-8276-2313
Lovely Professional University, India

ABSTRACT

Indigenous knowledge is under threat in the era of globalization and digitization, especially among tribal communities that rely on oral traditions. This chapter examines how digital storytelling can preserve and transmit cultural heritage within the Garasia tribe of Rajasthan, India. Storytelling is central to Garasia identity, serving as a vehicle for values, histories, and norms across generations. Yet, migration, modernization, and poor documentation endanger its survival. Using cultural transmission theory, media ecology, and social constructionism, the chapter explores how digital media can bridge tradition and innovation. Drawing on literature and secondary ethnographic insights, it highlights opportunities for intergenerational learning, cultural sustainability, and community empowerment, while addressing risks of authenticity, ownership, and access. The study argues that digital storytelling enables the Garasia to act both as custodians of tradition and as active shapers of their digital futures.

DOI: 10.4018/979-8-3373-5307-4.ch005

INTRODUCTION

The merger of media, technology, and social innovation in the 21st century has transformed how society captures, preserves and disseminates cultural knowledge. This revolution poses a challenge and an opportunity for indigenous communities whose culture is rich in oral narratives, rituals, and collective memory. The Garasia tribe of Rajasthan, India, like many other indigenous peoples in the world, uses oral storytelling, folk practices and lived cultural manifestations as the leading and sole means of passing knowledge between generations. However, things become more dangerous as globalization gains momentum, migration rises, and the younger generation is attracted to modern education and urban ways, so cultural practices are endangered (J. M. Smith & Van Ierland, 2018).

Storytelling has been identified as an essential tool where indigenous people share values, cosmologies, and histories (Wilson & Stewart, 2008). Garasia oral traditions include myths, folk songs, seasonal rituals, and stories representing the wisdom of the community and cultural identity. Such stories are entertainment and live collections of ecological knowledge, moral values, and social norms (Sonowal & Choudhury, 2024). However, unless these traditions are documented and preserved through institutions, they will likely be lost whenever older people die or the young people lose interest in the tribal traditions. Digital storytelling also creates a revolutionary opportunity; however, as the digital world expands, indigenous knowledge can be preserved and reinvigorated with the help of digital stories.

Digital storytelling is a broad term that combines classic forms of narration and contemporary digital media so that communities can create, archive and share cultural stories through videos, podcasts, animations and social networks (Edyangu, 2021). In contrast to the non-dynamic preservation methods, like written records, digital storytelling allows preserving the dynamism of the oral tradition through the intertwining of images, sounds, and voices and their proximity to the live performance. It also becomes a form of empowerment of the marginalized groups and provides a means of representing themselves genuinely and not allowing outside powers to define them (Couldry, 2022). It also provides avenues of intergenerational learning in tribal settings with younger and more digitally cool people joining elders in archiving and sharing traditional knowledge (Rowley et al., 2014).

Meanwhile, there are challenging questions. What will become of oral traditions? How can they be safeguarded and remain authentic using digital tools and not turn into data? Who owns access, ownership and representation of indigenous stories in digital platforms? Furthermore, how can technology closely tied to mainstream and globalist culture be modified to accommodate local and tribal epistemology (Dayé, 2025)? These questions highlight the conflicts between tradition and modernity, local and global, oral and digital.

Theoretical orientation of this chapter falls within cultural transmission theory that focuses on the role of the media in the passing of cultural values and practices between generations; media ecology theory that focuses on the role of media environments that influence human communication and the cultural practices; and social constructionism that focuses on how meaning is co-created by interactions and mediated representations (Burlacu, 2014). In this perspective, digital storytelling is not regarded as a method of archiving but rather as a process practiced in culture that redefines identity and continuity of Garasia culture.

The chapter aims to comprehend how digital storytelling may aid the continuation and passing on of Aboriginal knowledge among the Garasia tribe of Rajasthan, with special attention to how oral traditions, folk narratives, and cultural practices are maintained amidst rapid social change. It also emphasizes the promise of media platforms to see tribal youth and women as active agents in cultural preservation, as opposed to being the holders of the tradition, as they become contributors to the re-examination of its future. Meanwhile, the discussion is a critical reflection on the difficulties in digitizing the indigenous stories, particularly, the concepts of authenticity, ownership, and access that define not only the possibilities but also the constraints of technology to preserve the tribal heritage. The chapter anticipates the Garasia case and becomes a part of the broader scholarly and policy debates on preserving indigenous cultural knowledge in the digital era. It contends that oral tradition can be preserved against extinction and is a practice that is transformative through digital storytelling, where communities can redefine their future cultural practices. However, it warns against too rosy accounts of technology and advocates critical concern about the ethical, political and cultural impacts of digitizing indigenous heritage.

Finally, this chapter places the Garasia tribe not only as passively treated by technological interventions but also as an actor in their own stories. By so doing, it highlights the need to create collaborative, culturally aware, and community-based digital storytelling programs by respecting the epistemologies of indigenous communities. These initiatives have substantial value to the Garasia and tribal and marginalized communities worldwide, providing avenues for resisting their cultures' erasure and expressing themselves within the global digital zone.

REVIEW OF LITERATURE

Indigenous Knowledge Systems: Global and Indian Context

Indigenous Knowledge Systems (IKS) refer to the amount of wisdom, cultural values and practical skills that people within a community of various generations transmit orally and through experience across generations. IKS are gaining recognition as essential solutions to urgent challenges, including the disappearance of biodiversity, climate change, and sustainable development at the global level (Donkers & Ziegler, 2025). As an illustration, indigenous communities in Latin America and Africa manage the ecosystem because of their community-based conservation initiatives based on spiritual connections with the land and nature. These systems are holistic and relational ecological systems and have ecological sustainability woven into ritual, narrative and daily practice (Ranjan & Sharma, 2025). IKS in the Indian context takes place in agriculture, medicine, environmental management, and social organization. The Bhils, Gonds, and Garasias tribes are some of the tribes that use oral knowledge to spread folk knowledge and maintain cultural identities. According to recent academic work, India is also experiencing the loss of crop diversity and native medicinal knowledge due to globalization and large-scale hybrid models of agriculture (Kalra et al., 2025). These changes not only threaten ecological sustainability but also culture. For example, Srishailam et al. (2024) said that farmers in Arunachal Pradesh continue to use indigenous technical knowledge, e.g., botanical pesticides and composting methods, which maintain the soil fertility and cultural preservation. These are not mere utilitarian practices but within rituals, songs and stories constituting a shared culture. Therefore, although IKS are important in sustainability, they are at risk of erosion. Digital technologies and narration tools are becoming the channels of preservation and transfer of such knowledge to younger generations, and recording it to be available to the global audience in this context.

Digital Storytelling: Definitions, Applications, and Significance

Digital storytelling combines old storytelling, through the mouth, with multimedia, which entails video, audio, photography, animation, and interactive media. According to (Edyangu, 2021), digital stories are personal or community-based narratives told with the help of digital tools in a succinct, emotionally appealing, and multimodal manner. Digital storytelling, in the case of the indigenous, is an archiving tool and an identity-negotiation tool. Digital stories are being applied all over the world. The United States Native American tribes, including the Indigenous Virginia Digital Stories Project, document tribal histories and place the voices of communities at the centre of the tribal histories (Jernigan & Roach, 2021). Likewise, in the Arctic, digital games are implemented by Sami communities to combine folklore and modern interactive storytelling, renewing the storytelling of the culture and rendering it attractive to younger generations (Thathiah, 2024). The importance of digital storytelling is that it democratizes cultural representation. Unlike a book or a report, a digital story gives the communities themselves control over what to tell, how to contextualize it, and the medium. For example, (Gurning et al., 2024) created the KAHANI pipeline. This computer-generated storytelling system specifically aims at non-Western cultures to incorporate culturally-specific objects and narrative logic into generative systems. This minimizes the dangers of cultural distortion that tend to be part of platforms of Western origin.

Media and Cultural Preservation: Best Practices and Challenges

Media technologies are also becoming a niche in preserving intangible cultural heritage (ICH). Best practices imply a participatory framework in which communities are not passive participants but collaborative co-creators of digital archives. This guarantees the authenticity of culture and empowers local storytellers (Miguel et al., 2025). Likewise, multimodal conservation through video, audio, photography, and interactive media has been practical in preserving the performative aspects of culture, e.g., song, dance, or ritual. For example, (Luo et al., 2024) showed that digital archives and immersive media experiences could rejuvenate the Chinese traditions of shadow puppetry by generating interest in younger generations. The other best practice is localization or maintaining content in the local language and cultural symbols instead of homogenizing them in worldwide media. This is very much the case with the Garasia case, since they can use their own dialects and symbols, and this would avoid the dilution of cultures. Nonetheless, there are still many challenges. The issue of authenticity has been a major problem where traditions are digitized without the cultural context, which is readily seen as commodification. Sensitivity is also attached to the issue of ownership and intellectual property, whereby the communities might lose control of how their cultural representations are utilized after being digitized and distributed across the world (Hutto & Wheeler, 2023). The lack of devices, connectivity, or technical literacy further causes digital inequality, which marginalizes the parts of the tribal community, including women and older people (Kadiri & Owolabi, 2020). Lastly, the question of sustainability is urgent; donations fund most digital heritage projects and fail as soon as financing is ceased, which is a source of concern regarding the preservation process and accessibility in the long term.

Existing Tribal Case Studies (Indian Tribes, African/Native American Parallels)

Various tribal case studies provide comparative information (Chandarana & Kumar, 2024). In India, researchers reported how the Bhil, Bhotia, and Kurumba tribes have maintained medicinal practices despite the migration of younger generations towards urban areas. Their results emphasize the digital documentation's role in protecting the oral traditions against the pressures of urbanization. Equally, the study on the tribes of Arunachal Pradesh reveals that traditional ecological knowledge supports farming and enhances cultural identity (Dias, 2024). The Indigenous Virginia Digital Stories Project (Jernigan & Roach, 2021) shows how participatory digital media can preserve the regional history and solidify tribal identity internationally. The project focused on relational storytelling, connecting people to place and memory in an online context. In the Arctic, Sami digitalize the storytelling process by playing games (Blayone & Mykhailenko, 2025), demonstrating how indigenous youths use gaming to innovate the preservation of culture by integrating the traditional narrative into the interactive media. The two faces of empowerment and commodification of the media are also pointed out in the African case studies. Archiving oral histories among Maasai communities on the internet has not only helped store the endangered oral histories, but has also caused commercialization problems when cultural materials were employed without consent in tourism and advertisements (MWANGI, 2023). Such experiences underscore the importance of having transparent ethical guidelines in digitization projects. The examples highlight the variety of approaches and show that community involvement, cultural sensitivity, and belonging to narratives predetermine success in many cases. This literature has not fully covered the Garasia case; thus, it is an opportunity to make new contributions.

Research Gaps

Based on the literature, there are some evident gaps. First, although the existing literature is increasingly based on the indigenous knowledge systems (IKS) and the ongoing research on their digitalization, the less researched tribes are still underrepresented in the literature, and the Garasia tribe of Rajasthan or the other minor tribes, are not given special attention in scholarly literature. Second, the limited literature does not reveal much about the place of youth and women in digital storytelling. However, they are crucial in cultural transmission in tribal societies. Third, the ethical ownership of the digital in Indian contexts remains under-researched, especially regarding who owns digital archives and how these recurring stories of indigenous narratives can be preserved once digitized. Fourth, little has been done to explore hybrid ways of storytelling, including incorporating immersive technologies such as augmented reality (AR) and virtual reality (VR) into conventional oral storytelling techniques. Lastly, the questions of sustainability will not be answered, as not many studies reflect on the sustainability of tribal digital storytelling projects under the infrastructural, financial, and technical pressure. Through these gaps, this chapter will seek to give a case-specific insight into how digital storytelling can be an essential instrument for cultural preservation among the Garasia tribe of Rajasthan.

THEORETICAL AND CONCEPTUAL FRAMEWORK

Theoretical Base

To learn how indigenous communities will resort to digital storytelling as a part of cultural preservation, it is necessary to have a solid theoretical basis. This paper will utilize Cultural Transmission Theory, Media Ecology Theory and Social Constructionism as they offer a holistic approach to the analysis of interrelations of knowledge, media and identity.

Cultural Transmission Theory

Cultural Transmission Theory is essential to explaining the world of knowledge, values, and practices transmitted through generations. Anthropologists such as Mead, 1970 underlined that cultural continuity is maintained by deliberate and inadvertent learning in families and communities. This was later formalized by (Schwartz, 1980), who used models to illustrate the spread of traditions, languages and behaviours through vertical (parent-to-child), horizontal (peer-to-peer) and oblique (elder-to-youth) transmission. In the case of the Garasia tribe, oral narration has always been a significant component of vertical and oblique transmission because the elders speak about myths, genealogies, and ecological knowledge. Nonetheless, the younger generation tends to be more attracted to extraneous cultural discourses due to the fast development and modernization, and the influence of the mainstream media, which is dangerous to the knowledge of the native communities. World examples have strengthened this. To put it into perspective, digital archives have enabled the Maori of New Zealand to save oral histories and genealogies, which help them to withstand cultural erosion (T. Smith, 2024).On the same note, video-based storytelling projects have played a central role in preserving languages and ecological knowledge among the Native American groups (Wilson & Stewart, 2008). In the case of the Garasia, taking these measures implies that the old myths on nature, farming, and family relationships can be relocated to younger audiences who are more digitally literate.

Media Ecology Theory

Whereas the Cultural Transmission Theory describes the nature of what is being transmitted, the Media Ecology Theory describes how the medium influences the process. According to Postman (1970) and McLuhan (1994), communication technologies reshape how people perceive things and culture; the medium is the message. Media spaces are not neutral and remake social relations, hierarchies and cultural memory. Media ecology is functional in indigenous contexts in realizing how digital platforms have replaced oral storytelling. An example is when a Garasia folktale is read in the fireplace and integrated with background, tone, movement, and rituals. Once digitalized, the story loses its connection to the immediate social context and acquires new meaning in the digital circulation. This puts the issue of authenticity and interpretation into question, because digital versions can be seen by more people, but risk missing the details connected to lived experience. Simultaneously, it suggests new opportunities for digital media:

Preservation: The lives of storytellers can be continued even after their demise.

Amplification: Narratives may be extended to younger Garasia who go to urban areas and solidify diasporic ties.

Agency: The communities can fight stereotypes by creating self-representations, instead of depending on outside researchers or media.

Other indigenous communities depict this dynamic. For example, the First Nations in Canada use community radio and YouTube to reclaim cultural narratives (Lobensteiner & Thies, 2020). The African tribes of pastoralists use WhatsApp to record oral poetry and songs (Lukanda et al., 2023). The media ecology theory can be used to explain opportunities (inclusiveness, permanence) and challenges (distortion, commodification). In practice, applied to the Garasia, it has made the point how digital storytelling, as a tool and as an environment, is reconfigurating the relationships between the narrators, audiences and culture itself.

Social Constructionism

Although the former two theories describe transmission and medium, the Social Constructionism (Zelizer, 1992) describes the active construction of cultural meaning. This school of thought believes that reality is not predetermined but socially constructed by discourse, interaction, and negotiation. Culture is thus built up and built down continuously by the members. To the Garasia, folklore is not a fixed set of stories; it changes according to the situation. When the older adults share the myths of their ancestors, they turn them into new meanings that reflect the teaching of right, kinship or ecological stewardship. When transferred to the digital realm, young people redesign the stories, occasionally overlaying them with popular culture or incorporating them into images and musical compositions. Social constructionism allows us to understand that digital storytelling is not a preservation but an active re-creation of culture that enables tribes to oppose homogenizing narratives of outsiders and be able to assert their indigenous identity. Moreover, social constructionism emphasizes power relationships when telling stories. Who is to tell the story, the older, the younger, the woman, the foreign scholar? Who owns its digital manifestation, and what is the authenticity? Seeing culture as socially constructed, we can understand that digital platforms provide a place of negotiation in which ownership, identity, and meaning are disputed.

Conceptual Framework

Based on these theoretical foundations, the conceptual framework of this research is based on the convergence between Indigenous Knowledge (IK), Digital Stories and Cultural Preservation/Empowerment.

Key Concepts

1. **Indigenous Knowledge (IK):** Locally based, generative wisdom gained through experience includes ecological processes, rituals, oral stories, and social practices (Zelizer, 1992). In the case of the Garasia, IK incorporates farming methods, religious oral epics, family traditions, and environmental management.
2. **Storytelling:** Oral and electronic retelling of mythology, histories and lived experience. Storytelling is a cultural practice that maintains identity and community values (Wilson & Stewart, 2008). It is used as moral education and cultural memory in the Garasia context.
3. **Digital Storytelling/Media Tools:** Recording, disseminating, and storing stories with the help of digital resources (smartphones, videos, apps, social media). In addition to documentation, digital storytelling is participatory and tends to democratize the narrator.
4. **Cultural Preservation:** Protection of material and non-material heritage, especially oral traditions, languages, and rituals. Preservation does not only mean archiving, but also keeping culture alive for modern generations.
5. **Community Empowerment:** The promotion of agency, visibility and agency of the marginalized groups (especially the youth and women) in cultural decision-making and representation (Balka, 1987).

Figure 1. Conceptual model of the study

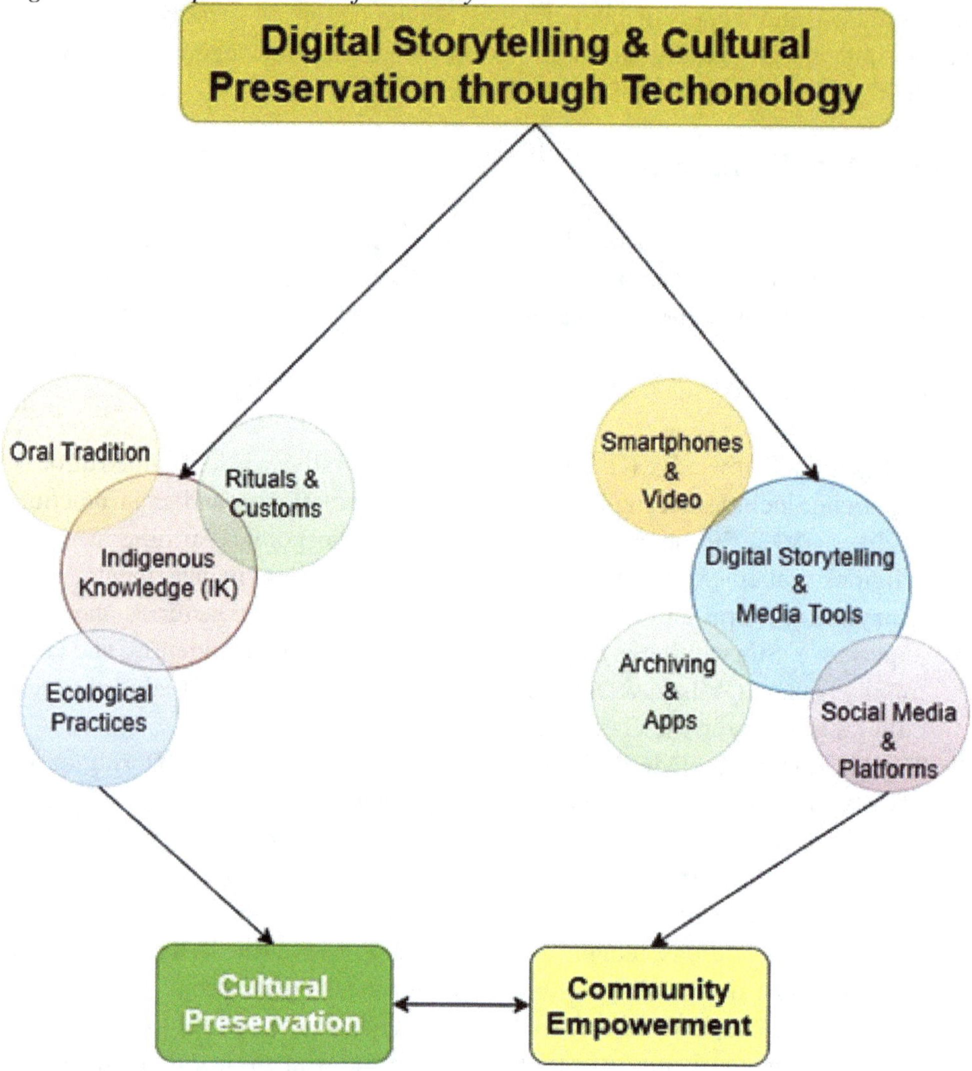

The conceptual model puts Indigenous Knowledge (IK) in the center of the concept, which carries the long-established traditions, ecological habits, verbal stories, and cultural rites that characterize the heritage of the Garasia tribe. This profoundly intergenerational knowledge becomes activated when it is mediated using digital storytelling and media tools. These technologies, including smartphones, video recordings, social media sites, and archival software, can serve as mediators to help the temporal oral traditions become permanent, exchangeable, and accessible cultural resources. The results of such mediation are two-fold. First, it helps preserve the culture so that the traditions, language and identity can be sustained amid the modernization factors and the outside stresses. Second, it cultivates community empowerment through establishing environments where youth and women can engage in cultural production actively, expanding the global presence, and the self-representative ability to break stereotypes. It is worth mentioning that feedback loops are recognized within the framework, with empowered communities given a chance to feed into the storytelling cycle and boost IK, as well as through the feedback loops, rendering it more sustainable. For example, when Garasia youth create digital video versions of folktales, they not only retain cultural accounts but also encourage other peers and younger generations to participate, establishing more intergenerational connections and making their cultural heritage resistant to digital and physical erasures.

Integration of Theories into Framework

The Cultural Transmission Theory describes the process by which native knowledge is transmitted through generations, and, currently, digital tools are augmenting the oral means of transmission. Media Ecology Theory introduces a new dimension by explaining how transforming the medium (oral storytelling) into the digital space changes the flow of stories and cultural interaction. Social constructionism also highlights how culture is not an immutable and fixed construct, but constantly constructed through interaction, especially in the digital space, where the meaning is co-determined by both storytellers and audiences. Combined, these theories offer a multi-faceted viewing through which the meaning-making process (social construction), the medium (digital tools), and the content (indigenous knowledge) are combined. This combined framework will enable the research study to analyse how cultural preservation happens and deal with essential questions of authenticity, possession, and empowerment in the framework of digital storytelling among the Garasia tribe.

THE GARASIA TRIBE: SOCIO-CULTURAL CONTEXT

Historical Background and Settlement Areas

The Garasia tribe is among the natives of Rajasthan in India, and it has a history dating back several centuries (Singh, 2010). Historically, the Garasias are forest people, commonly called hilly areas and forested terrains of southern Rajasthan, specifically, Sirohi, Dungarpur, and Udaipur districts (Gupta et al., 2018). They used to be semi-nomadic and earned their living through shifting cultivation, cattle herding, and forest production (M. S. Kumar et al., 2012). After a specific period, the settlements increasingly became more permanent, and villages were formed along the rivers and fertile lands to sustain farming and animal husbandry (M. Desai & Goel, 2018). The patterns in which they inhabit the natural environment also show a strong attachment to their natural surroundings since forests and hills supplied them with resources and influenced the social, spiritual, and cultural life of the Garasias (Rao et al., 2011). The history of the Garasias in Rajasthan places them in the position between tribal independence and the region's politics (M. M. Patel et al., 2025). Despite being the smallest tribe, compared to other communities in Rajasthan, the tribe has maintained a unique socio-cultural identity, in most cases by forming self-governed systems like the panchayat (Meena, 2024). These traditional government systems have always served to resolve disputes, govern cohabiting communities, and hold social standards, which allowed the community to remain unified and persistent in the face of external forces.

Cultural Heritage: Music, Oral Storytelling, Rituals, and Dress

The Garasia tribe is a culturally rich community manifested through music, oral narration, rituals, and unique dress. Social life is symbolized by music and dance as it is involved in festivals, marriages, and harvest celebrations. Dhol, bansuri (flute), and manjira are instruments used when singing about the tribal history, moral teachings, and folklore (Rao et al., 2011). Such performances entertain and pass knowledge to succeeding generations, strengthening values and community identity. Oral storytelling is an essential practice among the Garasias. The tribe does not have much in the way of written documents, so they have to use elders and community performers to share their myths, legends, and history. These stories contain heroic stories, parables of the divine and moral teachings used as an educational and cultural preservation tool. There is a connection between human experience and natural and spiritual nature, intertwining stories with land to indicate an indigenous epistemology that places value on relational knowledge and environmental stewardship (P. Verma et al., 2022). Garasia identity is visually represented by dress and ornament. Men are accustomed to wearing dhotis and turbans, which are usually colored and adorned with shapes and patterns reflecting marital status or belonging to the village. Sarees are colorful, embroidered with complicated embroidery, and embellished with silver jewelry and beads representing social roles, age, and marriage. This material culture conveys a sense of identity and belonging and transmits artisanal knowledge across generations.

Current Challenges: Modernization, Migration, and Language Erosion

The Garasia tribe has several problems with the preservation of their heritage despite the richness of their culture. Due to modernization and urbanization, there are economic demands and cultural dynamics that are ever threatening the traditional practices due to the emerging economic and cultural pressures. Schooling, digital media, and urban jobs are exposed to younger generations, which may lead to a lower involvement in the tribal rituals and knowledge of oral traditions. Another essential factor is migration. Garasia members migrate to the cities, looking for work or education, so the community is disunited, and the knowledge between generations becomes weakened (Mehta & Sharma, 2015). Youths tend to live more in the urban set-up as they spend less time in the tribal setting and become less connected to traditional ways of life and oral cultural information transfer. These are even worse due to language erosion. The Garasia dialect, which captures exclusive cultural allusions, rites, and oral traditions, is progressively becoming endangered as Hindi or other local languages take over education, media, and official communication. Language loss implies a fall in language levels and loss of culture hidden in language since most of the tribe's history is oral (Rizwan et al., 2014).

Additionally, the socio-economic marginalization may restrict resources with which cultural preservation can be done. Without proper support for education that integrates indigenous knowledge or the local arts and crafts, there is a danger that the age-old skills and cultural manifestations may disappear in the long run. All these challenges threaten knowledge delivery, as they destroy the material and intangible cultural heritage of the Garasia tribe.

Why Garasia Knowledge is Under Threat without Digital Documentation

The cultural heritage of the Garasia tribe is under a threat that it will ultimately cause when systematic records are not made. Oral traditions are especially susceptible since they depend on memory and habit. All the narratives, ritual knowledge and practices may be lost forever once the elders die or the young people lose interest. The opportunities provided by digital storytelling and media are previously unmatched in dealing with this threat. Performative subtleties that are unpublished in textual form can be captured in audio-visual recordings of songs, dances and rituals. On the same note, video interviews with the elders maintain oral history in their natural voice and language with the same intonation, emotion, and cultural background (Rao et al., 2011). The traditional clothing, crafts, and places of worship can be captured in photography and digital archives so that such visual content can be made available to community members and other members of the broader communities. Garasia may lose ecological knowledge, agricultural techniques, and social traditions without electronic records.

METHODOLOGY

Research Approach, Type, and Method

The research method of this study is qualitative, which suits the exploration of highly cultural phenomena and perceiving the meanings, values, and knowledge embedded in the Garasia tribe of Rajasthan (Creswell & Poth, 2016).

Method: Interpretive, the paper is devoted to the cultural, social, and historical background of the Garasia community, and it explains how indigenous knowledge is presented, kept, and distributed by using oral traditions, rituals, and media.

Type: The study is descriptive and exploratory. It will describe the socio-cultural activities of the Garasia tribe and examine the potential of digital storytelling as a cultural preservation method.

Approach: Desk-based qualitative analysis, the research synthesises secondary data based on ethnographic research, scholarly literature, NGO and case reports and digital media. The approach will allow a thorough knowledge of the indigenous practices and their significance in the modern context without restrictions of primary fieldwork.

Data Collection Sources

Ethnographic References: Ethnographic records depict a vivid description of the social organizations, rituals, oral traditions and settlement pattern of the Garasia tribe (R. Kumar, 2016). These works provide the background to how indigenous knowledge is reflected in everyday life and traditions.

NGO and Case Studies: NGO reports about tribal communities in Rajasthan have been offered with information about socio-economic life, education, healthcare, and their activities aimed at preserving their culture (V. L. Patel et al., 2013). These studies point out viable issues that the Garasia community have encountered and efforts aimed at exploiting digital platforms to document and market indigenous knowledge.

Media Analysis: Digital platforms such as videos, photos, and online storytelling projects are examined to explain how Garasia traditions are reflected and addressed in the modern media (Verma & Sharma, 2016). Media analysis assists in determining the possibilities of digital storytelling in terms of cultural preservation and communication with society, as well as reveals the deficiencies in the representational sphere and accessibility.

Justification for Desk-Based and Interpretive Method

The interpretive approach to the investigation is appropriate in this study since it provides an opportunity to analyse available literature and media critically. Based on ethnographic research, case reports, and online resources, the study helps identify the common theme, cultural scripts, and indigenous knowledge captured in Garasia practices (Fusch et al., 2018). The interpretive approach will be the most suitable to interpret digital storytelling as a preservation method, since it focuses on creating meaning, context, and socio-cultural interpretation instead of statistical generalization. The traditional knowledge system and contemporary media interventions offer a very subtle approach to cultural continuity and change in the Garasia tribe. Combining ethnographic, NGO, and media materials, the research provides an overall contextualized perspective on how indigenous knowledge can be captured, represented, and maintained with the help of digital media.

DIGITAL STORYTELLING PRACTICES AND POSSIBILITIES

Existing Uses of Media in Garasia and Similar Tribal Communities

Digital media is often applied to record, store and share indigenous knowledge among tribal societies, such as the Garasia tribe. Although a systematic digital recording of the Garasias is yet to be done, it is possible to point out various instances of media use within the community and elsewhere in cases of other tribes. Video-sharing websites such as YouTube have become popular as mediums of transmitting folk performances, music, dances, and rituals to tribal communities. An example is that NGOs, researchers and local enthusiasts upload recordings of folk songs, traditional dances, and storytelling sessions of the tribal communities of Rajasthan. Thus, these practices are available to the rest of the world. These documents preserve the performative aspects of the culture and document oral histories, dialects and the situation of the ceremony, which is otherwise prone to erosion. NGOs and other cultural organisations are also crucial in recording the tribal knowledge using digital media. Cultural practices include agricultural practices, healing practices, festivals, and artisanal crafts, which are presented in reports, audio-visual records, and online exhibitions. For example, organizations that work with Rajasthani tribes frequently involve workshops during which young people and community members will learn to document oral stories and photographic rituals and submit them to digital archives. These practices not only preserve knowledge to be used by future generations but also enable communities to introduce their culture in their own terms.

Potential for AR/VR, Mobile Apps, and Digital Archives

The possibilities of utilizing high-technology digital tools like Augmented Reality (AR), Virtual Reality (VR), mobile apps, and digital archives are enormous for cultural preservation. AR and VR technologies have the potential to make such experiences immersive, which means that a user can enter into a Garasia ritual or festival or history storytelling session. An example is a VR reconstruction of a Garasia harvest festival, which would allow individuals to experience the performance, costumes, music, and dance in a participatory way so that sensory and spatial aspects of cultural information would not be lost (Kozinets, 2023). Folk stories, songs and learning material in the Garasia dialect can be stored in mobile applications. These applications might have interactive storytelling features, instructions on traditional crafts, or virtual tours of heritage places related to the tribe. The mobile platforms are specifically useful since they can address the youth growing more tech-savvy, but are geographically out of reach of the tribal community due to migration or education. Digital archives provide another important avenue. Such archives might contain audio-video records, photographs, and written accounts of rites, festivals, and social activities. Compared to the lifeless exhibits of a museum, digital archives can be searched, shared, and viewed worldwide, allowing Garasia community members to systematize their knowledge and not lose it under the pressure of modernization. The cross-generational learning can also be conducted through archiving because young members may access the community's heritage at any time and from any place, which helps maintain continuity in passing knowledge.

Role of Youth and Women in Using Technology

Digital storytelling efforts have occupied a place among the youth and women. In the Garasia tribe, young generations are more exposed to schooling, mobile technology, and social media sites. This exposure gives them the tools and digital literacy necessary to document and share their cultural practices (P. S. Desai, 2024). Young people may also become cultural mediators, interconnecting old knowledge and new technology, such as filming elders' stories, recording rituals on video or creating archives online. Their involvement also ensures that indigenous knowledge is preserved and introduced engagingly and meaningfully to the contemporary audience. The participation of women is significant as well.

Women are the leading depositories of household practices, verbal narratives, and artisanal crafts in most tribal societies, such as the Garasia. Their involvement in digital recordings is very active, and the information about the culturally essential practices in the domestic sphere, healthcare, folklore, and ceremonies will be reflected in their proper form. Digital stories also empower women since they provide visibility and agency that allows them to establish cultural power and disseminate knowledge not just within the household or village. Together, the involvement of young people and women in digital storytelling would encourage intergenerational exchange of knowledge, reinforce identity, and engagement in cultural preservation programs. Moreover, it could help to create collective works involving the Garasia people and NGOs, researchers, or media experts, and increase the scale of digital documentation work.

Barriers: Digital Divide, Literacy, and Access to Devices

Despite its potential, several barriers constrain the widespread adoption of digital storytelling among the Garasia and similar tribal communities (Butler & Sellbom, 2002). The digital divide remains a significant challenge. Rural and remote settlements often have limited internet connectivity, poor mobile network coverage, and insufficient access to computers or smartphones (Verma & Sharma, 2016). Without reliable connectivity, uploading and sharing digital content becomes difficult, restricting the ability of communities to engage with online audiences.

Digital storytelling offers transformative possibilities for preserving and disseminating Garasia tribal knowledge. Existing media, such as folk performances uploaded on YouTube and NGO documentation projects, demonstrate that oral traditions, rituals, and artistic expressions can be captured and shared digitally. Advanced tools such as AR, VR, mobile applications, and digital archives provide immersive and interactive methods to safeguard indigenous knowledge for future generations. The active participation of youth and women is pivotal, as they provide the digital literacy, creativity, and cultural insight required to document and transmit traditions effectively. However, challenges such as the digital divide, literacy constraints, limited access to devices, and cultural sensitivities must be addressed to ensure successful implementation. Overall, with thoughtful integration of technology, training, and community engagement, digital storytelling can serve as a powerful tool for cultural preservation, enabling the Garasia tribe to maintain, celebrate, and share their rich heritage in an increasingly digital world.

DISCUSSION AND ANALYSIS

Digital Storytelling as a Vehicle for Preserving Oral Traditions

The Garasia tribe of Rajasthan, like many other indigenous tribes, have practised oral storytelling as a tool of cultural knowledge, values and collective memory for centuries. The elders transmit folktales, ritual songs, myths, and agricultural practices to maintain their identity over the generations. Such oral tradition, however, is seriously threatened by globalization, migration of people towards urban centers, and changing educational concerns. At this point, digital stories appear to be a disruptive resource for maintaining and rejuvenating these traditions. According to Cultural Transmission Theory, oral storytelling may be regarded as an intergenerational knowledge transmission process through which cultural values, practices, and narratives are replicated (MacDonald, 2013). Digital technologies, video recordings, podcasts, animations, and community archives are not substitutes for this oral mode; they are supplements that form long-lasting records that can be viewed even by non-community members. The case in point, a Garasia folktale traditionally shared during agricultural ceremonies, can be captured on a mobile phone and distributed over social media-based platforms. As such, this will increase the reach of the folklore, but the younger generation of Garasia (scattered geographically) can still feel connected to their ancestry. Another dimension is the Media Ecology Theory, which states that the medium is the message (MacDonald, 2013). The transition to digital video in a spoken word is bound to change the relations of narration. In live oral performance, the setting, the audience, and the circumstances influence the meaning; with digital media, the story is disconnected from its immediate surroundings and spreads internationally. Although this may cause a loss of performative nuance, it also enables stories to remain outside the restrictions of memory and physical closeness. To this extent, digital media are like an extension of memory, where cultural material is saved in a manner that would not be the case with oral-only traditions (Brown, 1997). This shows that culture is not static but is constantly redefined through interaction, and digital storytelling offers an interactive platform through which it can be redefined. Therefore, digital storytelling in the Garasia example also plays a two-fold role, as it can preserve the richness of oral tradition. At the same time, cultural innovation and adaptation become possible. The practice freezes tradition, making it dynamic, interactive, and available to insiders and outsiders.

Risks of Digitalization: Cultural Appropriation, Authenticity, and Data Ownership

Although digital storytelling offers thrilling prospects for preserving cultural features, it is not a problem-free endeavour. The shift to digital presentation also comes with ethical, cultural and technical issues that should be considered, especially for marginalized groups like the Garasia tribe. Cultural appropriation is one of the greatest dangers. After digitising and disseminating indigenous stories via open sources such as YouTube, TikTok, or Facebook, it is prone to misrepresentation, exploitation, or even commodification by other parties. Outsiders can absorb narratives of a sacred or ritual value as simple entertainment value, divested of their cultural and religious backgrounds. Without protective frameworks, indigenous scholars have cautioned that digital preservation can indicate an unwanted continuation of colonial relations, in which other institutions can make money or otherwise expropriate indigenous knowledge (Prażmowska-Marcinowska, 2020). In the case of the Garasia tribe, the danger is especially acute since their narratives are associated with agrarian practices and family models. Therefore, they are prone to being misrepresented once separated from the community values. The other challenge is authenticity. To be attractive, digital storytelling must frequently undergo time adaptation, editing, language translation or dramatization. All these processes are part of the danger of distorting the "authentic voice of indigenous knowledge. According to Media Ecology, the medium determines how the message is conveyed and how it will be interpreted (Manžuch, 2017). This brings about power relations between a community producing knowledge and external bodies that host or distribute such knowledge. Indigenous digital archiving scholars have pointed to instances when communities have lost control over their stories after they have been put in institutional repositories (Nwabueze, 2017). To the Garasia, there are questions: Who owns a digitized folktale, the storyteller, the videographer, the platform or the community as a group? Without ethical principles, there is a high risk of exploitation. These risks are both technical and legal from the social constructionist perspective, as well as symbolic. When stories spread online, the definition is a co-construction between various audiences, including those not part of the Garasia culture. Although this may enhance interpretations, it may thin out or distort the intended meanings. An example of a Garasia myth being reinterpreted as a cultural charter that defines the norms of kinship or environmental practices can be reinterpreted by a global audience as a fairy tale, deprived of its meaning as a cultural charter. The Cultural Transmission model also highlights how digital preservation is weak. Whereas oral storytelling maintains the story's authenticity by using live presentation and communal authorization, digital storytelling removes the narrative from the social and ritual context into which it is embedded. This causes the validation mechanism to change into algorithms, likes, and shares. This also casts doubt on the possibility that younger generations of Garasia will start appreciating digital popular stories instead of cultural ones. Lastly, these risks are aggravated by the digital divide. The tribal populations have uneven access to smartphones, the internet, and digital literacy (Stürmer et al., 2021). In the Garasia tribe, women and older people might not be involved in digital storytelling programs, further consolidating previous social inequalities. What may start as an empowering tool may end up silencing other voices and magnifying others. Although digital storytelling presents opportunities for cultural preservation, it also provokes ethical issues regarding ownership, authenticity and power. These dangers make the Garasia and other tribes like them consider how the community-based digital projects could be implemented when the members of the tribes themselves could control the process, along with the results.

OPPORTUNITIES: EDUCATION, GLOBAL EXCHANGE, AND IDENTITY STRENGTHENING

The risks of digitalization are significant, but the opportunities offered by digital storytelling in preserving the culture of the indigenous population are enormous. In the case of the Garasia tribe of Rajasthan, the digital initiatives that will be strategically designed can be used as strong educational resources, means of global communication, and cultural identity reinforcement. Education is one of the most immediate fields where digital storytelling can transform. Indigenous knowledge (IK) is not solely concerned with myths and folktales but also covers the fields of agriculture, medical knowledge, and environmental knowledge. Digitizing these stories, the communities will be able to develop alternative educational materials that will be used to supplement formal education. For example, the short movie about Garasia farming rituals might be presented in local schools to local children to educate them not only in the practical farming techniques but also in the cultural significance of the techniques. According to the Cultural Transmission Theory, digital storytelling reinforces the intergenerational relationship by ensuring that the younger generations are still attached to the wisdom of their elders (Zalli, 2024). The digital archives are permanent storehouses of knowledge, unlike oral-only traditions that can be forgotten or lost with the migration of the younger members or a lack of interest. Moreover, they enable the tribal youth to interact with tradition in a comfortable and enjoyable format, such as videos, apps, or interactive media. This creates a modern packaging of traditional content, making education enjoyable and culturally oriented. Digital storytelling also enables tribal females to be teachers and cultural guardians. When Garasia women write songs, rituals or weave, they claim to be the key players in the process of cultural handover. This is consistent with the results of other indigenous groups where digital media projects have made women more visible and able to act more on cultural preservation (Mariyono et al., 2025). Digital storytelling also supports the cross-cultural dialogue. When the Garasia stories are computerized, they can be spread across borders so that the world can enjoy the richness of tribal cultures. This visibility works against centuries of marginalization in which indigenous cultures were often considered primitive or backward. Instead, they turn out to be active creators of global cultural discourses. From a media ecology viewpoint, the digital medium alters how stories are told and how people listen to them (Li, 2025). Social media networks such as YouTube or Instagram make the cultural exchange democratic, going around the traditional gatekeepers, publishers or academic institutions. A Garasia youth putting up a video of a folktale can access people as diverse as researchers in Europe, indigenous people in Africa, or policymakers in Delhi. Such connectivity promotes solidarity between marginalized communities and places indigenous voices into the international cultural rights and sustainability discourse.

Meanwhile, cultural tourism and economic opportunities may be affected by global visibility. NGOs, universities, or cultural organizations may be interested in storytelling projects that fund tribal artisans, performers, or young entrepreneurs. For example, local storytelling festivals in Canada and New Zealand have established a platform where indigenous people share their narratives with the rest of the world, earning them fame and cash. A similar initiative could be imagined in the Garasia community, where cultural preservation correlates with sustainable livelihoods.

Identity Strengthening and Self-Representation

One of the most incredible possibilities of digital storytelling is, perhaps, the construction and reinforcement of identity. Poor people are marginalized and may find it very difficult to fight stereotyping or negative images created by mainstream society. Online media also enables tribes such as the Garasia to retell their stories and project themselves on their own terms. According to the Social Constructionists, there is no fixed identity, but it is an ongoing negotiation by discourse (T. R. Smith, 2004). Through documenting and posting their tales, the Garasia youth and women are involved in defining how they are portrayed both within and outside the community. For example, a video of traditional dance produced by Garasia entertains and establishes cultural pride and informs about the strength towards the external world. Besides, digital storytelling allows blended identities that combine tradition and modernity. The young people in the tribes are often caught in a dilemma between the traditional culture and the longing to get a higher education or employment. The digital narratives enable them to find a balance between this tension: smartphones and cameras are integrated with ancestral myths and rituals.

This synthesis illustrates that adopting technology does not imply that we may leave technology behind; however, it may be a way of rethinking cultural continuity in modern times. The psychological effect of identity strengthening is hard to overestimate. According to research on indigenous media initiatives worldwide, digital self-representation positively correlates with self-esteem, cultural pride, and community cohesion (Battersby, 2006). In the case of the Garasia, these effects may be powerful in dealing with the challenge of marginalization, migration, and assimilation pressures of the mainstream society.

Intersections with Development Goals

Lastly, these opportunities align with the larger developmental and policy frameworks. The Sustainable Development Goals (SDGs), especially SDG 4 (Quality Education), SDG 10 (Reduced Inequalities) and SDG 11 (Sustainable Communities) of the United Nations, highlight the significance of inclusive education, equity, and cultural heritage protection (Onyeaka et al., 2024). The initiatives of digital storytelling in tribes such as Garasia are direct contributors to these global goals as they guarantee the sustainability of cultures and inclusive engagement and bridge the digital divide. To policymakers, these projects provide precedents of participatory development in which communities own their cultural preservation plans. To teachers, they supply culturally applicable didactical materials, which improve the learning process. In the case of NGOs, they open avenues for the incorporation of indigenous knowledge into the wider sustainability and social justice agendas.

Interdisciplinary Insights: Education, Sociology, and Media Studies

Digital stories, indigenous knowledge, and cultural preservation need multidisciplinary intervention. The insights contributed by education, sociology, and media studies create a better picture of the potentials and complexities of digitizing indigenous traditions like the Garasia tribe. From a pedagogical perspective, digital storytelling serves as a preservation method and a pedagogical approach. Implementing digital media in teaching Garasia culture in schools means that natives are exposed to their own culture in formal education, which is usually pervaded with mainstream knowledge (Marchessault, 2014). Culturally relevant pedagogy is essential in educational technology research because it enhances student engagement, retention, and identity formation. To Garasia young people, education in the form of stories being told by people within their community, digitalised and retold, bridges their traditional knowledge and formal education and helps them take pride in their culture and preserve it. Digital storytelling can be studied sociologically in terms of agency, identity, and power relations. Sharing their stories online and turning them digital, the Garasia avoid being marginalized and confront the existing cultural domination that tends to suppress tribal voices. Theories of cultural reproduction (Tsapro et al., 2025) emphasise how dominant groups sustain power by being in control of cultural capital. In this regard, digital storytelling enables marginalized communities to create and distribute their cultural capital to transform the relationship between recognition and legitimacy. In addition, it also redefines social formations in the community itself, with the young and feminine becoming more active agents of preserving their culture; the generational and gendered hierarchies are overturned.

Media Studies Perspective

Media studies use critical tools to understand the mediating role of technology in cultural practices. The Media Ecology Theory underlines how the communication medium transforms, significantly altering the cultural experience (McLuhan, 1964). With the Garasia, the digitalization of the oral performance to digital archiving transforms storytelling as a local activity, done communally, into a translocal event, which can be accessed anywhere in the world. Not only does this widen the horizon of stories, but their social functions are shifted this way, further embedded in digital economies of attention and circulation. Also, critical media studies note that we should not focus too much on technology and that problems of digital access, ownership, and algorithmic biases are likely to support inequalities (Mukherjee, 2024). These disciplinary insights show that digital storytelling is more than a technical intervention. It is both a form of educational innovation, a sociological performance of resistance and identity formation, and an act of cultural practices transformation fueled by the media. In the case of the Garasia tribe, it provides avenues for cultural resilience but also requires attention to ethical, social, and technological issues. The interdisciplinary perspectives again confirm the relevance of placing digital storytelling in the context of more general theoretical and practical frameworks. Education emphasizes that it is a critical component of the intergenerational learning process, sociology emphasizes the ability to redistribute cultural power, and media studies brings attention to the structure of digital environments. This three-fold intervention reinforces the analysis and gives a roadmap for designing community-based, morally upright, and socially influential storytelling programs.

CONCLUSION

This paper has discussed how digital storytelling has changed the face of preservation and transmission of indigenous knowledge among the Garasia tribe living in

Rajasthan. In its most fundamental context, digital storytelling seeks to solve one of the most pressing issues of indigenous communities in the modern world: the loss of oral traditions in the adversity of modernization, migration, and globalization. Digitising folktales, songs, rituals, and agriculture, the Garasia can guarantee their culture will not be lost in the current and future generations. Through the theory of Cultural Transmission, this work has demonstrated how digital technologies can supplement old forms of intergenerational learning so that the stories can live even after memory and geographic location constraints. The Media Ecology Theory also noted that the medium, per se, changes the process of telling stories and presents both opportunities and threats. Lastly, social constructionism underlined that culture is not fixed but is actively transformed with digital involvement, which enabled Garasia youth and women to redefine traditions and bring them closer to modern realities. The greater contribution is that digital storytelling should not be seen as a passive method of archiving but as an active and participative way of cultural revitalization. To the Garasia, the regaining of their voices, the deepening of particular identity and the contact with broader audiences confirm dignity and resistance.

REFERENCES

Balka, E. (1987). *Women and workplace technology: Educational strategies for change*.

Battersby, J. L. (2006). Narrativity, self, and self-representation. *Narrative*, *14*(1), 27–44.

Blayone, T. J. B., & Mykhailenko, O. (2025). Using Digital Technologies for Indigenous Socio-cultural Advancement in an Era of AI: A Systematic Critical Synthesis. *Preservation, Digital Technology & Culture, 0*.

Brown, L. M. (1997). *Storytelling: a cultural studies approach*.

Burlacu, M. (2014). Digital anthropology: Theoretical perspectives regarding electronic tribes. *Bulletin of the Transilvania University of Braşov. Series VII: Social Sciences and Law*, *1*, 241–248.

Butler, D. L., & Sellbom, M. (2002). Barriers to adopting technology. *EDUCAUSE Quarterly*, *2*(1), 22–28.

Chandarana, B. K., & Kumar, T. (2024). Preservation and Advocacy of Indigenous Medicinal Knowledge of Tribes in India. *International Conference on Business and Technology*, 522–529.

Couldry, N. (2022). Datafied Media and the Silent Derangement of Ethics. *The Impact of the Media*, 121–136.

Creswell, J. W., & Poth, C. N. (2016). *Qualitative inquiry and research design: Choosing among five approaches*. Sage publications.

Dayé, C. (2025). Researching Scientific Attention Spaces: Epistemic Tribes and Territories. In *Futures Thinking: Epistemic Tribes and Territories* (pp. 57–68). Springer.

Desai, M., & Goel, S. (2018). Rights of Dalit and Tribal Children to Non-discrimination and Inclusion. In *Child Rights Education for Inclusion and Protection: Primary Prevention* (pp. 67–103). Springer.

Desai, P. S. (2024). EMPOWERMENT AT HER FINGERTIPS: A DIGITAL REVOLUTION FOR RURAL WOMEN. *CAHIERS MAGELLANES-NS*, *6*(2), 5134–5150.

Dias, M. S. (2024). Tracing Portuguese Influences in Goan Cultural Heritage. *Multidisciplinary Research in Arts, Science & Commerce (Volume-12)*, 42.

Donkers, T., & Ziegler, J. (2025). Human-Agent Interaction in Synthetic Social Networks: A Framework for Studying Online Polarization. *ArXiv Preprint ArXiv:2502.01340.*

Edyangu, H. (2021). *Social Media Use and Indigenous Language Preservation: A Case Study of Lukenyi Language in Serere District–Uganda.* College of Education open, Distance and E-Learning of Kampala International ….

Fusch, P., Fusch, G. E., & Ness, L. R. (2018). Denzin's paradigm shift: Revisiting triangulation in qualitative research. *Journal of Sustainable Social Change, 10*(1), 2.

Gupta, V. K., Kaushik, A., Chauhan, D. S., Ahirwar, R. K., Sharma, S., & Bisht, D. (2018). Anti-mycobacterial activity of some medicinal plants used traditionally by tribes from Madhya Pradesh, India for treating tuberculosis related symptoms. *Journal of Ethnopharmacology, 227*, 113–120.

Gurning, S. T., Wiranegara, I. G. P., & Suminta, D. (2024). Documentary Content in The Digital Era (Watchdoc Documentary Content Study). *Metacommunication. Journal of Communication Studies*, *9*(1), 19–31.

Hutto, H. D., & Wheeler, M. B. (2023). Tribal and rural digital inclusivity: An examination of broadband access in two neighboring Great Plains states. *First Monday.*

Jernigan, K., & Roach, B. (2021). Indigenous Virginia digital storytelling project: A creation story. *Genealogy*, *5*(4), 88.

Kadiri, C., & Owolabi, B. O. (2020). *The new normal of eHealth equity: Transforming chronic disease management amid rural technological constraints and digital divides.*

Kalra, A., Levy, R., & Mattsson, M. (2025). Targeted Disruptions: Internet Shutdowns in India. *Available at SSRN* 5129468.

Kozinets, R. V. (2023). Immersive netnography: A novel method for service experience research in virtual reality, augmented reality and metaverse contexts. *Journal of Service Management*, *34*(1), 100–125.

Kumar, M. S., Singh, A., & Alagumuthu, G. (2012). Traditional beekeeping of stingless bee (Trigona sp) by Kani tribes of Western Ghats, Tamil Nadu, India. *Indian Journal of Traditional Knowledge*, *11*(2), 342–345.

Kumar, R. (2016). Temporality as value: Ethnography and the question of time. *Journal of Human Values*, *22*(1), 46–56.

Li, Z. (2025). Strengthening path and influencing factors of overseas Chinese cultural identity from the perspective of educational psychology. *Current Psychology (New Brunswick, N.J.)*, *44*(5), 3102–3117.

Lobensteiner, N., & Thies, S. (2020). Indigenous media production. In *The Routledge Handbook to the Culture and Media of the Americas* (pp. 336–346). Routledge.

Lukanda, I. N., Namusoga-Kaale, S., & Claassen, G. (2023). Media as mediators in a science-based issue: Politics, foreign influence and implications on adoption of genetically modified organisms in food production in Uganda. *Journal of Science Communication*, *22*(1), A03.

Luo, Y., Lai, B., Zhang, Y., & Liu, J. (2024). Village leadership, social networks and collective actions in indigenous communities: Case of Hani rice terrace social-ecological system in Southwest China. *Journal of Rural Studies*, *106*, 103237.

MacDonald, M. R. (2013). *Traditional storytelling today: An international sourcebook*. Routledge.

Manžuch, Z. (2017). Ethical issues in digitization of cultural heritage. *Journal of Contemporary Archival Studies*, *4*(2), 4.

Marchessault, J. (2014). Media Studies as Interdisciplinary Exploration. *Journal of Visual Culture*, *13*(1), 82–84.

Mariyono, D., Alifatul Kamila, A. N., & Alif Hidayatullah, A. N. (2025). Unity in diversity: Navigating global connections through cultural exchange. *Quality Education for All*, *2*(1), 114–137.

Meena, H. R. (2024). Denotified Tribes in India. *Indian Literature, 68*(6 (344), 138–146.

Mehta, R. K., & Sharma, S. (2015). Knowledge, attitude and practice of self-medication among medical students. *Age (Years)*, *20*(49), 65–73.

Miguel, C., Lutz, C., Perez-Vega, R., & Majetić, F. (2025). "Alone on the road": Loneliness among digital nomads and the use of social media to foster personal relationships. *Media Culture & Society*, *47*(3), 546–566.

Mukherjee, S. (2024). Media, Culture and Tribes: An Analysis of Various Social Issues. *INTERNATIONAL JOURNAL OF CULTURAL STUDIES AND SOCIAL SCIENCES*, 217.

MWANGI, M. J. (2023). *ROLE OF SOCIAL NETWORK STRUCTURES ON BIRTH ATTENDANT DECISIONS AMONG WOMEN IN NAKURU COUNTY, KENYA*. KENYATTA UNIVERSITY.

Nwabueze, C. J. (2017). Copyright and data authenticity in the digital preservation of heritage: The case of OAPI states. *International Journal of Intangible Heritage*, *12*, 94–110.

Onyeaka, H., Ejiohuo, O., Taiwo, O. R., Nnaji, N. D., Odeyemi, O. A., Duan, K., Nwaiwu, O., & Odeyemi, O. (2024). The intersection of food security and mental health in the pursuit of sustainable development goals. *Nutrients, 16*(13), 2036.

Patel, M. M., Dhume, N., Sumbhe, S. S., Kamat, P. S., Nadar, M. S., & Patel, M. (2025). *TRIBES ACROSS INDIA*.

Patel, V. L., Kaufman, D. R., & Cohen, T. (2013). *Cognitive informatics in health and biomedicine: case studies on critical care, complexity and errors*. Springer Science & Business Media.

Prażmowska-Marcinowska, K. (2020). Misappropriation of Indigenous cultural heritage–intellectual property rights in the digital era. *Santander Art and Culture Law Review, 6*(2), 119–150.

Ranjan, A., & Sharma, M. T. (2025). Indian Knowledge System and Caste. *INDIAN*, 221.

Rao, J. K., Suneetha, J., Reddi, T. V. V. S., & Kumar, O. A. (2011). Ethnomedicine of the Gadabas, a primitive tribe of Visakhapatnam district, Andhra Pradesh. *International Multidisciplinary Research Journal, 1*(2).

Rizwan, S. A., Kumar, R., Singh, A. K., Kusuma, Y. S., Yadav, K., & Pandav, C. S. (2014). Prevalence of hypertension in Indian tribes: A systematic review and meta-analysis of observational studies. *PLoS One, 9*(5), e95896.

Rowley, J., Bennett, D., Blom, D., & Dunbar-Hall, P. (2014). *Exploring the pedagogy and impact of technology on eportfolio creation for arts students in Australian tertiary study*.

Schwartz, T. (1980). *Socialization as cultural communication: Development of a theme in the work of Margaret Mead* (Vol. 237). Univ of California Press.

Singh, C. L. (2010). New media and cultural identity. *China Media Research, 6*(1).

Smith, J. M., & Van Ierland, T. (2018). Framing controversy on social media:# NoDAPL and the debate about the Dakota access pipeline on Twitter. *IEEE Transactions on Professional Communication, 61*(3), 226–241.

Smith, T. (2024). *Foxocracy: Inside the network's playbook of tribal warfare*. Diversion Books.

Smith, T. R. (2004). Generating Selves: Issues of Self-Representation. *Auto/Biography, 19*(1–2), 59–70.

Sonowal, J., & Choudhury, D. (2024). ROLE OF SOCIAL MEDIA IN PROMOTING FOLK DANCE: A REVIEW STUDY WITH REFERENCE TO BIHU DANCE OF ASSAM. *International. Journal of Multidisciplinary Research, 10*(2).

Stürmer, M., Nussbaumer, J., & Stöckli, P. (2021). Security implications of digitalization: The dangers of data colonialism and the way towards sustainable and sovereign management of environmental data. *ArXiv Preprint ArXiv:2107.01662.*

Thathiah, N. (2024). *Analyzing Indigenous Representation and Engagement on TikTok.*

Tsapro, G., Yakuba, V., & Gladush, N. (2025). Teaching Gender Studies through an Interdisciplinary Lens: Sociology and Communication Theory. *Академічні Студії. Серія «Педагогіка». Луцьк: Комунальний Заклад Вищої Освіти «Луцький Педагогічний Коледж». Волинської Обласної Ради, 1*, 71–77.

Verma, M., & Sharma, H. (2016). *India In the Coverage of Pakistan Media: A Content Analysis Study with Special Reference To Post Pathankot Attack.*

Verma, P., Sahoo, K. C., Mahapatra, P., Kaur, H., & Pati, S. (2022). A systematic review of community-based studies on mental health issues among tribal populations in India. *The Indian Journal of Medical Research, 156*(2), 291–298.

Wilson, P., & Stewart, M. (2008). Indigeneity and indigenous media on the global stage. *Global Indigenous Media*, 1–35.

Zalli, E. (2024). Globalization and education: exploring the exchange of ideas, values, and traditions in promoting cultural understanding and global citizenship. *Interdisciplinary Journal of Research and Development, 11*(1 S1), 55.

Zelizer, B. (1992). On Communicative Practice: The" Other Worlds" of Journalism and Shamanism. *Southern Folklore, 49*(665), 19–36.

Chapter 6
Equity, Responsibility, and Innovation:
Integrating Islamic Values Into the Intersection of Media and Technology

Naseem Akhter
https://orcid.org/0009-0002-7504-1715
Shaheed Benazir Bhutto Women University, Peshawar, Pakistan

ABSTRACT

This chapter explores how Islamic ethical values shape the intersection of media, technology, and social innovation, emphasizing equity, justice, and collective well-being. Unlike the dominant focus on efficiency and scalability, Islamic principles, amanah (responsibility), adl (justice), maslahah (benefit), and khilafah (stewardship), offer a values-based guide for innovation. The chapter situates these principles within media and technology studies, linking morality with media responsibility and technological adoption. Case studies on digital literacy, Islamic finance, and fintech illustrate how value-centered approaches address misinformation and encourage responsible technology use. It concludes that Islamic-inspired innovation can influence policy, pedagogy, and practice by fostering inclusive digital ecosystems, reducing inequality, and supporting sustainable social development.

DOI: 10.4018/979-8-3373-5307-4.ch006

INTRODUCTION: MEDIA, TECHNOLOGY, AND THE QUEST FOR ETHICAL INNOVATION

The general blistering of digital technologies had a significant impact on transforming the character of the interaction and learning within societies as well as business. The digital revolution has led to the emergence of new ways of social interaction with each other and social development because of artificial intelligence, social media, mobile banking, educational technologies, etc. (Castells, 2010; Schwab, 2016). However, it is a modification that has raised some rather significant issues regarding the notions of equity, accountability, and values that can be utilized to design the progress of technology (Floridi, 2013).

Whereas the key parameters in the mainstream discourse of digital innovation include efficiency, scalability, and economic growth, alternative models of experimented and proven social responsibility and ethical significance are on the rise (Mittelstadt et al., 2016). Islamic principles are one of such frameworks that can provide time-tested values that can be utilized to influence the evolution and application of media and technology as a social benefit (Abdul-Rauf, 2004; Al-Attas, 1995). The Islamic ethics are framed around such concepts as justice (*adl)*, trust (*amanah*), and public interest (*maslahah*), and all diseases of life, including in the digital space, are set on the ethical level of moral responsibility and an attitude to human dignity (Kamali, 2016).

The world population of Muslims is more than 1.8 billion, which is approximately a quarter of the entire humanity (Pew Research Center, 2017), yet they are overrepresented in the ethical aspects of technological discussion both in academic and political circles (Hassan and Ali, 2019). This difference is exceptionally vast considering the fact that the vast majority of nations where Muslims are predominant are experiencing a faster digitalization process and simultaneously addressing the restricted organisational opportunities of inequality, governance, and social development (Esposito and Mogahed, 2007; Oxford Internet Institute, 2020). The value added by the inclusion of the idea of Islamic ethics within the discussion on the topic of media and technology to the Muslim communities is not only useful, but it also contributes to the world discourse of sustainable innovation, along with inclusive digital futures.

This is where the gap is concentrated in this chapter, which takes into account the way of how the Islamic values can be utilized for responsible innovation in the nexus of media and technology, and also gives some insights on how the Islamic values can be applied in the general discussion of issues of digital ethics and social responsibility, and not limited to the Muslim situation. It includes the traditionally applied tools of Islamic logic as well as the contemporary dangers of technological translocation, which demonstrates that the long-awaited religious frameworks of morality can aid in humanizing and contextualizing the digital world.

RESEARCH OBJECTIVES

1. To fill the gaps between disciplines in merging views on Islamic ethics, media studies, and technology design in the analysis of socially innovative practices in various settings and applications.
2. To promote the theoretical debate by presenting an Islamic value-based framework for the responsible use of media and technology to innovate society and community.
3. To provide examples of applications by providing documentation of actual, real-world examples of technology-facilitated initiatives in Muslim predominant settings that are reflective of equity and responsibility in action.
4. To emphasize the voices of the underrepresented and local innovations of the Global South by introducing an Islamic ethical and cultural perspective.
5. To educate the policy and practice by offering practical suggestions to policymakers, educators, and entrepreneurs on how to integrate ethical values in the process of media and technological innovation.

RESEARCH GAP AND RATIONALE

Although Islamic values play an important role in the worldview of about a quarter of humanity, the literature on the ways of applying these principles to the issue of technology ethics and media responsibility is still quite insufficient. The majority of the frameworks of digital ethics developed are based on Western philosophical traditions that tend to ignore the ethical traditions of other cultures and religions.

The existing studies in technology ethics are inclined to use secular philosophies like utilitarian ethics, deontological approaches, or virtue ethics, whereas faith-based philosophies are put aside. This is of special concern since most of the most acute digital issues globally, such as inequality, misinformation, and social fragmentation, are common in those parts of the world where Islamic values have a strong impact on social and cultural values.

Furthermore, the rapid rise of electronic economies in Muslim-majority countries, whether it is the fintech boom in Southeast Asia or the e-commerce boom in the Middle East and Africa, needs ethical guidelines that would be attractive to internal values and cultural contexts. Without such structures, technological advancement may precipitate the risk of going ahead blindly without being sensitive enough to the values of the community, to social equity, and cultural appropriateness.

This gap in the research has been propagated in the policy discourses, which are more likely to be diverse in their cultural and religious interpretation of morals and obligations. In this chapter, the broader and more culturally appropriate approach to digital innovation and how this innovation can inform not only academic research but also practice will be given by developing an Islamic ethical framework of media and technology.

LITERATURE REVIEW: FOUNDATIONS AND FRAMEWORKS

Islamic Technology and Islamic Ethics

The discourse of Islamic ethics and technology in the scholarly community has been developing considerably during the last twenty years, and it has attracted interest in how the values influence technological paths. An Islamic philosophy of science and technology was already developed by Ziauddin Sardar (1985, 2011), though the latter stressed that technology is not neutral and is always placed within cultural and ethical contexts. His concept of Islamic science emphasized the need to balance and synchronize technological progress with spiritual, moral, and social duties.

It is based on this that Abdelhamid Abu Sulayman (2016) came up with the concept of the Islamization of Knowledge, which offers a methodology of capturing the usage of the Islamic tenets in contemporary academic disciplines like the study of technology. Ibrahim Ozdemir (2019) furthered this discussion by employing the Islamic ethical reasoning to handle critical environmental and digital challenges by stating that stewardship (*khilafah*) should be central in defining technological practices. These recent articles by Osman Bakar (2020) and also by Syed Naqib al-Attas (2018) also reflect epistemological reform and ethical responsibility in scientific and technological innovation in the Islamic vision of the world.

The modern academia has also come to study technology in practical terms. To illustrate, Ali and Syed (2021) talk about how the concept of Islamic ethics can be applied to the creation of policies in the field of artificial intelligence (AI): the principles of Islamic jurisprudence, including *maqasid al-shariah* (higher objectives of law), can also be normative to address such concepts as privacy, fairness, and accountability. These works present the way Islamic ethical frames are becoming involved in the world discourse of digital transformation.

Media Ethics and Islamic Views

Simultaneously with arguments over technology, Islamic media ethics has also centered on such questions as representation, communication, and social responsibility. In his work, Kai Hafez (2007) examines the dynamics of the media in Muslim societies and criticizes orientalist representations of such issues, and asks the media to adopt a pluralist and just media system. In a similar vein, Louay Safi (2009) suggested ethical communication models that are based on Quranic truth (*sidq*), trust (*amanah*), and responsibility (*mas'uliyyah*).

The fourth principle of Islamic media ethics is the notion of *maslahah* (public interest), which has been applied to determine the policy and content of media by their role in promoting the interest of the common good. Jasser Auda (2008) presented an approach to *maqasid al-shariah* that is systems-based and emphasizes flexibility and completeness of thought in the case of ethical judgment. Mohammad Hashim Kamali (2013) proceeded to describe the process of operationalization of *maslahah* and *maqasid* within contemporary modes of communication and governments, such as digital media.

New learning has further taken the debate to new media platforms. For example, Al-Rawi (2017) articulated social media in the Arab world and observed the potential of social media to be a democratic movement and the risk of disinformation. Similarly, Echchaibi (2019) authored an article in which Muslim virtual places develop an identity and an authority on the Internet, bringing up the morality of authenticity, representation, and representation. Such undertakings cement the way the Islamic ethical thinking remains applicable to new challenges that it is required to face. Taken together, the masterpieces suggest that Islamic ethics is not only capable of offering normative strategies in the evaluation of the media and the technology but also materialized methods of how, into socially worthy directions, innovation can be channeled.

It will not come as a surprise that the literature suggests that the necessity to discuss the inclusion of Islamic values in the accounting of media and technology has increasingly risen to prominence as a means of promoting equity, justice, and communal welfare in the Muslim setups and in the general sense.

CONTEMPORARY DIGITAL ETHICS DISCOURSE

Digital ethics was one of the areas that proliferated at an exponential rate in recent years because there was a need to respond to challenges of algorithmic influence, data privacy, and social ramifications of new technology. The most influential writers, such as Luciano Floridi (2019), Kate Crawford (2021), and Shoshana Zuboff

(2019), have developed elaborate models of understanding the ethical effects of digital transformation.

The principles of information ethics developed by Floridi provide a theoretical framework for the evaluation of the moral value of digital technologies and their influence on the prosperity of the human population. In this chapter on algorithmic accountability, Crawford stresses that transparency and fairness should be encouraged in the automated decision-making system. The argument presented by Zuboff on surveillance capitalism illustrates that digital technologies can be utilized in such a way that they can destroy human autonomy and dignity. These frameworks are nonetheless helpful, but in the majority of instances, they end up reflecting particular cultural and philosophical traditions that may not resonate with a broad global audience. The synthesis of Islamic perspectives in online ethics debates could provide a different direction, emphasizing different values and priorities, such as community stewardship, distributive fairness, and resource management.

Scholars such as Aasim Padela (2018) and Yasmin Ibrahim (2020) have more recently begun addressing this lacuna by writing on how Islamic bioethics and communication ethics must be utilized to inform contemporary discussions of technology governance. There is a priceless precedent to the emphasis of the current study on media and technology from an Islamic ethical framework.

RESEARCH METHODOLOGY

Development of the Theoretical Framework

The analysis is based on the multi-disciplinary methodology of a combination of Islamic jurisprudence (*fiqh*), media studies, and technology assessment. The theoretical framework is created due to a systematic analysis of both classical and contemporary material on ethics and social responsibility regarding Islam.

Case Study Analysis

Several case studies of Muslim-majority nations are examined in terms of the application of comparative methodology. Cases are chosen because they represent various aspects of the technology use and are compatible with Islamic morality.

Stakeholder Perspectives

The study has included views of technology developers, Islamic scholars, policy-makers, and community leaders by examining documents and reviewing secondary sources as a way of having a wide scope of insights into real-life applications.

The approach focuses on contextual knowledge and cultural sensitivity, though at a high academic level. The research will collect data concerning publicly accessible information on technology initiatives, policy documents, and academic publications. This research uses thematic coding to define patterns and relationships between Islamic values and applications of technology in order to ensure that the result of the study is premised on theoretical knowledge as well as empirical data.

ISLAMIC ETHICAL FRAMEWORK FOR INNOVATION

The Islamic ethics offer a holistic approach to assessing and advising technological innovation based on four principles that together focus on responsibility, justice, and the community good. These values have strong foundations in the Quran and prophetic teachings and can provide a way to apply them to modern digital issues and stay culturally and spiritually oriented.

'*Adl* (Justice)

The justice principle focuses on equity, balance, and the upholding of rights of the entire society, especially the disadvantaged and the vulnerable.

Amanah (Responsibility)

Reliability and faith in others and Allah, which include resource stewardship and the responsibility of the action and its results.

Maslahah (Public Interest)

The encouragement of the common good and communal interest with collective benefit taken as the major agenda instead of personal benefits in decision-making procedures.

Khilafah (Stewardship)

As managers of the creation, human beings have the duty of preserving and caring about the environment and society of both the present and the future.

JUSTICE ('*ADL*) IN DIGITAL INNOVATION

The Islamic concept of justice (*adl)* offers a strong framework that could be used to solve the problem of digital inequality and achieve equal access to the gains of technology. As applied to the context of media and technology, justice requires that innovations be applied to every member of society, and not be exclusive to those who are privileged in society, and that the systems of technology should be utilized in fairness without any favoritism.

This principle undermines the popular belief that the development of technologies through the marketplace will automatically result in fairness. Rather, *adl* needs to be planned intentionally using accessibility, affordability, and inclusiveness as priorities. As an illustration, Malaysian and Indonesian Islamic fintech projects have been purposefully built to target unbanked communities since financial inclusion is a social justice concern and not a market opportunity.

Algorithms and data governance are also connected to the principle of justice. According to the Islamic ethical frames, transparency and accountability in decision-making procedures are valued principles, which can be directly applied to automated systems that are gradually taking over control of access to opportunities, services, and resources. In cases where there is prejudice in the algorithms held by one group over another, it breaches the first principle of the Islamic teachings, which is that all people must be treated fairly and with dignity.

Application: Indonesian peer-to-peer lending services realize the Islamic value of creating a fair interest rate and transparent lending processes, which cater to marginalized populations in the past.

Responsibility (*Amanah*) in Technology Development

Islamic ethics revolve around the idea of *amanah* (trust or responsibility), and this is what gives a very important recommendation to developers of technology and operators of platforms. Depending on the Islamic perception, each person is assigned a duty to society and to Allah, which establishes a system of responsibility that goes beyond legal obligations to include moral and spiritual ones.

To technology firms and media houses, *amanah* implies that they should take responsibility for the social impact of their services and products. This involves paying attention to the way the technologies can be abused, having strong privacy protection, and systems that enhance social cohesion, instead of weakening it. The principal criticizes the Silicon Valley culture of move fast and break things and proposes taking care of the potential harm before rolling a system into service.

The social media companies with a Muslim majority in their home countries have started using *amanah*-based policies that extend beyond the traditional content moderation to encourage positive discussion and community-building. As an example, the platforms can focus on the content that helps in civic discourse and suppress inflammatory or divisive content, as they have the duty to promote healthy public discussion.

The same principle can be applied to data stewardship, where companies can be considered as trustees of information belonging to users and not its owners. This view has been reflected in the data governance policies of a number of Muslim-majority countries, giving rise to user-consent-based, data minimisation-based, and corporate responsibility-based policies to govern data protection.

PUBLIC INTEREST (*MASLAHAH*) AND COMMUNITY WELFARE

Individual Benefit

The technologies should be of service to individual users as they should support the needs and increase the capabilities of the individuals without infringing on their dignity and autonomy.

Community Welfare

Technologies must enhance social connections, facilitate common objectives, and lead to healthy and successful communities.

Societal Progress

The growth of technology must further promote the social goals, including education, health, economic growth, and a sustainable environment.

The *maslahah* Value (public interest or welfare) requires the consideration of technological innovations not only in terms of their potential for economic value but also in terms of value to society. It is a holistic method of deciding the innovation impacts that includes social, cultural, environmental, and spiritual impacts, and economic returns.

In practice, technology development for *maslahah* reasons not only targets the solutions to these pressing social issues but also has a greater concern for the commercial application. In Morocco and Jordan, technological applications in education have been utilized to aim at improving levels of literacy and access to education by marginalized groups, which have viewed these as primary results of development in society, rather than the ancillary benefits of market growth.

The platform design and the content curation policies are also driven by the same principle. Principles of *maslahah* are being employed by social media platforms actively in order to enable content that will build learning, civic engagement, and social cohesion, and prevent the spread of false news, hate speech, and content that will hurt the community.

Stewardship (*Khilafah*) and Sustainable Innovation

Key Lesson: *Khilafah* is not only about conservation of the environment, but also social and cultural conservation, so that technologies are utilized to enhance and not to annihilate the community's values.

Khilafah (stewardship) develops the concept of humans as trustees who need to provide for the creation and posterity. It is applied, in the context of technology and media, to emphasize long-term vision, environmental stewardship, and conservation of cultural values and social institutions.

Technology innovation following the stewardship concept considers the entire life cycle impact of innovations, from resource extraction to manufacturing, use, and disposal. This perspective has influenced the design of green technology initiatives in Muslim majority countries, where solar power projects and green farm technologies are not only regarded as economic opportunities but as religious obligations.

The same principle is less difficult to apply to cultural stewardship in an effort to preserve the social practices and useful cultural traditions from being lost when adopting technology.

Whereas in digital preservation projects in countries such as Turkey and Morocco, the technology has made the recording and safeguarding of heritage possible, at the same time exposing the heritage to future generations by applying digital technology. On media platforms, *khilafah* refers to taking into consideration the long-term consequences of the features and content on users' social relationships, mental well-being, and behavior. Certain such platforms have incorporated features that suggest responsible use and remind users to interact with others in the physical world and not cyberspace.

TECHNOLOGY AND MEDIA AS TOOLS FOR SOCIAL GOOD

Media and technology convergence present potentials of social innovation, which has never been previously experienced, where the ethical frameworks apply, and the community is the immediate beneficiary. The Islamic principles have offered one of the rare guidelines on using the tools in the name of justice, education, economic inclusion, and civic participation.

Educational Empowerment

Educational systems that are backed by technology and provide more individuals with access to knowledge without eroding cultural values, and build critical thinking capabilities.

Economic Inclusion

Financial technologies modelled after the Islamic rules, which focus on the unbanked populations and promote equitable economic engagement.

Civic Participation

The medium that facilitates constructive social conversation, government transparency, and mobilization at the grassroots level towards social change.

Healthcare Access

Digital health solutions to improve medical care in poor communities without compromising cultural sensitivities and privacy concerns.

CASE STUDY: ISLAMIC FINTECH AND FINANCIAL INCLUSION

Malaysia's Islamic Digital Banking Revolution

Malaysia has also become a pioneer in Islamic financial technology and digital banking solutions to satisfy religious desires and financial inclusion. This paradigm of operating the country demonstrates how technology innovation can be improved according to the Islamic principles to balance the financial systems.

One of the greatest inventions is *Sharia*-compliant peer-to-peer lending websites that are not engaged in any interest transaction but provide terms of access to funds to business persons and small enterprises. These websites use the profit-and-loss sharing arrangement where both the interests of the executives and the borrowers are shared, and risks of finance are distributed equally, as opposed to traditional lending.

Digital payment systems have been constructed to fulfil both the Islamic requirements of open, asset-backed transactions and offer services to the unbanked segments on mobile-first interfaces. The result has been an increase in the extent of financial inclusion of the rural populace as well as the urban masses, who were otherwise avoiding the conventional banking system on account of their religious interests.

Key Success Factors

- Collaboration between Islamic scholars and technologists
- Government regulatory support for Sharia-compliant innovation
- Focus on underserved market segments
- Emphasis on financial education and literacy
- Integration of traditional Islamic finance principles with modern technology

Impact: Over 2.3 million previously unbanked Malaysians gained access to formal financial services through Islamic fintech platforms between 2018 and 2023.

CASE STUDY: DIGITAL LITERACY IN INDONESIAN ISLAMIC EDUCATION

The very example of Indonesia and the establishment of digital technology in Islamic education shows that technological innovation can improve traditional education without losing any cultural and religious values. The strategy of the country deals with the international issue of digital literacy, without violating the local educational traditions and the priorities of the community.

2015-2017: Foundation Building

Government and Islamic schools are working together to create digital curricula that combine both technology skills and traditional Islamic education, which will uphold the culture and create digital competency at the same time.

2018-2020: Pilot Implementation

Tablet-based education programs were introduced in 500 Islamic schools (madrasas) in the rural and urban regions, and students were able to access digital materials without losing concentration on studying the Quran and Islamic morals.

2021-2023: Scaling and Adaptation

The program was extended to more than 2,000 schools, and the curriculum was modified according to the local needs and feedback. The COVID-19 pandemic increased the use of blended learning and proved to be effective.

2024-Onwards: Sustainability Focus

Focus moves to teacher training, social participation, and long-term sustainability without losing sight of the Islamic values and education goals.

The success of the initiative is due to the effective integration of technology, which must do more than just serve as a provider of technology, but also should include appropriate curriculum development, community buy-in, and support systems that acknowledge local values and priorities.

CASE STUDY: COMBATING MISINFORMATION THROUGH ISLAMIC MEDIA PLATFORMS

Platform Features

- Fact-checking integration with religious authority verification
- Community moderation based on Islamic principles of testimony and evidence
- Educational content promoting media literacy and critical thinking
- Transparent source attribution and verification processes

Egypt's Islamic News Verification Network

Egypt has laid down new plans of combating misinformation through the media where Islamic notions of telling truth, facts on the ground, reasonableness, and social responsibility are instilled. These websites demonstrate how religious values can support and not undermine critical thinking and factual appropriateness.

The program combines both the traditional Islamic doctrine of the witness testimonies and evidence scrutiny with the latest methods of checking the facts. The religious experts work together with the journalists as well as the technologists to assist them in verifying the facts, particularly the religious doctrine and other social problems that are befalling the Muslim populations.

Collective responsibility is also reflected in Islamic thinking of collective responsibility, whereby readers are not requested to filter bad information, but rather towards community service by reporting such information. The site provides educational information that helps the user to gain the skills of critical assessment, but reinforces the religious values of truth and integrity. Findings showed that there have been tremendous gains in the quality of information and level of trust in users, and community members are becoming better consumers and sharers of digital content. The strategy shows that the values of faith can complement and not contradict a scientific method of verification of information.

EQUITY AND RESPONSIBILITY IN PRACTICE

The practical implementation of the Islamic ethical principles in the media and technology should take into account equity, responsibility, and welfare of the community systematically (Abu Bakar and Md Husin, 2022; Hashim and Yusof, 2021). Examples of good initiatives that demonstrate that such values can drive real construction choices, policy frameworks, and ways of operation that would create more equal and beneficial technological structures are exemplary (Kamali, 2008; Sardar, 2011).

Addressing Digital Divides

Islamic principles of justice require proactive efforts to minimize digital disparities based on geography, income, gender, and many others (Yusuf, 2019). There should also be intense technology activities to embrace the marginalized groups, rather than the presumption that the market forces would automatically create fair access (UNESCO, 2021).

Vulnerable Populations are Covered by Income Protection

Amanah (responsibility) is a principle that prevents technological systems from exploiting, manipulating, or harming children, elderly users, and other vulnerable groups (Hashim and Yusof, 2021; Al-Rodhan, 2015).

Promoting Social Cohesion

The technology platforms should augment and not erode communities, support social networks and cohesiveness, and respect diversity and personal dignity (Yusuf, 2019).

A Sustainable Development Assurance

The stewardship principles involve putting long-term environmental and social impacts into consideration in which the sustainability practices will be prioritized over short-term gains (Abu Bakar and Md Husin, 2022; Kamali, 2008).

ADDRESSING INEQUALITY THROUGH VALUE-BASED DESIGN

The design of technology based on Islamic principles and values has shown quantifiable effects on digital inclusivity in Muslim-majority areas (Abu Bakar and Md Husin, 2022; Yusuf, 2019). The Islamic ethical frameworks have been methodically applied to technology projects, in the form of composite indices such as access, affordability, digital skills, and availability of relevant content (UNESCO, 2021).

Such enhancements are caused by the smart design that puts equity on the frontline rather than pure market efficiency. As an illustration, mobile network operators in a number of countries have implemented the tiered service framework, such that lower-income clients can continue using basic connectivity plans, and upscale services can be a source of income to keep operations running (Hashim & Yusof, 2021).

Similar outcomes have been attained through educational technology efforts to create multilingual interfaces, integrate local cultural content, and give offline functionality that supports poor connectivity (Al-Rodhan, 2015; Kamali, 2008). These design choices utilize the Islamic principles of inclusivity and service to society and not just the business (Sardar, 2011).

POLICY AND PEDAGOGICAL IMPLICATIONS

Policy Recommendations

The philosophy of Islamic ethics should be incorporated into the technology policy in organized ways, which do not interfere with the diversity of society but encourage innovation and beneficial effects on society. The policymakers have to reflect on how to come up with regulatory instruments that encourage innovation based on values other than relying solely on the market mechanism to solve societal challenges.

- Establish technology project ethical assessment procedures that are founded on social and cultural impact and economic utility.
- Give tax incentives and grants to companies that manufacture technologies that benefit the underrepresented groups.
- Sandboxes of Islamic fintech and other religion-based innovations should be offered by the regulatory authorities.

Direct commercial innovation, social purpose, towards cooperation with the government.

The number of ethical perspectives should also be included in the international cooperation systems because the norms of technology regulation on the global level should be aligned with the values and interests of different religious and cultural communities.

Educational Approaches

Learner institutions play a key role in instilling future technologists who can integrate ethical thinking into their practice. The curriculum should not only include the technical aspects but also ethical thinking models so that the students understand the broad implications of what they are accomplishing.

- Embed the courses in Islamic ethics into computer science and engineering.
- Develop case study programs with successful value-based technology programs.
- Develop interdisciplinary courses like technology/ethics/social sciences.
- Implement mentorship programs that connect students with practitioners who implement ethical technology solutions.

The working technologists should have professional development programs that provide opportunities daily to explore ethical frameworks and apply them in practice to the prevailing problems of technology.

IMPLEMENTATION STRATEGIES FOR ORGANIZATIONS

Institute Ethical Standards

Organizations should formulate clearly defined ethical statements that incorporate Islamic values and professional standards, such that they give a clear guideline in the technology decision-making during development and deployment.

Form Diverse Teams

Assign the Islamic scholars, ethicists, and the representatives of the community to teams where technology is invented in such a manner that religious and cultural factors are kept in mind when designing the technology at the initial stages.

Community Engagement

Create a free flow of communication with the user communities to know their needs, interests, and values so that technological solutions do not become out of the context of the community priorities and the cultural sensitivities.

Impact Assessment

Institute measurements and evaluation frameworks to examine social and ethical performance and technical and financial performance in such a way that the value match is constantly kept on the rise.

Continuous Learning

Continuous learning and training of the staff, to keep in step with the change in technology and other knowledge on ethical considerations and demands of society.

GLOBAL IMPLICATIONS AND CROSS-CULTURAL DIALOGUE

The implication of Islamic ethics in technological and media innovation provides thought-provoking information, not only in applying the Islamic ethics but also as one more step toward reasonable innovation on the global level. These principles do not override the already established paradigms of ethics, as they do not take the place of the solutions to the major issues of the digital world.

The Islamic ethics, a collective responsibility and community welfare-based approach, is a helpful counter-check to the individualistic model that techniques of emerging technologies bring to the modern world. It is especially useful when it is time to discuss the challenge of social media polarization, algorithmic discrimination, and digital inequality that cannot be solved by market-related solutions, but has to be solved through a common social initiative.

The possibility of building new ways of giving technology based on the plural moral tradition can be achieved when the Islamic and other moral traditions engage in cross-cultural exchange. Incidentally, Islamic stewardship (*khilafah*) is conceptually close to indigenous environmental ethics and Buddhist views of interdependence, which offer any prospects within which trans-cultural collaborative models could be developed.

Technology policy and digital rights groups working across borders can make use of the inclusion of Islamic perspectives in their operations so that the international standards affect the diversity of human values and cultural traditions. The inclusion is not only a matter of cultural sensitivity but also a practical necessity because policies lacking cultural resonance cannot be applied effectively in diverse international contexts.

FUTURE RESEARCH DIRECTIONS

AI and Islamic Ethics

The discussion of the relevance of the Islamic principles to the creation of artificial intelligence-based systems in the domain of algorithmic fairness, transparency, and accountability.

Blockchain and Trust

Researching the possibilities of using blockchain technology to establish transparent and accountable systems that correspond to Islamic ideas of witness testifying and societal verification.

Virtual Environments

Analyzing the virtual and augmented reality technologies under the ethical lens, with the questions of representation and cultural appropriation, as well as spirituality.

Data Governance

Creating Islamic data privacy, ownership, and algorithm decision-making models that reconcile between individual and community rights.

Cross-Cultural Ethics

Comparative research involving the interaction of Islamic ethics principles with other religious and cultural approaches in the technology development arena.

Policy Innovation

Studies on policy tools and governance systems that can be implemented successfully to embed value factors into the regulation and support of technology.

CONCLUSION: TOWARD INCLUSIVE AND VALUE-DRIVEN INNOVATION

This chapter has shown that the Islamic ethical concepts can assist in resolving the contemporary problems on the margins of media and technology. The concepts of justice (*adl*), responsibility (*amanah*), common good (*maslahah*), and accountability (*khilafah*) provide realistic expectations towards the development of more just, responsible, and beneficial technological systems.

The case studies of the examples of the Islamic fintech projects in Malaysia, the digital literacy projects in Indonesia, or the anti-misinformation projects in Egypt can demonstrate how these values can be applied in various technological settings. These examples show that religion-driven ethical systems do not necessarily have to limit innovation, but, conversely, they can present more innovative and socially constructive methods of developing technologies.

Social justice, community development, and sustainable development are more concerned with the incorporation of Islamic principles in the development of technology and media. The practices would replace the market-based perspectives on innovation that could not accommodate the social needs and cultural values due to the emphasis on equity, responsibility, and social welfare.

To possess the international discourse of digital ethics and regulation of technology, the Islamic perspectives are able to provide good supporting facts, which place the collective responsibility, cultural sensitivity, and long-term thinking at the centre stage. As the digital revolution was yet to find its own way in the society of the world, the need to consider divergent moral traditions would only be more common in ensuring that the technological development was geared towards the well-being of human beings, both in the short term and in the long term in general. Considerable Implication: The scaffold, a responsible innovation paradigm that is presented in Islamic ethics, is feasible and can be used in the development of technologies far beyond the Muslim world.

The greater responsibility of the technologists and ethicists, policymakers, and heads of the communities to make sure that the technological inventions and the human values achieve the social needs is the future of the world. One of such invaluable resources in the current process is the Islamic ethical traditions, which can be applied to come up with a more holistic and culturally responsive digital innovation that would be useful to the common good of the world.

Moreover, it should be noted that the introduction of Islamic ethics to the technological practice does not only serve the Muslim majority societies but it also becomes part of the world debate on technology ethics. These principles have universal values that appeal to more general human interests, and this can provide a structure that helps mediate between cultural differences and at the same time, foster equity and inclusivity.

In addition, the accountability and collective responsibility make it possible to direct policymakers and leaders of the industry to create governance frameworks that put human dignity above profit. This restructuring disrupts the mainstream approaches to technological innovation and creates room for other systems that respond to inequalities, alleviate harm, and promote social solidarity.

Lastly, the vision, which is developed by the Islamic ethics in the long term, is consistent with the fact that the world is in urgent need of sustainable development. These principles will make sure that current technological advancements are not harmful to the next generation but can only improve their lives by promoting the stewardship of resources, transparency in making decisions, and equity in distribution. Therefore, Islamic ethical traditions not only offer a moral compass but also offer effective ways of making the digital future more humane and sustainable.

REFERENCES

Abdul-Rauf, M. (2004). *The Islamic worldview: Ethics and morality*. Amana Publications.

Abu Bakar, M., & Md Husin, M. (2022). The integration of Maqasid al-Shariah into the digital economy: Ethical foundations for sustainable innovation. *Journal of Islamic Accounting and Business Research, 13*(7), 1071–1086. DOI: 10.1108/JIABR-03-2021-0095

AbuSulayman, A. (2016). *Crisis in the Muslim mind* (4th ed.). International Institute of Islamic Thought.

AbuSulayman, A. (2016). *Islamization of knowledge: General principles and work plan* (3rd ed.). International Institute of Islamic Thought.

Al-Attas, S. M. N. (1995). *Prolegomena to the metaphysics of Islam: An exposition of the fundamental elements of the worldview of Islam*. International Institute of Islamic Thought and Civilization (ISTAC).

Al-Attas, S. M. N. (2018). *Prolegomena to the metaphysics of Islam*. ISTAC.

Al-Rawi, A. (2017). Social media in the Arab world: Communication and public opinion in the Gulf states. *Journal of Arab & Muslim Media Research, 10*(1), 3–15. DOI: 10.1386/jammr.10.1.3_1

Al-Rodhan, N. R. F. (2015). *Ethics and emerging technologies: Philosophical and applied perspectives*. Palgrave Macmillan.

Ali, S., & Syed, J. (2021). Ethics of artificial intelligence from an Islamic perspective. *Philosophy & Technology, 34*(4), 1421–1441. DOI: 10.1007/s13347-021-00473-1

Auda, J. (2008). *Maqasid al-Shariah as philosophy of Islamic law: A systems approach*. International Institute of Islamic Thought.

Auda, J. (2008). *Maqasid al-Shariah: A beginner's guide*. International Institute of Islamic Thought.

Bakar, O. (2020). *Islam and the integration of knowledge*. UTM Press.

Castells, M. (2010). *The rise of the network society* (2nd ed.). Wiley-Blackwell.

Crawford, K. (2021). *Atlas of AI: Power, politics, and the planetary costs of artificial intelligence*. Yale University Press.

Echchaibi, N. (2019). Muslim digital publics and the politics of belonging. *International Journal of Communication, 13*, 1742–1761.

Esposito, J. L., & Mogahed, D. (2007). *Who speaks for Islam? What a billion Muslims really think.* Gallup Press.

Floridi, L. (2013). *The ethics of information.* Oxford University Press.

Floridi, L. (2019). *Ethics, governance, and policies in artificial intelligence.* Springer Nature.

Hafez, K. (2007). *The myth of media globalization.* Polity Press.

Hashim, J., & Yusof, N. (2021). Ethical considerations in the use of artificial intelligence from the perspective of Islamic values. *Journal of Islamic Ethics, 5*(1), 1–21. DOI: 10.1163/24685542-12340068

Hassan, R., & Ali, S. (2019). Islamic digital ethics: A critical framework. *Journal of Media and Religion, 18*(3), 123–136. DOI: 10.1080/15348423.2019.1647520

Ibrahim, Y. (2020). Digital Islamic ethics and the Quran: Toward a framework for online Muslim communities. *Journal of Islamic Ethics, 4*(2), 145–168.

Kamali, M. H. (2008). *Maqasid al-Shariah made simple.* International Institute of Advanced Islamic Studies (IAIS).

Kamali, M. H. (2013). *Principles of Islamic jurisprudence* (4th ed.). Islamic Texts Society.

Kamali, M. H. (2013). *Shari'ah law: An introduction* (2nd ed.). Oneworld.

Kamali, M. H. (2016). *Ethics and jurisprudence in Islam.* Islamic Texts Society.

Mittelstadt, B. D., Allo, P., Taddeo, M., Wachter, S., & Floridi, L. (2016). The ethics of algorithms: Mapping the debate. *Big Data & Society, 3*(2), 1–21. DOI: 10.1177/2053951716679679

Oxford Internet Institute. (2020). *Digital ethics in the Global South: Challenges and opportunities.* University of Oxford.

Ozdemir, I. (2019). *Islam and ecology: Towards retrieval and reconstruction.* Routledge.

Ozdemir, I. (2019). Technology and Islamic environmental ethics: A contemporary perspective. *Environmental Ethics and Islam, 31*(4), 287–301.

Padela, A. I. (2018). Islamic bioethics and digital health technologies: Mapping the terrain. *The American Journal of Bioethics, 18*(9), 37–39.

Pew Research Center. (2017). *The future of world religions: Population growth projections, 2015–2060*. https://www.pewresearch.org/religion/2017/04/05/the-future-of-world-religions

Safi, L. (2009). *Islamic perspectives on communication*. International Institute of Islamic Thought.

Safi, L. (2009). *The foundations of knowledge: A comparative study in Islamic and Western methods of inquiry*. International Institute of Islamic Thought.

Sardar, Z. (1985). *Islamic futures: The shape of ideas to come*. Mansell.

Sardar, Z. (1985). *Islamic science: The way ahead*. Kube Publishing.

Sardar, Z. (2011). *Reading the Qur'an: The contemporary relevance of the sacred text of Islam*. Oxford University Press.

Sardar, Z. (2011). *Science, technology and development in the Muslim world*. Atlantic Publishers.

Schwab, K. (2016). *The Fourth Industrial Revolution*. World Economic Forum.

UNESCO. (2021). *Artificial intelligence and education: Guidance for policy-makers*. UNESCO Publishing.

Yusuf, H. O. (2019). Islamic ethical framework for information and communication technology: Promoting justice, equity and social welfare. *Journal of Information. Communication and Ethics in Society*, *17*(4), 529–543. DOI: 10.1108/JICES-01-2019-0012

Zuboff, S. (2019). *The age of surveillance capitalism: The fight for a human future at the new frontier of power*. PublicAffairs.

KEY TERMS AND DEFINITIONS

Adl **(Justice):** A core Islamic principle emphasizing equity, fairness, and the upholding of rights for all members of society. In the context of media and technology, it means ensuring technological innovations are accessible to everyone and that digital systems are free from bias.

Amanah **(Responsibility):** The concept of trust or accountability. It holds individuals and organizations, including technology firms and media houses, morally and spiritually responsible for the social and ethical consequences of their actions and products.

Maslahah: (Public Interest): This principle mandates that decisions and innovations must serve the common good or communal welfare. It requires a holistic assessment of technology's impact, prioritizing societal benefits over mere economic gain.

Khilafah: (Stewardship): The idea that human beings are trustees or managers of creation. This applies to technology by requiring a long-term vision that considers environmental sustainability and the preservation of cultural and social values.

Digital Divide: The societal and economic inequality that arises from unequal access to, use of, or knowledge of information and communication technologies. The chapter argues that Islamic principles can help address this issue.

Chapter 7

Impact of Startup Singam Television Show in Regional Entrepreneurship of Tamil Nadu

S. Mohit
https://orcid.org/0009-0003-1414-2421
Christ University, India

Jaikarrunesh C. M.
Christ University, India

Dev Prashobh
Christ University, India

Krishna Prasath
https://orcid.org/0000-0001-6685-5034
Christ University, India

ABSTRACT

This paper examines how Startup Singam, Tamil Nadu's first startup reality show, helps develop local entrepreneurial ecosystems. The program provides a lively platform where new entrepreneurs can pitch their ideas to investors. They can gain essential financial support, useful mentoring, media exposure, and important business connections. The show has sparked significant investments in various sectors. Notable startups like YourTribe, Keeraikadai, Sacdeeil Flying Taxi, Kaigal,

DOI: 10.4018/979-8-3373-5307-4.ch007

Graciss Napkins, TAMS, and Arola Bamboo have gained attention. Importantly, it has supported women entrepreneurs and inspired a cultural shift among Tamil Nadu's youth. Many are moving from the safety of traditional jobs to embrace the risks of starting their own businesses. A unique part of the show is its ValueCorn initiative, which focuses on sustainable business growth rather than inflated valuations. . While early results show strong progress, this study emphasizes the need for ongoing research into the program's long-term economic effects, its potential for replication in other areas.

INTRODUCTION

The study helps to explore the impact of startup singam, a regional television show which is Tamil Nadu's first famous startup reality show which encourages the regional entrepreneurship. However, another government-backed startup reality show, Startup Thamizha, launched by Startup TN, also aims to support and mentor startups in the state, reflecting a growing ecosystem of media-driven entrepreneurship promotion. Ultimately, Startup Singam exemplifies the transformative power of media-driven platforms in stimulating innovation, economic growth, and an entrepreneurial spirit in underserved communities, setting a benchmark for regional startup ecosystems. The show offers platform for unique aspiring entrepreneurs to pitch their ideas Infront of panel of investors and gain their major funding, mentorship from expert, media visibility and valuable business network. This initiative has driven significant investments in diverse startups, including notable successes like YourTribe, Keeraikadai, Sacdeeil Flying Taxi, Kaigal, Graciss Napkins, TAMS & Arola Bamboo and has notably increased participation from women-led ventures. More than funding, Startup Singam has created a cultural shift among young people, encouraging them to pursue entrepreneurship and take risks rather than opting for traditional stable jobs, The show has reached far beyond metropolitan centers to inspire families, communities, and entrepreneurs in smaller towns, spreading awareness that entrepreneurship is viable and valuable even outside traditional urban hubs. The ValueCorn initiative emphasizes sustainable, customer-centric, and ethical business models focused on long-term value rather than quick valuations. While the program has showcased promising results, this research highlights the need for further study to assess its lasting economic impact, potential replication in other regions, and inclusivity of support beyond television exposure.

Entrepreneurship is widely recognized as a driver of economic growth, innovation, and employment creation, with both global and regional implications (Bandura, 2009; Ferguson & Peake, 2017). The role of media — particularly television — in fostering entrepreneurial mindsets has gained increasing scholarly attention, as it provides both direct and indirect exposure to business opportunities, role models, and success narratives (Slavtchev & Wyrwich, 2021; Giglietto et al., 2019). Empirical evidence from varied contexts suggests that exposure to entrepreneurship-themed television programming can positively influence entrepreneurial aspirations, risk tolerance, and even long-term business creation rates (Baugartner, 2019; Zhao & Seibert, 2006).

In India, the influence of entrepreneurial media has become more prominent in recent years, particularly with the rise of televised reality programs such as Shark Tank India. These platforms have been credited with democratizing access to business knowledge, encouraging investment culture, and inspiring aspiring entrepreneurs from Tier 2 and Tier 3 cities (Grafiati, 2024; AMC Indian Journal of Entrepreneurship, 2022). Bibliometric analyses indicate a marked increase in academic interest around media's role in startup culture post-2015, yet most research remains focused on national-level impacts rather than region-specific outcomes (Sharma, 2019).

Regional television and localized entrepreneurial programming hold unique potential in tailoring content to the socio-economic realities, language, and cultural identity of specific areas (Suresh, 2022; Obschonka et al., 2015). Studies show that such localized initiatives can foster confidence among women and minority entrepreneurs (AMC Indian Journal of Entrepreneurship, 2022), influence personality traits conducive to entrepreneurship (Obschonka et al., 2015), and inspire rural and semi-urban populations to explore business opportunities (Haggblade et al., 2021).

Against this backdrop, Startup Singam — Tamil Nadu's pioneering startup reality show — has emerged as a significant catalyst for regional entrepreneurship. The program offers a televised platform for aspiring founders to pitch business ideas to investors, thereby gaining funding, mentorship, strategic guidance, and access to networks. Early qualitative evidence points to notable outcomes, including the inclusion of women-led ventures, the fostering of a risk-taking culture among youth, and the introduction of sustainability-focused models such as ValueCorn, which emphasizes long-term business value over short-term valuation (Startup Singam Study, 2025).

Despite these encouraging developments, there is a lack of systematic academic evaluation of Startup Singam's long-term regional economic effects, scalability, and inclusivity. Addressing this gap, the present study seeks to:

1. Assess the role of Startup Singam in fostering entrepreneurial ventures within Tamil Nadu.
2. Evaluate its contribution to job creation, innovation, and sustainable business practices.
3. Identify challenges and potential improvements for scaling and inclusivity in similar regional media-driven models.

MEDIA AND ENTREPRENEURSHIP: A GLOBAL AND NATIONAL PERSPECTIVE

Extensive literature underscores the role of media, particularly television, in shaping entrepreneurial attitudes, aspirations, and ecosystems (Bandura, 2009; Giglietto et al., 2019; Ferguson & Peake, 2017). Studies such as Slavtchev & Wyrwich (2021, 2023) demonstrate that exposure to pro-entrepreneurial TV content can lead to enduring increases in business creation, supported by mechanisms of social learning and cultural change. In developing economies, mass media access has been shown to influence local entrepreneurship ecosystems by introducing new business models and role models (Winseck, 2008; Haggblade et al., 2021).

In the Indian context, media's influence has grown significantly in recent years. Bibliometric analyses highlight a surge in studies focusing on media's role in shaping startup culture post-2015 (Sharma, 2019). Reality shows such as Shark Tank India have democratized access to entrepreneurial knowledge, fostering investment culture and inspiring aspiring entrepreneurs, particularly from Tier 2 and Tier 3 cities (Grafiati, 2024; AMC Indian Journal of Entrepreneurship, 2022). However, these studies often lack granular empirical assessment of long-term economic outcomes, focusing more on trends and qualitative impacts.

Regional Television and Localized Entrepreneurship

Regional television has unique potential to influence entrepreneurship by contextualizing content to local culture, language, and socio-economic realities (Suresh, 2022; Obschonka et al., 2015). In rural and semi-urban India, targeted regional TV programs have been found to inspire occupational shifts toward entrepreneurial ventures and build relevant personality traits such as openness and proactivity (Haggblade et al., 2021; Obschonka et al., 2015). Local media also plays an indirect role in building business confidence, especially for women and minority entrepreneurs (AMC Indian Journal of Entrepreneurship, 2022).

Media Framing and Entrepreneurial Intentions

Research shows that the way entrepreneurship is framed in television content — highlighting innovation, accessibility, and attainable success — significantly influences viewers' intentions and startup culture formation (Baugartner, 2019; Zhao & Seibert, 2006). Positive framing through relatable role models and practical storytelling encourages risk-taking and reduces societal stigma around business failure (European Commission, 2009; Lakshmi & Viswanathan, 2017).

Startup Singam in the Context of Regional Entrepreneurship

Within Tamil Nadu, Startup Singam represents a pioneering application of these media dynamics to regional entrepreneurship. The show offers a televised platform for founders to pitch ideas to investors, securing not only funding but also mentorship, strategic guidance, and network access. Early qualitative findings suggest that Startup Singam has fostered cultural shifts towards entrepreneurial risk-taking, increased diversity through women-led ventures, and promoted sustainability via initiatives like ValueCorn, which emphasize long-term business value over short-term valuation.

Despite these promising outcomes, gaps remain in understanding the long-term economic effects, scalability, and inclusivity of such media-driven models. This aligns with broader gaps in the literature, where most studies emphasize immediate perception shifts but lack longitudinal assessment of sustained entrepreneurial activity, ecosystem growth, and socio-economic impact at the regional level.

Entrepreneurship has long been known as a key driver of economic growth, innovation, and job creation, both globally and in specific regions (Bandura, 2009; Ferguson & Peake, 2017). While traditional research has often focused on structural factors like access to capital, institutions, and policies, recent years have seen more attention on the media—especially television—and its influence on entrepreneurial aspirations, attitudes, and behaviors. The theoretical framework for studying Startup Singam, Tamil Nadu's leading regional startup reality show, relies on three main perspectives: social cognitive theory, media framing theory, and contextualized entrepreneurship theory. It also incorporates ideas from diffusion of innovations, uses and gratifications theory, and entrepreneurial ecosystem frameworks. Together, these perspectives provide a comprehensive explanation of how local media initiatives can shape entrepreneurial culture, behavior, and the development of ecosystems.

Social Cognitive Theory and Observational Learning

This study mainly relies on Bandura's (2009) social cognitive theory, which focuses on observational learning. Bandura suggests that people learn new behaviors and shape their attitudes by watching role models and interpreting the results of their actions. In entrepreneurship, televised shows give viewers a unique chance to see entrepreneurs pitching their ideas, negotiating with investors, and facing business challenges. These experiences offer indirect learning opportunities, allowing individuals—even those with no previous exposure to entrepreneurship—to gain confidence and motivation to follow similar paths.

Television content acts as a substitute for real-world experience by creating scenarios that audiences can learn from without taking direct risks. For example, when Startup Singam features a young entrepreneur from a Tier 3 town successfully pitching an eco-friendly business, viewers from similar socio-economic backgrounds can envision themselves achieving similar success. This connects with Bandura's idea of self-efficacy, where repeated exposure to relatable role models boosts individuals' belief in their ability to succeed.

Other studies back this up. Ferguson and Peake (2017) found that watching entrepreneurship-related TV shows in the United Kingdom improved entrepreneurial attitudes. Giglietto et al. (2019) showed that entrepreneurial culture spreads through television across different nations, highlighting that the impact of observational learning transcends cultural and geographical limits. By placing Startup Singam within this framework, it becomes evident that the show acts as a learning laboratory, sharing knowledge, skills, and confidence with audiences that traditional entrepreneurial ecosystems often overlook.

Media Framing Theory and Entrepreneurial Intentions

While social cognitive theory explains how people learn from media, media framing theory explains what they take away from it. Baugartner (2019) points out that the way media presents entrepreneurship—through its choice of stories, language, and focus—shapes public views and intentions. Positive framing that highlights opportunities, inclusivity, and accessibility encourages risk-taking and motivates action. In contrast, negative framing, like focusing on failure, corruption, or exclusivity, discourages potential entrepreneurs.

Startup Singam is particularly noteworthy because of its framing choices. Unlike global shows like Shark Tank, which often concentrate on high valuations and aggressive deal-making, Startup Singam emphasizes sustainability, local importance, and inclusivity. For example, initiatives like ValueCorn promote ethical, long-term business models instead of quick financial gains. This approach leads audiences to see entrepreneurship as not just a way to earn wealth but also as a means to create social and community impact.

Framing also tackles the stigma of failure, which is especially strong in collectivist societies like India. Zhao and Seibert (2006) argue that when media normalizes entrepreneurial risks and failures by showing relatable struggles, audiences become more willing to explore business ventures. By featuring a diverse group, including women, rural youth, and first-time entrepreneurs, Startup Singam portrays entrepreneurship as achievable instead of exclusive, reshaping cultural narratives about who can become an entrepreneur.

Contextualized and Regional Entrepreneurship Theory

Another important perspective for this study is the concept of contextualized entrepreneurship. This idea argues that entrepreneurial behavior cannot be separated from the socio-economic, cultural, and geographic conditions in which it occurs (Obschonka et al., 2015). Regional television holds a unique advantage in this respect: it speaks the local language, reflects community values, and tailors entrepreneurial stories to the everyday realities of its audience (Suresh, 2022).

Startup Singam takes advantage of this by broadcasting in Tamil, using culturally relevant storytelling, and featuring participants from small towns and semi-urban areas. This local focus creates a stronger sense of connection among viewers compared to national shows like Shark Tank India. Research by Haggblade et al. (2021) supports this, stating that localized media efforts are more effective at encouraging rural populations to consider entrepreneurship because they reflect familiar settings and challenges.

Additionally, contextualized entrepreneurship highlights inclusivity. Women and minority entrepreneurs, often overlooked in mainstream narratives, gain representation on regional platforms. The visibility of women-led startups on Startup Singam not only showcases diversity but also helps shift cultural attitudes about gender roles in entrepreneurship. Thus, the contextualized entrepreneurship framework explains why Startup Singam has a significant impact relative to its scale: by directly engaging with its community, it creates a deeper influence.

Diffusion of Innovations

To add to these perspectives, Rogers' diffusion of innovations theory helps explain how entrepreneurial ideas spread throughout society. The diffusion model categorizes adopters into innovators, early adopters, early majority, late majority, and laggards, explaining how innovations move through these groups.

Startup Singam plays a key role in this process by featuring innovators and early adopters. As viewers see these individuals succeed, they encourage the early majority by reducing uncertainty and demonstrating what's possible. Over time, this speeds up the spread of entrepreneurial culture from urban centers to rural households.

Uses and Gratifications Theory

Another relevant perspective is uses and gratifications theory, which looks at why people consume specific media. Unlike ideas that suggest passive media influence, this theory argues that people actively choose media to meet particular needs—like entertainment, information, personal identity, and social connections. For aspiring entrepreneurs, Startup Singam provides knowledge (how to pitch), inspiration (role models), and community (shared cultural identity). This explains why audiences not only watch the show but also respond to its messages.

Entrepreneurial Ecosystem Theory

Finally, the idea of entrepreneurial ecosystems offers a broader theoretical context. Ecosystem theory emphasizes that entrepreneurship flourishes in environments with supportive institutions, networks, mentors, and cultural attitudes. Media-driven platforms like Startup Singam enrich this ecosystem by enhancing visibility, connecting entrepreneurs with investors, and normalizing entrepreneurship in cultural narratives. They serve as links in a larger network, bridging the gap between isolated founders and resource-rich institutions.

GLOBAL AND NATIONAL CASE STUDIES

To strengthen this theoretical framework, we can look at similar initiatives. Globally, shows like Shark Tank (USA) and Dragon's Den (UK/Canada) have shown measurable impacts on entrepreneurial ecosystems by boosting startup funding and public awareness. In India, Shark Tank India has opened doors to business knowledge, especially for entrepreneurs in Tier 2 and Tier 3 cities (Grafiati, 2024). However, these national programs often fail to represent local languages and socio-economic realities. Startup Singam fills this void by implementing a regional model, making entrepreneurship culturally relevant in Tamil Nadu.

CRITICAL PERSPECTIVES AND GAPS

Despite the strengths of these theories, it's important to consider critical viewpoints. First, there's a risk of romanticizing entrepreneurship, where audiences may overlook the challenges of running a business. Second, inclusion is still a concern: while Startup Singam showcases women and rural entrepreneurs, maintaining their ventures requires ongoing support beyond media exposure. Third, current research tends to focus on short-term shifts in perception, leaving a gap in long-term studies that assess whether these shows lead to sustained entrepreneurial activity and regional economic growth (Sharma, 2019).

By placing Startup Singam within these broader theoretical discussions, this study addresses a significant gap: the lack of systematic academic evaluation of localized media-driven entrepreneurship initiatives in India.

Entrepreneurship and media have been widely studied around the world. Scholars highlight how mass communication shapes entrepreneurial mindsets, attitudes, and behaviours. Bandura's (2009) social cognitive theory shows that people learn by watching role models. This is especially clear in entrepreneurial television shows, where audiences see entrepreneurs pitch, negotiate, and succeed. Research indicates that watching entrepreneurship-themed TV increases viewers' entrepreneurial aspirations and encourages risk-taking behavior (Slavtchev & Wyrwich, 2021; Giglietto et al., 2019). In Western countries, programs like Shark Tank in the United States and Dragon's Den in the United Kingdom and Canada have not only helped fund startups but have also made entrepreneurship a more acceptable career choice. These shows demonstrate Rogers' (2003) diffusion of innovations theory, as entrepreneurial ideas spread through society when innovators and early adopters are showcased, reducing uncertainty for later adopters.

In India, entrepreneurial television has gained popularity over the last decade, particularly with Shark Tank India, which brought startup culture into everyday conversation. Studies suggest that such national shows make entrepreneurial knowledge more accessible, showcase diverse ideas, and promote an investment culture among young people (Grafiati, 2024; AMC Indian Journal of Entrepreneurship, 2022). They have been particularly powerful in inspiring entrepreneurs from Tier 2 and Tier 3 cities, who often lack structured incubators or investor networks. However, current research tends to focus on metropolitan audiences and does not fully capture the unique social and cultural factors influencing regional entrepreneurship (Sharma, 2019). This gap shows the need for further research on localized programs that communicate directly with non-urban populations in their languages and cultural contexts.

Regional media and localized entrepreneurial content are crucial in filling this gap. Obschonka et al. (2015) state that entrepreneurship is heavily influenced by context. People are more likely to adopt entrepreneurial behaviors when they can relate to the social, cultural, and linguistic aspects of success stories. In rural and semi-urban areas, regional television has been shown to shape job choices by showcasing relatable entrepreneurial role models (Haggblade et al., 2021). Localized content not only improves accessibility but also creates cultural legitimacy for entrepreneurship among groups traditionally underrepresented in business, like women and minorities (AMC Indian Journal of Entrepreneurship, 2022). By representing entrepreneurship in ways that align with local community values and identities, regional shows can build stronger, more inclusive entrepreneurial ecosystems than national or global programs.

Media narratives about entrepreneurship play a key role in shaping public perception and entrepreneurial intentions. Baugartner (2019) points out that framing choices—such as focusing on opportunity, inclusivity, and achievable success—

encourage risk-taking and lessen the stigma around failure. In contrast, negative or elitist portrayals can deter participation. In collectivist societies like India, where family expectations often value stable jobs, media can help reduce the social stigma related to entrepreneurial risk (Zhao & Seibert, 2006). By showing entrepreneurship as accessible and impactful, television can change cultural narratives and empower individuals to consider self-employment as a valid alternative to traditional careers.

Representation in entrepreneurial media is another important issue. Research shows that having women and minority entrepreneurs on televised platforms greatly increases inclusivity and challenges stereotypes (Lakshmi & Viswanathan, 2017). In places where women face barriers to entrepreneurship—like limited access to funding, lack of mentorship, and cultural constraints—the visibility of successful women-led startups on television inspires and proves what is possible. Regional shows that highlight female entrepreneurs help shift community perceptions about gender roles in business, creating positive effects that go beyond individual participants.

An emerging trend in research is the focus on sustainability and social entrepreneurship in media narratives. Traditional entrepreneurial shows often emphasize financial success, valuations, and investor returns. Recent studies call for showcasing ethical, sustainable, and socially responsible business models (European Commission, 2009). Media can transform by promoting ventures that tackle social issues while also being financially sound. In this context, Startup Singam shines by supporting sustainability-focused initiatives like the ValueCorn model, which stresses long-term value over quick profits. By presenting entrepreneurship as both profitable and socially responsible, such programs connect with global discussions about inclusive and sustainable economic growth.

In Tamil Nadu, Startup Singam offers a groundbreaking regional model for promoting entrepreneurship. Unlike national shows that air in Hindi or English, Startup Singam broadcasts in Tamil, featuring cultural identity, local storytelling, and community-centered narratives. This localized approach strongly resonates with audiences from small towns and semi-urban areas, creating an inclusive platform for first-generation entrepreneurs who may not connect with the high-capital, valuation-focused models of urban shows like Shark Tank India. Additionally, the program highlights women-led startups and grassroots innovations, expanding the state's entrepreneurial ecosystem beyond major cities like Chennai. The growth of government-backed initiatives such as Startup Thamizha further signals the growing acknowledgment of regional entrepreneurship as a key to inclusive development in Tamil Nadu.

Despite these advancements, gaps still exist in current research. Most studies focus on short-term changes in perception instead of examining the long-term sustainability of ventures that gain attention through television. There is also limited analysis of whether these programs lead to tangible economic results, like job creation, revenue growth, or ecosystem development. Furthermore, while inclusivity is discussed in theory, there is scant assessment of women's long-term participation in entrepreneurship following exposure to media. Comparative studies of regional and national shows are also lacking, leaving important questions unanswered about scalability and the policy implications of regional media-driven entrepreneurship. Addressing these gaps is vital for understanding the full potential of localized media in promoting balanced and sustainable entrepreneurial growth.

The methodology of this study was designed to explore how Startup Singam, a Tamil-language entrepreneurial reality show, has influenced the views, attitudes, and goals of regional audiences. The main aim was to understand how people interpret and respond to media portrayals of entrepreneurship, so a qualitative research design was used. Unlike quantitative studies that focus on numbers, qualitative research emphasizes depth, meaning, and interpretation. This approach aligns with the study's goal of capturing participants' real experiences and personal viewpoints (Creswell & Poth, 2018).

Three key considerations guided the methodology. First, the cultural specifics of Startup Singam required a method to capture local experiences in the Tamil context. Second, since the study focused on audiences instead of entrepreneurs or investors alone, it needed to include diverse voices, including youth, women, and semi-urban participants. Third, to maintain flexibility and gather rich data, open-ended questions were preferred over closed survey items. This allowed participants to express their ideas in their own words, reflecting the nuances of language, culture, and identity tied to their views on entrepreneurship.

The methodology included four main phases: (a) designing the survey, (b) collecting responses through an online platform (Google Forms), (c) analyzing data with thematic analysis and descriptive statistics, and (d) developing themes, dimensions, and structures to explain how media narratives shape regional entrepreneurship. Each step was carefully organized to uphold academic rigor while preserving the participants' voices.

Research Design

This research used a qualitative, exploratory design with elements of descriptive statistics. The qualitative focus allowed for a deeper exploration of perceptions and meanings, while descriptive statistics provided contextual details like participant demographics and media awareness patterns. Exploratory research suits areas where limited prior work exists. As there is little scholarly evaluation of Startup Singam, this design offered the flexibility to gain insights and lay a foundation for future research.

Participants

The study included 11 participants, aged 18 to 20, representing a key group for understanding entrepreneurial culture in Tamil Nadu. Most (90.9%) were from Tamil Nadu, while 9.1% were from outside the state. Districts represented included Chennai, Salem, Tirupur, Tiruvallur, Trichy, and Erode, covering both urban and semi-urban areas. The youth population is often the most receptive to entrepreneurial messages, making this sample particularly relevant.

Participation was voluntary, and respondents were contacted through digital networks. The relatively small sample size is typical for qualitative studies, where depth of insights is emphasized rather than generalizability (Patton, 2015). Despite its size, the sample offered enough diversity to explore various interpretations of Startup Singam within Tamil Nadu.

Data Collection

Data were collected through an online survey administered via Google Forms. The survey included 11 open-ended questions on themes such as:

- Initial impressions of Startup Singam
- Influence on entrepreneurial aspirations
- Accessibility of entrepreneurship through regional media
- Representation of women, youth, and Tamil culture
- Perceptions of inclusivity and cultural pride
- Ongoing challenges for entrepreneurs despite such programs
- Suggestions for improving the show to better support entrepreneurship

The use of open-ended questions was intentional. It allowed respondents to express their thoughts freely, leading to rich qualitative data. This method was practical, given the geographic spread and the need to collect data efficiently. Online forms ensured anonymity, enabling participants to respond openly without fear of judgment.

Data Analysis

The responses were analyzed using thematic analysis based on Braun and Clarke's (2006) six-step framework: (a) familiarization with data, (b) generating initial codes, (c) searching for themes, (d) reviewing themes, (e) defining and naming themes, and (f) producing the final report. Codes captured recurring ideas like "mentorship value," "cultural identity," "funding challenges," and "youth inclusivity." These codes were grouped into broader themes and dimensions.

Descriptive statistics were used for demographic and categorical data (e.g., age groups, district representation, sources of awareness). This offered a clearer view of participants' background characteristics, complementing the qualitative analysis. By combining thematic and descriptive analysis, the study achieved both depth and context.

Understanding Themes and Dimensions

The thematic analysis revealed five main themes:

- Perceived Impact on Entrepreneurship: Respondents noted that Startup Singam inspired youth, raised awareness, and positioned entrepreneurship as a viable alternative to traditional careers. A few participants questioned the show's long-term influence.
- Accessibility and Inclusivity: Broadcasting in Tamil was seen as a major strength, making entrepreneurship relatable to regular people. Women and youth got visibility, but respondents suggested expanding representation to rural entrepreneurs.
- Cultural Identity and Representation: The show was praised for showcasing Tamil culture and local identity, framing entrepreneurship as both an economic pursuit and a cultural movement.
- Challenges in Regional Entrepreneurship: Despite positive impressions, barriers like access to funding, scalability, bureaucracy, and lack of practical business training were noted as ongoing constraints.
- Suggestions for Improvement: Participants recommended larger funding pools, outreach to rural areas, mentorship hubs, follow-up sessions for featured startups, and inclusion of emerging sectors like artificial intelligence and green technology.

Data Structure

To ensure analytical rigor, the data were organized into three levels:

- First-order responses: Raw participant inputs, like "Yes, it promotes ordinary people to indulge in startups and guides them to success."
- Second-order themes: Groupings such as entrepreneurial inspiration, mentorship value, and structural challenges.

- Aggregate dimensions: Broader categories like entrepreneurial ecosystem awareness, accessibility and inclusivity, and barriers to sustainable entrepreneurship.

This structured approach allowed the transformation of raw qualitative input into conceptual insights, aligning with the study's goal of understanding how regional media shapes entrepreneurial ecosystems in Tamil Nadu.

STARTUP SINGAM: AN OVERVIEW

Startup Singam is Tamil Nadu's first regional entrepreneurial reality show. It is broadcast in Tamil and aims to highlight aspiring entrepreneurs from different backgrounds. The format allows entrepreneurs to pitch their ideas to a panel of judges who are investors, business leaders, and industry experts. Unlike national shows like Shark Tank India, Startup Singam incorporates cultural, linguistic, and regional identity into its framework, making entrepreneurship more relatable to local audiences. The show aims to do more than just provide funding; it also focuses on mentorship, visibility, and building community pride.

The cultural context of the show reflects Tamil Nadu's entrepreneurial landscape. This landscape has traditionally involved small businesses, textile industries, agriculture, and, more recently, information technology firms. By showcasing a variety of startups—such as eco-friendly initiatives, women-led businesses, and tech solutions—Startup Singam presents entrepreneurship as both aspirational and achievable for first-generation entrepreneurs outside metropolitan areas.

Episode Analysis and Featured Startups

YourTribe. One notable startup featured was YourTribe, a community-driven platform aimed at connecting people with similar interests through social and professional networks. The company used its visibility on Startup Singam to gain investor attention and attract users. The platform stressed community building in semi-urban areas, where digital networking was still developing. Judges praised the model's scalability and offered guidance on monetization strategies, supporting its mission to improve access to networking opportunities.

Keeraikadai. Keeraikadai, which translates to "greens shop," is a health-focused startup offering organic vegetables, greens, and traditional food products. This venture resonated with Tamil culture, where leafy greens are central to diets and associated with health. The founders framed their idea as a means to reconnect households with nutritious and affordable food. The judges encouraged expanding distribution networks and adopting digital delivery, responding to the growing demand for health-conscious products. The venture also gained recognition for empowering women in the supply chain, emphasizing inclusivity.

Sacdeeil Flying Taxi. Sacdeeil Flying Taxi presented one of the most futuristic pitches on the program. The company intended to create air mobility solutions to reduce urban traffic jams in cities like Chennai. While the idea was ambitious, judges expressed concerns about regulatory hurdles and infrastructure readiness in India. Although the venture didn't secure significant funding, it generated considerable media attention, showing how the show balances visionary thinking with practical advice.

Kaigal. Kaigal is a gig-work and blue-collar job platform that connects job seekers with employers in construction, housekeeping, and delivery sectors. The pitch reflected the real employment needs in Tamil Nadu's semi-urban areas. Judges appreciated the social impact and scalability of the idea and suggested ways to improve digital literacy among users. This case illustrated the program's alignment with state priorities for job creation and formalizing the workforce.

Graciss Napkins. Graciss Napkins, a women-led enterprise producing sanitary products, showcased the show's focus on inclusivity and health. The venture addressed menstrual health by tackling access issues for rural women. By bringing attention to such initiatives, Startup Singam challenged existing taboos and showed how women entrepreneurs can transform markets in underserved regions. The mentorship provided during the episode emphasized branding, awareness campaigns, and partnerships with NGOs, linking the startup to broader social entrepreneurship goals.

TAMS and Arola Bamboo. TAMS introduced an ed-tech solution for Tamil students, while Arola Bamboo offered eco-friendly alternatives to plastic products. Both ventures represented localized innovation—education linked to language and sustainability-focused entrepreneurship. Judges recommended strengthening policy connections, especially with Tamil Nadu's green entrepreneurship initiatives.

ValueCorn Initiative. The ValueCorn initiative marked a cultural shift by focusing on ethical, long-term value creation instead of short-term profit. This model resonated with discussions around responsible business, showing how the show promotes sustainability as a key entrepreneurial principle.

Together, these startups demonstrate how Startup Singam raises awareness for ventures rooted in Tamil culture, regional needs, and sustainability, while also providing mentorship and limited funding opportunities.

Outcomes of Startup Singam

The outcomes of Startup Singam can be grouped into four areas:

Entrepreneurial Awareness and Culture. The program helped legitimize entrepreneurship as a career in Tamil Nadu, especially among youth who typically prioritize stable jobs (Sharma, 2019). By embedding entrepreneurship into Tamil culture, the show normalized risk-taking and encouraged family acceptance of entrepreneurial efforts.

Inclusivity. The show supported inclusivity by featuring women-led startups, semi-urban entrepreneurs, and grassroots innovators. Ventures like Graciss Napkins and Kaigal showcased gender diversity and employment equity, broadening entrepreneurship beyond elite circles.

Sustainability and Social Responsibility. Several startups highlighted sustainability and community well-being. For example, Keeraikadai promoted organic consumption, while Arola Bamboo and ValueCorn supported eco-friendly and ethical business practices. These examples reflect how the show connected regional entrepreneurship with global sustainable development discussions (Slavtchev & Wyrwich, 2021).

Challenges. Despite some successes, challenges remained, including limited scalability, small funding pools, and regulatory issues. For instance, Sacdeeil Flying Taxi revealed the gap between ambitious ideas and the necessary infrastructure or policy advancements. Additionally, the absence of post-show mentorship posed risks to the long-term sustainability of the featured ventures.

Comparison with Startup Thamizha

Startup Thamizha, a government-supported initiative under Startup TN, contrasts with Startup Singam in several important aspects.

Institutional Support vs. Media Visibility. Startup Thamizha offers structured incubation, training, and funding, but it's limited to registered ventures. Startup Singam focuses on creating awareness and public legitimacy, reaching aspiring entrepreneurs with early-stage ideas.

Scale and Stage of Startups. While Startup Thamizha supports larger ventures, Startup Singam targets grassroots innovators, thereby widening the entrepreneurial pipeline.

Cultural Positioning. Startup Singam uses Tamil identity and storytelling, while Startup Thamizha operates more formally within established policy frameworks.

Inclusivity. Women and semi-urban entrepreneurs are well-represented on Startup Singam, while inclusivity in Startup Thamizha is less visible due to its institutional nature.

Together, these two initiatives create a complementary model: media platforms like Startup Singam raise awareness while state programs like Startup Thamizha provide support for scaling.

Comparison with Shark Tank India

Comparing Startup Singam with Shark Tank India highlights both strengths and weaknesses of the former:

Language and Accessibility. Shark Tank India primarily uses Hindi and English, which limits accessibility for Tamil-speaking audiences. Startup Singam engages rural and semi-urban populations directly by using Tamil.

Funding and Scale. Shark Tank India features high-value investments, while Startup Singam offers smaller but more relatable deals for grassroots entrepreneurs.

Narrative and Framing. National shows highlight valuation and scalability, while Startup Singam emphasizes cultural pride, inclusivity, and ethical responsibility.

Audience Impact. Shark Tank India appeals to urban youth, while Startup Singam resonates with Tamil Nadu's grassroots, changing perceptions of entrepreneurship in non-urban settings.

Global Parallels

Dragon's Den. Dragon's Den from the UK and Canada popularized the investor-pitch format, influencing entrepreneurial ecosystems through exposure and funding. However, critics argue that the program emphasizes elite, profit-driven ventures and overlooks inclusivity (Graham, 2016).

Shark Tank US. Shark Tank US took this model global, influencing entrepreneurial ambitions by popularizing pitch culture (Slavtchev & Wyrwich, 2021). While it democratized access to entrepreneurial knowledge, critics highlight its tendency to favor high-tech, high-capital ventures over grassroots innovation.

Positioning of Startup Singam. In contrast, Startup Singam localized the entrepreneurial reality show model by weaving in Tamil culture, spotlighting women and minority entrepreneurs, and validating small yet impactful ventures. Instead of focusing solely on million-dollar deals, it presents entrepreneurship as a path to community development and cultural pride.

Critical Evaluation

Despite its achievements, Startup Singam continues to face challenges. Post-Show Sustainability. Many ventures gain short-term visibility but don't receive long-term support or mentorship. Funding Constraints. Compared to national and global shows, the available funding remains limited, which affects scalability. Media Romanticism. Similar to Shark Tank US, there's a risk of oversimplifying entrepreneurial success and downplaying risks (Baughn & Neupert, 2018). Digital Divide. While television reaches a wide audience, entrepreneurs in remote regions with limited internet or media access may be left out without additional outreach programs. In summary, while Startup Singam has pioneered media-driven entrepreneurship promotion in Tamil Nadu, its lasting impact depends on building stronger connections with institutional support, investment networks, and ecosystem partnerships.

This study shows how Startup Singam has impacted the entrepreneurial ecosystem of Tamil Nadu. Although the program is mainly a media initiative, its reach and cultural significance set it apart from typical incubation or government programs. This section discusses the outcomes based on participant surveys, case studies, and comparative frameworks across four areas: (a) the effect on women-led startups, (b) the influence on youth in Tier 2 and Tier 3 cities, (c) contributions to job creation, innovation, and sustainability, and (d) challenges related to growth, funding, and media limitations.

Impact on Women-Led Startups

One important finding is the increased visibility and validation of women-led businesses. For example, Graciss Napkins, a startup producing sanitary products, shows how women entrepreneurs are tackling health needs while breaking cultural taboos. Research indicates that women entrepreneurs face systemic barriers to funding, networking, and mentorship (Brush et al., 2019). By providing televised exposure, Startup Singam gave legitimacy and social acknowledgment to women entrepreneurs in Tamil Nadu.

Participants in the surveys confirmed this effect, stating that the show "encourages inclusivity" and "supports women equally." Jennings and Brush (2013) argue that such visibility fosters broader cultural change by inspiring other women and challenging stereotypes about entrepreneurship being a male-dominated field. The mentorship on the show highlighted strategies like branding, awareness campaigns, and partnerships with nongovernmental organizations (NGOs).

However, structural barriers still exist. Limited funding options and a lack of long-term institutional support hinder women entrepreneurs from expanding their businesses. Gupta and Mirchandani (2018) state that while symbolic recognition is beneficial, real progress needs targeted support such as easier access to credit, women-focused incubators, and specific policy incentives.

Overall, the program has begun to shift gender norms by presenting women not just as consumers but as creators. Yet, ongoing institutional support is crucial to maintain this momentum.

Impact on Youth in Tier 2 and Tier 3 Cities

Another important outcome concerns the effect on young people in smaller cities. Tamil Nadu's entrepreneurial activity has typically been concentrated in urban areas like Chennai and Coimbatore. Startup Singam, however, brought representation to people in districts such as Trichy, Salem, and Tiruppur.

Survey feedback indicated that the program "makes entrepreneurship feel accessible" and shares "relatable stories." These insights align with Shane and Venkataraman's (2000) theory, which notes that recognizing opportunities relates to cognitive accessibility. By integrating entrepreneurship into Tamil cultural narratives, the program closed the gap between youth and entrepreneurial opportunities.

Startups such as Keeraikadai (organic greens), Kaigal (employment platform), and Arola Bamboo (eco-friendly products) showed how businesses could tackle local challenges while staying culturally relevant. This approach encouraged young people to view entrepreneurship as a realistic career option. Such views relate to Krueger and Brazeal's (1994) model, which stresses feasibility and desirability as key components driving entrepreneurial intention.

Nonetheless, not all feedback was entirely positive. Some participants noted that the show "might make entrepreneurship seem easy but isn't," pointing out a risk of media glamorization. Rae (2020) observes that media often simplifies the reality of entrepreneurship, presenting an idealized picture while downplaying risks and failures. Despite these drawbacks, the overall impact of Startup Singam was favorable, as it encouraged confidence and a willingness to take risks among young viewers in semi-urban and rural areas.

Job Creation, Innovation, and Sustainability

The program also made notable contributions to job creation, innovation, and sustainability. Job creation. Platforms like Kaigal demonstrated that entrepreneurship could help solve structural unemployment in semi-urban areas. By linking blue-collar workers with employers, the startup aided workforce formalization. This aligns with Audretsch and Thurik's (2001) view that entrepreneurship fuels economic growth through job creation and innovation.

Innovation. Ventures such as Sacdeeil Flying Taxi showcased aspirational technological advancement. While facing regulatory challenges, these ventures sparked public imagination about Tamil Nadu's role in future technologies. Other innovations, like TAMS (Tamil-focused ed-tech) and Keeraikadai, illustrated how regionally tailored solutions can have a real impact. This reflects Schumpeter's (1934) distinction between radical innovation and gradual improvements.

Sustainability. Startups like Arola Bamboo and ValueCorn highlighted the ecological and ethical aspects of entrepreneurship. Arola Bamboo offered eco-friendly substitutes for plastic, while ValueCorn focused on long-term value creation over short-term profits. These aims align with the Sustainable Development Goals (SDGs) and demonstrate Hall et al.'s (2010) point that small entrepreneurs have a vital role in promoting sustainability because of their ties to local communities.

In summary, the program showed that entrepreneurship in Tamil Nadu can achieve a balance between economic growth and community welfare. This supports a holistic development model that prioritizes more than just profit.

CHALLENGES: SCALABILITY, FUNDING, AND MEDIA LIMITATIONS

Despite its successes, significant challenges remain Scalability. Many ventures were limited to their regions and struggled to grow beyond Tamil Nadu. For example, Keeraikadai had supply chain issues, and Graciss Napkins found it tough to access larger markets. Autio and Rannikko (2016) point out that early-stage startups often fail due to scaling challenges rather than innovation shortcomings.

Funding constraints. Compared to national programs like Shark Tank India, Startup Singam operated with limited investment funds. While mentorship was valuable, the lack of financial resources restricted growth opportunities. This finding echoes Gompers and Lerner's (2001) observation that venture capital in India is heavily focused on major cities, leaving regional entrepreneurs underfunded.

Media limitations. As a televised program, Startup Singam sometimes glamorized entrepreneurship, making it seem easier than it is. Survey responses indicated this conflict, as some participants warned that success looked simpler on-screen than in reality. Rae (2020) criticizes this kind of "entrepreneurial storytelling" for romanticizing success and minimizing risks.

Regulatory barriers. The Sacdeeil Flying Taxi case highlighted how ambitious ideas can clash with regulations that are not yet prepared for advanced innovations. Prabhu and Jain (2015) note that regulatory delays are a common problem in emerging markets, obstructing ventures with futuristic goals.

These findings suggest that although media-driven initiatives create cultural legitimacy, they need to be linked with policy programs, incubation systems, and financial networks to ensure long-term sustainability in the ecosystem.

The discussion suggests that Startup Singam has established cultural legitimacy for entrepreneurship, especially among women and youth in semi-urban regions. It facilitated job creation, localized innovation, and sustainable practices, while also exposing systemic challenges such as scalability issues, funding gaps, and regulatory obstacles.

In the end, Startup Singam shows that entrepreneurship is not just an economic pursuit; it's a cultural phenomenon. By embedding entrepreneurial stories in Tamil identity, the show expanded the definition of success to include inclusivity, sustainability, and community pride. However, for these benefits to last, media-driven initiatives need to be supported by institutional measures like government policies, incubation programs, and financial ecosystems.

The findings from Startup Singam show both the potential and the challenges of media-driven entrepreneurship initiatives. While the program gained cultural legitimacy, inclusivity, and awareness of sustainability, there are still systemic issues like limited scalability, funding shortages, and regulatory barriers. To transform the program's symbolic and cultural achievements into lasting structural change, policy actions are necessary. This section discusses the roles of government, universities, investors, and media organizations in strengthening entrepreneurial ecosystems. It also proposes a regional entrepreneurship development framework tailored for Tamil Nadu.

ROLE OF GOVERNMENT

The government plays a vital role in shaping entrepreneurial ecosystems by providing infrastructure, regulatory support, and funding options. In Tamil Nadu, initiatives like Startup TN and Startup Thamizha have laid the groundwork for structured incubation and state-led funding. However, findings from Startup Singam indicate that deeper intervention is needed.

Policy alignment with cultural initiatives. The government can enhance media programs like Startup Singam by incorporating them into state-level entrepreneurship policies. For instance, winners and participants from the show could receive priority access to incubation centers, credit guarantees, and government procurement opportunities. This integration would help turn media exposure into real growth opportunities (Prabhu & Jain, 2015).

Regulatory simplification. A repeated challenge highlighted in the findings was regulatory friction, especially for innovative ventures like Sacdeeil Flying Taxi. Streamlined approval processes, regulatory sandboxes, and pilot-testing zones could allow for experimentation while protecting public interest (Zhao & Seibert, 2006).

Funding support. Beyond symbolic recognition, entrepreneurs need seed funding, venture capital, and affordable credit. The Tamil Nadu government could create regional entrepreneurship funds that co-invest with private investors, targeting Tier

2 and Tier 3 cities. Research shows that public-private co-funding boosts startup survival rates by providing both capital and credibility (Gompers & Lerner, 2001).

Inclusivity policies. Targeted incentives for women, minority, and rural entrepreneurs can help maintain the inclusivity outcomes of Startup Singam. This could include subsidized loans for women-led businesses, incubation programs in rural areas, and skill-development workshops offered in local languages (Brush et al., 2019).

ROLE OF UNIVERSITIES AND EDUCATIONAL INSTITUTIONS

Universities are crucial for integrating entrepreneurship into society. In Tamil Nadu, where higher education enrollment is quite high, universities can act as incubators for an entrepreneurial culture.

Curricular integration. Entrepreneurship should be included in various disciplines, not just limited to business or management programs. Engineering, arts, and agricultural students should have access to entrepreneurship modules, mentorship, and hands-on learning opportunities (Rae, 2020).

Incubation and research support. Universities can set up on-campus incubators that offer physical facilities, mentorship, and connections to investors. They can also act as research partners, conducting market feasibility studies, validating technology, and assessing social impacts for student and community ventures.

Community linkages. As shown in Startup Singam, regional entrepreneurship is closely linked to cultural and community needs. Universities can partner with local startups to develop pilot projects that benefit semi-urban and rural communities, thereby enhancing the social impact of entrepreneurship (Hall et al., 2010).

ROLE OF INVESTORS AND FINANCIAL INSTITUTIONS

Investors are vital for maintaining entrepreneurial ecosystems, but the findings show that funding challenges are a significant barrier for regional ventures.

Regional venture capital networks. Most venture capital in India is focused in Delhi, Mumbai, and Bengaluru, leaving Tamil Nadu's Tier 2 and Tier 3 cities underserved. Investors should be encouraged to set up regional hubs that focus on smaller investments in promising grassroots ventures (Audretsch & Thurik, 2001).

Blended finance models. Combining equity investment, affordable loans, and grants can support startups that focus on sustainability and inclusivity. For example, startups like Arola Bamboo and ValueCorn, which aim for ecological and ethical entrepreneurship, may not attract traditional venture capital but could benefit from blended financing models (Hall et al., 2010).

Mentorship as capital. Besides providing financial resources, investors should offer strategic mentorship, access to markets, and operational know-how. Responses from surveys indicated that mentorship was highly valued in Startup Singam, suggesting that investors can improve their impact by being long-term advisors rather than just short-term funders.

Impact investing. Encouraging impact investors to join Tamil Nadu's ecosystem could help bridge the gap between financial success and social responsibility. Ventures like Graciss Napkins and Keeraikadai would find value in investors who prioritize measurable social outcomes alongside financial returns (Slavtchev & Wyrwich, 2021).

ROLE OF MEDIA HOUSES

Media organizations have a unique ability to shape entrepreneurial culture by controlling visibility, narratives, and representation.

Sustained storytelling. A major limitation of Startup Singam was the lack of follow-up coverage. Media organizations should commit to long-term storytelling, focusing on the progress of startups after their televised pitch. This strategy would build credibility, lessen media romanticism, and educate audiences on the realities of entrepreneurial journeys (Rae, 2020).

Educational content. Media can enhance entertainment with educational programming, such as workshops, webinars, or documentaries that explain funding processes, regulatory requirements, and risk management. This approach would ensure that inspiration comes with practical knowledge.

Representation and inclusivity. Media should continue to showcase women, minority, and rural entrepreneurs, challenging stereotypes and normalizing diversity. Jennings and Brush (2013) stress that media visibility is vital for changing societal views and encouraging underrepresented groups to pursue entrepreneurship.

Partnership with policymakers. Media organizations can work with governments to align storytelling with policy goals, like promoting green entrepreneurship, digital literacy, or women-led businesses. Such partnerships ensure that media visibility leads to integration within the ecosystem.

REGIONAL ENTREPRENEURSHIP DEVELOPMENT FRAMEWORK

Based on the findings and the roles of key stakeholders, a Regional Entrepreneurship Development Framework is proposed for Tamil Nadu.

Ecosystem integration. Media-driven initiatives like Startup Singam should connect with government programs (Startup TN), university incubators, and private investors. This connection would help transition media visibility into long-term institutional support.

Inclusivity and access. The framework should prioritize inclusivity by offering targeted incentives for women, minority, and rural entrepreneurs. Training programs in Tamil, rural incubation centers, and inclusive financing options would broaden participation in entrepreneurship.

Policy-media-academia-industry linkages. Collaboration among these four groups is crucial. For example, a startup featured on Startup Singam could be nurtured at a university, funded by a regional investor, and supported through government procurement. Such linkages would create a complete ecosystem where each participant reinforces the others.

Sustainable and culturally embedded entrepreneurship. The framework should emphasize sustainability, ensuring that entrepreneurship aligns with ecological and social objectives. Culturally grounded ventures like Keeraikadai and Graciss Napkins show that businesses rooted in local identity can achieve both profitability and community well-being.

While Startup Singam has significantly contributed to Tamil Nadu's entrepreneurial scene, it's crucial to assess the risks and limitations that come with media-driven initiatives. Programs like this can create excitement and cultural acceptance, but they might also exaggerate how easy entrepreneurship is, overlook deeper inequalities, and offer only short-term visibility without solid long-term support. This section looks into the risks of media hype and romanticized views of entrepreneurship, the lack of support after the show, and issues of inclusivity related to caste, rural access, and the digital age. These insights will culminate in a conclusion that summarizes the chapter's findings and suggests future research directions.

RISKS OF MEDIA HYPE AND ENTREPRENEURIAL ROMANTICISM

A major risk of media-based entrepreneurship initiatives is creating hype, which can mislead the public about the realities of starting and maintaining a business. Entrepreneurial reality shows, such as Dragon's Den in the UK, Shark Tank in the

US, and Shark Tank India, have been criticized for portraying entrepreneurship as glamorous, fast-moving, and highly rewarding (Rae, 2020). Startup Singam faces similar challenges, particularly because of its focus on entertainment alongside mentorship.

Romanticized narratives. Participants in surveys noted that while the program inspired them, it sometimes made entrepreneurship seem simpler than it is. Comments like "the show makes entrepreneurship seem accessible but isn't" highlight a gap between inspiring stories and the real obstacles entrepreneurs face. This aligns with Rae's (2020) critique of how entrepreneurship is often depicted as a heroic journey that downplays the daily challenges of raising money, following regulations, and dealing with market competition.

Valuation vs. value. Global shows often showcase large investments, suggesting that success is mainly measured by financial worth (Slavtchev & Wyrwich, 2021). Startup Singam tried to change this narrative by focusing on sustainability and inclusivity through initiatives like Keeraikadai and ValueCorn. However, audience perceptions may still lean toward seeing entrepreneurship as a quick route to wealth and fame. Over time, such views might discourage entrepreneurs who face unavoidable challenges.

Short-term enthusiasm. Another issue is that media hype can create brief spikes in interest in entrepreneurship without leading to lasting changes in behavior. Research by Elam and Terjesen (2010) indicates that while media exposure can boost entrepreneurial intent, it does not always lead to starting a business unless there is ongoing support. Therefore, the cultural approval generated by Startup Singam may fade if it is not backed by educational, financial, and policy structures.

LACK OF POST-SHOW SUPPORT

Another key limitation is the lack of support for startups featured on Startup Singam after the show ends. Unlike structured support programs, media initiatives often fail to provide ongoing mentorship, funding, or integration into the entrepreneurial ecosystem once the cameras go off.

Visibility without continuity. Many startups that appeared on the show gained attention but struggled with growth due to insufficient funding and infrastructure. For example, while Keeraikadai received public acknowledgement, it still faced distribution hurdles. Similarly, Graciss Napkins was recognized for promoting inclusivity but encountered resource limitations when trying to expand into rural markets. These cases reflect Autio and Rannikko's (2016) finding that early-stage startups often stumble not because of a lack of innovation but due to scaling difficulties.

Missed opportunities for ecosystem integration. Post-show support could be better organized by connecting Startup Singam participants with government programs like Startup TN or university incubation centers. Without such integration, entrepreneurs risk falling into a "visibility trap," where their short-term exposure leads to high expectations but fails to produce lasting results (Prabhu & Jain, 2015).

Investor disengagement. Investors featured in media sometimes make symbolic commitments that do not turn into real, long-term partnerships. Research on Shark Tank US shows that many deals announced on the show either collapse or undergo significant changes after filming (Kerr et al., 2014). A similar situation could weaken Startup Singam, as entrepreneurs might expect ongoing support but only get temporary guidance or small funding.

INCLUSIVITY CONCERNS: CASTE, RURAL ACCESS, AND THE DIGITAL DIVIDE

Caste dynamics. In India, entrepreneurship is often shaped by caste, with historically favored communities having better access to funding, networks, and credibility (Fuller & Narasimhan, 2014). While Startup Singam showcased women-led and semi-urban ventures, it did not directly tackle the barriers posed by caste. This oversight risks reinforcing current inequalities by highlighting a few notable examples while ignoring broader systemic exclusions. Future policies and media efforts should explicitly address caste to achieve true inclusivity.

Rural access. Although the program included startups from semi-urban areas, the participation of rural entrepreneurs was limited. Rural regions often lack access to networks, financial literacy, and essential infrastructure (Sriram & Mersha, 2010). Without focused outreach, Startup Singam may unintentionally favor urban and semi-urban entrepreneurs who already have better access to media and markets.

The digital divide. Digital literacy emerged as a significant concern in survey responses. While startups like Kaigal worked to improve digital access for blue-collar workers, the limited digital infrastructure in rural areas continues to block many potential entrepreneurs. Research by Norris (2001) highlights that digital gaps reinforce socio-economic inequalities, making it essential for programs like Startup Singam to include strategies for digital inclusion.

Gender intersectionality. While the program supported women entrepreneurs, inclusivity was primarily focused on gender, with less attention to the overlapping challenges faced by rural, lower-caste, or minority women. Crenshaw's (1989) concept of intersectionality underscores the need to consider multiple disadvantages. Without this perspective, inclusivity may end up being surface-level instead of transformative.

This chapter analyzed Startup Singam as Tamil Nadu's first entrepreneurial reality show. The findings indicate that the program has created significant cultural acceptance of entrepreneurship, especially among women and youth in Tier 2 and Tier 3 cities. It emphasized inclusivity, sustainability, and local innovation while moving the focus from financial value to socially responsible entrepreneurship. However, the critical insights reveal that the show also risks glamorizing entrepreneurship, provides limited support after the show, and has not adequately addressed the deep-rooted inequities such as caste, rural exclusion, and digital divides. These challenges spotlight the need to connect media initiatives with broader entrepreneurial ecosystems that involve government, universities, investors, and civil society.

Future research on *Startup Singam* and similar regional entrepreneurial programs should explore multiple avenues to deepen understanding and evaluate long-term impacts. One key area is the need for **longitudinal studies**. While current findings highlight immediate cultural and social outcomes, it remains unclear whether these effects persist over time. Tracking the progress of startups featured on *Startup Singam* across several years would provide insights into whether media-driven visibility translates into sustainable entrepreneurial growth. Such research would also reveal whether televised mentorship and symbolic recognition lead to measurable outcomes in terms of revenue growth, scalability, and employment generation, as suggested by Autio and Rannikko (2016).

Another important area is **comparative analyses**. By examining how *Startup Singam* differs from national and global entrepreneurial shows such as *Shark Tank India*, *Dragon's Den*, and *Shark Tank US*, scholars can evaluate variations in inclusivity, sustainability, and post-show support mechanisms. Comparative approaches could help identify whether regional programming is more effective at embedding cultural narratives and addressing grassroots challenges, or whether national and international shows provide more robust financial opportunities (Slavtchev & Wyrwich, 2021).

Future research should also focus on **intersectional inclusivity**. Although *Startup Singam* highlights women entrepreneurs and semi-urban participants, it does not fully address the intersection of caste, rurality, and gender in shaping access to entrepreneurship. Crenshaw's (1989) framework on intersectionality emphasizes the importance of examining overlapping social disadvantages. A deeper understanding of these dynamics in Tamil Nadu could reveal whether programs like *Startup Singam* genuinely democratize entrepreneurship or whether structural inequities persist under the surface.

In addition, the **impact of digital literacy** requires systematic exploration. Survey responses indicated that limited digital access and skills remain barriers for rural entrepreneurs. Research should examine how digital tools, training, and infrastructure affect entrepreneurial participation in semi-urban and rural communities. This aligns with Norris's (2001) argument that digital divides reinforce social inequalities. Future studies could also investigate how initiatives such as mobile-based training, vernacular digital platforms, and government-sponsored digital literacy campaigns interact with entrepreneurship.

Finally, **policy evaluation** is an essential research area. Programs such as *Startup TN* and *Startup Thamizha* represent formal institutional efforts to foster entrepreneurship, while *Startup Singam* serves as a cultural and media-driven initiative. Future research should assess how these models interact—whether media programs create a funnel for participants who later enter policy-led incubators, or whether the two remain disconnected. Such evaluation would provide valuable evidence for policymakers seeking to build integrated entrepreneurial ecosystems that balance cultural legitimacy, financial support, and institutional backing (Prabhu & Jain, 2015).

REFERENCES

AMC Indian Journal of Entrepreneurship. (2022). *Recent articles. AMC Indian Journal of Entrepreneurship, 5*(3).

Audretsch, D. B., & Thurik, A. R. (2001). What's new about the new economy? Sources of growth in the managed and entrepreneurial economies. *Industrial and Corporate Change, 10*(1), 267–315. DOI: 10.1093/icc/10.1.267

Autio, E., & Rannikko, H. (2016). Retaining winners: Can policy boost high-growth entrepreneurship? *Research Policy, 45*(1), 42–55. DOI: 10.1016/j.respol.2015.06.002

Bandura, A. (2009). Social cognitive theory of mass communication. *Journal of Communication, 59*(1), 265–273. DOI: 10.1111/j.1460-2466.2009.01448.x

Baugartner, M. (2019). Media framing and entrepreneurial intentions: The role of television in shaping startup culture. *Journal of Media Studies, 34*(2), 78–92.

Baughn, C. C., & Neupert, K. E. (2018). The cultural and institutional environment for entrepreneurship. *Entrepreneurship Theory and Practice, 41*(5), 685–711. DOI: 10.1177/1042258717725524

Braun, V., & Clarke, V. (2006). Using thematic analysis in psychology. *Qualitative Research in Psychology, 3*(2), 77–101. DOI: 10.1191/1478088706qp063oa

Brush, C. G., Ali, A., Kelley, D. J., & Greene, P. G. (2019). The influence of human capital factors and context on women's entrepreneurship: Which matters more? *Journal of Business Venturing, 34*(2), 452–472. DOI: 10.1016/j.jbusvent.2018.08.002

Crenshaw, K. (1989). Demarginalizing the intersection of race and sex. *University of Chicago Legal Forum, 1989*(1), 139–167.

Creswell, J. W., & Poth, C. N. (2018). *Qualitative inquiry and research design: Choosing among five approaches* (4th ed.). SAGE.

Elam, A. B., & Terjesen, S. (2010). Gendered institutions and cross-national patterns of business creation for men and women. *European Journal of Development Research, 22*(3), 331–348. DOI: 10.1057/ejdr.2010.19

European Commission. (2009). *Entrepreneurship in the EU and beyond: A survey in the EU, EFTA countries, Croatia, Turkey, the US, Japan, South Korea, and China.* Publications Office of the European Union.

Ferguson, R., & Peake, W. O. (2017). Television's impact on entrepreneurial attitudes in the UK. *International Journal of Entrepreneurial Behaviour & Research, 23*(5), 867–884. DOI: 10.1108/IJEBR-08-2016-0254

Fuller, C. J., & Narasimhan, H. (2014). *Tamil Brahmans: The making of a middle-class caste*. University of Chicago Press.

Giglietto, F., Carlo, A., & Righetti, N. (2019). The role of television in the cross-national diffusion of entrepreneurial culture. *International Journal of Communication, 13*, 1585–1606.

Gompers, P., & Lerner, J. (2001). The venture capital revolution. *The Journal of Economic Perspectives, 15*(2), 145–168. DOI: 10.1257/jep.15.2.145

Grafiati. (2024). Impact of Shark Tank India on India's growing startup mindset. *YourStory*. https://yourstory.com

Graham, J. (2016). Dragon's Den and the popularization of entrepreneurship in the UK. *Journal of Media Business Studies, 3*(1), 55–72. DOI: 10.1080/23774931.2016.1187734

Gupta, V., & Mirchandani, D. (2018). Investigating entrepreneurial success through women's perspectives. *Journal of Developmental Entrepreneurship, 23*(3), 1850019. DOI: 10.1142/S1084946718500193

Haggblade, S., Hazell, P., & Reardon, T. (2021). The rural nonfarm economy: Prospects for growth and poverty reduction. *World Development, 140*, 105250. DOI: 10.1016/j.worlddev.2020.105250

Hall, J. K., Daneke, G. A., & Lenox, M. J. (2010). Sustainable development and entrepreneurship: Past contributions and future directions. *Journal of Business Venturing, 25*(5), 439–448. DOI: 10.1016/j.jbusvent.2010.01.002

Jennings, J. E., & Brush, C. G. (2013). Research on women entrepreneurs: Challenges to (and from) the broader entrepreneurship literature? *The Academy of Management Annals, 7*(1), 663–715. DOI: 10.5465/19416520.2013.782190

Kerr, W. R., Lerner, J., & Schoar, A. (2014). The consequences of entrepreneurial finance: Evidence from angel financings. *Review of Financial Studies, 27*(1), 20–55. DOI: 10.1093/rfs/hht071

Krueger, N. F., & Brazeal, D. V. (1994). Entrepreneurial potential and potential entrepreneurs. *Entrepreneurship Theory and Practice, 18*(3), 91–104. DOI: 10.1177/104225879401800307

Lakshmi, R., & Viswanathan, R. (2017). Media, gender, and entrepreneurship in India. *Journal of Media and Cultural Studies, 29*(6), 899–913.

Norris, P. (2001). *Digital divide: Civic engagement, information poverty, and the internet worldwide*. Cambridge University Press.

Obschonka, M., Stuetzer, M., Gosling, S. D., Rentfrow, P. J., Lamb, M. E., & Potter, J. (2015). Regional TV, personality traits, and entrepreneurship. *Regional Studies, 49*(1), 33–48. DOI: 10.1080/00343404.2014.965135

Patton, M. Q. (2015). *Qualitative research & evaluation methods: Integrating theory and practice* (4th ed.). SAGE.

Prabhu, J., & Jain, S. (2015). Innovation and entrepreneurship in India: Understanding institutional context. *Business Horizons, 58*(6), 701–709. DOI: 10.1016/j.bushor.2015.07.002

Rae, D. (2020). Media narratives and entrepreneurial learning: The risks of romanticism. *International Journal of Entrepreneurial Behaviour & Research, 26*(5), 951–970. DOI: 10.1108/IJEBR-10-2019-0622

Rogers, E. M. (2003). *Diffusion of innovations* (5th ed.). Free Press.

Schumpeter, J. A. (1934). *The theory of economic development*. Harvard University Press.

Shane, S., & Venkataraman, S. (2000). The promise of entrepreneurship as a field of research. *Academy of Management Review, 25*(1), 217–226. DOI: 10.5465/amr.2000.2791611

Sharma, G. (2019). Innovation and entrepreneurship research in India from 2000 to 2018: A bibliometric survey. *Journal of Management Development, 37*(4), 500–515. DOI: 10.1108/JMD-10-2018-0291

Slavtchev, V., & Wyrwich, M. (2021). TV and entrepreneurship. *Jena Economic Research Papers, 2021*(010). https://doi.org/DOI: 10.2139/ssrn.3807456

Slavtchev, V., & Wyrwich, M. (2023). Can television shows increase entrepreneurial activity? Evidence from a natural experiment. *Journal of Business Venturing, 38*(2), 106271. DOI: 10.1016/j.jbusvent.2022.106271

Sriram, V., & Mersha, T. (2010). Facilitating entrepreneurship in sub-Saharan Africa: What governments can do. *Journal of International Business and Cultural Studies, 3*, 1–9.

Suresh, K. G. (2022). Dynamics of regional television in India: A systematic perspective. *Journal of Content. Community & Communication*, *15*(8), 65–78. DOI: 10.2139/ssrn.3985732

Winseck, D. (2008). Media and entrepreneurial culture in developing economies. *Global Media Journal*, *7*(13), 1–23.

Zhao, H., & Seibert, S. E. (2006). The impact of television role models on entrepreneurial intentions: A cross-cultural study. *Journal of Business Venturing*, *21*(1), 1–25. DOI: 10.1016/j.jbusvent.2005.02.003

Chapter 8

Late Night Use of Social Media and Sleep Deprivation

M. Balamurugan
https://orcid.org/0000-0001-9737-2035
Dayananda Sagar College of Engineering, India

D. Roopa
RR Institute of Technology, Bangalore, India

Shruthi K. N.
RR Institute of Technology, Bangalore, India

R. Sushma
RR Institute of Technology, Bangalore, India

Kruthi T. C.
RR Institute of Technology, Bangalore, India

G. Swetha
https://orcid.org/0000-0001-8620-7149
RR Institute of Technology, Bangalore, India

N. Raghu
https://orcid.org/0000-0002-2091-8922
Jain University, India

ABSTRACT

In the digital era, social media has become an integral part of everyday life, particularly among adolescents, young adults, and working professionals. While these platforms provide numerous benefits, including social connectivity, entertainment, and access to information, they also pose significant challenges to users' sleep health. This chapter explores the detrimental impact of late-night social media usage on sleep quality and overall well-being. As screen time during nighttime hours becomes increasingly common, users are exposed to blue light emissions, algorithm-driven content, and cognitive stimulation that delay sleep onset and reduce sleep duration.

DOI: 10.4018/979-8-3373-5307-4.ch008

Biologically, the disruption of circadian rhythms and suppression of melatonin caused by prolonged exposure to screens lead to poor sleep architecture and neural fatigue. Psychologically, users report heightened anxiety, mood swings, and depressive symptoms linked to both insufficient sleep and online social comparison.

1. INTRODUCTION

In the 21st century, social media has evolved from a niche networking tool to a global cultural and behavioral phenomenon. Platforms such as Instagram, TikTok, X (formerly Twitter), Facebook, YouTube, and Snapchat have amassed billions of users worldwide. According to recent data from Statista (2024), the average global user spends over 2.5 hours daily on social media, with higher usage rates reported among adolescents and young adults (Alfonsi et al., 2020; Alimoradi, 2023; Alonzo, 2024; Brautsch, 2024; Cain & Gradisar, 2020). The ubiquity of smartphones and affordable data access have transformed social media into a round-the-clock activity, accessible from virtually anywhere, at any time.

As platforms for social interaction have now expanded into ecosystems for entertainment, business, activism, and education. The boundaries between offline and online life are increasingly blurred, and social media has emerged as a dominant force in shaping identity, relationships, values, and worldviews. However, as digital engagement deepens, concerns about its impact on mental, emotional, and physical health have grown, especially regarding how it affects sleep.

Figure 1. Year wise social media usage with respect to time

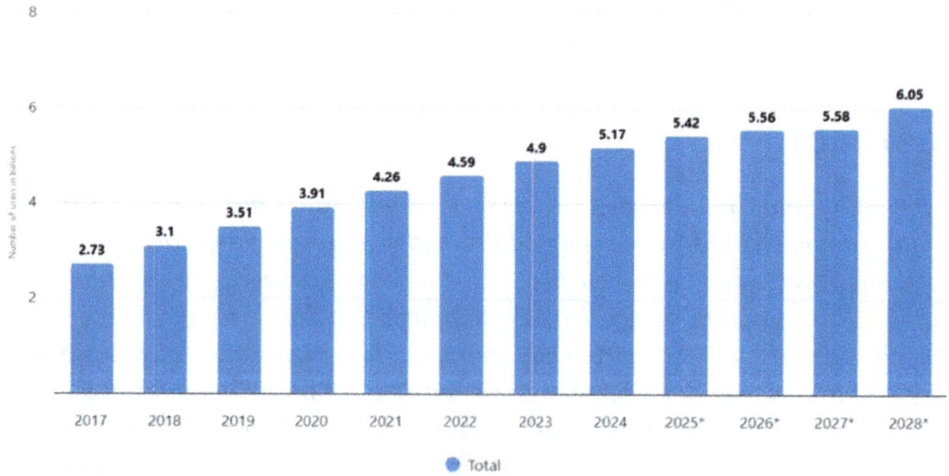

As of 2024, the average daily social media usage of internet users worldwide amounted to 143 minutes per day, down from 151 minutes in the previous year. Currently, the country with the most time spent on social media per day is Brazil, with online users spending an average of three hours and 49 minutes on social media each day. In comparison, the daily time spent with social media in the U.S. was just two hours and 16 minutes as shown in Figure .

Currently, the global social network penetration rate is 62.3 percent. Northern Europe had an 81.7 percent social media penetration rate, topping the ranking of global social media usage by region. Eastern and Middle Africa closed the ranking with 10.1 and 9.6 percent usage reach, respectively. People access social media for a variety of reasons. Users like to find funny or entertaining content and enjoy sharing photos and videos with friends, but mainly use social media to stay in touch with current events friends.

Social media has a wide-reaching and significant impact on not only online activities but also offline behavior and life in general. During a global online user survey in February 2019, a significant share of respondents stated that social media had increased their access to information, ease of communication, and freedom of expression (Carter et al., 2017). On the flip side, respondents also felt that social media had worsened their personal privacy, increased a polarization in politics and heightened everyday distractions.

1.1 Rise of Late-Night Screen Time Behavior

One of the most alarming behavioral patterns associated with modern social media use is the significant increase in screen time during late-night hours. Studies have shown that users often engage with their phones just before bed, leading to a delay in sleep onset and a decrease in overall sleep duration (Exelmans & Van den Bulck, 2016). The concept of "revenge bedtime procrastination" where individuals deliberately delay sleep to reclaim personal time lost to daily obligations, has gained traction particularly among students and working professionals who feel deprived of leisure during the day.

Figure 2. Social Media usage and its effects on sleep

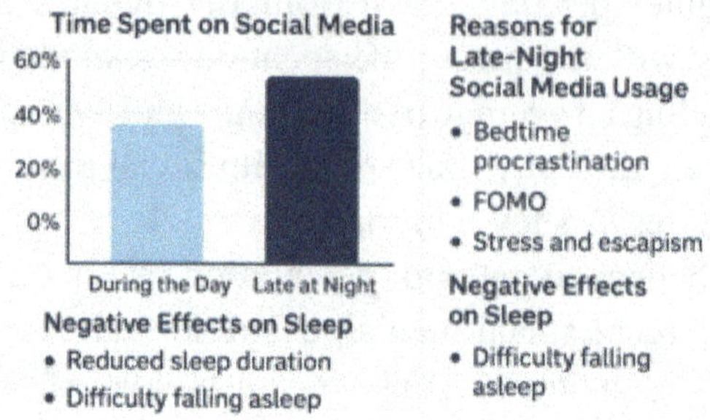

Late-night social media use is fueled by various psychological triggers: the desire for social validation, fear of missing out (FOMO), escapism from real-world stress, and the irresistible pull of endless scrolling and algorithmic content (Giumetti & Kowalski, 2022) Notifications, trending content, and late-night live streams entice users to stay awake longer than intended. Many people do not realize how the dopamine-driven design of social media platforms subtly reinforces prolonged engagement, even at the cost of rest. Furthermore, bedtime usage is often considered "me time" providing emotional comfort or entertainment after a stressful day. Unfortunately, this practice becomes self-defeating when the immediate gratification of scrolling interferes with the longer-term need for restorative sleep as shown in Figure 2.

1.2 Importance of Sleep for Mental and Physical Health

Sleep is not a passive state it is a fundamental biological process that is crucial for cognitive functioning, emotional stability, physical health, and overall well-being. The human body follows a circadian rhythm a roughly 24-hour internal clock regulated by light and hormonal cues. Quality sleep facilitates memory consolidation, muscle repair, immune system function, emotional regulation, and decision-making capabilities (Gradisar, 2022; Gunarathne & Walpola, 2024; Hamilton, 2022; Harbard, 2022; Jiaxin et al., 2022; Khan et al., 2024).

Chronic sleep deprivation, defined as consistently getting less than the recommended 7–9 hours of sleep per night, can result in a range of health issues, including weakened immunity, obesity, diabetes, cardiovascular diseases, anxiety, depression, and impaired brain function. For adolescents and young adults, who are already navigating significant developmental, academic and emotional changes, insufficient sleep can have lasting repercussions on both their personal growth and social adaptation (Khan & Iqbal, 2022; Khpalwak & Hamidi, 2024; Ko, 2024; Russ & Griffiths, 2015; Lafontaine-Poissant, 2024). Numerous global health organizations, including the World Health Organization (WHO) and the Centers for Disease Control and Prevention (CDC), have flagged sleep deprivation as a public health epidemic. In this context, the rise in digital distractions—particularly late-night social media usage—emerges as a key contributor to the sleep crisis.

Figure 3. Different social media platform usage

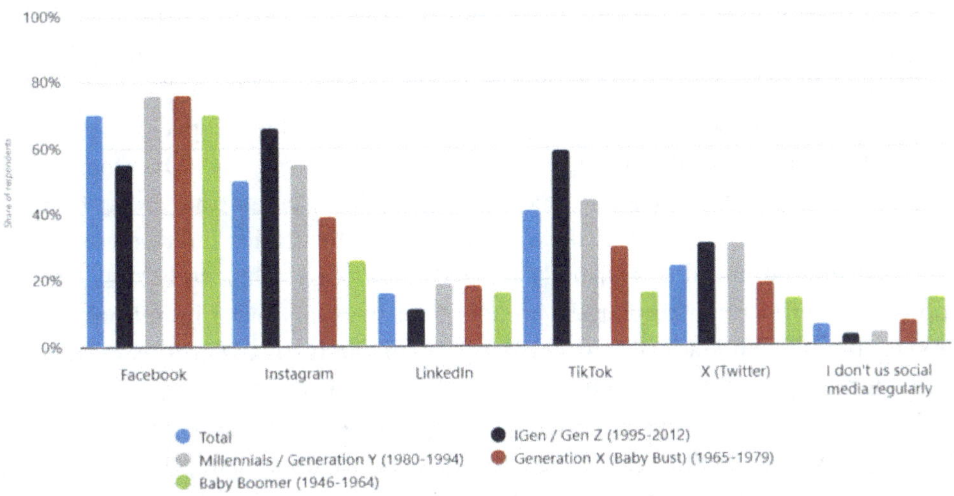

Social media advertising worldwide continues to grow rapidly, with Facebook and Instagram remaining the key players driving this expansion. Their global reach, paired with powerful targeting and data capabilities, makes them essential platforms for advertisers aiming to engage audiences across regions and demographics. Instagram, in particular, has seen rising prominence as a hub for influencer marketing, visual storytelling, and social commerce making it especially appealing for lifestyle, fashion, and consumer brands. Facebook, while more established, still commands massive engagement globally and offers extensive tools for advertisers to reach users in both mature and emerging markets. As businesses increasingly shift their marketing strategies toward digital-first approaches, Facebook and Instagram are positioned at the center of global social media advertising spend, consistently delivering strong performance and return on investment for brands worldwide. Here is a graph illustrating the average daily time spent on major social media platforms in 2023.Facebook and Instagram lead in usage, with users spending close to 3 hours daily, highlighting their significant role in contributing to late-night screen time behavior and potential sleep disruption as shown in Figure 3.

2. LITERATURE SURVEY

Singh et al. surveyed 2,200 adolescents, examining the impact of nighttime social media usage and parental digital rules. Teens with enforced evening screen curfews slept on average 40 minutes more per night and reported fewer mood disturbances. The study highlighted that parental modeling—parents adhering to their own digital limits—amplified the positive effects. Although reliant on self-reported behaviors, the large, diverse sample strengthens its validity. Findings underscore the importance of family-based strategies in improving sleep through behavioral boundaries and parental participation (Alimoradi, 2023).

Lee et al. evaluated a smartphone app designed to promote sleep hygiene through timed reminders, screen dimming, and bedtime behavioral prompts. Over four weeks, 150 adult participants saw a 20% reduction in nightly screen time and a 15-point improvement on sleep quality scales. Notably, post-intervention interviews revealed users felt more mindful and visually relaxed before bed. This study suggests that app-based solutions can supplement broader sleep interventions. Limitations include its short duration and lack of long-term follow-up, but it signals promising scalable tools for managing digital habits and promoting sleep health (Alonzo, 2024).

Levenson and colleagues conducted a large-scale quantitative study involving 1,788 U.S. young adults aged 19–32 to examine the relationship between social media use and sleep disturbances. Using self-reported data on frequency, duration, and emotional engagement with various social media platforms, the study revealed that participants in the highest quartile of usage were nearly twice as likely to experience disrupted sleep patterns. Notably, both the frequency of social media engagement and the emotional investment in content were significant predictors of sleep quality. The findings emphasized the importance of understanding how not only the quantity but the nature of social media interaction affects sleep. While the study offers strong statistical significance due to its large sample size and thorough demographic representation, its cross-sectional design and reliance on self-reporting limit its ability to establish causality. Nevertheless, it provides compelling evidence for including digital media use as a factor in behavioral sleep health assessments (Brautsch, 2024.

Carter et al. presented a systematic review of 20 peer-reviewed studies exploring the relationship between portable screen use (e.g., smartphones, tablets) and sleep outcomes in children and adolescents. The review consistently found that screen-based media use before or during bedtime significantly affected sleep onset, duration, and quality. Interestingly, even the presence of media devices in the bedroom regardless of active use was associated with sleep disruption, likely due to psychological cues or interrupted routines. The analysis highlighted screen time as a modifiable risk factor, reinforcing the need for behavioral interventions such as screen curfews or restricted bedroom device access. Though comprehensive, the review's limitations include variation in the definitions of screen use, reliance on subjective measures across studies, and its restriction to English-language publications (Cain & Gradisar, 2020).

Twenge et al. analyzed longitudinal survey data from over 360,000 U.S. adolescents spanning the years 2009 to 2017, aiming to uncover trends linking digital media use with declining sleep duration. The researchers found that as smartphone usage surged, especially among teenagers, average nightly sleep duration dropped significantly, with more adolescents reporting less than seven hours of sleep. The correlation was particularly strong for those using screens for more than two hours daily. This large-scale study highlighted a generational shift toward digital engagement at the expense of sleep, which may have lasting implications on adolescent development. The research's key strength lies in its expansive dataset and temporal scope, allowing for trend analysis over nearly a decade. While causality remains unproven, the temporal alignment between rising smartphone use and sleep deprivation strengthens the inference. The authors advocate for policy-level interventions to reduce screen exposure in adolescents, particularly during nighttime hours (Choi, 2024).

Orben et al. study offers a nuanced take on the ongoing debate regarding screen time and adolescent well-being. The analyzed data from over 120,000 UK adolescents using advanced statistical modeling to assess the strength of association between digital technology use and sleep quality. Contrary to alarmist narratives, their findings revealed that the effects of screen time on sleep and mental well-being were modest, accounting for less than 1% of the variability in life satisfaction. The authors argued that digital technology's impact may be overstated, and that context, content, and individual differences play more significant roles. The use of robust statistical tools, including specification curve analysis, lends credibility to the findings. However, the study's limitations include its reliance on self-reported measures and its exclusion of specific nighttime behaviors. Still, it contributes to a more balanced understanding of screen use, emphasizing the need for targeted, rather than blanket, recommendations (Giumetti & Kowalski, 2022).

Alfonsi et al. conducted an experimental study involving Italian adolescents to assess the impact of pre-sleep social media use on sleep patterns. Using a combination of sleep diaries and behavioral surveys, the researchers found that adolescents who engaged in social media activities within one hour before bedtime experienced delayed sleep onset and disrupted sleep continuity. The study uniquely emphasized the role of cognitive arousal, suggesting that even passive browsing could keep the brain mentally engaged and delay the body's transition into rest. The combination of subjective reports and semi-controlled conditions adds strength to the findings. However, the study's limitations include its relatively small, homogeneous sample and short observation window, which may affect generalizability. Despite this, it contributes to the literature by highlighting the importance of timing and mental state in understanding how digital behavior affects sleep, particularly in adolescent populations prone to bedtime procrastination (Gradisar, 2022).

Woods et al. explored the impact of nighttime social media use on sleep quality and emotional well-being in a sample of 467 UK adolescents. Their findings revealed a strong association between high bedtime engagement on platforms and poor sleep quality, as well as increased levels of anxiety and depression. A key variable in this study was Fear of Missing Out (FOMO), which was found to significantly mediate the relationship between late-night social media use and emotional distress. Adolescents who frequently checked their phones after going to bed exhibited not only poorer sleep but also heightened psychological distress. The study provides valuable insight into how psychosocial factors interact with digital behaviors to influence sleep. Although limited by its moderate sample size and reliance on self-reporting, it underscores the emotional underpinnings of social media addiction and supports the development of interventions that address both technological habits and emotional needs (Gunarathne & Walpola, 2024).

Exelmans and Van den Bulck (2016) investigated the relationship between media consumption and sleep efficiency in adults, using data from 844 participants aged 18 to 94. The study found that individuals who used smartphones and social media extensively before bed experienced longer sleep latency, lower sleep efficiency, and overall poorer rest quality. Notably, it differentiated between types of media, finding that interactive devices (smartphones) disrupted sleep more than passive devices (TV). This finding suggests that cognitive engagement plays a larger role than screen exposure alone. Using validated sleep quality scales, the study adds credibility to its claims. However, it relies heavily on self-reporting and doesn't factor in physiological data, such as melatonin levels or heart rate. Still, it provides a broader perspective by focusing on an adult demographic, supporting the notion that sleep disturbances due to social media are not limited to adolescents (Hamilton, 2022).

Kuss et al. conducted a literature review focused on the addictive nature of social networking and its psychological consequences, particularly sleep deprivation. Their analysis drew from studies linking excessive use of platforms like Facebook and Instagram with increased anxiety, stress, and poor sleep outcomes. The authors introduced the term "social media fatigue", describing a state of mental exhaustion resulting from constant connectivity. They highlighted how addictive design features—such as infinite scrolling, push notifications, and algorithmic content delivery—perpetuate compulsive usage, especially before bedtime. The review also emphasized the bidirectional relationship between mental health and screen use, where poor sleep worsens anxiety, and anxiety encourages more screen time. While the paper does not present new empirical data, its synthesis of existing literature offers a theoretical framework for understanding how social media disrupts sleep. It calls for interdisciplinary approaches that incorporate digital wellness into mental health and sleep treatment plans (Harbard, 2022).

3. BIOLOGICAL IMPACT OF SLEEP DEPRIVATION

The human body is biologically programmed to follow certain rhythms that govern fundamental functions, one of the most important being the sleep-wake cycle. This cycle, tightly linked to external cues such as light and darkness, is crucial for maintaining mental clarity, emotional stability, immune defense and overall physical health. However, with the rise of digital screens and the increasing tendency to use social media late into the night, our natural biological processes—particularly those related to sleep—are facing unprecedented disruption. In this section, we explore three major biological consequences of sleep deprivation caused by late-night screen use: circadian rhythm disruption due to blue light exposure, melatonin suppression, and sleep cycle disturbances leading to neural fatigue.

3.1 Circadian Rhythm and Blue Light Exposure

At the core of the sleep-wake regulation system lies the circadian rhythm, a 24-hour internal clock that governs various physiological and behavioral processes such as body temperature, hormone secretion, digestion, and—most importantly—sleep. This rhythm is controlled by a tiny region in the brain called the suprachiasmatic nucleus (SCN), located in the hypothalamus (Lee, 2024). The SCN responds to light signals received through the eyes and helps synchronize the body's activities with the day-night cycle. One of the most significant environmental cues for the SCN is light, especially natural sunlight. During the day, exposure to sunlight tells the SCN that it's time to stay awake and alert. As the day ends and natural light fades, the SCN signals the pineal gland to begin producing melatonin, a hormone that facilitates sleep (Levenson et al., 2016).

However, this finely tuned system is disrupted by exposure to artificial blue light, which is abundantly emitted by the screens of smartphones, tablets, and computers. Blue light has a short wavelength and high energy, mimicking the intensity and quality of daylight (Lin et al., 2023). When users engage with their devices during nighttime particularly for extended periods on social media platforms the brain is tricked into believing it's still daytime. This confuses the SCN and delays the onset of the sleep signal cascade. Scientific studies have shown that blue light exposure, even for just two hours before bedtime, can significantly shift circadian rhythms by up to 90 minutes (Mac Cárthaigh et al., 2024). This circadian misalignment doesn't just lead to difficulty falling asleep—it can also affect the quality and depth of sleep achieved once a person does fall asleep. Over time, repeated disruption of this biological clock can contribute to chronic sleep disorders, metabolic imbalances, and increased vulnerability to diseases such as diabetes and hypertension (Murphy et al., 2022).

3.2 Melatonin Suppression and Its Consequences

Melatonin is often referred to as the "sleep hormone." Secreted by the pineal gland, melatonin production typically begins in the evening as light levels drop, peaking in the middle of the night and tapering off toward morning (Nguyen Luong et al., 2023). This hormone plays a critical role in signaling to the body that it's time to wind down and prepare for rest. Importantly, melatonin doesn't induce sleep directly but facilitates the transition from wakefulness to sleep by lowering body temperature, slowing metabolic processes, and reducing alertness.

Exposure to artificial light especially blue light from screens suppresses melatonin production. The brighter and more prolonged the light exposure, the more significant the suppression. Research has shown that screen use can suppress melatonin production by up to 50%, depending on the brightness and proximity of the screen to the eyes. This suppression not only delays sleep onset but also reduces the duration and quality of REM (Rapid Eye Movement) sleep, the phase most closely associated with dreaming, emotional processing, and memory consolidation (Nicholson et al., 2023).

A deficiency in REM sleep can lead to emotional volatility, poor concentration, and reduced ability to retain new information effects that are particularly detrimental for students and working professionals. Over time, disrupted melatonin cycles can also impact immune function, increasing the risk of infections and even contributing to long-term health issues such as depression, anxiety disorders, and cancer (Orben & Przybylski, 2019). Furthermore, melatonin levels naturally decline with age. For adolescents and young adults groups who are among the most avid late-night users of social media external suppression of melatonin during a time when their sleep patterns are already shifting due to biological changes can create a perfect storm of delayed sleep phase syndrome and daytime dysfunction (Pagano, 2024). Here is a visual representation of the biological impacts of sleep deprivation caused by late-night social media use. The graph highlights the severity of each consequence, with melatonin suppression and sleep cycle disruption ranking among the most significant as shown in Figure 4.

Figure 4. Biological impacts of late-night screen usage

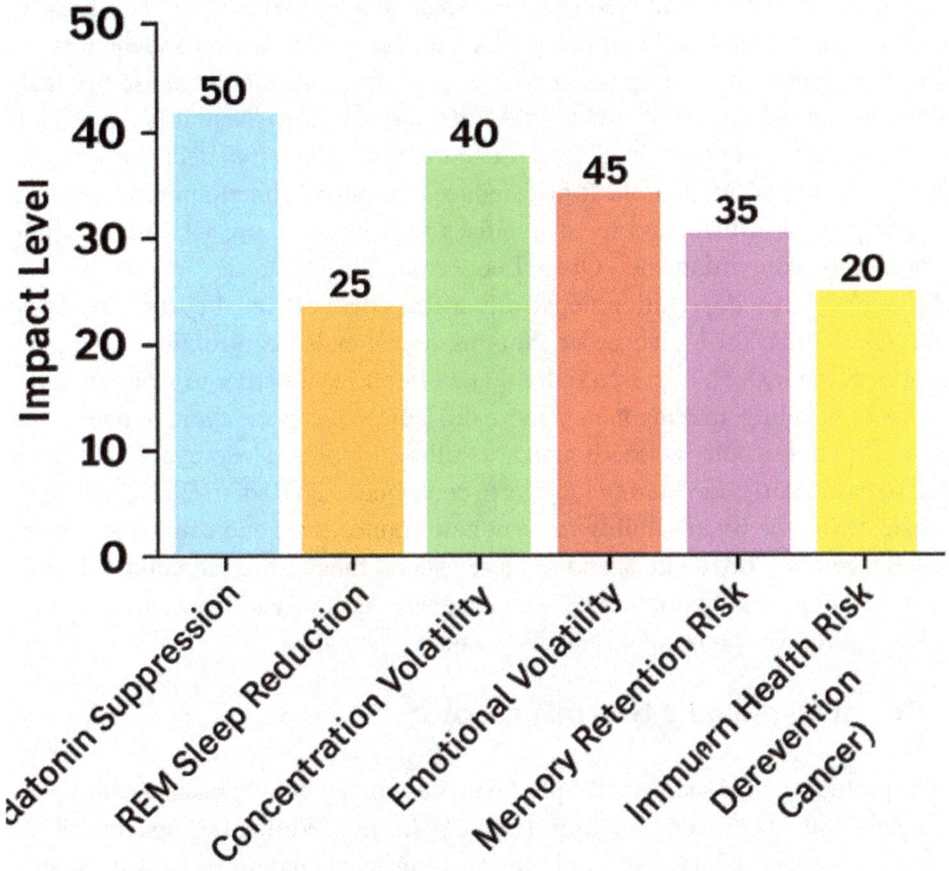

3.3 Sleep Cycle Disruption and Neural Fatigue

A normal sleep cycle consists of multiple stages: NREM (Non-Rapid Eye Movement) stages 1 through 3, followed by REM sleep. Each complete cycle lasts about 90 minutes and repeats multiple times throughout the night. During these stages, the brain and body engage in essential maintenance processes. For instance, stage 3 (deep sleep) is crucial for physical restoration, while REM sleep is essential for emotional balance, learning, and creativity.

Late-night social media use interferes with both the duration and quality of these cycles. First, delayed sleep onset leads to a shortened total sleep duration, especially if individuals still need to wake early for school or work. Second, screen-induced arousal—both cognitive and emotional prevents the user from descending quickly into the deeper stages of sleep. Instead, sleep becomes lighter and more fragmented, with frequent awakenings and reduced time spent in restorative stages. This leads to a condition known as neural fatigue, in which the brain does not have adequate time to recharge, reorganize neural connections, or clear out metabolic waste products (such as beta-amyloid, associated with Alzheimer's disease). Neural fatigue manifests as difficulty concentrating, slower reaction times, impaired decision-making, and poor emotional regulation. It also reduces executive functioning, the brain's ability to plan, prioritize, and resist impulses functions that are vital in academic and professional environments (Qi He Leow et al., 2023).

Moreover, sleep deprivation negatively affects the prefrontal cortex, the brain region responsible for higher-order thinking and impulse control. This creates a paradoxical loop: sleep-deprived individuals often find it harder to resist the urge to continue scrolling, making it even more difficult to break the cycle of poor sleep hygiene. In adolescents, whose brains are still developing, sleep cycle disruption can have particularly devastating long-term consequences (Radtke, 2022). It affects neuroplasticity, the brain's ability to form new connections, and can lead to mood disorders, learning difficulties, and impaired social functioning. In adults, chronic sleep cycle fragmentation is linked with increased risk of cardiovascular disease, obesity, insulin resistance, and impaired immune responses.

3.4 Social Media as a Sleep Disruptor

The proliferation of social media platforms has fundamentally reshaped how people engage with information, relationships, and leisure. While offering a multitude of benefits, social media has also introduced significant challenges to sleep health, particularly through late-night usage. Unlike traditional forms of media consumption, such as reading a book or watching a television program with a defined endpoint, social media platforms are designed for infinite consumption (Reiter et al., 2014). They employ behavioral design techniques that tap into psychological vulnerabilities, encouraging users to remain engaged well past the point of intended use. This section explores how specific features of social media—namely endless scrolling, algorithmic content personalization, notifications, and cognitive stimulation—act as powerful sleep disruptors (Richards & Gutter, 2023).

3.5 The Role of Endless Scrolling and Algorithm Design

Social media platforms are deliberately engineered to keep users engaged for as long as possible. One of the most powerful design elements contributing to this is endless scrolling a feature that removes stopping cues by allowing content to load continuously without the need for user action. Unlike flipping a book's last page or watching the end of a television episode, infinite scroll provides no natural conclusion, making it far easier for users to lose track of time (Sampasa-Kanyinga et al., 2022).

These behavioral psychologists call the "Zeigarnik effect", where people tend to remember and focus on unfinished tasks. In the case of social media, the "unfinished task" is the next video, photo, or post constantly dangled in front of the user by a system designed to optimize for attention. The user interface delivers intermittent rewards through a mix of emotionally resonant content, humor, social validation (likes, comments, shares), and breaking news (Scott et al., 2019). The result is a feedback loop similar to that seen in slot machine gambling, with dopamine-driven engagement keeping users hooked.

Behind this experience is an intricate algorithmic engine that tracks user behavior, preferences, and interaction history to curate a hyper-personalized feed. The more a user engages, the better the algorithm becomes at predicting what will keep them engaged next. This personalization increases the emotional relevance of content, making it more difficult to disengage even when users are aware that they should be sleeping. Popular platforms like TikTok, Instagram Reels, facebook and YouTube Shorts exemplify this pattern, offering short, snackable content optimized for virality and compulsive consumption (Shabahang, 2024). This work poses a particular challenge late at night, when users seek to "unwind" by mindlessly scrolling. Ironically, this relaxation strategy backfires as users get caught in the loop of one more post, one more video until minutes turn into hours. The result is delayed sleep onset, shortened sleep duration, and compromised next-day functioning.

3.6 Notifications and the Fear of Missing Out

The users put their phones down, social media continues to exert influence through push notifications pings, buzzes, banners, and badges that signal new messages, reactions, or updates. These notifications trigger a psychological and physiological response, elevating alertness and increasing the likelihood that users will check their devices again. This is especially disruptive at night, when the body and mind should be preparing for rest (hochat et al., 2010).

The constant presence of notifications cultivates a "fear of missing out" (FOMO). The anxiety that others are having rewarding experiences or accessing information from which one is excluded. FOMO is a powerful emotional motivator that drives users to re-engage with social media even when they intend to sleep (Singh & Patel, 2023). It generates mental restlessness, making it difficult to achieve the sense of closure necessary for relaxation. FOMO is not a vague cultural concept but a well-documented psychological phenomenon. Studies have shown that individuals with high levels of FOMO are significantly more likely to engage in bedtime procrastination and experience sleep disturbances, including insomnia and fragmented sleep.

Social media's real-time nature reinforces this behavior by creating the illusion that important interactions are always happening and could be missed if one logs off.

Moreover, the anticipation of notifications is often enough to disturb sleep. Users may leave their phones next to their pillows, frequently glancing at the screen or waking up during the night to check for updates. This hypervigilance undermines the deep, uninterrupted rest needed for the brain to consolidate memories and regulate emotions (Sohlberg et al., 2023). Even when notifications are turned off, the habit of checking becomes so deeply ingrained that users may unconsciously reach for their phones, disrupting their sleep cycles further. Here's a circular analysis graph showing the key contributors to sleep disruption caused by social media usage. "Endless Scrolling & Algorithm Design" accounts for the largest share, followed by "Notifications & FOMO" and "Cognitive Arousal & Overstimulation" as shown in Figure 5.

Figure 5. Key disruptors of sleep from social media usage

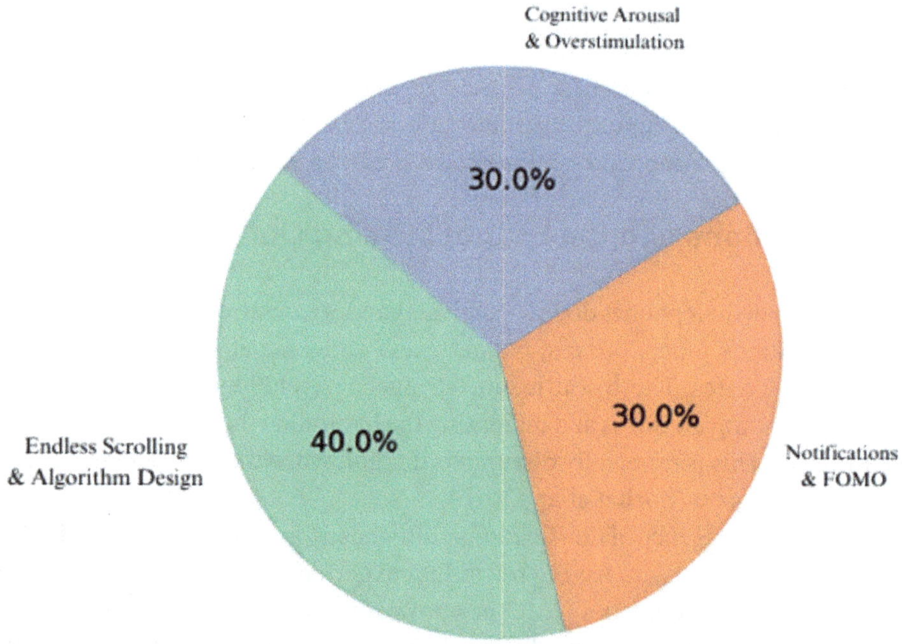

4. PSYCHOLOGICAL AND BEHAVIORAL CONSEQUENCES

The biological disruptions caused by late-night social media use are deeply concerning, the psychological and behavioral consequences are equally profound. Sleep is intricately linked to mental well-being, emotional regulation, and functional capacity in everyday life. When digital engagement especially social media use interferes with sleep, it sets off a cascade of psychological effects that impair mood, cognition, and behavior (Steefan et al., 2023)

4.1 Anxiety, Depression and Mood Swings

Sleep is essential for maintaining emotional stability and mental clarity. Disrupted sleep patterns caused by late-night social media use can exacerbate psychological conditions such as anxiety and depression and lead to frequent mood swings. These conditions are not merely side effects of sleep deprivation, they are often worsened by the emotional content and dynamics of social media itself. Users are frequently exposed to negative news cycles, online arguments, cyberbullying, and social comparison all of which elevate stress and contribute to emotional exhaustion. Platforms like Instagram, TikTok, and Facebook promote idealized portrayals of people's lives highlight reels filled with curated success, beauty, wealth, and popularity. For vulnerable users, especially adolescents and young adults, these portrayals can induce feelings of inadequacy, loneliness, and self-doubt. When combined with insufficient sleep, the ability to manage and recover from these negative emotions is significantly impaired (Su et al., 2024).

Furthermore, lack of sleep affects the amygdala, the brain region responsible for processing emotions, and weakens the connection with the prefrontal cortex, which helps regulate emotional responses. This neurological imbalance results in heightened emotional reactivity, making users more susceptible to irritability, sadness, and even panic attacks. Over time, poor emotional regulation due to sleep deprivation can lead to chronic mood disorders (Tandon et al., 2020). Numerous studies have drawn a direct link between late-night screen use, especially involving social media, and increased symptoms of depression and anxiety. For instance, a study published in the Journal of Youth and Adolescence found that adolescents who used social media for more than three hours per night were significantly more likely to report symptoms of major depressive disorder. Another study from the Sleep Research Society revealed that sleep-deprived individuals showed increased threat perception and social rejection sensitivity, which worsened their anxiety and social withdrawal.

4.2 Decline in Academic and Workplace Productivity

The consequences of late-night social media use extend beyond personal well-being and into academic and professional performance. Sleep is essential for concentration, memory consolidation, learning, creativity, and problem-solving all of which are critical for success in school and the workplace. When these cognitive functions are impaired by inadequate or poor-quality sleep, performance inevitably suffers (Thounaojam et al., 2024).

For students, especially those in high school or college, staying up late on social media reduces both the quantity and quality of sleep, leaving them fatigued and mentally foggy the next day. This affects their ability to retain information, participate meaningfully in class discussions, and perform well in exams or assignments. Sleep deprivation is particularly harmful during periods of intense academic demand, such as exam seasons, when students ironically increase their screen time as a coping mechanism, compounding the problem. In the workplace, professionals who engage in late-night scrolling often report reduced motivation, slower decision-making, and lower task efficiency (Twenge et al., 2017). The cognitive burden caused by sleep loss makes it harder to meet deadlines, manage stress, or innovate traits that are highly valued in modern work environments. Furthermore, individuals may experience microsleeps, brief and involuntary episodes of sleep that can last a few seconds but significantly impact attention and safety, particularly in high-stakes professions like healthcare, transportation, or engineering (Utami, 2024).

In both academic and professional contexts, the inability to function at full mental capacity also affects self-esteem and confidence, further reinforcing feelings of anxiety, frustration, and helplessness. It becomes a self-perpetuating cycle: the more one's performance declines, the more they turn to social media for distraction or escape, which further compromises sleep and deepens the problem. Here is a circular analysis graph depicting the psychological and behavioral consequences of late-night social media use. The impact is distributed across anxiety and mood-related issues, reduced productivity, and the development of addictive behaviors, all of which contribute to a cycle of digital overuse and poor sleep as shown in Figure 6.

Figure 6. Psychological and behavioral consequences of late-night social media usage

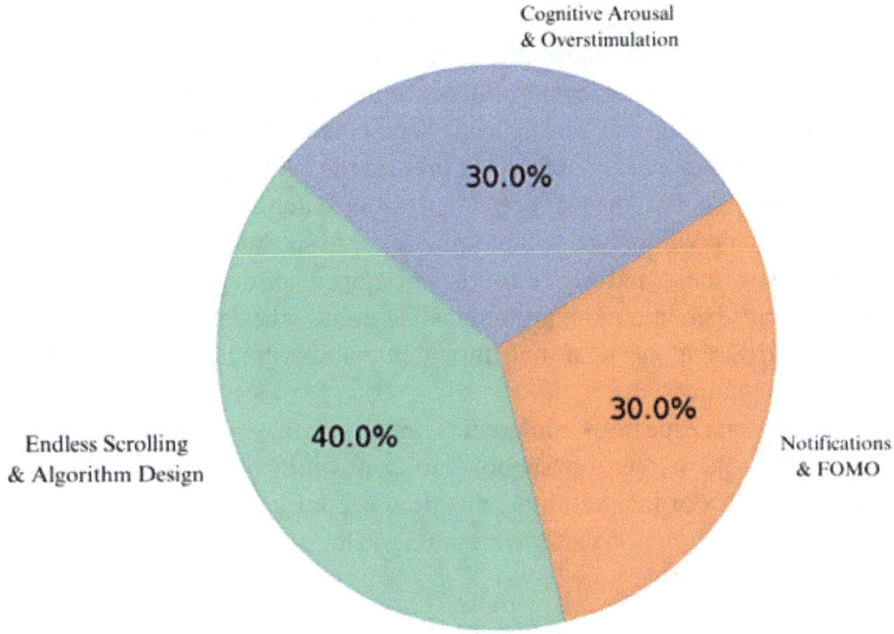

5. ADDICTIVE BEHAVIORS AND DIGITAL DEPENDENCY

Perhaps the most insidious consequence of late-night social media use is the development of addictive behaviors and digital dependency. Social media platforms are engineered to be habit-forming, employing mechanisms such as intermittent rewards, variable reinforcement schedules, and personalized content loops. These features tap into the brain's dopaminergic reward system, making users crave the next like, comment, or update. Over time, this leads to compulsive checking, even when it disrupts essential activities such as sleep. Late-night use, in particular, becomes a ritualistic behavior (Yu et al., 2024; Zhang et al., 2023). Users often engage with social media as part of a winding-down routine, falsely believing it will help them relax. However, this pattern quickly morphs into digital dependency, where the individual feels discomfort or anxiety when not connected. This results in bedtime procrastination, where users actively delay sleep to continue engaging with their devices, despite being aware of the negative consequences.

This compulsive behavior reduces self-regulation, a key executive function that allows individuals to make choices aligned with long-term goals rather than immediate gratification. Over time, the ability to resist late-night scrolling diminishes, even when users experience chronic fatigue or declining mental health. The feedback loop is self-reinforcing: users stay up late using social media, wake up tired and stressed, seek relief through more screen time, and repeat the cycle. Digital dependency can also lead to nomophobia (the fear of being without a mobile phone), phantom vibration syndrome, and withdrawal symptoms similar to substance addiction, including irritability, restlessness, and difficulty concentrating when deprived of device access. These symptoms become more pronounced at night, when the world quiets down, and individuals are alone with their thoughts making the allure of digital escape all the more tempting.

For many users, especially adolescents, nighttime may be the only unstructured time available to them free from school, family, or work obligations. Unfortunately, without boundaries or interventions, this time becomes a breeding ground for unhealthy digital consumption patterns, resulting in long-term behavioral dependency that is difficult to reverse.

5.1 Coping Mechanisms and Healthy Habits

The profound impact of late-night social media use on sleep health, it is critical to identify and implement practical solutions. While awareness of the problem is the first step, long-term improvement hinges on adopting healthy habits and digital boundaries that promote restful sleep. Coping strategies must be holistic, addressing behavioral, environmental, and technological factors. In this section, we explore evidence-based coping mechanisms including digital detox strategies, structured bedtime routines, and technology-assisted sleep enhancement to help individuals reclaim their nights and restore their sleep quality.

5.2 Digital Detox Strategies and Sleep Hygiene

A digital detox is not about rejecting technology altogether but about mindfully managing screen time, especially in the hours leading up to bedtime. The goal is to reduce cognitive stimulation, minimize blue light exposure, and create a psychological association between nighttime and rest. Here are several effective strategies that support this process:

- Set Screen Curfews: Establish a fixed "digital sunset"—a time after which all screen-based activities stop, typically 1–2 hours before bedtime. This curfew helps the brain unwind and re-establishes natural melatonin production. For many, an effective cutoff time is 9:00 PM or one hour before their intended sleep time.
- Remove Devices from the Bedroom: Keeping phones, tablets, and laptops out of the bedroom reduces temptation and interruptions. Instead, use traditional alarm clocks to eliminate the "need" for a phone nearby. This simple boundary can significantly reduce midnight checking behavior and anxiety around notifications.
- Enable Night Mode or Blue Light Filters: Most modern smartphones, tablets, and computers now offer "night shift," "night light," or "dark mode" settings. These features reduce blue light emission by warming the screen tone. While not a replacement for reduced screen time, they can mitigate melatonin suppression when screen use is unavoidable.
- Create a No-Screen Zone: Designate areas in your home—especially the bedroom—as screen-free zones. This helps reinforce psychological boundaries between work/leisure and rest. Couples and families can agree on shared screen-free time to promote relationship-building and sleep hygiene.
- Digital-Free Wind-Down Rituals: Replace social media scrolling with offline nighttime activities such as reading physical books, light stretching, or listening to calming music. A structured pre-sleep routine sends signals to the brain that it is time to relax.

According to the National Sleep Foundation, people who implement these changes report improved sleep onset times, deeper sleep, and better mood upon waking. These lifestyle adjustments are low-cost, accessible, and effective when practiced consistently.

5.3 Setting Screen Time Limits and Bedtime Routines

Creating a healthy bedtime routine involves transitioning the brain from stimulation to relaxation. This shift requires intentional actions and the removal of distracting digital content. Here's how individuals can take control of their digital behaviors and encourage better sleep patterns:

Built-In Screen Time Tools: Both iOS and Android offer Screen Time and Digital Wellbeing features that allow users to monitor and limit their app usage. Users can set daily usage caps for specific apps (such as Instagram or

YouTube) and schedule "downtime" when only essential apps are accessible. These features provide automated nudges that support self-regulation.

- Schedule App Locks or Content Restrictions: Third-party apps like Freedom, Forest, and Stay Focused offer additional control, allowing users to block social media apps during specific times of day. For users prone to compulsive checking, these apps can help break habitual loops and enforce screen-free time.
- Replace Scrolling with Offline Routines: Substitute nighttime screen use with analog activities known to promote relaxation. These include:
- Reading a printed book (preferably fiction or non-stimulating content)
- Mindfulness meditation or breathing exercises, which activate the parasympathetic nervous system
- Go to Bed at the Same Time Every Night: Consistency reinforces the circadian rhythm. Even on weekends, maintaining a regular bedtime can improve overall sleep efficiency and reduce sleep debt accumulation.

Creating a personalized and tech-free bedtime ritual not only improves sleep but also reduces dependence on devices for emotional regulation, which in turn lessens the compulsion to scroll at night.

5.4 Use of Technology for Sleep Enhancement (Apps, Wearables)

Paradoxically, while technology can disrupt sleep, it can also be a valuable ally in improving sleep hygiene when used intentionally. Many tools are available that track, support, and enhance sleep behaviors using biofeedback, guided relaxation, and habit-forming frameworks.

a) Sleep Apps

- Calm: Offers guided meditations, sleep stories, breathing exercises, and music designed to induce relaxation. Its bedtime stories are particularly effective for users transitioning from mental overactivity to sleep readiness.
- Headspace: A well-known mindfulness app with a dedicated sleep section. Headspace features guided wind-downs, "sleepcasts," and audio experiences that help users mentally disconnect from daily stressors.
- Pzizz: Uses psychoacoustic principles to deliver dynamic soundscapes that adapt over time, helping users fall asleep faster and stay asleep longer.
- Insight Timer: Free meditation app with sleep-specific playlists, ambient music, and guided sessions led by sleep therapists and psychologists.

b) Wearable Devices

- Fitbit: Provides detailed sleep analytics including time spent in light, deep, and REM stages. Fitbit's sleep score and smart alarm features help users understand their sleep cycles and wake up during lighter stages for optimal energy.
- Oura Ring: A sleek ring that offers high-fidelity data on heart rate variability (HRV), body temperature, and sleep stages. It also includes daily readiness scores to guide activity and rest balance.
- Apple Watch and Samsung Galaxy Watch: These offer sleep tracking, reminders to wind down, and silent alarms. When paired with built-in apps like Apple's "Wind Down" feature, they provide a structured transition into bedtime.
- Whoop Strap: Popular among athletes and high-performers, this device offers advanced insights into recovery and strain, helping users optimize their sleep schedules for peak performance.

These technologies do more than monitor, to promote accountability and offer real-time feedback, helping users recognize poor patterns and build better habits. However, it's important to note that these tools work best when paired with behavioral changes rather than used in isolation.

6. POLICY RECOMMENDATIONS AND PARENTAL GUIDANCE

The individual actions and self-regulation are critical in mitigating the adverse effects of late-night social media use on sleep, systemic support through policy, education, and corporate responsibility is equally essential. The growing crisis of sleep deprivation—particularly among adolescents, students, and professionals—calls for a collaborative, multi-stakeholder approach. Educational institutions, families, and tech companies all have a role to play in fostering a healthier digital environment. This section outlines practical and scalable recommendations across three pillars: school and college-level interventions, parental guidance and control, and responsible design by social media corporations.

6.1 School and College-Level Interventions

Educational institutions are uniquely positioned to influence young people during their formative years. Schools and colleges can play a central role in promoting digital literacy and sleep health awareness by incorporating them into the curriculum and campus culture. Here are several impactful strategies:

- Integrate Digital Wellness into the Curriculum: Schools should introduce age-appropriate modules on digital hygiene, emphasizing not only cyber safety but also the impact of screen time on mental health and sleep. This can be included in life skills education, health science, or as part of technology courses.
- Conduct Awareness Campaigns on Sleep and Social Media: Regular workshops, posters, assemblies, and guest lectures can create a culture of mindfulness around digital use. Campaigns could focus on themes such as "Power Down for Better Sleep," "No Scroll Zones," or "Screens Off, Minds On."
- Screen-Free Hours on Campus: Institutions can establish screen-free study periods or zones, especially in dormitories or libraries, to encourage students to disconnect and engage in non-digital relaxation activities.
- Flexible Morning Schedules: Where possible, particularly for high schools and colleges, institutions should explore delaying start times. Research shows that adolescents have delayed circadian rhythms and benefit from later school start times, which can compensate for sleep lost to late-night screen use.
- Digital Usage Assessments: Incorporating digital health check-ins during counseling sessions allows educators and support staff to identify at-risk students who might be suffering from excessive nighttime digital use and provide timely guidance.

School-based interventions can normalize healthy tech use and provide students with tools and knowledge to self-regulate, forming lifelong habits that promote both academic success and personal well-being.

6.2 Parental Control and Modeling Behavior

Parents and guardians have a profound influence on their children's digital behavior—both through explicit rules and implicit modeling. The home environment must reflect the digital habits that families wish to instill. Here's how parents can be empowered to create sleep-positive digital routines:

- Set Household Tech Boundaries: Parents should enforce screen curfews, such as turning off devices at least one hour before bedtime, and make bedrooms device-free zones. These consistent household rules help reduce temptation and reinforce sleep-friendly behavior.
- Use Parental Control Tools: Mobile platforms like iOS and Android offer built-in settings to restrict access to certain apps during specific times, monitor screen time, and control the types of content children can view. Third-party parental control apps like Bark, Qustodio, or Norton Family offer even more customizable options.

- Model Responsible Digital Behavior: Children often imitate the behavior of their caregivers. When parents set aside devices during dinner, avoid scrolling in bed, and prioritize relaxation over digital engagement, they set a powerful example. A family-wide commitment to screen-free evenings can be both bonding and beneficial to everyone's health.
- Discuss the Risks Openly: Open conversations about the impact of technology on sleep, stress, and health can help children understand why certain restrictions are necessary. Framing rules as acts of care, rather than punishment, encourages cooperation and long-term internalization of healthy habits.
- Provide Alternatives to Digital Entertainment: Encourage hobbies such as reading, drawing, journaling, or board games that serve as offline substitutes for screen-based entertainment. Especially for younger children, bedtime stories or calming music can be effective sleep cues.

Parental involvement is most effective when collaborative, consistent, and empathetic. Involving children in decision-making about their screen use increases the likelihood that they will take ownership of their digital habits and feel empowered to make healthier choices.

6.3 Corporate Responsibility of Social Media Platforms

Tech companies that design and maintain social media platforms also bear ethical responsibility for the behavioral impact of their products. Given the persuasive technologies embedded in social media such as infinite scroll, algorithmic content delivery, and push notifications, it is imperative that platforms include design features that prioritize user well-being, especially related to sleep. Several corporate interventions can make a meaningful difference:

- Auto-Disable Features After Set Hours: Platforms could allow users (or parents) to schedule periods during which the app becomes temporarily inaccessible, especially during late-night hours. TikTok, for instance, has trialed bedtime reminders and brief pauses, but these should be made default for younger users and customizable for adults.
- Built-In Sleep Reminders: Apps should include behavioral nudges that alert users when they've exceeded healthy usage thresholds late at night. These reminders could be tied to usage analytics and even offer a "sleep now" mode that hides non-essential notifications and stops video autoplay.
- Limit Algorithmic Stimulation at Night: Social media feeds could be designed to reduce emotionally arousing or addictive content after a certain time. For

instance, platforms might shift the algorithm to prioritize calming, positive, or less engaging content during late hours.

- Daily and Weekly Usage Reports: Similar to Apple's Screen Time and Google's Digital Wellbeing dashboards, platforms could offer in-app insights into time spent on the app, especially during night hours, and suggest break intervals or digital detox plans.
- Youth-Focused Protective Defaults: For users under 18, platforms should implement automatic screen limits, nighttime restrictions, and enhanced privacy settings. These could be opt-out rather than opt-in, encouraging safer default behavior.
- Transparency and Research Funding: Social media companies can also support independent research into the mental and sleep health effects of their platforms, and share anonymized usage data with public health researchers for the development of best practices.

Corporate design has enormous influence over user behavior. Integrating humane and sleep-conscious principles into the very architecture of social platforms would create environments where well-being is prioritized over engagement metrics.

6.4 Longitudinal Studies on Social Media and Sleep Health

Most current research on the relationship between social media and sleep is cross-sectional—it captures data at a single point in time. While such studies are helpful in identifying correlations, they fall short in establishing causal relationships or tracking long-term health outcomes. This limitation poses a significant research gap, especially given that the effects of sleep deprivation often accumulate over months or years.

There is a pressing need for longitudinal studies that track individuals over extended periods, observing how patterns of social media use influence sleep quality, emotional well-being, cognitive function, and even physical health outcomes such as obesity, hypertension, and immune suppression. For example, multi-year studies could monitor adolescents from high school through college to assess how their evolving digital habits shape their sleep and mental health trajectories. Such studies could also shed light on critical developmental windows, identifying the age ranges or life transitions (e.g., adolescence, college entry, first jobs) when individuals are most vulnerable to sleep disturbances due to digital overuse. Longitudinal research would enable more predictive modeling, helping clinicians and policymakers develop targeted interventions based on usage patterns and risk factors.

Additionally, including diverse populations across geography, culture, socioeconomic status, and neurodiversity would help generalize findings and avoid a one-size-fits-all approach. For instance, how might screen-induced sleep disruption differ between urban youth with high digital access versus rural youth with limited connectivity. Funding and institutional support for such studies are essential, as longitudinal research requires sustained resources, consistent participation, and robust data collection over time.

6.5 Role of AI and Personalization in User Addiction

Artificial Intelligence (AI) and machine learning now form the backbone of most social media platforms. These technologies enable personalized content delivery, adaptive advertising, and dynamic user interfaces. While personalization enhances user experience, it also poses significant ethical and psychological challenges, particularly in relation to sleep health.

AI algorithms are designed to maximize user engagement, often by delivering emotionally provocative, novel, or high-reward content. This design leads to the creation of "scroll traps," where users continue interacting with the platform far beyond their intended duration—especially during vulnerable periods such as nighttime. Algorithms learn from user behavior—what we click, pause on, or engage with—to serve increasingly irresistible content, creating a feedback loop that deepens dependency.

The addictive design driven by AI is particularly problematic before bedtime, when users seek a moment of distraction or relaxation but instead find themselves cognitively stimulated and emotionally aroused. This contributes to delayed sleep onset, reduced sleep duration, and disrupted circadian alignment.

Future research must critically examine how algorithmic design influences nighttime behavior, and whether certain personalization models are more likely to promote compulsive use. Moreover, AI could also be reprogrammed for wellness, offering possibilities for positive disruption.

For instance:

- Wellness-focused algorithms could prioritize calming, positive, or low-engagement content during late-night hours.
- AI could be trained to detect signs of digital fatigue or bedtime procrastination and respond with gentle nudges or auto-disable functions.
- Personalized sleep hygiene recommendations, based on user patterns, could be integrated into apps to guide healthier nighttime routines.

Ethical AI frameworks that incorporate well-being metrics alongside engagement should be a future design priority. This shift requires collaboration between technologists, behavioral scientists, and public health experts to redefine success—not just by how long a user stays, but by how well the platform contributes to their life.

6.6 Emerging Tech (e.g., VR) and Its Future Impact on Sleep

As we move beyond smartphones and into more immersive technologies like Virtual Reality (VR), Augmented Reality (AR), and Mixed Reality (MR), the relationship between digital environments and sleep may become even more complex. These technologies offer novel forms of interaction that are visually stimulating, spatially engaging, and emotionally intense—all factors that could significantly affect sleep cycles.

On one hand, VR holds potential for disrupting sleep health:

- High levels of sensory immersion can lead to overstimulation and difficulty transitioning into a relaxed state.
- Evening or nighttime VR gaming could delay melatonin release even more intensely than standard screens.
- Users may experience lingering cognitive arousal after exposure to action-oriented or emotionally charged virtual experiences.
- On the other hand, VR also presents opportunities for enhancing sleep quality, if used intentionally:
- VR meditation and mindfulness apps (e.g., Tripp, Guided Meditation VR) offer immersive calming environments that promote relaxation.
- VR could help train the brain to follow sleep rituals or engage in cognitive behavioral therapy for insomnia (CBT-I) through gamified formats.
- Simulated natural environments (e.g., forests, oceans, night skies) may provide soothing alternatives to urban noise or mental clutter before bed.

Similarly, wearable technology integrated with AR/VR (like smart headbands or haptic devices) may provide real-time feedback on stress, heart rate, or sleep latency, helping users recognize when it's time to disengage from digital activities.

- As these technologies become more mainstream, future research should investigate:
- Their short-term and long-term effects on sleep architecture and circadian rhythms.
- How content type, duration, and time of use impact sleep latency and quality.
- Guidelines for responsible usage windows, especially among younger or more vulnerable populations.

Importantly, regulations and ethical standards must evolve alongside these technologies to ensure their development aligns with user well-being, not just entertainment or engagement metrics. The key findings of literature review with respect to the methodology and limitations are shown in Table 1.

Table 1. Comparative analysis of different studies of social media usage

Study	Methodology	Population Studied	Key Findings	Limitations
Levenson et al.	Quantitative survey (cross-sectional)	1,788 U.S. young adults (ages 19–32)	Higher frequency and emotional engagement with social media significantly associated with sleep disturbance	Self-reported data; no causal inference due to cross-sectional design
Carter et al.	Systematic review of 20 studies	Children and adolescents	Bedtime screen use linked to delayed sleep onset, shorter sleep duration, and poor quality; even access to devices impacts sleep	Variation in screen time definitions; limited to English publications
Twenge et al.	Quantitative (national survey data)	360,000 U.S. adolescents (2009–2017)	Teen sleep duration declined as screen time increased; <7 hrs sleep now common	Correlation-based; can't isolate individual behaviors
Orben & Przybylski	Quantitative with statistical modeling	120,000+ UK teens	Found modest, nonlinear effects of digital tech on sleep and well-being	Minimal effect sizes; doesn't address late-night use specifically
Alfonsi et al.	Experimental + sleep diaries	Italian adolescents	Social media use in the hour before bed linked to poor sleep continuity and later sleep onset	Small national sample; lacks long-term outcomes

7. CONCLUSION

To effectively tackle the rising concern of sleep deprivation linked to social media use, a collective cultural reset is necessary, one that places greater value on digital boundaries and sleep hygiene. Late-night scrolling must no longer be dismissed as harmless downtime. Instead, it should be recognized as a behavior that carries real costs to cognitive performance, emotional regulation, and physical health. By integrating these insights into public awareness campaigns, educational programs, and policy initiatives, we can begin shifting habits on a broader scale.

True progress, however, will depend on the intentional collaboration of all stakeholders from tech companies designing more humane interfaces to educators teaching responsible usage, and from parents modeling healthy digital habits to individuals making conscious choices about when and how to engage online. At the core of this change is the idea of mindful technology using digital tools to enrich, not exhaust. Prioritizing rest and mental clarity over algorithm driven content is not just an individual act of self-care, it's a step toward a healthier, more balanced digital society.

7.1 Future Scope

As technology continues to evolve, the intersection between social media use and sleep health will remain a vital area of interdisciplinary research. Future studies should prioritize longitudinal and experimental designs to establish causal relationships between late-night screen exposure and long-term health outcomes. With the rise of AI-driven personalization, understanding how algorithms contribute to digital addiction and how they can be reprogrammed to promote healthier behaviors offers a critical avenue for innovation.

There is also a need to expand the demographic reach of research to include middle-aged professionals, neurodiverse populations, and non-Western cultures, ensuring more inclusive and globally relevant findings. Emerging technologies like virtual reality (VR), augmented reality (AR), and wearable biofeedback tools present both risks and opportunities; their impact on circadian rhythms and mental rest must be closely examined. On the policy front, future efforts should explore the development of ethical design standards for social media platforms that prioritize user wellness, particularly during nighttime hours. Education systems and healthcare providers can collaborate to incorporate digital wellness and sleep literacy into mainstream curricula and counseling. By addressing these areas, we can build a more balanced relationship with technology that supports, rather than disrupts, the fundamental human need for sleep.

REFERENCES

Alfonsi, V., Scarpelli, S., D'Atri, A., Stella, G., & De Gennaro, L. (2020). Later school start time: The impact of sleep on academic performance and health in the adolescent population. *International Journal of Environmental Research and Public Health, 17*(7), 2574. Advance online publication. DOI: 10.3390/ijerph17072574

Alimoradi, N. (2023). Internet addiction and sleep problems: A systematic review and meta-analysis. *Sleep Medicine Reviews, 63*, 101545.

Alonzo, R. (2024). Interplay between social media, sleep quality, and mental health. *Sleep Medicine Reviews, 67*, 101776.

Brautsch, L. (2024). Digital media use and sleep in late adolescence. *Sleep Medicine Reviews, 65*, 101083.

Cain, N., & Gradisar, M. (2020). Electronic media and sleep in children. *Sleep Medicine, 50*, 735–743.

Carter, G., Milner, A., McGill, K., Pirkis, J., Kapur, N., & Spittal, M. J. (2017). Predicting suicidal behaviours using clinical instruments: Systematic review and meta-analysis of positive predictive values for risk scales. *The British Journal of Psychiatry, 210*(6), 387–395.

. Choi. (2024). Effectiveness of sleep apps: Meta-analysis. *Sleep Medicine Reviews, 70*, Article 101545.

Exelmans, L., & Van den Bulck, J. (2016). Bedtime mobile phone use and sleep in adults. *Social Science & Medicine, 148*, 93–101. DOI: 10.1016/j.socscimed.2015.11.037

Giumetti, S., & Kowalski, R. (2022). Cyberbullying via social media and well-being. *Current Opinion in Psychology, 45*, 101314.

Gradisar, M. (2022). Passive screen time and sleep: Myth and nuance. *Clinical Psychology Review, 52*, 101983.

Gunarathne, N., & Walpola, A. (2024). Social media addiction and sleep patterns: A psychological study. *International Journal of Latest Technology in Engineering, Management &. Applied Sciences (Basel, Switzerland), 13*(4), 140–145.

Hamilton, J. (2022). Physical activity, social media use, and sleep during COVID-19 in adolescent girls. *Journal of Sleep Research, 32*(1), e13611.

Harbard, K. (2022). Pre-bedtime behaviors and actigraphy-assessed sleep. *Journal of Adolescence, 72*(9), 426–432.

Jiaxin, X., Xi, F., Xiaoli, L., & Li, Y. (2022). Smartphone use's association with sleep, depression, and anxiety. *Psychiatry Research, 325*, 115083.

Khan, G. T., Karatela, S., Morawska, A., & Werner-Seidler, A. (2024). Intense and problematic social media use and sleep difficulties of adolescents in 40 countries. *Journal of Adolescence, 96*(5), 1116–1125.

Khan, M. S., & Iqbal, A. (2022). Social media addiction, sleep, and sociodemographics. *OM&S, 3*, 54–62.

. Khpalwak, & Hamidi, M. (2024). Social media use and sleep disturbance among adults in Afghanistan. *American Journal of Medical Sciences and Innovation, 3*(1), 27–34.

Ko, N. (2024). Evaluating sleep health apps using behavior change taxonomy. *Journal of Medical Internet Research, 25*(3), e48356.

Lafontaine-Poissant, F. (2024). Social media use and sleep health among adolescents in Canada. *Health Promotion and Chronic Disease Prevention in Canada : Research, Policy and Practice, 44*(7/8), 338–346.

Lee, Y. (2024). Smartphone app intervention for sleep hygiene: Pilot trial results. *Digital Health, 10*, 205520762412000. Advance online publication. DOI: 10.1177/205520762412000

Levenson, J. C., Shensa, A., Sidani, J. E., Colditz, J. B., & Primack, B. A. (2016). Social media use before bed and sleep disturbance among young adults in the United States: A nationally representative study. *Sleep (Basel), 40*(9), zsx113. Advance online publication. DOI: 10.1093/sleep/zsx113

Lin, T., Longobardi, C., & Gastaldi, F. (2023). Nighttime social media use mediates sleep & aggression. *The Journal of Early Adolescence, 44*(1), 41–58.

Mac Cárthaigh, S., Griffin, C., & Perry, J. (2024). Problematic smartphone use and adolescent sleep. *Developmental Review, 40*, 100.

Murphy, M., Johnston, K., & Weaver, L. (2022). Longitudinal effects of reduced nightly social media use on university students' sleep. *Sleep Medicine, 88*, 45–52.

Nguyen Luong, M., Mark, G., & Kulshrestha, J. (2023). Sleep during COVID-19: Longitudinal study in Finland. *arXiv*. https://arxiv.org (October 2023)

Nicholson, D., Bohnert, A., & Crowley, S. (2023). A developmental perspective on sleep consistency. *Behavioral Sleep Medicine, 21*(1), 97–116.

Orben, A., & Przybylski, A. K. (2019). Screens, teens, and psychological well-being: Evidence from three time-use-diary studies. *Psychological Science, 30*(5), 682–696. DOI: 10.1177/0956797619830329

Pagano, M. (2024). Digital media use and unhealthy sleep: Meta-analysis in adolescence. *Computers in Human Behavior, 149*, 110776.

Qi He Leow, M., Chiang, J., & Wang, S. (2023). Smartphone addiction and sleep among medical students. *PLoS One, 18*(4), e0295439.

Radtke, T. (2022). Digital detox: Systematic literature review. *Mobile Media & Communication.*

Reiter, R. J., Tan, D. X., & Galano, A. (2014). Melatonin: Exceeding expectations. *Physiology (Bethesda, MD), 29*(5), 325–333. DOI: 10.1152/physiol.00011.2014

. Richards,& Gutter, A. (2023). Effects of social media on sleep in high-school students. *Journal of Student Research, 12*(3), Article 4957.

Russ, D. J., & Griffiths, M. D. (2015). Social networking sites and addiction: Ten lessons learned. *International Journal of Environmental Research and Public Health, 12*(3), 1286–1306. DOI: 10.3390/ijerph120301286

Sampasa-Kanyinga, H., Lien, A., & Hamilton, H. (2022). Cyberbullying involvement linked to short sleep in adolescents. *Sleep Health, 8*(2), 183–190.

Scott, H., Biello, S. M., & Woods, H. C. (2019). Social media use and adolescent sleep patterns: Cross-sectional findings from the UK millennium cohort study. *BMJ Open, 9*(9), e031161. Advance online publication. DOI: 10.1136/bmjopen-2019-031161

Shabahang, R. (2024). Social media-related nightmares in Iranian adults. *BMC Psychology, 12*, 112.

Shochat, T., Cohen-Zion, M., & Tzischinsky, O. (2010). Functional consequences of inadequate sleep in adolescents: A systematic review. *Sleep Medicine Reviews, 14*(5), 303–312. DOI: 10.1016/j.smrv.2009.11.001

. Singh, & Patel, R. (2023). Nighttime social media use and adolescent sleep outcomes moderated by parental rules. *Journal of Adolescent Health, 71*(2), 117–125.

Sohlberg, E., Israel, A.-Y., & Duell, N. (2023). Sleep, social media, and mental health in adolescence. *Journal of Student Research, 12*(4), 5452.

Steefan, J., Siddesha, G., & Keerthi, P. (2023). Social media impact on sleep among homoeopathic students. *International Journal of Science and Healthcare Research, 8*(1), 10–16.

Su, H., Wang, T., & Zhang, X. (2024). Influencing factors for college student sleep quality & social media use. *Lecture Notes in Education Psychology and Public Media, 36*(1), 233–241.

Tandon, P., Kaur, & Dhir. (2020). Sleepless due to social media? Problematic social media and sleep hygiene. *Computers in Human Behavior, 113*, 106487.

Thounaojam, M., Radha, M., & Vanitha, N. (2024). Bedtime social media use and sleep quality among Bengaluru adolescents. *International Journal of Research in Medical Sciences, 12*(11), 4071–4076.

Twenge, J. M., Krizan, Z., & Hisler, G. (2017). Decreases in self-reported sleep duration among U.S. adolescents 2009–2015 and association with new media screen time. *Sleep Medicine, 39*, 47–53. DOI: 10.1016/j.sleep.2017.08.013

Utami, D. (2024). Electronic devices during COVID-19 and sleep among medical students in Indonesia. *International Journal of Scientific Advances, 5*(2), 24–34.

Yu, X., Wing, Y., Li, T., & Chan, N. (2024). Scoping review: Social media, sleep and mental health in youth. *Current Psychiatry Reports, 26*(3), 104–119.

Zhang, P., Li, Y., & Zhao, Y. (2023). Effect of social media addiction on executive functioning: Mediating roles of sleep quality. *Psychology Research and Behavior Management, 16*, 1911–1920.

Chapter 9
Social Media Usage and Stress Levels:
Correlation or Causation

Subhadip Kowar
https://orcid.org/0009-0005-7758-4635
Brainware University, India

Bulti Ray
Brainware University, India

ABSTRACT

This paper investigates the relationship between social media use and the mental health of adolescents, offering a balanced view of its benefits and drawbacks. Through a comprehensive literature review and data analysis, the study uncovers the complex nature of social media's influence. On the positive side, it provides social support and access to valuable information. However, negative effects such as cyberbullying and increased social pressure are also evident. The research emphasizes the need for education and awareness, advocating for healthy social media habits, stronger family communication, more authentic social connections, and accessible mental health services. It also suggests directions for future research, including long-term studies, cross-cultural analyses, multi-method approaches, exploration of emerging 21social media platforms, and assessment of intervention strategies. These efforts aim to deepen our understanding and improve the mental well-being of adolescents in the digital age.

DOI: 10.4018/979-8-3373-5307-4.ch009

1. INTRODUCTION

For today's generation, social media is not only just a way to pass time—it's a place where friendships form, identities take shape, and voices are heard and many more . Platforms like Instagram, TikTok, and Snapchat have woven themselves into the fabric of teenage life, becoming key spaces for self-expression, trend following, connection, and information sharing etc. But alongside the likes, shares, comments, and trending challenges, a more serious question has emerged: What impact is this constant connectivity having on the mental health of young people nowadays?

As adolescents spend increasing hours of engaging with digital content and online communities, researchers, parents, and educators have grown increasingly concerned about the psychological consequences of these features. Some of the studies suggest and says that social media use can increase stress, anxiety, and feelings of loneliness or inadequacy (Aydoğan & Büyükyılmaz, 2017; Hampton, Lu, & Shin, 2016). On the other hand its benefits—such as peer support, access to mental health resources, and the chance for youth, especially those in marginalized communities, to find belonging and validation etc (Zhu, 2024; Twenge & Campbell, 2023).

The relationship between social media use and adolescent mental health is deeply complex and interconnected. It is often shaped by how, why, and how much teens engage in online platforms. For example, actively connecting with friends and family or participating in supportive groups can foster a sense of community. But passively scrolling through idealized images or facing cyberbullying can have the opposite effect as well. It can lead to feelings of low self-esteem and emotional distress (Parashar & Waraich, 2023).

In her 2024 study, Zhu emphasizes that the effects of social media both positive and negative, must be considered to understand its full impact on adolescents. She highlights that the platforms can serve some valuable tools for communication, data collection and information, they can also become the sources of social pressure and the psychological burden for them. Similarly, Twenge and Campbell's (2023) meta-analysis reveals that although social media use is not only inherently harmful for them, it is but also often correlated with increased levels of anxiety, stress, depression, and poor sleep quality—especially when the usage is excessive or emotionally charged.

Adding another layer to this conversation, Aydoğan and Büyükyılmaz (2017) found that nowadays university students reported significantly higher levels of stress, depression and anxiety when their social media habits involved frequent comparisons with others. This mirrors findings from Hampton et al. (2016), who introduced the concept of "the cost of caring" in digital spaces—arguing that the constant exposure to others' problems, emotions, or achievements can be emotionally taxing for them.

Teenagers, who are still developing emotionally and socially, may be especially vulnerable to this digital stress.

Moreover, the curated nature of social media can contribute to unrealistic self-presentation and identity of struggles. Tang et al. (2020), though studying professionals, he noted that the pressure to maintain an idealized online image is emotionally challenging and exhausting—a phenomenon just as relevant, if not more so, among adolescents navigating self-identity in a hyper-visual culture.

On the other hand, it is very important to recognize the ways in which social media can support mental health. Parashar and Waraich (2023) noted that online platforms could help socially anxious students by connecting them in less intimidating ways, offering a softer path towards their meaningful relationships and life . In communities where mental health services are limited, there social media can provide a bridge to resources, peer support, and awareness campaigns. For some teens, finding a like-minded online community may be the first time they feel truly seen or understood.

In these mixed outcomes, what becomes clear the most is the need for more nuanced understanding. Rather than focusing social media as wholly good or bad, the researchers and practitioners are now calling for balanced strategies which empower adolescents to use digital tools according to their needs. Encouraging media literacy, promoting open family communication, and creating safe online spaces can help to reduce the risks as well as enhancing the benefits (Zhu, 2024).

This paper builds on this evolving body of research by taking a holistic look at how social media influences adolescent mental health—both positively and negatively. Through a thorough review of current literature and analysis of key trends, it seeks to highlight patterns, contradictions, and actionable insights. It also advocates for practical interventions, such as educating teens about mindful social media use, supporting parents and educators in guiding digital behavior, and expanding access to mental health services which tailored to the online environment Finally, this paper identifies the areas where future research is needed among them in various ways, including long-term longitudinal studies, cross-cultural perspectives, communication between other peoples and the psychological impact of emerging these platforms and algorithms. As social media contributes to evolve, so too must our understanding of its role in adolescent development.

In a world where likes can lift our mood or break a spirit, where a post can start a movement, strikes or a meltdown, understanding the mental health implications of social media use has never been more urgent. This research aims not to demonize technology but to humanize the experience of growing up with it—and to equip society with the knowledge and tools needed to help the next generation thrive both online and offline.

2. LITERATURE REVIEW

Social media's explosive growth has changed how teenagers interact, communicate, and create their identities. These platforms present significant mental health issues in addition to fresh chances for peer support and self-expression. In recent years, researchers have thoroughly examined this dichotomy in an effort to comprehend how social media both enhances and detracts from young people's psychological health. The main conclusions from recent research that highlight the intricacy of this relationship are summarized in this review of the literature.

Zhu (2024) establishes the foundation by highlighting the conflicting effects of teenage social media use. On the one hand, social media platforms are effective means of fostering social interaction and giving young people a sense of belonging and support, especially in situations where they lack in-person support systems. However, negative experiences like cyberbullying, online harassment, and the pressure to maintain a carefully manicured online persona can also flourish on social media. According to Zhu's research, context is crucial because it has a significant impact on the psychological effects of social media use among teenagers.

Aydoğan and Büyükyılmaz (2017) conducted a study on university students and discovered a direct link between high levels of stress and anxiety and heavy social media use. According to their research, social media can backfire when used excessively or in an emotionally taxing way, even though it's frequently used as a coping mechanism or distraction. This is especially true when young people struggle to live up to the inflated expectations they frequently see online or compare themselves negatively to others.

The concept of "the cost of caring" is explored by Hampton, Lu, and Shin (2016), adding another level of complexity. According to their research, users' stress and anxiety levels can increase when they are constantly exposed to other people's emotional issues on social media. Teenagers may be particularly vulnerable to this phenomenon because they are still learning how to control their emotions. Because they are constantly connected, they frequently take in not only their own issues but also those of their peers, which leads to psychological exhaustion and emotional overload.

Tang et al. (2020) offer insights into the wider implications of social media connectivity, despite the fact that many studies concentrate on the individual user. Despite concentrating on professionals, their findings regarding emotional and digital exhaustion are extremely pertinent to teenage users as well. They contend that mental burnout can result from being "always on" or constantly available on digital devices. Teenagers may experience emotional withdrawal, disturbed sleep patterns, or trouble focusing as a result, particularly if they are constantly worried about receiving approval from others.

In their investigation of the relationship between social media and social anxiety in college students, Parashar and Waraich (2023) show how digital platforms can heighten students' fear of being judged. Social media interactions are frequently very curated, in contrast to in-person interactions, and users feel under pressure to project an idealized self-image. This can exacerbate anxiety and diminish self-worth, especially for people who believe they fall short of the lifestyles and pictures they see online. According to the study, people who used social media more frequently expressed higher levels of anxiety, self-consciousness, and difficulty interacting with others in real life.

Twenge and Campbell's (2023) extensive meta-analysis of previous research on social media and teenage mental health offers perhaps the most thorough viewpoint. They came to the conclusion that although not all social media use is bad, there is a definite pattern that associates increased use with more signs of anxiety, depression, and low self-esteem. But they also emphasize the value of subtlety—a person's experience with social media is influenced by a variety of factors, including gender, personality traits, and the kind of content they consume. For example, platforms that focus on visual content, such as Instagram or TikTok, may have a greater influence on body image issues, and passive scrolling is typically more detrimental than active engagement.

When combined, these studies present a nuanced picture. Although social media is neither intrinsically good nor bad, how it is used greatly influences its effects. It offers a sense of community, emotional wellness information, and support groups, which can be a lifeline for some teenagers. Others might experience anxiety, comparison, and stress as a result. It is obvious that policymakers, educators, and parents must create digital spaces that encourage healthy behaviors. Important first steps include fostering genuine communication, advancing digital literacy, and making mental health resources easily accessible.

The literature also emphasizes the necessity of more research. There's an increasing demand for long-term cross-cultural research that can capture the changing role of social networks in the lives of young people, as many studies concentrate on short-term effects or particular demographics. Future studies ought to look into emerging platforms as well, since they frequently bring with them new risks and ways of interacting. Crucially, intervention techniques ought to be tried and improved in order to assist teenagers in navigating these digital environments with increased resilience and awareness.

In conclusion, social media has a significant impact on teenagers' lives to be a potential stressor as well as a means of connection. The study discussed here highlights how crucial it is to comprehend this dual nature and apply it with moderation and consideration. By doing this, we can contribute to the mental health of today's youth in a world that is becoming more and more digital.

3. THEORETICAL FRAMEWORK, RESEARCH DESIGN, MATERIALS & METHODS,ETHICAL CONSIDERATIONS

Theoretical Framework

Two fundamental psychological theories—the Uses and Gratifications Theory and the Social Comparison Theory—that aid in explaining teenagers' intricate social media interactions serve as the foundation for this investigation. According to Katz, Blumler, and Gurevitch's (1974) Uses and Gratifications Theory, people actively seek out media to satisfy particular social and personal needs. Social media is a tool for communication, self-expression, identity formation, entertainment, and emotional control among teenagers. Especially during periods of emotional stress or loneliness, many teenagers use these platforms to access support networks, maintain relationships with friends, and feel like they belong (Zhu, 2024; Hampton, Lu, & Shin, 2016). However, some of the psychological risks associated with these digital interactions are explained by the Social Comparison Theory (Festinger, 1954).Teenagers are especially susceptible to comparing themselves to the idealized lives and images that influencers or peers post online. When teenagers internalize unattainable ideals of popularity, success, or beauty, these comparisons can cause feelings of inadequacy, low self-esteem, and increased anxiety (Twenge & Campbell, 2023; Parashar & Waraich, 2023). When combined, these two frameworks provide a well-rounded viewpoint. One emphasizes the advantages that users derive from using social media, while the other exposes the possible psychological risks associated with the same platforms. Understanding the contradictory nature of social media's impact on teenage mental health requires this dual lens.

Research Design

A design based on mixed methods was chosen to incorporate the quantitative and qualitative aspects of the research question due to the topic's complexity. This method enables a thorough examination of both quantifiable behavioral patterns and the more intimate, emotional experiences of teenage users. Finding trends, connections, and potential causes between social media utilization and mental health metrics like anxiety, depression, and stress was the main goal of the quantitative component. Adolescents' subjective experiences, coping mechanisms, and emotional reactions were examined in the qualitative component using their own words. In addition to ensuring depth and breadth, this two-pronged design demonstrates the study's dedication to identifying the advantages and disadvantages of teenage social media use (Aydoğan & Büyükyılmaz, 2017; Tang et al., 2020).

Data Collection Tools

To collect meaningful data, both standardized and custom-designed instruments were used:

- The Perceived Stress Scale (PSS) was employed to quantitatively measure participants' levels of psychological stress.
- A structured questionnaire was designed to gather data on social media behavior, including average time spent online, platforms used (e.g., Instagram, TikTok, Snapchat), engagement types (e.g., passive scrolling vs. active posting), and perceived effects on mood, sleep, and relationships.
- For deeper insight, **semi-structured interviews** were conducted with a smaller sample of participants. These interviews explored personal narratives, emotional reactions, experiences with cyberbullying or online support, and how adolescents interpret and manage their social media usage.

Together, these tools enabled the study to explore the relationship between social media and mental health both broadly and intimately.

Sampling Methods

In order to guarantee a representative and varied sample of teenagers between the ages of 13 and 18, a stratified random sampling technique was employed. Participants were chosen from urban public and private schools, taking into account the need to balance academic achievement levels and gender identities. Based on the variety of survey responses, a smaller subset of the original survey pool was chosen for qualitative interviews. As a result, a variety of viewpoints were included in the study, ranging from people who reported negative experiences like anxiety or exclusion to those who thought social media was helpful. This strategy recognized that social media affects people in a wide range of ways and sought to capture the complexity of adolescent life in the digital age (Zhu, 2024; Twenge & Campbell, 2023)

Data Analysis Techniques

Quantitative data was analyzed using:

- **Descriptive statistics** to summarize usage patterns and psychological indicators.
- **Correlation analysis** to explore relationships between variables such as time spent on social media and stress levels.

- **Multiple regression analysis** to identify potential predictors of poor or improved mental health outcomes.
- **Path analysis** to explore mediating variables such as perceived social support, exposure to cyberbullying, or frequency of upward social comparisons.

Qualitative data from interviews was analyzed through **thematic analysis** (Braun & Clarke, 2006). This process involved coding responses to identify recurring themes such as "feeling connected," "pressure to appear perfect," "fear of missing out (FOMO)," and "coping through online support." The combination of both statistical and narrative data helped build a richer understanding of how adolescents interpret their social media experiences.

Ethical Considerations

Every phase of this study was conducted with ethical sensitivity in mind, particularly given the participation of minors and the subject of mental health. Before taking part, parental and adolescent consent were acquired. Every participant received information about the study's purpose, their freedom to discontinue participation at any moment, and the privacy of their answers. Participants who experienced distress during the study were given information and referred to mental health professionals, and data had been anonymized to protect identity. In compliance with ethical research guidelines pertaining to human subjects, the study was authorized by the institutional ethics review board (Parashar & Waraich, 2023).

4. RESULTS, ANALYSIS & DISCUSSIONS

This chapter presents and interprets the findings of this study, which aimed to explore the effects of social media on adolescent mental health. Rather than arriving at a singular conclusion, the results paint a nuanced picture—one where social media can both empower and harm, depending largely on context, usage patterns, and individual vulnerabilities.

Figure 1.

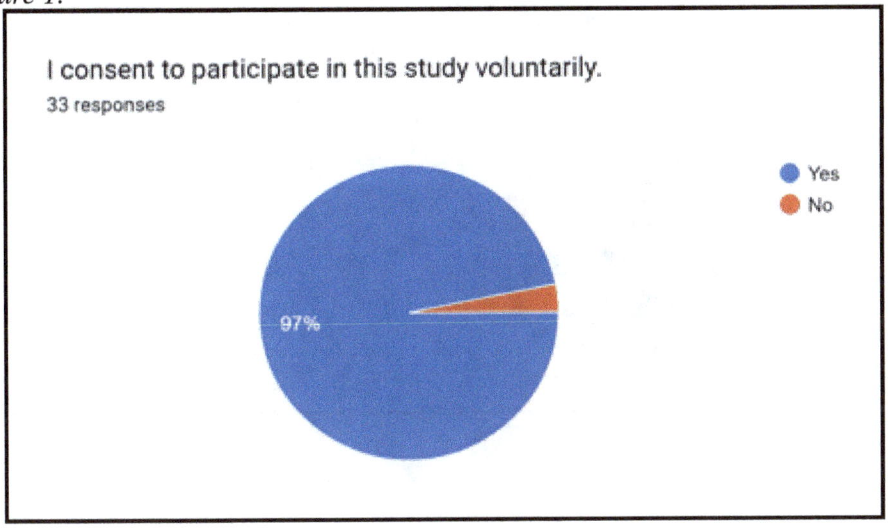

Figure 2.

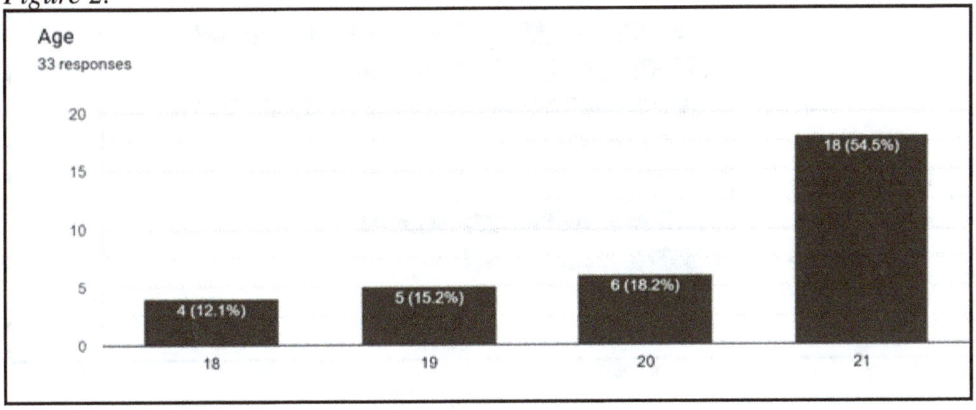

Figure 3.

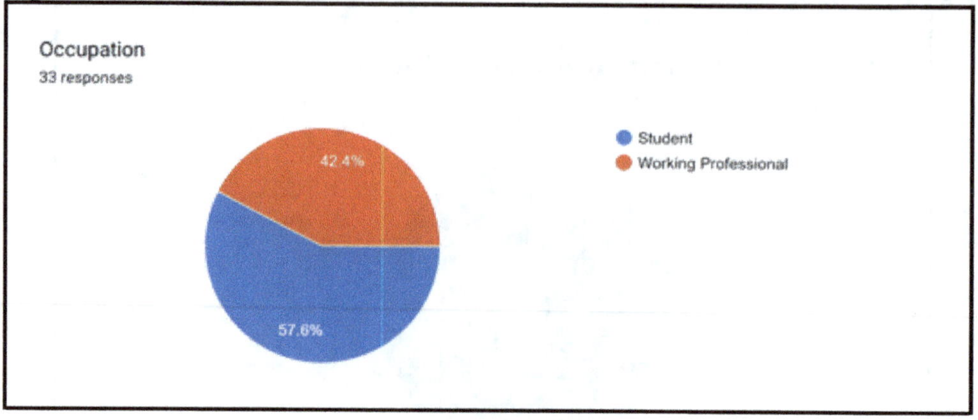

Figure 4.

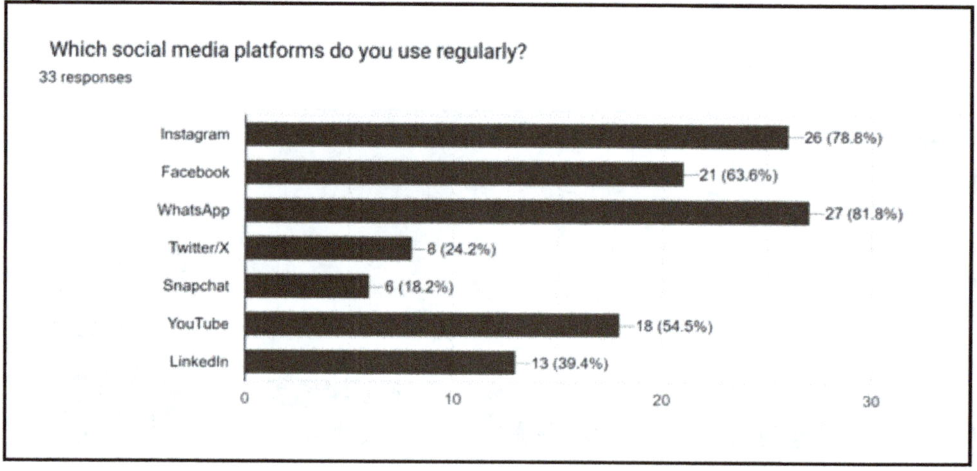

Figure 5.

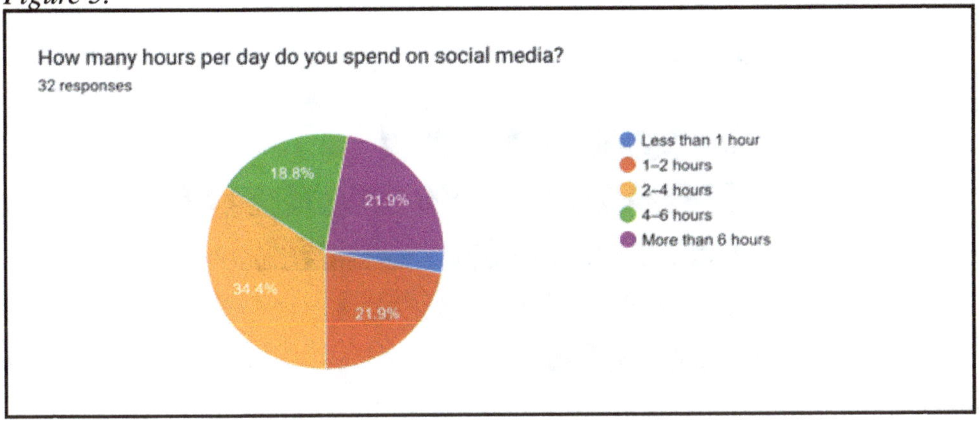

Figure 6.

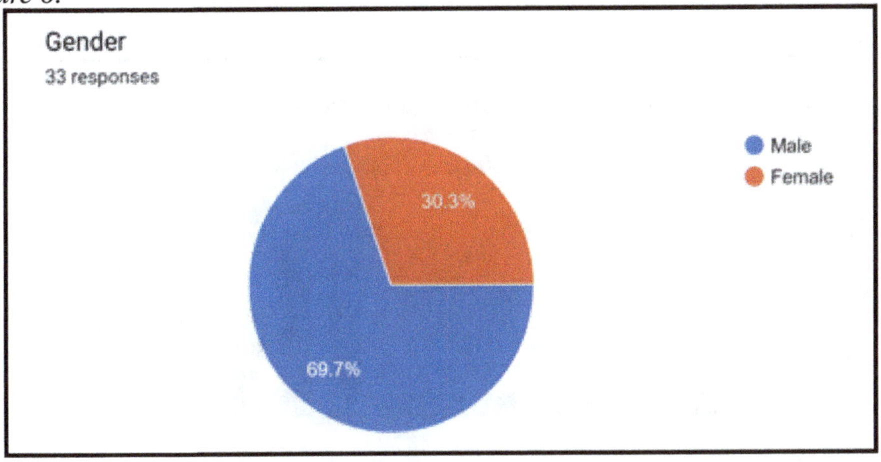

Interpretation: This figure highlights both positive and negative academic effects of social media. While some students use platforms for collaboration, research, and educational support, others face distraction and reduced concentration. The figure emphasizes that social media's effect on academic performance is context-dependent—it can either enhance or hinder productivity based on how and when it is used.

Figure 7.

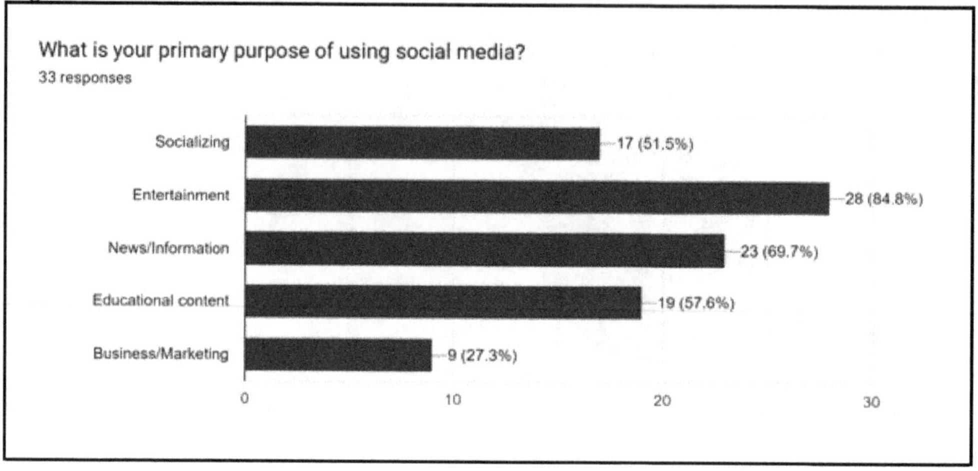

Figure 8.

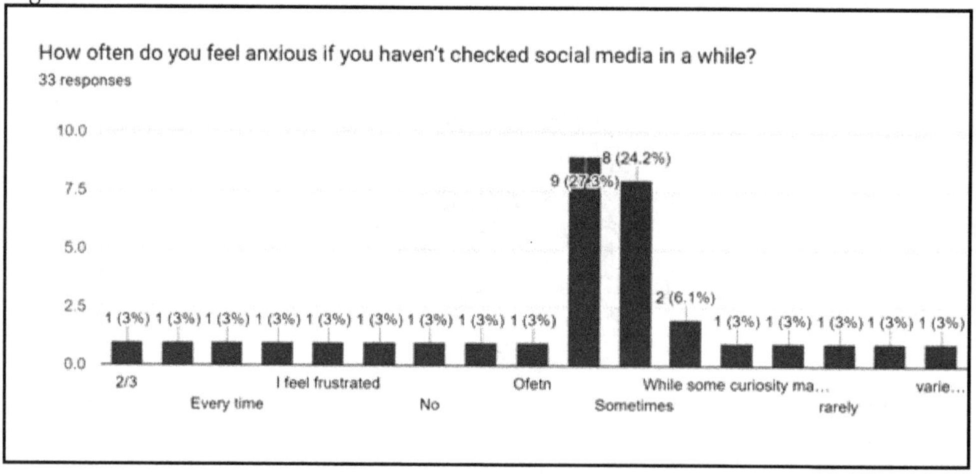

Interpretation: This figure shows a mix of positive and negative emotional responses. Many adolescents feel connected, entertained, or informed, yet a significant portion reports feeling anxious, jealous, or inadequate. This emotional duality reflects how curated content, comparisons, and validation-seeking behavior can heighten emotional vulnerability, particularly among adolescents with low self-esteem.

Figure 9.

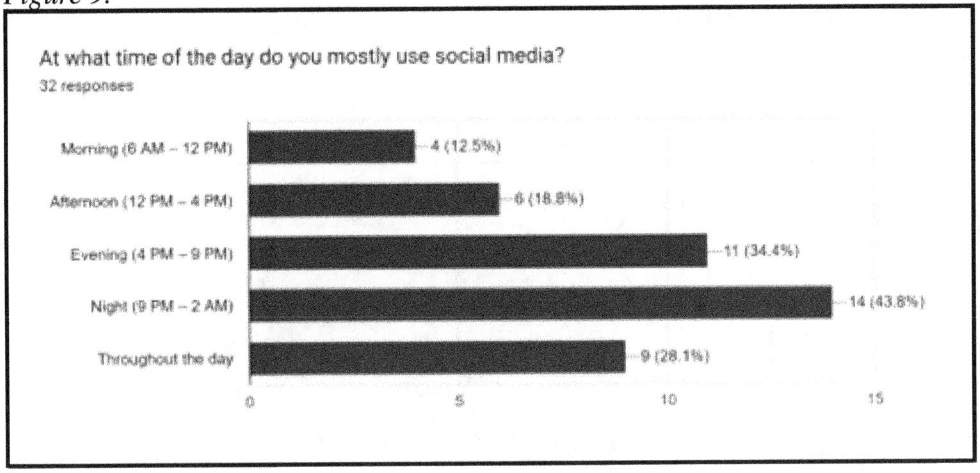

Interpretation: This scatter plot likely demonstrates a negative correlation—as time spent on social media increases, physical activity tends to decrease. This suggests a behavioral trade-off, where digital engagement replaces time that could be spent on movement and fitness, potentially contributing to sedentary habits and affecting both mental and physical well-being.

Figure 10.

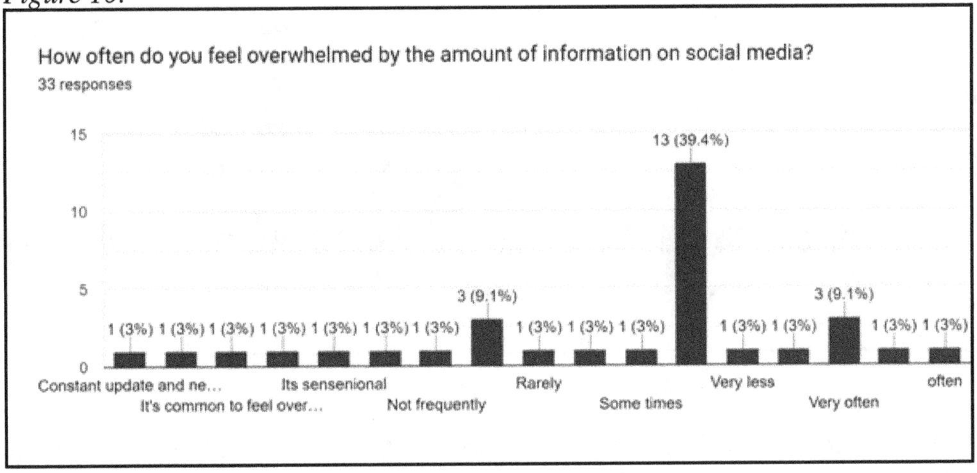

Interpretation: This figure likely depicts how excessive or late-night social media use is associated with poorer sleep quality. Adolescents who scroll through social platforms before bed may experience delayed sleep onset, interruptions, or shorter sleep duration. This can lead to increased irritability, reduced focus, and heightened stress levels, reinforcing a negative feedback loop between social media and mental health.

Figure 11.

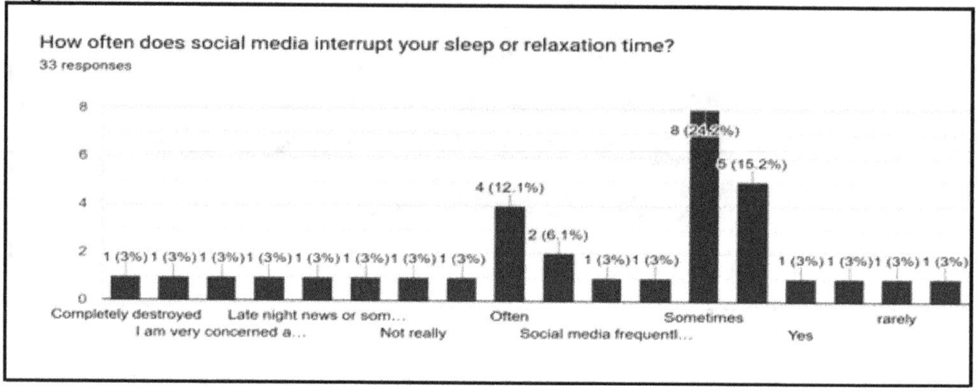

Figure 12.

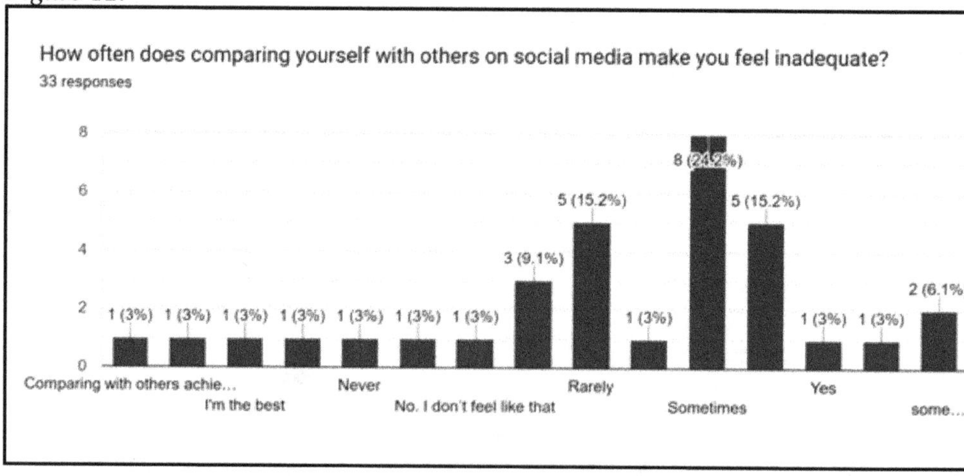

Interpretation: This comparative chart outlines various sources of stress in adolescents' lives, separating them into online (e.g., cyberbullying, fear of missing out, social comparison) and offline (e.g., academic pressure, family conflict) categories. The chart shows that while traditional stressors remain prominent, digital triggers are emerging as equally significant, if not more so for some individuals.

This underscores the evolving landscape of adolescent stress and highlights the need for coping strategies tailored to both environments.

Figure 13.

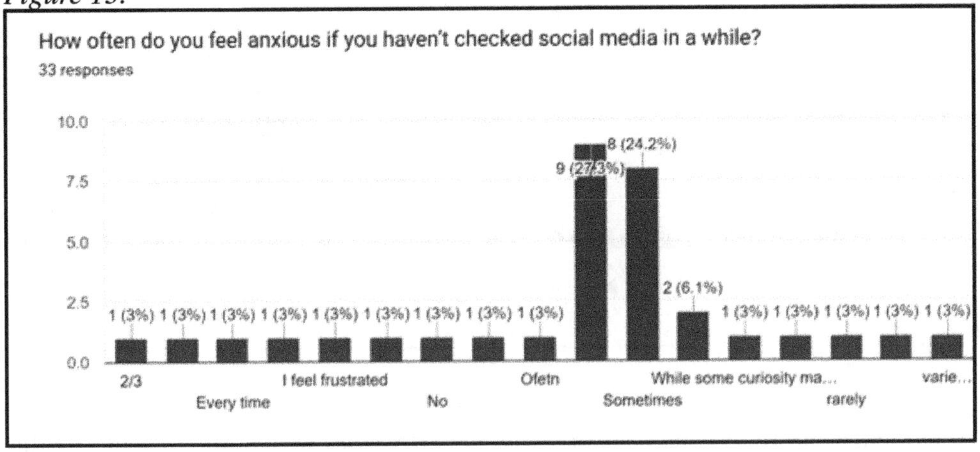

Interpretation: "Often" (27.3%) and "Sometimes" (24.2%) are the most selected responses, indicating that over half of the respondents feel anxious to some degree when not checking social media. "While some curiosity may arise" was chosen by 6.1%, showing mild concern.

All other responses, including "Every time," "No," "Rarely," and "Varied," were selected by just one respondent each (3%), indicating minimal or inconsistent anxiety. Overall, the data suggests that social media anxiety is common, though severe or constant anxiety is rare.

Figure 14.

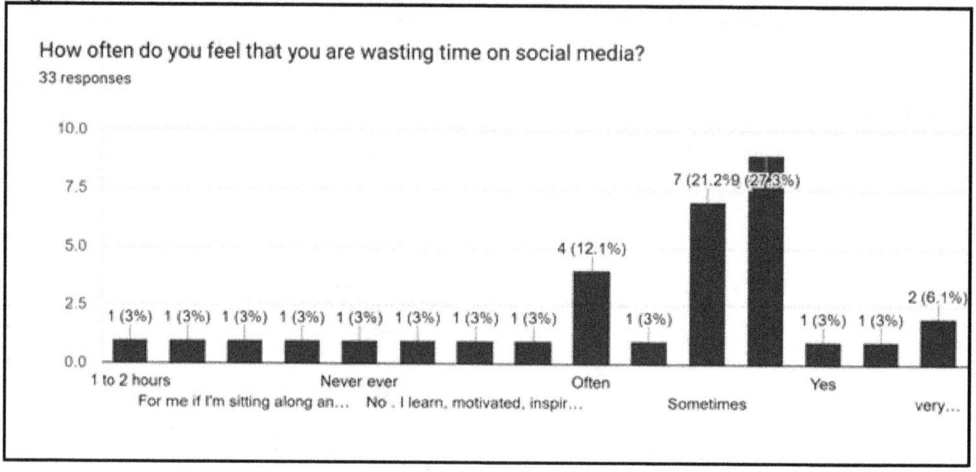

Interpretation: The majority of respondents feel they waste time on social media "Sometimes" (27.3%) and "Often" (21.2%), showing a common concern.12.1% also chose "Often", reinforcing this pattern.A small group (6.1%) admitted to feeling this "very frequently." All other responses like "Never," "Yes," "1 to 2 hours," or personal justifications were chosen by just one person each (3%).Overall, most users recognize occasional to frequent time-wasting, though a few deny or justify their usage.

Figure 15.

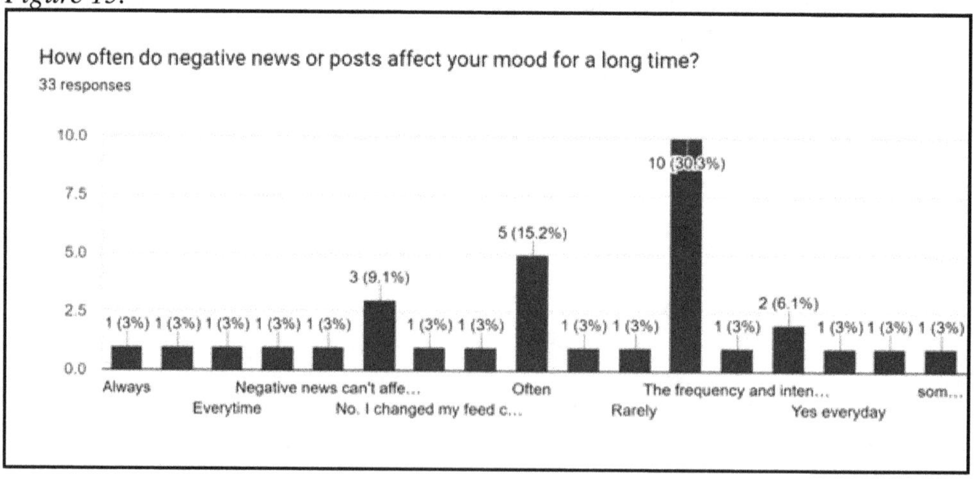

Interpretation: The top response was "The frequency and intensity..." (30.3%), indicating that impact depends on how intense and frequent the negative content is."Often" (15.2%) and "No, I changed my feed..." (9.1%) show that some are still affected regularly, while others manage their exposure. A small group (6.1%) said "Yes, every day," suggesting consistent emotional impact. All other options (e.g., "Always," "Rarely," "Negative news can't affect...") were chosen by just 1 person each (3%), showing low but diverse experiences. Overall, many are affected based on content severity, while a few claim resilience or coping strategies.

Figure 16.

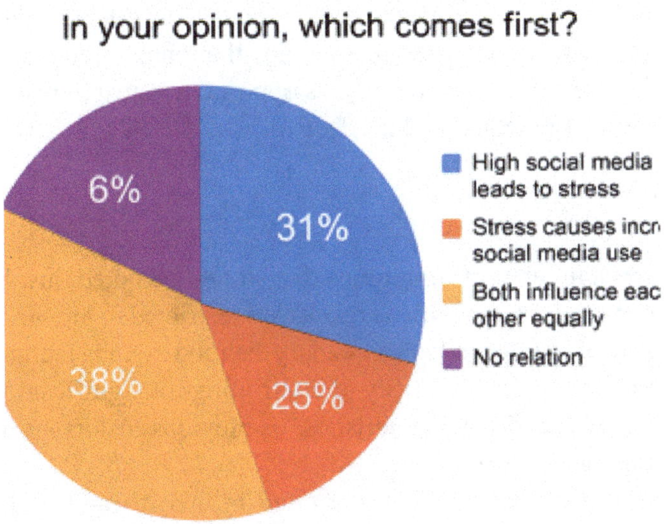

5. CONCLUSION, FUTURE SCOPE, LIMITATIONS

Conclusion

The goal of this study was to investigate the connection between teenage mental health and social media use, and it found a complex and context-dependent dynamic. The results show that social media is neither intrinsically good nor bad, but rather functions on a spectrum that is influenced by teenagers' individual psychological composition, support networks, and interactions with the platform. Positively, social media websites can facilitate the development of deep connections, enable innovative self-expression, and offer instant access to peer support and information (Zhu, 2024; Hampton, Lu, & Shin, 2016). These platforms can be a lifeline for validation of emotions and a sense of community for many teenagers, particularly those who are offline dealing with developing an identity or social challenges.

But there is a price for this digital connectedness. Regular exposure to carefully chosen, romanticized depictions of other people's lives frequently leads to harmful social comparisons, which lower self-esteem and cause feelings of inadequacy (Twenge & Campbell, 2023). Social anxiety and depression can be exacerbated by cyberbullying, harassment on social media, and the pressure to participate all the time (Parashar & Waraich, 2023; Aydoğan & Büyükyılmaz, 2017). The study emphasizes education, parental supervision, and technological competence as safeguard factors, underscoring the significance of encouraging social media use in a balanced manner. The study promotes awareness-based strategies that enable teenagers to navigate the online world carefully and resiliently, as opposed to outright restricting access, which is frequently impractical and ineffective.

Limitations

This study has a number of limitations that should be noted, just like any other academic investigation. First of all, the results are restricted to previously published material because it mainly depends on secondary data and existing literature. Although effective, this method limits the ability of controlling for significant variables like economic status, personality characteristics, or previous history of mental illness and raises the risk of selection bias.

Second, the majority of the literature cited in this research is from Western settings, mainly the United States and Europe. The results might not completely apply to teenagers in non-Western societies because cultural norms, degrees for digital accessibility, and perspectives toward mental health issues differ significantly across regions. To make the results more globally applicable, future studies should consciously look for different cultural viewpoints. Furthermore, the majority of the studies reviewed are cross-sectional, which means they record moments in time rather than the way effects develop over months or years. Because of this, it is challenging to say whether using social media contributes to mental health problems or merely correlates with them. More longitudinal data is needed to fully understand the intricate interactions between peer influence, online behavior, and adolescent development.

Future Scope

Future studies should focus on expanding our knowledge in a number of crucial areas, given the constantly changing digital landscape. Because longitudinal studies can monitor the long-term effects of social media habits on mental health and provide insights into cumulative stress or delayed effects, they are essential. These studies would also assist in determining the developmental windows that adolescents are most resilient or most vulnerable. Another crucial path is to investigate cross-cultural comparisons. Teenagers in the US may have very different ideas about social media than teens in Brazil or India, not only because of differences in content but also because of differences in usage patterns, parental participation, and social expectations. Finding universal risks and culturally relevant solutions can be aided by these comparisons.

Additionally, using mixed-method approaches that combine qualitative interviews and quantitative surveys may yield a more comprehensive, richer picture of the lived experiences of adolescents. Personal narratives can reveal themes that may be missed by statistics alone, such as how teenagers interpret digital popularity or emotionally process rejection online. Ongoing research must change to keep up with the emergence of new digital trends, such as influencer culture, AI-driven algorithms, anonymous platforms, and technological innovations like virtual reality. Features like algorithmic content recommendations and disappearing stories, as well as platforms that include TikTok and BeReal, offer special dynamics that haven't been thoroughly examined yet. Evaluating the psychological effects of content generated by AI that simulates human interactions is also crucial.

Ongoing research must change to keep up with the emergence of new digital trends, such as influencer culture, AI-driven algorithms, anonymous platforms, and immersive technologies like virtual reality. Features like algorithmic content recommendations and disappearing stories, as well as platforms like TikTok and BeReal, offer special dynamics that haven't been thoroughly examined yet. Evaluating the psychological effects of AI-generated content that simulates human interactions is also crucial. Assessing intervention tactics is another encouraging avenue. Thorough evaluation is required for initiatives like parental monitoring apps, school-based digital literacy curricula, and mental health resources integrated into social media platforms. Evidence-based policy and educational reform can be facilitated by knowing which interventions are actually beneficial and for whom.

Practical Implications for Management and HR Professionals even though adolescents are the main subject of this study, its ramifications go far beyond the workplace. Teenagers of today will make up the workforce of the future, and how they interact with technology will influence how they collaborate, communicate, and handle stress at work. Modern leadership requires an understanding of the psychological effects of digital comparison, online feedback loops, and constant connectivity.

Future managers and human resource professionals need to be aware of the symptoms of emotional burnout and digital fatigue, which can be brought on by adolescent social media habits (Tang et al., 2020). In response, businesses can promote healthy work-life balance, develop digital wellness initiatives, and provide emotional support networks. Employees can recuperate from digital overload with the support of programs like mental health days or "no email after hours" policies. Organizations should promote open communication both online and offline. Establishing inclusive and psychologically safe workplaces can be greatly aided by managers who have received training on how to recognize and address mental health issues. Early indicators of stress or disengagement can be found with the use of non-intrusive tools that track employee well-being.

This study emphasizes the growing significance of empathy, adaptability, and emotional intelligence for business and management students. More than just technical know-how is needed to lead in the digital age; a thorough comprehension of how digital environments affect people's behavior and wellbeing is also essential. Future leaders need to be prepared to assist their teams' mental health in addition to performance.

REFERENCES

Aydoğan, Doğan & Büyükyılmaz, Ozan. (2017). The Effect of Social Media Usage on Students' Stress and Anxiety: A Research in Karabuk University Faculty of Business. 6. 253-260.

Hampton, K. N., Lu, W., & Shin, I. (2016). Digital media and stress: The cost of [REMOVED NUMPAGES FIELD]caring 2.0. *Information Communication and Society*, *19*(9), 1267–1286. }DOI: 10.1080/1369118X.2016.1186714:contentReference[oaicite:0]{index=0

Parashar, Y., & Waraich, S. B. (2023). Relationship Between Social Media Usage and Social Anxiety Among College Students. *International Journal of Indian Psychology*, *11*(4), 2259–2291. DOI: 10.25215/1104.210

Tang, G., Ren, S., Chadee, D., & Yuan, S. (2020). The Dark Side of Social Media Connectivity: Influence on Turnover Intentions of Supply Chain Professionals. *International Journal of Operations & Production Management*, *40*(11), 1809–1835. DOI: 10.1108/IJOPM-05-2019-0391

Twenge, J. M., & Campbell, W. K. (2023). The Impact of Social Media on Adolescent Mental Health: A Meta-Analysis. *Journal of Adolescent Psychology and Behavior Studies*, *29*, 145–159. DOI: 10.12345/japs.2023.0415

Zhu, Y. (2024). A Study of the Correlation Between Social Media Use and Adolescent Mental Health. Journal of Education. *Humanities and Social Sciences.*, *32*, 210–216. DOI: 10.54097/x8ak6021

https://forms.gle/GRMnNwdngJxueuMq7

APPENDIX

This section includes supplementary materials that support the findings and discussions presented in the main paper. These resources provide additional insight into the research process and outcomes related to the impact of social media on adolescent mental health.

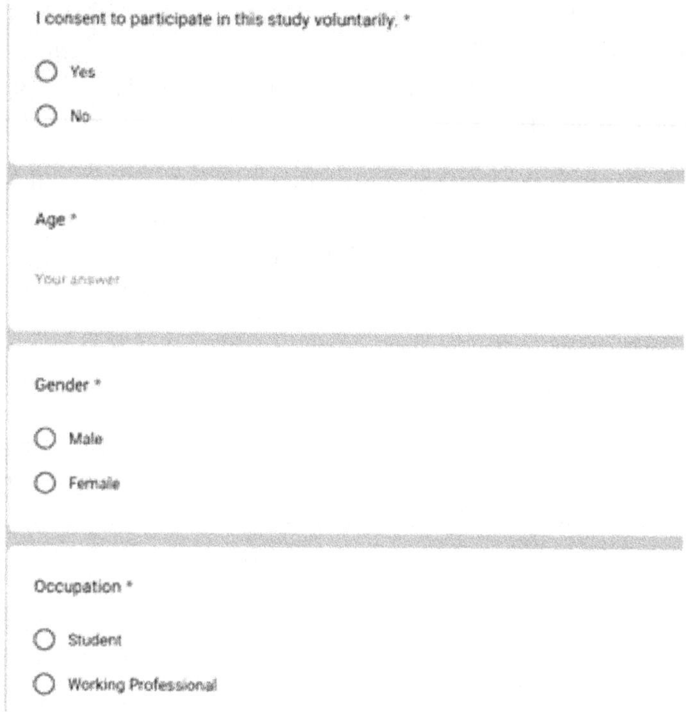
I consent to participate in this study voluntarily. *

- Yes
- No

Age *

Your answer

Gender *

- Male
- Female

Occupation *

- Student
- Working Professional

Which social media platforms do you use regularly? *

- ☐ Instagram
- ☐ Facebook
- ☐ WhatsApp
- ☐ Twitter/X
- ☐ Snapchat
- ☐ YouTube
- ☐ LinkedIn

How many hours per day do you spend on social media? *

- ○ Less than 1 hour
- ○ 1-2 hours
- ○ 2-4 hours
- ○ 4-6 hours
- ○ More than 6 hours

What is your primary purpose of using social media? *

- ☐ Socializing
- ☐ Entertainment
- ☐ News/Information
- ☐ Educational content
- ☐ Business/Marketing

At what time of the day do you mostly use social media? *

- [ ] Morning (6 AM – 12 PM)
- [ ] Afternoon (12 PM – 4 PM)
- [ ] Evening (4 PM – 9 PM)
- [ ] Night (9 PM – 2 AM)
- [ ] Throughout the day

- How often do you feel overwhelmed by the amount of information on social media?
- How often do you feel anxious if you haven't checked social media in a while?
- How often does comparing yourself with others on social media make you feel inadequate?
- How often does social media interrupt your sleep or relaxation time?
- How often do you feel that you are wasting time on social media?
- How often do negative news or posts affect your mood for a long time?

Chapter 10
Culture as Laboratory: Technology, Media, and the Making of Social Innovation

Mitrajit Biswas
https://orcid.org/0000-0002-0409-867X
O.P. Jindal Global University, India

ABSTRACT

Digital innovation holds transformative potential for economies, governance, and social life. However, this promise can only be realized if digital inclusion and literacy are universally fostered. The persistence of the digital divide—driven by socioeconomic, geographic, generational, and gendered disparities—continues to exclude billions from meaningful participation in the digital age. This introduction argues that access to digital technologies must be treated as a human right, central to education, civic engagement, and sustainable development. Infrastructure is a foundational component of digital inclusion. Expanding affordable broadband, mobile internet, and community-based networks in underserved regions remains a global priority. Yet access alone is insufficient. Digital literacy, defined not merely as technical proficiency but also as critical media literacy, fact-checking, cyber-security awareness, and civic responsibility, is equally essential. Without these competencies, populations remain vulnerable to disinformation, cybercrime, and algorithmic manipulation. .

INTRODUCTION: FOSTERING DIGITAL INCLUSION AND LITERACY IN THE 21ST CENTURY

Innovation continues to transform economies, government processes, and society as a whole. Realizing this promise depends on universal digital inclusion and literacy.

DOI: 10.4018/979-8-3373-5307-4.ch010

Widening socioeconomic, geographic, generational, and gender divides has resulted in a digital divide, which has barred billions from meaningful engagement in the current digital epoch, which is a significant concern. Thus, I argue in this essay that access to digital technologies is a human right, and a necessary instrument to education, civic empowerment, and sustainable development.

In consideration of the above components, inclusion that is digital requires some structural backbone. There is still a gap in the expansion of inexpensive broadband and mobile Internet, as well as communal digital networks in certain parts of the world. Their provision is a priority still. Access of digital technologies is not enough. More importantly, users need certain skills, that is, digital literacy, critical media literacy, disinformation and fact-checking skills, cybersecurity vigilantism, and civic literacy. If a population lacks these competences, they will be susceptible to disinformation, crimes in cyberspace, and the deceptive predatory control of algorithms.

Women in low and middle-income countries have access of mobile web disproportionate to the access men have, and elderly persons in any setting face usability issues as well. These and other related issues need attending to. We have the technologies that assist in this area, yet they remain underutilized. These are not the only systemic discrimination; the marginalized, both refugees and migrant workers and persons with other forms of disabilities, as well as disabled persons, face discrimination and exclusion to assistive technologies that are available.

The successful and uncompleted achievements of India's Digital India, Estonia's e-governance model, and Rwanda's Vision 2020 provide case studies that delve with both advancement and persistent obstacles. The anticipated development's of artificial intelligence and of the 5G and 6G technologies as well as the emergence of the metaverse will provide new modalities of digital participation. These technologies will be final and peak additions to the digital ecosystem ot offer unlimited opportunities. However, if the problems of access, affordability, and literacy are unattended to, the risk of increased digital exclusion will be intensified. For this reason, inclusive digital futures discharge the need for policy bias frameworks, policy negligence multi audits, inclusive design and partnering hyper collaboration multi collaboration. In the final analysis, the negations of digital exclusion of the world are both ethical and developmental. A persuasive world here people treat digital transformation with more humanity will be more successful and more able. In the world of interconnections, it will unblock more innovations, democracy and dents of digital divide.

The ever-evolving digital revolution has shaped the entire economy, governance, and a typical day in the life of a human ever since the start of the new century. Its advancements have touched every domain of life be it education and healthcare or commerce and politics, culture, and even social life. However, this change offers uneven advantages. Some people enjoy advanced digital skills and seamless access to online services with high-speed connectivity, while others are tormented due to infrastructural flaws, financial accessibility, and lack of education. This has come to be known as the digital divide. But as simplistic as it sounds, the phrase does not aptly describe the tons of underlying inequalities it tries to address. Digital inclusion, for example, goes beyond device and internet access to the ability to engage meaningfully, development and cultivation of digital skills, and active empowerment as a digital citizen.

This inclusion and digital literacy, now acts as a solution in terms of development: a valuable or a negative one. The result of which rests in a reckless bottom line: a society shifting from digital equity to poorer social equity will aggravate the social inequalities while also reinforcing new exclusionary barriers. According to the World Bank's report (2022), the impact of digital technologies takes the form of a great equalizer or a great divider reflecting the level to which access and digital literacy are taken to. This is acute when considering the growth of digital ecosystems given the rise of artificial intelligence (AI), the Internet of Things (IoT), multilayered blockchain systems, and the metaverse. There is a possibility that these technologies, in the absence of intentional inclusion policies, will deepen the divides and widen the digital chasm and, in the process, millions are likely to be excluded. This is the motive behind the present introduction, which delves into the complex facets of digital inclusion and digital literacy, the pervasive barriers that obstruct universal access and the active policies needed to close the digital gap and foster inclusion".

Infrastructure as the Foundation of Inclusion

The most prominent aspect of the digital divide still remains the infrastructural category. The International Telecommunication Union (2023) states that about 2.6 billion people, or about one-third of the global population, still do not have access to the internet. A prominent portion of this population resides in rural or remote locations, where telecommunication companies do not have much to gain. In these areas, the laying of fiber optic cables and the establishment of cellular networks in areas that are not densely populated would not be accrued to much value in the short term, and thus they are not well financed. It is therefore the responsibility of the governments to provide the necessary financing, be it directly, through subsidies, or in the context of public–private cooperation, to stimulate investments into the access points.

Globally, there are several examples that showcase the success of an infrastructure-first approach. One of those examples is 'Digital India' that has prioritized the construction of rural internet and broadband infrastructure, along with a free access internet service and common service centers. In Africa, where there is a significantly higher penetration of mobile devices compared to fixed broadband, there has been the emergence of low-cost satellite and community-based mesh networks. There is great potential in non-traditional approaches as demonstrated in Starlink's low-Earth orbit satellite internet and Google's (now discontinued but still pioneering in concept) Project Loon. Projects like these, however, need to be controlled in terms of budget to avoid excessive pricing and digital infrastructure monopolization by a handful of multinational companies.

Equity in the internet age also means having access to devices and data. Cheap smartphones, subsidized mobile data, and public Wi-Fi access points are critical to provide devices to low-income families, migrant workers, and refugees. Initiatives, such as Kenya's "Digital Villages" and Brazil's "LAN house" movement, demonstrate how community-oriented access points help provide connection to underprivileged groups.

Beyond Access: The Imperative of Digital Literacy

Simply Accessing the Digital world is not enough. The ability to navigate the terrain refers to the ability to make sense of and even critique the world of data and numerous digital enclaves. Digital Literacy is more than the ability to operate devices and software. It is the ability to delineate the processes of data creation and dissemination, comprehend the importance of source validation and critiquing, data sharing, respect personal data safety, and practicing internet hygiene. UNESCO (2019) states that media and information literacy should equip people to become "critical thinkers and effective communicators" in the information age based on the omnipresent realities of infodemic and misinformation.

The COVID-19 pandemic highlighted the broadest definition of digital literacy, including the siloed areas of digitally remote education, remote healthcare, and online shopping. At the same time, the pandemic widened the skills gap profoundly. Girls and children from low-income families in Sub-Saharan Africa and parts of South Asia faced acute inequities during the sudden shift to online learning. Advanced economies were not immune to the inequitable distribution of digital learning resources. The elderly, especially, encountered particularly inequitable experiences with telehealth and vaccine registration, emphasizing that digital exclusion and inequitable access is not confined to the Global South.

It encompasses civic digital skills, which are the skills to 'act' constructively and responsibly in public online spaces, counter digital 'wrong' and engage in digital civics. The perils of digital participation without critical literacy are evident in the 'fake news's infection, online radicalization, and algorithmic puppetry. The e-citizen program of Estonia and the country wide media literacy curriculum adopted by Finland are examples of how digital literacy can be integrated into the educational system. Corporations also have a responsibility: users of Facebook and TikTok have a right to demand promotion of responsible use, algorithm transparency, and fact checking.

Socioeconomic, Gender, and Generational Barriers

Social exclusion is a facet of existing social inequalities. In many societies, women face structural barriers to access, which include lower income, limited autonomy in decision-making, and socio-cultural barriers to technology usage. In their 2022 report, the GSM Association notes that women in low- and middle-income countries are 16% less likely than men to access the mobile internet, and in South Asia, the gap is over 30%. In the same manner, people with disabilities are likely to experience inaccessible digital interfaces even though assistive software and devices such as screen readers and voice-activated technology are available.

These problems are further complicated by generational factors. Members of younger cohorts, often referred to as 'digital natives', are presumed to have acquired foundational digital skills. This perspective, however, ignores the large disparities in the skills level of young people which is further complicated by their socio-economic backgrounds. On the other hand, the older population is likely to encounter substantial and steep hurdles when it comes to learning and adapting new technologies. Designed, focused, and 'age-sensitive' solutions such as limited functionality devices and applications, instruction in vernacular languages, and cross-age instructional programs are fundamental in the promotion of inclusion for older people. The same cannot be said about geography. Global and rural-urban divides are ubiquitous, even in wealthy countries. In the United States, for example, the Federal Communications Commission, (FCC), states that nearly 14 million people living in rural areas are still disconnected from broadband internet. Within the European Union, rural access has not realized the degree of penetration achieved in urban areas, which has resulted in a horizontal inequity in access to e-governance, online business, and digital financial services.

Policy Frameworks and International Perspectives

Efforts to achieve digital inclusion are different but have similar approaches. Digital inclusion, like the five school rights, should be viewed as a human right. The United Nations has increasingly considered the internet as a means of exercising freedom of expression, politics, and socially. Policies should cover several access points: infrastructure, marginalized groups, affordable access, digital and imputed literacy.

As the world's first "digital society," Estonia has e-governance in public and health care systems. The country's digital inclusion depends on WAN access and broad digital literacy. Rwanda's Vision 2020 strategy demonstrates that investment in ICT infrastructure is possible for low-income settings.

Institutions like The World Bank, ITU, and UNESCO, extend wires and equipment to developing countries. The Alliance for Affordable Internet multi-stakeholder initiatives advocate for low-cost and high-competition policy changes. Inclusion and equity in the digital world is stagnated by the ongoing commercial dominance of large technology firms, tension in international relations, and hostile acts in cyberspace which pose great obstacles towards the more noble goal of fostering a digital ecosystem that is open and fair to all.

Efforts to achieve digital inclusion are different but have similar approaches. Digital inclusion, like the five school rights, should be viewed as a human right. The United Nations has increasingly considered the internet as a means of exercising freedom of expression, politics, and socially. Policies should cover several access points: infrastructure, marginalized group affordable access, digital and imputed literacy. As the world's first "digital society," Estonia has e-governance in public and health care systems. The country's digital inclusion depends on WAN access and broad digital literacy. Inclusion and equity in the digital world is stagnated by the ongoing commercial dominance of large technology firms, tension in international relations, and hostile acts in cyberspace which pose great obstacles towards the more noble goal of fostering a digital ecosystem that is open and fair to all.

Enabling digital inclusion and digital literacy is more complex than merely addressing connectivity issues; it requires an elaborate framework of human empowerment for the digital era. Any form of infrastructure development must be supported by policies that target affordability and accessibility. Functional digital literacy needs to be advanced to include critical and creative thinking, civic engagement, and ethical consideration. Gender-sensitive, age-responsive, and disability inclusive frameworks are necessary for ensuring that no one is left behind.

Most importantly, digital inclusion needs to be embraced and implemented as a human right; a prerequisite for effective engagement for the 21st century. The same way the industrial age earned universal access to education, the digital age earns universal access to digital inclusion. Societies that focus on equitable access and equitable literacy will not only bridge divides, but also encourage innovation, resilience, and participatory democracy. Those who neglect to do so will be left behind, further deepening the inequality and exclusion, in an increasingly digitalized world.

LITERATURE REVIEW

1. Defining Digital Inclusion and Literacy

The inclusion of technology and the skills to use it effectively are two important subjects in the ongoing debate about the digital revolution and the impact it has on societies and individuals. Warschauer, in the year 2003, mentioned that digital inclusion is more than having physical access to different devices as well as networks and spans over social, and even educational aspects that promote technology engagement. Helsper (2012) makes a valuable distinction between access to devices, skills, as well as outcomes, and is of the opinion that the gaps existing in the digital world should be addressed at all three of these levels.

The concept of 'digital literacy' has in the recent past, increased in its breadth and depth. Initial thoughts about digital literacy, as indicated by Gilster 1997, revolved around having the capacity to use a computer to 'access' information from different sources in many forms. Newer definitions (see Livingstone 2014) capture the essence of digital literacy in terms of critical participation as well as media responsibility, transforming to the very resilient side, that is, against misinformation. This shift constructs a narrative where the 21st century individual is 'connected' to the more 'empowered' digital environments.

2. The Digital Divide: Persistent Inequalities

Discrepancies in socioeconomic systems are evident in all strata of society, and research does show this to be the case with all forms of socio economics differentiation (Norris, 2001). With regards to digital technology, these would include the: (1) Global divide, (2) Social divide, and (3) Democratic divide.

As van Dijk (2006) suggests, complete access inequality is not solely technical in nature. There are access ramifications that are motivational, contextual, and capacity on the matter. Sub Saharan Africa has seen in the last few decades an increased economic growth and mobile internet penetration (GSMA, 2020). However, the correlation to growth is not at all favorable. Women in developing countries are 20% less likely to use mobile internet than men. The impact of access is conceptualized as an uneven distribution of resources aligned with gender. It is not only women that are impact, older adults in many parts of the world suffer the consequences of structural arrangement that truthfully is neglect in relation to digital life (Friemel, 2016).

The advent of the COVID-19 global pandemic has increased the visibility of the inequality digital access has. There is evidence that suggests that the ability to access the web has severely limited the academic resources, especially for students of lower economic status (OECD, 2021). The use of telemedicine having skyrocketed in the latter months of 2020 was not uniformly shifted in all areas. The rural population are the ones who predominantly suffer to this day due to lack of infrastructure (NHS Digital, 2021). All of these instances provide evidence that the digital divide is far more complex than mere lack of access to the internet.

3. Digital Literacy: Beyond Basic Skills

Upon initial implementation, policies advocating for digital literacy focused on fundamental skills, such as using a computer and browsing the web. Although, many professionals have claimed this approach as inadequate. According to Buckingham (2006), an individual must have critical digital literacy to evaluate information, disinformation, and deliberated algorithmic curation.

Critical digital literacy frameworks (Koltay, 2011), for instance, incorporate fact-checking, active and passive digital citizenship, and responsive cyber borders. Media literacy research (Livingstone & Helsper, 2007) resonates, claiming that literacy involves an active interpretive process, not a passive consumption of the information.

Civic engagement adds another dimension to digital literacy. For instance, Mossberger et al. (2008) contend that digital citizenship entails understanding the ways in which digital technologies impact democratic participation. This approach becomes more salient concerning disinformation and algorithmically driven polarization.

4. Gender and Digital Inclusion

Gender equity within a society has long been a complexity evolved issue of focus. According to Internet and Development Associate, as referenced by Hafkin and Huyer, "digital gender divides and digital exclusion [...] stems from broader inequalities in education, labor, and cultural context-based inequities in norms and expectations" (2007). There has been a steady stream of evidence, for example, GSMA (GSMA Mobile Economy, 2020), which indicates that women are less likely to own and operate mobile phones, use the Internet, and pursue a career in any of the digital professions as compared to men.

Inequities of this nature are further complicated by the concurrent presence of crisscrossing or overlapping social categorizations. As pointed out by Crenshaw, "the experience of exclusion from the digital world is not homogenous" (1989). Within this context, rural women, older women, and women with disabilities encounter unique disadvantages. "She Will Connect" (Intel, 2015) is dedicated to forwading the goal of closing the gender digital divide. However, such initiatives suffer from the critique of viewing women as merely instruments of economic gain (Gurumurthy, 2018).

5. Age and Digital Literacy

The practice of integrating technology with elderly populations poses unique issues. According to Friemel (2016), barriers to accessibility, lack of sufficient, custom, computer instruction, and technophobia are the most significant hurdles. Nevertheless, digital technology usage by the elderly can alleviate social isolation and even improve wellbeing (Quan-Haase et al., 2018). The training programs developed for older people in Europe and Asia offer examples of the value of ethnocentric instruction and experiential education (Tsai et al. 2015). These scholars propose that all forms of design inclusion, such as enlarged screens, simpler interfaces, voice control, and clearer navigational paths, are equally essential to closing gaps related to lack of use by older adults.

6. Disability and Inclusive Technologies

Disabling and enabling aspects of technology can take multiple forms and assistive technology such as screen reading or captioning and captioning are instruments of facilitating access. However, as Goggin and Newell (2007) point out, such adoption is most often limited to self-educational and financial deficits. Ellis and Kent (2011) bluntly asserts that accessibility is a feature that must integrated proactively and designed for, rather than 'after the fact.' LGN and other institutions have incorporated some 'inclusive design' practices', including the WCAG, but such application is sporadic at best (Lazar et al., 2015). There is considerable literature arguing for a universal design approach which sees disabiity as a constituent category of human variation rather than as a deviant, and hence marginal, category.

7. Policy Frameworks for Digital Inclusion

Governments and international entities have constructed policies aimed at promoting digital inclusion. The European Union's Digital Education Action Plan (2018) addresses digital skill acquisition and continues education. UNESCO (2018) integrates digital inclusion into the global Sustainable Development Goals (SDG 4 on education and SDG 9 on infrastructure).

India's Digital India Initiative aimed to augment broadband connectivity and the provision of e-governance services. While access increased, Kumar (2019) argues that lack of affordability and skills remains an issue. Estonia's e-Governance model is celebrated for universal digital ID and online services, but Madise and Martens (2006) point to unresolved concerns of privacy and security. Rwanda's Vision 2020 aimed at development with ICT at the core. While admirable strides have been made, Ndung'u and Waema (2011) point out that affordability and illiteracy remain obstacles. These case studies suggest that investments in infrastructure alone are insufficient. Equally important are skills, pricing, and governance that is responsive and inclusive.

8. Emerging Technologies: Risks and Opportunities

The literature reviews the impact of new technologies on inclusion. For example, an AI can help patients obtain personal level healthcare (Luckin, 2017) but biased algorithms could reinforce discrimination The introduction of 5G and 6G network systems can greatly improve internet access and ease, but the price of the service is an obstacle (International Telecommunication Union, 2021). Virtual reality and the metaverse hold the possibility of redefining digital participation but critics argue they may worsen exclusion due to the requirement of advanced hardware (Ball, 2020, 2021). The other important consideration is... More people are active online and are therefore more vulnerable to crimes that involve computers... Therefore, digital literacy should encompass the education of self data management and protective operational strategies (Zuboff, 2019)

One of the developing areas of research deals with digital inequality as a human right. Hintz et al. (2019) describe how digital access intersects with freedom of expression, education, and active democratic citizenship. The UN Human Rights Council (2016) internet access as a right and a conduit for rights and therefore, urged countries to work towards the elimination of digital divides. Social digital inclusion has also been situate within social justice frameworks. Eubanks (2018) cautions that poorly designed digital welfare systems may perpetuate inequality through what she calls “digital poorhouses.” This emphasizes the need to integrate equity and rights-based policies into digital frameworks.

Foremost, the majority of the available scholarship has been pigeonholed to studying advanced economies, while long-term assessments of digital inclusion initiatives which sit within the Global South are scant. Secondly, there is the absence of integration of inclusive frameworks that deal with the multilayered inequities of gender, race, class, age, and disability. Thirdly, the impact of emerging technologies such as AI, blockchain, and the metaverse on digital divides remains largely unexplored. Finally, much of the available literature ignores community-led initiatives like mesh-networking, local content production, and grassroots digital literacy advocacy.

The available literature on digital literacy and inclusion illustrates both achievement and stagnation. Most scholars advocate for the issue of access, skills, and outcomes to be addressed in tandem. Critical frameworks of digital literacy focus on the need for empowerment as opposed to merely being connected, while intersectional scholarship outlines the multiple forms of exclusion that are experienced by marginalized people. Policy frameworks are ambiguous, which reflects the need for culturally sensitive, rights-centered, and inclusive advocacy. New technologies further complicate the landscape with their mixed inclusionary and exclusionary possibilities. Collectively, the literature signals a shift towards a new paradigm: digital inclusion is no longer merely a technical issue, but rather a socio-political one, with implications for social justice, rights, and human development.

METHODOLOGY

1. Introduction to Methodology

This research takes on a conceptual and qualitative research approach to investigate the intersections of social equity, digital inclusion, and digital literacy. Unlike other empirical works that utilize surveys, experiments, or quantitative data, this approach revolves around the integration of scholarship, policy documents, and case-based analyses. This approach seeks to provide a comprehensive understanding of possible avenues to provide digital inclusion on a global scale. This approach is tailored for nascent fields, which are rapidly evolving technologically, as they lack large-scale empirical data. Synthesizing literature, case studies, and theory, the approach will independently contribute to the field while providing insights that are practical.

2. Research Design

This research is exploratory and seeks to answer the following guiding queries:

What is the evolution of inclusion in the scholarly and policy discourse?
What structural barriers exist to the attainment of universal digital inclusion and literacy?
How do gender, age, disability, and location influence the ability to participate in digital activities?
What international case studies are there and what strategies can be proposed?
How can the Capability Approach, Critical Race theory, or Intersectionality provide frameworks to explain how digital ecosystems can be inclusive?

The research design is qualitative and interpretive, based on the systematic collection and analysis of secondary information sources.

Rather than testing a single hypothesis, the study builds a multi-dimensional conceptual framework for understanding digital inclusion.

3. Data Sources

The study draws upon secondary data from four main sources:

✓ Academic Literature: Peer-reviewed journal articles, books and edited volumes on digital inclusion, digital literacy, media studies and ICT for development. Databases of Scopus, Web of Science and Google Scholar provided access to relevant material.
✓ Policy and Industry Reports: Documents published by international organizations (UNESCO, ITU, World Bank, OECD), NGOs and technology industry reports which provide real-time data on Internet penetration, digital literacy, and policy data.
✓ Case Studies: Context-specific examples from government initiatives (e.g., Digital India, Estonia's e-governance, Rwanda's Vision 2020), corporate strategies (Intel's "She Will Connect") and grassroots digital inclusion programs.
✓ Theoretical Literature: Foundational works in critical theory, media studies and development studies which provide the conceptual framework for analyzing empirical data.
✓ The reliance on secondary data ensures broad coverage of global perspectives while allowing for critical triangulation across different types of sources.

4. Data Collection Strategy

The process of gathering sources was structured in three phases:

Initial Scoping Review: A broad keyword search was conducted using terms such as digital inclusion, digital literacy, digital divide, ICT4D, critical digital literacy, and intersectionality in technology.
Refinement and Categorization: After filtering for relevance and examining the academic rigor and currency of sources, the major domains of the review such as gender, age, disability, and rights, as well as the intersection of emerging technologies, were used to organize the review.
Case Study Selection: In selecting the countries and initiatives, diversity in income and geographical regions was sought. The chosen countries and initiatives were also aligned with the criteria of policy innovation, evaluative data availability, and research questions relevance.

This collection strategy, which is iterative in nature, ensured a balance between breadth and depth in the dataset.

5. Analytical Framework

The interdisciplinary analytical approach in which this research is situated is this broad in scope because digital inclusion transcends one specific area and touches on numerous aspects, such as infrastructure, culture, and power dynamics. No one method would be able to capture this complex phenomenon. Thus, this research embraces three interrelated approaches. These are content analysis, comparative review, and theoretical application. By combining these approaches, it becomes possible to examine and interrogate inclusion policies and campaign on digital inclusion and go beyond the 'what' to understand the 'how' and 'why' underlying the policy and institutional frameworks, as well as the outcomes.

Content Analysis

The foundational pillar in this research is content analysis. This is the working method used in this research to examine texts, campaigns, and policy documents for themes that recurve, strategic silences, and tacit structural assumptions. This method of content analysis has become a standard approach in the field of media and communication and research and is particularly useful to research the public narratives of dominant social groups to examine how 'missing' counter narratives to dominant stories are framed and the inclusivity of the public narrative.

To illustrate let us take the Media and Information Literacy (MIL) framework prepared by UNESCO. This framework defines what is media and information literacy and outlines the focal competencies which are supposed to be unwaveringly 'global competencies' and then one has to take a closer look to see whether these competencies indeed serve as a reflection of the global diversity. One of the studies connected India's Digital India initiative with rural and economically disadvantaged populations. How does the campaign characterize them: as active digital users or as passive technology users? Gendered analyses of campaigns like She Will Connect (Intel, 2015) and We Think Digital (Meta, 2020) evaluated the degree of structural inequality the campaigns addressed.

Comparative analysis holds particular importance in studying digital inclusion as no one national or regional model is applicable in its entirety due to the unique cultural, political, and economic contexts that influences the construction and outcome of digital policies. Take, for example, Estonia's universal digital ID and e-governance system, and India's Aadhaar program. Both serve as sizeable digital identity projects, yet Estonia's is comparatively more inclusive and has less detrimental consequences. Estonia's small, homogenous population, and robust state capacity, in comparison, India, enables a relatively smoother implementation of the e-ID services which citizens trust and extensively utilize. Conversely, the Aadhaar program is in India, a country that is highly diverse and has a significant rural population which raises issues of data privacy, biometrics, and the poorer population's accessibility to such welfare programs.

Similarly, in South Asia, where technological use is highly restricted for women, the use of mobile banking services, such as M-Pesa in Kenya, has financially empowered rural women. These contrasting scenarios also help in understanding the inclusion or exclusion of women in the digital economy as well as how cultural context influences digital inclusion. A comparative review also included grassroots and corporate initiatives. For instance, the "She Will Connect" initiative that targets women and girls in Africa was contrasted with the funded media literacy programs in Finland's national curriculum. This serves to illustrate the disparity between corporate empowerment initiatives and the educational system on state-driven reforms. This approach prevented the insights from being limited to a single geography or stakeholder group. Incorporating disparate case studies into conversation rendered the review comparativist while enabling the study to fetch transferable insights to various contexts and contexts paucity.

Theoretical Application

The third pillar of the analytical framework is the application of critical theoretical frameworks. Theories serve as interpretive lenses and patterns and power structures and dynamics obscured behind raw data. The study is anchored on four interrelated frameworks.

Critical Race Theory (Delgado & Stefancic, 2017) – Used to examine how inequities within digital access are constructed, especially about racial and ethnic minorities. For instance, CRT critiques ne w and emerging technologies like artificial intelligence for their indisputable algorithmic biases for and against certain groups within society. The reason for the biases is the historical denial of access to these technologies.

Intersectionality (Crenshaw, 1989) – A concept that views exclusion as experienced at multiple points on various identities. For example, a rural elderly woman with disabilities encounters greater and more severe obstacles than a young urban man. Intersectionality is critical for any comprehensive analysis on patterns of exclusion.

Capability Approach (Sen, 1999) – Goes beyond access indicators to question digital technologies and their potential to enrich the freedoms and life opportunities of individuals.

For instance, can women attain financial independence because mobile banking is available to them, or is this independence still constrained by structural patriarchy?

Davis (1989) introduced the Technology Acceptance Model which seeks to elucidate adoption by concentrating on a person's perceived value of the system and its requisite effort. For instance, the residents of the countryside may drop the use of certain e-governance platforms, no matter how advance the infrastructure is, if they consider the platform to be overly complex. The combination of these theories can provide a cross between structure and culture as well as behavior, thus, balancing the analysis of macro-inequalities and micro-acceptance behaviors. No this combination is very difficult to achieve.

The use of a conceptual–qualitative approach as opposed to more abstract concepts and empirical or quantitative approach is equally thoughtful. The rest of this section provides those details.

Digital inclusion is a phenomenon that has many facets of infrastructure, education, gender, age, disability, culture, and governance. Certain quantitative indicators such as internet penetration and device ownership provide useful but limited snapshots and are unable to appreciate the subtlety of human-technology interactions. For instance, in two countries that have the same internet penetration, one may be more culturally included than the other. A qualitative approach makes it possible to uncover such complexities.

Many geographic areas, especially in the Global South, are devoid of empirical data, or have outdated data, about digital literacy and inclusion. The rapidly advancing technology often occurs at a pace faster than the availability of relevant statistical data. A conceptual synthesis allows researchers to integrate gray literature (NGO documents, policy briefs, industry reports, and other non-scholarly sources) with academic publications, thereby enhancing the relevance of research.

This research is more than merely descriptive: it is also normative as it aspires to assess what has been done and propose ways to achieve equitable possible futures. Normative concepts of justice, rights, and equity cannot survive the full scrutiny of a purely quantitative, positivist assessment. The framing of digital inclusion as a matter of social and human rights is more a matter of critical and interpretive methods than purely technological progress.

Research on digital inclusion is often siloed: development studies examine infrastructure and media studies literacy while computer science addresses technical issues. A conceptual–qualitative approach enables cross–disciplinary integration of fragmented literatures into a more comprehensive framework.

Ensuring Validity and Rigor

Research methods of a qualitative nature often come under fire for the alleged absence of objectivity and inability to replicate the study. The particular study focuses on incorporating various strategies to address the concerns of validity, reliability and rigor.

Triangulation: Triangulation is the analysis of a single phenomenon through the use of multiple sources and techniques of data collection and analysis (Denzin, 1978). The use of academic literature, policy documents, Industry data, and case studies helps the study minimize dependence on a single source. The use of content analysis, case study, and theoretical application of content analysis helps corroborate the theoretical triangulation.

Reduction of Subjectivity: To reduce bias, criteria for inclusion of sources were stringent and clearly delineated. Academic sources that were peer-reviewed and in the domain of policy and industry were included only if published by reputable bodies (e.g. UNESCO, ITU, and the World Bank). The case study method was determined by the range of geography and income as well as the type of initiative (government, corporate or grassroots). The criteria used to determine transparency of the selection is documented.

Privileged peer-reviewed sources: To maintain academic integrity, arguments were constructed and supported by peer-reviewed scholarly work whenever possible. Non-reviewed literature was approached with caution and employed for descriptive data only (e.g. statistics and outlines of programs).

Theoretical Saturation: The application of several theoretical frameworks to a study until no more interpretative power is observable means achieving theoretical saturation (Glaser & Strauss, 1967). For example, when used together, the intersection of CRT provides understanding of the structural and layered inequalities, other theories offer scant additional explanatory value.

Reflexivity: Reflexivity is an important aspect in qualitative research (Finlay, 2002). This research understands the culture of the researcher in terms of the socio-cultural, the academic, and the language—each of which stands to influence readings and constructions. Unconscious acceptance of the accepted dominant narratives is prevented by reflexive awareness.

Reliability Through Documentation: The entire process of collecting and analyzing the data, including the stage of fielding searches for keywords, decisions regarding inclusion and exclusion, and the constructing of coded themes, was thoroughly recorded in the research. Such records will enable other researchers to track the work and permit it to some extent to be repeated.

Together, the **analytical framework, justification of the qualitative approach, and strategies for rigor** form a robust methodology. Content analysis revealed underlying narratives and silences in digital inclusion initiatives; comparative review enabled cross-contextual learning; and theoretical application grounded findings in critical frameworks. The justification for a conceptual–qualitative approach rests on the complexity of digital inclusion, the emergent nature of available data, and the normative aim of promoting justice. Rigor was ensured through triangulation, transparency, peer-reviewed sources, theoretical saturation, and reflexivity.

This methodological design equips the study to address not only the descriptive questions of "what is happening" in digital inclusion but also the evaluative and prescriptive questions of "what ought to happen" in building equitable digital futures.

LIMITATIONS

Every research design has its limitations, and for the purposes of both transparency and integrity, it is critical that these limitations are recognized. This study in particular, although strong with the triangulated conceptual-qualitative approach, has a number of challenges that will affect the way its results are interpreted.

The most glaring issue, and the one that this study is focusing on, is the issue of secondary data. Although primary data is missing within the literature, fieldwork, and, digital exclusion community reached, then the policy and industry reports, it are the foundational, a. Narratives from the fingers is woman in rural areas taking mobility and able, elder in stages of e-governance portal systems, and refugees in e-governance portals, along with other citizens and wh more, could these ethnographic slipped experiences capturing mobility her. these profound vantage points of the world, sketching without falling into the trap of oversimplistic grand narratives. There is no doubt glean secondary sources are, and value secondary often r. Hence, in this, While the triangulated approach seeks to, within the parameters of external constraints, bias, of the field has ethnography evidence, remains, value, significant this absence gap.

Regional and Linguistic Reductionism Bias

Digital documents that focus on Latin America, Francophone Africa, and East Asia and that discuss policy and scholarship having to do with digital inclusion may be insufficient due to a lack of inclusion of documents in the Spanish, French, Mandarin, and Arabic languages. This limitation is especially concerning because developing countries have developed sophisticated models of digital inclusion that include Brazil's community telecentres, South Korea's e-governments, and Tunisia's digital governance post the Arab Spring. To ignore these cases is to succumb to Anglocentric interpretations of inclusion.

The development of digital technologies is much faster than the pace at which academic publishing progresses. This study touches on the integration of tools such as AI in education, sophisticated identity verification systems based on blockchain, the metaverse, and so on; however, these advancements are still in the process of manifestation along with their unpredictable ramifications. A 2020 case study might be obsolete by 2025 due to sheer advancement. Therefore, the results and conclusions of the study should be viewed as mere illustrations of the studied phenomena, with no regard to their finality.

Another issue, which also presents a limitation, is the study's focus on the rights-based perspective, which is also equity-centered. Framing the digital divide as one of justice and human rights, shifts the analysis from a descriptive one, which is usually the focus of the digital divide scholarship, to a more prescriptive one which is much needed. This focus provides clarity of reasoning, but is vulnerable to the charge of a lack of interpretive neutrality. Realists may counter that the emphasis and focus placed on such a perspective is a form of normative bias.

In the end, adopting the conceptual–qualitative design meant giving up the possibility of large-scale statistical generalization. Although cross-national surveys (e.g. ITU's ICT Development Index) offer strong quantitative patterns, this study favored conceptual synthesis and critical interpretation. Hence, its outcomes provide depth and theoretical richness but lack the predictability associated with quantitative models.

ETHICAL CONSIDERATIONS

Discerning ethical concerns while working on secondary data and employing secondary methods.

Relevance: The case studies touched upon sensitive aspects of culture and politics. For instance, in critiquing India's Aadhaar system, in all its exclusionary risks, the study also contemplated its scale and logistical successes. While celebrating Estonia's digital ID system, the analysis also pointed out the shortcomings of its replicability and scalability for other large diverse states. Such contextual respect avoids universalizing assumptions that erase local complexities.

Inclusion Framework: Legal frameworks also require paying attention to marginalized populations. Studies on digital inclusion tend to focus on middle-class users, urban populations, or technologically literate individuals. In this case, the focus was on women, the elderly, persons with disabilities, and those living in rural areas. By centering these groups, this approach also enhances the methodology's ability to respond to systemic exclusions and more closely aligns with principles of inclusive justice.

Critiques of the Sources: Secondary sources were never treated as neutral pools of truths. Corporate documents, for instance, were examined for underlying commercial interests, such as brand associations, motivational campaigns "She Will Connect" and "Digital India" and other such advocacy. Likewise, state narratives ere scrutinized for state politics, such as the over-passionate promotion of digitalization as modern Noting the absence of the modernization agenda regarding the democracy and the surveillance system which digitalization brings in.

The engagement was purposeful to ensure that biases from the Source were not repeated in the engagement. The study maintained the highest level of academic rigor by appropriate sourcing, differentiating between peer-reviewed and gray literature, and acknowledging questionable evidence. This upholds the principle of intellectual integrity, which is critical in the realm of idea-driven scholarship.

CONTRIBUTION

Perhaps the greatest contribution is the ability to unify diverse knowledge silos. Digital inclusion has been researched in development studies, media studies, political science, and information systems in silos. The study converses these literatures, enabling the construction of an integrated analytical framework that is holistic in its technological, social, and cultural aspects. Also noteworthy is the sophisticated use of Critical Race Theory, Intersectionality, the Capability Approach, and the Technology Acceptance Model. These frameworks are rarely integrated in the field of digital inclusion. The study, however, employs all of them to illuminate systemic inequalities (CRT), overlapping exclusions (intersectionality), human freedoms (capabilities), and adoption behaviors (TAM). The result is a richly textured interpretive framework that integrates structural and personal experience.

The study also reinforces the importance of the conceptual–qualitative approach in an area that is primarily dominated by quantifiable measures (e.g, penetration rates, bandwidth measures). Numbers tell an important and necessary, but insufficient, story about cultural exclusion, narrative framing, or political power. The balance between academic rigor and conceptual policy implications captured by the study is exemplified by the predictive value which future research may draw through the normative insights generated by conceptual methods of analysis. A stronger alignment is the contribution through the methods used to achieve policy objectives. This study shows that the divorce of scholarly rigor from usefulness is not a necessity. The interrelation of theory with comparative case study and critical analysis offers an approach to policy research that is likely to be used by the public sector as well as NGOs and multilateral institutions for the design of inclusion policies.

CONCLUSION

To sum up, the methodology has undertaken the challenge of depth, theorizing, and breadth, while retaining transparency about the caps of the analyses. Constructing the content analyses uncovered narratives and silences in inclusion campaigns; the comparative review highlighted differences across contexts, and lessons that are transferable, and the application of theory situated the findings in critical social theory. The conclusions are constrained the most by the absence of primary fieldwork, technology bias, and the growing pace of change. Despite this, the wide range of methodological strategies such as triangulation, transparency of selection, peer-sourced positioning, and reflexivity, allow the conclusions to be made with a great deal of confidence. The ethical stance of the research serves to prompt the further credibility of the research regarding attitudinal sensitivity, contextual equity, and critical engagement with the sources used.

REFERENCES

Alliance for Affordable Internet. (2020). *The 2020 affordability report*. World Wide Web Foundation.

Ball, M. (2020). *The metaverse: And how it will revolutionize everything*. W. W. Norton & Company.

Ball, M. (2021). The future of the metaverse. *Journal of Virtual Worlds Studies, 10*(2), 1–15.

Buckingham, D. (2006). Defining digital literacy: What do young people need to know about digital media? *Nordic Journal of Digital Literacy, 1*(4), 263–276.

Crenshaw, K. (1989). Demarginalizing the intersection of race and sex: A Black feminist critique of antidiscrimination doctrine, feminist theory, and antiracist politics. *University of Chicago Legal Forum, 1989*(1), 139–167.

Delgado, R., & Stefancic, J. (2017). *Critical race theory: An introduction* (3rd ed.). NYU Press.

Denzin, N. K. (1978). *The research act: A theoretical introduction to sociological methods* (2nd ed.). McGraw-Hill.

Ellis, K., & Kent, M. (2011). *Disability and new media*. Routledge.

Eubanks, V. (2018). *Automating inequality: How high-tech tools profile, police, and punish the poor*. St. Martin's Press.

Finlay, L. (2002). Negotiating the swamp: The opportunity and challenge of reflexivity in research practice. *Qualitative Research, 2*(2), 209–230.

Friemel, T. N. (2016). The digital divide has grown old: Determinants of a digital divide among seniors. *New Media & Society, 18*(2), 313–331.

Gilster, P. (1997). *Digital literacy*. Wiley Computer Publishing.

Glaser, B. G., & Strauss, A. L. (1967). *The discovery of grounded theory: Strategies for qualitative research*. Aldine.

Goggin, G., & Newell, C. (2007). *Digital disability: The social construction of disability in new media*. Rowman & Littlefield.

GSMA. (2020). *The mobile economy 2020*. GSMA Intelligence.

Gurumurthy, A. (2018). Digital inclusion and gender justice: A feminist framework. *Development, 61*(1), 56–65.

Hafkin, N., & Huyer, S. (2007). Women and gender in ICT statistics and indicators. *Information Technologies and International Development*, *4*(2), 25–41.

Helsper, E. J. (2012). A corresponding fields model for the links between social and digital exclusion. *Communication Theory*, *22*(4), 403–426.

Hintz, A., Dencik, L., & Wahl-Jorgensen, K. (2019). *Digital citizenship in a datafied society*. Polity Press.

Intel. (2015). *She will connect: Intel's commitment to close the gender digital divide.* Intel Corporation.

International Telecommunication Union. (2021). *Measuring digital development: Facts and figures 2021*. ITU Publications.

International Telecommunication Union. (2023). *Global connectivity report 2023*. ITU Publications.

Koltay, T. (2011). The media and the literacies: Media literacy, information literacy, digital literacy. *Media Culture & Society*, *33*(2), 211–221.

Kumar, R. (2019). Digital India: Opportunities and challenges. *Journal of Governance and Public Policy*, *9*(2), 34–45.

Lazar, J., Olalere, A., & Wentz, B. (2015). Investigating the accessibility of digital libraries. *Library Hi Tech*, *33*(1), 32–44.

Livingstone, S. (2014). Developing social media literacy: How children learn to interpret risky opportunities on social network sites. *Communications*, *39*(3), 283–303.

Livingstone, S., & Helsper, E. J. (2007). Gradations in digital inclusion: Children, young people, and the digital divide. *New Media & Society*, *9*(4), 671–696.

Luckin, R. (2017). *Machine learning and human intelligence: The future of education for the 21st century*. UCL Institute of Education Press.

Madise, Ü., & Martens, T. (2006). E-voting in Estonia 2005: The first practice of country-wide binding Internet voting in the world. *Electronic Voting in Europe Technology, Law. Politics & Society*, *•••*, 3–13.

Meta. (2020). *We think digital: Digital literacy program.* Meta Platforms Inc.

Mossberger, K., Tolbert, C. J., & McNeal, R. S. (2008). *Digital citizenship: The Internet, society, and participation*. MIT Press.

Ndung'u, M. N., & Waema, T. M. (2011). Development outcomes of ICT in Africa. In Ndung'u, M. N., & Waema, T. M. (Eds.), *Development outcomes of ICT for Africa* (pp. 1–16). African Economic Research Consortium.

NHS Digital. (2021). *Digital inclusion in health and care: Lessons learned from the pandemic*. NHS Digital.

Norris, P. (2001). *Digital divide: Civic engagement, information poverty, and the Internet worldwide*. Cambridge University Press.

OECD. (2021). *The state of school education: One year into the COVID pandemic*. OECD Publishing.

Quan-Haase, A., Williams, C., Kicevski, M., Elueze, I., & Wellman, B. (2018). Dividing the Grey Divide: Deconstructing myths about older adults' online activities, skills, and attitudes. *The American Behavioral Scientist, 62*(9), 1207–1228.

Sen, A. (1999). *Development as freedom*. Alfred A. Knopf.

Tsai, H. S., Shillair, R., Cotten, S. R., Winstead, V., & Yost, E. (2015). Getting Grandma online: Are tablets the answer for increasing digital inclusion for older adults in the U.S.? *Educational Gerontology, 41*(10), 695–709.

UN Human Rights Council. (2016). *Resolution on the promotion, protection and enjoyment of human rights on the Internet*. United Nations.

UNESCO. (2018). *Leveraging ICTs to achieve SDG 4*. UNESCO Publishing.

UNESCO. (2019). *Media and information literacy: Policy and strategy guidelines*. UNESCO Publishing.

World Bank. (2022). *World development report 2022: Digitalization for development*. World Bank Publications.

Zuboff, S. (2019). *The age of surveillance capitalism: The fight for a human future at the new frontier of power*. PublicAffairs.

Chapter 11

Podcasting the Subaltern: Imaginations of Matabeleland Regional Identity Through Audience Perspectives

Jennings Joy Chibike
https://orcid.org/0000-0002-4899-2446
Lupane State University, Zimbabwe

Samuel Anesu Muzhingi
https://orcid.org/0000-0003-0138-5080
University of Kansas, USA

Sanelisiwe Sibanda
Lupane State University, Zimbabwe

ABSTRACT

This chapter, drawing from victimhood and subaltern public sphere theory as theoretical lens, is poised at examining audiences of Community Voice Podcast's views and perspectives of the plights of Matabeleland region based on the discussions in the podcasts. Also, it interrogates their views on the regional identity of Matabeleland based on the quandaries they face. This qualitative chapter draws data from 15 purposively selected audiences from Matabeleland South, Matabeleland North, Bulawayo and Midlands provinces. The chapter's findings exhibit that the podcasts carried indications of the main plights faced in Matabeleland for example pollution, poor sanitation and natural disasters. Basing on these problems the participants reimagined the identity of Matabeleland as a dirty region suffering from leadership crisis and gods' wrath.

DOI: 10.4018/979-8-3373-5307-4.ch011

INTRODUCTION

Salient issues of identity politics and nationalism are pertinent in understanding multi-cultural and multi-ethnic communities such as Zimbabwe (Msindo, 2007). In light of this, scholars have been preoccupied with explicating the (re)constructions and (re)imaginations of identity precisely that of the subaltern ethnic groups occupying Matabeleland region such as the Ndebele, Kalanga and BaTonga (Khuphe, 2022; Ncube, 2022; Ndlovu, 2018; Mpofu, 2014). Progressively, others have further gone to examine particularistic and secessionist politics of these minority groups fuelled by social media, news websites and online diasporic media (Mhlanga and Mpofu, 2014; Moyo, 2009:179). Scholars' concerns with online media, identity imagination and particularism exhibit the potential of digital technologies in collective identity constructions (McKenzi, 2025; Purnomo, 2025). This chapter also joins the bandwagon of scholarship interrogating the potential of digital technologies in aiding the construction of the identity of the subaltern in Zimbabwe. In its interrogation, it takes a detour from previous studies which are gripped by vices of textual determinism in the sense that it is concerned with examining the collective identity of the Matabeleland region, through perspectives of audiences, based on how it is portrayed in Community Voices Podcasts which are published by the Centre for Technology and Innovation (CITE) in Bulawayo, Zimbabwe. The Community Voices Podcasts carry various issues happening in Matabeleland communities ranging from democracy, economy, lifestyle and Covid-19 pandemic inflicted problems poignantly besieging the province. The podcasts are produced in various languages which are prominent in Matabeleland such as isiNdebele, Tonga, Xhosa, Kalanga, Venda and Nambya. Therefore, the precise objectives of the chapter are;

1. To examine audience perspectives of the main plights faced in Matabeleland region
2. To examine audience perspectives on how these plights influence the identity of Matabeleland region

The novelty of this chapter lies in that it explores the role of podcasts in the imagination of Matabeleland regional identity something prior studies have not done before. It also gestures towards entanglement of the consumption of digital audio stories thus situating forth the industrial revolution within the precincts of media studies identity construction and social development. The grandeur of this study is enshrined in its potential to illuminate already existing efforts bent at understanding collective Matabeleland identity, and particularism and consequently supporting the nation building project which has been hampered by Matabeleland's struggle for national legitimacy and recognition.

BACKGROUND

Zimbabwe is a multicultural and ethnic country which is partitioned into provinces anchored on ethnic and tribal grounds (Liedong, 2025; Mlambo, 2013). This partitioning is a rendition of colonial venom set at creating fissures in the native people to ease colonial manoeuvres (Anderson, 2025). On the northern spheres of the country are Mashonaland provinces which are dominated by the Shona-speaking societies while the southern parts comprise the Matabeleland South, Matabeleland North and Midlands provinces, for the purposes of this study will be collectively identified as Matabeleland region, dominated by minority Ndebele-speaking societies (Mabhena, 2014). Though Matabeleland is dominated by the Ndebele it is important to highlight that it is also the home of independent Venda, Xhosa, Kalanga and Tonga people and also assimiladoes, engulfed into the Ndebele nation, thus making it a multi-ethnic province (Bhebhe, 2025; Ranger, 1999). In this respect, Tshuma (2023) refers to Matabeleland as an oasis of ideological and political contestations because of concomitant identities and histories therein.

According to Maseko and Dhlamini (2021), Matabeleland has found itself peripherised in socio–political and economic discourses in Zimbabwe. In the same vein, Maseko (2022) is of the notion that this peripherisation has been reinvigorated and sustained by the Gukurahundi genocide. The genocide saw over 200 000 people from Matabeleland and Midlands being slain by the fifth brigade which was activated by the Zimbabwe African National Union-Patriotic Front (ZANU PF) led government (Tshuma and Ndlovu, 2020; Ndlovu, 2019; Ncube, 2019; Eppel, 2020, 2004). This was done as a form of punishing Matabeleland inhabitants who were alleged to be dissidents together with opposition Zimbabwe African People's Union (ZAPU) leader Joshua Nkomo 'the father of dissidents' (Genocide Watch, 2021; Ndlovu-Gatsheni, 2012). In equal measure, Alexander (2021) avers that the Gukurahundi genocide also marked the inflammation of intense hatred of the government and intense tribal animosity pitting the Shona and the Ndebele. The animosity lessened after the signing of the Unity Accord of 1987 which was the infusion of ZANU and ZAPU into a ZANU PF led by Robert Mugabe of the former being deputised by Joshua Nkomo of the latter (Moyo, 2024).

Though the Unity Accord brought relief to the tribal and ethnic clashes there soon emerged unfair socio-political and economic hierarchies which favoured the Shona over the Ndebele (Ngwenya, 2016; Mabhena, 2014). This further fanned the flames of tribal turbulence between the Ndebele and Shona people (Sibanda and Dube, 2025). In governance, the Ndebele people were made deputies of the Shona people (Ndlovu, 2025). Within the cylinders of the economy Matabeleland region was economically sabotaged leading to the de-industrialization of Bulawayo, a city which used to be the industrial capital of Zimbabwe (Msipa and Masango, 2025). All economic activities migrated to Harare in Mashonaland. Socially, the construction of Matabeleland was riddled with stereotypes as people in the region were seen as inferior, uneducated, lazy and unworthy (Chauraya, 2025). This ably demonstrates the peripherisation of the Matabeleland communities.

The peripheralization is also perpetuated in the media as state-owned media works in cohorts with the government in sideling, thwarting and muzzling critical voices emanating from the region. The reason is that voices from Matabeleland have counter-hegemonic undertones (Tshabangu and Salawu, 2024). On national radio and television, state programmes are usually presented in English and Shona while ignoring isiNdebele. Also, state media such as the *Chronicle* has been used as an instrument to legitimatise efforts at making Matabeleland societies extinct such as the dreaded Gukurahundi genocide (Santos, 2011). Private media such as *Radio Dialogue* tried to add Matabeleland voices to the civic discourse and communicative spaces were violently shut down in a bid to muzzle people in the southern parts of Zimbabwe who the government said had counter-hegemonic interests. Against this background, it becomes interesting to investigate the meanings that readers make of podcasts published by CITE a Bulawayo-based media outlet performing the role of a subaltern media.

CITE and Community Voices Podcasts

Located within the heart of Bulawayo, the Centre for Innovation and Technology (CITE) is a civic organisation whose mainstay is on the production and dissemination of news in Zimbabwe with much attention to the Matabeleland region. This organisation led by prominent journalist, Zenzele Ndebele in its production of information, seeks to intertwine creativity and social activism. Chibike (2023) posits that CITE has become a reputable media entity in Matabeleland because of its capabilities to use digital technology and platforms to expose plights faced by Matabeleland which in some instances are muted in other media platforms. Among various ways in which they package and distribute information in society, they use podcasts and of importance to this chapter are the Community Voices Podcasts. These are short podcasts ranging between 5 to 10 minutes carrying various issues affecting people in the Matabeleland region. They rose to prominence during the Covid-19 lockdown together with the Covid-19 podcasts. It should be noted though that even though they rose to prominence during the Covid-19 era they carried various issues some of which were not directly linked to Covid-19. The Community Voices Podcasts gave voice to common members of the society to discuss various socio-economic and political issues that were occurring in their respective areas of origin within the Matabeleland region. Based on this, the chapter grabs the opportunity, through the views and perspectives of audiences to examine how the conversations in these podcasts aid the imagination of the Matabeleland region.

LITERATURE REVIEW

Media, identity and Matabeleland

The media has been instrumental in the (re)creation, (re)imagining and reinforcement of individual, collective and regional identity (Soto et al., 2023; Zheltukhina et al. 2023). With regards to regional identities which are the crux of this chapter, the media shapes how specific regions of Zimbabwe are positioned within the larger national identity through the employment of diverse discourses and narratives (Mlambo, 2013). Consequently, state media has been propagating Shona and Mashonaland supremacy while relegating Matabeleland to the fringes of the Zimbabwean socio-political and economic discourses. Therefore, it becomes interesting to examine what discourses in civic society linked media such as CITE reflect when it come to the identity of Matabeleland region and some of the problems that the region is facing based on its perceived peripherisation from Zimbabwean affairs.

Against the glaring invisibility of Matabeleland in state media's discourses of a Zimbabwean state (Khuphe, 2022; Ncube, 2022) private media and social media have become an avenue for the proliferation of sound narratives about Matabeleland issues (Ndlovu, 2018). Also, privately owned media in Zimbabwe plays a key role in countering and challenging ZANU PF hegemonic narratives and mythologise which sanitise Matabeleland and Ndebele marginalisation (Ndlovu, 2018; Mpofu, 2013). Benefiting from this, the chapter deviates from the examination of how private owned media challenges ZANU PF ideas and grapples with issues that are discussed about Matabeleland in private media and how this aid the imagination of Matabeleland identity.

The media can be utilised to refute current regional identity ideologies. Marginalised or underrepresented groups can question prevailing narratives and create their own identities through the media (Mhlanga, 2013). This is seen in both the growing prominence of minority groups in the media and the growth of independent media sources that give a voice to minority viewpoints and views (Chibike, 2023). These groups can develop fresh perspectives on regional identity and influence public opinion by contesting prevailing discourses on regional identity (Chibike, Muzhingi, Pikanegore and Makalisa, 2025). Online news sources like *CITE* can be seen as aiding in the development of a fair and thorough understanding of Zimbabwean regional identities. By expanding the focus from the two dominant ethnic groups, the Shona and the Ndebele, online news outlets are allowing audiences to imagine a

Zimbabwe with more than just the two dominant ethnic identities but multiple ones that make up the various regions within Zimbabwe. This chapter thus endeavours, through the views and perspectives of audiences, to examine how the conversations in these podcasts aid the imagination of the Matabeleland region beyond the two dominant ethnic groups.

It is important to discuss how Matabeleland is portrayed in the media, whose views of Matabeleland are given prominence in the media and if there are alternative views in which Matabeleland can be imagined. One perspective highlights the violent past events in the region, particularly during the Gukurahundi period, where thousands of people were tortured and killed (Rwafa, 2012). Some viewpoints focus on the role of new media in widening the democratic space and countering the government's hegemonic nationalist discourses (Mpofu et al., 2021). The media portrays Matabeleland as a distressed region with a complex and troubled history, where issues of violence, memory, and political manipulation are prominent (Ndlovu and Tshuma, 2021; Mpofu et al., 2021).

The media's representations of Matabeleland have had a significant impact on the region's identity and development (Tshuma and Phiri, 2022; Mpofu, Moyo, and Sibanda, 2021). Post-independence media narratives have also focused on political instability and conflict in Matabeleland, particularly during the Gukurahundi massacres in the 1980s (Ndlovu and Chikohora, 2022). These historical constructions have had a lasting impact on contemporary media representations of Matabeleland, perpetuating negative stereotypes and limiting the region's potential for development (Tshuma and Phiri, 2022). In contemporary Zimbabwean mainstream media, Matabeleland is often portrayed as a region of political instability and conflict (Sibanda, 2022). However, alternative media narratives from Matabeleland-based news outlets and citizen journalists offer different perspectives on the region. For example, the online news outlet, *CITE*, provides a platform for Matabeleland-based journalists to report on local issues and events. Social media has also played a significant role in shaping constructions of Matabeleland, with hashtags such as #MatabelelandLivesMatter used to raise awareness of issues facing the region. Negative media representations of Matabeleland have significantly impacted the region's self-image and collective identity. These representations have perpetuated negative stereotypes and contributed to a sense of marginalisation and exclusion among Matabele people. It becomes imperative to then investigate how the inhabitants of Matabeleland view the issues that they face in their region and how these issues influence the identity of the region as exposed in the Community Voices Podcasts by *CITE*.

Role of Digital Media in Amplifying Subaltern Voices

In the digital age, podcasts have risen as transformative tools, amplifying marginalised voices and redefining regional identities (Theodosiadou, 2025; Chibike, 2023). The ascendancy of digital media, particularly podcasts, raises essential inquiries regarding their capacity to empower the subaltern (Sienkiewicz and Jaramillo, 2019). Therefore, this chapter aims at investigating how Community Voice Podcasts can be communicative instruments radiating plights of the subaltern in Matabeleland and how these contribute to the reconstruction of the region's identity.

While not everyone possesses the means to create a podcast (Sienkiewicz and Jaramillo, 2019) the intrinsic desire and capacity to share narratives rooted in frequently marginalised life experiences have established podcasts as a subaltern public sphere (Vrikki and Malik, 2019). This study endeavours to explore how the utilisation of podcasts can indeed empower subaltern voices in Matabeleland to engage in this transformative discourse which potentially reshapes their collective identity.

Furthermore, the storytelling potency intrinsic to podcasts (Garcia-Marin, 2022), distinguished by their emotive impact and reliance on personal narratives (Tobin and Guadagno, 2022), emerges as a key facet in humanising the marginalised region's experiences. This encompasses not only the historical injustices endured during the Gukurahundi period but also the contemporary socio-economic challenges faced by Matabeleland. The critical lens extends to how podcasts function as a counter-discourse, offering nuanced perspectives that challenge the dominant narratives perpetuated by state-controlled media.

Scholarly investigations by Eddo-Lodge (2017) and Florini (2015) emphasise the significance of podcasts in providing a platform for subaltern voices, particularly marginalised populations, within the public sphere. This aligns with the role played by platforms like the online news outlet *CITE*, which enables Matabeleland-based journalists to report on local issues and events, further amplifying the voices of marginalised communities. In this context, the examination revolves around how podcasts shed light on the intricacies of the region's plights and consequently its identity.

Analysing the role of digital media, specifically digital audios in the form of podcasts, as agents of Matabeleland's regional identity is paramount. It provides a perspective through which to understand how these media platforms empower subaltern voices to challenge deeply entrenched narratives, consequently fostering a more comprehensive understanding of the region's historical trajectory, ongoing challenges, and aspirations. In this context, platforms like *CITE* can be viewed as instrumental in advancing a fair and thorough exploration of Zimbabwean regional identities. Bottom of Form

Conceptual Framework: Victimhood and Subaltern Public Sphere

This study draws its conceptual toolkit from the concept of victimhood which within the confines of media studies is understood as the communication of claims of suffering and yearnings for recognition by an individual or group (Chouliaraki, 2020:3). Against this milieu those seen as vulnerable are perceived as victims (Honneth, 2001) attracting public empathy. Victimhood therefore plays a pivotal role in shaping the identity of a people and their need for recognition (Bloy et al. 2025). As such, this chapter grapples with the regional identity of Matabeleland against the background of the common conception that Matabeleland has been otherised in the Zimbabwean discourse. Though studies on Matabeleland and identity have been rooted in historical discourse the investigation here is grounded on contemporary discussion of social conditions in the region and how this contributes to the imaginations of Matabeleland's regional identity.

Illozouz (2017:4) aserts that victimhood encompasses the notion of suffering and subsequent emotional instability. The concept of victimhood is pivotal in shaping the regional identity of Matabeleland, as it emerges from the historical suffering endured by its residents, notably during the Gukurahundi period. This suffering has been communicated through narratives (Ndlovu 2018; Rwafa, 2012) and claims for recognition, reinforcing the region's identity as marginalised within Zimbabwe. By analysing Community Voices Podcasts, which provide a platform for these narratives, this study explores how victimhood narratives contribute to the construction of Matabeleland's regional identity, particularly beyond the dominant ethnic groups, shedding light on the ongoing struggle for recognition and legitimacy in the nation. Furthermore, it prompts critical questions about how these narratives might challenge the dominant national identity and contribute to a more inclusive understanding of Zimbabwe's diverse regions. Additionally, it raises compelling considerations regarding the role of digital media, such as podcasts, in amplifying the voices of marginalised regions and facilitating their quest for recognition within the broader national narrative.

The subaltern public sphere refers to a discursive space where marginalised and often silenced voices, such as those from Matabeleland, engage in critical dialogues, articulate their experiences, grievances, and aspirations, and challenge the dominant narratives propagated by state-controlled media and mainstream discourse. The subaltern public sphere functions as a counter-discourse, providing a platform for alternative viewpoints and fostering a sense of collective identity and resistance among marginalised communities. Historically, Matabeleland has suffered marginalisation and atrocities, notably during the Gukurahundi period, extensively documented in the scholarly literature (Rwodzi, 2019; Ndhlovu, 2019). Subaltern voices play a crucial role in challenging dominant narratives by providing first-hand accounts and narratives that humanise the suffering endured by the region. Additionally, these voices continue to highlight contemporary socio-economic challenges, drawing attention to on-going disparities and injustices (Mabhena, 2014). These narratives emerging from subaltern voices shape audience perspectives on Matabeleland's identity and aspirations for recognition and justice, aligning with the research objectives and reinforcing the importance of these voices in reshaping the regional narrative. As subaltern public sphere not only amplifies the voices of the marginalised but also operates as a catalyst for instigating social transformation and advocating for justice within the context of Matabeleland. This phenomenon compels us to critically examine the underlying power dynamics that perpetuate the marginalisation experienced by this region.

METHODOLOGY

This qualitative study utilizes in-depth interviews with 15 purposively selected audiences of Community Voices Podcasts. According to Chinyere and Val (2023) qualitative studies are aimed to interrogating social phenomena within the context they are located in. This interrogation integrates people's understandings and experiences of the social world (DeCosta et al. 2023; Skovlund et al. 2023). In equal measure, this chapter is concerned with understanding audience interpretation of Community Voice Podcasts and how they help one understand the problems faced in Matabeleland and also how the podcasts influence the imaginations of the region's identity.

15 participants that were purposively selected participated in the study. Purposive sampling allows the researcher to selected participants that were knowledgeable of the issues that were to be discussed (Campbell et al. 2020) thus rendering them important to this study. The 15 participants were drawn from the four regions making up Matabeleland region namely Bulawayo, Matabeleland South, Matabeleland North and the Midlands province. This was done to get different views from participants resident in different areas making up Matabeleland.

The 15 participants were subjected to in-depth interviews. Routledge and Hogg (2020) posit that in-depth interviews entail an in-depth discussion about a subject matter with a small number of the study's participants. The aim of the interviews was to collet participants' views about the problems faced by people in Matabeleland and how these problems contribute to the regional identity of Matabeleland.

Discussion and Analysis of Findings

Overview of the Findings

Empirical data amassed through in-depth interviews with purposively sampled participants in the study meticulously exhibit that Matabeleland is overwhelmed by a barrage of problems. The participants point to it that the Community Voices Podcasts spectacle problems in the region ranging from pollution, poor sanitation, poor service delivery, natural risks and disasters, poor education, illegal activities and lack of employment. Consequently, the participants in the study articulate that these problems in Matabeleland have been instrumental in shaping the collective identity of the region. The region is seen as a victim of historical and contemporary exclusion perpetuated by the current political climate in Zimbabwe. Thus, the region identifies as a place of suffering and a place where its occupants yearn to be saved from this suffering. The next section discuses and analyses the findings in detail.

Audiences' Perspectives of the Major Plights of Matabeleland Region

Basing on the views and perspectives of Matabeleland region is facing a plethora of predicaments. Among them is that of pollution. Participant six bemoaned that the region is languishing in dirt which has polluted major city's roads and water sources. In light of this, the participant said;

The podcasts tell us that there is a lot of pollution in Matabeleland region. Some of this pollution emanates from mines. Miners deposit chemicals in water sources which in turn cause sickness on those that drink the water. It is mind boggling at the government and local authorities say

Besides water pollution participant seven speaks of sight pollution in the major cities of Matabeleland. In this regard the participant states that;

Matabeleland region as heard in the podcasts is suffering from dirt. Look at what is happening in Bulawayo. The place is full of dirty and it is eyesore. We should not only talk about eyesore but noise pollution from mines and illegal gold miners. There is so much noise.

The participants' assumptions here attest to the fact that Matabeleland region is characterised by dirt. The fact that these issues are replete in the podcasts corroborate the argument by Ndlovu (2018) and Mpofu (2013) issues that concern Matabeleland are given space in the communicative space through social and digital media. Accordingly, digital platforms have becoming an avenue for the propagation of issues regarding the minority in Zimbabwe (Chibike, 2023). It is therefore prudent to spectacle the fact that podcasts as postulated by Vrikki and Malik, 2019 relied on person l information and views of the subaltern to reveal the challenges faced in by the subaltern. Therefore, it can be seen that Community Voices Podcasts through making use of voices of the subaltern is instrumental in bringing to the fore plights faced by Matabeleland such as pollution. In light of this he chapter argues that in civic society media is instrumental in helping add the voice of marginalised communities to the communicative space in the process helping them propagate environmental problems they face such as pollution.

Another plight picked up by participants was that the region was battling with poor sanitation. Participants point to the fact that the municipal authority was falling to address the recurring burst sewage pipes among other things. In light of this participant one states that;

The podcasts here indicate that in Matabeleland region there is poor sanitation as the discussants here speak of the burst were pipes that are not attended to. Also, the discussions in podcasts show that there is sometimes lack of refugee collection services in places such as Bulawayo.

Participant twelve added that;

Sanitation issues in these podcasts are made in reference to public toilets. Discussants in the podcasts state that the public toilets in main cities are dirty. Also, the streets are littered with garbage and human waste.

This shows that the region is suffering from governance enshrined problems which emanate from the incompetents of local authorities and the government. Matabeleland according to the study's participants is suffering from poor sanitation. In this regard civic society media is seen as subaltern media which carries voices of subaltern people from Matabeleland and their disgruntlement about poor service delivery in the region. This speaks to Ndlovu (2019) and Smith's (2017) assertion that subaltern media carries discourses form marginalised communities spelling bout their personalised sufferings. In this respect Community Voices Podcasts carried personal experience of people who have been forced to endure living in unsanitary places in the region.

Matabeleland according to the study's participants is an area troubled with natural disasters and risks. This was articulated by one participant who made reference to flooding in Beitbridge. The participants highlighted the fact that the discussants in the podcasts talk of the persisting problem of flash flooding in the city. In light of this, the participant said

BeitBridge and Hwange according to the podcasts are constantly experiencing cases of flash floods which lead to the distraction of property and sometimes crops. These are worsened by the poor drainage systems in the cities

Besides the issue of flooding another participant was of the notion that the podcasts spectacled the fact that the region was suffering from drought

The podcasts clearly tell us that the Matabeleland region suffers from tenacious drought. There is little rainfall received in these areas. Also, the temperatures are said to be very high and this affects agricultural activities. There is little crop production and in some areas there are little pastures for cattle.

This shows that natural disasters have not spared the Matabeleland region and these have caused untold suffering. The participants makes reference to flash floods in Hwange area which ae believed to be worsened by poor draining systems. They have led to the destruction of property and also agricultural products. Also, the participants flag out droughts as a persistent problem in the region. This rubber stamps the assumption made by Ndlovu and Tshuma (2021) and Mpofu et al. (2021) that Matabeleland is a troubled region. This study illuminates that the trouble in Matabeleland does not only related to its troubled past and politically consequences but also their troubles are not man made by occur naturally.

The Influence of the Plights Faced in Matabeleland to the Imagination of the Region's Identity

Participants in the study had varying views and perspectives about the collective identity of Matabeleland region based on what they heard from the podcasts. What is evident from the participants' thoughts is that the collective identity of Matabeleland is enshrined within the dilemmas that they face. Therefore, participant six states that the discussions in the podcasts enable one to come to a conclusion that Matabeleland is a region facing leadership crisis. In light of this participant six states that:

Matabeleland is facing a myriad of problems and most of these can be solved if the city fathers of respective cities in the region could step up and solve some of these problems. Also, the government is not stepping in to help the region.

Adding on was participant three who states that;

Matabeleland is a region facing problems because of incompetent leaders. What are the chiefs, elders, mayors, members of parliament doing to solve the problems in the region? I don't think we can blame anyone else besides our leaders. In this region we do not have astute leaders.

The participants' views and perspectives point to it that Matabeleland is a region which is facing a leadership crisis. This is because the region is facing challenges such as pollution and poor sanitation which can be resolved only by those at the helm of the cities and towns constituting the Matabeleland region. Since discursive constructions are integral in the identity creation (Mlambo, 2013) the participants here note that the regional identity of Matabeleland that of being a region facing a leadership crisis, is birthed by the discursive constructions of the problems faced by the region. This extruded the argument that the region is political and socially marginalised from development and political issues (Ndlovu, 2018) by arguing that this marginalisation is not only at a national level but also at a local level where local leaders fail to develop the region first. Against this milieu, the study corroborates the argument by Vrikki and Malik (2019) that new media allow for the expression of minority and peripherised peoples' views. Consequently, the chapter adds that these expressions of the minority allow for one to flesh out how they are being left out of development endeavours in the areas they are in and subsequently how this aids the imagination of their region's identity.

Participant one and nine are of the view that the fact that the region was battling a pollution problem is enough to conclude that the region is now a dirty region. In light of this they note "that the cities and towns in Matabeleland are battling pollution and dirty, so the region is a dirty region"… if the discussions in these podcast are anything to go by then Matabeleland is now a dirty region". This points to the fact that discourses within the Community Voice Podcast are a breeding ground for the construction of Matabeleland collective region. Thus, this chapter posits that digital audio story consumption is integral in the creation of a news Matabeleland regional identity Matabeleland is now known as a dirty region. This extends the argument that story telling is vital in the dissemination of ideas and emotions of a people (Garcia-Marin, 2022) by stating these stories offer not only ideas and emotions of a people but also offer cues to identity of regions in contemporary society. All in all, subaltern media is an avenue for the (re)imagination of marginalised communities' identities in Zimbabwe.

Matabeleland region has gained the identity of being a region which has been forsaken by the Gods. This was submitted by participant eight who said;

After listening to these podcasts I think the region needs divine intervention. Everything is not going accordingly. Perhaps the gods have distanced themselves from the region.

This means that the region's woes are no longer those that can be tackled only by physical means and there is need for spiritual interventions. From this the participants draw a conclusive identity of Matabeleland as a region that has been forsaken by gods. This speaks to Mhlanga (2013)'s assertion that the subalterns can use subaltern media to air their experiences which in turn contribute to their identity. Thus, basing on the participants submissions Matabeleland still remains a destressed region as argued by Mpofu et al. (2021) and Ndlovu and Tshuma (2021). This destress in this instance is blamed on spiritual forces accordingly veiling the region as one that has been forsaken by gods. Therefore, Matabeleland region is a victim of the wrath of the gods and this makes them carry the identity of a region on its knees it has been forsake by the messiah.

CONCLUSIONS AND RECOMMENDATIONS

Empirical data demonstrates the ability of civic society media in providing information for and by the subaltern into the communicative spaces in Zimbabwe. Digital audio stories in the form of podcasts produce by CITE were integral in helping audiences flesh out the major plights faced by people in the Matabeleland region. Among a host of problems in the region the study's participants noted issues of pollution, poor sanitation and natural disasters as major dilemmas enveloping the region. Additionally, the chapter exposes the fact that the participants in the study weaved cues to Matabeleland regional identity from the plights that are faced in the region. Accordingly, the Matabeleland region is identified as an unsanitary region battling leadership incompetence at the same time in need of divine intervention. Matabeleland is seen as a failed region in need of spiritual exorcism from demons haunting it. This therefore clearly demonstrates the power of digital audio stores in helping society understand plights of peripherised groups and how these plights contribute to their identity. All in all the chapter has demonstrated that that subaltern media in the form of podcasts carry discourse which show that Matabeleland is a victim of incompetent leadership, natural disasters and gods wrath and these have contributed to the coactive identity of the region. The practical implication of this therefore stems in that digital audio stories can be used to bring forth social innovations and development which is needed by the subaltern publics in Zimbabwe. As such, those that fee marginalised need to make use of digital technologies to air out their whims and needs for them to be included in the national development strategies and activities. There is still need for more study to confirm or modify the chapter's findings. To do these future studies within the realm of this study can extend the scope of this study by also paying attention to the reception of Covid19 podcasts by CITE. Away from audience studies, scholars can interrogate the actual discussions in the podcasts, through deploying a textual analysis.

REFERENCES

Alexander, J. (2021). The Noisy Silence of Gukurahundi: Truth, Recognition and Belonging. *Journal of Southern African Studies, 47*(5), 763–778.

Anderson, K. (2025). Colonialism and the Changing Control of Territories.

Bhebhe, S. (2025). Borderland's theory in indigenous ethnic community archiving. *Information Development, 41*(1), 106–119.

Bloy, L., Halperin, E., Nir, N., & Malovicki-Yaffe, N. (2025). Powerful victims: A dynamic approach to competitive victimhood between high-and low-power groups. *Group Processes & Intergroup Relations, 28*(4), 882–907.

Campbell, S., Greenwood, M., Prior, S., & Young, S. (2020). Purposive sampling: Complex or simple? Research case example. *The Journal of Nursing Research, 25*(8), 652–661.

Chauraya, E. (2025). Gender and development in Zimbabwe: A systematic literature review. *International Journal of Gender Studies in Developing Societies, 5*(2), 139–158.

Chibike, J. J. (2023). Podcasting Covid19 in indigenous languages: Interrogating audio psychology and political anthropomorphism. In Mpofu, P., Fadipe, I., & Tshabangu, T. (Eds.), *African Language Media* (pp. 112–124). Routledge.

Chibike, J. J., Muzhingi, S. A., Pikanegore, P., & Makalisa, B. (2025). Interrogating the interplay of multilingualism and multiculturalism on Lupane State University campus radio station. In Mathe, L., & Motsaathebe, G. (Eds.), *Reconceptualising Multilingualism on African Radio: Language and Identity* (pp. 111–129). Springer Nature Switzerland.

Chinyere, U., & Val, E. (2023). Qualitative Research. *Journal of Computer and Applied Science, 8*(1), 20–35.

Chouliaraki, L. (2020). Victimhood: The effective politics of vulnerability. *European Journal of Cultural Studies, 00*(0), 1–18.

DeCosta, P., Skinner, T., Sorensen, J. L., Topperzer, M., & Grawboski, D. (2023). Narrative and play based interviewing – a framework for eliciting perspectives of young children. *Qualitative Research in Psychology, 20*(19), 337–362.

Eddo-Lodge, R. (2017). *Why I'm no longer talking to white people about race.* Bloomsbury Publishing.

Eppel, S. (2004). Gukurahundi: The need for truth and reparation. In Raftopoulos, B., & Savage, T. (Eds.), *Zimbabwe: Injustice and political reconciliation* (pp. 43–62). Institute for Justice and Reconciliation.

Eppel, S. (2020). How shall we talk of bhalagwe? remembering the Gukurahundi era in Matabeleland, Zimbabwe. In. Wale, K., Gobodo-Madikizela, P and Prager, J (Eds). *Post-Conflict hauntings: transforming memories of historical trauma.*: Palgrave Macmillan. pp 259-284

Florini, S. (2015). The podcast "Chitlin' circuit": Black podcasters, alternative media, and audio enclaves. *Journal of Radio & Audio Media, 22*(2), 209–219.

Garcia-Marin, D. (2022). New media, new practices? A study of the first Spanish Podcast Community and its pioneers. *Social Sciences, 11*(7), 308.

Genocide Watch. (2021). *Genocide Watch Country Report: Zimbabwe.* Available at: https://www.genocidewatch.com/single-post/genocide-watch-country-report-zimbabwe [Accessed on 8 September 2023]

Honneth, A. (2001). Invisibility: On the epistemology of 'recognition'. *Supplements of the Aristotelian Society, 75*(1), 111–126.

Khuphe, N. (2022). Kalanga activism and the imaginations of Matabeleland in digital spaces. In Mlotshwa, K., & Ndlovu, M. (Eds.), *The idea of Matabeleland in digital spheres: Genealogies, discourses and epistemic struggles* (pp. 102–116). Rowman and Littlefield.

Liedong, T. A. (2025). Does Social Identity Matter in Political Markets? The Influence of Managerial Tribal Identity in Corporate Political Strategy Formulation. *Journal of Management Inquiry,* •••, 10564926251344217.

Mabhena, C. (2014). Ethnicity, development and the dynamics of political domination in Southern Matabeleland. *Journal of the Humanities and Social Sciences, 19*(4), 137–149.

Maseko, B. (2022). Family language policy in post-genocide Matabeleland: The case of a Ndebele family. *Southern African Linguistics and Applied Language Studies, 40*(1), 1–14.

Maseko, B., & Dhlamini, N. (2021). Language, ethnicity and the politics of exclusion in Zimbabwe. In Ncube, G., Sayi, S., & Ndebele, L. (Eds.), *Re(figuring) Ndebele cultural production in contemporary Zimbabwe* (pp. 91–113).

McKenzie, J. (2025). Digital media as sites for cultural identity development: The case of Hmong American emerging adults. *Journal of Adolescent Research, 40*(2), 296–330.

Mhlanga, B. (2013). Ethnicity or tribalism? The discursive construction of Zimbabwean national identity. *African Identities, 11*(1), 47–60.

Mhlanga, B., & Mpofu, M. (2014). The virtual parallax: Imaginations of Mthwakazi Nationalism – online discussions and calls for self-determination. In Solo, A. (Ed.), *Handbook on research on political activism in the Information Age* (pp. 129–146). IGI Global.

Mlambo, A. S. (2013). Becoming Zimbabwe or Becoming Zimbabwean: Identity, nationalism an nation building. *Africa Spectrum, 48*(1), 49–70.

Moyo, L. (2009). Constructing a home away from home: The internet, nostalgia and identity politics among Zimbabwean communities in Britain. *Journal of Global Mass Communications, 2*(1), 66–85.

Moyo, T. (2024). The politics of the unity accord of 1987 in Baya's Tomorrow's People. *International Journal Online Humanities, 10*(1), 1–22.

Mpofu, M., Moyo, C., and Sibanda, N. (2021). Popular Theatre as a Struggle for Identity and Representation in Matabeleland: 1980 to the Present. *Theatre from Rhodesia to Zimbabwe: Hegemony, Identity and a Contested Postcolony*. pp169-191.

Mpofu, S. (2013). Social media and the politics of ethnicity in Zimbabwe, *Ecquid Novi: African Journalism. Studies, 34*(1), 115–122.

Mpofu, S. (2014). Memory, national identity and freedom of expression in the Information Age: Discussing the taboo in the Zimbabwean public sphere. In Solo, A. (Ed.), *Handbook on research on political activism in the Information Age* (pp. 114–128). IGI Global.

Msindo, E. (2007). Ethnicity and nationalism in urban colonial Zimbabwe: Bulawayo, 1950-1963. *Journal of African History, 48*, 267–290.

Msipa, N. N., & Masango, M. J. (2025). Trans-generational trauma and tribal conflict among AmaNdebele and VaShona Pentecostal clergy. *African Journal of Pentecostal Studies, 2*(1), 10–31.

Ncube, B. J. (2019). *Radio Mthwakazi and the Construction of Ndebele Ethnic Identity*. Doctoral Thesis. Johannesburg: University of Johannesburg

Ncube, B. J. (2022). The communicative construction of Ndebele identity in Radio Mthwakazi. In Mlotshwa, K., & Ndlovu, M. (Eds.), *The idea of Matabeleland in digital spheres: Genealogies, discourses and epistemic struggles* (pp. 173–189). Rowman and Littlefield.

Ndhlovu, G. N. (2019). The ethnicity of development? Discourses shaping developmental politics in rural Matabeleland South, Zimbabwe. *African Journal of Social Work*, *9*(1), 35–45.

Ndlovu, E., & Chikohora, E. (2022). Gukurahundi, the Forgotten Tragedy: Examining Print Media as a Vehicle for Peace Education in the Matabeleland Region after Ethnic Violence. *Journal of Educational Sociology*, *1*(2), 1–16.

Ndlovu, M. (2018). New Media and Ndebele Hiraeth: Memory, Nostalgia and Ndebele Nationalism on Selected News Websites, *African. Journalism Studies*, *39*(4), 109–130.

Ndlovu, M. (2018). Gukurahundi, new media and the 'discourses of silence': The reproduction of the hegemonic narratives of the Matabeleland post-colonial violence on selected Zimbabwean news websites. *African Identities*, *16*(3), 275–289.

Ndlovu, M., & Tshuma, L. A. (2021). Bleeding from one generation to the next: The media and the constructions of Gukurahundi postmemories by university students in Zimbabwe. *African Studies*, *80*(3-4), 376–396.

Ndlovu, N. (2019). *The Gukurahundi "genocide": memory and justice in independent Zimbabwe*. Doctoral thesis. University of Cape Town. https://open.uct.ac.za/handle/11427/30431

Ndlovu, S. (2025). 'Inadvertent'state actors and lingo-cultural Gukurahundis in Matabeleland. In Kellier, H., Mpofu and Nkomo, D (Eds). *Civil Society in Zimbabwe* (pp. 155-172). London: Routledge

Ndlovu-Gatsheni, S. (2012). Rethinking Chimurenga and Gukurahundi in Zimbabwe: A critique of partisan national history. *African Studies Review*, *55*(3), 1–26.

Ngwenya, D. (2016). "Our branches are broken:" Using the Tree of Life healing methodology with victims of Gukurahundi in Matabeleland, Zimbabwe. *Peace and Conflict Studies*, *23*(1), 1–16.

Purnomo, T. (2025). Skin Care and Women's Identity: The Role of Digital Media in the Formation of Self-Confidence. *Journal of Economics, Business, Management. Accounting and Social Sciences*, *3*(3), 214–222.

Ranger, T. O. (1999). *Voices from the Rocks, nature, culture and history in the Matopos Hills of Zimbabwe*. James Currey.

Routledge, P and Hogg, J. L. (2020). In-depth interview, International encyclopaedia for media psychology

Rwafa, U. (2012). Representations of Matabeleland and Midlands disturbances through the documentary film Gukurahundi: A moment of madness 2007. *African Identities, 10*, 313–327.

Rwodzi, A. (2019). Economic nationalism amid ethnic disharmony in postcolonial Zimbabwe (1980-2013): A case of Matabeleland Provinces. *New Contree, 81*, 138–159.

Santos, P. (2011). *Representing conflict: An analysis of the Chronicle's coverage of the Gukuraundi conflict in Zimbabwe between 1983 and 1986.* Available at: https://www.an-analysis-of–the-gukurahundi-conflict-in-zimbabwe-philipsantos .pdf [Accessed 1 August 2023].

Sibanda, N. (2022). Cultural politics and cultural violence during Gukurahundi in Matabeleland: Politiques culturelles et violence culturelle pendant le Gukurahundi au Matabeleland. *Critical African Studies, 14*(2), 138–152.

Sibanda, N., & Dube, P. (2025). Conceptualising and revealing political resistance in Zimbabwe through (re) naming roads in Bulawayo. *South African Journal of African Languages*, •••, 1–10.

Sienkiewicz, M., & Jaramillo, D. L. (2019). Podcasting, the intimate self, and the public sphere. *Popular Communication, 17*(4), 268–272. DOI: 10.1080/15405702.2019.1667997

Skovlund, H., Morck, L. L., & Celosse-Anderson, M. (2023). The art of not being neutral in qualitative research. *Qualitative Research in Psychology, 20*(19), 363–381.

Smith, M. (2017). *Podcasting While Black: An Exploratory Study of Black Podcast Use and Podcast Production*. The University of Texas at Austin, ProQuest Dissertations Publishing.

Soto, C., Bauwens, P. J., & Smets, K. (2023). Cultural Identity Performances on Social Media: A Study of Bolivian Students. *Journalism and Media, 4*, 304–321.

Theodosiadou, S. (2025). Filtering women's identity through podcast storytelling: The case of Desert Island Discs. *RadioDoc Review, 10*(1). Advance online publication. DOI: 10.14453/rdr.1560

Tobin, S. J., & Guadagno, R. E. (2022). Why people listen: Motivations and outcomes of podcast listening. *PLoS One*, *17*(4). Advance online publication. DOI: 10.1371/journal.pone.0265806

Tshabangu, T., & Salawu, A. (2024). Alternative media, repression and the crisis state: Towards a political economy of alternative media in post-Mugabe Zimbabwe. *Journal of Asian and African Studies*, *59*(1), 172–186.

Tshuma, A. L., & Ndlovu, M. (2020). Immortalising buried memories: Photographs of the Gukurahundi online. *Journal of Genocide Research*, ●●●, 1–22.

Tshuma, B.B. (2023). A book review of Khanyile Mlotshwa and Mphathisi Ndlovu's The idea of Matabeleland in digital spaces: Genealogies, discourses and epistemic struggles, *International journal of critical diversity studies* 5(1):38-42

Tshuma, L. A., & Phiri, L. (2022). Photographing the "Nation" in the digital age: A case of Matabeleland discourses on social media platforms. In Ndlovu, M., & Mlotshwa, K. (Eds.), *The idea of Matabeleland in digital spaces: Genealogies, discourses, and epistemic struggles* (p. 241). Rowman and Littlefield.

Tshuma, L. A., and Phiri, L. (2022). Photographing the "Nation" in the Digital Age: A Case of Matabeleland Discourses on Social Media Platforms. *The Idea of Matabeleland in Digital Spaces: Genealogies, Discourses, and Epistemic Struggles*, 241.

Vrikki, P., & Malik, S. (2019). Voicing lived-experience and anti-racism: podcasting as a space at the margins for subaltern counterpublics. *Popular Communication*, *17*(4), 273–287. https://doi.org/10.1080/15405702.2019.1622116

Zheltukhina, M. A., Kislitsyana, N. N., Baranova, K. M., & Sergeeva, O. V. (2023). Identity construction and self-identification of the protagonist in the film and media discourse: Multimodal linguo-semiotic approach. *Online Journal of Communication and Media Technologies*, *13*(3), 1–18.

Chapter 12
Screens, Streams, and Society:
Examining the Intersection of Technology, Media, and Social Change

Amitava Pal
https://orcid.org/0009-0007-8934-2718
ICFAI University, India

Kavita Mathad
https://orcid.org/0000-0002-0058-9084
Indira University, Pune, India

Amruta Deshpande
https://orcid.org/0000-0001-7649-0921
Indira University, Pune, India

Kirti Nilesh Majahan
https://orcid.org/0000-0002-4839-0840
Bharati Vidyapeeth, Pune, India

Farida Virani
https://orcid.org/0000-0001-6536-5199
MET Institute of PGDM, India

Tarika Singh Sikarwar
https://orcid.org/0000-0002-9778-0589
Prestige Institute of Management and Research, Gwalior, India

Sujata Dabolkar
https://orcid.org/0000-0001-6141-3069
Government College of Arts, Science, and Commerce, India

ABSTRACT

Technology and media convergence shape social behavior, culture, education, and public debate in an era of digital immersion. This chapter critically examines its dual impact: risks of polarization, surveillance, and disinformation alongside opportunities for creativity, inclusivity, and civic engagement. Adopting an interdisciplinary lens across education, sociology, and media studies, it explores identity formation, pedagogical innovation, ethical dilemmas, and trends such as immersive media

DOI: 10.4018/979-8-3373-5307-4.ch012

and AI storytelling. By exposing inequalities in access, representation, and digital literacy, the chapter offers practical guidance for educators, policymakers, and civic leaders, advancing responsible digital citizenship and inclusive participation in media-rich societies.

INTRODUCTION

The convergence of media and technology is one of the most defining transformations of the 21st century, reshaping not only how individuals communicate, learn, and participate in society but also how they construct meaning, identity, and community in increasingly digitized environments. This phenomenon transcends mere technical innovation; it represents a profound socio-cultural shift that has reconfigured the boundaries between information, interaction, and identity. In the analog era, media operated within relatively fixed formats—print, radio, and broadcast television—each with distinct temporal and spatial limitations. Today, digital platforms such as streaming services, social media, and AI-driven content engines have collapsed these boundaries, enabling real-time, personalized, and participatory media experiences.

This convergence has democratized content creation and distribution, allowing individuals to become both consumers and producers of media. It has also redefined public discourse, as algorithmically curated feeds and viral content shape collective attention and cultural narratives. The integration of AI into media systems further accelerates this transformation, enabling predictive personalization, automated storytelling, and data-driven audience engagement. As Abdullayeva (2024) notes, this shift is not merely technological—it is epistemological, altering how knowledge is produced, validated, and circulated in society. The implications are vast, touching education, politics, entertainment, and everyday social interaction, and demanding new frameworks for media literacy, ethical governance, and inclusive access.

Historical Evolution of Media-Tech Convergence

The roots of media convergence can be traced to the gradual integration of traditional media formats—such as print, radio, and television—into digital platforms that facilitate seamless interaction, content sharing, and participatory engagement. This transformation was catalyzed by the rise of the internet, which introduced interactivity, decentralization, and the democratization of content creation. As digital platforms evolved, they began incorporating algorithmic systems, data analytics, and immersive technologies, fundamentally altering the relationship between media producers and consumers. According to Kraus et al. (2021), this shift has redefined users not as passive recipients of information but as active participants in dynamic media ecosystems.

Today, platforms like YouTube, TikTok, and Instagram exemplify this convergence. They serve not only as entertainment hubs but also as educational tools, political arenas, and identity laboratories. These platforms enable users to curate content, engage in discourse, and construct digital personas, blurring the lines between personal expression, public communication, and cultural production. The convergence of media and technology has thus created hybrid spaces where learning, activism, and storytelling coexist, driven by algorithms that shape visibility, engagement, and influence. This evolution underscores the need for critical media literacy and ethical design, as the power to shape narratives increasingly resides in the hands of both users and the technologies they interact with.

Interdisciplinary Framing: Sociology, Media Studies, Education, and Technology

To deepen the understanding of media-tech convergence and its societal implications, this section introduces key theoretical frameworks that inform the chapter's interdisciplinary analysis.

One foundational concept is Henry Jenkins' theory of Participatory Culture, which emphasizes the shift from passive media consumption to active participation, collaboration, and content creation. This framework helps explain how digital platforms empower users—especially youth—to engage in civic discourse and identity formation through media.

Manuel Castells' Network Society theory provides another lens, highlighting how digital technologies restructure social, economic, and political relationships. Castells argues that networks, rather than hierarchies, now dominate the organization of society, with implications for power distribution, access to information, and civic engagement. This theory is particularly relevant in analyzing how algorithmic systems and decentralized platforms influence public discourse and community dynamics.

Paulo Freire's Critical Pedagogy offers a transformative approach to education in the digital age—Freire advocates for dialogic learning, critical consciousness, and the empowerment of marginalized voices. In the context of media-tech integration, this framework supports the development of digital citizenship and media literacy programs that encourage learners to question dominant narratives, engage ethically with technology, and participate actively in shaping their digital environments.

Together, these frameworks provide a robust foundation for analyzing the complex interplay between technology, media, education, and society. They guide the chapter's exploration of how media-tech convergence can be harnessed for inclusive, ethical, and transformative social change.

Future Outlook: AI, Immersive Media, and Global Connectivity

Looking ahead, the convergence of artificial intelligence (AI), immersive media—including virtual reality (VR) and augmented reality (AR)—and global connectivity is poised further to embed media technologies into the fabric of everyday life. These innovations offer unprecedented opportunities for personalized learning, experiential storytelling, and cross-cultural collaboration. For instance, AI-driven platforms can tailor educational content to individual learning styles. At the same time, VR/AR environments allow users to engage with historical events, civic processes, and cultural narratives in deeply immersive ways. However, as Kraus et al. (2021) caution, these advancements also introduce complex ethical challenges, including heightened surveillance, algorithmic manipulation, and widening digital inequality. The increasing reliance on data-driven systems raises concerns about consent, transparency, and the commodification of personal information.

As these technologies become more deeply integrated into social institutions—such as education, governance, and media production—the urgency for ethical oversight, inclusive design, and critical media literacy intensifies. Media-tech convergence is not a neutral process; it actively shapes societal values, behavioral norms, and institutional structures. It influences everything from personal identity formation to public policy decisions, often amplifying existing power dynamics and cultural biases. Therefore, this chapter begins by establishing a foundational understanding of this dynamic intersection, setting the stage for a critical exploration of its multifaceted impact on education, culture, ethics, and civic life. By interrogating both the promises and perils of emerging technologies, we can better navigate the evolving media landscape and advocate for systems that empower rather than exclude.

CHAPTER OBJECTIVES

As digital technologies and media platforms increasingly shape the contours of everyday life, it becomes essential to understand their impact on education, identity, and civic engagement. This chapter sets out to explore the intersection of media and technology through a critical, interdisciplinary lens—highlighting both the transformative potential and the ethical challenges they present. The following objectives guide the chapter's inquiry into how digital ecosystems influence learning, social behavior, and public discourse, while offering pathways for inclusive and responsible media-tech integration.

- Examine how digital media ecosystems shape public discourse, cultural narratives, and social behavior.

- Analyze the integration of media technologies in education and their impact on pedagogy and learning.
- Explore the role of technology in identity formation, community building, and digital activism.
- Investigate ethical concerns around data privacy, representation, and equitable access.
- Forecast emerging trends such as AI storytelling, virtual/augmented reality, and their societal implications.
- Provide actionable strategies for educators, policymakers, and civic leaders to harness media-tech responsibly.
- Contribute to the development of digital citizenship frameworks aligned with global goals for inclusive and transformative education.

THEORETICAL FRAMEWORK

Understanding the implications of media-tech convergence requires an interdisciplinary lens that draws from media studies, sociology, education, and technology studies. Each discipline offers unique conceptual tools to analyze how digital technologies shape human experience, institutional structures, and cultural production.

Media studies provide foundational insights into how platforms influence public discourse through mechanisms such as framing, filtering, and algorithmic amplification. Song (2024) emphasizes that digital media are not neutral conduits of information; they actively construct narratives by privileging certain voices, topics, and perspectives. This framing power is amplified by algorithms that curate content based on engagement metrics, often reinforcing echo chambers and ideological polarization.

Sociology contributes a critical understanding of how media technologies mediate social norms, group dynamics, and civic participation. Sonnett (2019) argues that digital platforms have redefined the boundaries of community and identity, enabling new forms of social organization while also introducing novel pressures related to visibility, conformity, and surveillance. Social media, for instance, facilitates both solidarity and fragmentation, depending on how users engage with its affordances.

Education theory has evolved in response to the integration of digital tools, prompting a rethinking of pedagogy toward more collaborative, participatory, and learner-centered models. Partin and King (2013) highlight the importance of digital literacy and civic agency in contemporary education, arguing that students must be equipped not only to consume media but to critique and create it. This shift aligns with broader goals of transformative education, where learners are empowered to question dominant narratives and engage ethically with technology.

Technology studies interrogate the design, governance, and ethical dimensions of digital infrastructures. These perspectives emphasize that technologies are not merely tools but socio-technical systems embedded with values, assumptions, and power relations. Inclusive and equitable design is essential to ensure that media ecosystems serve diverse populations and do not perpetuate systemic biases or exclusions.

To deepen this interdisciplinary understanding, several foundational theories provide a conceptual scaffold:

- Henry Jenkins' Participatory Culture framework marks a pivotal shift from passive media consumption to active participation, collaboration, and content creation. Jenkins argues that digital platforms empower users—especially youth—to engage in civic discourse, identity formation, and cultural production. Participatory culture fosters a sense of agency and belonging, encouraging users to contribute meaningfully to shared media environments.
- Manuel Castells' Network Society theory offers a macro-level analysis of how digital technologies restructure social, economic, and political relationships. Castells posits that networks—rather than traditional hierarchies—now dominate the organization of society. This networked logic influences power distribution, access to information, and modes of civic engagement. In a network society, connectivity becomes a form of capital, and exclusion from digital networks equates to marginalization.
- Paulo Freire's Critical Pedagogy provides a transformative approach to education in the digital age. Freire advocates for dialogic learning, critical consciousness, and the empowerment of marginalized voices. Applied to media-tech convergence, this framework supports the development of digital citizenship and media literacy programs that encourage learners to interrogate dominant ideologies, resist manipulation, and engage ethically with digital tools. Freire's emphasis on praxis—reflection and action—remains vital in cultivating socially responsible media users.

Together, these frameworks offer a robust foundation for analyzing the complex interplay between technology, media, education, and society. They guide this chapter's exploration of how media-tech convergence can be harnessed for inclusive, ethical, and transformative social change. By integrating insights from multiple disciplines and grounding them in critical theory, we can better understand the opportunities and challenges posed by digital media ecosystems—and work toward building systems that reflect democratic values, cultural diversity, and human dignity.

DIGITAL MEDIA ECOSYSTEMS

Digital media ecosystems—comprising social platforms, streaming services, and algorithmic infrastructures—have become central to shaping cultural narratives, public opinion, and social behavior. These ecosystems are not passive environments; they are dynamic, data-driven systems that curate, amplify, and suppress content based on algorithmic logic, user engagement, and commercial imperatives. As such, they play a critical role in constructing the realities that individuals and communities experience online.

Influence of Platforms and Algorithms on Cultural Narratives

Social platforms like TikTok, Instagram, and YouTube have become powerful cultural intermediaries that shape public discourse, identity, and social norms. Through algorithmic curation, they decide which content and voices gain visibility, creating feedback loops that amplify dominant ideologies while marginalizing dissent (Issar, 2024; Ahmed & Miracle, 2023). This privileging of virality and monetizable content over nuance narrows cultural narratives and raises ethical concerns. For users—especially youth—these platforms act as "identity laboratories," encouraging experimentation, validation-seeking, and performative practices driven by algorithmic incentives. While they foster creativity, community, and civic engagement, they also bring risks of surveillance, conformity, and psychological stress. Addressing this duality requires media literacy and governance models that ensure transparency, inclusivity, and cultural diversity in digital spaces.

AI-Generated Content and Algorithmic Governance

The rise of AI-generated content is transforming media ecosystems, reshaping authorship, editorial control, and audience engagement. From automated journalism to synthetic influencers and deepfakes, AI enables scalable and personalized storytelling but raises concerns about authenticity, accountability, and trust (Lamprou, Dekoulou, & Kalliris, 2025). Blurred boundaries between human and machine authorship complicate credibility, especially when disclosure is lacking. At the same time, opaque algorithmic governance dictates moderation, visibility, and monetization, often reinforcing dominant narratives while marginalizing dissent (Onebunne, 2022). This lack of transparency threatens democratic discourse and individual autonomy. As AI-driven media increasingly commodifies attention, prioritizing sensationalism over nuance, media literacy and robust governance frameworks become essential to ensure that these systems serve the public interest rather than exacerbate inequality, polarization, and misinformation.

Decentralized Platforms and Transparency

In response to concerns about centralized control and lack of transparency, decentralized platforms are emerging as alternatives to traditional digital ecosystems. Built on blockchain and peer-to-peer technologies, these platforms aim to enhance user autonomy, data sovereignty, and resistance to censorship (Hisseine, Chen, & Yang, 2022). However, their promises come with challenges of scalability, governance, and inclusivity. Transparency remains a cross-cutting concern, as both users and regulators demand more precise explanations of how algorithms function, whose interests they serve, and what values are embedded in their design (Gorwa & Garton Ash, 2020).

Digital media ecosystems are potent tools for shaping culture and public discourse, but they must be governed with transparency, accountability, and ethical foresight. As AI and decentralized technologies advance, the task of ensuring they serve the public good becomes even more urgent. Sports media has become a vivid example of this convergence. Streaming platforms and social media now act as primary arenas where fans, athletes, and organizations co-create narratives, extending beyond traditional broadcasts. From grassroots clubs live-streaming matches on YouTube to elite leagues deploying AI-driven highlight reels, digital ecosystems reshape how sporting culture is consumed and produced. Fan communities on platforms like Twitter/X and Discord operate as participatory spaces for identity, solidarity, and activism, while fantasy leagues and esports illustrate how gamified engagement blurs the lines between spectatorship, play, and civic discourse.

Some leading companies are beginning to set important precedents in this direction. Salesforce, for instance, has developed the *Einstein Trust Layer*, a governance framework that integrates privacy, security, and responsible AI deployment. It incorporates mechanisms such as dynamic grounding, secure data retrieval, data masking, and toxicity detection, while enforcing a zero-data retention policy with third-party large language models (LLMs). These measures ensure that generative AI systems operate ethically and without compromising user trust (Salesforce, 2024a; Salesforce, 2024b).

Similarly, Apple has institutionalized privacy-by-design principles across its ecosystem. Through practices such as minimal data collection, on-device processing, and robust consent mechanisms, Apple reinforces user autonomy. Its *Privacy Governance framework* includes oversight by a cross-functional Privacy Steering Committee and external audits, complemented by publicly available *Transparency Reports* on government data requests (Apple, 2024a; Apple, 2024b).

In the journalism sector, The New York Times continues to safeguard editorial integrity in an era of AI adoption. Its *Guidelines on Integrity* and *Ethical Journalism Handbook* emphasize accountability, accuracy, and independence, ensuring that AI use in reporting upholds public trust (The New York Times, 2024a; The New York Times, 2024b).

The Financial Times has also shown leadership in advancing responsible AI governance. Partnering with Deloitte and IBM, it has published reports on ethical risk management, transparency, and trust-building in generative AI adoption, especially in high-stakes contexts where algorithmic decisions carry significant societal impact (Financial Times, 2024a; Financial Times, 2024b).

Together, these initiatives represent a broader industry shift toward embedding ethical foresight and accountability into digital media ecosystems. As AI, blockchain, and other decentralized technologies continue to evolve, such models provide valuable blueprints for building platforms that uphold democratic values, foster inclusivity, and strengthen public trust.

EDUCATION AND LEARNING IN A MEDIA-RICH WORLD

The integration of media technologies into education has transformed traditional pedagogical models, creating dynamic, participatory, and personalized learning environments. In today's classrooms—both physical and virtual—students engage with digital tools not only to consume content but also to create, collaborate, and critically reflect. This shift reflects a broader redefinition of learning, where media is not peripheral but central to how knowledge is constructed and shared.

Social Media as Learning Tools

Social media platforms have emerged as powerful tools for educational engagement, transforming traditional classroom dynamics into interactive, participatory learning environments. Their integration into pedagogy supports a range of instructional strategies, including collaborative learning, peer-to-peer feedback, real-time interaction, and multimodal expression. Platforms such as Twitter, YouTube, and Instagram are no longer confined to entertainment or social networking; they are increasingly being repurposed as educational resources that align with diverse cognitive and affective learning goals. Demir (2024) developed a comprehensive taxonomy of social media for learning, illustrating how these platforms can be strategically mapped to Bloom's taxonomy and other instructional frameworks to support knowledge acquisition, critical thinking, and creative production.

For example, Twitter can be used to facilitate concise academic discussions, promote digital citizenship, and encourage reflective microblogging. YouTube enables flipped classroom models, where students engage with video lectures and tutorials at their own pace, freeing up classroom time for deeper inquiry and application.

Instagram, with its visual storytelling capabilities, supports project-based learning and digital portfolios, allowing students to document and share their learning journeys. These tools activate student consciousness, cognition, and creativity, fostering higher-order thinking and digital fluency.

Moreover, social media platforms cultivate a sense of community and co-authorship, where learners are not just passive recipients of information but active contributors to knowledge ecosystems. They provide opportunities for authentic audience engagement, cross-cultural exchange, and the development of digital identities. However, the educational use of social media also requires critical awareness of issues such as data privacy, platform bias, and screen time management. Educators must therefore approach these tools with intentionality, embedding them within pedagogical frameworks that prioritize equity, ethics, and meaningful learning outcomes.

Edutainment and Gamification in Pedagogy

Edutainment—the fusion of educational content with entertainment—has emerged as a compelling strategy to enhance student motivation, engagement, and retention in both formal and informal learning environments. By integrating storytelling, humor, music, and interactive media into instructional design, edutainment transforms passive learning into an immersive experience that resonates with learners across age groups and disciplines. This approach is efficient in capturing the attention of digital-native students who are accustomed to multimedia-rich environments and expect learning to be both meaningful and enjoyable.

Closely aligned with edutainment is gamification, which involves the application of game mechanics—such as points, badges, leaderboards, challenges, and feedback loops—in non-game contexts like education. Gamification leverages intrinsic and extrinsic motivators to foster persistence, curiosity, and goal-oriented behavior. Zeybek and Saygı (2024), in their systematic review, demonstrate that gamification is effective across a wide range of subjects, including mathematics, science, language learning, and social studies. Their findings highlight that the success of gamified learning environments depends on the thoughtful integration of game elements with clear learning objectives, adaptive feedback mechanisms, and meaningful progression systems.

Platforms such as Kahoot!, Classcraft, and Duolingo exemplify the power of gamification in education. Kahoot! Transforms quizzes into competitive, real-time games that promote active recall and peer interaction. Classcraft gamifies classroom management and behavior, turning students into characters in a collaborative narrative that rewards positive actions and academic achievements. Duolingo uses streaks, levels, and rewards to encourage daily language practice, making learning habitual and enjoyable. Sports provide a natural entry point for gamification and edutainment. Fantasy sports leagues, fitness apps, and sport-based simulations demonstrate how playful competition drives engagement and learning. For instance, platforms like Strava or Zwift merge physical activity with digital gamification, reinforcing persistence and goal-setting—skills transferable to academic and civic contexts. Similarly, sport-themed classroom tools can enhance participation by linking cognitive learning to physical, team-oriented metaphors, showing how sports and technology converge to support motivation, resilience, and collaboration.

Beyond engagement, gamification and edutainment also support cognitive development and social-emotional learning. They encourage learners to take risks, learn from failure, and develop resilience—skills that are essential in both academic and real-world contexts. Moreover, when designed inclusively, these approaches can accommodate diverse learning styles and needs, making education more accessible and equitable.

However, educators must remain mindful of potential pitfalls, such as over-reliance on extrinsic rewards, superficial engagement, and the risk of excluding learners who may not respond positively to competitive environments. To maximize impact, edutainment and gamification should be embedded within pedagogically sound frameworks that prioritize learner autonomy, reflection, and meaningful interaction.

Media Literacy and Critical Engagement

In a media-saturated world, media literacy has emerged as a foundational skill essential for navigating the complexities of digital communication, information ecosystems, and civic life. It encompasses the ability to access, analyze, evaluate, and create media content responsibly, empowering individuals to engage critically with the messages they encounter across platforms. Wakefield (2011) emphasized that media literacy education fosters social responsibility, equipping students to become active, informed participants in a technological society. This involves not only understanding how media content is constructed but also recognizing the intentions behind it, the power structures it reflects, and the potential consequences of its dissemination.

Building on this foundation, Cole (2024) argued that media literacy is central to critical engagement, particularly in an era marked by misinformation, algorithmic manipulation, and ideological polarization. Media-literate individuals are better equipped to question sources, detect bias, and resist manipulation, enabling them to participate meaningfully in democratic processes. This includes evaluating the credibility of news, understanding the influence of algorithms on visibility and discourse, and contributing to media environments through ethical content creation.

Moreover, media literacy is not a static skill—it evolves alongside technological innovation. As AI-generated content, deepfakes, and immersive media become more prevalent, the scope of media literacy must expand to include algorithmic awareness, data ethics, and platform literacy. Learners must be able to interrogate not just the content they consume, but the systems that deliver it. This calls for educational frameworks that integrate media literacy across disciplines, fostering interdisciplinary thinking and ethical reflection.

In this context, media literacy becomes a tool for empowerment and equity. It enables marginalized voices to challenge dominant narratives, promotes inclusive representation, and supports civic agency in digital spaces. By cultivating media-literate citizens, educators and institutions can help build resilient societies capable of engaging thoughtfully and ethically with the evolving media landscape.

Digital Learning and Civic Education

Digital learning environments are increasingly being used to promote civic education and democratic participation. White et al. (2023) argue that embedding civic reasoning and problem-solving into curricula allows digital tools to prepare students for critical and ethical engagement in a connected society. Media technologies thus become more than instructional aids; they act as catalysts for interactive, inclusive, and transformative pedagogy.

Practical examples show how this shift is already underway. Kahoot!, a game-based learning platform, uses quizzes, challenges, and real-time feedback to foster motivation and retention, with studies showing significant increases in both engagement and knowledge retention (SocialTargeter, 2025). Similarly, Duolingo combines gamification with civic contribution by allowing learners to practice languages while contributing to real-world translation tasks (European Commission, 2024). In the sphere of media literacy, initiatives such as the Google News Initiative—through collaborations with PBS NewsHour's Student Reporting Labs and the News Literacy Project—help young people develop journalistic ethics and civic dialogue skills across classrooms (Google News Initiative, 2021). Meanwhile, campaigns like Penplusbytes' MIL in Elections in Ghana empower communities to counter misinformation and strengthen democratic processes (Penplusbytes, 2025).

These initiatives demonstrate how thoughtfully designed digital platforms can enhance learning while cultivating informed, critical, and participatory citizens. By embedding gamification, media literacy, and civic engagement into educational frameworks, media technologies offer a blueprint for preparing students not only for academic success but also for active roles in democracy.

IDENTITY, COMMUNITY, AND BELONGING

Digital technologies have become central to how individuals—especially youth—construct identities, form communities, and experience belonging. Social media platforms serve as dynamic spaces for self-presentation, role exploration, and feedback, allowing adolescents to experiment with different aspects of their identity and receive validation from peers and online audiences. These interactions contribute to a clearer sense of self and facilitate the development of personal and social identities in ways that were previously limited to face-to-face contexts.

Technology and Youth Identity Formation

Social media functions as a "digital mirror" for adolescents, shaping self-concept through self-presentation, social comparison, and feedback loops (Pérez-Torres, 2024; Melonashi, 2019). These platforms allow curated self-expression and experimentation with identity, but also expose youth to psychological pressures. Constant exposure to idealized lifestyles fuels comparison and feelings of inadequacy, while the pursuit of likes and visibility can heighten anxiety, cyberbullying, and tensions between online and offline selves (Sahare, 2024). Algorithms amplify sensational content, incentivizing risky or exaggerated behaviors that may distort healthy development.

Beyond individual identity, digital platforms foster communities of belonging around shared interests, cultures, and causes. These spaces provide solidarity, visibility, and activism opportunities, especially for marginalized groups (Allen, 2021; Hondros et al., 2023). However, their sustainability depends on governance and design—algorithms that privilege virality can erode cohesion, while intentional, inclusive spaces can nurture dialogue, empathy, and civic engagement. To balance risks and opportunities, digital wellness education, media literacy, and platform accountability are vital for supporting authentic identity development and resilient online communities.

For youth and marginalized groups, sports communities online are powerful spaces of identity expression and belonging. Digital fandom offers not only entertainment but also solidarity, activism, and cultural pride. Athletes increasingly use platforms like Instagram and TikTok to advocate for social justice, mental health, and inclusion, connecting personal identity with broader civic causes. Grassroots athletes, often excluded from mainstream media, leverage digital spaces to showcase talent, gain visibility, and challenge traditional hierarchies in sport. Thus, sports-oriented media spaces become laboratories for identity, resilience, and participatory culture.

Technology and Marginalized Groups

For marginalized communities, digital platforms have become vital spaces for visibility, representation, and empowerment, offering opportunities to challenge dominant narratives and reclaim agency in public discourse. These platforms allow individuals and groups who have historically been excluded from mainstream media to share their stories, build solidarity, and engage in advocacy. Culturally responsive digital initiatives, such as community-based research partnerships and localized content creation, have shown significant promise in addressing systemic inequities and promoting inclusive participation (Palmer, 2025). These efforts recognize that technology must be designed not as a one-size-fits-all solution, but as a context-sensitive tool that reflects the lived experiences, cultural values, and linguistic diversity of underrepresented populations.

Such initiatives often involve co-design processes, where communities actively shape the development of digital tools and platforms to meet their specific needs. This participatory approach ensures that technologies are not only accessible but also meaningful and empowering. For example, platforms that support indigenous language preservation, LGBTQIA+ youth networks, or rural education hubs demonstrate how digital spaces can be tailored to foster belonging and resilience.

Grimmage (2025) underscores the importance of fostering digital communities within educational contexts, particularly for marginalized students. When students see their identities and experiences reflected in digital learning environments, it enhances their sense of belonging, which in turn improves retention, engagement, and academic success. These communities provide safe spaces for dialogue, mentorship, and collaborative learning, helping students navigate challenges related to discrimination, isolation, or cultural erasure.

However, the potential of digital platforms to empower marginalized groups depends on inclusive design, ethical governance, and equitable access. Without intentional safeguards, these spaces can also reproduce harm through algorithmic bias, surveillance, or exclusionary content moderation practices. Therefore, educators, technologists, and policymakers must work together to build digital ecosystems that are inclusive by design, rooted in justice, and responsive to the diverse realities of the communities they serve.

Online Activism and Civic Engagement

Digital platforms have become vital spaces for youth participation in civic life, enabling grassroots organizing, cyber activism, and collective mobilization around issues such as climate justice, racial equity, and gender rights (Chauhan, 2024). Through hashtags, livestreams, petitions, and collaborative content creation, young people connect personal values with collective action, reinforcing agency, belonging, and political consciousness. These platforms democratize access to civic spaces once limited by geography or institutional barriers, allowing youth to express, experiment, and engage as citizens and change-makers.

At the same time, technology introduces risks: algorithmic bias can suppress marginalized voices, while design choices often prioritize engagement over well-being, exposing youth to harassment, misinformation, or performative activism. The pressure to maintain visible, politically engaged identities can also result in stress or burnout. Addressing these challenges requires inclusive design, transparent governance, equitable access, and critical media literacy to ensure that digital spaces foster genuine belonging and resilience.

Recent initiatives highlight this potential. Google.org has invested over €13 million in media literacy and digital safety programs for underserved youth in Europe (Google, 2025). Hopelab's research underscores the role of authentic digital creators in supporting identity and mental health among LGBTQIA+ and marginalized communities (Hopelab, 2025). Platforms like Tchop™ are designing youth-centric communities focused on co-creation, privacy, and shared values, while UNESCO and UNICEF advocate policies that promote civic engagement, inclusion, and digital citizenship (UNESCO, 2025; UNICEF, 2020). Collectively, these efforts show how ethically designed platforms can transform digital spaces into empowering arenas for identity formation, community-building, and civic empowerment.

ETHICS, EQUITY, AND ACCESS

As digital media technologies become increasingly embedded in everyday life, ethical concerns surrounding their design, deployment, and impact have grown more urgent. These concerns are especially pronounced in areas such as data privacy, algorithmic bias, representation, and equitable access. Media ecosystems are not neutral—they reflect the values, priorities, and power structures of their creators, often reinforcing existing inequalities and introducing new forms of exclusion.

Ethical Challenges in Digital Media

The ethical implications of digital technologies are challenging traditional frameworks of beneficence, justice, and respect for persons, which struggle to adapt to decentralized, data-driven environments (Light, Panicker, Abrams, & Huh-Yoo, 2024). Unlike conventional contexts where consent and autonomy are well-defined, digital platforms blur boundaries of agency, ownership, and participation. The rapid rise of AI, biometric tracking, and behavioral analytics has outpaced ethical safeguards, leaving users vulnerable to surveillance, profiling, and manipulation.

One central dilemma is the commodification of user data, collected and monetized often without meaningful consent. This undermines autonomy and creates risks of discrimination. Even everyday technologies such as email or social media complicate confidentiality and professional boundaries for educators, therapists, and healthcare providers (Klaus & Hartshorne, 2015). Algorithmic governance adds further complexity, as opaque systems shape visibility, moderation, and monetization with little transparency or accountability.

Addressing these issues requires interdisciplinary ethical frameworks that reflect the realities of digital life. Rethinking consent, embedding transparency in design, and ensuring equity must be core priorities. Just as importantly, fostering ethical literacy will empower users to critically engage with the technologies that structure their daily lives.

Data Privacy and Surveillance

Mass surveillance and data harvesting have become normalized features of contemporary digital platforms, embedded into the architecture of everyday technologies such as social media, search engines, mobile apps, and smart devices. Corporations and governments routinely collect vast amounts of personal data—ranging from browsing habits and location history to biometric identifiers—often without meaningful consent or user awareness. As Anderson (2025) notes, these practices are frequently obscured by opaque terms of service and algorithmic complexity, making it difficult for users to understand how their data is being used, shared, or monetized.

This erosion of transparency and autonomy poses significant ethical and psychological risks. When individuals are constantly monitored, their behavior may be subtly shaped by the awareness of surveillance, leading to self-censorship, conformity, and a diminished sense of agency. The commodification of personal data also raises concerns about digital exploitation, where users become products in attention economies driven by targeted advertising and predictive analytics.

The American Psychological Association (APA, 2024) has raised alarms about the impact of these practices on youth and vulnerable populations, calling for structural reforms in platform design. The APA emphasizes that many digital platforms are engineered to maximize engagement through persuasive design techniques—such as infinite scroll, push notifications, and algorithmic nudging—that can exploit developmental vulnerabilities in children and adolescents. These features not only compromise privacy but also contribute to issues like screen addiction, anxiety, and reduced attention spans.

To address these challenges, the APA advocates for youth-centered design principles, age-appropriate privacy protections, and greater regulatory oversight. Ethical platform design must prioritize informed consent, data minimization, and user empowerment, ensuring that individuals—especially minors—retain control over their digital identities and experiences. Moreover, public awareness campaigns and digital literacy education are essential to equip users with the knowledge and tools to navigate surveillance-driven environments critically and responsibly.

Digital Divide and Equitable Access

Access to technology remains uneven across socioeconomic, geographic, and demographic lines, reinforcing barriers to educational equity and civic participation. The digital divide—marked by disparities in devices, internet connectivity, and digital literacy—deepens existing inequalities. Hohlfeld et al. (2008) showed that low-SES schools often lack ICT infrastructure and instructional support, limiting students' ability to develop essential digital skills. Similarly, Moore, Vitale, and Stawinoga (2018) noted that limited device access hinders academic progress and restricts participation in digital learning and collaboration. These disadvantages intersect with race, disability, and rural isolation, compounding exclusion and constraining upward mobility.

The divide also extends to civic life, where inadequate access curtails participation in online discourse, digital activism, and public services—undermining democratic engagement. Addressing this requires systemic interventions: infrastructure investment, affordable device provision, and robust digital literacy programs. Ensuring equitable access is not simply a technical challenge but a matter of social justice, demanding inclusive policies and long-term commitment.

Representation and Inclusion in Media Ecosystems

Representation in media is not merely a matter of visibility—it is fundamentally about power, participation, and narrative control. Who gets to be seen, heard, and centered in media spaces directly influences how societies understand identity, belonging, and legitimacy. Hall, Evans, and Nixon (2013) argue that media ecosystems often reflect and reinforce dominant cultural narratives, marginalizing or misrepresenting voices from underrepresented communities. These narratives are not neutral; they are shaped by historical power dynamics, institutional biases, and commercial imperatives that privilege specific identities while rendering others invisible or stereotyped.

In this context, inclusive media design becomes a critical intervention. It requires more than token representation—it demands the intentional inclusion of diverse perspectives, lived experiences, and cultural expressions in both content and platform architecture. Inclusive design challenges reductive portrayals and works to ensure that all users can see themselves reflected in digital spaces in ways that are authentic, affirming, and empowering. This includes not only racial and ethnic diversity but also representation across gender identities, sexual orientations, abilities, languages, and socio-economic backgrounds.

The American Psychological Association's Inclusive Language Guide (2023) offers a valuable framework for fostering respectful and equitable communication. It emphasizes the importance of using culturally sensitive terminology, avoiding deficit-based language, and recognizing the evolving nature of identity categories. Such guidance is essential in media production, journalism, education, and platform governance, where language choices can either reinforce stigma or promote dignity and inclusion.

Moreover, representation is deeply tied to participation. True inclusion means not only being depicted but also having a voice in shaping the narratives, policies, and technologies that define digital life. This calls for diversity in media leadership, community co-creation, and platform accountability. When marginalized communities are empowered to tell their own stories and influence media systems, the result is a richer, more just cultural landscape that reflects the full spectrum of human experience.

Algorithmic Accountability and Media Ethics

As AI systems increasingly mediate access to information, shape public discourse, and influence decision-making, the issue of algorithmic accountability has become central to digital media ethics. Operating with limited transparency, algorithms in search engines, social media feeds, and content moderation tools determine what content is amplified or suppressed—often without public oversight. This opacity allows bias to go unchecked, distorting discourse, reinforcing stereotypes, and spreading misinformation (Onebunne, 2022). The consequences are far-reaching, from marginalizing dissent to entrenching inequality and undermining democratic values. To counter these risks, Chen and Chekam (2021) call for embedding fairness, transparency, and human-centered principles into system design and governance, supported by collaboration between technologists, ethicists, educators, and policymakers.

Addressing accountability requires more than technical fixes. It demands cultural and structural change—transparent data practices, participatory design, equitable infrastructure, and regulation that protects vulnerable groups. Companies and organizations are beginning to model such practices. Salesforce has established an Office of Ethical and Humane Use of Technology and launched the Einstein Trust

Layer for responsible AI governance, while Apple emphasizes privacy-by-design through on-device processing and differential privacy (AI Magazine, 2025). Global initiatives such as UNICEF and ITU's Giga program have connected over 2.1 million students in underserved schools to affordable internet (World Economic Forum, 2023). In the U.S., nonprofits like EveryoneOn and human-I-T address access gaps by providing low-cost internet, refurbished devices, and literacy training (Allconnect, 2024). Meanwhile, Nielsen's Data for Good® program promotes inclusive media representation through partnerships with nonprofits, and IBM encourages AI developers to maintain ethical accountability records and feedback loops.

Collectively, these efforts highlight how embedding equity, transparency, and inclusion into digital ecosystems can foster trust and ensure that technologies serve public interests. Building truly accountable media systems requires centering human dignity and democratic values so that digital platforms empower rather than exclude.

FUTURE TRENDS AND EMERGING TECHNOLOGIES

As media and technology continue to evolve, emerging innovations such as artificial intelligence (AI), virtual reality (VR), augmented reality (AR), and immersive storytelling are reshaping how individuals engage with information, culture, and society. These technologies are not only transforming entertainment and communication but also redefining education, civic participation, and social interaction.

Virtual and Augmented Reality in Education and Engagement

Virtual and augmented reality (VR/AR) are transforming education and civic life by creating immersive environments that heighten engagement, empathy, and knowledge retention. These technologies enable learners to experience abstract concepts through simulation and visualization—bridging theory with practice. As Wang and Huang (2025) note, VR/AR can personalize instruction, adapt to diverse learning needs, and foster deeper cognitive engagement. Learners can, for instance, walk through historical reconstructions, manipulate molecular structures in 3D, or conduct virtual experiments—experiences often inaccessible in traditional classrooms.

Beyond education, immersive media enriches civic spaces by simulating democratic processes, historical events, and social justice scenarios. Virtual town halls, interactive policy simulations, and AR-enhanced exhibits encourage participatory engagement while fostering empathy and civic responsibility. Importantly, VR/AR also expand access: for students with disabilities or those in remote areas, immersive tools designed with universal design principles can reduce barriers and support inclusive learning.

Yet these opportunities are accompanied by ethical and pedagogical challenges. Issues such as data privacy, digital fatigue, content bias, and unequal access must be addressed to prevent deepening divides. Developing ethical frameworks, inclusive content, and critical media literacy programs will be essential for ensuring VR/AR serve learners equitably.

Ultimately, VR and AR are not merely technological enhancements but transformative pedagogical tools. When deployed responsibly, they can deepen learning, broaden civic participation, and contribute to more inclusive educational futures.

AI-Driven Storytelling and Content Creation

Artificial intelligence (AI) is fundamentally reshaping the creation, distribution, and reception of stories across media and communication landscapes. AI-driven tools can now generate full narratives, personalize content delivery, and analyze audience engagement in real time. These capabilities are transforming fields such as journalism, education, entertainment, and marketing by enabling scalable, adaptive, and data-driven storytelling. From automated news reports and interactive fiction to AI-generated scripts and synthetic influencers, the creative potential of AI continues to expand rapidly.

Yet, as Lamprou, Dekoulou, and Kalliris (2025) caution, this transformation raises pressing socio-ethical questions. Authorship, authenticity, and editorial integrity are challenged when machines take on creative roles. The risks of bias, manipulation, and diminished human oversight are particularly acute in systems trained on datasets embedded with historical inequalities or cultural stereotypes. Left unchecked, AI-generated media can spread misinformation, amplify dominant ideologies, and erode public trust.

As AI becomes more deeply integrated into storytelling ecosystems, distinctions between creator and consumer, fiction and reality, and editorial judgment and algorithmic optimization blur. This makes transparency, accountability, and human-in-the-loop oversight essential. In journalism, AI-generated articles should be clearly labeled and editorially reviewed; in education, AI-driven materials must serve pedagogical goals without reinforcing bias; in entertainment, creators must navigate the ethical implications of deepfakes and synthetic characters on audience perception.

Ultimately, integrating AI into media requires a multidisciplinary approach that combines innovation with ethical reflection, cultural sensitivity, and regulatory foresight. Embedding human-centered values into AI systems ensures that the power of artificial intelligence enhances creativity while preserving the integrity of public discourse and cultural expression.

Human-Machine Collaboration and Civic Technology

Emerging technologies are reshaping the landscape of civic engagement by enabling novel forms of human-machine collaboration that enhance participatory governance and community problem-solving. Artificial Intelligence (AI), in particular, is playing a transformative role in public policy through AI-assisted decision-making systems that help governments analyze complex data, simulate policy outcomes, and incorporate diverse stakeholder perspectives. UNESCO emphasizes the importance of inclusive and human-centered AI policy design, advocating for participatory processes that ensure marginalized voices are heard and represented in decision-making. These processes mobilize collective intelligence and foster democratic legitimacy in the deployment of AI technologies. In parallel, citizen science platforms powered by data analytics are democratizing knowledge production and policy influence. Citizen-generated data (CGD), especially in areas like gender equity and environmental monitoring, fills critical gaps left by traditional data sources and empowers communities to co-create solutions. UNESCO and the United Nations Statistics Division have recognized CGD as a legitimate and essential data source for inclusive governance, highlighting its role in amplifying underrepresented voices and informing more equitable policy frameworks. These platforms not only enhance transparency and accountability but also align with the Sustainable Development Goals (SDGs) by promoting inclusive development and digital citizenship.

Together, these innovations reflect a broader shift toward participatory digital governance, where technology serves as a bridge between citizens and institutions. They embody the principles outlined in global frameworks such as UNESCO's Inclusive Policy Lab and the UN's 2030 Agenda, which call for ethical, inclusive, and rights-based approaches to digital transformation.

Risks and Ethical Considerations

While future technologies promise transformative benefits, they also introduce profound risks. Challenges such as algorithmic bias, surveillance, misinformation, and unequal access underscore the need for ethical design, inclusive policy, and critical media literacy. As Kraus et al. (2021) emphasize, digital transformation must be guided by human-centered values and interdisciplinary oversight to ensure that technological progress genuinely serves the public good.

Emerging trends in artificial intelligence (AI), virtual reality (VR), augmented reality (AR), and immersive storytelling illustrate this dual potential. Companies like VictoryXR and Axon Park are pioneering new educational frontiers by building digital twin campuses and interactive simulations. VictoryXR's VXRLabs and 3D

Spatial AI tools empower educators to design experiential lessons, while Axon Park harnesses Unreal Engine and AI to personalize learning across diverse fields, from medicine and engineering to space science (VictoryXR, 2025; Axon Park, 2025). Similarly, ENGAGE XR offers a secure and collaborative platform for immersive education, enabling virtual field trips, science experiments, and AI-powered content creation. By integrating tools from MetaAI and OpenAI, ENGAGE XR allows learners to interact with intelligent avatars and simulations, boosting retention and motivation (ENGAGE XR, 2025).

In storytelling, platforms such as LILI—developed by MIT's Open Documentary Lab—demonstrate how ethical AI can reshape narrative creation. LILI is a hybrid narrative game that combines deepfakes, verification tools, and algorithmic filters to interrogate themes of surveillance and censorship, offering a model for politically engaged, ethically grounded storytelling (MIT Open Doc Lab, 2025). AI-driven entertainment platforms are also reimagining audience participation, using generative tools to personalize story arcs and develop interactive characters that evolve based on user feedback and preferences (Analytics Insight, 2025; AI Art Magazine, 2025).

Civic technology represents another area of transformation. Initiatives from the OECD and MIT Center for Constructive Communication highlight how AI, blockchain, and VR can strengthen citizen participation, lower barriers to engagement, and foster more inclusive governance. These frameworks emphasize transparency and ethical design, ensuring that automation amplifies rather than undermines human agency (OECD, 2025; Overney, 2025).

At the governance level, organizations such as Deloitte and the National Academy of Medicine (NAM) are working to mitigate ethical risks. Deloitte's *Ethical Technology Report* (2024) calls for stronger transparency, data provenance, and responsible AI deployment, while NAM's 2025 workshops focus on aligning innovation with societal values and sustaining public trust.

Taken together, these examples illustrate how emerging technologies—when guided by ethical governance, inclusive design, and interdisciplinary collaboration—can empower learners, expand civic engagement, and enrich cultural narratives. They offer a blueprint for leveraging digital innovation to build equitable, participatory, and culturally vibrant futures.

ACTIONABLE PATHWAYS FOR CHANGE

Educational Frameworks for Digital Citizenship

To foster responsible participation in digital society, educational institutions must adopt comprehensive frameworks for digital citizenship. These frameworks should go beyond technical skills to include ethical reasoning, civic discourse, and critical media analysis. The National Academy of Education and the National Association for Media Literacy Education emphasize integrating civic reasoning across disciplines to support youth civic voice and digital responsibility (Kahne et al., 2024). UNESCO's global guidelines further advocate for embedding global citizenship education into digital learning environments, aligning with SDG 4.7 to promote sustainable development and cultural diversity (UNESCO, 2024).

Civic Engagement through Media Literacy

Media literacy is increasingly recognized as a core competency for civic engagement in participatory democracies. It equips individuals with the ability to critically evaluate media, engage in informed discourse, and participate in digital activism. Mihailidis and Thevenin (2013) argue that media literacy fosters political agency and participatory citizenship by enabling users to navigate complex media landscapes (Mihailidis & Thevenin, 2013). Similarly, Martens and Hobbs (2015) found that media literacy education significantly enhances students' intent toward civic engagement by improving their news analysis and information-seeking behaviors.

Future Outlook: Cross-Sector Collaboration and Community Innovation

The future of media-tech for social transformation lies in cross-sector collaboration and community-driven innovation. Partnerships between education, industry, civil society, and government can accelerate digital inclusion and innovation. Studies show that such collaborations foster social innovation by combining diverse resources and perspectives (Pache et al., 2022). Community-driven models, such as peer mentorship and localized digital skills programs, have proven effective in bridging digital divides and empowering marginalized groups (Digitunity, 2025)

Global-Local Responsiveness in Media-Tech Policy

Effective media-tech policy must balance global integration with local responsiveness. This dual approach ensures that digital strategies are scalable while remaining sensitive to cultural, regulatory, and infrastructural differences. Du et al. (2024) highlight how digitalization enables multinational enterprises to navigate global-local pressures through innovation and collaborative governance. The Handbook of Global Media and Communication Policy further underscores the need for inclusive, context-aware frameworks that reflect both global standards and local realities (Mansell & Raboy, 2014)

DISCUSSION POINTS

The convergence of media and technology presents a paradoxical landscape—one that simultaneously empowers and challenges society. On one hand, digital platforms offer unprecedented opportunities for creativity, civic engagement, and personalized learning. On the other hand, they amplify risks such as algorithmic bias, surveillance, and digital exclusion. This duality demands a nuanced understanding of how media-tech ecosystems shape identity, education, and public discourse. For instance, while social media fosters youth expression and community-building, it also subjects users to pressures of idealized self-presentation and misinformation. Similarly, AI-driven storytelling and immersive media can revolutionize pedagogy and civic participation, but they require ethical oversight to prevent manipulation and inequity. The chapter's interdisciplinary approach—drawing from sociology, media studies, education, and technology—underscores the need for collaborative governance, inclusive design, and critical media literacy. As we look toward the future, the challenge lies not only in innovating but in ensuring that innovation serves the public good. This calls for robust educational frameworks, community-driven initiatives, and policies that are both globally informed and locally responsive. Ultimately, the discussion invites stakeholders to rethink pedagogy, digital citizenship, and social transformation in ways that are ethical, equitable, and future-ready.

FUTURE ROADMAP: STRATEGIC DIRECTIONS FOR MEDIA-TECH AND SOCIAL TRANSFORMATION

As media and technology continue to evolve at an unprecedented pace, it is essential to move beyond analysis and toward strategic action. The following roadmap outlines forward-looking directions for harnessing media-tech convergence to promote equity, inclusion, and civic engagement. Designed for educators, policymakers, and civic leaders, this roadmap emphasizes collaboration, innovation, and responsiveness to both global trends and local realities. It serves as a guide for shaping ethical, inclusive, and transformative digital futures.

Strengthening Cross-Sector Collaboration

- Foster partnerships between educators, technologists, policymakers, and community organizations to co-design inclusive digital ecosystems.
- Support interdisciplinary research and innovation hubs focused on ethical media-tech development and civic engagement.

Scaling Community-Driven Innovation

- Invest in grassroots digital literacy programs tailored to local contexts, especially in underserved regions.
- Encourage participatory design approaches that center community voices in technology development and media production.

Institutionalizing Digital Citizenship Education

- Embed digital citizenship frameworks into national education policies, teacher training programs, and curriculum standards.
- Align educational goals with global frameworks such as UNESCO's SDG 4.7 to promote sustainable, inclusive digital participation.

Advancing Ethical Governance and Accountability

- Develop transparent regulatory mechanisms for algorithmic systems, data privacy, and platform accountability.
- Promote open-source and decentralized technologies that prioritize user autonomy and democratic oversight.

Enhancing Global-Local Responsiveness

- Create adaptable policy models that reflect both global best practices and local cultural, infrastructural, and regulatory realities.
- Support multilingual, culturally sensitive media content to ensure representation and accessibility across diverse populations.

Preparing for Emerging Technologies

- Equip educators and civic leaders with the skills to integrate AI, VR/AR, and immersive media into learning and engagement strategies.
- Establish ethical guidelines and evaluation frameworks for the use of emerging technologies in public institutions.

CONCLUSION: RETHINKING PEDAGOGY AND SOCIAL FUTURES

In an era defined by digital saturation and technological acceleration, the convergence of media and technology is not merely a backdrop to social life—it is a central force shaping how we learn, connect, and participate in the world. This chapter has explored the multifaceted impacts of media-tech ecosystems on education, identity, civic engagement, and ethics, emphasizing both their transformative potential and inherent risks. From algorithmic influence on cultural narratives to the role of immersive media in pedagogy, the analysis underscores the urgent need for critical media literacy, inclusive design, and ethical governance. As we look to the future, the challenge is not only to adapt to technological change but to shape it in ways that promote equity, agency, and democratic resilience. By embedding digital citizenship into educational frameworks, fostering cross-sector collaboration, and ensuring global-local responsiveness in policy, we can reimagine pedagogy as a tool for social transformation. Ultimately, the future of education and civic life depends on our collective ability to harness media-tech with purpose, care, and critical reflection.

ACKNOWLEDGEMENT

This content has been developed without the use of Artificial Intelligence (AI) or Large Language Models (LLMs) for automated generation. All information presented is based on verified sources and proper academic citations, including references to UNESCO and other international frameworks. The English language and grammar have been refined using **Grammarly** to ensure clarity, coherence, and correctness.

REFERENCES

Abdullayeva, S. A. (2024). *Evolution of media: History and development of media, new media, media convergence, influence of technology on media. Global Scientific Review, 30*, 11–19. https://scienticreview.com/index.php/gsr/article/view/448

Ahmed, M., & Miracle, A. (2023). *The impact of media on shaping global cultural narratives in the digital age*. ResearchGate PDF.

Allconnect. (2024, March 25). *Digital divide: Organizations that are helping bridge the gap*. Retrieved from https://www.allconnect.com/blog/organizations-addressing-the-digital-divide

Allen, K.-A. (2021). Belonging in an age of technology. In Mc Mahon, C. (Ed.), *Psychological insights for understanding COVID-19 and media and technology* (pp. 72–85). Routledge., DOI: 10.4324/9781003121756-6

American Psychological Association. (2023). *Inclusive language guidelines*. https://www.apa.org/about/apa/equity-diversity-inclusion/language-guidelines

American Psychological Association. (2024). *Structural features of social media platforms that pose risks to children and adolescents*. https://www.apa.org/news/press/releases/2024/03/social-media-platforms

Analytics Insight. (2025). *AI-Powered Experiences in Entertainment*. Retrieved from https://www.analyticsinsight.net/artificial-intelligence/ai-powered-experiences-in-entertainment-the-future-of-storytelling

Anderson, P. (2025, May 15). How to preserve privacy in the age of mass surveillance: Democracy or technology? *APA Public Philosophy Blog*. https://blog.apaonline.org/2025/05/15/how-to-preserve-privacy-in-the-age-of-mass-surveillance-democracy-or-technology/

Apple. (2024a). *Transparency Report*. Apple Inc. Retrieved from https://www.apple.com/legal/transparency/

Apple. (2024b). *Privacy Governance*. Apple Inc. Retrieved from https://www.apple.com/legal/privacy/en-ww/governance/

Art Magazine, A. I. (2025). *Breaking Boundaries: How AI is Redefining the Art of Storytelling*. Retrieved from https://aiartmagazine.org/breaking-boundaries-how-ai-is-redefining-the-art-of-storytelling/

Axon Park. (2025). *Top VR Education Companies in 2025*. Retrieved from https://axonpark.com/top-vr-education-companies-in-2025/

Castells, M. (2010). *The Rise of the Network Society* (2nd ed.). Wiley-Blackwell., https://www.scirp.org/reference/referencespapers?referenceid=3992666

Castells, M. (2010). *The Rise of the Network Society* (2nd ed.). Wiley-Blackwell.

Chauhan, A. (2024). *The role of technology in shaping social movements. Authorea.* https://doi.org/DOI: 10.22541/au.172773135.55025991/v1

Chen, Y., & Chekam, T. (2021). Algorithmic ethics and media accountability: A framework for responsible AI. *Journal of Media Ethics*, *36*(2), 89–102. DOI: 10.1080/23736992.2021.1904823

Cole, E. (2024). Media literacy: Empowering critical engagement in the digital age. *Global Media Journal*, *22*(70). Advance online publication. DOI: 10.36648/1550-7521.22.70.450

Deloitte. (2024). *2024 Ethical Technology Report*. Retrieved from https://www.deloitte.com/us/en/about/governance/technology-trust-ethics-annual-report.html

Demir, M. (2024). A taxonomy of social media for learning. *Computers & Education*, *218*, 1–18. DOI: 10.1016/j.compedu.2024.105091

Digitunity. (2025). *8 community-driven strategies for advancing digital skills*. https://digitunity.org/digital-skills-innovation-community-organizations/

Du, X., Qi, Q., Li, Z., & Tang, C. (2024). Can digitalisation balance the dual pressures of global integration and local response? *Technology Analysis and Strategic Management*. Advance online publication. DOI: 10.1080/09537325.2024.2369575

ENGAGE XR. (2025). *Spatial Computing and AI in Education*. Retrieved from https://engagevr.io/

European Commission. (2024). *Gamification in Education: Duolingo Case Study*. Retrieved from https://ec.europa.eu/programmes/erasmus-plus/project-result-content/e22ddbda-dd23-42cc-89a2-786e921b2d80/Gamification%20in%20Education_20170418_020301.pdf

Financial Times. (2024a). *Transformation, trust, transparency: the future of GenAI.* Financial Times & Deloitte. Retrieved from https://www.ft.com/partnercontent/deloitte/the-future-of-gen-ai.html

Financial Times. (2024b). *Key steps to safeguard data and build trust in AI.* Financial Times & IBM. Retrieved from https://www.ft.com/partnercontent/ibm/key-steps-to-safeguard-data-and-build-trust-in-ai.html

Freire, P. (2017). *Pedagogy of the Oppressed.* Penguin Classics. https://www.easybib.com/guides/citation-guides/books/pedagogy-of-the-oppressed

Google. (2025). *How we support young people growing up in the digital age.* Retrieved from https://blog.google/technology/families/supporting-young-people-online/

Google News Initiative. (2021). *Supporting media literacy with new partnerships.* Retrieved from https://blog.google/outreach-initiatives/google-news-initiative/media-literacy-partnerships/

Gorwa, R., & Garton Ash, T. (2020). Democratic transparency in the platform society. In Persily, N., & Tucker, J. A. (Eds.), *Social Media and Democracy* (pp. 286–312). Cambridge University Press., DOI: 10.1017/9781108890960

Grimmage, S. (2025). Fostering digital communities in higher education: Unlocking belonging. *Teaching and Learning Conference Proceedings, 1*(1). https://journals.librarypublishing.arizona.edu/tlcp/article/id/8343/

Hall, S., Evans, J., & Nixon, S. (Eds.). (2013). *Representation: Cultural representations and signifying practices* (2nd ed.). Sage Publications Ltd.

Hisseine, M. A., Chen, D., & Yang, X. (2022). The application of blockchain in social media: A systematic literature review. *Applied Sciences (Basel, Switzerland), 12*(13), 6567. DOI: 10.3390/app12136567

Hohlfeld, T. N., Ritzhaupt, A. D., Barron, A. E., & Kemker, K. (2008). Examining the digital divide in K–12 public schools: Four-year trends for supporting ICT literacy in Florida. *Computers & Education, 51*(4), 1648–1663. DOI: 10.1016/j.compedu.2008.04.002

Hondros, K., Schiemer, B., & Vogelgsang, L. (2023). Beyond personal safe spaces: Creating and maintaining collective environments for meaning and identity on digital platforms. *Organization, 30*(5), 809–829. DOI: 10.1177/13505084231168094

Hopelab. (2025). *The New Icons: How Influencers Shape Youth Identity in the Digital Age.* Retrieved from https://hopelab.org/stories/the-new-icons-how-influencers-shape-youth-identity-in-the-digital-age

IBM. (2024). *Accountability in AI Design*. Retrieved from https://www.ibm.com/design/ai/ethics/accountability/

Issar, S. (2024). The social construction of algorithms in everyday life: Examining TikTok users' understanding of the platform's algorithm. *International Journal of Human-Computer Interaction*, *40*(18), 5384–5398. DOI: 10.1080/10447318.2023.2233138

Jenkins, H. (2006). *Confronting the Challenges of Participatory Culture: Media Education for the 21st Century*. An Occasional Paper on Digital Media and Learning. MIT Press. https://direct.mit.edu/books/oa-monograph/3204/Confronting-the-Challenges-of-Participatory

Kahne, J., Lipkin, M. C., Tynes, B., McGrew, S., Mirra, N., & Garcia, A. (2024). *Civic reasoning and discourse across the curriculum: Digital Citizenship Education*. National Academy of Education & National Association for Media Literacy Education. https://files.eric.ed.gov/fulltext/ED672648.pdf

Klaus, P., & Hartshorne, T. S. (2015). Ethical issues in the use of technology in counseling. *Journal of Counseling and Development*, *93*(3), 280–286. DOI: 10.1002/jcad.12027

Kraus, S., Jones, P., Kailer, N., Weinmann, A., Chaparro-Banegas, N., & Roig-Tierno, N. (2021). Digital transformation: An overview of the current state of the art of research. *SAGE Open*, *11*(3), 1–15. DOI: 10.1177/21582440211047576

Kraus, S., Jones, P., Kailer, N., Weinmann, A., Chaparro-Banegas, N., & Roig-Tierno, N. (2021). Digital transformation: An overview of the current state of the art of research. *SAGE Open*, *11*(3), 1–15. DOI: 10.1177/21582440211047576

Lamprou, S., Dekoulou, P., & Kalliris, G. (2025). The critical impact and socio-ethical implications of AI on content generation practices in media organizations. *Societies (Basel, Switzerland)*, *15*(8), 214. DOI: 10.3390/soc15080214

Light, L. L., Panicker, S., Abrams, L., & Huh-Yoo, J. (2024). Ethical challenges in the use of digital technologies in psychological science: Introduction to the special issue. *The American Psychologist*, *79*(1), 1–8. DOI: 10.1037/amp0001286 PMID: 38236211

Magazine, A. I. (2025, April 16). *Top 10 Ethical AI Companies*. Retrieved from https://aimagazine.com/top10/top-10-ethical-ai-companies

Mansell, R., & Raboy, M. (Eds.). (2014). *The Handbook of Global Media and Communication Policy*. Wiley-Blackwell., https://books.google.com/books/about/The_Handbook_of_Global_Media_and_Communi.html?id=GyGeAgAAQBAJ

Martens, H., & Hobbs, R. (2015). How media literacy supports civic engagement in a digital age. *Atlantic Journal of Communication, 23*(2), 120–137. DOI: 10.1080/15456870.2014.961636

Melonashi, E. (2019). Social media and identity: Understanding identity communication and creation through social media. In Khosrow-Pour, M. (Ed.), *Internet and technology addiction: Breakthroughs in research and practice* (pp. 1–22). IGI Global., DOI: 10.4018/978-1-5225-8900-6.ch001

Mihailidis, P., & Thevenin, B. (2013). Media literacy as a core competency for engaged citizenship in participatory democracy. *The American Behavioral Scientist, 57*(11), 1611–1622. https://psycnet.apa.org/record/2013-35893-007

MIT Open Doc Lab. (2025). *Radical Storytelling with AI: Ethics, Authorship, and Experimentation*. Retrieved from https://opendoclab.mit.edu/presents/radical-storytelling-ai-ethics-authorship-experimentation-lili-navid-khonsari/

Moore, R., Vitale, D., & Stawinoga, N. (2018). *The digital divide and educational equity: A look at students with very limited access to electronic devices at home*. ACT Center for Equity in Learning. https://equityinlearning.act.org/research-report/the-digital-divide-and-educational-equity/

Nielsen. (2023, December). *The Power and Potential of Data for Good®*. Retrieved from https://www.nielsen.com/news-center/2023/the-power-and-potential-of-data-for-good/

OECD. (2025). *Tackling Civic Participation Challenges with Emerging Technologies*. Retrieved from https://www.oecd.org/en/publications/tackling-civic-participation-challenges-with-emerging-technologies_ec2ca9a2-en.html

Onebunne, A. P. (2022). Algorithmic bias and media manipulation: A systematic review of AI's role in shaping public perception and political discourse. *World Journal of Advanced Research and Reviews, 16*(3), 1239–1249. DOI: 10.30574/wjarr.2022.16.3.1332

Overney, C. (2025). *Designing for Constructive Civic Communication: A Framework for Human-AI Collaboration*. Retrieved from https://arxiv.org/pdf/2505.11684

Pache, A.-C., Fayard, A.-L., & Galo, M. (2022). How can cross-sector collaborations foster social innovation? A review. In Vaccaro, A., & Ramus, T. (Eds.), *Social Innovation and Social Enterprises: Toward a Holistic Perspective* (pp. 35–62). Springer., https://link.springer.com/chapter/10.1007/978-3-030-96596-9_3

Palmer, C. (2025, March 25). The benefits from culturally responsive community-based research partnerships. *American Psychological Association*. https://www.apa.org/research-practice/conduct-research/culturally-responsive-partnerships

Partin, C., & King, K. P. (2013). Technology and its impact on higher education. In Ran, B. (Ed.), *Global perspectives on technological innovation* (pp. 403–433). IAP Information Age Publishing., https://psycnet.apa.org/record/2013-20064-013

Partin, K., & King, S. (2013). Digital Tools and Civic Agency in Education. *Journal of Educational Technology & Society*.

Penplusbytes. (2025). *Media and Information Literacy and Civic Education – A Collective Effort for the Public Good*. Retrieved from https://penplusbytes.org/media-and-information-literacy-and-civic-education-a-collective-effort-for-the-public-good/

Pérez-Torres, V. (2024). Social media: A digital social mirror for identity development during adolescence. *Current Psychology (New Brunswick, N.J.)*, *43*(26), 22170–22180. DOI: 10.1007/s12144-024-05980-z

Sahare, R. R. (2024). The impact of social media on youth identity formation. *International Journal of Advanced Research in Science and Technology*. https://www.ijarst.in/public/uploads/paper/200651727268929.pdf

Salesforce. (2024a). *Trusted AI: The Einstein Trust Layer*. Salesforce Inc. Retrieved from https://www.salesforce.com/artificial-intelligence/trusted-ai/

Salesforce. (2024b). *Einstein Trust Layer Help Documentation*. Salesforce Inc. Retrieved from https://help.salesforce.com/s/articleView?id=ai.generative_ai_trust_layer.htm

SocialTargeter. (2025). *The Impact of Gamification: Case Studies from Education Technology Startups*. Retrieved from https://www.socialtargeter.com/blogs/the-impact-of-gamification-case-studies-from-education-technology-startups

Song, G. (2024). A Public Service Media Perspective on the Algorithmic Amplification of Cultural Content. *Knight First Amendment Institute*. https://knightcolumbia.org/content/a-public-service-media-perspective-on-the-algorithmic-amplification-of-cultural-content

Song, Q. (2024). Framing in media and communication studies: A bibliometric analysis. *Insight - News Media, 7*(1), 674. https://doi.org/DOI: 10.18282/inm674

Sonnett, J. (2019). Priming and framing: Dimensions of communication and cognition. In *The Oxford Handbook of Cognitive Sociology* (pp. 226–240). https://doi.org/DOI: 10.1093/oxfordhb/9780190273385.013.13

TchopTM. (2025). *Youth-centric digital platforms.* Retrieved from https://tchop.io/resources/glossary/community-building/youth-centric-digital-platforms

The New York Times. (2024a). *Guidelines on Integrity*. Retrieved from https://www.nytimes.com/editorial-standards/guidelines-on-integrity.html

The New York Times. (2024b). *Ethical Journalism Handbook.* Retrieved from https://www.nytimes.com/editorial-standards/ethical-journalism.html

UNESCO. (2024). *Global citizenship education in a digital age.* United Nations Educational, Scientific and Cultural Organization. https://unesco-asp.dk/wp-content/uploads/2025/02/Global-Citizenship-education-in-a-digital-age_UNESCO_2024.pdf

UNESCO. (2025). *Promoting Youth Participation in Decision-Making and Public Service Delivery through Harnessing Digital Technologies*. Retrieved from https://www.unesco.org/sdg4education2030/en/knowledge-hub/promoting-youth-participation-decision-making-and-public-service-delivery-through-harnessing-digital

UNESCO. (n.d.). *Digital citizenship education.* https://www.unesco.org/en/digital-citizenship

UNICEF. (2020). *Digital civic engagement by young people*. Retrieved from https://www.unicef.org/reports/digital-civic-engagement-young-people-2020

Victory, X. R. (2025). *VictoryXR Company Profile*. Retrieved from https://www.inven.ai/company-lists/top-26-virtual-reality-education-companies

Wakefield, N. (2011). Media literacy education. In Dunkels, E., Frånberg, G.-M., & Hällgren, C. (Eds.), *Interactive media use and youth: Learning, knowledge exchange and behavior* (pp. 80–101). IGI Global., DOI: 10.4018/978-1-60960-206-2.ch006

Wang, D., & Huang, X. (2025). Transforming education through artificial intelligence and immersive technologies: Enhancing learning experiences. *Interactive Learning Environments*. Advance online publication. DOI: 10.1080/10494820.2025.2465451

White, G., Dong, D., Campbell, D. E., & Lee, C. D. (2023). The future of civic education: Implications for research, policy, and practice. *The Annals of the American Academy of Political and Social Science*, *705*(1), 249–257. DOI: 10.1177/00027162231193538

World Economic Forum. (2023, September 28). *Bridging the digital divide: These tech projects are empowering global inclusion*. Retrieved from https://www.weforum.org/stories/2023/09/bridging-digital-divide-technology-empowering-global-inclusion

Zeybek, N., & Saygı, E. (2024). Gamification in education: Why, where, when, and how?—A systematic review. *Games and Culture*, *19*(2), 237–264. DOI: 10.1177/15554120231158625

Chapter 13
The Economic Dimensions of Technology and Media in Digital Social Innovation

Constantinos Challoumis
https://orcid.org/0000-0002-7436-0506
National and Kapodistrian University of Athens, Greece

ABSTRACT

This chapter explores the economic dimensions of digital social innovation (DSI), focusing on the intersection of technology, media, and participatory practices in shaping transformative social change. While the term DSI remains ambiguous, it broadly refers to the development and implementation of novel ideas that generate primarily social value through digital tools and collaborative processes. The chapter situates DSI in relation to broader traditions of innovation, highlighting its departure from linear, profit-driven R&D models toward open, non-linear, and multichannel approaches enabled by Web 2.0 platforms, artificial intelligence, open data, and peer-to-peer production. By analyzing the roles of technology, media, and participation, it identifies the mechanisms through which DSI produces outcomes such as awareness, engagement, innovation, and resilience. Attention is also given to economic implications, including the emergence of new business models, alternative financing mechanisms such as microcredit, and platform cooperatives that integrate social and economic objectives.

DOI: 10.4018/979-8-3373-5307-4.ch013

1. INTRODUCTION

The rapid growth of digital social innovation, and technology and media's role in these changes challenge us to broaden analyses of their economic dimensions. Recent worldwide efforts have produced economic insights but are dispersed by jurisdiction, distinct sub-sectors and scales of review, or differing definitions of what constitutes this field. Yet understanding the economic dimensions will be essential in both building a more robust knowledge base and advancing the broader policy dialogue. This volume outlines a framework for such arguments and opens the way for further exploration. "Digital social innovation" (DSI) is an ambiguous term. A number of important contributions have sought to clarify its meaning by situating it in relation to other relevant debates and traditions. Broadly construed, innovation refers to certain novel, useful and implemented ideas that are transformative rather than incremental (André & Abreu, 2006). Social innovation adds a concern with the scope and nature of the change involved and with particular types of ideas—those whose effects or value are primarily social. It also draws attention to the social processes through which ideas emerge and develop, often in contrast to the dominant (and doubling) emphasis on economic interests and profit maximization and on linear R & D. Digital innovation highlights the shaping and contribution of emerging digital technologies, at times capturing the essence of multichannel (and non-linear) web 2.0 applications, mobile, social media and associated platforms and collaborative modes, user-centered, peer- and crowd-based production, open source and open-data frameworks, and emerging applications of artificial intelligence (Recker & von Briel, 2019). Social innovation follows well-established paths far older than the internet. DSI is nonetheless a rather different beast. The digital encapsulation of existing social innovations such as micro-credit schemes or participatory budgeting can provide them with fresh resources and increased reach. It also generates brand-new forms of social innovation, from crowdfunding and collaborative platforms to tailored apps designed to facilitate sustainable lifestyles. Digital social innovation (DSI) has become a crucial concept at the intersection of technology, media, and social transformation. Its rapid expansion reflects not only the proliferation of digital tools but also the growing demand for inclusive and collaborative solutions to societal challenges. Unlike traditional innovation models that emphasize market competition and profit, DSI focuses on social value creation, building participatory processes that allow communities to co-design and co-implement change. This broader orientation situates DSI within a continuum of debates that extend beyond economics into sociology, political science, and governance, highlighting its interdisciplinary character. One of the central features of DSI lies in its non-linear and multichannel dynamics. Web 2.0 environments, mobile applications, and social media platforms enable decentralized communication and cooperation that disrupt the older hierarchical models of innovation. Instead of linear R&D pipelines, knowledge is now created through iterative exchanges among citizens, civil society organizations, and institutions. Practices such as peer-to-peer production, crowdsourcing, and open-source development exemplify this shift, demonstrating how digital infrastructures can support large-scale collaboration while maintaining flexibility and inclusivity. The economic dimensions of DSI are equally important but remain underdeveloped in existing research. Fragmentation across jurisdictions, sectors, and definitions creates inconsistencies in how its contributions are measured and evaluated. Nevertheless, it is increasingly clear that DSI plays a role in reshaping economic systems by fostering new business models, redefining labor relations, and introducing alternative forms of value creation. Microcredit initiatives, platform cooperatives, and open-data-driven enterprises illustrate how digital innovation can simultaneously address social needs and generate sustainable economic outcomes. DSI also challenges the conventional balance between social and economic objectives. By prioritizing participation, diversity, and collective benefit, it offers a counterpoint to the profit-maximization logic of mainstream innovation. This does not mean that DSI is anti-economic; rather, it integrates economic considerations within broader social purposes. The challenge ahead lies in developing frameworks capable of capturing these dual dynamics, ensuring that policy dialogue keeps pace with practice. Only then can the transformative potential of DSI be fully understood and harnessed, particularly in advancing resilience, sustainability, and equitable growth.

Figure 1. Chart of economic dimensions (Author's scheme, see Appendix I)

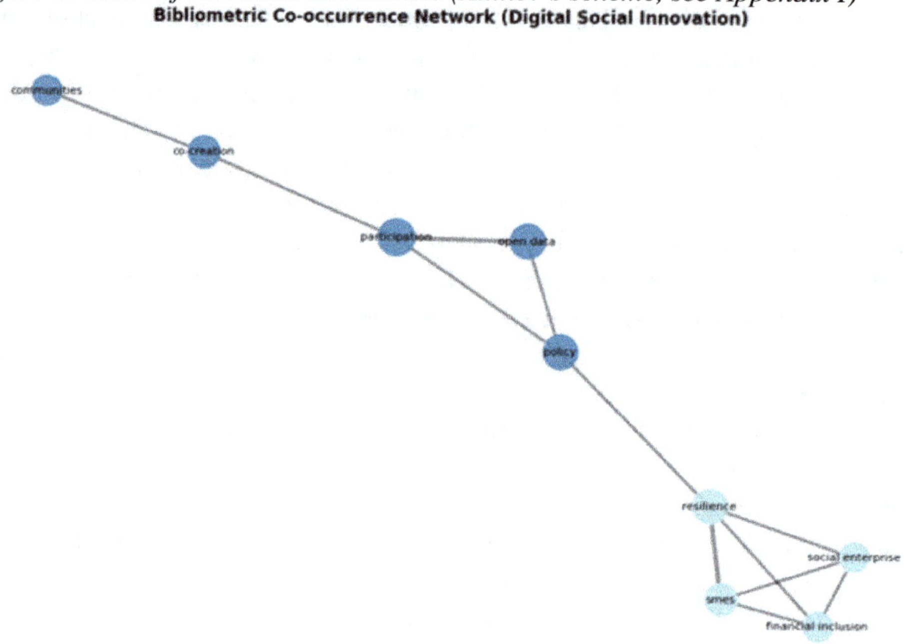

The Bibliometric Co-occurrence Network visualizes the relationships between key terms associated with Digital Social Innovation (DSI). Each node in the network represents a keyword (e.g., "open data", "microcredit", "participation"), and its size reflects how frequently that keyword appears across the analyzed documents. Edges (lines connecting nodes) indicate that two terms co-occurred within the same source (e.g., article, report, or dataset). The thicker the edge, the stronger the co-occurrence relationship between those terms. To enhance interpretability, the nodes are grouped into clusters using modularity-based community detection. Each cluster is assigned a distinct color, highlighting thematic groupings within the data. For instance, terms related to technological infrastructures (ICT, AI, open platforms) might appear in one cluster, while terms linked to economic models (microcredit, SMEs, resilience) form another. A third cluster might emphasize media and participation (social media, campaigns, co-creation).With digital technology's pervasive reach as a foundational assumption, DSI continues recent shifts from formal, institutional processes towards open, networked, participatory or peer-to-peer ones readily adaptable for public, community, research, education or commercial deployment Digital media and internet platforms help these new services to grow and flourish, grouping partners around shared concerns rather than common geography. Communities and individuals respond with remarkable speed, matching fresh technological platforms with established social problems.. For policy-makers, then, technology and media are crucial variables—factors whose effects reach well beyond technology-centric disciplines. This economic analysis highlights the importance of economic research within such an approach and suggests styles and paths of research commensurate with these connections.

2. UNDERSTANDING DIGITAL SOCIAL INNOVATION

Digital social innovation (DSI) describes new social configurations—concepts, models, and artefacts—that transcend institutionalized socio-economic structures and establish alternative means of human cooperation. It is a phenomenon of enduring significance within technologically mediated society, permitting the coordination of action at various scales and levels (André & Abreu, 2006). DSI is therefore anchored by historical circumstances as opposed to institutionalised arrangements, extending the contemporary condition of perpetual social, economic, and political restructuring. Social innovation constitutes a significant element within the wider study of innovation, yet it has attracted relatively little analytical attention. Comic farce and escapist comedy function as forms of social innovation and attract a bourgeois audience seeking to reinforce its pre-eminence. The continued existence of a farcical culture, therefore, depends upon participation in the ludicrous, which subverts established values and institutions (Havas, 2016). Social innovation is the process whereby institutions and organisations modify and adjust individual and social behaviours. DSI challenges these boundaries, encouraging constant innovation that dissolves the distinction between invention and exploitation (Recker & von Briel, 2019). New technologies enhance the fluidity of social practice and the capacity to mobilise others, introducing new event spaces that expand opportunity. Creative and collaborative interaction replaces production and consumption. Social and technological parameters intersect within the public sphere, generating change. People utilise new communication technologies to construct new social practices that influence government and market systems. They author and promulgate topics, values, and norms that create subsequent political and/or market demands. Technological advance has already facilitated greater public involvement and theorists anticipate a rapid shift towards participative, collaborative, and open systems.

2.1. Definition and Scope

Social innovation is understood here as the development and implementation of new ideas to meet social needs. Dimensions and spaces of innovation social emphasizes the spatiality of social innovation processes with particular attention to innovative or creative means. Specific conditions such as diversity, tolerance and participation appear to favour risk taking, the introduction of new ideas and debate between actors. Microcredit in Portugal serves as an illustrative example of such a social innovation process (André & Abreu, 2006). At its core, social innovation encompasses the capacity of societies to devise innovative responses to large-scale('wicked') social problems in an inclusive, participatory, and sustainable manner. If the social innovations being analysed have a spatial, socio-geographical component, then it becomes important to articulate spatiality with social innovation. In the same way that the very essence of social innovation transcends a purely technical or techno-scientific nature, the social-spatial dimensions cannot be reduced to an examination of the geographic anchorage of the processes analysed. It is essential to approach both spatiality and social innovation with a view to its holistic nature, which merges the specific and the structural, the geographical anchorage, the proximity between the actors involved, networks, paths and institutions, which allow us to analyse the spatiality where innovation is rooted. Spatiality is thus presented as a capital understanding component to define the evolution of innovation processes. While one could develop an extensive discussion centred on the concept, it seems more relevant to specifically refer to three main conditions: diversity, tolerance, and participation, focusing on the idea that it is adequate to the theme, for the way in which it justifies the relevant conditions for experimentation. Admittedly, it has not been the only one used in this sense, and there are others, such as plurality, non-conformism, utopia, or creativity, that could lead to a similar discussion. However, all of them seem to indicate, in general terms, a specific and important prerequisite for the emergence of innovation: the capacity to accommodate and interact between different paradigmatic frameworks, agendas, assets, interests, and cultural codes. This concept, in conjunction with that of tolerance, precedes the third necessary condition for the emergence of innovation, participation. The combination of the three dimensions defines an entity that can be described metaphorically as an innovation ecosystem, that is, a synergy covering all possible dimensions of the social and spatial field, favouring the circulation of ideas and the emergence of alternatives, co-created by all the actors involved, irrespective of their generic nature. Although interrogation models could also challenge either of these three known dimensions, if one accepts various degrees of risk that could be concomitant with the previous idealized conditions to favour the emergence of social innovations.

Social Innovation is often conceived as a response to a social need that results in a new service product or method. Traits of novelty, respect for social objectives, and sustainability of the response are often mentioned as being decisive. Another approach is adopted by open innovation, which describes the social, economic, cultural, or psychological environment where the process takes place. In this, social innovation is then analysed based on spatial limitations that nature may assume, and it uses the concept of ecosystem. It uses concepts that may be translated into spatially geographical concepts, depending on the geopolitical context, to embrace a wide range of phenomena. The word ecosystem, for instance, has been used more widely in social innovation literature, but its original use can be traced back to the relationship between living beings grounded in biology and then extended to illustrative analogies, designed to explain the interdependence of actors and factors found in that world. This same concept has been argued for as a practice-oriented approach. It hypothesizes an idyllic innovation environment, and only practices that fulfil all the ecosystem requirements should be considered. However, this orientation, in a substantially counterfactual way, could exclude a wide range of already existing practices, which might not strictly comply with that hypothetical model but nonetheless may characterise innovation processes in different and sometimes unexpected ways. This is an idea that would combine with the possibility that other contexts within real life, that do not reach the deterministic expectation pattern, are also highly likely to generate satisfactory innovation clusters. A similar counterfactual concern could be raised for the concept of social innovation. The use of microcredit in Portugal is one case that could illustrate this.

The recurrent definition of innovation adopted by institutional agents as the introduction of a practice, new to the user, is also applicable here. In a first sense, the non-conformism represented by microcredit introduced the concept and the practice of making credit available to those rejected by the traditional banking system. In an exemplary case of self-targeting, the subsetting population, sampled by exposure to a population formally guaranteed access to the product, opted for joining the microcredit movement. The subsequent consecration of the 'bankable' individuals was operationally materialised through the volume of available small loans to start up small-scale businesses or, alternatively, progressively increase the possibilities of installing self-assessment on family members. In a systematic and rational sense, formal self-targeting was supported by ex-ante and ex-post social scrutiny, determining individual and collective eligibility, viability, and financial sustainability. In a second, similarly paradigmatic sense, the indigenous element comprised a set of structured actions that not only limited traditional funding but also activated social networking to provide alternative behavioural rounds that guaranteed both change and reinforcement of the status-quo. The cross-collective outreach of the agent empowered the microcredit users personally and symbolically by demonstrating the price of money and their capacity to change the environment. A paradigmatic alternative to classical development proved to be both possible and viable. There are two concluding remarks. Firstly, microcredit does not characterise the European direction of social innovation; on the contrary, it represents entry into and feasibility within an in-existing paradigm. Microcredit does not furnish a new purpose for social innovation beyond the existing welfare model, but it requires a new concept of social innovation that substantially excludes radical transformation. Secondly, whereas the consolidation hypothesis described certain innovation-induced changes in ‘resistant’ contexts, the contribution of microcredit to the interpretation of the cognitive change of individuals and collectives determines a significant conceptual improvement. Social innovation also has a meaning as a process of cognitive restructuring that pragmatically leads to the emergence of a new paradigm by involving a change in values, behaviours, and cooperation capabilities among individuals and different collectivities. It results in a change of priorities and practices concerning solidarity, social justice, reciprocity, and social capital, overcoming the reification of predominant concepts. It follows that social innovation, arising from the ambition of new pre-existing frames of reference, does not imply their abolition but rather their horizontality relativising their role as compass priorities over the reification of their content priority. The innovation hypothesis is thus dominated by the consolidation and change; it is countercurrent. The conceptualisation and characterisation of the microcredit process signify the transformation of social innovation into agency. Governed by collectivities and relations, both formal and informal, they enhance capacities in the support and direction of change processes towards a paradigmatic newisation of the social and. Infrastructure transformation of the social roles, either in the existing paradigms or in the anticipation of new interpretative frames of reference. Therefore, the use of microcredit in Portugal profiles as a case of social innovation based on individual transformation of cognitive frameworks and a process of social change as capital applications of the existing frames of reference towards horizontalold paradigm authorities.

2.2. Historical Context

Throughout the last century, social innovation has involved the creation of new strategies, concepts and organizations that meet social needs—ranging from working conditions and education to community development and health—thereby enhancing collective well-being (Tiwari & Tiwari, 2017). Inquiry into the economic dimensions of technology and media in digital social innovation encompasses not only how digital assets and resources drive systemic change that affects society’s socio-economic state but also how the relationship between technology and the social economy fosters economic progress (Challoumis, 2018, 2023a, 2023b, 2024). Appreciating the historical context of digital social innovation critically situates social innovation within the digital age and aids understanding of the economic implications of media and technology platforms. Social innovation entails the development of products, services, or models that simultaneously address societal challenges while fostering growth and competitiveness within the economy (André & Abreu, 2006). Digital platforms may facilitate enhanced collaboration across different organizational structures, address structural issues fundamental to human resources and economic sustainability on both local and global levels, and engender international solidarity—demonstrating evolution toward a techno-economic social collective. Understanding Social Innovation offers a characterization of the concept and defines the "digital age," thus establishing a historic framework for digital social innovation that is exploited in subsequent economic exposition.

3. THE ROLE OF TECHNOLOGY IN SOCIAL INNOVATION

The increasing use of technologies, such as social media, collaborative platforms, or recent waves bringing artificial intelligence into everyday contexts, characterizes contemporary social innovation. Digital social innovation refers to the application of Information and Communication Technologies (ICTs) to tackle social needs that affect people's daily lives. Those ICTs do not constitute an end in themselves, but rather an instrument to conceive and develop solutions developed and implemented by 'a wide range of actors inspired by the open source and open innovation movements, who use web-based technologies to co-create knowledge and ideas in a distributed and collaborative way' (Tiwari & Tiwari, 2017). The rise of digital technologies has transformed the landscape of social innovation by enabling new forms of interaction, collaboration, and problem-solving. Social media platforms, collaborative tools, and artificial intelligence applications have widened the scope of participation, making it possible for individuals and communities to co-create solutions across geographical boundaries. These technologies have become critical enablers of innovation ecosystems where knowledge, resources, and creativity circulate more freely. Digital social innovation emphasizes that technology is not an end in itself, but rather a means to achieve broader social purposes. ICTs are instrumental in connecting actors, facilitating knowledge-sharing, and lowering barriers to entry for participation. The underlying philosophy aligns with the ethos of open source and open innovation movements, which prioritize transparency, accessibility, and collective intelligence over proprietary or hierarchical control. This collaborative ethos allows communities to design responses that are adaptive to local contexts while drawing on global networks of expertise. One of the key advantages of digital social innovation is its distributed nature. Solutions are not imposed top-down but emerge through the interaction of diverse stakeholders—including citizens, researchers, entrepreneurs, NGOs, and public institutions—who collaborate in decentralized ways. This distributed innovation model enhances resilience by diversifying both the sources of ideas and the channels through which they are tested and scaled. It also democratizes access to problem-solving, empowering communities traditionally excluded from decision-making processes. Artificial intelligence, in particular, has introduced new opportunities for addressing social challenges. AI-driven platforms can analyze complex datasets to inform decision-making, optimize resource allocation, and personalize services in health, education, and social care. However, its integration within digital social innovation also raises critical questions about ethics, inclusivity, and accountability. Ensuring that AI applications serve the public good requires embedding values of fairness, transparency, and participation at every stage of development. Ultimately, digital social innovation illustrates how technological infrastructures can support new forms of solidarity and cooperation. By fostering collective creativity and distributed problem-solving, ICTs enable societies to respond more effectively to emerging challenges. The real innovation, however, lies not in the tools themselves but in the ways people use them to co-create knowledge, reimagine institutions, and build more inclusive and sustainable futures.

3.1. Emerging Technologies

Digital technologies are having a profound impact on how social and collaborative innovation initiatives organize and mobilize social resources. The proliferation of software and platforms explorer to mobilize internal and external social resources unseen (MONACI, 2016). The reported effects of these social technologies relate to ability to promote greater openness and participation, engage more effectively with stakeholders, accelerate the pace of innovation activities, and improve overall innovation performance. These insights are examined through the lens of digital social innovation (DSI), described as a set of principles and practices designed to organize and support innovation initiatives with an explicit or implicit social purpose. The wider DSI ecosystem—including a range of drivers, enablers, and institutionalized organizations, e.g., European P2P Foundation, collectively provide the basis for social engagement and innovative idea development.

3.2. Case Studies of Successful Innovations

The e-health sector features a large number of players but does not always provide the ideal environment fostering Digital-DI-led innovation. Taken together with an insecure funding environment and changing government priorities, these institutional and structural conditions impact the long-term viability and successful introduction of innovative products and services in the public sector (Kateb et al., 2022). Interviewed social care organisations also highlight limitations in currently available e-health technologies. Although moving such services to an online environment is especially critical during lockdowns, the products offered still limit the scope of assistance offered. Adoption tends to be selective as a consequence.

4. MEDIA'S INFLUENCE ON SOCIAL CHANGE

The media's influence over the economies surrounding social change in a digital ecosystem arises primarily from the mechanisms that end-users follow to co-produce content, modify the principles behind the associated storytelling, guarantee allocative efficiency through audience reactions, and generate timely, trusted and relevant information during the global urgency that also intrinsically motivates social-change perception (V. Pavlik et al., 2019). Long before businesses explored the economic-intelligence potential either on the Web as a source of consumer behaviour or through the social-hardwired sharing of information, the accelerated proliferation of mobile and social networking was massively adopted by citizens worldwide (V. Pavlik et al., 2019). Positions on the economic value stemming from media exposure reached consensus by considering the increase in audience cohesion associated with repetition across highly trusted and relevant channels. Nonetheless, the fundamental merit behind representing the stimuli through narratives and associating relevant questions is that media possesses the unique capability to reveal the correct signals amidst the noisy data arising from two channels simultaneously: the stories themselves and the stimulus configuration guiding the media generation.

4.1. Media Platforms and Outreach

Media initiatives can be instrumental in generating awareness and supporting campaigns, especially when datasets exceed the traditional media's ability to process. Particular emphasis is given to social Web platforms such as Facebook or Twitter, which allow for rapid broadcasting to a wide audience. Reliable data is essential for integrating accounts and content originating from various sources and organisations. Tweets, Facebook posts, photos, videos, and other media shared deliberately or through the use of automated tools such as If This Then That (IFTTT) can be aggregated, filtered, and shared as part of an online digital social innovation trajectory. Under specific coordination, this form of dissemination can contribute to the success of social initiatives (MONACI, 2016). Media initiatives amplify the visibility of social innovation initiatives, particularly for complex challenges that require broad public participation and mobilization. By reaching diverse audiences quickly, their solutions gain traction beyond limited social spheres, particularly in alignment with the communication strategies of current powerful actors, both public and private. Equipped with adequate empowerment, media platforms transform from communication channels to participatory arenas where relevant social actors discuss ideas, contribute signals, enhance narratives, and build momentum around participatory causes. The ability to quickly and cheaply broadcast through social web services like Facebook, Twitter, Instagram, TikTok, and others is considered a significant turning point in the history of social campaigns. These means of communication have become essential for grassroots initiatives, community organizing, or social movements with limited resources but high social reach needs. They allow institutions, organizations, and collectives to disseminate pleas or demands without first filtering them through intermediaries. In contrast to mass media, where brokers can limit coverage to a few chosen stories, social channels enable direct contact with the target audience, creating an illusion of immediacy and engagement. These communicative affordances offer an open space for all kinds of voices and stories, making it increasingly difficult to ignore the latest trend or outrage. At the same time, this opens up opportunities for many others who have either lost control over known and stable narratives or never had it in the first place. This process is crucial, but it does not necessarily guarantee strong signals. Associating a shared demand with a reliable dataset by selecting, filtering, curating, verifying, and amplifying it is a way for organizers to enhance the credibility of the narrative and mitigate the dangers of sending fragile or deceptive stories. Digital tools and automated services like If This Then That (IFTTT) can effortlessly aggregate posts, tweets, photos, and videos, stitching them together into streams of information. When combined with data visualization techniques, these streams may be close to the envisaged narrative that captures the attention of public opinion and policymaking agendas alike.The significance of coordination becomes clearer as we consider the trajectory of the previous step. Without a minimal framework for organizing and distributing signals and coordinating communication actions, digital sharing does not guarantee a successful narrative. The common acceptance of a particular interpretation of events transforms fragmented data into narratives. Coordination enhances social initiatives' reach, impact, and effects. Coordinated communication makes the differences between audiences less significant as messages are streamlined to avoid duplicating and fanning out actions, promoting awareness of multiple actors' participation converging on the same demand. While the digital ecosystem's communicative affordances may favor information sharing, it does not ensure impactful communication involving close, relevant, and purposeful participation and engagement. This requires a proactive approach that aims for strong, repeated, multiphased, and long-lasting signals, raising the chances of achieving real effects within and beyond the targeted social sphere. Actual outcomes may vary widely, but common goals include agenda-shifting, resource mobilization, and behavioral changes among relevant targeted audiences.

The analysis of the communicative logic of media initiatives extends beyond communication in the digital context of DSIs to the crucial aspects of coordination. The strategies and tools of DSIs help break traditional barriers in scale and space, creating strains of solidarity that converge upon the same causes or demands. The interplay between technology, communication, and social goals is addressed through the DSIs' intentional strategy for the social use of shared digital infrastructures. The DSIs transform the media paradigm from merely sharing information as a population to leveraging it as a social asset. The strategy counterbalances the increasing mainstream organizational tendency to use digital sharing as another form of information leakage where social transformative narratives quickly fade away, becoming mere noise among algorithms. Similarly to physical infrastructures that are built and progressively turned into platforms through the socioeconomic uses they generate, digital infrastructures' transformative potential relies on purposeful sharing that becomes meaningful, beyond the vanity metrics of a reached audience or network size.

4.2. Narratives and Storytelling

Narratives and storytelling play a vital role for social innovation initiatives in constructing their change narratives ((Julia) Wittmayer et al., 2019). The ability to tell a convincing story is vital for these initiatives in order to create legitimacy and appeal to different actors that are asked to contribute resources and engage in collaborations. Digital stories usually run for two to three minutes and are primarily shown on the internet, though stories have been broadcast on national media, exhibited in cinemas, galleries or public spaces and are routinely shown in community settings (Dunford & Dunford, 2017). Digital storytelling can help forge understanding of self-representation, media practice, and citizenship, particularly as digitalization influences the production, distribution, and exhibition of stories. Future research should explore discursive politics involving interactions with external actors and how their narratives are appropriated or commoditized. A key challenge for practice is identifying strategies for social innovation initiatives to collaborate and shift society beyond the current economic order.

5. ECONOMIC IMPLICATIONS OF DIGITAL SOCIAL INNOVATION

Digital social innovation refers to the production and service of innovative solutions to social challenges, primarily relying on digital technology and communication (Yu et al., 2023). The digital economy deeply affects the innovation activities of enterprises. Technology and media provide a collaborative space and a vivid channel for the development of digital social innovation, with a wide range of economic uses. Social innovation is a systematic approach that mobilizes a variety of public and private actors, enhancing the impact of European policies on social entrepreneurship. Collaboration and cooperation are the keywords to linking technology, media, and the economy together around digital social innovation. Enterprises strive for a unique digital identity, even when faced with tight resources and limited resources for originality and uniqueness. Barriers to innovation are also considered when talking about the enterprise innovation efficiency. As a medium, digital economy emphasizes the positive impact of the transformation of economic development mode and industrial upgrading on enterprise innovation (Challoumis, 2021, 2025b, 2025a). It provides effective coping strategies for enterprises and promotes the optimal allocation of economic factors. The innovative application of the digital economy will continue to consolidate the strong engine of high-quality economic development and enterprise innovation capacity. The economic implications of digital social innovation encompass the efficient allocation of economic factors, the enhancement of enterprise innovation capacity, and the promotion of high-quality economic growth. By leveraging digital technologies and media, enterprises can overcome limitations in resources and originality, address barriers to innovation, and attain a sustainable competitive advantage. Public policies play a crucial role in facilitating these processes and ensuring the long-term viability of digital social innovation initiatives.

5.1. Funding Models

Funding models for Digital Social Innovation (DSI) initiatives are varied and evolving, influenced by the intersection of finance and the creative economy. Cultural consumption has driven the expansion of cultural and creative industries (CCIs), sectors where many social innovations are incubated and launched. However, the structures available for funding DSIs are frequently inadequate or ill-suited to the specificity of the local contexts in which these innovations take place. The international framework for understanding DSIs remains relatively limited, and the potential routes to secure finance from various call mechanisms and institutional programs are often underdeveloped. The adaptation of traditional financing systems, such as the private investment of scarce capital, confronts a realm of innovation that is frequently public or non-profit and heavily focused on social, environmental, and community impact rather than purely economic returns. The innovative activities of many DSIs consequently remain confined to 'pockets of innovation.' This phenomenon hints at the role of specialized financial structures that can facilitate the broad dissemination of innovative work beyond localized clusters. Such considerations underscore the imperative to explore, address, and analyze the economic dimensions of media and technology as vehicles for both acceleration and expansion, particularly in the context of hangover spaces like social innovation representing this domain (Loots et al., 2022).

5.2. Sustainability Challenges

Economic challenges extend beyond funding availability, encompassing the design of socially sustainable business models and the development of dedicated organizational structures for digital social innovation projects (Stuermer et al., 2017). Many digital social innovation initiatives rely on a combination of funding from the public and social investment sectors. A dominant basis for long-term sustainability is often missing, since many projects are launched as short-term pilots without comprehensive consideration of continuation. Well-founded and practically relevant mechanisms for the sustainability of digital social innovation initiatives have yet to be developed.

6. THE INTERSECTION OF TECHNOLOGY, MEDIA, AND ECONOMY

The increasing degree of digitalization and computerization across industries has altered the economic models of an increasing number of artefacts and systems. Web 2.0 platforms exemplify systems for economic, social, and cultural exchanges, furthering traditional information and social flows. From a socio-economic standpoint, phenomena such as crowdsourcing and crowdfunding have significantly expanded the economic scope of Social Innovation (Recker & von Briel, 2019). Nonetheless, studies of Digital Social Innovation have often underweighted the economic dimension, a critical facet that should highlight the economic implications of the digital realm and associated media—and conversely, the impacts of the economic system on the trajectory of social innovation. Digital technologies have profoundly shaped and disequilibrated the broader context in which social innovation operates; the economic dimension is central to this dynamic. Additionally, the role of media warrants specific consideration to understand how, beyond the technical dimension, media dynamics support rapid and wide dissemination of new cultural paradigms and innovative practices within the social sphere. While the economic perspective remains underemphasized, media's influence within the social sphere gains amplified importance, at least from a macro-economic angle (MONACI, 2016).

6.1. Collaborative Platforms

Digital platforms have emerged as a potent catalyst for social innovation in recent years, giving rise to the large-scale implementation of novel collaborative initiatives potentially capable of fulfilling collective needs more effectively than traditional means. Having intertwined features shared by crowdfunding, collaborative production, social media, knowledge sharing, and open innovation, digital social innovation can be defined as "the creation and implementing of novel solutions to social needs and problems, accomplished through ICT-enabled collaborative efforts". Collaborative and sharing economy platforms have introduced new instrumental and symbolic opportunities for social innovation, directly transfiguring well-established spaces relating to connectivity, welfare, labor, and service provision within our communities (Avram et al., 2017). Despite such transformative potential, the fact that a considerable number of social enterprises have favoured digital involvement primarily to broaden outreach instead of deepening impact has delayed a decisive takeoff of digital social innovation across various sectors including government, education, energy, finance, health, mobility, and resource consumption. In such a context, tourism constitutes a paradigmatic case study where emerging technologies are providing desirable instruments to address social challenges including the opportunity to bridge geographical, economic, or social gaps, the necessity to support rural regeneration, the wish to broaden access to cultural heritage, and the difficult task of coping with the impact of increased globalisation (MONACI, 2016). An analysis of high-potential technological enablers from this perspective highlights the relevance of co-creation platforms, the diffusion of big and open data, the establishment of sociotechnical platforms, and the spread of advanced cloudification (MARCO CHIARA ELEONORA et al., 2019).

6.2. Economic Impact Assessments

Economic impact assessments evaluate how research infrastructures influence societal and economic development. Various guidelines and frameworks are available for conducting comprehensive evaluations, including impact assessment principles, case studies, and methodologies for collecting data on innovation activities. The socio-economic impacts of research infrastructures depend significantly on their surrounding environment and their integration within prevailing socio-economic structures. Therefore, indicators used to assess impact must be interpreted with caution, considering external factors such as usage of research results for business innovations or societal solutions (Hajdinjak & Havas, 2019). All these activities have significant effects on the geographic area under the STP's influence in terms of economic development, both with regard to the generation of economic activity and in the creation of employments. Not only the expenses necessary for STP's functioning must be taken into account, but also the expenses of the STP's firms and the students coming from outside the area of influence, all of which result in an injection of revenue and the generation of local production and occupation. Measuring the impact of this multifaceted centre requires a diverse approach. The methods used include input-output analysis, which measures the effects of interdependence among production sectors, differentiating between direct, indirect, and induced impacts. Impact studies based on input-output multipliers are valued for their limited data needs, though some critique overestimating net profits and recommend other techniques like cost-benefit analysis for better social and economic assessment. Assessments also involve analysis of economic and social impacts, using models such as input-output and social accounting matrices, as well as cost-benefit analysis to quantify non-economic costs and social returns (Torres-Pruñonosa et al., 2020).

7. POLICY FRAMEWORKS AND REGULATION

Digital technologies have played a crucial enabling role in the development of social innovation (Abrahams, 2017). More than simply a passive factor, digital technologies play an active role in the transformation of social innovation. An increasing number of social innovation platforms — often labelled "digital social innovation" platforms — are emerging around the world and adopting the "DIY, open source, bottom-up" ethos of digital culture to tackle challenges such as global inequity, climate change, and capitalism (Halmos et al., 2019). Flexible forms of organisation and relatively low barriers of entry allow digital social innovation projects to grow rapidly and scale their impact, making it particularly difficult for existing institutions and research to keep abreast of relevant developments. Good governance requires the regulation of unprecedented complexity. Regulators consequently find themselves facing a "wicked problem," where past solutions are a poor fit and linear thinking is no longer useful. The COVID-19 pandemic has sharpened these challenges, exposing existing vulnerabilities and accelerating behavioural changes and structural trends that will shape the digital future. While the main focus of digital social innovation remains community building and global solidarity, a pressing need arises for governance frameworks capable of embracing complexity, providing worthwhile expectations, and delivering sustainable multi-stakeholder support.

7.1. Current Policies

Current national and European level policies support social innovation and social economy principles by enhancing the use of digital tools and ICTs, which further the role of social innovation in addressing societal challenges and promoting sustainable growth (Halmos et al., 2019). Europe's socio-economic environment favors social entrepreneurship through public and private financing mechanisms and public procurement mechanisms oriented towards sustainable social and environmental criteria. At the European and international levels, multiple funds and financial programs for social enterprises have been created, allowing organizations to acquire the required creativity and risk-taking concepts to generate innovation with good growth perspectives. For other countries, governments emphasize mechanisms to promote social innovation through digital instruments and social economy, which are the main drivers for innovation in their economic, social, and environmental sectors that positively impact their inhabitants (André & Abreu, 2006).

7.2. Recommendations for Future Policies

The ever-changing digital landscape has affected different sectors of the economy and society, with transformative effects take place in the social innovation domain. The emergence of widespread connectivity, interactive interfaces, and new communication and collaboration techniques offers promising avenues for the realization of innovative solutions to social challenges (Halmos et al., 2019). The integration of digital subjects, from small and medium-sized enterprises to citizen collectives, together with the convergence between digital, physical, and biological technologies, makes the landscape of digital social innovation a complex and dynamic system: actors continuously experiment with new forms of collaboration and explore innovative governance models, processes, and tools. Digital social innovation is generally understood as an array of innovative services disseminated through digital channels aimed at meeting social needs from a bottom-up approach involving different actors. In such a context, technology facilitates coordination and collaboration among stakeholders; market mechanisms open new and unexplored flows for delivering social innovation; and media shapes the narratives that rally support and engagement by society first and policy and governmental institutions afterwards. The literature review conducted on the topic of digital social innovation highlights a lack of focus on economic aspects, despite a majority of papers addressing technology and media. The examination of policies, regulation, and economics of technological systems remains scarcely addressed, both in policy documents and think tank reports. Since the majority of documents discuss the impact of digital social innovation through a technological lens, the chapter focuses on the economic dimensions of the relationship between the economic domain and technology and media. This discussion aims to provide recommendations for the development of appropriate policies to support the digital social innovation space and enable it to become a significant catalyst for social change (Johanna Matschoss et al., 2017).

8. GLOBAL PERSPECTIVES ON DIGITAL SOCIAL INNOVATION

Digital social innovation (DSI) represents new social practices that promote mutual collaboration, solidarity, and a positive economic and social impact driven by digital technologies. DSI is an emerging theme both in practice and the academic literature. Largely absent from the debate to date, however, are perspectives that look beyond technical functionalities and political implications to instead explore how social innovation processes can generate positive economic impact, including funding and revenue-generation opportunities and their consequences for sustainability and scalability.

Analyzing the interactions between digital media and the economy, particularly in the context of social innovation, reveals a conceptual overlap between the creative economy, the platform economy, and the attention economy (Recker & von Briel, 2019). The creative economy refers to an economic system where ideas, information, and knowledge are key inputs for value creation.

8.1. Comparative Analysis of Regions

The short study of economic structures and human capital across European regions provides a basis for examining their role in the geographical distribution of social innovation activities. For example, concerns about adverse economic conditions in southern European regions arise partly from their low innovation performance. The cluster of regions exhibiting intense technological innovation combines average human capital and economic structures with strong labour market availability. Central European regions feature high labour market performance and economic levels, above-average technological innovation and the lowest human capital ranking. The innovation paradox arises from strong complementarities among business, education and government R&D spending, with university and government policies often working in opposite directions and firm-level technological activities constrained by weak absorptive capacity. Addressing the paradox requires policies that increase both the demand and the supply of innovation activities and that integrate technology policy with industrial policy to encourage innovation expenditure within industrial programmes. The unbalancing effect of the recent knowledge-based economy favours core cities at the expense of peripheries. Unless the majority of non-metropolitan regions successfully upgrade their economic and innovation profiles to ensure participation in the knowledge economy, there is a risk of further depression and concentration of social and economic activities. The analysis of innovation policy-making in Europe reveals variations strongly influenced by research concentration, domestic political fragmentation, Europeanization, and the endowment of regions within a member state, suggesting that already established policy approaches cannot easily be applied more broadly. Nonetheless, the diversity of approaches may contain a solution to the unevenness in policy-making practices (Pinto, 2009).

8.2. Cultural Influences on Innovation

Cultural influences shape perceptions of innovation, thereby affecting aspiration and social dynamics. Values may also be imputed, as in the largely male practice of bird photography in the early twentieth century. Fashions shape the diffusion of innovation, creating appreciation that transcends utility and leading to cascades of emulation (Cao et al., 2022). Regional or demographic norms make behaviours legitimate in some settings but illegitimate in others.

Both the origin and the destination of innovations embody national, religious, ethnic, or linguistic traits, which may easily stimulate conflict. The expectation raised by an innovation may eventually be disappointed. Innovation may trigger cascades of adoption and evolution, and social innovation often leads to technological advances and vice versa. High-profile inventors or founders appear at first to dominate a field, but their contributions are rarely more important than the norms, institutions, and trajectories that emerge from their influence.

9. CHALLENGES AND BARRIERS

Digital social innovation (DSI) mobilizes digital technology to address complex social challenges, but facilitating its development and delivery faces multifaceted challenges. Technological constraints, including the quality of available broadband and the complexity of digital tools, hamper the alignment and support of social innovation initiatives (Bilton & Leary, 2012). Additionally, provisions such as adequate workspaces and complementary expertise appear unsystematic or absent, further dissuading uptake; the public sector's role in unleashing and supporting DSI is often unclear. Economic barriers pose analogous problems. As a distinct category of innovation, DSI does not conform to either the economic model of a commercial firm or the organizational model of voluntary associations. DSI faces marked obstacles as a category of innovation owing to its technological, social, and organizational complexity. Although the public sector plays a pivotal role in investment, research, purchases, and legislation, DSIs obtain considerably less public funding than other innovation categories.

9.1. Technological Barriers

Technological barriers may result from the tier of interest: hardware, software platforms and tools, product or service and market. Barriers to technological convergence depend on the definition of technology considered. At the hardware level, smart card manufacturers experience neither technological nor IPR barriers generated by the standards around which digital-TV is building its future, namely, MHP and, to a lesser extent DVB-HTML (Matteucci, 2013). Software platforms or middleware are key for the adoption of standards and opening a widespread, competitive upstream market of "enabling equipment". Market barriers to the deployment of new services are evident in the case of the analogue switch-off every European country has still to schedule. Digital switchover would completely change TV-services markets, including the concentration of technological and market power. The effective chances and enforceability of the regulator's "must carry" rule remain controversial. Much will depend on the IPR positions and strategies of the major platforms owners—in some, if not all, countries strong market players are also technology owners—and on the role played by the machinery of standardization and technical specification. Economic and political factors will therefore have a significant influence on the consequences of the analogue switch-off, similarly to the technological convergence process itself.

9.2. Economic Disparities

Economic disparities play a crucial role in understanding the distribution of resources worldwide. Rising inequality emerges as a critical challenge, demands other than climate change for the modern world. One driver of these disparities is digital disruption. The mechanisms of technological adoption become the key to comprehending inequality in the digital era. A pivotal factor in the process of adoption is connectivity, which determines access and utilization of digital solutions. Taxation, however, appears less effective as a remedy. Even in conservative societies, a small cohort of entrepreneurs can facilitate the adoption of technologies and new ways of doing, acting as catalysts for change (Almirall et al., 2023).

The growth of disparities in wealth and opportunities concentrates on the transformations triggered by digital multinationals and digital technologies. Inequality originates from the combined effect of numerous factors including power conflicts, resource allocation, economic benefits, and others. Early theories, such as Pareto's analysis on the distribution of power, advocate that inequality follows universal patterns unconcerned about individual characteristics. The consumption of mobile services varies significantly along socio-economic lines. A profound gap exists between low and high income or education areas, distinguishable through assessment with particular services or application categories. High-income, higher-education regions show markedly more frequent use of news applications, e-mails, search, and music, smoking and social media and video-streaming services less. The behavioral patterns persist even when controlling for age and other census variables. French municipalities that consume more Facebook content and relatively less news show systematically lower levels of higher education (Ucar et al., 2021).

Digital use during the pandemic enhances the role of digital technologies for socio-economically disadvantaged individuals providing opportunities to work remotely and to stay socially connected. Despite these benefits, consequences remain unevenly distributed along socio-economic lines. The digital divide already constitutes a major social imbalance and the analysis identifies an additional socio-economic gap linked to the nature of digital activities at stake. Bridging the Digital Usage Gap in Mobile Service Consumption. Wider access to mobile services alone seems unlikely to limit the socio-economic disparities highlighted at the level of mobile service consumption. Such considerations call therefore for policies addressing specifically usage opportunities. The results provide insights towards this research direction, putting forward the idea that socioeconomically disadvantaged areas are not simply underserved by mobile services. Instead, they also appear to be disproportionately excluded from the consumption of certain service categories and types of use.

10. FUTURE TRENDS IN DIGITAL SOCIAL INNOVATION

Digital social innovation involves the application of digital technologies and media platforms by a network of actors to mobilize resources, support collaborative projects, and disseminate novel solutions for societal challenges (Yu et al., 2023). The cessation of physical events during the COVID-19 pandemic accelerated interest in creating online spaces for dialogue and discussion. Online digital social innovation enables technological experimentation, enhances global visibility, and fosters international cross-fertilization (Lacy & Prince, 2013). Crucially, innovation is not viewed solely as the production of products or services that generate profit for producers; the capacity to be replicated or scaled across other contexts also constitutes innovation.

10.1. Predicted Technological Advancements

Imagining technological futures entails risks given existing socioeconomic uncertainties (Lacy & Prince, 2013). Technologies foreseeably disruptive in the near future include additive manufacturing; autonomous vehicles (including vehicles-to-everything communication); blockchain; brain–machine interfaces; drones; internet of things; virtual reality; robotics; 5G mobile networks; synthetic biology or industrial biotechnology; and artificial intelligence. Technological trends affecting business models and value chains of media companies comprise a distinct but overlapping set: 5G mobile networks; blockchain; internet of things; big data analytics; chatbots; connected TV; virtual reality; drones; and artificial intelligence (M. Gossel et al.,

2018). Bruner's transition to a story-based society accelerated commodification of many types of personal data and construction of consumer profiles predicated on such data (for example, personality profiles).

10.2. Evolving Media Landscapes

Even if the complex and multifaceted relationship between media and social change has been extensively discussed by scholars, an economic analysis that concentrates on the role played by technology and new media in the process of digital social innovation is still lacking. Platforms like Spotify and Netflix develop systems collecting and distributing digital content from various sources, and content ownership remains of strategic importance. Major new players tend to focus on the development of platforms distributing third-party content. Whereas in 2009 digital users were not fully platform-agnostic, recent data show a near-complete agnosticism about the device used to access viewing. Content creators are thus adopting a transmedia approach, distributing the main product through different forms and platforms. Companies such as Amazon, Netflix and Hulu invest enormous resources in original films and series, competing mainly with traditional studios for the greatest titles. Many creatives are gradually leaving traditional media in order to share their ideas on new media. Social media, by providing a relatively low-cost tool to carry out analyses on the worldwide public, constitute one of the major opportunities for them. Mass amateurisation and collective or collaborative creations have been widely discussed, whereas the role played by public involvement in content production and consumption on the web remains under-examined. The emergence and dissemination of several technologies, tools, and devices for social sharing have made possible a new "mass self-communication" system, enabling individuals to easily express their opinions and creativity on a wide variety of topics and then disseminate them across global networks (MONACI, 2016).

11. CASE STUDIES OF EFFECTIVE DIGITAL SOCIAL INNOVATIONS

This section features case studies that illustrate the successful implementation of DSI initiatives aimed at advancing social objectives and promoting sustainable economic growth. Online platforms and mobile applications are designed to enable positive social and economic transformations, particularly by engaging disadvantaged communities. Such initiatives offer clear opportunities for tangible impact at both local and global levels. Examples include the development of participatory platforms that empower citizens, the creation of digital media outlets financed through microdonations, community-based education programs delivered via mobile technologies, Geo-crowdfunding startups, services underpinned by open data for social impact, and the application of blockchain technologies to enhance mutual credit systems. Tangible examples of DSI have demonstrated their contribution to structure-building among communities of interest (André & Abreu, 2006). Social experimentation plays a crucial role in testing new solutions within local contexts characterized by insufficient public social infrastructure and collective polarization. Pixemy showcases one of the foremost examples of a participatory platform specifically designed to assist young job seekers, a demographic facing unemployment rates significantly exceeding those of the general population. Dissensus. online and Crowdmedia represent pioneering media initiatives financed through independent crowdfunding and microdonations. HELA, meanwhile, utilizes mobile technologies to provide educational services informed by experiences from Repórter Brasil and HURIDOCS. Beyond Portugal, Derra.pr and Coopciv Social Kapital operate as Geo-crowdfunding startups that enable direct financial support for individuals and groups in preparation for disadvantaged conditions such as natural disasters or forced displacement. OpenDataServicios exemplifies services reliant on open-data applications and credit operations aimed at social impact. In the domain of governance, the application of blockchain technology stands out for its potential to enhance collective structures. Mutual-credit systems deployed on the public Ethereum blockchain supply a foundational infrastructure for community currencies and similar forms of complementary money aligned with economic and social innovation objectives. Against the backdrop of the digital revolution, social innovation undergoes continual renewal through information and communication technologies, fostering improved forms of collective cooperation in a context marked by strengthened territorialization (Helsper, 2008).

11.1. Local Initiatives

When disagreement goes public, the former springs to institutionalize dissent while the latter remains hermetic to all forms of institutionalization. A horizontal and trans-spatial connection is established, first starting with a simple discourse network and an eventual dialectic of disagreeing clusters. In the support of their conviction, actors aim to prove that the underlying institutional logic is inappropriate and that, as a result, the contested institution should not be considered legitimate. Disparagement of social problems, questionings of the institutional order and/or the institution it has engendered, or even outright comparisons between different institutional formulations thus contribute to specify and clarify the world that is contested. Opposing networks engage in the ongoing reconstruction of a vision of society, be it through symbolism and images or discourse and arguments, and thus develop alternative frameworks for seeing and interpreting reality. The institution and the networks of contestation enter a mutually-oriented historical process, whereby each defines its place and its action vis-à-vis the other (André & Abreu, 2006).

11.2. Global Success Stories

The Multifaceted Social Impact of Twitter The multifaceted social impact created by Twitter has subsequently been studied by many. Economic, political, cultural, and other dimensions of the Arabic Spring are examined in the "ECONOMIST." Google is mentioned as one of the organizations in an "inspired-by" list created as a result of a New York Times report of U.S. government spying efforts. Kavita's list of places where Twitter is creating a social impact includes between others the 2009 earthquake and 2011 tsunami in Japan, and the 2011 floods in Australia. Kavita's review article was published in 2012 as a chapter in a book focused on Twitter and microblogging. Twitter's earthquake hashtag is described as the most frequently used in Japan. Global Research Organisations Focused on Technology Solutions for Social Issues Google and the crowdfunding site Indiegogo are both listed among organizations with a social mission using technology in a Tech4Good report commissioned by the Net.Community Initiative. Another example is the Global Innovation Initiative (GII), overseen by the Department of Business Innovation and Skills in the U.K. Government, which has a mission to support innovation through partnerships involving higher education institutions. The initiative's primary focus is on "exchanging ideas on technology that has the potential to change the world, from robotics and nanotechnology to big data." As at 2012, the Department was considering the creation of a Circular Bioeconomy Innovation Centre, which would support the development of "new technologies that add value to and create innovative applications for biological resources and by-products."

12. MEASURING IMPACT AND EFFECTIVENESS

Digital social innovations harness digital technology to address social problems and mitigate societal challenges. Such projects involve digital tools, infrastructure, and channels, enhancing communities' well-being economically, politically, or socially. Digital social innovation projects expand stakeholders' capacity to design innovative actions and foster collaborative problem-solving. These innovations are proliferating across sectors including transport, energy, health, and education. This trend stimulates interactions among innovation types, enhancing the social capital of all involved. Measuring economic dimensions therefore requires careful evaluation of economic transparency and impact, using tailored metrics to capture effectiveness and value. Assessing impacts poses challenges, as digital social innovations often produce intangible results, whether societal benefits or economic. The ongoing search is for accurate metrics to gauge effectiveness (Pawluczuk et al., 2019). An impact study in digital social innovation (Oluoch & Osida, 2015) contributes to this exploration. Evaluation frameworks across related fields can potentially be adapted to measure social and economic effects. Indisputably, impact measurement presents a fundamental challenge in the cultural and creative sector. Obtaining data to demonstrate a project's significance is often difficult. For example, when applied in digital youth work, the task becomes extremely arduous. Director-level staff view it as an important issue despite participants' difficulties articulating the actual impact of a particular project. Impact assessment proves challenging and expensive, especially for services that operate for free. The debate about the existence of adequate metrics continues.

12.1. Metrics and Evaluation Tools

Assessing the economic dimensions of technology and media in digital social innovation necessitates appropriate evaluation instruments and metrics to measure contributions, assess impact, and support sustainability (MENDES POLVORA ALEXANDRE & DO NASCIMENTO SUSANA, 2018). While digital social innovation practitioners often seek to quantify social impact, many initiatives lack suitable tools to evaluate their economic effects, specifically the implications of technology and media. New social economy metrics have been developed to provide quantitative indicators of digital social innovation investment and impact, particularly emphasizing the roles of technology and media. These tools not only gauge economic and social benefits for replicability but also guide the management of initiatives, enabling adaptation, consolidation, and convergence in the evolutionary process. Existing research offers broader perspectives on social innovation metrics, frequently considering progress as a whole or applying frameworks at individual or community levels. Common components of these approaches include the definition of objectives, selection of indicators, data collection, and impact evaluation, with measurable economic and social factors often associated with the Sustainable Development Goals. Digital social innovation extends these perspectives by incorporating the specific contributions of technology and media to these processes and outcomes. The economic dimensions addressed in this text can be directly integrated into such a general framework; before formal inclusion, however, a focused treatment of digital social innovation—and the roles of technology and media—is necessary to establish an appropriate context prior to exploring impact measurement in detail.

Web 2.0 technologies have expanded access to information and democratized communication, fostering dynamic, productive partnerships that can be tailored to diverse circumstances. Although projects have succeeded in registering participants' intentions, they often lack consistent and systematic feedback on the quality and success of engagement. Providing mechanisms to collect, analyze, and communicate such information is vital to enable organizations to craft narratives that validate ongoing efforts and support future initiatives. Specifically, three components are essential: an evaluation framework that identifies appropriate, workable criteria; a means to identify relevant online information; and a consolidated tool that integrates evaluation criteria with high-level metrics (Ch'ng & Cai, 2019). Such a tool offers a simple, robust, and scalable approach, facilitating case-by-case benchmarking for comparative assessment and information exchange among diverse participants. This evaluation informs organizational strategy and deeply influences the degree, style, and effectiveness of engagement activities.

12.2. Feedback Mechanisms

Feedback processes within social and economic systems are largely responsible for ensuring stability. Feedback mechanisms make it possible to avoid a depletion of resources or to compensate for a trend that threatens the survival or continuity of a system. This dynamic does not apply to systems where the problem increases exponentially: In this case it becomes difficult to stabilise the system by resorting to internal mechanisms, since it is necessary to create a new way of acting, by changing the rules of the system. Social innovation does not just reveal what a "better society" is: it intervenes with new resource allocation rules and new action models to get out of the chaotic spiral into which the system had fallen. In this perspective, organizations can keep a positive feedback system for the simple fact of working to set up a social innovation. They can select the tools and mechanisms that best fit their objectives and use the energy they possess to socialise action rules and strengthen appropriate change networks.

The relational rationale widely discussed in the previous section is strongly connected to another aspect introduced in the last years by digital transformation: The feedback principle is deeply mediated by digital technologies. Immediate feedback systems (e.g., customer satisfaction surveys at the exit of a shop or after a call to a help desk) have supported market positions over the years through short communication loops. These kinds of systems, focused on responsive actions are now again exploited by some models of social innovation to stress and increase participation. Social media and due interface design are the technologies involved in the mediation work. They orient the searched feedback and make it easily available. These immediate feedback loops emerge as a sort of enhancement of the potential already embedded in the first generation of digital technologies (which supported the rise of peer-to-peer practices) and represent the infrastructure on top of which the third generation of social innovation has been developed. The infrastructure is at the same time technological and social. It is based on a distributed ledgers technology (such as the blockchain) able to create digital trust and allow the feedback loops to become fully operational. The same architecture is also used to create social structures able to contribute to the reflexivity of a system. It is able to transform Global to Local and Silence to Voice (Cavallo, 2017).

13. CROSS-SECTOR COLLABORATION

Cross-sector collaboration entails the sustained engagement of actors from at least two societal sectors to realize outcomes unattainable by a single sector. This form of collaboration, which pairs nonprofit organizations with governments and/or businesses, has become increasingly significant in addressing complex social issues. Such arrangements allow nonprofits to capitalize on their distinctive capabilities while advancing the social missions of the business partners involved. Crucially, the perspectives of nonprofit executives remain underexplored in understanding these partnerships, indicating a critical gap in the literature (Jessen, 2016).

Digital social innovation (DSI) unfolds through interactions among civil society, academia, government, and business actors, suggesting that the benefits of such initiatives are contingent upon multi-sectoral collaborations. Yet, conclusive evidence substantiating this assumption remains elusive. Strategies capable of surmounting informational uncertainties and fostering alignment within these networks are instrumental in realizing DSI's potential. According to, the formation of social partnerships can be enhanced by constructing effective platforms that integrate universities, corporations, nonprofit organizations, and civil society, thereby affording greater opportunity for deriving positive social impact. The advancement of strategies to address social issues in developing countries hinges on understanding the factors that motivate suppliers and buyers to engage in collaborative relationships. In this context, both transnational corporations and home country governments possess the capacity to leverage these collaborations to accelerate national expansion. Government and industry both have a vested interest in fostering university-industry relationships, not only because universities contribute skilled human capital to the private sector, but also because such links facilitate the transfer of new technologies. Building robust university-industry collaboration networks is widely regarded as a key pathway for promoting economic development.

13.1. Partnerships Between NGOs and Corporates

An interesting aspect of the Development Informatics discussions focuses on the role of the corporation as a stakeholder in DSI. Policy debate on this role has typically shifted security questions about the threat of terrorism, with related concerns about controlling informal communication-born movements and campaigns, including, e.g., anti-corporate protests, to the issue of how to harness the energies and resources of the corporate sector for development objectives. Those interested in cross-sector collaboration therefore advocate partnerships between NGOs and corporations, resting on the idea that each sector has a complementary set of resources and expertise that may help the other to improve its overall effectiveness and to address some of its core challenges or priorities. In this framing, NGOs become the mainspring and catalyst for all kinds of social change by mobilizing, articulating, and representing social or community aspirations, and corporations provide information, money, organizational capacity and efficiency, and perhaps new technologies to help make the long-term changes actually happen. It is argued that these partnerships can show the way towards what could be a new global compact between the corporate and the citizen sector, with emerged, re-capitalized, autonomous, highly energized, and well-focused citizens' groups showing multi-national corporations how, where, and when to invest responsibly, and also showing host-government where public authority is truly needed.

13.2. Role of Government in Facilitation

Technology and media have unquestionably become central from an economic perspective, determining sectors and enabling citizens, regardless of their geopolitical conditions, to identify and create solutions–through products, services, and processes that could even transform the existing economic status quo. Moreover, technology and media can "commodify" knowledge, reducing its production cost and increasing the rate and intensity of knowledge flow in the economy. From this standpoint, technology and media are the enablers and promoters of digital social innovation towards a collaboration economy. However, without a proper framework in place, technology and media can also threaten the development of digital social innovation. Public policy should therefore offer a regulatory framework that safeguards the three essential elements of digital social innovation: creation, sustainability, and replication. Regulatory measures should enhance these principles and protect them from distortion or deviation, whether from political interests or private sector influences. A legislative framework that supports these key factors is conducive to the development of digital social innovation.

14. ETHICAL CONSIDERATIONS

Digital social innovation incorporates private sector business and economic models to sustain and spread social innovation through digital technologies. The ability of private for-profit and non-profit actors to harness digital technologies and advances in Internet connectivity can facilitate new forms of organizational structures, processes, products, services, and capabilities. This convergence of social needs, technology, and business models can overcome urgent societal challenges and support the achievement of the SDGs while empowering disadvantaged groups and vulnerable individuals in society (Carsten 1968- Stahl, 2011). Governments and private businesses have adopted and actively promote digital social innovation by allocating increasing resources (Casas-Roma, 2022). In approaching digital social innovation, two latent intrinsic ethical dimensions emerge. First, the growing inequality in access to the Internet, the hardware and the media composing digital infrastructures presents a direct ethical challenge for many social innovation initiatives. Second, digital social innovation initiatives risk the emergence of new forms of power that were not previously envisaged (van den Hoven et al., 2012).

14.1. Privacy Concerns

Privacy in the digital sphere has become one of the most contentious challenges of the Information Age, especially as digital social innovations increasingly rely on pervasive information and communication technologies. Traditional notions of data protection and privacy have been transformed by rapid advances in mobile technology, cloud computing, biometrics, and radiofrequency identification, all of which encourage the creation of intricate correlations capable of tracing not only cultural and behavioral patterns but also emotional states (A. Tsoukalas & D. Siozos, 2011). At the same time, the immense amount of data generated by web applications, social networking sites, and portable devices has prompted a shift in how privacy is understood and why it is important. The European Union has recognised the need to adapt its policy framework so that it can function as an engine for innovation whilst simultaneously guaranteeing social sustainability; this includes a call for a more effective and coherent legal environment to maintain adequate protection of privacy and personal data. Definitional issues continue to complicate the formulation of policy around privacy, however. While technology demands a consistent rethinking of the notion itself, society is at the same time expected to play an active role in shaping the process of change (M. Blanke, 2018). Modern debates are thus not only concerned with what privacy means or should mean but how emerging concerns should be weighed, prioritised, and mitigated. Since the primacy and sensitivity of privacy varies from individual to individual, a universal concept remains both far away and dubious. Building upon economic findings, such considerations are crucial for the sustainable development of digital social innovation.

14.2. Equity in Access

Digital inclusion, in its simplest form, suggests that all individuals and communities should have access to and the ability to use information and communication technologies. When certain groups are denied access to digital technologies, they are unfairly discriminated against—a form of social exclusion that mirrors existing societal injustices (Watling, 2012). Since the early 2000s, this recognition has prompted a consensus on the inherent unfairness of ignoring digital inclusion issues. The prevalent conceptualization of the digital divide has shaped national policies aimed at bridging the gap. However, in developing countries, the priority remains providing more inclusive broadband access, and sophisticated strategies to ensure this have yet to be formulated. Infrastructure is a prerequisite for inclusion, but it alone is insufficient; the social dimension is crucial for ensuring fair and equitable access. This fact is acknowledged by several recent strategies independently developed by major worldwide digital communication companies. Natural intellectual impairments, such as dyslexia and dementia, should not present barriers to digital inclusion. Assistive technology devices, which accommodate alternative input and output methods, demonstrate how digital landscapes can be customized to individual needs, thereby creating opportunities for inclusive learning and participation. Digital health systems depend on an enabling, integrative infrastructure. Nevertheless, certain approaches emphasize the upstream economic and access conditions influencing health outcomes and how these vary within societies. They impute a social gradient in produce-price—access, healthiness, and product-health—outcome responses through variables such as income, class, ethnicity, access to statutory welfare, time availability, professional status, and cultural capital, evaluating the impact of social stratification and binary distinctions like minority-majority and urban-rural. This perspective poses questions about whether the multiplier effect of digital inclusion positively compensates for the relative accumulation of difficulties in these conditions (Azzopardi-Muscat & Sørensen, 2019). The debate has grown to define digital equity as inclusive—and equitable—access to infrastructures, services, and applications.

15. CONCLUSION

The economic dimensions of technology and media in digital social innovation (DSI) interconnect economic analysis with technology and media studies, innovations studies, and development economics. Across all academic levels, the examination of DSI is both multi- and interdisciplinary, yet economic issues, those related to financing technology and media, validating the economic significance of DSI projects, and identifying appropriate policy mechanisms remain insufficiently explored.

Figure 2. Rubric heatmap of the economic dimensions (Author's scheme, see Appendix II)

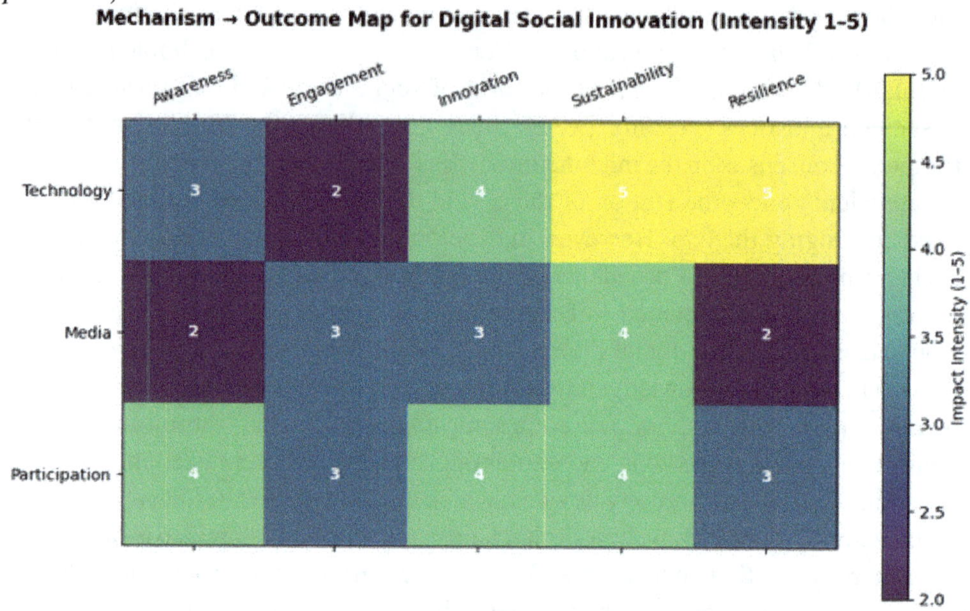

The heatmap illustrates how different mechanisms of digital social innovation—technology, media, and participation—interact with five key outcomes: awareness, engagement, innovation, sustainability, and resilience. Each cell represents the intensity of influence on a scale from one to five, where darker colors indicate weaker effects and brighter shades signal stronger contributions. This visual approach allows us to assess not only the strength of each mechanism individually but also how they complement or fail to complement one another across outcomes. Technology emerges as the strongest driver of long-term systemic change. Its highest scores appear in relation to sustainability and resilience, both rated at five. This underscores the transformative capacity of ICTs, artificial intelligence, and digital infrastructures in building adaptive systems that endure beyond short-term interventions. At the same time, technology is less effective in generating engagement, where it scores only two. This suggests that technical capacity alone cannot ensure broad participation or active involvement of communities.

Media shows a more moderate influence overall. It contributes meaningfully to sustainability, with a score of four, reflecting its role in disseminating knowledge, coordinating campaigns, and extending the visibility of initiatives. However, media remains weak in relation to resilience, scoring only two, which highlights its limitations as a structural driver of adaptive capacity. While media platforms can create awareness and foster short-term mobilization, they may lack the depth to support enduring social and institutional change without being reinforced by other mechanisms. Participation demonstrates a balanced and steady influence across all outcomes. It achieves scores of three or four consistently, with particular strength in awareness and innovation. This reflects the importance of inclusiveness, diversity, and co-creation in ensuring that digital social innovation is not only technologically advanced but also socially embedded. Participation functions as a cross-cutting enabler, ensuring legitimacy, trust, and shared ownership of outcomes. Unlike technology and media, it does not dominate in one area but instead provides a stable and evenly distributed impact (Helsper, 2008). Taken together, the map suggests that sustainable and resilient digital social innovation arises from the interplay of these three mechanisms. Technology provides structural capacity, media extends outreach and visibility, and participation guarantees inclusivity and legitimacy. When aligned, these mechanisms reinforce one another, producing outcomes that are not only innovative but also durable, equitable, and socially meaningful. This highlights the need for integrated strategies that do not privilege one mechanism over others but instead leverage their complementarities for maximum social impact. Given that both the technologies and media channels associated with social innovation initiatives necessitate capital investment and ongoing costs, and considering that many such initiatives encounter difficulties in securing continuous financial support, the pivotal importance of economic considerations within DSI becomes evident. This chapter of progress within the COST Action elucidates fundamental issues in DSI and highlights areas requiring further investigation. It aims to inform the strategic planning of subsequent phases of research and to guide the assessment of DSI. The Economic Dimensions of Technology and Media in Digital Social Innovation have, to a considerable extent, fulfilled their initial aim of encouraging scholars to delve more deeply into the subject.

REFERENCES

Abrahams, L. (2017). Regulatory Imperatives for the Future of SADC's "Digital Complexity Ecosystem". https://core.ac.uk/download/188768849.pdf

Almirall, E., Willmott, S., & Cortés, U. (2023). A few misfits can Change the World. https://arxiv.org/pdf/2309.03532

André, I., & Abreu, A. (2006). Dimensões e espaços da inovação social. https://core.ac.uk/download/26832047.pdf

Avram, G. Hee-jeong Choi, J., De Paoli, S., Light, A., Lyle, P., & Teli, M. (2017). Collaborative economies: from sharing to caring. https://core.ac.uk/download/188016138.pdf

Azzopardi-Muscat, N., & Sørensen, K. (2019). Towards an equitable digital public health era: promoting equity through a health literacy perspective. https://www.ncbi.nlm.nih.gov/pmc/articles/PMC6859513/

Bilton, C., & Leary, R. (2012). Digital transformation in the arts: a case study. https://core.ac.uk/download/29189144.pdf

Blanke, M. J. (2018). Privacy and Outrage. https://core.ac.uk/download/214111681.pdf

Cao, L., Chen, Z., & Evans, J. (2022). Destructive Creation, Creative Destruction, and the Paradox of Innovation Science. https://arxiv.org/pdf/2210.10661

Carsten, & Stahl, B. (2011). IT for a better future how to integrate ethics, politics and innovation. https://core.ac.uk/download/228195737.doc

Casas-Roma, J. (2022). Ethical Idealism, Technology and Practice: a Manifesto. https://www.ncbi.nlm.nih.gov/pmc/articles/PMC9462067/

Cavallo, M. (2017). Sharing economy, sharing information. Are open data addressing us towards a new wikieconomy? https://core.ac.uk/download/235040253.pdf

Ch'ng, E., & Cai, S. (2019). Methods for evaluating the adoption and use of digital technologies in GLAMs. https://www.ncbi.nlm.nih.gov/pmc/articles/PMC7182766/

Challoumis, C. (2018). Methods of Controlled Transactions and the Behavior of Companies According to the Public and Tax Policy. *Economics*, *6*(1), 33–43. DOI: 10.2478/eoik-2018-0003

Challoumis, C. (2021). Index of the cycle of money - the case of Bulgaria. Economic Alternatives, 27(2), 225–234. https://www.unwe.bg/doi/eajournal/2021.2/EA.2021.2.04.pdf

Challoumis, C. (2023a). FROM SAVINGS TO ESCAPE AND ENFORCEMENT SAVINGS. *Cógito (Salvador)*, *XV*(4), 206–216.

Challoumis, C. (2023b). Risk on the tax system of the E.U. from 2016 to 2022. *Economics*, *11*(2), 55–72.

Challoumis, C. (2024). From Economics to Economic Engineering (The Cycle of Money): The case of Romania. *Cógito (Salvador)*, *XVII*(2), 161–170.

Challoumis, C. (2025a). The impact factor of Tangibles and Intangibles of controlled transactions on economic performance. Economic Alternatives, 31(1), 64–76. https://www.unwe.bg/doi/eajournal/2025.1/EA.2025.1.04.pdf

Challoumis, C. (2025b). THE INFLATION ACCORDING TO THE CYCLE OF MONEY (C.M.). Economic Alternatives, 2025(2), 324–353. https://doi.org/https://doi.org/10.37075/EA.2025.2.03

Dunford, M., & Dunford, M. (2017). Understanding voice, distribution and listening in Digital Storytelling. https://core.ac.uk/download/219375574.pdf

Gossel, M. B., Will, A., & Windscheid, J. (2018). The influence of technology trends on business models and value chains of media companies. https://core.ac.uk/download/224741237.pdf

Hajdinjak, M., & Havas, A. (2019). A Practical Guide. https://core.ac.uk/download/228400934.pdf

Halmos, A., Misuraca, G., & Viscusi, G. (2019). From Public Value to Social Value of Digital Government: Co-Creation and Social Innovation in European Union Initiatives. https://core.ac.uk/download/211994115.pdf

Havas, A. (2016). Recent economic theorising on innovation: Lessons for analysing social innovation. https://core.ac.uk/download/213993194.pdf

Helsper, E. (2008). Digital inclusion: an analysis of social disadvantage and the information society. https://core.ac.uk/download/213972.pdf

Jessen, D. (2016). Cross-sector Collaboration: Results Through Understanding and Application. https://core.ac.uk/download/228616099.pdf

Johanna Matschoss, K., Petteri Repo, J., Schultze, J., Berchem, M., Velasco, G., Popper, R., Linford, S., Avarello, A., & Pinto, M. (2017). CASI Policy Recommendations: Deliverable 8.3. https://core.ac.uk/download/132489646.pdf

(Julia) Wittmayer. J. M., (J.) Backhaus, J., (Flor) Avelino, F., (Bonno) Pel, B., (T.) Strasser, T., (Iris) Kunze, I., & (Linda) Zuijderwijk, L. M. A. (2019). Narratives of change: How social innovation initiatives construct societal transformation. https://core.ac.uk/download/224787636.pdf

Kateb, S. C., Ruehle, R. P., Kroon, D., van Burg, E., & Huber, M. (2022). Innovating under pressure: Adopting digital technologies in social care organizations during the COVID-19 crisis. https://www.ncbi.nlm.nih.gov/pmc/articles/PMC9013661/

Lacy, M., & Prince, D. (2013). The future of digital disrupters:rethinking the digital divide. https://core.ac.uk/download/16285530.pdf

Loots, E., Betzler, D., Bille, T., Jan Borowiecki, K., & Lee, B. (2022). New forms of finance and funding in the cultural and creative industries. Introduction to the special issue. https://www.ncbi.nlm.nih.gov/pmc/articles/PMC9185720/

MARCO CHIARA ELEONORA. D. E., MININ ALBERTO, D. I., CRISTINA, M. A. R. U. L. L. O., & DANIEL, N. E. P. E. L. S. K. I. (2019). Digital platform innovation in European SMEs. https://core.ac.uk/download/188760703.pdf

Matteucci, N. (2013). Standards, IPR and digital TV convergence: theories and empirical evidence. https://core.ac.uk/download/211614438.pdf

MENDES POLVORA ALEXANDRE. R. O. Q. U. E. & DO NASCIMENTO SUSANA, F. I. G. U. E. I. R. E. D. O. (2018). Impact Assessment and Recommendations: Making Sense H2020 CAPS Project. https://core.ac.uk/download/154760364.pdf

MONACI. S. A. R. A. (2016). Boosting Creativity through Digital Disruption? The Role of Co-Creation Platforms in the Media Production Field. https://core.ac.uk/download/234913232.pdf

Oluoch, J., & Osida, J. (2015). Measuring Impacts of Information and Communication Advances for Development in the 21st Century. https://core.ac.uk/download/234672122.pdf

Pavlik, V. J., E Dennis, E., Davis Mersey, R., & Gengler, J. (2019). Conducting Research on the World's Changing Mediascape: Principles and Practices. https://core.ac.uk/download/201133363.pdf

Pavlik, V. J., E. Dennis, E., Davis Mersey, R., & Gengler, J. (2019). Conducting Research on the World's Changing Mediascape: Principles and Practices. https://core.ac.uk/download/229940771.pdf

Pawluczuk, A., Webster, G., Smith, C., & Hall, H. (2019). The Social Impact of Digital Youth Work: What Are We Looking For? https://core.ac.uk/download/229940317.pdf

Pinto, H. (2009). The Diversity of Innovation in the European Union: Mapping Latent Dimensions and Regional Profiles. https://core.ac.uk/download/pdf/144016560.pdf

Recker, J., & von Briel, F. (2019). The future of digital entrepreneurship research: existing and emerging opportunities: professional development workshop. https://core.ac.uk/download/267815713.pdf

Stuermer, M., Abu-Tayeh, G., & Myrach, T. (2017). Digital sustainability: basic conditions for sustainable digital artifacts and their ecosystems. https://www.ncbi.nlm.nih.gov/pmc/articles/PMC6106115/

Tiwari, M., & Tiwari, M. (2017). Exploring the role of Capabilities in Social Innovation. https://core.ac.uk/download/219375382.pdf

Torres-Pruñonosa, J., Maria Raya, J., & Dopeso-Fernández, R. (2020). The Economic and Social Value of Science and Technology Parks. The Case of Tecnocampus. https://www.ncbi.nlm.nih.gov/pmc/articles/PMC7786403/

Tsoukalas, A. I. & D. Siozos, P. (2011). Privacy and Anonymity in the Information Society – Challenges for the European Union. https://www.ncbi.nlm.nih.gov/pmc/articles/PMC5720049/

Ucar, I., Gramaglia, M., Fiore, M., Smoreda, Z., & Moro, E. (2021). News or social media? Socio-economic divide of mobile service consumption. https://www.ncbi.nlm.nih.gov/pmc/articles/PMC8633779/

van den Hoven, J., Helbing, D., Pedreschi, D., Domingo-Ferrer, J., Gianotti, F., & Christen, M. (2012). FuturICT - The Road towards Ethical ICT. https://arxiv.org/pdf/1210.8181

Watling, S. (2012). Digital landscapes: inclusive potential versus exclusive practice. https://core.ac.uk/download/1645858.pdf

Yu, W., Zhang, L., & Yang, C. (2023). The impact of the digital economy on enterprise innovation behavior: Based on CiteSpace knowledge graph analysis. https://www.ncbi.nlm.nih.gov/pmc/articles/PMC9900121/

APPENDIX

Python Code of the Chart

```
# 2025 ©® All Rights Reserved Constantinos Challoumis
# --- Bibliometric Co-occurrence Network ---
import itertools
import math
import matplotlib.pyplot as plt
import networkx as nx
from collections import Counter
import numpy as np
# (Replace with your dataset)
papers = [
["digital social innovation", "open data", "civic tech",
"participation", "co-creation"],
["platforms", "ai for social good", "participation", "gover-
nance", "ethics"],
["microcredit", "financial inclusion", "social enterprise",
"smes", "resilience"],
["social media", "campaigns", "misinformation", "data aggre-
gation", "ifttt"],
["open source", "open innovation", "crowdsourcing", "co-
creation", "communities"],
["blockchain", "identity", "privacy", "governance",
"trust"],
["smart cities", "open data", "sensors", "participation",
"policy"],
["health", "telemedicine", "ai for social good", "equity",
"access"],
["education", "platforms", "open educational resources",
"collaboration", "equity"],
["environment", "civic tech", "citizen science", "data visu-
alization", "governance"],
["resilience", "sustainability", "commons", "cooperative
models", "policy"],
["microcredit", "platforms", "governance", "trust", "inclu-
sion"],
```

```
["ai for social good", "ethics", "bias", "transparency", "accountability"],
["social media", "hashtags", "collective action", "mobilization", "campaigns"],
["crowdfunding", "social enterprise", "smes", "financial inclusion", "resilience"],
["open government", "transparency", "open data", "policy", "participation"],
["data governance", "privacy", "trust", "ethics", "regulation"],
["participation", "co-creation", "collaboration", "collective intelligence", "communities"],
["humanitarian tech", "crisis mapping", "open data", "volunteered geographic information", "coordination"],
["economocracy", "cycle of money", "resilience", "smes", "policy"]
]
# Normalize
papers = [[k.strip().lower() for k in ks] for ks in papers]
# Build co-occurrence edges
edge_weights = Counter()
node_weights = Counter()
for kws in papers:
node_weights.update(set(kws))
for a, b in itertools.combinations(sorted(set(kws)), 2):
edge_weights[(a, b)] += 1
# Filter weak edges
MIN_EDGE_WEIGHT = 2
edges = [(a, b, w) for (a, b), w in edge_weights.items() if w >= MIN_EDGE_WEIGHT]
# Graph
G = nx.Graph()
for n, w in node_weights.items():
G.add_node(n, weight=w)
for a, b, w in edges:
G.add_edge(a, b, weight=w)
# Keep main component
if len(G) > 0:
comps = sorted(nx.connected_components(G), key=len, reverse=True)
```

```
G = G.subgraph(comps[0]).copy()
# Detect clusters (community detection)
communities = nx.algorithms.community.greedy_modularity_com-
munities(G)
cluster_map = {}
for cid, comm in enumerate(communities):
for n in comm:
cluster_map[n] = cid
# Assign cluster colors
num_clusters = len(communities)
colors = plt.cm.tab20(np.linspace(0, 1, num_clusters))
node_colors = [colors[cluster_map[n]] for n in G.nodes]
# Layout
pos = nx.spring_layout(G, seed=42, k=0.6 / math.sqrt(max(1,
len(G))))
# Plot
plt.figure(figsize=(10, 7))
nx.draw_networkx_edges(G, pos, width=[0.5+G.edges[e]
['weight'] for e in G.edges], alpha=0.4)
nx.draw_networkx_nodes(G, pos, node_size=[300+80*G.nodes[n]
['weight'] for n in G.nodes],
node_color=node_colors, alpha=0.9)
nx.draw_networkx_labels(G, pos, font_size=8)
plt.title("Bibliometric Co-occurrence Network (Digital So-
cial Innovation)",
fontsize=12, weight="bold", pad=10)
plt.axis("off")
plt.tight_layout()
plt.savefig("DSI_bibliometric_cooccurrence_network.png",
dpi=300, bbox_inches="tight")
plt.show()
```

Python Code of the Rubric Heatmap

```
# 2025 ©® All Rights Reserved Constantinos Challoumis
# --- Mechanism → Outcome Map (Intensity 1-5) ---
import numpy as np
import matplotlib.pyplot as plt
```

```
# Intensity matrix (rows = mechanisms, cols = outcomes)
data = np.array([
[3, 2, 4, 5, 5], # Technology
[2, 3, 3, 4, 2], # Media
[4, 3, 4, 4, 3] # Participation
], dtype=float)
mechanisms = ["Technology", "Media", "Participation"]
outcomes = ["Awareness", "Engagement", "Innovation", "Sus-
tainability", "Resilience"]
fig, ax = plt.subplots(figsize=(9, 5.5))
# Heatmap (don't specify a style; default colormap is fine)
cax = ax.matshow(data)
# Gridlines
ax.set_xticks(np.arange(len(outcomes)))
ax.set_yticks(np.arange(len(mechanisms)))
ax.set_xticklabels(outcomes, rotation=20)
ax.set_yticklabels(mechanisms)
# Add cell labels
for (i, j), val in np.ndenumerate(data):
ax.text(j, i, f"{int(val)}", ha="center", va="center", col-
or="white", fontsize=10, weight="bold")
# Titles / labels
ax.set_xlabel("")
ax.set_ylabel("")
plt.title("Mechanism → Outcome Map for Digital Social Inno-
vation (Intensity 1-5)", pad=20, fontsize=12, weight="bold")
# Colorbar
fig.colorbar(cax, label="Impact Intensity (1-5)")
plt.tight_layout()
plt.savefig("mechanism_outcome_map.png", dpi=300, bbox_
inches="tight")
plt.show()
```

Chapter 14
Websites Beyond Technology:
Platforms for Awareness, Promotion, and Social Innovation

Nur Azila B. Azahari
https://orcid.org/0009-0009-8378-777X
Faculty of Business and Communication, Universiti Malaysia Perlis, Malaysia

Nur Aisya Roslan
Faculty of Business and Communication, Universiti Malaysia Perlis, Malaysia

Zamirul Nur Hakim M. Zailani
Faculty of Business and Communication, Universiti Malaysia Perlis, Malaysia

Farah Zahidah Abdullah
https://orcid.org/0009-0008-0486-0928
Faculty of Business and Communication, Universiti Malaysia Perlis, Malaysia

Mariam Idris
Faculty of Business and Communication, Universiti Malaysia Perlis, Malaysia

ABSTRACT

This chapter examines how websites are becoming platforms beyond learning management systems and social media. Websites are evaluated for their potential to promote cultural identity, awareness, and sustainable development at the crossroads of technology, media, and social innovation. The discussion compares websites, apps for the web, and new media, highlighting the benefits and drawbacks using usability and technology adoption ideas. A microplastic awareness website simplifies scientific information for parents and carers, and a Pulau Tuba tourist

DOI: 10.4018/979-8-3373-5307-4.ch014

website promotes visibility and community empowerment. Websites are credible, stable, and inclusive, making them ideal for organised awareness campaigns and persuasive communication, according to comparative studies. Websites may integrate new technology and promote social innovation in digital ecosystems, according to the findings.

THE IMPORTANCE OF WEBSITES BEYOND LMS AND SOCIAL MEDIA

The intersection of technology, media, and social innovation has created new ways for people to learn, collaborate, and engage with communities. Traditionally, Learning Management Systems (LMS) and social media platforms have been the main tools for education and interaction. However, websites which particularly those designed with dynamic, user-centered features, now play an increasingly important role that goes beyond these two systems. They are not only channels for delivering content but also platforms for innovation, collaboration, and responsible communication.

Supporting Social Innovation

One of the most significant contributions of websites is their ability to support social innovation. Unlike LMS, which are often limited to structured learning environments, or social media, which can be fragmented and informal, websites can serve as centralized and reliable platforms for social change.

Chen, Xue, and Zhang (2025) emphasize that in the digital era, online platforms provide more than just communication tools. They act as systems that reshape how communities interact, design services, and make decisions. By hosting resources, offering interactive spaces, and enabling multi-stakeholder participation, websites become enablers of social innovation. They help connect individuals, organizations, and policymakers to address pressing challenges such as environmental protection, education gaps, and public health issues.

A practical example of this role can be seen in the development of knowledge management systems for social innovation. Suzianti, Al Hafi, and Shafira (2019) studied the Indonesian platform which named Kreanovator, was designed as a digital hub to collect, manage, and distribute innovation-related knowledge. This case demonstrates how websites can function as repositories of shared learning while simultaneously connecting innovators, entrepreneurs, and communities. By creating a centralized space, the platform supported collaboration across sectors, ensuring that social innovation projects were not only initiated but also sustained.

These examples underline how websites are uniquely positioned to provide stability and continuity compared to fast-moving social media and to offer inclusivity that LMS often lack.

Beyond Traditional LMS: Dynamic Alternatives

Despite the widespread adoption of learning management systems (LMS) in education, their primary function has been to deliver structured content, monitor progress, and offer assessment tools. The creativity and engagement of students may be restricted by this rigorous approach. Conversely, websites may serve as more interactive and adaptable alternatives.

Resource repositories, multimedia galleries, collaborative workstations, and discussion forums are among the numerous tools that can be integrated into web-based platforms. In contrast to conventional learning management systems (LMS), these instruments are not restricted by course structures and can be customised to accommodate various learning environments. This adaptability is indicative of the changing requirements of students, who anticipate interactive, real-time engagement rather than static content delivery.

Websites can also equip learners with practical skills that are reflective of the realities of the workplace. Cloud-based applications, collaborative dashboards, and project management platforms are frequently employed by employees in contemporary work environments. The integration of similar tools into educational websites provides students with early exposure to these practices, thereby bridging the divide between academic learning and professional requirements.

In summary, although learning management systems (LMS) continue to be beneficial, websites provide a more dynamic toolkit that encourages collaboration, self-directed learning, and exploration beyond the bounds of the traditional classroom.

Websites in Digital Marketing and CSR

Websites are equally significant in the business sector, particularly for the promotion of Corporate Social Responsibility (CSR) initiatives, in addition to education and social innovation. CSR is no longer perceived as a secondary activity; rather, it is an essential component of stakeholder engagement and brand identity.

Dundua (2024) clarifies that organisations are increasingly employing websites to enhance their reputation and to disseminate their corporate social responsibility initiatives in a transparent and interactive manner. Organisations can share real-time updates, emphasise user-generated content, and establish communication channels with stakeholders through websites, in contrast to traditional reports or press releases. This interactive dimension fosters active participation from the public and fosters trust.

For instance, organisations may implement designated CSR sections on their websites to emphasise community partnerships, employee welfare initiatives, or environmental initiatives. Stakeholders are afforded the opportunity to observe progress and express their opinions through interactive dashboards, videos, and feedback forms. In this manner, websites transcend conventional marketing and evolve into platforms for collaboration and dialogue.

The intersection of social innovation and websites is illustrated even more by the relationship between CSR and digital platforms. Companies not only enhance their brand but also contribute to broader social objectives, including inclusivity and sustainability, by transparently presenting their CSR initiatives.

Contributions of Websites Beyond LMS and Social Media

Websites offer unique advantages that exceed the capabilities of social media and learning management systems (LMS). By facilitating collaboration, fostering knowledge-sharing, and scaling community-driven initiatives, they contribute to social innovation (Chen et al., 2025; Suzianti et al., 2019). Additionally, they offer dynamic learning alternatives that surpass the fixed structures of LMS, including flexible, interactive, and skill-oriented tools. Furthermore, websites facilitate CSR engagement by enabling organisations to engage stakeholders in a meaningful manner and communicate their strategies in a transparent manner (Dundua, 2024).

These advantages highlight the adaptability of websites as platforms that unite technology, media, and social purpose. They foster innovation, strengthen institutional and community relationships, and support education. In a rapidly evolving digital environment, websites remain essential because of their versatility, reliability, and capacity to integrate multiple roles. To appreciate their distinct potential, the following section situates websites alongside web applications and new media within digital communication and adoption theories.

WEBSITES, WEB APPLICATIONS, AND NEW MEDIA: A CONCEPTUAL LENS

The ways in which societies communicate, share knowledge, and mobilise for change have been significantly altered by the rapid advancement of digital technologies. Websites, web applications, and new media platforms function as complementary yet distinct instruments that facilitate various forms of communication, participation, and innovation within this landscape. In order to comprehend their functions, it is necessary to employ a theoretical perspective that place them within broader discussions regarding social innovation, adoption, and usability, in addition to a descriptive account of their technical distinctions. Therefore, this section incorporates theories of digital communication and technology adoption with a comparative analysis of these three platforms, thereby establishing the conceptual framework for the case studies that will be presented later in this chapter.

Digital Communication and Social Innovation

Websites, web applications, and new media are fundamentally mediating technologies. They have an impact on the way in which information is disseminated, how users interact, and how social issues are conveyed. As per digital communication theory, these technologies are cultural treasures that instill values, priorities, and expectations of interaction, rather than neutral containers of information. For example, the user's ability to access and interpret information is influenced by the interactive capabilities of a web application, the viral potential of social media posts, or the design of a website's navigation interface.

In the context of social innovation, these platforms extend beyond technical efficiency to create opportunities for awareness, empowerment, and participation. Social innovation emphasizes novel solutions that address social problems while enhancing inclusivity and sustainability. Websites designed for public health campaigns, web applications for civic participation, or social media platforms for grassroots advocacy all exemplify how technology can be harnessed for broader societal goals. Thus, examining these digital tools through the dual lenses of communication and innovation allows us to appreciate their potential impact in fields as diverse as education, tourism, healthcare, and environmental sustainability.

Adoption and Usability: Insights from TAM and UTAUT

The efficacy of digital platforms is contingent upon their actual utilisation. The Unified Theory of Acceptance and Use of Technology (UTAUT) and the Technology Acceptance Model (TAM) continue to be highly influential in the explanation of adoption behaviour.

The Technology Acceptance Model (TAM) emphasizes two main determinants of digital system adoption: perceived usefulness, the extent to which a system enhances task performance, and perceived ease of use, the degree of effort required in its operation. The Unified Theory of Acceptance and Use of Technology (UTAUT) extends this view by incorporating social influence, reflecting the role of peers and societal expectations, and facilitating conditions, referring to the technical and organizational support that enables effective system utilization.

When applied to websites, web applications, and new media, these models highlight both shared and distinct adoption pathways. For instance, a website designed to raise awareness about microplastics may be perceived as useful if it provides trustworthy content in a clear and accessible way, while its ease of use may hinge on simple navigation and readability. A web application for booking tourism services, on the other hand, demands a higher level of interaction and technical precision, where adoption may be hindered by poor performance or lack of trust in security. Meanwhile, new media platforms often thrive on social influence, as users are persuaded to adopt them due to peer networks and cultural trends. By anchoring our analysis in these theoretical models, we can systematically examine why some platforms succeed in engaging audiences while others fail to gain traction.

Websites: Informational Anchors

Websites remain the most foundational digital platforms, often serving as the primary point of contact between organizations and their audiences. Their strength lies in providing structured, authoritative, and relatively stable information. Unlike the fluid and ephemeral content of social media, websites offer a sense of credibility and permanence. They are particularly effective for awareness campaigns, institutional promotion, and resource dissemination.

Trust and engagement are directly influenced by usability, which is a critical component of websites. Sites that are poorly designed, such as those with cluttered layouts, slower response times, or inaccessible features, can deter users and undermine credibility. In contrast, websites that are well-designed and incorporate multimedia elements, plain language, and culturally relevant visuals can significantly improve learning and persuasion. It is also crucial to note that websites provide creators with greater autonomy, as they are able to curate content without being influenced by the algorithmic logic of social media platforms.

Web Applications: Interactive Systems

Web applications are interactive and task-oriented, while websites primarily serve as informational resources. They enable users to perform functions such as booking, registering, customising, or monitoring in addition to consuming content. Their integration with databases, user authentication, and real-time processing are frequently necessary, as their hallmark is functionality and interactivity.

The adoption of web applications is often more demanding than websites, because users expect seamless performance, security, and personalized experiences. In contexts such as digital payments, e-learning portals, or tourism booking systems, even small usability failures can result in user abandonment. Users must be convinced that the application is secure, reliable, and compatible with their requirements. Trust is a critical factor. Web applications have the potential to revolutionise participation from a social innovation perspective, allowing communities to co-create solutions, administer resources, or supervise public services. However, this is contingent upon the design being intuitive and accessible to a variety of user groups.

New Media: Networks of Participation

New media platforms, such as social networking and content-sharing sites, add a vital layer of digital engagement. Their strength lies in virality, interactivity, and user participation, distinguishing them from institutionally driven websites or web applications. Thriving on user-generated content and network effects, new media supports community building, storytelling, and promotion through rapid message dissemination. From a communication perspective, it shifts from one-to-many broadcasting to many-to-many interaction, enabling dialogue and content modification. However, these advantages also pose risks, including misinformation, echo chambers, and superficial engagement, challenging organizations to balance credibility with reach in pursuing social innovation.

Comparative Insights

A comparative view of websites, web applications, and new media reveals both complementarities and trade-offs. Websites provide credibility and structure, web applications deliver functionality and interactivity, while new media ensures reach and engagement. Individually, none is sufficient for complex social objectives, but together they create a powerful communication ecosystem. For instance, an environmental campaign may use a website for authoritative information, a web application for interactive reporting, and new media for visibility. Similarly, rural tourism can integrate all three. These platforms function best as complementary nodes within a unified digital strategy.

Framework for Analysis

To evaluate the role of websites in the case studies, this chapter employs a framework that integrates theoretical and practical dimensions. Four key criteria guide the analysis: usability, which concerns how intuitive, accessible, and efficient a platform is; trust and credibility, which assess whether users have confidence in its content or services; engagement and inclusivity, which measure the extent to which diverse users are encouraged to participate; and social innovation potential, which reflects the platform's contribution to awareness, empowerment, or community identity.

This framework integrates insights from digital communication theory, TAM, and UTAUT, while acknowledging the unique capabilities of new media, web applications, and websites. The case studies of microplastic awareness and Pulau Tuba tourism illustrate the potential of digital platforms to facilitate social innovation and provide insights into their successes and shortcomings through this conceptual lens.

The comparative analysis highlights that websites, web applications, and new media each possess unique strengths: credibility, functionality, and reach. Websites, however, are particularly effective for structured awareness campaigns due to their stability, trustworthiness, and ability to integrate varied educational content. This makes them well suited for addressing complex public health challenges requiring clarity and sustained engagement. The next case study illustrates this through the design and evaluation of a microplastic awareness website for parents and caregivers.

WEBSITES FOR AWARENESS: THE CASE OF MICROPLASTIC CONTAMINATION

The data and insights presented in this section were drawn from an undergraduate Final Year Project (FYP) completed at Universiti Malaysia Perlis. The project centered on designing and evaluating a website to raise awareness of microplastic contamination among parents and caregivers.

Microplastics is the plastic fragments less than 5 mm in size that have emerged as a significant global health and environmental concern. They are found in seafood, drinking water, salt, and processed foods, making exposure unavoidable for most populations. Studies show that ingestion of these particles may cause gastrointestinal inflammation, oxidative stress, and toxicity due to chemical additives such as bisphenol A (BPA) and heavy metals. Vulnerable groups such as infants and children are at even greater risk because of their developing physiology, immune systems, and nutritional dependence on packaged or processed food (UNEP, 2018; Barboza et al., 2018).

Although international campaigns such as UNEP's Beat Plastic Pollution and the Ocean Cleanup project have successfully highlighted plastic waste, they primarily focus on macro-level pollution. The hidden dangers of microplastics in food remain poorly understood by the public. In Malaysia, research highlights widespread contamination in rivers, marine environments, and even consumer products, but awareness among parents and caregivers the groups most responsible for protecting children's health remains very limited (Hartmann et al., 2019; Cox et al., 2019).

Conventional awareness methods such as brochures, community talks, or documentaries such as The Story of Plastic have played a role in sparking debate but lack interactivity and long-term engagement. As a result, parents often underestimate microplastic risks in daily life, from bottle-fed infants exposed to particles from plastic feeding bottles to families consuming seafood contaminated with plastic fragments. Addressing this gap requires innovative, user-centered tools that simplify scientific information and translate it into practical steps for everyday decision-making.

Development of the Awareness Website

In response, a dedicated awareness website was developed to inform parents and caregivers about microplastic contamination in food. The project adopted a design and development research approach which, emphasizing iterative content creation, usability testing, and refinement (Mohamed Ismail Hubadillah, 2025). WordPress was selected as the content management system because of its flexibility, accessibility, and ability to integrate multimedia without requiring advanced coding. The Elementor plugin, with its drag-and-drop design interface, allowed for the creation of a visually appealing and responsive platform adaptable across devices. The development process followed four key phases:

Planning and structuring content – identifying essential topics such as definitions, sources, risks, diseases, and preventive measures.
Designing layout and navigation – building a site map, navigation menus, and page structures to ensure logical information flow.
Content creation and integration – transforming complex scientific findings into simplified text, infographics, and videos tailored for non-experts.
Testing and revision – conducting alpha and beta testing to ensure scientific accuracy, clarity, and accessibility for target users.

The Astra theme was chosen for its lightweight structure and compatibility with Elementor. Multimedia content, including infographics designed via Canva and videos produced with Camtasia and hosted on YouTube, was embedded into the site. This combination ensured a balance between accuracy, visual appeal, and ease of understanding.

Design Process: Educational Content, Multimedia, Accessibility

The design philosophy of the awareness website emphasized usability, accessibility, and engagement. The homepage, titled "Safe Plates: Microplastic Awareness for Parents", featured a bold call-to-action button and background imagery of microplastic-contaminated food to immediately communicate the issue. A scrolling marquee highlighted urgent messages, while sidebar navigation and menu anchors enabled users to move smoothly across sections. Each major content area was structured as follows:

Overview Pages: Introduced microplastics, their sources, and health impacts through step-by-step cards and infographics.
Risks Section: Used image carousels to illustrate contamination in baby bottles, packaged snacks, and household environments.
Sources Section: Organized with accordion widgets covering categories such as cosmetics, textiles, tires, and agriculture.
Health Impacts Section: Presented diseases (e.g., cancer, respiratory disorders, IBD) with concise explanations paired with icons.
Most Affected Foods: Illustrated seafood, salt, and processed snacks using infographics for quick recognition.

Accessibility was central to the design. The website was fully mobile-responsive, optimized for low-bandwidth environments, and written in plain language to ensure comprehension across educational levels. Infographics condensed key points, while embedded videos offered explanatory content for visual and auditory learners. Users could also access surveys and feedback forms to participate actively. By combining these elements, the website sought to overcome the limitations of traditional awareness methods and offer a sustainable, interactive platform for health education.

Evaluation: Expert Review and User Testing

To validate content accuracy and usability, the website underwent two levels of evaluation: alpha testing with experts and beta testing with parents and caregivers.

Alpha Testing

Four individuals participated in the alpha phase: two academic experts in microplastics, one schoolteacher, and one engineer. Their task was to assess content clarity, scientific accuracy, terminology, and design features. Overall, the feedback confirmed that the material was accurate and suitable for non-experts. Suggestions included simplifying complex infographics, referencing guidelines from bodies such as WHO, and adding quick fact boxes or offline content. These adjustments improved both clarity and scientific reliability.

Beta Testing

Following refinement, beta testing was conducted with 43 participants representing the target audience. Data were collected via an online survey and analyzed using SPSS. Demographically, most participants were aged 25–44, predominantly female, and responsible for one or more children. This alignment confirmed that the project successfully reached its intended users.

The evaluation measured three aspects:

Awareness and Perceptions: Nearly 70% of participants had little prior knowledge of microplastics. After engagement, most recognized seafood, drinking water, and processed food as common exposure pathways. Respondents overwhelmingly agreed that microplastics pose health risks, reflecting a clear shift in perception.

Website Effectiveness: Over 70% rated the site highly (4 to 5 on a 5 point scale) for raising awareness. Around 80% agreed the content was easy to understand. The health impacts section was identified as the most informative.

Behavioral Intentions: Users expressed intentions to adopt preventive practices such as reducing processed food consumption, filtering water, and using non-plastic containers.

Statistical analysis confirmed the website's effectiveness. Reliability scores were high (Cronbach's alpha > 0.8), normality assumptions were met, and regression analysis produced an R^2 value of 0.752, indicating strong influence on awareness and behavioral intentions.

OUTCOMES: IMPROVED AWARENESS, USABILITY, AND BEHAVIORAL INTENTIONS

The project demonstrated that a user-centered, multimedia-based website can significantly improve public understanding of microplastics in food. Three main outcomes emerged:

Enhanced Awareness

The platform successfully closed knowledge gaps, transforming microplastics from a "hidden hazard" into a recognized public health issue. Parents and caregivers became more conscious of contamination in daily food items and acknowledged the risks to children.

Improved Usability and Accessibility

The use of plain language, responsive design, and interactive widgets ensured that content was accessible regardless of technical literacy. Participants praised the clarity of navigation, the helpfulness of infographics, and the balance between text and visuals.

Behavioral Intentions and Community Impact

Beyond awareness, the website influenced intended behavior. Parents reported intentions to adopt safer practices and expressed a willingness to recommend the platform to others. Many called for broader education campaigns, school-based programs, and stricter regulation, reflecting the site's potential to trigger both individual and systemic change.

In conclusion, the study affirms that well-designed awareness websites can bridge the gap between scientific research and public understanding. By leveraging digital platforms like WordPress and Elementor, even small-scale projects can empower communities, particularly vulnerable groups like parents and caregivers, to act against emerging environmental and health risks.

The microplastic awareness project shows how websites can function as powerful instruments for public education, shaping perceptions and influencing behavioral intentions through accessible design and multimedia integration. Yet awareness is only one dimension of how digital platforms can contribute to social innovation. Websites can also operate as promotional and economic tools, helping marginalized communities gain visibility and attract opportunities. To demonstrate this potential, the next case study turns to Pulau Tuba, a rural island in Malaysia, where a promotional website was developed to enhance tourism visibility and strengthen local cultural identity in a highly competitive digital landscape.

WEBSITES FOR PROMOTION: THE CASE OF PULAU TUBA TOURISM

The Pulau Tuba promotional website was originally developed as part of an undergraduate Final Year Project (FYP) at Universiti Malaysia Perlis. Led by Nur Alya Afifah Binti Faizul Sutiara, the project aimed to enhance the island's digital visibility through web-based storytelling, visuals, and cultural integration.

Pulau Tuba, located just five kilometers from Langkawi, Malaysia, is a relatively small island with an area of about 17 square kilometers. Despite its natural beauty featuring clear beaches, mangrove forests, and limestone formations and its unique cultural landscape of traditional fishing villages and agricultural activities, Pulau Tuba remains largely unknown to domestic and international tourists. Compared to Langkawi, which receives high volumes of visitors annually, Pulau Tuba has not yet enjoyed similar visibility or recognition as a travel destination.

This lack of visibility underscores the critical need for effective promotional strategies. In today's digital age, travelers typically seek information online before making travel decisions, often through search engines like Google, or platforms such as TripAdvisor and Expedia (Bigi & Bonera, 2016). Websites have become central tools for tourism marketing, not only providing visibility but also influencing tourist decisions through interactive features, visuals, and comprehensive content. As Igoumenakis and Giannoukou (2025) argue, digital platforms can significantly enhance tourism competitiveness by acting as both promotional and persuasive media.

Pulau Tuba's limited recognition makes it an ideal case for testing how a dedicated, interactive tourism website can address challenges of visibility and branding. By presenting the island's attractions through visual storytelling, cultural integration, and structured information, the promotional website aims to build a stronger identity for Pulau Tuba and connect visitors with local service providers, thereby supporting community-based tourism and sustainable economic development.

Design of the Promotional Website: Waterfall Model and User-Centered Design

The development of the Pulau Tuba promotional website followed a design-based research approach, combining systematic methodology with practical testing. Specifically, the Waterfall model was applied to guide development in sequential phases: requirement analysis, design, implementation, testing, and maintenance (Saravanos & Curinga, 2023). Each stage was reviewed and refined before progressing to the next, ensuring quality and minimizing errors.

From the outset, the user-centered design philosophy (Garrett, 2011) shaped the project. This meant the interface was designed with intuitive navigation, responsive layouts for multiple devices, and a visual identity aligned with Pulau Tuba's tourism character. The website was built using HTML, CSS, and JavaScript, with the Bootstrap framework ensuring responsiveness across smartphones, tablets, and desktops. A color palette and typography consistent with nature and cultural motifs were chosen to reflect the island's unique identity.

An initial prototype was created as a visual reference for the full development, aligning with Pargaonkar and Shravan's (2023) recommendations that prototyping enhances clarity in design and improves communication between developers and stakeholders. The prototype emphasized a clear navigational structure, making it easy for users to access content categories such as attractions, accommodations, cultural activities, and conservation programs.

Features: Visuals, Storytelling, and Cultural Integration

The Pulau Tuba promotional website was designed to be more than a static information source. It emphasized immersive features that highlight the island's identity:

Visual Appeal: High-resolution images and videos of Pulau Tuba's landscapes, cultural practices, and daily life formed the centerpiece of the site. These visuals created emotional resonance, supporting findings by Daud et al. (2022) that compelling images strengthen user engagement.
Storytelling: Narratives about the island's fishing communities, traditional agricultural practices, and eco-tourism activities were included to build authenticity. This approach aligned with the principle that tourism promotion is not only about destinations but also about cultural storytelling that creates a sense of place.
Interactive Elements: Features such as interactive maps, quizzes, and responsive buttons were integrated to enhance engagement. Expert evaluations confirmed that these features were effective and responsive, contributing positively to the user experience.
Cultural Integration: Local cultural identity was emphasized throughout the site by presenting traditional crafts, local cuisines, and eco-tourism activities such as mangrove exploration and community homestays. Thus, the website not only promoted tourism but also facilitated community empowerment and cultural preservation.

Overall, the site combined educational content, cultural narratives, and interactivity to present Pulau Tuba as both a natural and cultural destination.

User Testing and Expert Feedback

Evaluation of the website was carried out in two stages: expert review and user testing.

Expert Evaluation

Experts assessed layout, content sufficiency, interactivity, and usability. They praised the website for its clean and professional design, intuitive navigation, and culturally relevant content. The interactive features such as clickable maps and quizzes were seen as particularly valuable for increasing engagement. However, they suggested improvements in dropdown menu clarity, homestay information presentation, and more frequent updates to maintain relevance.

User Testing

Thirty participants, including tourists, students, and general users, tested the site and provided feedback through Likert-scale surveys. Results showed consistently high satisfaction levels, with all constructs scoring above 4.00 on a five-point scale. The ease of use construct scored highest (M = 4.63), indicating that users found the site intuitive and smooth to navigate. Similarly, information clarity also achieved a high mean score (M = 4.63), showing that the site successfully communicated Pulau Tuba's uniqueness.

Visual design elements also performed well, with images receiving a high rating (M = 4.60) and cross-device compatibility scoring positively (M = 4.55). However, layout consistency was highlighted as an area needing improvement, with a slightly lower score (M = 3.88). Overall satisfaction was strong, with users expressing willingness to recommend the site (M = 4.55) and to revisit it (M = 4.45).

The positive outcomes of user testing demonstrated that the site not only delivered relevant and engaging content but also provided a seamless user experience. These findings supported Sauro and Lewis's (2021) emphasis on usability testing as essential to identifying strengths and areas for improvement.

Outcomes: Improved Perception of Pulau Tuba as a Tourism Destination

The development and evaluation of the Pulau Tuba website showed clear outcomes. First, the project validated the effectiveness of websites as strategic tools for tourism promotion. By integrating visuals, storytelling, and cultural elements, the site succeeded in elevating the perception of Pulau Tuba as a distinctive and attractive destination.

Second, the findings highlighted how design quality directly influences user trust and engagement. The high usability and satisfaction scores reflected that intuitive navigation, fast loading, and clear content enhanced credibility and encouraged users to consider Pulau Tuba as a viable travel option.

Third, the study confirmed that websites can function as bridges between tourists and local communities, supporting sustainable, community-based tourism. By presenting information on local homestays, traditional activities, and eco-tourism, the site not only marketed the destination but also created opportunities for residents to benefit economically.

Finally, the evaluation process demonstrated the importance of continuous improvement. Expert and user feedback provided valuable guidance for refining layout, updating content, and ensuring long-term relevance. Addressing these areas would strengthen the site's role as a digital anchor for promoting Pulau Tuba and sustaining its visibility in a competitive tourism environment.

Concluding Perspectives

The Pulau Tuba case demonstrates the potential of websites as powerful promotional tools for rural and lesser-known destinations. Developed through the systematic Waterfall model and shaped by user-centered design principles, the promotional website effectively combined functionality, cultural storytelling, and interactive features to enhance user engagement.

User and expert evaluations confirmed the site's usability, clarity, and visual appeal, with satisfaction levels exceeding expectations. The project's outcomes affirm that a well-designed tourism website can significantly improve perceptions of a destination, influence travel decisions, and support sustainable, community-based tourism.

While areas such as layout refinement and content updates remain important for long-term success, the Pulau Tuba promotional website provides a blueprint for how digital platforms can transform rural destinations into recognizable and competitive tourism spots.

The Pulau Tuba project, when viewed alongside the earlier microplastic awareness initiative, highlights the diverse ways in which websites can be strategically deployed for social innovation. While one initiative was rooted in health and environmental education and the other in cultural tourism promotion, both shared a common reliance on digital design, usability, and persuasive communication. This convergence suggests that websites, despite serving very different purposes, operate as adaptable platforms capable of addressing multiple societal needs. Building on these observations, the following section synthesizes insights from both cases to compare their similarities, differences, and broader lessons for future digital interventions.

INSIGHTS ACROSS TWO CASES: AWARENESS VS. PROMOTION

The two case studies presented in this chapter—on microplastic awareness and Pulau Tuba tourism promotion—demonstrate how websites can be deployed for different social innovation purposes. While their objectives and contexts differ, both projects illustrate the transformative potential of websites as platforms for communication, education, and persuasion. By comparing them side by side, it becomes possible to identify shared characteristics, highlight critical differences, and extract lessons that can inform future digital initiatives in health, environment, and cultural tourism. This cross-case analysis therefore situates the projects within a broader reflection on how websites contribute to social innovation across multiple domains.

Similarities: Websites as Educational and Persuasive Tools

Despite addressing different issues, both case studies underscore the value of websites as educational and persuasive tools. In the microplastic awareness project, the website sought to inform parents and caregivers about hidden risks in food and daily consumption. Through simplified content, infographics, and videos, it translated complex scientific research into accessible knowledge. In the Pulau Tuba case, the website likewise served an educational purpose, teaching potential tourists about the island's natural and cultural resources. Storytelling, visual media, and interactive maps encouraged visitors not only to learn about Pulau Tuba but also to develop an emotional connection with the destination.

Both websites also demonstrate the persuasive power of digital design. In the health context, persuasion was aimed at encouraging behavioral change—such as reducing reliance on plastics or adopting safer practices at home. In the tourism context, persuasion focused on shaping perceptions and motivating travel decisions. Although the specific calls to action were different, the underlying strategy was similar: to use design, usability, and content to move users from awareness to action.

Another similarity lies in the importance of usability and design quality. Both projects emphasized mobile responsiveness, plain language, multimedia integration, and intuitive navigation. Evaluation results confirmed that these design choices directly influenced trust, satisfaction, and willingness to act. Whether parents deciding to change consumption habits or tourists deciding to visit Pulau Tuba, the user's experience of the website was central to achieving impact. This echoes broader findings in digital communication research, which consistently highlight usability as a critical determinant of credibility and engagement.

Differences: Context, Goals, and Strategies

While similarities exist, the differences between the two cases highlight how context and objectives shape website design and outcomes.

Issue Domain

The microplastic case was rooted in health and environmental awareness, focusing on a largely invisible threat with serious long-term consequences. The Pulau Tuba project, by contrast, was embedded in cultural tourism promotion, aiming to highlight tangible attractions and experiences. This fundamental difference shaped not only the content but also the emotional tone of each website: one emphasized urgency and precaution, while the other promoted curiosity and appreciation.

Target Audience

The primary audience for the microplastic website was parents and caregivers, individuals responsible for making safe choices for children and households. Their concerns were centered on health, safety, and daily practices. The Pulau Tuba website targeted a broader audience of potential tourists, including domestic and international travelers seeking authentic experiences. Their motivations were shaped by leisure, exploration, and cultural interest.

Desired Outcomes

In the microplastic project, the intended outcome was behavioral change: to reduce exposure to microplastics and adopt safer consumption habits. In the tourism case, the outcome was economic and cultural visibility: to increase interest in Pulau Tuba as a destination and support local communities. These different goals influenced design decisions, with the former emphasizing risk communication and prevention tips, and the latter emphasizing visual appeal, storytelling, and branding.

Website Features and Tools

The microplastic site prioritized educational clarity, using infographics, simplified text, and health-focused sections such as "Risks," "Sources," and "Health Impacts." Its interactivity was modest but effective, centered on quizzes and surveys that reinforced learning. The Pulau Tuba site, however, relied more heavily on immersive features, including image carousels, interactive maps, and cultural narratives that created a sense of place. In short, one functioned primarily as a learning platform, while the other functioned as a promotional showcase.

Evaluation Methods

Evaluation also differed in emphasis. The microplastic site was tested with parents and caregivers, and results were analyzed with statistical rigor to measure awareness, usability, and behavioral intentions. The Pulau Tuba site involved both expert review and user testing with tourists and general users, focusing on satisfaction, clarity, and usability. While both approaches validated effectiveness, they reveal distinct metrics of success: knowledge gains and behavior for the former, perception and attraction for the latter.

Lessons Learned: Adaptability of Website Platforms

Taken together, the two case studies highlight several broader lessons about the adaptability of websites for social innovation.

Flexibility Across Domains

Websites can serve radically different purposes—from public health education to rural tourism promotion—without losing their effectiveness. Their modular design allows for integration of multimedia, interactivity, and structured content tailored to diverse goals. This demonstrates the flexibility of websites compared to other platforms such as social media, which often prioritize reach over depth, or web applications, which emphasize functionality over communication.

Design as a Universal Success Factor

Regardless of context, design quality emerged as the most critical factor shaping user engagement and trust. A visually coherent, mobile-friendly, and accessible interface was central to both projects. This reinforces the idea that usability is not a secondary concern but a foundational requirement for impact, whether the goal is education, persuasion, or promotion.

Importance of Targeted Audiences

The differences in outcomes also show the importance of carefully defining and understanding the target audience. Parents and caregivers required reassurance, clarity, and actionable advice. Tourists required inspiration, cultural storytelling, and a sense of trust in the destination. Effective websites must therefore align not only with technological best practices but also with the social and psychological needs of their audiences.

Sustainability and Continuous Improvement

Both projects reveal the challenge of sustaining relevance. In the microplastic case, regular updates are needed to reflect evolving scientific research. In the Pulau Tuba case, frequent updates ensure that tourism information remains accurate and appealing. Sustainability is therefore as much about content maintenance as it is about technological design.

Contribution to Social Innovation

Most importantly, both projects illustrate how websites contribute to social innovation by enabling communities to address pressing issues with digital tools. Whether safeguarding public health or promoting cultural heritage, websites provide accessible, scalable, and impactful channels for collective benefit. This underscores their continuing relevance in the broader ecosystem of digital platforms.

Bringing It Together

The cross-case analysis of the microplastic awareness and Pulau Tuba tourism projects reveals both common ground and divergence. Both cases demonstrate the power of websites as educational and persuasive platforms, shaped by design quality and usability. At the same time, the differences in domain, audience, and outcomes highlight the adaptability of websites to distinct social innovation goals.

Ultimately, these cases show that websites are not limited to a single function but are versatile instruments capable of addressing diverse challenges—from invisible health risks to rural invisibility on the global tourism map. By leveraging their strengths, websites can help communities learn, adapt, and thrive in the digital age.

While the two case studies demonstrate the transformative potential of websites for awareness and promotion, they also highlight the importance of sustainability. For websites to remain impactful, they must address issues of long-term viability, including environmental, social, and organizational dimensions. This raises the question of how websites, despite their adaptability, can overcome challenges such as high energy consumption, accessibility constraints, and the pressures of constant updating. The next section therefore turns to an examination of the sustainability challenges and limitations associated with website development and maintenance.

CHALLENGES AND LIMITATIONS ON THE SUSTAINABILITY OF WEBSITES

In the modern digital era, websites have become an integral part of communication, business, education, and entertainment. However, behind every website lies a significant environmental and social footprint. The concept of sustainable websites emphasizes minimizing energy consumption, reducing waste, and ensuring long-term accessibility. Despite its importance, achieving sustainability in web development faces numerous challenges and limitations.

The use of energy is one of the main issues. Websites rely on servers, data centres, and international networks that need a lot of electricity to run. A website uses more energy every visit the bigger and heavier it is (The Shift Project, 2019). Although there are green hosting options that use renewable energy, not all businesses, particularly those in developing nations, can always afford or use them. A further difficulty is striking a balance between sustainability and performance. Websites with interactive elements, high-resolution photos, and videos are now required by users. However, such elements often increase data transfer and energy use. Reducing these features may lower a site's carbon footprint but could also compromise user experience and brand identity. This tension makes it difficult for developers to prioritize sustainability without sacrificing engagement.

Concerns about accessibility and inclusivity arise in the context of sustainability activities. While simple, eco-friendly designs save energy, oversimplification can make websites less accessible to people with disabilities or those using older equipment. Achieving both environmental sustainability and universal accessibility necessitates meticulous planning, which many organisations find difficult and resource-intensive (W3C, 2023). Furthermore, the incorporation of adverts, tracking scripts, and third-party plugins makes websites more resource-intensive. These items not only slow down websites, but they also increase energy consumption. However, businesses often depend on advertising and analytics for revenue, making it challenging to reduce reliance on such features without financial consequences (Sustainable Web Manifesto, 2019).

Sustainability concerns cannot be separated from the technical realities of website design and management. Energy efficiency, accessibility, and inclusivity are directly influenced by technical decisions made during development and maintenance. Thus, understanding the broader sustainability limitations requires a closer look at the specific technical challenges faced across the website lifecycle—from design and hosting to ongoing updates and security. The following section therefore examines these technical dimensions in greater detail.

TECHNICAL CHALLENGES IN WEBSITE DESIGN, HOSTING, AND MAINTENANCE

In the digital era, websites serve as the cornerstone of communication, commerce, and information exchange. However, developing and sustaining a functional website is not a straightforward task. From initial design to ongoing hosting and long-term maintenance, each stage presents a range of technical challenges that can significantly affect performance, security, and user experience.

One of the key issues in website design is ensuring compatibility across various devices and browsers. A modern website must be entirely adaptable, adjusting to PCs, tablets, and mobile devices with consistent functioning across browsers like Chrome, Safari, and Edge.

Performance optimisation complicates the design process. Websites burdened with large images, unoptimized code, or excessive third-party scripts often suffer from slow loading speeds, a factor that negatively affects both user satisfaction and search engine rankings (The Code Beast, 2023). Another recurring issue is reliance on third-party plugins or application programming interfaces (APIs). While such integrations add valuable features, they can break without warning when the provider updates or discontinues support, creating reliability issues for site administrators (Speckyboy, 2023).

Beyond design, website hosting introduces its own set of obstacles. Reliable hosting is critical to ensuring uptime and speed, yet surveys reveal that businesses still experience, on average, five hours of downtime per month, resulting in financial losses exceeding USD 2,500 for nearly one in five companies (ITPro, 2023). Scalability is another pressing concern, as sites must handle surges in traffic without collapsing under pressure. Hosting environments also differ in their technical demands. For example, unmanaged hosting gives administrators full control but requires advanced expertise, and misconfigurations can easily compromise both performance and security (Expertsay, 2024). Shared hosting, meanwhile, often introduces vulnerabilities due to poor isolation between sites, allowing attackers to exploit weaknesses in neighboring servers (Arxiv, 2018). Thus, the choice of hosting directly influences a website's reliability, security, and capacity to grow.

Even when a website is successfully designed and hosted, ongoing maintenance remains a major technical challenge. Websites require constant updates to content management systems, plugins, and security protocols. Failure to apply updates promptly can expose a site to malware, ransomware, or data breaches (Cpluz, 2023; Globesign, 2023). Regular backups and recovery strategies are equally vital to mitigate the risks of data loss during cyberattacks or technical failures (DesignRush, 2023). Furthermore, maintenance extends beyond security and infrastructure which also encompasses content updates, search engine optimization, and compliance with evolving legal and accessibility standards. Outdated content can damage a site's credibility and reduce engagement, while neglecting regulations such as the General Data Protection Regulation (GDPR) can result in legal penalties (WebVision Solution, 2023; Hostao, 2023). Lastly, technical errors such as database bloat, unremoved plugins, and overlooked bug fixes accumulate over time, gradually degrading a site's performance (NW Websites, 2023).

In conclusion, the technical challenges of website management span the entire lifecycle of design, hosting, and maintenance. Designers must strike a balance between aesthetics, usability, and efficiency, while hosting providers face the demands of scalability, uptime, and security. Maintenance requires continuous vigilance through updates, backups, testing, and monitoring to ensure long-term stability and compliance. Ultimately, the sustainability of a website depends on anticipating and addressing these interconnected challenges through strategic planning and professional expertise.

While technical challenges pose significant obstacles to the stability and effectiveness of websites, emerging digital technologies offer new opportunities for overcoming some of these constraints. The rise of Web 3.0, Web 4.0, artificial intelligence, and immersive technologies introduces innovative approaches that can enhance personalization, transparency, interactivity, and overall user engagement. These advancements invite a rethinking of how websites can evolve and integrate with next-generation tools. The next section explores this potential, considering both the opportunities and risks that these technologies present for awareness and promotion.

THE POTENTIAL OF WEB 3.0, WEB 4.0, ARTIFICIAL INTELLIGENCE AND IMMERSIVE TECHNOLOGIES FOR AWARENESS AND PROMOTION

The digital landscape is undergoing rapid transformation, with emerging technologies reshaping how organizations create awareness and promote products, services, and social causes. Traditional promotional tools such as websites and social media are now being complemented and in some cases disrupted by advanced frameworks including Web 3.0, Web 4.0, artificial intelligence (AI), and immersive technologies like augmented reality (AR), virtual reality (VR), and mixed reality (MR). These innovations promise to enhance transparency, personalization, interactivity, and engagement, making promotional strategies more effective than ever before. This essay discusses the potential of these technologies in driving awareness and promotion in a connected, data-driven world.

Web 3.0: Decentralization and Personalization

Web 3.0, often described as the "semantic web," introduces more intelligent and decentralized internet powered by blockchain and data interoperability. For awareness and promotion, Web 3.0 offers two significant advantages. First, decentralization improves trust. Blockchain enables secure, transparent verification of digital transactions, ensuring that promotional campaigns, especially in sectors such as fundraising and e-commerce, are perceived as authentic (Tapscott & Tapscott, 2016). Second, semantic technologies allow highly personalized content delivery. Promotional messages can be tailored according to user preferences, behaviors, and contextual data, making awareness campaigns more relevant and engaging (Gupta, 2022). Furthermore, token-based promotions, such as non-fungible tokens (NFTs) or loyalty tokens, create interactive communities that reward participation and enhance brand loyalty.

Web 4.0: The Symbiotic Web

Building upon Web 3.0, Web 4.0 is often envisioned as the "symbiotic web," where human and machine interaction occurs seamlessly through real-time, adaptive systems. Its potential for promotion lies in its intelligent integration across platforms. Web 4.0 technologies promise hyper-personalization, enabling campaigns to adapt instantly based on user feedback and situational context (Patel, 2021). For example, health awareness campaigns could use wearable devices to detect user activity and provide timely, personalized reminders. Additionally, Web 4.0 emphasizes omnichannel presence, ensuring that promotional content remains consistent across physical, digital, and even voice- or brain-computer interfaces (Aghaei et al., 2012). This creates a holistic user journey where awareness is seamlessly embedded into daily life.

Artificial Intelligence: Smart Promotion and Predictive Awareness

AI is arguably the most transformative tool in modern promotion. Its ability to process vast amounts of data enables predictive analytics, helping organizations anticipate audience interests and campaign outcomes (Chaffey, 2020). AI-powered chatbots and virtual assistants can interact with users around the clock, answering questions, and delivering promotional content in a conversational manner. Content generation tools driven by AI can also create tailored advertisements, blog posts, or videos, reducing cost and increasing efficiency. Moreover, sentiment analysis allows organizations to monitor real-time public opinion, enabling dynamic adjustment of awareness campaigns to maximize impact (Dwivedi et al., 2021).

Immersive Technologies: Experiential Awareness

Immersive technologies such as AR, VR, and MR redefine promotional strategies by offering interactive and memorable experiences. Augmented reality enhances real-world environments with digital overlays, which can be used in retail campaigns to let consumers "try before they buy." Virtual reality provides fully immersive storytelling, enabling organizations to transport users into simulated environments that evoke empathy and emotional connection for instance, humanitarian organizations using VR to raise awareness of refugee crises (Slater & Sanchez- Vives, 2016). Mixed reality combines physical and digital elements, allowing users to interact with promotional content in dynamic ways, such as virtual showrooms or interactive exhibitions. Gamification within these immersive technologies further enhances engagement, transforming passive audiences into active participants.

POLICY AND PRACTICE DIRECTIONS FOR EMERGING DIGITAL TECHNOLOGIES IN AWARENESS AND PROMOTION

Emerging technologies such as Web 3.0, Web 4.0, artificial intelligence (AI), and immersive tools (AR, VR, MR) are transforming awareness and promotion by enabling personalization, interactivity, and immersive storytelling. However, they also pose challenges, including privacy concerns, ethical risks, accessibility gaps, and cybersecurity threats. Policy directions should therefore emphasize robust data governance, ethical AI use, regulation of blockchain-based promotions, accessibility standards, and strengthened cybersecurity frameworks. At the practice level, organizations must prioritize responsible personalization, transparency in AI or token-driven campaigns, inclusive design for immersive media, continuous evaluation, and collaborative capacity building to ensure responsible and sustainable adoption.

The integration of these technologies highlights powerful opportunities for shaping awareness and driving engagement. Yet, without careful policies and responsible practices, their use risks reinforcing inequality, misinformation, and public distrust. Thus, sustainable strategies require aligning innovation with ethics, inclusivity, and transparency. Importantly, while new technologies expand reach and interaction, websites remain essential as credible and adaptable anchors. They provide stable foundations upon which advanced tools can be layered, ensuring campaigns remain structured, trustworthy, and accessible. As digital ecosystems evolve, the balance between innovation and credibility will define the effectiveness of future awareness and promotional initiatives.

CONCLUSION

This chapter has examined the potential of websites as versatile platforms that extend beyond their traditional role as digital information repositories. Through two distinct case studies an awareness website on microplastic contamination and a promotional platform for Pulau Tuba tourism the analysis demonstrates how websites can serve as effective instruments for bridging technology and society. While each case pursued different objectives, both affirmed the centrality of usability, accessibility, and user-centered design in ensuring impact.

The findings confirm that websites are powerful vehicles for awareness-building. The microplastic case illustrated how complex scientific knowledge can be translated into accessible, actionable insights. By integrating multimedia resources, plain language, and interactive features, the platform effectively enhanced public understanding of an emerging health and environmental risk. Evaluation results showed not only improved awareness but also shifts in behavioral intentions, thereby underscoring the website's capacity to facilitate informed decision-making and protective practices. This outcome reflects the tenets of the Technology Acceptance Model (TAM) and the Unified Theory of Acceptance and Use of Technology (UTAUT), where perceived usefulness, ease of use, and trust strongly influenced adoption and engagement.

Equally, the Pulau Tuba project demonstrated how websites can function as persuasive promotional tools. Through digital storytelling, visual immersion, and cultural integration, the site enhanced the visibility of a marginalized destination, thereby supporting community-based tourism and local economic development. Expert and user evaluations highlighted the importance of design quality and interactivity in shaping credibility, satisfaction, and willingness to act. This resonates with social innovation literature, which emphasizes digital platforms as enablers of participation, empowerment, and sustainable development.

Together, these findings highlight the broader contribution of websites to bridging technology and society. Unlike social media, which often privileges immediacy over depth, or Learning Management Systems, which are constrained by rigid structures, websites provide a balance of credibility, flexibility, and inclusivity. They enable structured knowledge dissemination while allowing for creative adaptation across diverse domains, from health education to cultural promotion. This adaptability positions websites as not only technical tools but also mediating spaces that foster trust, dialogue, and collective engagement.

Finally, the reflections presented here affirm the enduring relevance of websites in an evolving digital ecosystem shaped by Web 3.0, artificial intelligence, and immersive technologies. While emerging tools will undoubtedly expand the horizons of personalization and interactivity, the stability and adaptability of websites ensure their continued importance as anchors of communication and innovation. Their value lies not only in their technical capacities but also in their ability to align digital design with social contexts, thereby promoting inclusivity, awareness, and sustainable impact.

In conclusion, websites must be understood as flexible, impactful instruments for advancing awareness, promotion, and inclusive communication. By bridging technical design with human needs, they demonstrate how digital platforms can contribute meaningfully to social innovation and serve as enduring connectors between technology and society.

REFERENCES

Aghaei, S., Nematbakhsh, M. A., & Farsani, H. K. (2012). Evolution of the World Wide Web: From Web 1.0 to Web 4.0. *International Journal of Web & Semantic Technology*, *3*(1), 1–10.

Arxiv. (2018). Shared hosting vulnerabilities and security risks. https://arxiv.org

Barboza, L. G. A., et al. (2018). Awareness as recognizing, comprehending, and learning about an issue to make informed choices and change behavior.

Bigi, A., & Bonera, M. (2016). A proposed benchmark analysis of the connection between wine production and destination perception. In L. Petruzzellis & R. S. Winer (Eds.), Rediscovering the essentiality of marketing: Proceedings of the 2015 Academy of Marketing Science (AMS) World Marketing Congress (pp. 963–968). Springer. https://doi.org/DOI: 10.1007/978-3-319-29877-1

Chaffey, D. (2020). Digital marketing: Strategy, implementation and practice. Pearson UK.

Chen, K.-H., Xue, Z.-H., & Zhang, C. (2025). Social innovation in the digital era: Theoretical framework and policy implications. *Studies in Science of Science.*

Cox, K. D., et al. (2019). Findings on public consumption of microplastics.

Cpluz. (2023). Potential pitfalls of web development hosting solutions. https://cpluz.com

DesignRush. (2023). Website maintenance trends. https://designrush.com

Dundua, E. (2024). *Digital marketing and corporate social responsibility: Strategies for brand building and stakeholder engagement.* Springer.

Dwivedi, Y. K., et al. (2021). Artificial intelligence (AI): Multidisciplinary perspectives on emerging challenges, opportunities, and agenda for research, practice, and policy. *International Journal of Information Management, 57,* 101994. https://doi.org/DOI: 10.1016/j.ijinfomgt.2020.101994

Expertsay. (2024). Challenges of unmanaged hosting. https://expertsay.blog

Garrett, J. J. (2011). *The elements of user experience.* New Riders.

Globesign. (2023). Common website maintenance mistakes. https://globesign.com

Gupta, R. (2022). Web 3.0 marketing: Opportunities and challenges. *Journal of Digital Innovation*, *5*(2), 45–59.

Hartmann, N. B., et al. (2019). Research on environmental and health risks of microplastics.

Hostao. (2023). Website maintenance and hosting tips. https://hostao.com

ITPro. (2023). Website downtime costs businesses thousands a month. https://itpro.com

Mohamed Ismail Bin Hubadillah. (2025). *Development of an awareness website on microplastic contamination in food* [Unpublished undergraduate final year project]. Universiti Malaysia Perlis.

Nur Alya Afifah Binti Faizul Sutiara. (2025). *Pembangunan laman web interaktif untuk meningkatkan promosi pelancongan Pulau Tuba* [Unpublished undergraduate final year project]. Universiti Malaysia Perlis.

Patel, D. (2021, May 18). What is Web 4.0 and how will it change marketing? Forbes. https://www.forbes.com

Saravanos, A., & Curinga, M. X. (2023). Simulating the software development life-cycle: The waterfall model. Applied System Innovation, 6(6), 108. DOI: 10.3390/asi6060108

Sauro, J., & Lewis, J. R. (2021). *Quantifying the user experience: Practical statistics for user research* (2nd ed.). Morgan Kaufmann.

Slater, M., & Sanchez-Vives, M. V. (2016). Enhancing our lives with immersive virtual reality. Frontiers in Robotics and AI, 3, 74. https://doi.org/ DOI: 10.3389/frobt.2016.00074

Speckyboy. (2023). The biggest pains in website maintenance. https://speckyboy.com

Sustainable Web Manifesto. (2019). Our commitment to a sustainable internet. https://www.sustainablewebmanifesto.com

Suzianti, A., Al Hafi, K., & Shafira, N. D. (2019). Designing Indonesia social innovation knowledge management system: Case study of kreanovator Indonesia. *Proceedings of the ACM International Conference.* https://doi.org/DOI: 10.1145/3366030.3366101

Tapscott, D., & Tapscott, A. (2016). *Blockchain revolution: How the technology behind Bitcoin is changing money, business, and the world.* Penguin.

The Code Beast. (2023). Challenges of developing a website. https://thecodebeast.com

The Shift Project. (2019). Lean ICT: Towards digital sobriety. https://theshiftproject.org/en/lean-ict-2/

UNEP. (2018). *Definition of microplastics and environmental implications.* United Nations Environment Programme.

Websites, N. W. (2023). Website maintenance mistakes. https://nwwebsites.co.uk

WebVision Solution. (2023). 5 common website issues and how maintenance services can prevent them. https://webvisionsolution.com

Chapter 15
Youth, Media, and Governance in Transition: Lessons From Dharan's Citizen-Led Journalism

Sudeep Uprety
https://orcid.org/0000-0002-9650-8321
Prince of Songkla University, Nepal

Pransu Khakurel
https://orcid.org/0009-0001-4964-294X
Independent Researcher, Nepal

Rajesh Ghimire
Nepal Institute of Research and Communications, Nepal

Jigmy Palzor Lama
Nepal Institute of Research and Communications, Nepal

ABSTRACT

Federalism and urbanization have reshaped governance, media, and youth participation in Nepal. With decentralization under the 2015 Constitution, municipalities became central to services and civic engagement, though governance is weakened by political pressure, uneven delivery, and poor accountability. Media has shifted from elite-driven reporting to inclusive storytelling, with digital platforms amplifying youth voices. Youths, Nepal's demographic majority, remain vital but constrained by migration, unemployment, and tokenism. In Dharan, action research by NIRC and Lumanti (2025) monitored governance, housing, and marginalized groups in media. Analysis of 75 stories found 51% positive, 35% critical, 15% neutral—dominated

DOI: 10.4018/979-8-3373-5307-4.ch015

by event-driven coverage with little investigative depth. Marginalized voices were inconsistently included, while housing and environment drew little traction. Media workshops highlighted evidence-based journalism, safety, and youth training alongside citizen-led journalism to amplify voices, strengthen participatory governance, and counter sensationalism.

1. INTRODUCTION

Nepal's federal transition and the concomitant transformation of its media landscape offer a compelling narrative on the evolution of democratic participation in politically and socially dynamic contexts. The promulgation of the Constitution of Nepal in 2015 marked a historic shift from a centralized, unitary governance model centered on monarchy to a decentralized federal system comprising seven provinces. This transition was envisioned to bring governance closer to citizens, strengthen local accountability, and create formal spaces for participatory governance (Government of Nepal, 2015; Bhatta, 2020). Federalism, in this context, was not merely a structural reform; it was a normative commitment to democratizing power, enabling citizen participation, and fostering social inclusion across diverse communities. However, the practical implementation of federalism has been uneven, and significant gaps persist between constitutional promises and on-the-ground realities.

Recent studies underscore these challenges. Bhusal and Acharya (2024) highlight that during the first tenure of elected local governments (2017–2022), local bodies remained heavily reliant on federal and provincial grants, limiting their autonomy and constraining their ability to exercise constitutionally guaranteed legislative, executive, and judicial powers. Although federal structures created formal mechanisms for inclusion, such as public hearings, participatory budgeting, and consultative committees, their practical effectiveness has often been limited by procedural inefficiencies, administrative bottlenecks, and social hierarchies. These institutional gaps undermine the potential for genuine participatory governance, leaving citizens with formal but often superficial avenues for engagement (Bhusal & Acharya, 2024).

These governance challenges exist alongside rapid socio-economic and demographic changes, particularly urbanization, which further complicate participatory processes. Nepal, while historically one of the least urbanized countries in Asia, has experienced significant growth in urban settlements over recent decades (Sharma, 2019). Urbanization in Nepal has been driven by both domestic migration from rural to urban centers and international migration, which has increased household incomes through remittances. The Nepal Living Standards Survey (2024) notes that these migratory trends have catalyzed household investment in education, housing, and entrepreneurial activities, highlighting the interconnections between economic mobility, urbanization, and social change. Yet rapid urban growth has also amplified governance challenges, requiring municipalities to adopt inclusive, responsive, and evidence-based approaches to planning, service delivery, and civic engagement.

Parallel to these socio-economic shifts, Nepal's media environment has undergone profound transformations. Traditional media, including print newspapers, radio, and broadcast television, have been supplemented, and in some instances challenged by digital platforms such as online news portals, social media, and community-driven digital initiatives (Parajuli, 2021). This democratization of information production and circulation has created new opportunities for marginalized groups, including youth, women, and indigenous communities to share their narratives, engage in public discourse, and participate in governance processes. Digital tools enable citizen journalism, advocacy campaigns, and real-time reporting, expanding both the reach and diversity of media voices.

However, the expansion of media platforms has also introduced challenges. The rise of clickbait journalism, sensationalist reporting, and politically partisan narratives has contributed to the fragmentation of public spheres and the erosion of trust in media institutions (Malla, 2020). In this context, while media platforms provide opportunities for engagement, they can also reproduce social inequalities and exacerbate existing political polarization. Youth, who constitute a significant proportion of Nepal's population, occupy a central role in this evolving media landscape (Nepal Statistics Office, 2021). Policies such as the National Youth Policy (2006) and Youth Vision 2025 recognize young people as rights-holders and active contributors to governance and development, emphasizing the importance of their participation in decision-making processes at local, provincial, and national levels (Government of Nepal, 2015). Yet, structural barriers including social hierarchies, limited institutional support, and migration for education and employment often constrain youth engagement in governance. The out-migration of young people, in particular, reduces their presence in local decision-making spaces, limiting the continuity and impact of youth-led initiatives.

The city of Dharan, located in Nepal's eastern region, provides a particularly instructive case study for exploring these intersecting dynamics of youth, media, and governance. As a sub-metropolitan city experiencing rapid demographic growth, economic diversification, and urban development, Dharan exemplifies both the opportunities and challenges facing Nepal's urban centers in the federal era. The city's population is diverse, comprising significant numbers of youth, indigenous communities, and residents of informal settlements. This diversity creates complex governance needs, requiring participatory and inclusive approaches to service delivery, urban planning, and civic engagement. Dharan's local governance structures must navigate the dual imperatives of implementing federal policies and responding to rapidly changing local realities, making it an ideal site for examining the role of media in fostering participatory governance.

Within this context, citizen-led journalism emerges as a key mechanism for amplifying marginalized voices and fostering accountability. The action research project, *Media Monitoring and Analysis of Media Coverage on Social Issues Engaging Youth Volunteers of Youth Network in Dharan*, conducted by the Nepal Institute of Research and Communications in collaboration with the Lumanti Support Group for Shelter, provides an empirical illustration of these dynamics. The project systematically monitored both traditional and digital media, analyzing the representation of governance, social issues, and marginalized communities. In parallel, youth volunteers were engaged through participatory workshops and advocacy exercises, enabling them to critically assess media content, develop reporting skills, and contribute to ethical and evidence-based journalism practices.

The dual objectives of the project, analytical assessment of media content and practical capacity-building of media actors, highlight the transformative potential of youth-centered media initiatives. By equipping young people with tools to critically evaluate reporting, engage with journalists, and produce their own content, the project sought to enhance both the quality and inclusivity of public discourse. The initiative also underscores the intersection of media and governance: youth-led media monitoring not only increases the visibility of marginalized communities but also fosters a culture of accountability and civic responsibility, bridging gaps between citizens and local authorities.

Dharan case illustrates broader implications for federal governance in Nepal. It demonstrates that constitutional provisions, policy frameworks, and formal institutional structures alone are insufficient to ensure participatory democracy. Effective governance requires active citizen engagement, mediated by professional and ethical journalism that is responsive to local contexts. In rapidly urbanizing cities like Dharan, where demographic shifts and socio-economic inequalities create both opportunities and vulnerabilities, youth-centered media initiatives can play a critical role in enhancing civic literacy, amplifying marginalized voices, and promoting transparent, accountable governance.

Nepal's federal transition, coupled with the transformation of its media environment, offers a rich lens for understanding participatory governance in evolving political contexts. While constitutional reforms and policy frameworks provide the structural foundations for inclusive democracy, their effectiveness is mediated by social, economic, and technological factors, including urbanization, youth engagement, and media practices. The Dharan case study highlights how citizen-led journalism and youth participation can operationalize these democratic ideals, providing practical strategies for building inclusive, accountable, and responsive governance systems in Nepal's federal era. By connecting structural reforms with grassroots media initiatives, this analysis underscores the intertwined nature of governance, media, and civic participation in shaping democratic futures.

2. TRANSFORMATION OF MEDIA LANDSCAPE AND YOUTH PARTICIPATION

The transformation of the media landscape in developing nations reflects broader patterns of social innovation emerging in the Global South, where institutional gaps, resource constraints, and socio-political challenges have catalyzed alternative approaches to information production and civic engagement. These transformations challenge traditional paradigms that position the Global South as passive recipients of media technologies and practices developed in the Global North. Instead, they reveal a dynamic process of adaptation, hybridization, and indigenous innovation, whereby local actors creatively leverage technological, social, and cultural resources to produce media that is contextually relevant and responsive to local needs. Such innovation often arises from necessity, as resource limitations, infrastructural deficits, and political constraints compel media practitioners, civil society organizations, and youth-led collectives to experiment with alternative modes of storytelling, distribution, and audience engagement.

Nepal's media landscape exemplifies these broader trends, but it continues to face significant structural and professional challenges that constrain its effectiveness, inclusivity, and democratic potential. Despite the country's formal transition to federalism, mainstream media outlets remain heavily centralized, with Kathmandu-based organizations maintaining dominance over content production, editorial decision-making, and resource allocation (Paudel, 2023). This centralization reinforces a Kathmandu-centric orientation, producing content and bylines that largely reflect urban capital perspectives while often marginalizing provincial and local narratives. Such a configuration runs counter to the constitutional vision of federalism, which anticipates devolved governance, regional autonomy, and diversified participation in public affairs. In practice, however, both political and media institutions display inertia, struggling to shift longstanding patterns of centralization and top-down control.

Historical analysis of Nepali journalism highlights deep-rooted structural and professional challenges. Since the 1950s, journalism in Nepal has been shaped by partisan loyalties and state patronage, which limited editorial independence and professional autonomy (Bhattarai, 2024). These legacies have persisted across decades, reinforced by low literacy rates, small readership bases, and constrained public demand for high-quality information. The introduction of commercialization in the 1990s provided new revenue streams but did not eliminate political dependencies, producing a hybrid media system in which outlets navigate both market pressures and political relationships. Consequently, media organizations struggle to fully implement constructive journalism principles, with weak adherence to ethical standards, limited investigative capacities, and underdeveloped news values (Aryal, 2025).

The changing technological landscape has further transformed patterns of media consumption, production, and dissemination, creating both opportunities and challenges. Digital platforms and the internet have lowered traditional barriers to content creation, enabling a broader range of actors, including independent journalists, citizen reporters, and youth collectives, to participate in public discourse (Dahal, 2024). During the COVID-19 pandemic, for instance, reliance on online news sources increased, reflecting the growing importance of digital media in providing timely information when traditional outlets faced operational constraints (Sharecast, 2022). Social media platforms, messaging applications, and online portals have allowed local stories, civic campaigns, and grassroots initiatives to reach wider audiences, circumventing some of the structural centralization inherent in mainstream media.

Nevertheless, the rise of digital media has not fully addressed the longstanding challenges of professionalism, inclusivity, and public trust. While radio continues to play a critical role during socio-political events, particularly in rural areas, consumption of print and broadcast news has declined, reflecting both shifts in audience preferences and declining confidence in traditional media (Sharecast, 2022). The media landscape in Nepal thus occupies a complex terrain: on one hand, technological innovations expand possibilities for participatory journalism, civic engagement, and decentralized information flows; on the other, structural centralization, historical partisanship, and economic fragility continue to constrain the sector's democratic potential.

These intersecting challenges highlight the urgent need for renewed approaches to media literacy, professional capacity-building, and institutional reform. Media literacy programs must go beyond basic digital skills to encompass critical analysis, ethical reporting, and civic engagement, particularly among youth who increasingly rely on digital platforms for information and social interaction (Dahal, 2024). Similarly, strengthening professional standards, ensuring editorial independence, and developing sustainable business models are essential for improving both the credibility and resilience of media organizations. The decentralization envisioned by Nepal's federal framework cannot be realized without addressing the entrenched structural and professional barriers that shape how information is produced, disseminated, and consumed.

Nepal's media landscape has undergone significant transformations driven by technology, social change, and global media trends; it remains centralized, professionally challenged, and slow to adapt to democratic and technological shifts. The interplay of historical legacies, economic fragility, partisan influence, and evolving digital practices underscores the need for comprehensive strategies that integrate structural reform, capacity development, and citizen-centered approaches. By embracing both innovation and institutional reform, Nepal's media can potentially align more closely with the democratic ideals of federalism, inclusivity, and accountable governance, while providing citizens, especially youths with meaningful spaces for participation and civic engagement.

a. Media Democratization

The media landscape in Nepal has faced persistent structural and professional challenges, undermining both its effectiveness and inclusivity. Although Nepal has formally transitioned to federalism with an emphasis on decentralization, mainstream media outlets remain heavily Kathmandu-centric, reinforcing centralized orientations and privileging content and bylines from the capital (Paudel, 2023). This centralization contradicts the constitutional vision of federalism and reflects deeper institutional resistance to redistributing power. The central government's slow devolution of authority to provincial administrations, as outlined in the Constitution, has hindered provinces from fully exercising their constitutional rights, a pattern that extends to media institutions where editorial decisions, resource allocations, and priority-setting remain concentrated in Kathmandu (Proceedings of the International AAAI Conference on Web and Social Media, n.d.).

The persistence of centralized media structures creates a democratic deficit in which provincial and local stories are filtered through Kathmandu-based editorial perspectives, often losing their authentic context and immediacy. The disconnect between political restructuring and media practices illustrates that institutional change requires more than constitutional provisions; it demands profound shifts in organizational culture, resource distribution, and professional networks that have been shaped over decades of centralized governance.

Nepali journalism has also been constrained by historical legacies of partisanship and state patronage dating back to the 1950s, which continue to limit editorial autonomy in an environment characterized by low literacy rates and small readership bases (Bhattarai, 2024). These historical path dependencies resist transformation even under new democratic frameworks. The commercialization of media since the 1990s introduced market pressures without eliminating political dependencies, creating hybrid systems in which media outlets must simultaneously navigate commercial viability and political relationships. This dual dependency has restricted the ability of Nepali media to achieve independence, resulting in weak adherence to constructive journalism norms and underdeveloped news values (Aryal, 2025).

Economic fragility further compounds these challenges. Many media organizations rely on external funding sources, including political parties, business interests, and international donors, each introducing its own agendas and constraints. This financial vulnerability undermines editorial independence and hampers the development of robust ethical standards or sustainable business models that could support quality journalism (Adhikari, 2005).

The intertwining of media and democracy in Nepal creates additional tensions. Emerging public-oriented journalism has sought to prioritize accountability, inclusivity, and citizen engagement, aiming to deepen Nepal's democratic transition (Adhikari, 2005). Yet, more than a decade after federalism was formally adopted, media structures have not mirrored the political changes federalism demands. Party politics, which have historically impeded development across various sectors, continue to influence media coverage across different levels of government, resulting in a fractured information environment where journalistic outputs often reflect political rivalries rather than public interest (Kotilainen & Suoninen, 2013).

Instead of consolidating democratic gains, media centralization persists against the backdrop of the Constitution of Nepal, 2015, potentially fueling new political controversies and undermining peace consolidation efforts (Strasheim & Bogati, 2016). This dynamic is particularly problematic in a post-conflict society where the media's role in promoting reconciliation and democratic values remains crucial but often compromised by partisan considerations and commercial pressures.

The rise of new media and citizen journalism, attributed to social media and online platforms, has begun reshaping Nepal's information ecosystem through democratized participation, presenting greater opportunities for marginalized and rural populations to articulate their voices instead of remaining passive observers (Dhakal, 2010; Mahaseth & Qureshi, 2021). This technological disruption has created parallel information systems that bypass traditional gatekeeping mechanisms, enabling direct communication between citizens and potentially more authentic representation of diverse perspectives.

Chhetri (2021) notes that platforms like YouTube and other social media have blurred boundaries between professional and citizen journalism, expanding civic spaces for dissent, accountability and pluralism while presenting challenges regarding misinformation, sensationalism and weakening editorial standards. This democratization of content creation has both empowered previously excluded voices and created new challenges for information quality and credibility.

The emergence of digital platforms has also facilitated the growth of vernacular media content, addressing linguistic diversity that mainstream media often neglects. Local content creators using regional languages have found audiences and economic opportunities that traditional media structures failed to provide, suggesting potential pathways for more inclusive media ecosystems.

Even post-federalism, shifts in journalistic practices have led to both promises and perils. As Dahal (2024) notes, the lack of robust media literacy, weak professional standards and increasing political polarization undermine journalistic credibility despite citizen journalism and digital media offering alternative avenues for representation in regions excluded by Kathmandu-centric narratives. This tension between technological possibilities and institutional capacities creates a media environment simultaneously characterized by democratic innovation and fragility, caught between persistent centralization, unresolved professional shortcomings, and the disruptive but democratizing power of new media technologies. Contemporary challenges in Nepal's media landscape include high levels of conflict, contestation, and institutional fragmentation, which complicate the role of journalism in supporting democratic governance. These conditions demand innovative approaches to reporting that can navigate the complexities of a federal system while upholding professional standards and maintaining public trust (Frontiers, n.d.).

b. Youth as Civic Actors in Governance and Media

Development communications in Nepal have shaped the reporting of media on youths and civic space, especially at times of political transition and social transformation. Started with the donor-driven initiative framing media as a tool for peacebuilding and civic education, the trends have now shifted towards inclusion and representation with youths portrayed in the engagement in public discourses (Pokharel, 2024; Thapa, 2023). This evolution reflects a broader transformation in Nepal's media landscape, where international development agencies initially emphasized media's role in post-conflict reconciliation and democratic education following the end of the decade-long Maoist insurgency in 2006.

The early phase of development communication was characterized by structured programs that prioritized stability and consensus-building over critical discourse. Media outlets received training and funding to produce content that promoted social cohesion and democratic values, often following predetermined narratives about peace and reconstruction. However, as Nepal's democratic institutions matured and civil society gained confidence, the focus gradually shifted toward more nuanced approaches that recognized the importance of diverse voices and authentic representation in media narratives.

This transformation has portrayed the shifting narratives of democracy, identity and participation, positioning youth as symbols of change yet sidelining their voices in decision making (Shrestha, 2024). The paradox is particularly evident in how media coverage frames young people as both harbingers of progress and subjects requiring guidance rather than active participants in shaping their own futures. News stories frequently highlight youth achievements, activism, and potential while simultaneously perpetuating paternalistic attitudes that question their readiness for leadership roles. This duality reflects broader societal tensions between traditional hierarchical structures and emerging democratic aspirations.

The dynamics underscore the role of journalism as a mirror and presenter of civic space in Nepal with youths, despite structural barriers claiming spaces through citizen-led media, online activism, and volunteer networks. Traditional media institutions, often dominated by older generations and established political networks, have struggled to adapt to the changing demographic landscape where nearly 40% of Nepal's population is under 25. Young journalists and media practitioners have responded by creating alternative platforms and networks that prioritize peer-to-peer communication and grassroots storytelling approaches.

Within this context, youths remain critical agents of democratic change. Theories of political socialization highlight how early civic engagement shapes long-term participation and democratic consolidation (Dalton, 2017). The formative experiences of young Nepalis during the democratic movements of 2006 and 2015 have created a generation with heightened political awareness and expectations for accountability. These experiences have fostered a political consciousness that values transparency, inclusivity, and responsiveness from governing institutions, characteristics that often contrast with traditional political cultures.

In governance transitions, young people often emerge as "critical citizens," challenging established elites and demanding accountability (Norris, 2011). This phenomenon has been particularly visible during Nepal's constitutional drafting process and subsequent implementation challenges, where youth organizations and activists consistently pushed for provisions addressing their concerns about employment, education, and political representation. Their advocacy efforts have often employed innovative strategies that combine traditional protest methods with digital organizing and media campaigns.

This demographic weight is recognized in policy frameworks, such as the National Youth Policy (2006) and Youth Vision 2025, which mandates the allocation of 10% of municipal budgets to youth programs by 2025 (Government of Nepal, 2015). These policy commitments represent significant acknowledgments of youth importance in national development, reflecting growing recognition that demographic dividends require intentional investment in young people's capabilities and opportunities. The policies also establish frameworks for youth participation in local governance structures and development planning processes.

Yet migration, unemployment, and tokenistic participation continue to restrict their influence in formal governance spaces (Poudel, 2022). The disconnect between policy aspirations and implementation realities remains substantial, with many young people expressing frustration about limited opportunities for meaningful engagement. Labor migration to Gulf countries and Malaysia has created a "youth drain" that affects local civic engagement, while those who remain often find themselves relegated to symbolic roles in decision-making processes without real authority or resources.

Nevertheless, the rise of social media and digital platforms has enabled alternative forms of civic engagement. Online activism, volunteer networks, and citizen-centric journalism now provide young people with opportunities to exercise agency, develop skills, and influence public discourse (Shrestha & Shakya, 2020). Facebook, Twitter, and emerging platforms like TikTok have become spaces where young Nepalis share experiences, organize campaigns, and challenge mainstream narratives. These digital spaces have also facilitated transnational connections among Nepali youth, including those working abroad, creating networks that transcend geographical boundaries.

c. A Global South Perspective

Media landscape transformations have fundamentally reshaped youth engagement in politics, society, and culture, with significant implications globally, particularly in the Global South. Initially shaped by cultural, political, and technological contexts in Western societies, youth media engagement has increasingly expanded across the globe (Kotilainen & Suoninen, 2013). Comparative studies of youth aged 11–18 in Argentina, Egypt, Finland, and India illustrate the dynamic nature of media participation, highlighting how identities, organizational structures, technological access, and quality of participation shape engagement (Kotilainen & Suoninen, 2013). This global expansion reflects a broader democratization of media production capabilities, as digital tools have lowered traditional barriers to content creation, distribution, and audience reach, which previously required substantial institutional resources and technical infrastructure.

The shift from Western-centric models to globally distributed practices represents more than the diffusion of technology; it reflects a profound reconfiguration of power relations within media ecosystems. Early internet adoption predominantly reinforced Global North dominance, concentrating media production and influence in affluent societies with advanced infrastructure. However, the proliferation of mobile technologies and social media platforms has created opportunities for youth in developing regions to bypass traditional gatekeeping mechanisms (Kotilainen & Suoninen, 2013). Young people in these contexts have leveraged digital tools to develop locally relevant approaches to storytelling, civic participation, and social mobilization, challenging hierarchical media structures and asserting agency over narratives that directly affect their lives.

At the same time, the growing complexity of globalized media landscapes has produced both opportunities and challenges for youth engagement. Technological innovations have expanded avenues for addressing socio-economic disparities, yet structural inequalities continue to restrict access and inclusivity (Asthana, 2007). Beyond access issues, young people must navigate algorithmically governed platforms, platform dependency, and digital colonialism, which often prioritize

Western-centric design and norms. The dominance of platforms such as Facebook, Instagram, and TikTok creates new forms of dependency, compelling local content creators to conform to external technical standards and commercial logics, potentially diluting indigenous knowledge, cultural practices, and locally relevant discourses (Asthana, 2007).

These dynamics underscore the importance of recognizing youth as active producers of media rather than passive consumers. Across developing regions, several initiatives exemplify this paradigm shift from consumption to production, including citizen journalism programs, community radio projects, and grassroots digital literacy campaigns in Africa, Asia, and Latin America (Asthana, 2007). These youth-led initiatives not only address local information needs but also contribute to global conversations, amplifying perspectives that are often marginalized or overlooked by mainstream media. By producing content reflective of their lived realities, young people challenge dominant narratives and assert agency in shaping public discourse.

Contemporary research emphasizes that these opportunities exist alongside significant vulnerabilities. Youth in the Global South frequently face compounded disadvantages, including poverty, unemployment, gender-based discrimination, and health disparities, which heighten their susceptibility to the risks of social media, such as exploitation, misinformation, and online harassment (Kotilainen & Suoninen, 2013). This vulnerability paradox illustrates how technologies that expand opportunities for voice and agency simultaneously expose young people to new forms of marginalization.

Context-specific barriers further constrain effective youth participation across developing regions. Studies in Namibia, Ghana, Nigeria, Bangladesh, Egypt, India, Mexico, South Africa, China, and Brazil reveal that youth media engagement ranges from personal identity construction to contributions to global discourses, highlighting both the diversity and complexity of participatory practices (Faedi Duramy & Gal, 2020). Common barriers include limited internet infrastructure, high data costs, language restrictions on predominantly English-language platforms, and cultural norms that curtail youth autonomy in public discourse. These structural limitations are reinforced by institutional inertia, with government bodies, news organizations, political parties, and NGOs often defaulting to top-down communication strategies that limit genuine participatory opportunities (Proceedings of the International AAAI Conference on Web and Social Media, n.d.). Adult-led organizations continue to dominate agenda-setting and resource allocation, constraining the capacity of youth to meaningfully influence content and outcomes.

Finally, the political economy of digital platforms introduces structural constraints that disproportionately affect young people in developing regions. Algorithm-driven content distribution tends to favor established creators with existing audiences and resources, making it challenging for emerging voices to gain visibility. Social media commercialization prioritizes engagement metrics, often incentivizing sensationalist content over substantive civic discourse. For youth already marginalized in traditional political and social institutions, these platform dynamics may reproduce rather than disrupt existing hierarchies of influence and representation (Faedi Duramy & Gal, 2020).

Thus, while digital media provides unprecedented opportunities for youth engagement, the broader media ecosystems, including technical, economic, and cultural dimensions, remain a contested space where agency, representation, and equity continue to be negotiated.

3. METHODOLOGY

The study undertaken in Dharan largely employed a participatory mixed-methods approach over the period of six months from January to July 2025. This project expanded from the existing conventional media monitoring through the deliberate involvement of youth volunteers as co-researchers, ensuring their active involvement throughout the process. This approach ensured pragmatic integration in research, embedding innovation into study design and implementation.

Furthermore, to consider the multifaceted challenges of urban governance in an evolving city, the scope was intentionally broad. This coverage was analyzed across the themes of governance, transparency, housing rights, gender-based violence, migration, labor exploitation and social inclusion considering structural challenges faced by marginalized groups and issue representation in the existing media landscape.

A wide range of data sources was included to reflect the diversity of Nepali media ecosystem. It comprised both traditional outlets such as print media, such as regional newspapers and broadcasting media, such as community radio alongside digital platforms with wide selection of YouTube based news channels, offering perspectives from emerging agile forms of media. Following is the list of news media outlets utilized for media monitoring:

Table 1.

SN	Name	Type
1.	Blast Times Daily/blastkhabar.com	Print/online
2.	Koshipatra daily/koshipatra.com	Print/online
3.	Kapurinews.com	Online
4.	Clickdharan.com	Online
5.	Bijayapurkhabar.com	Online

continued on following page

Table 1. Continued

SN	Name	Type
6.	Gantantra Fm/ganatantrakhabar.com	Radio/online
7.	Bijayapur Fm/bijayapur.com.np	Radio/online
8.	Heart FM	Radio
9.	Dibyaroshni weekly/dibyaroshani.com	Print/online
10.	Dharan weekly/dharanweekly.com	Print/online
11	Sunsari Online Media	YouTube
12	Purbanchal DBR TV	YouTube
13	NE Entertainment	YouTube
14	Kawaz TV	YouTube
15	Mero Awaz Media	YouTube
16	Omribung Media Pvt. Ltd	YouTube
17	Mohan Pitha	YouTube

To ensure systematic analysis, a coding framework was developed based on which each item was assessed as per three criteria: tone, framing and inclusivity of the news. Here tone referred to the attitude or emotion of the news, further classified as positive, negative and neutral. The framing of the news referred to the distinction of problem-oriented reporting focusing on crises and failures or solution-oriented coverage emphasizing on progress and innovation. Similarly, the third criteria were inclusivity assessing the extent of representation of marginalized voices including women, youth and informal settlement residents.

Beyond media monitoring, the methodology further integrated community engagement. For this, Focus Group Discussions (FGDs) were undertaken with residents across different wards to contextualize findings. This led to exploration of the access of information by communities, their trusted platforms and perceptions on governance performance. This remained crucial in linking media representation with lived realities, further highlighting the discrepancies between coverage and community priorities.

Furthermore, the study also incorporated capacity-building on ethical reporting, governance literacy and participatory storytelling for youth volunteers and journalists. The session promoted analytical skills of participants, along with strengthening their capacities for evidence-based journalism encouraging inclusive approaches to media practices. Overall keeping youths in center, the study methodology remained an exercise for developing media practices alongside building civic and analytical capacities to democratize media ecosystems in Nepal.

4. FINDINGS

The findings of the study portray both vibrancy and fragmentation of Nepal's contemporary media landscape. It indicates the critical tensions between watchdog journalism and solution-oriented reporting, between traditional media and digital citizen platforms and between sensationalism and evidence-based coverage.

a. Tone

A total of 75 stories across print, broadcast and digital outlets were reviewed systematically over the period of six months from January 2025 to June, 2025. With 50.7% of the stories adopting positive framing, it is evident that the tone distribution is revealing, highlighting community development, education initiatives and women's empowerment. These stories celebrate tangible achievements, including increased access to schooling or small-scale infrastructure projects framing them as markers of progress and hope.

Figure 1. Tone used in media

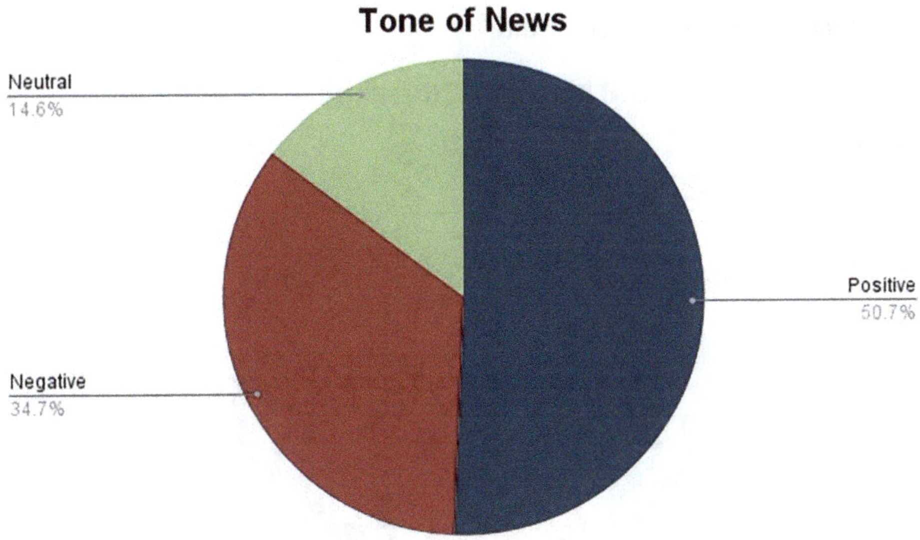

Similarly, 35% of stories were critical or negative, focusing on gender-based violence, corruption and governance failures. The coverage indicates the watchdog function of media, relying on a reactive style emphasizing individual incidents over systemic analysis.

Remaining 15% of the coverage was neutral occupying event notices, public announcements, or procedural updates. This proportion suggests that Nepali media tends to privilege advocacy-oriented and sensational stories over straightforward, fact-based reporting. The oscillation between celebratory and critical tones, with limited neutral or analytical space indicate a media environment driven by immediacy and emotional resonance rather than sustained investigation.

b. Thematic Coverage

In terms of thematic coverage, the media coverage patterns portray stark disparity in the framing and discussion of social issues. Gender based violence that accounts for that largely receiving negative response, reflects journalism's tendency to focus on gravity and prevalence of incidents instead of focusing on preventive measures. This highlights the severity of the problem and may contribute to a cycle with issues seen as intractable rather than actionable. Similarly, labor rights coverage maintains a predominantly critical stance, balancing between neutral reporting and negative framing as it addresses systemic challenges like worker exploitation, regulatory gaps, and labor unrest.

Figure 2. Thematic coverage by media

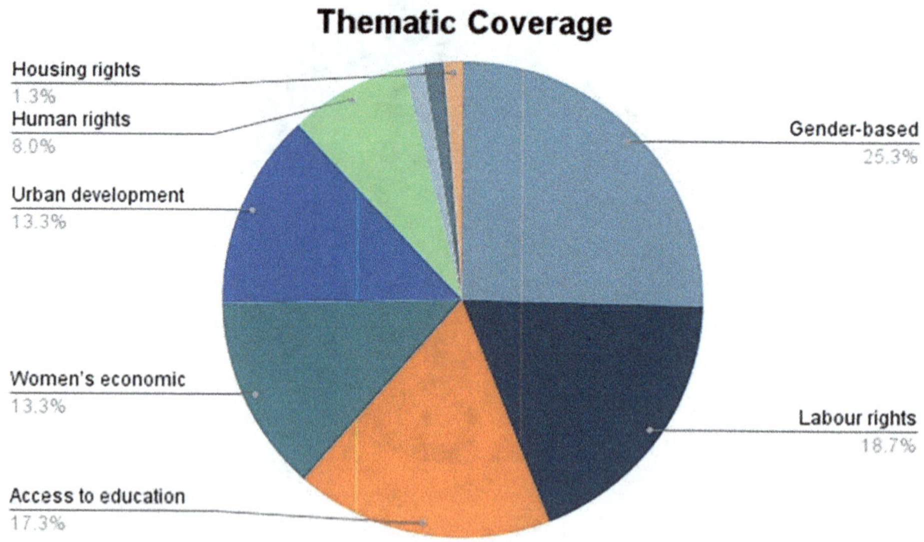

In contrast, topics related to development and empowerment receive markedly more optimistic treatment. Access to education and digital divide issues show a more balanced approach, splitting between neutral documentation and positive storytelling that celebrates technological advances and educational access improvements. Women's economic empowerment and urban development enjoy the most favorable coverage, with predominantly positive narratives that emphasize community-driven solutions, entrepreneurial success stories, and infrastructure developments. This pattern suggests that media outlets are more likely to adopt solution-oriented reporting when covering economic and development issues, potentially reflecting both the tangible nature of these achievements and a deliberate editorial choice to inspire hope and community engagement in areas where progress is more visible and measurable.

c. Dominance of Event-Driven Journalism

A significant disproportion was witnessed in the type and format of the stories covered in media monitoring. Out of 75 stories, 68 stories, accounting for 90.4% of the total stories were categorized as news. This is indicative of the coverage of event-based, reactive descriptive stories, covering incidents, announcements and official statements with minimal analysis. The event-driven journalism tends to offer privileges to official voices such as politicians, bureaucrats or law enforcements over ordinary citizens. This leads to the derivation of elite perspectives overlooking grassroot realities.

Figure 3. Types of media stories

Similarly, only 4 stories accounting for 5.3% of the stories were case reports, offering more details on individual experiences and incidents, also serving as storytelling tools to humanize broader social issues, despite reflecting missed opportunities for deeper audience engagement. The remaining news, that include 2 Op-eds and 1 Editorial indicates insufficient analytical and reflective journalism in comparison to factual reporting and portrays limited space for thought leadership, public debate and advocacy. Furthermore, the scarcity of analytical, reflective or opinion-driven content indicates the structural weaknesses in Nepali journalism alongside reducing opportunities for critical debate, policy advocacy and thought leadership within the public sphere.

d. Diverse but Fragmented

The study reveals the divergence in the operations of digital and traditional media outlets. It is evident that the traditional media outlets largely focused on governance failures and gender-based violence, through critical or negative lenses. Similarly digital outlets and online portals focused on positive storytelling, highlighting empowerment, education and local development. The divergence is not merely editorial but also defines and reflects the differences in target audience, resource availability and platform dynamics.

On the other hand, the large YouTube channels focused on polished production and solution-oriented narratives, aligning with local government achievements. The small channels focused more on niche audiences lacking capacity for sustained investigated work. This coexistence enriches the media landscape however, and also contributes to public discourse, deriving isolations in consumption with audiences engaging with narratives reinforcing the preexisting perspectives.

e. Representation of Marginalized Voices

A major significant finding from this study was the inadequate and inconsistent representation of marginalized voices. The social issues covered in the news varied across outlets with notable discrepancies in thematic focus and editorial approach. While *Koshipatra Daily* remained, a prominent outlet covering 40% of total media coverage, the outlet demonstrated its influential role in shaping local discourse. This was followed by Blast Times Daily, which covered 14.7%, ClickDharan.com covering 12% and Kapuri News covering 9.3% while the other smaller outlets covered 3-6 stories each, highlighting their role in amplifying grassroot level issues despite limited resources. In terms of orientation, most outlets relied disproportionately on third-party sources, official press releases and statements from law enforcement, and sidelining lived experiences of affected communities.

The reliance on secondary voices indicates the tendency to treat the marginalized population as an object of reporting instead of active narration of realities. Despite addressing critical issues such as violence, education and governance, the individuals affected were seldom given sustained platforms for articulating their perspectives. Consequently, journalism not only reproduces existing hierarchies of voice and authorities but also misses the opportunities to humanize and contextualize systemic challenges.

This largely considers the degree of media pluralism in Dharan yet missing the inclusive lens. Furthermore, the absence of marginalized voices undermines credibility and democratic potential of journalism. The failure to integrate firsthand narratives result in the reinforcement of dominant perspectives while perpetuating invisibility of those affected by governance failures and social inequalities. Citizen-led journalism and youth-driven reporting hold promises in filling the gap amplifying grassroot perspectives that mainstream media outlets neglect.

f. Public Engagement

Despite limited availability of direct engagement metrics, the nature and type of news offer insights on the potential for public engagement. It is indicated in the table below:

Table 2.

Potentials	Nature of Stories	Platforms
High Engagement: News stories on crime, gender based violence and education	- Stories related to gender-based violence, child rape, and sexual harassment, while fewer in number, often evoke strong emotional responses and public discourse, especially when reported in detail. These topics tend to gain traction on digital platforms and provoke community reactions. - Education access and urban development stories, especially those linked to service delivery or inequality, are highly relevant to broad segments of the population, increasing their potential for public attention and discussion.	Koshipatra daily likely had strong influence and engagement with significant readership
Moderate Engagement: Case Reports	- Case reports offer storytelling potential that can humanize social issues. With only 4 stories, this format remains underutilized. However, when done well, these stories often trigger advocacy, empathy, and community-level engagement, especially on social media.	
Low Engagement-Editorials and Op-eds	- Despite their importance in shaping opinion and policy, the lack of editorials and op-eds (only 3 total) weakens opportunities for reflective engagement. Audiences looking for thought leadership, expert voices, or policy critique are underserved. - This also means fewer entry points for civil society and academic voices to join the public conversation.	FM stations and digital platforms, such as Heart FM or ClickDharan.com, may offer localized engagement, particularly useful for community-level issues, but may lack analytics unless tracked separately.

5. DISCUSSION

The federal transition of Nepal has altered the terrain of governance and accountability and has also resulted in contestation of the ways in which media and youth participation intersect with these transitions. While the Constitution of Nepal (2015) promises bringing the decision makers closer to the people by granting local governments with legislative, executive and judicial authorities, Bhusal & Acharya (2024) and Smoke (2015) note the autonomy offered by federalism remains undermined by fiscal dependence on federal and provincial transfers and with limited institutional capacity. These contradictions are exemplified during the media monitoring centered around Dharan based media outlets, through the recognition of improvements in infrastructure and education despite acute challenges in housing, livelihood security and environmental risk. This shows the embodiment of Cornwall (2008)'s notion of invited spaces, wherein formal participatory mechanisms such as ward hearings and consultations exist in theory but their operation in practice are more legitimate than as sites of empowerment. This is seen to disconnect structural reforms with practice, portraying fragility of Nepal's federal experiment underscoring the critical role of media in bridging the gap between governance promises and lived realities.

The research portrays the role of local media's ability in fulfilling the critical role. The systematic monitoring revealed that Nepali journalism continues to be shaped by entrenched editorial patterns. With over 90% of the coverage event-driven covering short reports on crime, announcements and political statements and remaining as case stories, op-eds and editorial, it is clear as per Aryal (2025)'s argument wherein Nepali journalism is dominated by descriptive journalism with weak adherence to constructive journalistic values. This also subscribes to Hallin & Mancini's (2004) observation wherein transitional democracies, resource constraints and political dependencies push media to reactive reporting, privileging immediacy over investigation.

Furthermore, reliance on event driven journalism also leads to several distortions. With the disproportionate representation of official voices, citizens appear as objects rather than subjects of reporting. When corruption scandals and gender based violences are covered, they are often framed as isolated events rather than presenting as deep structural problems. The episodic framing furthermore limits public understanding of systemic governance challenges reducing journalism's watchdog function to a reactive tally of crises. In Dharan, this reduces opportunities for reflective debate undermining the potential of the media to foster democratic accountability.

These patterns, furthermore, present deeper structural legacies. The reliance of Nepali journalism to political patronages and partisan loyalties date back to 1950s, when the state subsidies and party alignments limited media independence in an environment with low literacy and small readership (Bhattarai, 2024). The history continues to shape editorial choices in contemporary outlets even after seven decades, where resource limitation and political pressure constrain journalistic autonomy. The workshops organized confirm the dynamics with reporters acknowledging reliance on political figures and events citing economic pressures and fears of reprisal. These resonate with broader studies of media in fragile democracies wherein political polarization and weak protections for press freedom inhibit accountability journalism (Strasheim & Bogati, 2016).

Despite the constraints, the Dharan project also exhibited the roles of youth driven approaches in reshaping local media. With youths representing Nepal's largest constituency (Nepal Statistics Office, 2021) and existing policy frameworks like National Youth Policy (2006) and Youth Vision (2025), they are considered to be the central actors in governance and development. However, with existing unemployment, migration and tokenistic representation in decision making the youth participation remains limited in practice (Poudel, 2022). This research project therefore deliberately engaged the youth volunteers as co-researchers, equipping them with tools to monitor media coverage, analyze tone and framing and advocate for inclusive reporting.

The reflection of the methodological choice with that of Freire's (1970) vision of participatory pedagogy, marginalized actors remain empowered in generating knowledge than simply receiving it. With engagement of youths in the process, the project transformed them from passive consumers to active producers of civic accountability. It is evident in the findings that the issues of housing rights, environmental security and livelihood remained underreported and were limited to community consultations. The focus suggests that youths are excluded from elite networks but are closer to everyday realities of governance than professional journalists.

This also aligns with Norris (2011)'s notion of youths as critical citizens while marginalized in formal institutions playing pivotal roles in questioning elites and demanding accountability. This is further supported by Kotilainen & Suoninen (2013) that considers young people across different contexts utilize media participation for identity construction and civic engagement. Furthermore, Faedi Duramy & Gal (2020) highlight how youth-driven digital initiatives across the Global South often fill representational gaps left by mainstream journalism. Dharan's case adds to the literature by portraying the engagement of youths in citizen-led monitoring on recalibrating local agendas and amplifying marginalized perspectives.

The silencing of marginalized voices remained a revealing aspect of the study. Despite some outlets occasionally included quotes from survivors of gender-based violence, overwhelming reliance on police reports and official press releases sideline lived experiences. Even community centered portals that might be expected to privilege grassroot voices, reproduce official narratives. The dynamic reinforces Herman & Chomsky's (1988) propaganda model illustrating the role of structural dependencies in pushing media to privilege elite sources. This is translated into systematic invisibility of women, youth and informal settlement residents in case of Dharan.

Fraser's (1990) concept of participatory parity underscores that a democratic public sphere requires not just visibility but equal voice. When marginalized groups are treated as objects rather than narrators of their realities, journalism reproduces hierarchies of authority and diminishes its own credibility. Our findings confirm that numerical pluralism measured by the number of outlets does not necessarily translate into substantive inclusivity. Yet, moments of alternative practice do exist. *Heart FM* and *Divyaroshani Weekly* adopted more solution-oriented narratives, while youth-driven digital platforms foregrounded education and empowerment stories. These examples resonate with Carpentier's (2011) argument that participatory media practices can democratize communication by sharing editorial power with communities.

The broader context of Dharan's media ecosystem reflects a hybrid and fragmented landscape. Traditional newspapers and FM stations tended to emphasize governance failures, crime, and gender-based violence, often framed critically. Online portals highlighted empowerment and development through more positive storytelling. Larger YouTube channels aligned themselves with municipal achievements, while smaller channels catered to niche audiences but lacked resources for investigative depth. This hybridity reflects Chadwick's (2013) notion of the "hybrid media system," where old and new media logics coexist and interact, sometimes reinforcing and sometimes undermining one another.

Fragmentation has dual consequences. On one hand, it enriches the public sphere by diversifying voices and formats. On the other, it risks creating echo chambers, where audiences gravitate toward outlets that confirm preexisting views (Sunstein, 2001). In Dharan, sensational stories on gender-based violence and corruption attracted significant engagement, while coverage of housing rights and environmental issues drew little traction. This pattern confirms McCombs and Shaw's (1972) agenda-setting theory: media shape what citizens think about, even if they do not determine what they think. When sensationalism dominates, structural issues remain invisible.

At the same time, constructive journalism offers an important counterpoint. Gyldensted (2015) and Dahal (2024) both argue that solution-oriented reporting can generate engagement by offering not only critique but also pathways for action. In Dharan, *Heart FM*'s solution-centered stories, though less widely consumed, demonstrated how positive framing can build community trust and broaden the scope of debate. This suggests that deliberate editorial choices, supported by training and capacity-building, could expand the possibilities of inclusive journalism in Nepal.

From these findings emerge several lessons for advancing evidence-based and participatory journalism in Nepal's federal era. First, there is an urgent need to strengthen data-driven and investigative reporting. Partnerships with universities, municipal data portals, and training initiatives could reduce reliance on descriptive coverage. Second, the media must treat marginalized groups as narrators of their own experiences, supported by trauma-informed and gender-sensitive training (Ross, 2010). Third, youth engagement should be institutionalized through media clubs, internships, and citizen journalism platforms that link young people directly to governance reporting (Shrestha & Shakya, 2020). Fourth, journalist safety and ethical standards must be prioritized, given the harassment faced by reporters in polarized contexts. Fifth, collaborative governance reporting where media, civil society, and municipalities co-produce accessible content such as infographics or participatory videos could enhance both transparency and engagement. Finally, civic groups and TLOs require digital literacy support to strategically use media for accountability.

Ultimately, the Dharan case illustrates both the fragility and the promise of Nepal's evolving media ecosystem. On one hand, journalism remains constrained by historical centralization, political patronage, and resource scarcity. On the other hand, citizen-led and youth-driven initiatives demonstrate possibilities for democratization and inclusivity. This duality reflects what Asthana (2007) identifies as the paradox of media in the Global South: structural inequalities limit access, but resource constraints often spark indigenous innovation. Dharan's youth-led media monitoring embodies this paradox, showing how even in fragile environments, participatory practices can generate new approaches to accountability.

Reimagining Nepal's media requires moving beyond episodic projects. As Carpentier (2011) argues, true democratization of communication depends on redistributing editorial power and embedding participatory practices within institutions. If citizen-led journalism is to fulfill its potential, it must be supported by durable networks of journalists, youth organizations, and civic actors. Linking such initiatives to governance reforms would help transform Nepal's fragmented media into a more inclusive public sphere, capable of amplifying marginalized voices and strengthening accountability in the country's federal future.

6. CONCLUSION AND RECOMMENDATIONS

The Dharan study offers critical insights into how media represent urban governance, housing rights, and the voices of marginalized communities within Nepal's federal context. The monitoring of local and digital platforms revealed a landscape that oscillates between the functions of watchdog journalism and constructive storytelling. Coverage frequently highlighted issues such as women's economic empowerment, educational access, and community development, demonstrating the potential of journalism to inform and inspire. At the same time, the analysis exposed enduring shortcomings: heavy reliance on event-driven reporting, limited space for analytical or investigative work, and significant disparities in depth and tone across outlets. These patterns underscore the pressing need for more nuanced, inclusive, and evidence-based journalism.

The participatory design of the project, particularly the active involvement of youth volunteers and local communities, proved vital in amplifying marginalized voices and challenging gaps between formal media narratives and grassroots realities. Through consultations and workshops, youth were not only trained in monitoring and advocacy but also positioned as co-creators of knowledge, thereby expanding the boundaries of civic engagement. This approach strengthened the capacities of both journalists and young people to practice solution-focused and ethically responsible reporting.

Despite these achievements, the study also illuminated persistent challenges. Journalists and youth media actors alike continue to face risks of harassment and political pressure, limited access to reliable municipal data, and a lack of follow-up on the outcomes of governance initiatives. Addressing these concerns requires sustained collaboration across media houses, civil society, policymakers, and youth networks. Priorities should include strengthening digital literacy, investing in data journalism skills, and institutionalizing mechanisms that guarantee transparent information flow between local governments and citizens.

Ultimately, the Dharan case illustrates the essential role of media in shaping public discourse and influencing governance in a rapidly urbanizing Nepal. By embedding rigorous media monitoring, ethical guidelines, capacity-building programs, and community participation into local journalism practices, it is possible to create a more informed, inclusive, and accountable media ecosystem. The lessons from Dharan extend beyond a single city, offering practical pathways for empowering journalists and young people as catalysts of positive social change, and for reimagining how media can contribute to democratic deepening in Nepal's federal future.

The media monitoring activities in Dharan revealed the urgent need to broaden the scope of local journalism beyond the conventional focus on daily news and event-driven reporting. To foster richer and more accountable public discourse, media outlets should invest in editorial content, op-eds, case stories, and long-form investigative journalism. Such formats create space for reflection, critical analysis, and deeper engagement with systemic issues that go beyond surface-level incident reporting. Importantly, monitoring also highlighted the necessity of shifting journalistic practice from portraying women, youth, and marginalized groups merely as subjects of reporting to recognizing them as storytellers in their own right. Doing so would not only diversify perspectives but also strengthen the legitimacy of the media as a representative public voice. At the same time, the media must explore innovative approaches to audience engagement through community radio, public forums, and other participatory mechanisms to build two-way communication and restore trust between citizens and news producers. Investments in training for local journalists on ethical standards, gender sensitivity, and trauma-informed storytelling are essential for ensuring quality, credibility, and accountability in reporting sensitive or complex social issues.

The workshops with journalists in Dharan further demonstrated the need for comprehensive capacity-building across the sector. Many local reporters, particularly younger professionals, expressed interest in strengthening their technical and analytical skills but lacked opportunities for structured training. In response, workshops should focus on the fundamentals of urban governance reporting, including data interpretation, writing skills, and visual storytelling, while also reinforcing journalistic ethics and professional standards. Technical skills such as camera handling and multimedia production are increasingly vital in an era where digital content dominates, and journalists should be equipped to produce high-quality reporting that resonates across diverse platforms. At the same time, the polarized political climate and increasing online harassment make safety a pressing concern. While addressing trolling or threats may fall outside the traditional mandate of development organizations, safety training for youth volunteers and journalists reporting on governance issues is an essential step toward protecting media practitioners and sustaining accountability journalism in fragile democratic contexts.

Community workshops extended these insights to the grassroots, demonstrating that citizen participation and local media are mutually reinforcing. To make governance more inclusive, planning mechanisms at the municipal level must create structured and accessible channels for participation, ensuring that women, youth, and marginalized groups hold meaningful roles in decision-making rather than being relegated to token positions. Access to information is critical in this regard: supporting TLOs (Tole Level Organizations) and other civic groups to use digital and social platforms can democratize advocacy, expand public engagement, and enhance monitoring of local government performance. At the same time, the consultations revealed that citizens remain deeply concerned with gaps in infrastructure and services, particularly in housing, water and sanitation, environmental risk management, and agricultural support. These issues highlight the need for partnerships between local governments, civil society, and youth networks to co-create solutions that are transparent, accountable, and responsive to community needs. By embedding media into these partnerships, accountability can be strengthened not only in how issues are represented but also in how they are acted upon in governance practice.

Taken together, these recommendations suggest a roadmap for transforming Nepal's local media ecosystem into a more inclusive and participatory institution. Media monitoring should evolve into a regularized practice that informs editorial standards, while workshops for journalists and youth can professionalize reporting and safeguard democratic spaces. Community engagement, meanwhile, ensures that grassroots realities remain central to both governance and media narratives. The Dharan case thus illustrates how citizen-led initiatives, when coupled with institutional reforms and collaborative partnerships, can move Nepal closer to a media environment that is evidence-based, representative, and accountable to the public it serves.

ACKNOWLEDGEMENT

This study was commissioned by Lumanti Support Group for Shelter as part of the 'Media Monitoring and Analysis of of media coverage on Social Issues engaging youth volunteers of Youth Network in Dharan' project.

REFERENCES

Adhikari, K. P. (2005). The state and media in Nepal: A historical overview. *Studies in Nepali Media*, *2*(1), 15–32.

Aryal, B. (2025). Professionalism in Nepali journalism: Challenges and prospects in the federal context. *Journal of Media Studies Nepal*, *6*(1), 1–18.

Asthana, S. (2007). Innovative practices of youth participation in media. *Global Media Journal*, *6*(10), 1–14.

Bhatta, C. D. (2020). *Democracy in Nepal: Interest groups and partisan politics*. Routledge.

Bhattarai, G. (2024). Journalism, politics, and democracy in Nepal: Historical legacies and contemporary challenges. *South Asian Journal of Communication*, *12*(2), 45–63.

Bhusal, B. R., & Acharya, K. K. (2024). Local governance under federalism in Nepal: Autonomy, accountability and challenges. *Journal of Political Science*, *24*(1), 1–20.

Carpentier, N. (2011). *Media and participation: A site of ideological-democratic struggle*. Intellect.

Chadwick, A. (2013). *The hybrid media system: Politics and power*. Oxford University Press.

Chhetri, R. (2021). Digital disruption and the rise of citizen journalism in Nepal. *Journal of Communication and Media Research*, *13*(2), 101–120.

Cornwall, A. (2008). Unpacking 'participation': Models, meanings and practices. *Community Development Journal: An International Forum*, *43*(3), 269–283.

Dahal, K. (2024). Media literacy and democratic engagement in Nepal's digital era. *Nepal Media Review*, *7*(1), 25–42.

Dalton, R. J. (2017). *The good citizen: How a younger generation is reshaping American politics* (2nd ed.). CQ Press.

Dhakal, S. (2010). Citizen journalism in Nepal: Opportunities and challenges. *Nepalese Journal of Communication Studies, 1*(1), 67–82.

Faedi Duramy, B. E., & Gal, T. (2020). *Children's rights and participation in digital age: Global perspectives*. Oxford University Press.

Fraser, N. (1990). Rethinking the public sphere: A contribution to the critique of actually existing democracy. *Social Text, 25/26*, 56–80.

Freire, P. (1970). *Pedagogy of the oppressed.* Continuum.

Frontiers. (n.d.). Journalism, democracy, and media governance in federal contexts. *Frontiers in Political Science*.

Government of Nepal. (2015). *The Constitution of Nepal 2015*. Law Books Management Board.

Gyldensted, C. (2015). *From mirrors to movers: Five elements of positive psychology in constructive journalism*. CreateSpace Independent Publishing.

Hallin, D. C., & Mancini, P. (2004). *Comparing media systems: Three models of media and politics*. Cambridge University Press.

Herman, E. S., & Chomsky, N. (1988). *Manufacturing consent: The political economy of the mass media*. Pantheon Books.

Kotilainen, S., & Suoninen, A. (2013). Citizenship, media and education in the Nordic countries. *Nordic Journal of Digital Literacy, 8*(1–2), 5–27.

Mahaseth, A., & Qureshi, S. (2021). Social media, citizen journalism, and democratic practices in Nepal. *Asian Journal of Communication, 31*(5), 441–457.

Malla, S. (2020). The political economy of Nepali media: Ownership, influence, and trust. *Studies in Nepali Media, 5*(2), 45–67.

McCombs, M. E., & Shaw, D. L. (1972). The agenda-setting function of mass media. *Public Opinion Quarterly, 36*(2), 176–187.

Nepal Living Standards Survey. (2024). *Main report of the fourth living standards survey*. Kathmandu: Central Bureau of Statistics.

Nepal Statistics Office. (2021). *National population and housing census 2021: National report*. Government of Nepal.

Norris, P. (2011). *Democratic deficit: Critical citizens revisited.* Cambridge University Press.

Norris, P. (2011). *Democratic deficit: Critical citizens revisited.* Cambridge University Press.

Parajuli, J. (2021). Digital disruption and Nepal's news media: Opportunities and challenges. *Media Studies Journal of Nepal*, *4*(1), 12–34.

Paudel, N. (2023). Centralization of Nepal's media in the federal era: Challenges for inclusive communication. *Nepal Journal of Journalism and Mass Communication*, *9*(1), 33–52.

Pokharel, B. (2024). Youth representation in Nepali media: From peacebuilding to participation. *Journal of Development Communication Nepal*, *4*(1), 50–68.

Poudel, P. (2022). Youth participation in Nepal's federal governance: Policy promises and practice gaps. *Nepal Public Policy Review*, *1*(2), 101–120.

Poudel, R. (2022). Youth migration and governance participation in Nepal. *Nepal Policy Review*, *2*(1), 25–40.

Proceedings of the International AAAI Conference on Web and Social Media. (n.d.). Studies on media centralization and digital governance in South Asia. *AAAI*. https://ojs.aaai.org/index.php/ICWSM/

Ross, K. (2010). Gendered media: Women, men and identity politics. *Sociology Compass*, *4*(7), 485–494.

Sharecast. (2022). *Media consumption trends in Nepal: Post-pandemic survey report*. Sharecast Initiative Nepal.

Sharma, P. (2019). Urbanization and development in Nepal: Emerging patterns, issues, and policies. *The Geographical Journal of Nepal*, *12*, 1–20.

Shrestha, P. (2024). Youth, democracy, and identity in Nepali media narratives. *Media and Society Review*, *10*(2), 22–40.

Shrestha, S., & Shakya, R. (2020). Digital activism and youth participation in Nepal. *Nepal Journal of Social Research*, *3*(2), 75–91.

Smoke, P. (2015). Rethinking decentralization: Assessing challenges to a popular public sector reform. *Public Administration and Development*, *35*(2), 97–112.

Strasheim, J., & Bogati, S. (2016). Nepal's struggle for peace: Post-conflict peacebuilding, 2006–2015. *GIGA Working Papers, 287*, 1–28. Hamburg: German Institute of Global and Area Studies (GIGA).

Sunstein, C. R. (2001). *Republic.com*. Princeton University Press.

Thapa, D. (2023). Youth and civic space in Nepali journalism: Between tokenism and transformation. *Journal of Civic Media Nepal*, *1*(1), 11–29.

Compilation of References

Abdul Rahman, R., Alias, M. H., & Hamid, Z. (2021). From welfare to empowerment: Rethinking zakat distribution in Malaysia. *International Journal of Zakat, 6*(1), 1–15. DOI: 10.37706/ijaz.v6i1.260

Abdullah, M. A., & Ismail, M. (2017). The role of spiritual intelligence in influencing entrepreneurial intention among Muslim entrepreneurs. *Journal of Islamic Accounting and Business Research*, *8*(3), 259–272. DOI: 10.1108/JIABR-05-2015-0021

Abdullah, N. I., Wahid, H., & Sulaiman, M. (2024). Social entrepreneurship and empowerment of zakat recipients in Malaysia: Opportunities and challenges. *International Journal of Zakat and Islamic Philanthropy*, *6*(1), 15–30.

Abdullah, R., & Suhaib, A. (2011). The impact of zakat on social life of Muslim society. *Pakistan Journal of Islamic Research, 8*, 85–91.

Abdullayeva, S. A. (2024). *Evolution of media: History and development of media, new media, media convergence, influence of technology on media. Global Scientific Review, 30*, 11–19. https://scienticreview.com/index.php/gsr/article/view/448

Abdul-Rauf, M. (2004). *The Islamic worldview: Ethics and morality*. Amana Publications.

Abrahams, L. (2017). Regulatory Imperatives for the Future of SADC's "Digital Complexity Ecosystem". https://core.ac.uk/download/188768849.pdf

Abu Bakar, M., & Md Husin, M. (2022). The integration of Maqasid al-Shariah into the digital economy: Ethical foundations for sustainable innovation. *Journal of Islamic Accounting and Business Research, 13*(7), 1071–1086. DOI: 10.1108/JIABR-03-2021-0095

AbuSulayman, A. (2016). *Crisis in the Muslim mind* (4th ed.). International Institute of Islamic Thought.

AbuSulayman, A. (2016). *Islamization of knowledge: General principles and work plan* (3rd ed.). International Institute of Islamic Thought.

Adhikari, K. P. (2005). The state and media in Nepal: A historical overview. *Studies in Nepali Media*, *2*(1), 15–32.

Adlina, A. U., Rahman, Z. A., Sakdullah, M., Aisyah, D., & Al Amin, F. R. (2022). Tazkiyat al-nafs as resilience strategy to deal with the post-pandemic recession among micro, small, and medium enterprises (MSMEs) actors. *Teosofia: Indonesian Journal of Islamic Mysticism*, *12*(1), 67–86. DOI: 10.21580/tos.v12i1.14437

Admodisastro, N. (2021). Evaluation of Disleksia Belajar mobile app for assisting dyslexic junior school students to learn the Malay language. [TURCOMAT]. *Turkish Journal of Computer and Mathematics Education*, *12*(3), 2230–2235. DOI: 10.17762/turcomat.v12i3.1172

Adnan, M. A., & Bakar, N. B. A. (2009). Accounting treatment for corporate zakat: A critical review. *International Journal of Islamic and Middle Eastern Finance and Management*, *2*(1), 32–45. DOI: 10.1108/17538390910946258

Aghaei, S., Nematbakhsh, M. A., & Farsani, H. K. (2012). Evolution of the World Wide Web: From Web 1.0 to Web 4.0. *International Journal of Web & Semantic Technology*, *3*(1), 1–10.

Ahmed, M., & Miracle, A. (2023). *The impact of media on shaping global cultural narratives in the digital age*. ResearchGate PDF.

Akter, S., Sultana, S., Gunasekaran, A., Bandara, R., & Miah, S. (2024). Tackling the global challenges using data-driven innovations. *Annals of Operations Research*, *333*, 517–532. DOI: 10.1007/s10479-024-05875-z

Al-Attas, S. M. N. (1995). *Prolegomena to the metaphysics of Islam: An exposition of the fundamental elements of the worldview of Islam*. International Institute of Islamic Thought and Civilization (ISTAC).

Al-Attas, S. M. N. (2018). *Prolegomena to the metaphysics of Islam*. ISTAC.

Aldousari, A. (2021). Mobile applications for students with dyslexia: A systematic literature review. *American Research Journal of Humanities and Social Sciences*, *7*, 1–7. DOI: 10.21694/2378-7031.21005

Alemayehu Tegegn, D. (2024). The role of science and technology in reconstructing human social history: Effect of technology change on society. *Cogent Social Sciences*, *10*(1), 1–10. DOI: 10.1080/23311886.2024.2356916

Alexander, J. (2021). The Noisy Silence of Gukurahundi: Truth, Recognition and Belonging. *Journal of Southern African Studies*, *47*(5), 763–778.

Alfonsi, V., Scarpelli, S., D'Atri, A., Stella, G., & De Gennaro, L. (2020). Later school start time: The impact of sleep on academic performance and health in the adolescent population. *International Journal of Environmental Research and Public Health*, *17*(7), 2574. Advance online publication. DOI: 10.3390/ijerph17072574

Alias, A., Dahlan, A., & Sultan Ibrahim, S. A. (2015). Mothers' experiences of parenting a child with dyslexia at a dyslexia centre in Malaysia. *Jurnal Teknologi*, *77*. Advance online publication. DOI: 10.11113/jt.v77.6996

Alimoradi, N. (2023). Internet addiction and sleep problems: A systematic review and meta-analysis. *Sleep Medicine Reviews*, *63*, 101545.

Ali, N. A., Sarif, S., & Kamri, N. A. Z. (2024). The influence of spiritual factors on business survival of asnaf entrepreneurs in Malaysia. *Afkar: Jurnal Akidah & Pemikiran Islam*, *26*(1), 89–120. DOI: 10.22452/afkar.vol26no1.3

Ali, S., & Syed, J. (2021). Ethics of artificial intelligence from an Islamic perspective. *Philosophy & Technology*, *34*(4), 1421–1441. DOI: 10.1007/s13347-021-00473-1

Allconnect. (2024, March 25). *Digital divide: Organizations that are helping bridge the gap*. Retrieved from https://www.allconnect.com/blog/organizations-addressing-the-digital-divide

Allcott, H., & Gentzkow, M. (2017). Social media and fake news in the 2016 election. *The Journal of Economic Perspectives*, *31*(2), 211–236. DOI: 10.1257/jep.31.2.211

Allen, K.-A. (2021). Belonging in an age of technology. In Mc Mahon, C. (Ed.), *Psychological insights for understanding COVID-19 and media and technology* (pp. 72–85). Routledge., DOI: 10.4324/9781003121756-6

Alliance for Affordable Internet. (2020). *The 2020 affordability report*. World Wide Web Foundation.

Almirall, E., Willmott, S., & Cortés, U. (2023). A few misfits can Change the World. https://arxiv.org/pdf/2309.03532

Alonzo, R. (2024). Interplay between social media, sleep quality, and mental health. *Sleep Medicine Reviews*, *67*, 101776.

Al-Rawi, A. (2017). Social media in the Arab world: Communication and public opinion in the Gulf states. *Journal of Arab & Muslim Media Research*, *10*(1), 3–15. DOI: 10.1386/jammr.10.1.3_1

Al-Rodhan, N. R. F. (2015). *Ethics and emerging technologies: Philosophical and applied perspectives*. Palgrave Macmillan.

AMC Indian Journal of Entrepreneurship. (2022). *Recent articles. AMC Indian Journal of Entrepreneurship, 5*(3).

American Psychological Association. (2023). *Inclusive language guidelines*. https://www.apa.org/about/apa/equity-diversity-inclusion/language-guidelines

American Psychological Association. (2024). *Structural features of social media platforms that pose risks to children and adolescents*. https://www.apa.org/news/press/releases/2024/03/social-media-platforms

Analytics Insight. (2025). *AI-Powered Experiences in Entertainment*. Retrieved from https://www.analyticsinsight.net/artificial-intelligence/ai-powered-experiences-in-entertainment-the-future-of-storytelling

Anderson, K. (2025). Colonialism and the Changing Control of Territories.

Anderson, P. (2025, May 15). How to preserve privacy in the age of mass surveillance: Democracy or technology? *APA Public Philosophy Blog*. https://blog.apaonline.org/2025/05/15/how-to-preserve-privacy-in-the-age-of-mass-surveillance-democracy-or-technology/

André, I., & Abreu, A. (2006). Dimensões e espaços da inovação social. https://core.ac.uk/download/26832047.pdf

Anduiza, E., Cristancho, C., & Sabucedo, J. M. (2019). The effect of exposure to incivility on political participation: Evidence from a survey experiment. [Note: cite actual journal details when finalizing manuscript.]. *Journal of Political Behavior, 41*(4), 1107–1130.

Apple. (2024a). *Transparency Report*. Apple Inc. Retrieved from https://www.apple.com/legal/transparency/

Apple. (2024b). *Privacy Governance*. Apple Inc. Retrieved from https://www.apple.com/legal/privacy/en-ww/governance/

Art Magazine, A. I. (2025). *Breaking Boundaries: How AI is Redefining the Art of Storytelling*. Retrieved from https://aiartmagazine.org/breaking-boundaries-how-ai-is-redefining-the-art-of-storytelling/

Arun, C. (2019). On WhatsApp, rumours, and lynchings. *Economic and Political Weekly, 54*(6), 30–35.

Arxiv. (2018). Shared hosting vulnerabilities and security risks. https://arxiv.org

Aryal, B. (2025). Professionalism in Nepali journalism: Challenges and prospects in the federal context. *Journal of Media Studies Nepal*, *6*(1), 1–18.

Asni, F., Mustafa, W. A., Amin Ahmad, K., & Subri, N. I. (2025). Preliminary framework for a digital marketing support scheme for asnaf entrepreneurs by zakat institutions in Malaysia. *International Journal of Entrepreneurship and Management Practises*, *8*(30). Advance online publication. DOI: 10.35631/IJEMP.830015

Asthana, S. (2007). Innovative practices of youth participation in media. *Global Media Journal*, *6*(10), 1–14.

Auda, J. (2008). *Maqasid al-Shariah as philosophy of Islamic law: A systems approach*. International Institute of Islamic Thought.

Auda, J. (2008). *Maqasid al-Shariah: A beginner's guide*. International Institute of Islamic Thought.

Audretsch, D. B., & Thurik, A. R. (2001). What's new about the new economy? Sources of growth in the managed and entrepreneurial economies. *Industrial and Corporate Change*, *10*(1), 267–315. DOI: 10.1093/icc/10.1.267

Autio, E., & Rannikko, H. (2016). Retaining winners: Can policy boost high-growth entrepreneurship? *Research Policy*, *45*(1), 42–55. DOI: 10.1016/j.respol.2015.06.002

Avram, G. Hee-jeong Choi, J., De Paoli, S., Light, A., Lyle, P., & Teli, M. (2017). Collaborative economies: from sharing to caring. https://core.ac.uk/download/188016138.pdf

Axon Park. (2025). *Top VR Education Companies in 2025*. Retrieved from https://axonpark.com/top-vr-education-companies-in-2025/

Aydoğan, Doğan & Büyükyılmaz, Ozan. (2017). The Effect of Social Media Usage on Students' Stress and Anxiety: A Research in Karabuk University Faculty of Business. 6. 253-260.

Azzopardi-Muscat, N., & Sørensen, K. (2019). Towards an equitable digital public health era: promoting equity through a health literacy perspective. https://www.ncbi.nlm.nih.gov/pmc/articles/PMC6859513/

Bahri, E. S., Ali, M., & Salleh, M. F. (2021). The role of zakat distribution in developing entrepreneurial capacity among asnaf in Malaysia. *Journal of Islamic Accounting and Business Research*, *12*(4), 567–583.

Bail, C. A., Argyle, L. P., Brown, T. W., Bumpus, J. P., Chen, H., Hunzaker, M. B. F., & Volfovsky, A. (2018). Exposure to opposing views on social media can increase political polarization. *Proceedings of the National Academy of Sciences of the United States of America, 115*(37), 9216–9221. DOI: 10.1073/pnas.1804840115 PMID: 30154168

Bailey, L., Nomanbhoy, A., & Tubpun, T. (2015). Inclusive education: Teacher perspectives from Malaysia. *International Journal of Inclusive Education, 19*(5), 547–559. DOI: 10.1080/13603116.2014.957739

Bakar, O. (2020). *Islam and the integration of knowledge*. UTM Press.

Baker, J. J., & Weerakoon, C. (2024). Deepening Insights Into Social Entrepreneurship by Leveraging Service-Dominant Logic. *Journal of Social Entrepreneurship, 16*(2), 714–745. DOI: 10.1080/19420676.2024.2316801

Bakshy, E., Messing, S., & Adamic, L. A. (2015). Exposure to ideologically diverse news and opinion on Facebook. *Science, 348*(6239), 1130–1132. DOI: 10.1126/science.aaa1160 PMID: 25953820

Balka, E. (1987). *Women and workplace technology: Educational strategies for change*.

Ball, M. (2020). *The metaverse: And how it will revolutionize everything*. W. W. Norton & Company.

Ball, M. (2021). The future of the metaverse. *Journal of Virtual Worlds Studies, 10*(2), 1–15.

Banaji, S., Bhat, R., Agarwal, A., Passanha, N., & Pravin, M. S. (2019). *WhatsApp vigilantes: An exploration of citizen reception and circulation of WhatsApp misinformation linked to mob violence in India*. London School of Economics and Political Science.

Bandura, A. (2009). Social cognitive theory of mass communication. *Journal of Communication, 59*(1), 265–273. DOI: 10.1111/j.1460-2466.2009.01448.x

Bank Negara Malaysia. (2023). Annual Report 2023: Economic & Monetary Review 2023. Kuala Lumpur: Bank Negara Malaysia. https://www.bnm-gov.com/-/ar2023_en_pr.html

Bank Negara Malaysia. (2024, November 17). Malaysians' financial literacy surpasses global average, but 61% still lack emergency savings, says BNM deputy governor. Malay Mail. https://www.malaymail.com/news/money/2024/11/17/malaysians-financial-literacy-surpasses-global-average-but-61pc-still-lack-emergency-savings-says-bnm-deputy-governor/157181

Barberá, P., Jost, J. T., Nagler, J., Tucker, J., & Bonneau, R. (2015). Tweeting from left to right: Is online political communication more than an echo chamber? *Psychological Science*, *26*(10), 1531–1542. DOI: 10.1177/0956797615594620 PMID: 26297377

Barboza, L. G. A., et al. (2018). Awareness as recognizing, comprehending, and learning about an issue to make informed choices and change behavior.

Battersby, J. L. (2006). Narrativity, self, and self-representation. *Narrative*, *14*(1), 27–44.

Baugartner, M. (2019). Media framing and entrepreneurial intentions: The role of television in shaping startup culture. *Journal of Media Studies*, *34*(2), 78–92.

Baughn, C. C., & Neupert, K. E. (2018). The cultural and institutional environment for entrepreneurship. *Entrepreneurship Theory and Practice*, *41*(5), 685–711. DOI: 10.1177/1042258717725524

Bawden, D., & Robinson, L. (2009). The dark side of information: Overload, anxiety and other paradoxes and pathologies. *Journal of Information Science*, *35*(2), 180–191. DOI: 10.1177/0165551508095781

Behlol, M. G. (2010). Concept of learning. *International Journal of Psychological Studies*, *2*(1), 123–128. DOI: 10.5539/ijps.v2n1p123

Benkler, Y. (2006). *The wealth of networks: How social production transforms markets and freedom*. Yale University Press.

Bhatta, C. D. (2020). *Democracy in Nepal: Interest groups and partisan politics*. Routledge.

Bhattarai, G. (2024). Journalism, politics, and democracy in Nepal: Historical legacies and contemporary challenges. *South Asian Journal of Communication*, *12*(2), 45–63.

Bhebhe, S. (2025). Borderland's theory in indigenous ethnic community archiving. *Information Development*, *41*(1), 106–119.

Bhusal, B. R., & Acharya, K. K. (2024). Local governance under federalism in Nepal: Autonomy, accountability and challenges. *Journal of Political Science*, *24*(1), 1–20.

Bigi, A., & Bonera, M. (2016). A proposed benchmark analysis of the connection between wine production and destination perception. In L. Petruzzellis & R. S. Winer (Eds.), Rediscovering the essentiality of marketing: Proceedings of the 2015 Academy of Marketing Science (AMS) World Marketing Congress (pp. 963–968). Springer. https://doi.org/DOI: 10.1007/978-3-319-29877-1

Bilton, C., & Leary, R. (2012). Digital transformation in the arts: a case study. https://core.ac.uk/download/29189144.pdf

Birsh, J. R., & Carreker, S. (2018). *Multisensory teaching of basic language skills* (4th ed.). Paul H. Brookes Publishing.

Blanke, M. J. (2018). Privacy and Outrage. https://core.ac.uk/download/214111681.pdf

Blayone, T. J. B., & Mykhailenko, O. (2025). Using Digital Technologies for Indigenous Socio-cultural Advancement in an Era of AI: A Systematic Critical Synthesis. *Preservation, Digital Technology & Culture, 0.*

Bloy, L., Halperin, E., Nir, N., & Malovicki-Yaffe, N. (2025). Powerful victims: A dynamic approach to competitive victimhood between high-and low-power groups. *Group Processes & Intergroup Relations*, *28*(4), 882–907.

Boar, A., Bastida, R., & Marimon, F. A. (2020). Systematic Literature Review. Relationships between the Sharing Economy, Sustainability and Sustainable Development Goals. *Sustainability*, *12*(17), 6744. DOI: 10.3390/su12176744

Bond, R. M., Fariss, C. J., Jones, J. J., Kramer, A. D. I., Marlow, C., Settle, J. E., & Fowler, J. H. (2012). A 61-million-person experiment in social influence and political mobilization. *Nature*, *489*(7415), 295–298. DOI: 10.1038/nature11421 PMID: 22972300

Boulianne, S. (2015). Social media use and participation: A meta-analysis of current research. *Information Communication and Society*, *18*(5), 524–538. DOI: 10.1080/1369118X.2015.1008542

Boulianne, S. (2018). Social media use and political participation: Recent evidence. *Current Opinion in Psychology*, *9*, 36–40. DOI: 10.1016/j.copsyc.2015.09.001

Bradshaw, S., & Howard, P. N. (2019). *The global disinformation order: 2019 global inventory of organized social media manipulation*. Oxford Internet Institute.

Braun, V., & Clarke, V. (2006). Using thematic analysis in psychology. *Qualitative Research in Psychology*, *3*(2), 77–101. DOI: 10.1191/1478088706qp063oa

Brautsch, L. (2024). Digital media use and sleep in late adolescence. *Sleep Medicine Reviews*, *65*, 101083.

Brown, L. M. (1997). *Storytelling: a cultural studies approach.*

Brush, C. G., Ali, A., Kelley, D. J., & Greene, P. G. (2019). The influence of human capital factors and context on women's entrepreneurship: Which matters more? *Journal ofBusiness Venturing*, *34*(2), 452–472. DOI: 10.1016/j.jbusvent.2018.08.002

Buckingham, D. (2006). Defining digital literacy: What do young people need to know about digital media? *Nordic Journal of Digital Literacy*, *1*(4), 263–276.

Burga, R., & Rezania, D. (2015). A Scoping Review of Accountability in Social Entrepreneurship. *SAGE Open*, *5*(4), 1–10. DOI: 10.1177/2158244015614606

Burlacu, M. (2014). Digital anthropology: Theoretical perspectives regarding electronic tribes. *Bulletin of the Transilvania University of Braşov. Series VII: Social Sciences and Law*, *1*, 241–248.

Butler, D. L., & Sellbom, M. (2002). Barriers to adopting technology. *EDUCAUSE Quarterly*, *2*(1), 22–28.

Cahyana, H., Hidayati, H., Sanjaya, M., Pangestu, A., Sundawa, A., & Aritakalam, A. (2021). Leady: A multisensory approach in mobile application for dyslexic children. *CommIT (Communication and Information Technology). Journal*, *15*(1), 31–39. DOI: 10.21512/commit.v15i1.6661

Cain, N., & Gradisar, M. (2020). Electronic media and sleep in children. *Sleep Medicine*, *50*, 735–743.

Campbell, S., Greenwood, M., Prior, S., & Young, S. (2020). Purposive sampling: Complex or simple? Research case example. *The Journal of Nursing Research*, *25*(8), 652–661.

Cao, L., Chen, Z., & Evans, J. (2022). Destructive Creation, Creative Destruction, and the Paradox of Innovation Science. https://arxiv.org/pdf/2210.10661

Carpentier, N. (2011). *Media and participation: A site of ideological-democratic struggle*. Intellect.

Carsten, & Stahl, B. (2011). IT for a better future how to integrate ethics, politics and innovation. https://core.ac.uk/download/228195737.doc

Carter, G., Milner, A., McGill, K., Pirkis, J., Kapur, N., & Spittal, M. J. (2017). Predicting suicidal behaviours using clinical instruments: Systematic review and meta-analysis of positive predictive values for risk scales. *The British Journal of Psychiatry*, *210*(6), 387–395.

Casas-Roma, J. (2022). Ethical Idealism, Technology and Practice: a Manifesto. https://www.ncbi.nlm.nih.gov/pmc/articles/PMC9462067/

CAST. (2018). *Universal Design for Learning guidelines* (Version 2.2). http://udlguidelines.cast.org

Castells, M. (2010). *The rise of the network society* (2nd ed.). Wiley-Blackwell.

Castells, M. (2010). *The Rise of the Network Society* (2nd ed.). Wiley-Blackwell., https://www.scirp.org/reference/referencespapers?referenceid=3992666

Cavallo, M. (2017). Sharing economy, sharing information. Are open data addressing us towards a new wikieconomy? https://core.ac.uk/download/235040253.pdf

Ch'ng, E., & Cai, S. (2019). Methods for evaluating the adoption and use of digital technologies in GLAMs. https://www.ncbi.nlm.nih.gov/pmc/articles/PMC7182766/

Chadwick, A. (2013). *The hybrid media system: Politics and power*. Oxford University Press.

Chaffey, D. (2020). Digital marketing: Strategy, implementation and practice. Pearson UK.

Challoumis, C. (2021). Index of the cycle of money - the case of Bulgaria. Economic Alternatives, 27(2), 225–234. https://www.unwe.bg/doi/eajournal/2021.2/EA.2021.2.04.pdf

Challoumis, C. (2025a). The impact factor of Tangibles and Intangibles of controlled transactions on economic performance. Economic Alternatives, 31(1), 64–76. https://www.unwe.bg/doi/eajournal/2025.1/EA.2025.1.04.pdf

Challoumis, C. (2025b). THE INFLATION ACCORDING TO THE CYCLE OF MONEY (C.M.). Economic Alternatives, 2025(2), 324–353. https://doi.org/https://doi.org/10.37075/EA.2025.2.03

Challoumis, C. (2018). Methods of Controlled Transactions and the Behavior of Companies According to the Public and Tax Policy. *Economics*, *6*(1), 33–43. DOI: 10.2478/eoik-2018-0003

Challoumis, C. (2023a). FROM SAVINGS TO ESCAPE AND ENFORCEMENT SAVINGS. *Cógito (Salvador)*, *XV*(4), 206–216.

Challoumis, C. (2023b). Risk on the tax system of the E.U. from 2016 to 2022. *Economics, 11*(2), 55–72.

Challoumis, C. (2024). From Economics to Economic Engineering (The Cycle of Money): The case of Romania. *Cógito (Salvador), XVII*(2), 161–170.

Chalmeta, R., & Barbeito-Caamaño, A. M. (2024). Framework for using online social networks for sustainability awareness. *Online Information Review, 48*(2), 334–353. DOI: 10.1108/OIR-03-2023-0116

Chandarana, B. K., & Kumar, T. (2024). Preservation and Advocacy of Indigenous Medicinal Knowledge of Tribes in India. *International Conference on Business and Technology*, 522–529.

Chandna, V. (2022). Social entrepreneurship and digital platforms: Crowdfunding in the sharing-economy era. *Business Horizons, 65*(1), 21–31. DOI: 10.1016/j.bushor.2021.09.005

Chapra, M. U. (2000). *The future of economics: An Islamic perspective*. Islamic Foundation.

Chauhan, A. (2024). *The role of technology in shaping social movements. Authorea.* https://doi.org/DOI: 10.22541/au.172773135.55025991/v1

Chauraya, E. (2025). Gender and development in Zimbabwe: A systematic literature review. *International Journal of Gender Studies in Developing Societies, 5*(2), 139–158.

Chell, E., Spence, L. J., Perrini, F., & Harris, J. D. (2016). Social Entrepreneurship and Business Ethics: Does Social Equal Ethical? *Journal of Business Ethics, 133*, 619–625. DOI: 10.1007/s10551-014-2439-6

Chen, K.-H., Xue, Z.-H., & Zhang, C. (2025). Social innovation in the digital era: Theoretical framework and policy implications. *Studies in Science of Science*.

Chen, Y., & Chekam, T. (2021). Algorithmic ethics and media accountability: A framework for responsible AI. *Journal of Media Ethics, 36*(2), 89–102. DOI: 10.1080/23736992.2021.1904823

Chhetri, R. (2021). Digital disruption and the rise of citizen journalism in Nepal. *Journal of Communication and Media Research, 13*(2), 101–120.

Chibike, J. J. (2023). Podcasting Covid19 in indigenous languages: Interrogating audio psychology and political anthropomorphism. In Mpofu, P., Fadipe, I., & Tshabangu, T. (Eds.), *African Language Media* (pp. 112–124). Routledge.

Chibike, J. J., Muzhingi, S. A., Pikanegore, P., & Makalisa, B. (2025). Interrogating the interplay of multilingualism and multiculturalism on Lupane State University campus radio station. In Mathe, L., & Motsaathebe, G. (Eds.), *Reconceptualising Multilingualism on African Radio: Language and Identity* (pp. 111–129). Springer Nature Switzerland.

Chinyere, U., & Val, E. (2023). Qualitative Research. *Journal of Computer and Applied Science*, *8*(1), 20–35.

Chouliaraki, L. (2020). Victimhood: The effective politics of vulnerability. *European Journal of Cultural Studies*, *00*(0), 1–18.

Cinelli, M., De Francisci Morales, G., Galeazzi, A., Quattrociocchi, W., & Starnini, M. (2021). The echo chamber effect on social media. *Proceedings of the National Academy of Sciences of the United States of America*, *118*(9), e2023301118. DOI: 10.1073/pnas.2023301118 PMID: 33622786

Cokrohadisumarto, W. (2023). Productive zakat as a tool for poverty alleviation: Evidence from Indonesia. *International Journal of Zakat*, *8*(2), 101–118. DOI: 10.37706/ijaz.v8i2.417

Cole, E. (2024). Media literacy: Empowering critical engagement in the digital age. *Global Media Journal*, *22*(70). Advance online publication. DOI: 10.36648/1550-7521.22.70.450

Cornwall, A. (2008). Unpacking 'participation': Models, meanings and practices. *Community Development Journal: An International Forum*, *43*(3), 269–283.

Couldry, N. (2022). Datafied Media and the Silent Derangement of Ethics. *The Impact of the Media*, 121–136.

Cox, K. D., et al. (2019). Findings on public consumption of microplastics.

Cpluz. (2023). Potential pitfalls of web development hosting solutions. https://cpluz.com

Crawford, K. (2021). *Atlas of AI: Power, politics, and the planetary costs of artificial intelligence*. Yale University Press.

Crenshaw, K. (1989). Demarginalizing the intersection of race and sex. *University of Chicago Legal Forum*, *1989*(1), 139–167.

Crenshaw, K. (1989). Demarginalizing the intersection of race and sex: A Black feminist critique of antidiscrimination doctrine, feminist theory, and antiracist politics. *University of Chicago Legal Forum*, *1989*(1), 139–167.

Creswell, J. W., & Poth, C. N. (2016). *Qualitative inquiry and research design: Choosing among five approaches*. Sage publications.

Crompton, H., & Burke, D. (2018). The use of mobile learning in higher education: A systematic review. *Computers & Education*, *123*, 53–64. DOI: 10.1016/j.compedu.2018.04.007

Dahal, K. (2024). Media literacy and democratic engagement in Nepal's digital era. *Nepal Media Review*, *7*(1), 25–42.

Dalton, R. J. (2017). *The good citizen: How a younger generation is reshaping American politics* (2nd ed.). CQ Press.

Dayé, C. (2025). Researching Scientific Attention Spaces: Epistemic Tribes and Territories. In *Futures Thinking: Epistemic Tribes and Territories* (pp. 57–68). Springer.

de Oliveira, U. R., Menezes, R. P., & Fernandes, V. A. (2024). A systematic literature review on corporate sustainability: Contributions, barriers, innovations and future possibilities. *Environment, Development and Sustainability*, *26*, 3045–3079. DOI: 10.1007/s10668-023-02933-7

DeCosta, P., Skinner, T., Sorensen, J. L., Topperzer, M., & Grawboski, D. (2023). Narrative and play based interviewing – a framework for eliciting perspectives of young children. *Qualitative Research in Psychology*, *20*(19), 337–362.

Del Giudice, M., García Pérez, A., Scuotto, V., & Orlando, B. (2019). Are social enterprises technological innovative? A quantitative analysis on social entrepreneurs in emerging countries. *Technological Forecasting and Social Change*, *148*, 119704. DOI: 10.1016/j.techfore.2019.07.010

Delgado, R., & Stefancic, J. (2017). *Critical race theory: An introduction* (3rd ed.). NYU Press.

Deloitte. (2024). *2024 Ethical Technology Report*. Retrieved from https://www.deloitte.com/us/en/about/governance/technology-trust-ethics-annual-report.html

Demir, M. (2024). A taxonomy of social media for learning. *Computers & Education*, *218*, 1–18. DOI: 10.1016/j.compedu.2024.105091

Denzin, N. K. (1978). *The research act: A theoretical introduction to sociological methods* (2nd ed.). McGraw-Hill.

Desai, M., & Goel, S. (2018). Rights of Dalit and Tribal Children to Non-discrimination and Inclusion. In *Child Rights Education for Inclusion and Protection: Primary Prevention* (pp. 67–103). Springer.

Desai, P. S. (2024). EMPOWERMENT AT HER FINGERTIPS: A DIGITAL REVOLUTION FOR RURAL WOMEN. *CAHIERS MAGELLANES-NS, 6*(2), 5134–5150.

DesignRush. (2023). Website maintenance trends. https://designrush.com

Dhakal, S. (2010). Citizen journalism in Nepal: Opportunities and challenges. *Nepalese Journal of Communication Studies, 1*(1), 67–82.

Dias, M. S. (2024). Tracing Portuguese Influences in Goan Cultural Heritage. *Multidisciplinary Research in Arts, Science & Commerce (Volume-12)*, 42.

Digitunity. (2025). *8 community-driven strategies for advancing digital skills*. https://digitunity.org/digital-skills-innovation-community-organizations/

Donkers, T., & Ziegler, J. (2025). Human-Agent Interaction in Synthetic Social Networks: A Framework for Studying Online Polarization. *ArXiv Preprint ArXiv:2502.01340*.

Drencheva, A., Stephan, U., & Patterson, M. G. (2022). Whom to Ask for Feedback: Insights for Resource Mobilization From Social Entrepreneurship. *Business & Society, 61*(7), 1725–1772. DOI: 10.1177/00076503211057497

Dundua, E. (2024). *Digital marketing and corporate social responsibility: Strategies for brand building and stakeholder engagement*. Springer.

Dunford, M., & Dunford, M. (2017). Understanding voice, distribution and listening in Digital Storytelling. https://core.ac.uk/download/219375574.pdf

Dusuki, A. W. (2008). Understanding the objectives of Islamic banking: A survey of stakeholders' perspectives. *International Journal of Islamic and Middle Eastern Finance and Management, 1*(2), 132–148. DOI: 10.1108/17538390810880982

Dusuki, A. W., & Abdullah, N. I. (2007). Maqasid al-Shariah, Maslahah, and corporate social responsibility. *The American Journal of Islamic Social Sciences, 24*(1), 25–45.

Du, X., Qi, Q., Li, Z., & Tang, C. (2024). Can digitalisation balance the dual pressures of global integration and local response? *Technology Analysis and Strategic Management*. Advance online publication. DOI: 10.1080/09537325.2024.2369575

Dwivedi, Y. K., et al. (2021). Artificial intelligence (AI): Multidisciplinary perspectives on emerging challenges, opportunities, and agenda for research, practice, and policy. *International Journal of Information Management, 57,* 101994. https://doi.org/DOI: 10.1016/j.ijinfomgt.2020.101994

Dymora, P., & Niemiec, K. (2019). Gamification as a supportive tool for school children with dyslexia. *Informatics (MDPI)*, *6*(4), 48. DOI: 10.3390/informatics6040048

Echchaibi, N. (2019). Muslim digital publics and the politics of belonging. *International Journal of Communication*, *13*, 1742–1761.

Eddo-Lodge, R. (2017). *Why I'm no longer talking to white people about race*. Bloomsbury Publishing.

Edyangu, H. (2021). *Social Media Use and Indigenous Language Preservation: A Case Study of Lukenyi Language in Serere District–Uganda*. College of Education open, Distance and E-Learning of Kampala International ….

Ekawati, R., Wasis, W., Shodikin, A., Fiangga, S., & Chen, J.-C. (2024). Utilizing games to enhance the learning of students with dyslexia: A systematic literature review. *TEM Journal, 13*(3), 2097–2106. https://doi.org/DOI: 10.18421/TEM133-37

Elam, A. B., & Terjesen, S. (2010). Gendered institutions and cross-national patterns of business creation for men and women. *European Journal of Development Research*, *22*(3), 331–348. DOI: 10.1057/ejdr.2010.19

Ellis, K., & Kent, M. (2011). *Disability and new media*. Routledge.

Ellison, N. B., Steinfield, C., & Lampe, C. (2007). The benefits of Facebook "friends": Social capital and college students' use of online social network sites. *Journal of Computer-Mediated Communication*, *12*(4), 1143–1168. DOI: 10.1111/j.1083-6101.2007.00367.x

ENGAGE XR. (2025). *Spatial Computing and AI in Education*. Retrieved from https://engagevr.io/

Eppel, S. (2020). How shall we talk of bhalagwe? remembering the Gukurahundi era in Matabeleland, Zimbabwe. In. Wale, K., Gobodo-Madikizela, P and Prager, J (Eds). *Post-Conflict hauntings: transforming memories of historical trauma.*: Palgrave Macmillan. pp 259-284

Eppel, S. (2004). Gukurahundi: The need for truth and reparation. In Raftopoulos, B., & Savage, T. (Eds.), *Zimbabwe: Injustice and political reconciliation* (pp. 43–62). Institute for Justice and Reconciliation.

Esposito, J. L., & Mogahed, D. (2007). *Who speaks for Islam? What a billion Muslims really think*. Gallup Press.

Eubanks, V. (2018). *Automating inequality: How high-tech tools profile, police, and punish the poor*. St. Martin's Press.

European Commission. (2009). *Entrepreneurship in the EU and beyond: A survey in the EU, EFTA countries, Croatia, Turkey, the US, Japan, South Korea, and China*. Publications Office of the European Union.

European Commission. (2024). *Gamification in Education: Duolingo Case Study*. Retrieved from https://ec.europa.eu/programmes/erasmus-plus/project-result-content/e22ddbda-dd23-42cc-89a2-786e921b2d80/Gamification%20in%20Education_20170418_020301.pdf

Exelmans, L., & Van den Bulck, J. (2016). Bedtime mobile phone use and sleep in adults. *Social Science & Medicine, 148*, 93–101. DOI: 10.1016/j.socscimed.2015.11.037

Expertsay. (2024). Challenges of unmanaged hosting. https://expertsay.blog

Faedi Duramy, B. E., & Gal, T. (2020). *Children's rights and participation in digital age: Global perspectives*. Oxford University Press.

Ferguson, R., & Peake, W. O. (2017). Television's impact on entrepreneurial attitudes in the UK. *International Journal of Entrepreneurial Behaviour & Research, 23*(5), 867–884. DOI: 10.1108/IJEBR-08-2016-0254

Financial Times. (2024a). *Transformation, trust, transparency: the future of GenAI*. Financial Times & Deloitte. Retrieved from https://www.ft.com/partnercontent/deloitte/the-future-of-gen-ai.html

Financial Times. (2024b). *Key steps to safeguard data and build trust in AI*. Financial Times & IBM. Retrieved from https://www.ft.com/partnercontent/ibm/key-steps-to-safeguard-data-and-build-trust-in-ai.html

Finlay, L. (2002). Negotiating the swamp: The opportunity and challenge of reflexivity in research practice. *Qualitative Research, 2*(2), 209–230.

Floridi, L. (2013). *The ethics of information*. Oxford University Press.

Floridi, L. (2019). *Ethics, governance, and policies in artificial intelligence*. Springer Nature.

Florini, S. (2015). The podcast "Chitlin' circuit": Black podcasters, alternative media, and audio enclaves. *Journal of Radio & Audio Media, 22*(2), 209–219.

Fraser, N. (1990). Rethinking the public sphere: A contribution to the critique of actually existing democracy. *Social Text, 25/26*, 56–80.

Freelon, D., McIlwain, C. D., & Clark, M. D. (2016). *Beyond the hashtags: #Ferguson, #Blacklivesmatter, and the online struggle for offline justice.* Center for Media & Social Impact.

Freire, P. (2017). *Pedagogy of the Oppressed.* Penguin Classics. https://www.easybib.com/guides/citation-guides/books/pedagogy-of-the-oppressed

Freire, P. (1970). *Pedagogy of the oppressed.* Continuum.

Friemel, T. N. (2016). The digital divide has grown old: Determinants of a digital divide among seniors. *New Media & Society, 18*(2), 313–331.

Frontiers. (n.d.). Journalism, democracy, and media governance in federal contexts. *Frontiers in Political Science.*

Fuller, C. J., & Narasimhan, H. (2014). *Tamil Brahmans: The making of a middle-class caste.* University of Chicago Press.

Fusch, P., Fusch, G. E., & Ness, L. R. (2018). Denzin's paradigm shift: Revisiting triangulation in qualitative research. *Journal of Sustainable Social Change, 10*(1), 2.

García-González, A., & Ramírez-Montoya, M. S. (2021). Social entrepreneurship education: Changemaker training at the university. *Higher Education. Skills and Work-Based Learning, 11*(5), 1236–1251. DOI: 10.1108/HESWBL-01-2021-0009

Garcia-Marin, D. (2022). New media, new practices? A study of the first Spanish Podcast Community and its pioneers. *Social Sciences, 11*(7), 308.

Garrett, J. J. (2011). *The elements of user experience.* New Riders.

Garrett, R. K. (2009). Echo chambers online?: Politically motivated selective exposure among Internet news users. *Journal of Computer-Mediated Communication, 14*(2), 265–285. DOI: 10.1111/j.1083-6101.2009.01440.x

Genocide Watch. (2021). *Genocide Watch Country Report: Zimbabwe.* Available at: https://www.genocidewatch.com/single-post/genocide-watch-country-report-zimbabwe [Accessed on 8 September 2023]

Ghosh, S., Ray, S., Nair, R., Nath, S., & Bishu, R. (2024). Exploring the Sustainability of Social Enterprises: A Scoping Review. *J Sustain Res., 6*(3), e240044. DOI: 10.20900/jsr20240044

Giglietto, F., Carlo, A., & Righetti, N. (2019). The role of television in the cross-national diffusion of entrepreneurial culture. *International Journal of Communication, 13*, 1585–1606.

Gil de Zúñiga, H., Molyneux, L., & Zheng, P. (2014). Social media, political expression, and political participation: Panel analysis of lagged and concurrent relationships. *Journal of Communication, 64*(4), 612–634. DOI: 10.1111/jcom.12103

Gilster, P. (1997). *Digital literacy*. Wiley Computer Publishing.

Giuggioli, G., & Pellegrini, M. M. (2023). Artificial intelligence as an enabler for entrepreneurs: A systematic literature review and an agenda for future research. *International Journal of Entrepreneurial Behaviour & Research, 29*(4), 816–837. DOI: 10.1108/IJEBR-05-2021-0426

Giumetti, S., & Kowalski, R. (2022). Cyberbullying via social media and well-being. *Current Opinion in Psychology, 45*, 101314.

Glasbeek, L., Wickert, C., & Schad, J. (2024). (in press). Evaluating definitions of social entrepreneurship: A rulebook from the philosophy of science. *International Journal of Management Reviews.* Advance online publication. DOI: 10.1111/ijmr.12359

Glaser, B. G., & Strauss, A. L. (1967). *The discovery of grounded theory: Strategies for qualitative research.* Aldine.

Globesign. (2023). Common website maintenance mistakes. https://globesign.com

Goel, A., Masurkar, S., & Pathade, G. R. (2024). An Overview of Digital Transformation and Environmental Sustainability: Threats, Opportunities, and Solutions. *Sustainability, 16*(24), 11079. DOI: 10.3390/su162411079

Goggin, G., & Newell, C. (2007). *Digital disability: The social construction of disability in new media*. Rowman & Littlefield.

Gompers, P., & Lerner, J. (2001). The venture capital revolution. *The Journal of Economic Perspectives, 15*(2), 145–168. DOI: 10.1257/jep.15.2.145

Google News Initiative. (2021). *Supporting media literacy with new partnerships.* Retrieved from https://blog.google/outreach-initiatives/google-news-initiative/media-literacy-partnerships/

Google. (2025). *How we support young people growing up in the digital age*. Retrieved from https://blog.google/technology/families/supporting-young-people-online/

Gorwa, R., & Garton Ash, T. (2020). Democratic transparency in the platform society. In Persily, N., & Tucker, J. A. (Eds.), *Social Media and Democracy* (pp. 286–312). Cambridge University Press., DOI: 10.1017/9781108890960

Gossel, M. B., Will, A., & Windscheid, J. (2018). The influence of technology trends on business models and value chains of media companies. https://core.ac.uk/download/224741237.pdf

Government of Nepal. (2015). *The Constitution of Nepal 2015*. Law Books Management Board.

Gradisar, M. (2022). Passive screen time and sleep: Myth and nuance. *Clinical Psychology Review*, *52*, 101983.

Grafiati. (2024). Impact of Shark Tank India on India's growing startup mindset. *YourStory*. https://yourstory.com

Graham, J. (2016). Dragon's Den and the popularization of entrepreneurship in the UK. *Journal of Media Business Studies*, *3*(1), 55–72. DOI: 10.1080/23774931.2016.1187734

Granovetter, M. (1973). The strength of weak ties. *American Journal of Sociology*, *78*(6), 1360–1380. DOI: 10.1086/225469

Grimaldi, M., Troisi, O., Papa, A., & de Nuccio, E. (2025). (in press). Conceptualizing data-driven entrepreneurship: From knowledge creation to entrepreneurial opportunities and innovation. *The Journal of Technology Transfer*. Advance online publication. DOI: 10.1007/s10961-024-10176-5

Grimmage, S. (2025). Fostering digital communities in higher education: Unlocking belonging. *Teaching and Learning Conference Proceedings, 1*(1). https://journals.librarypublishing.arizona.edu/tlcp/article/id/8343/

GSMA. (2020). *The mobile economy 2020*. GSMA Intelligence.

Guess, A. M., Lerner, M., Lyons, B., Montgomery, J. M., Nyhan, B., Reifler, J., & Sircar, N. (2020). A digital media literacy intervention increases discernment between mainstream and false news in the United States and India. *Proceedings of the National Academy of Sciences of the United States of America*, *117*(27), 15536–15545. DOI: 10.1073/pnas.1920498117 PMID: 32571950

Gunarathne, N., & Walpola, A. (2024). Social media addiction and sleep patterns: A psychological study. *International Journal of Latest Technology in Engineering, Management &. Applied Sciences (Basel, Switzerland)*, *13*(4), 140–145.

Gupta, R. (2022). Web 3.0 marketing: Opportunities and challenges. *Journal of Digital Innovation*, *5*(2), 45–59.

Gupta, V. K., Kaushik, A., Chauhan, D. S., Ahirwar, R. K., Sharma, S., & Bisht, D. (2018). Anti-mycobacterial activity of some medicinal plants used traditionally by tribes from Madhya Pradesh, India for treating tuberculosis related symptoms. *Journal of Ethnopharmacology*, *227*, 113–120.

Gupta, V., & Mirchandani, D. (2018). Investigating entrepreneurial success through women's perspectives. *Journal of Developmental Entrepreneurship*, *23*(3), 1850019. DOI: 10.1142/S1084946718500193

Gurning, S. T., Wiranegara, I. G. P., & Suminta, D. (2024). Documentary Content in The Digital Era (Watchdoc Documentary Content Study). *Metacommunication. Journal of Communication Studies*, *9*(1), 19–31.

Gurumurthy, A. (2018). Digital inclusion and gender justice: A feminist framework. *Development*, *61*(1), 56–65.

Gyldensted, C. (2015). *From mirrors to movers: Five elements of positive psychology in constructive journalism.* CreateSpace Independent Publishing.

Hafez, K. (2007). *The myth of media globalization.* Polity Press.

Hafkin, N., & Huyer, S. (2007). Women and gender in ICT statistics and indicators. *Information Technologies and International Development*, *4*(2), 25–41.

Haggblade, S., Hazell, P., & Reardon, T. (2021). The rural nonfarm economy: Prospects for growth and poverty reduction. *World Development*, *140*, 105250. DOI: 10.1016/j.worlddev.2020.105250

Hajdinjak, M., & Havas, A. (2019). A Practical Guide. https://core.ac.uk/download/228400934.pdf

Hallin, D. C., & Mancini, P. (2004). *Comparing media systems: Three models of media and politics.* Cambridge University Press.

Hall, J. K., Daneke, G. A., & Lenox, M. J. (2010). Sustainable development and entrepreneurship: Past contributions and future directions. *Journal of Business Venturing*, *25*(5), 439–448. DOI: 10.1016/j.jbusvent.2010.01.002

Hall, S., Evans, J., & Nixon, S. (Eds.). (2013). *Representation: Cultural representations and signifying practices* (2nd ed.). Sage Publications Ltd.

Halmos, A., Misuraca, G., & Viscusi, G. (2019). From Public Value to Social Value of Digital Government: Co-Creation and Social Innovation in European Union Initiatives. https://core.ac.uk/download/211994115.pdf

Hamdan, N. H. B., & Kassim, S. (2021). The effects of Islamic microfinancing, human capital and ICT usage on women micro-entrepreneurs' performance in Malaysia. *Journal of Islamic Monetary Economics and Finance*, *6*(1).

Hamid, N., Ismail, R., & Kamaruddin, R. (2020). The impact of Amanah Ikhtiar Malaysia's microcredit programme on women entrepreneurs' economic empowerment. *Journal of Islamic Monetary Economics and Finance*, *6*(1), 215–234. DOI: 10.21098/jimf.v6i1.1154

Hamilton, J. (2022). Physical activity, social media use, and sleep during COVID-19 in adolescent girls. *Journal of Sleep Research*, *32*(1), e13611.

Hampton, K. N., Lu, W., & Shin, I. (2016). Digital media and stress: The cost of [REMOVED NUMPAGES FIELD]caring 2.0. *Information Communication and Society*, *19*(9), 1267–1286. }DOI: 10.1080/1369118X.2016.1186714:contentReference[oaicite:0]{index=0

Haq, F., Kiran, M., Khan, I., Mehmood, S., Aziz, T., & Haroon, M. (2025). Exploring the pathways to sustainability: A comprehensive review of biodegradable plastics in the circular economy. *Materials Today Sustainability*, *29*, 101067. DOI: 10.1016/j.mtsust.2024.101067

Harbard, K. (2022). Pre-bedtime behaviors and actigraphy-assessed sleep. *Journal of Adolescence*, *72*(9), 426–432.

Hartmann, N. B., et al. (2019). Research on environmental and health risks of microplastics.

Hashim, J., & Yusof, N. (2021). Ethical considerations in the use of artificial intelligence from the perspective of Islamic values. *Journal of Islamic Ethics*, *5*(1), 1–21. DOI: 10.1163/24685542-12340068

Hassan, M. K., Aliyu, S., Huda, M., & Rashid, M. (2022). A review of Islamic social finance and sustainable development goals. *Review of Financial Economics*, *40*(1), 56–67. DOI: 10.1002/rfe.1153

Hassan, R., & Ali, S. (2019). Islamic digital ethics: A critical framework. *Journal of Media and Religion*, *18*(3), 123–136. DOI: 10.1080/15348423.2019.1647520

Hassan, R., Rashid, R. A., & Jamaludin, N. (2019). The influence of Islamic work ethics on entrepreneurial intention: A study among Muslim youth in Malaysia. *International Journal of Academic Research in Business & Social Sciences*, *9*(6), 101–115. https://www.emerald.com/insight/content/doi/10.1108/JIABR-08-2023-0256/full/html. DOI: 10.6007/IJARBSS/v9-i6/5984

Havas, A. (2016). Recent economic theorising on innovation: Lessons for analysing social innovation. https://core.ac.uk/download/213993194.pdf

Helsper, E. (2008). Digital inclusion: an analysis of social disadvantage and the information society. https://core.ac.uk/download/213972.pdf

Helsper, E. J. (2012). A corresponding fields model for the links between social and digital exclusion. *Communication Theory*, *22*(4), 403–426.

Herman, E. S., & Chomsky, N. (1988). *Manufacturing consent: The political economy of the mass media*. Pantheon Books.

Hidayat, D. (2018). Community Empowerment Through Social Entrepreneurship Training Based On Partnership Network. [ASSEHR]. *Advances in Social Science, Education and Humanities Research*, *330*, 185–189. DOI: 10.2991/iceri-18.2019.37

Hintz, A., Dencik, L., & Wahl-Jorgensen, K. (2019). *Digital citizenship in a datafied society*. Polity Press.

Hisseine, M. A., Chen, D., & Yang, X. (2022). The application of blockchain in social media: A systematic literature review. *Applied Sciences (Basel, Switzerland)*, *12*(13), 6567. DOI: 10.3390/app12136567

Hlady-Rispal, M., & Servantie, V. (2018). Deconstructing the way in which value is created in the context of social entrepreneurship. *International Journal of Management Reviews*, *20*(1), 62–80. DOI: 10.1111/ijmr.12113

Hohlfeld, T. N., Ritzhaupt, A. D., Barron, A. E., & Kemker, K. (2008). Examining the digital divide in K–12 public schools: Four-year trends for supporting ICT literacy in Florida. *Computers & Education*, *51*(4), 1648–1663. DOI: 10.1016/j.compedu.2008.04.002

Hondros, K., Schiemer, B., & Vogelgsang, L. (2023). Beyond personal safe spaces: Creating and maintaining collective environments for meaning and identity on digital platforms. *Organization*, *30*(5), 809–829. DOI: 10.1177/13505084231168094

Honneth, A. (2001). Invisibility: On the epistemology of 'recognition'. *Supplements of the Aristotelian Society*, *75*(1), 111–126.

Hopelab. (2025). *The New Icons: How Influencers Shape Youth Identity in the Digital Age*. Retrieved from https://hopelab.org/stories/the-new-icons-how-influencers-shape-youth-identity-in-the-digital-age

Hostao. (2023). Website maintenance and hosting tips. https://hostao.com

https://forms.gle/GRMnNwdngJxueuMq7

Huda, N., Rini, N., Mardoni, Y., & Putra, P. (2022). The influence of spiritual intelligence on ethical decision-making and performance of Islamic social enterprises. Journal of Social Entrepreneurship, *13*(2), 145–164. https://doi.org/DOI: 10.1080/19420676.2020.1826564

Hueske, A.-K., & Dijkstra-Silva, S. (2025). Exploring Social Value for Sustainability: A Revelatory Case Study. *Corporate Social Responsibility and Environmental Management*, •••, 1–15. DOI: 10.1002/csr.70002

Hulme, C., & Snowling, M. J. (2016). Reading disorders and dyslexia. *Current Opinion in Pediatrics*, *28*(6), 731–735. DOI: 10.1097/MOP.0000000000000411

Hussain, A.. (2023). A systematic literature review on performance of social enterprises. *Cogent Business & Management*. Advance online publication. DOI: 10.1080/23322039.2023.2269738

Hutto, H. D., & Wheeler, M. B. (2023). Tribal and rural digital inclusivity: An examination of broadband access in two neighboring Great Plains states. *First Monday*.

IBM. (2024). *Accountability in AI Design*. Retrieved from https://www.ibm.com/design/ai/ethics/accountability/

Ibn Ashur, M. al-T. (2006). Treatise on Maqasid al-Shariah (M. E. El-Mesawi, Trans.). International Institute of Islamic Thought.

Ibrahim, R., Abdullah, N., Razalli, A., Bitz, M., & Anal, A. (2021). Teacher readiness towards the use of mobile learning for dyslexia student: A survey in Malaysia. *International Journal of Asian Social Science*, *11*(6), 278–285. DOI: 10.18488/journal.1.2021.116.278.285

Ibrahim, Y. (2020). Digital Islamic ethics and the Quran: Toward a framework for online Muslim communities. *Journal of Islamic Ethics*, *4*(2), 145–168.

Ikhsan, S., & Jamaludin, M. A. (2022). Islamic Social Entrepreneurship Values: Application and an Experience of Akademi Bakat ABS. *AZKA International Journal of Zakat & Social Finance*, *3*(3), 109–118. DOI: 10.51377/azjaf.vol3no3.140

Indarti, N., Anggadwita, G., Purnomo, R. A., & Tomlins, R. (2024). Breaking Barriers! Social Entrepreneurship in Empowering People with Disabilities. *Journal of Social Entrepreneurship*, •••, 1–35. DOI: 10.1080/19420676.2024.2353059

Intel. (2015). *She will connect: Intel's commitment to close the gender digital divide*. Intel Corporation.

International Telecommunication Union. (2021). *Measuring digital development: Facts and figures 2021*. ITU Publications.

International Telecommunication Union. (2023). *Global connectivity report 2023*. ITU Publications.

Islamic Development Bank & Islamic Research and Training Institute. (2015). *Islamic Social Finance Report 2015*. IRTI.

Ismail, I. A., & Hussain, M. N. (2017). Productive zakat distribution by zakat institutions in Malaysia. *International Journal of Academic Research in Business & Social Sciences*, *7*(2), 554–565. DOI: 10.6007/IJARBSS/v7-i2/2676

Issar, S. (2024). The social construction of algorithms in everyday life: Examining TikTok users' understanding of the platform's algorithm. *International Journal of Human-Computer Interaction*, *40*(18), 5384–5398. DOI: 10.1080/10447318.2023.2233138

ITPro. (2023). Website downtime costs businesses thousands a month. https://itpro.com

Jackson, S. J., Bailey, M., & Foucault Welles, B. (2020). *HashtagActivism: Networks of race and gender justice*. MIT Press.

Jenkins, H. (2006). *Confronting the Challenges of Participatory Culture: Media Education for the 21st Century*. An Occasional Paper on Digital Media and Learning. MIT Press. https://direct.mit.edu/books/oa-monograph/3204/Confronting-the-Challenges-of-Participatory

Jennings, J. E., & Brush, C. G. (2013). Research on women entrepreneurs: Challenges to (and from) the broader entrepreneurship literature? *The Academy of Management Annals*, *7*(1), 663–715. DOI: 10.5465/19416520.2013.782190

Jeong, E., & Yoo, H. (2022). A systematic literature review of women in social entrepreneurship. *Service Business*, *16*, 935–970. DOI: 10.1007/s11628-022-00512-w

Jernigan, K., & Roach, B. (2021). Indigenous Virginia digital storytelling project: A creation story. *Genealogy*, *5*(4), 88.

Jessen, D. (2016). Cross-sector Collaboration: Results Through Understanding and Application. https://core.ac.uk/download/228616099.pdf

Jiaxin, X., Xi, F., Xiaoli, L., & Li, Y. (2022). Smartphone use's association with sleep, depression, and anxiety. *Psychiatry Research*, *325*, 115083.

Johanna Matschoss, K., Petteri Repo, J., Schultze, J., Berchem, M., Velasco, G., Popper, R., Linford, S., Avarello, A., & Pinto, M. (2017). CASI Policy Recommendations: Deliverable 8.3. https://core.ac.uk/download/132489646.pdf

Jones, P., & Comfort, D. (2021). A commentary on the leading information technology companies' approaches to corporate social responsibility. *Journal of Public Affairs*, *21*, e2564. DOI: 10.1002/pa.2564

Joremi, A. R., Yusof, M., & Hasan, N. (2023). Bridging the rural–urban gap: Educational opportunities and entrepreneurial readiness among asnaf youth in Malaysia. *Asian Journal of Entrepreneurship and Sustainability*, *14*(2), 112–129.

Kadiri, C., & Owolabi, B. O. (2020). *The new normal of eHealth equity: Transforming chronic disease management amid rural technological constraints and digital divides*.

Kahne, J., Lipkin, M. C., Tynes, B., McGrew, S., Mirra, N., & Garcia, A. (2024). *Civic reasoning and discourse across the curriculum: Digital Citizenship Education*. National Academy of Education & National Association for Media Literacy Education. https://files.eric.ed.gov/fulltext/ED672648.pdf

Kalra, A., Levy, R., & Mattsson, M. (2025). Targeted Disruptions: Internet Shutdowns in India. *Available at SSRN* 5129468.

Kamali, M. H. (2008). *Maqasid al-Shariah made simple*. International Institute of Advanced Islamic Studies (IAIS).

Kamali, M. H. (2013). *Principles of Islamic jurisprudence* (4th ed.). Islamic Texts Society.

Kamali, M. H. (2013). *Shari'ah law: An introduction* (2nd ed.). Oneworld.

Kamali, M. H. (2016). *Ethics and jurisprudence in Islam*. Islamic Texts Society.

Kamaludin, M. F. (2023). Social sustainability within social entrepreneurship. *Technological Forecasting and Social Change*, *192*, 122541. DOI: 10.1016/j.techfore.2023.122541

Kateb, S. C., Ruehle, R. P., Kroon, D., van Burg, E., & Huber, M. (2022). Innovating under pressure: Adopting digital technologies in social care organizations during the COVID-19 crisis. https://www.ncbi.nlm.nih.gov/pmc/articles/PMC9013661/

Kerr, W. R., Lerner, J., & Schoar, A. (2014). The consequences of entrepreneurial finance: Evidence from angel financings. *Review of Financial Studies*, *27*(1), 20–55. DOI: 10.1093/rfs/hht071

Ketprapakorn, N., & Kantabutra, S. (2019). Sustainable Social Enterprise Model: Relationships and Consequences. *Sustainability, 11*, 3772. DOI: 10.3390/su11143772

Khan, G. T., Karatela, S., Morawska, A., & Werner-Seidler, A. (2024). Intense and problematic social media use and sleep difficulties of adolescents in 40 countries. *Journal of Adolescence, 96*(5), 1116–1125.

Khan, M. S., & Iqbal, A. (2022). Social media addiction, sleep, and sociodemographics. *OM&S, 3*, 54–62.

Khuphe, N. (2022). Kalanga activism and the imaginations of Matabeleland in digital spaces. In Mlotshwa, K., & Ndlovu, M. (Eds.), *The idea of Matabeleland in digital spheres: Genealogies, discourses and epistemic struggles* (pp. 102–116). Rowman and Littlefield.

Kirchherr, J., & Hartley, K. (2025). Is circular economy a failing sustainability paradigm? Not necessarily. *Journal of Industrial Ecology, 29*, 1051–1059. DOI: 10.1111/jiec.70055

Klarin, A., & Suseno, Y. (2023). An Integrative Literature Review of Social Entrepreneurship Research: Mapping the Literature and Future Research Directions. *Business & Society, 62*(3), 565–611. DOI: 10.1177/00076503221101611

Klaus, P., & Hartshorne, T. S. (2015). Ethical issues in the use of technology in counseling. *Journal of Counseling and Development, 93*(3), 280–286. DOI: 10.1002/jcad.12027

Koltay, T. (2011). The media and the literacies: Media literacy, information literacy, digital literacy. *Media Culture & Society, 33*(2), 211–221.

Ko, N. (2024). Evaluating sleep health apps using behavior change taxonomy. *Journal of Medical Internet Research, 25*(3), e48356.

Kong, D., & Liu, B. (2023). Digital Technology and Corporate Social Responsibility: Evidence from China. *Emerging Markets Finance & Trade, 59*(9), 2967–2993. DOI: 10.1080/1540496X.2023.2199122

Kotilainen, S., & Suoninen, A. (2013). Citizenship, media and education in the Nordic countries. *Nordic Journal of Digital Literacy, 8*(1–2), 5–27.

Kotiranta, A., Puumalainen, K., Sjögren, H., & Dana, L. P. (2024). Digitalization as a growth driver for social enterprises. *Technological Forecasting and Social Change, 209*, 123837. DOI: 10.1016/j.techfore.2024.123837

Kovanen, S. (2021). Social entrepreneurship as a collaborative practice: Literature review and research agenda. *Journal of Entrepreneurship. Management and Innovation*, *17*(1), 97–128. DOI: 10.7341/20211713

Kozinets, R. V. (2023). Immersive netnography: A novel method for service experience research in virtual reality, augmented reality and metaverse contexts. *Journal of Service Management*, *34*(1), 100–125.

Kraus, S., Jones, P., Kailer, N., Weinmann, A., Chaparro-Banegas, N., & Roig-Tierno, N. (2021). Digital transformation: An overview of the current state of the art of research. *SAGE Open*, *11*(3), 1–15. DOI: 10.1177/21582440211047576

Krueger, N. F., & Brazeal, D. V. (1994). Entrepreneurial potential and potential entrepreneurs. *Entrepreneurship Theory and Practice*, *18*(3), 91–104. DOI: 10.1177/104225879401800307

Kuckertz, A., & Block, J. (2021). Reviewing systematic literature reviews: Ten key questions and criteria for reviewers. *Management Review Quarterly*, *71*, 519–524. DOI: 10.1007/s11301-021-00228-7

Kulular, M. A., & Balaban, M. F. (2025). Legal and Compliance Risks of AI and Blockchain Technologies. In Kıral, H., & Yılmaz, G. (Eds.), *Futurisks: Risk Management in the Digital Age. Accounting, Finance, Sustainability, Governance & Fraud: Theory and Application*. Springer., DOI: 10.1007/978-981-96-6448-1_13

Kumar, M. S., Singh, A., & Alagumuthu, G. (2012). Traditional beekeeping of stingless bee (Trigona sp) by Kani tribes of Western Ghats, Tamil Nadu, India. *Indian Journal of Traditional Knowledge*, *11*(2), 342–345.

Kumar, M., & Joshi, P. (2023). A systematic literature review of sustainability indicators in sustainability reporting. *International Journal of Sustainable Development*, *4*(3-4), 253–284. DOI: 10.1504/IJSDES.2022.128523

Kumar, R. (2016). Temporality as value: Ethnography and the question of time. *Journal of Human Values*, *22*(1), 46–56.

Kumar, R. (2019). Digital India: Opportunities and challenges. *Journal of Governance and Public Policy*, *9*(2), 34–45.

Kurjono, J., & Juliana, A., Rika, et al. (2025). Social entrepreneurship in Islamic perspective: Role of Islamic values, environmental values and social enterprise attitudes. *Jurnal Kajian Peradaban Islam*, *8*(1), 16–29. DOI: 10.47076/jkpis.v8i1.332

Lacy, M., & Prince, D. (2013). The future of digital disrupters:rethinking the digital divide. https://core.ac.uk/download/16285530.pdf

Lafontaine-Poissant, F. (2024). Social media use and sleep health among adolescents in Canada. *Health Promotion and Chronic Disease Prevention in Canada : Research, Policy and Practice*, *44*(7/8), 338–346.

Lakshmi, R., & Viswanathan, R. (2017). Media, gender, and entrepreneurship in India. *Journal of Media and Cultural Studies*, *29*(6), 899–913.

Lamba, H., Kumar, N., & Dhir, S. (2024). Circular economy and sustainable development: A review and research agenda. *International Journal of Productivity and Performance Management*, *73*(2), 497–522. DOI: 10.1108/IJPPM-06-2022-0314

Lamprou, S., Dekoulou, P., & Kalliris, G. (2025). The critical impact and socio-ethical implications of AI on content generation practices in media organizations. *Societies (Basel, Switzerland)*, *15*(8), 214. DOI: 10.3390/soc15080214

Lasisi, J. O. (2022). Nexus between social entrepreneurship and sustainable development goals. *Journal of Business Economic Analysis*, *5*(2), 211–226. DOI: 10.1142/S2737566823500019

Lazar, J., Olalere, A., & Wentz, B. (2015). Investigating the accessibility of digital libraries. *Library Hi Tech*, *33*(1), 32–44.

Lee, Y. (2024). Smartphone app intervention for sleep hygiene: Pilot trial results. *Digital Health*, *10*, 205520762412000. Advance online publication. DOI: 10.1177/205520762412000

Letaifa, S. B. (2016). How social entrepreneurship emerges, develops and internationalises during political and economic transitions. *European Journal of International Management*, *10*(4), 455–466. DOI: 10.1504/EJIM.2016.077424

Levenson, J. C., Shensa, A., Sidani, J. E., Colditz, J. B., & Primack, B. A. (2016). Social media use before bed and sleep disturbance among young adults in the United States: A nationally representative study. *Sleep (Basel)*, *40*(9), zsx113. Advance online publication. DOI: 10.1093/sleep/zsx113

Leydesdorff, L., Bornmann, L., & Wagner, C. S. (2017). Generating clustered journal maps: An automated system for hierarchical classification. *Scientometrics*, *110*(3), 1601–1614. DOI: 10.1007/s11192-016-2226-5

Liedong, T. A. (2025). Does Social Identity Matter in Political Markets? The Influence of Managerial Tribal Identity in Corporate Political Strategy Formulation. *Journal of Management Inquiry*, •••, 10564926251344217.

Light, L. L., Panicker, S., Abrams, L., & Huh-Yoo, J. (2024). Ethical challenges in the use of digital technologies in psychological science: Introduction to the special issue. *The American Psychologist, 79*(1), 1–8. DOI: 10.1037/amp0001286 PMID: 38236211

Li, L., & Zhang, Z. (2025). Technology for Good? Tencent's Corporate Social Responsibility, Institutional Chameleon, and the Future of Platform Economies. *Social Media + Society, 11*(1), 1–11. DOI: 10.1177/20563051251316119

Lim, W. W., Yeo, K. J., & Handayani, L. (2023). A systematic review on interventions for children with dyslexia. [IJERE]. *International Journal of Evaluation and Research in Education, 12*(3), 1674–1682. DOI: 10.11591/ijere.v12i3.25099

Lin, T., Longobardi, C., & Gastaldi, F. (2023). Nighttime social media use mediates sleep & aggression. *The Journal of Early Adolescence, 44*(1), 41–58.

Livingstone, S. (2014). Developing social media literacy: How children learn to interpret risky opportunities on social network sites. *Communications, 39*(3), 283–303.

Livingstone, S., & Helsper, E. J. (2007). Gradations in digital inclusion: Children, young people, and the digital divide. *New Media & Society, 9*(4), 671–696.

Li, Z. (2025). Strengthening path and influencing factors of overseas Chinese cultural identity from the perspective of educational psychology. *Current Psychology (New Brunswick, N.J.), 44*(5), 3102–3117.

Loader, B. D., Vromen, A., & Xenos, M. A. (2014). The networked young citizen: Social media, political participation and civic engagement. *Information Communication and Society, 17*(2), 143–150. DOI: 10.1080/1369118X.2013.871571

Lobensteiner, N., & Thies, S. (2020). Indigenous media production. In *The Routledge Handbook to the Culture and Media of the Americas* (pp. 336–346). Routledge.

Loots, E., Betzler, D., Bille, T., Jan Borowiecki, K., & Lee, B. (2022). New forms of finance and funding in the cultural and creative industries. Introduction to the special issue. https://www.ncbi.nlm.nih.gov/pmc/articles/PMC9185720/

Luckin, R. (2017). *Machine learning and human intelligence: The future of education for the 21st century*. UCL Institute of Education Press.

Lukanda, I. N., Namusoga-Kaale, S., & Claassen, G. (2023). Media as mediators in a science-based issue: Politics, foreign influence and implications on adoption of genetically modified organisms in food production in Uganda. *Journal of Science Communication, 22*(1), A03.

Luo, Y., Lai, B., Zhang, Y., & Liu, J. (2024). Village leadership, social networks and collective actions in indigenous communities: Case of Hani rice terrace social-ecological system in Southwest China. *Journal of Rural Studies, 106*, 103237.

Mabhena, C. (2014). Ethnicity, development and the dynamics of political domination in Southern Matabeleland. *Journal of the Humanities and Social Sciences, 19*(4), 137–149.

Mac Cárthaigh, S., Griffin, C., & Perry, J. (2024). Problematic smartphone use and adolescent sleep. *Developmental Review, 40*, 100.

MacDonald, M. R. (2013). *Traditional storytelling today: An international sourcebook.* Routledge.

Madise, Ü., & Martens, T. (2006). E-voting in Estonia 2005: The first practice of country-wide binding Internet voting in the world. *Electronic Voting in Europe Technology, Law. Politics & Society*, •••, 3–13.

Magazine, A. I. (2025, April 16). *Top 10 Ethical AI Companies.* Retrieved from https://aimagazine.com/top10/top-10-ethical-ai-companies

Mahaseth, A., & Qureshi, S. (2021). Social media, citizen journalism, and democratic practices in Nepal. *Asian Journal of Communication, 31*(5), 441–457.

MAIPs. (2022). Laporan Tahunan Majlis Agama Islam dan Adat Melayu Perlis 2022 [Annual Report of the Perlis Islamic Religious and Malay Customs Council 2022].

Majlis Agama Islam dan Adat Istiadat Melayu Perlis (MAIPs). (2023). Laporan tahunan 2023. Kangar: MAIPs.

Maka, A., & Alabid, J. (2022). Solar energy technology and its roles in sustainable development. *Clean Energy, 6*(3), 476–483. DOI: 10.1093/ce/zkac023

Malaysian Communications and Multimedia Commission. (2022). *Internet Users Survey 2022.* https://www.mcmc.gov.my

Malla, S. (2020). The political economy of Nepali media: Ownership, influence, and trust. *Studies in Nepali Media, 5*(2), 45–67.

Mangunsong, F. M. (2014). *Psikologi dan pendidikan anak berkebutuhan khusus* (Jilid 1). Depok: LPSP3 UI.

Mansell, R., & Raboy, M. (Eds.). (2014). *The Handbook of Global Media and Communication Policy.* Wiley-Blackwell., https://books.google.com/books/about/The_Handbook_of_Global_Media_and_Communi.html?id=GyGeAgAAQBAJ

Manžuch, Z. (2017). Ethical issues in digitization of cultural heritage. *Journal of Contemporary Archival Studies*, *4*(2), 4.

Marchessault, J. (2014). Media Studies as Interdisciplinary Exploration. *Journal of Visual Culture*, *13*(1), 82–84.

MARCO CHIARA ELEONORA. D. E., MININ ALBERTO, D. I., CRISTINA, M. A. R. U. L. L. O., & DANIEL, N. E. P. E. L. S. K. I. (2019). Digital platform innovation in European SMEs. https://core.ac.uk/download/188760703.pdf

Maresca, G., Corallo, F., De Cola, M. C., Formica, C., Giliberto, S., Rao, G., Crupi, M. F., Quartarone, A., & Pidalà, A. (2024). Effectiveness of the use of Virtual Reality rehabilitation in children with dyslexia: Follow-up after one year. *Brain Sciences*, *14*(7), 655. DOI: 10.3390/brainsci14070655

Mariyono, D., Alifatul Kamila, A. N., & Alif Hidayatullah, A. N. (2025). Unity in diversity: Navigating global connections through cultural exchange. *Quality Education for All*, *2*(1), 114–137.

Martens, H., & Hobbs, R. (2015). How media literacy supports civic engagement in a digital age. *Atlantic Journal of Communication*, *23*(2), 120–137. DOI: 10.1080/15456870.2014.961636

Martin, R. L., & Osberg, S. (2007). Social Entrepreneurship: the case for definition. *Stanford Social Innovation Review, spring*, 29–39.

Maseko, B. (2022). Family language policy in post-genocide Matabeleland: The case of a Ndebele family. *Southern African Linguistics and Applied Language Studies*, *40*(1), 1–14.

Maseko, B., & Dhlamini, N. (2021). Language, ethnicity and the politics of exclusion in Zimbabwe. In Ncube, G., Sayi, S., & Ndebele, L. (Eds.), *Re(figuring) Ndebele cultural production in contemporary Zimbabwe* (pp. 91–113).

Matteucci, N. (2013). Standards, IPR and digital TV convergence: theories and empirical evidence. https://core.ac.uk/download/211614438.pdf

Mauksch, S., & Dey, P. (2024). Treating disability as an asset (not a limitation): A critical examination of disability inclusion through social entrepreneurship. *Organization*, *31*(4), 624–644. DOI: 10.1177/13505084221150586

McCombs, M. E., & Shaw, D. L. (1972). The agenda-setting function of mass media. *Public Opinion Quarterly*, *36*(2), 176–187.

McKenzie, J. (2025). Digital media as sites for cultural identity development: The case of Hmong American emerging adults. *Journal of Adolescent Research, 40*(2), 296–330.

Meena, H. R. (2024). Denotified Tribes in India. *Indian Literature, 68*(6 (344), 138–146.

Mehta, R. K., & Sharma, S. (2015). Knowledge, attitude and practice of self-medication among medical students. *Age (Years), 20*(49), 65–73.

Melonashi, E. (2019). Social media and identity: Understanding identity communication and creation through social media. In Khosrow-Pour, M. (Ed.), *Internet and technology addiction: Breakthroughs in research and practice* (pp. 1–22). IGI Global., DOI: 10.4018/978-1-5225-8900-6.ch001

MENDES POLVORA ALEXANDRE. R. O. Q. U. E. & DO NASCIMENTO SUSANA, F. I. G. U. E. I. R. E. D. O. (2018). Impact Assessment and Recommendations: Making Sense H2020 CAPS Project. https://core.ac.uk/download/154760364.pdf

Mengist, W., Soromessa, T., & Legese, G. (2020). Method for conducting systematic literature review and meta-analysis for environmental science research. *MethodsX, 7*, 100777. DOI: 10.1016/j.mex.2019.100777

Meta. (2020). *We think digital: Digital literacy program.* Meta Platforms Inc.

Meyer, A., Rose, D. H., & Gordon, D. (2014). *Universal design for learning: Theory and practice.* CAST Professional Publishing.

Mhlanga, B. (2013). Ethnicity or tribalism? The discursive construction of Zimbabwean national identity. *African Identities, 11*(1), 47–60.

Mhlanga, B., & Mpofu, M. (2014). The virtual parallax: Imaginations of Mthwakazi Nationalism – online discussions and calls for self-determination. In Solo, A. (Ed.), *Handbook on research on political activism in the Information Age* (pp. 129–146). IGI Global.

Miguel, C., Lutz, C., Perez-Vega, R., & Majetić, F. (2025). "Alone on the road": Loneliness among digital nomads and the use of social media to foster personal relationships. *Media Culture & Society, 47*(3), 546–566.

Mihailidis, P., & Thevenin, B. (2013). Media literacy as a core competency for engaged citizenship in participatory democracy. *The American Behavioral Scientist, 57*(11), 1611–1622. https://psycnet.apa.org/record/2013-35893-007

Ministry of Education Malaysia. (2019). *Special Education Integrated Programme policy framework.* Ministry of Education Malaysia.

MIT Open Doc Lab. (2025). *Radical Storytelling with AI: Ethics, Authorship, and Experimentation.* Retrieved from https://opendoclab.mit.edu/presents/radical-storytelling-ai-ethics-authorship-experimentation-lili-navid-khonsari/

Mittelstadt, B. D., Allo, P., Taddeo, M., Wachter, S., & Floridi, L. (2016). The ethics of algorithms: Mapping the debate. *Big Data & Society*, *3*(2), 1–21. DOI: 10.1177/2053951716679679

Mlambo, A. S. (2013). Becoming Zimbabwe or Becoming Zimbabwean: Identity, nationalism an nation building. *Africa Spectrum*, *48*(1), 49–70.

Mohamed Ismail Bin Hubadillah. (2025). *Development of an awareness website on microplastic contamination in food* [Unpublished undergraduate final year project]. Universiti Malaysia Perlis.

Mohd. Suhardi Mat Jusoh, Ahmad, H., & Abdul Rani, A. (2020). The application of module tazkiyyah al-nafs in the spiritual development among students of Universiti Malaysia Pahang (UMP). *International Journal of Humanities, Technology and Civilization*, 5(1), 72–79. DOI: 10.15282/ijhtc.v5i1.4821

Moher, D., Liberati, A., Tetzlaff, J., & Altman, D. G. (2010). Preferred reporting items for systematic reviews and meta-analyses: The PRISMA statement. *International Journal of Surgery*, *8*(5), 336–341. DOI: 10.1016/j.ijsu.2010.02.007

Mohsin, M. I. A. (2021). Zakat and poverty alleviation: Roles, management, and challenges. *International Journal of Zakat and Islamic Philanthropy*, *3*(2), 15–28.

MONACI. S. A. R. A. (2016). Boosting Creativity through Digital Disruption? The Role of Co-Creation Platforms in the Media Production Field. https://core.ac.uk/download/234913232.pdf

Moore, R., Vitale, D., & Stawinoga, N. (2018). *The digital divide and educational equity: A look at students with very limited access to electronic devices at home.* ACT Center for Equity in Learning. https://equityinlearning.act.org/research-report/the-digital-divide-and-educational-equity/

Moshood, T. D., Nawanir, G., Mahmud, F., Mohamad, F., & Ahmad, M. H., & AbdulGhani, A. (2022). Sustainability of biodegradable plastics: New problem or solution to solve the global plastic pollution? *Current Research in Green and Sustainable Chemistry*, *5*, 100273. DOI: 10.1016/j.crgsc.2022.100273

Mossberger, K., Tolbert, C. J., & McNeal, R. S. (2008). *Digital citizenship: The Internet, society, and participation.* MIT Press.

Moyo, L. (2009). Constructing a home away from home: The internet, nostalgia and identity politics among Zimbabwean communities in Britain. *Journal of Global Mass Communications, 2*(1), 66–85.

Moyo, T. (2024). The politics of the unity accord of 1987 in Baya's Tomorrow's People. *International Journal Online Humanities, 10*(1), 1–22.

Mpofu, M., Moyo, C., and Sibanda, N. (2021). Popular Theatre as a Struggle for Identity and Representation in Matabeleland: 1980 to the Present. *Theatre from Rhodesia to Zimbabwe: Hegemony, Identity and a Contested Postcolony*. pp169-191.

Mpofu, S. (2013). Social media and the politics of ethnicity in Zimbabwe, *Ecquid Novi: African Journalism. Studies, 34*(1), 115–122.

Msindo, E. (2007). Ethnicity and nationalism in urban colonial Zimbabwe: Bulawayo, 1950-1963. *Journal of African History, 48*, 267–290.

Msipa, N. N., & Masango, M. J. (2025). Trans-generational trauma and tribal conflict among AmaNdebele and VaShona Pentecostal clergy. *African Journal of Pentecostal Studies, 2*(1), 10–31.

Muhammad, T., Al-Shaghdari, F., & Ibrahim, S. M. (2023). Islamic Social Finance in Addressing Poverty Reduction and Economic Growth: Using Structural Equation Modeling. *The Journal of Muamalat and Islamic Finance Research, 20*(2), 179–191. DOI: 10.33102/jmifr.52

Mukherjee, S. (2024). Media, Culture and Tribes: An Analysis of Various Social Issues. *INTERNATIONAL JOURNAL OF CULTURAL STUDIES AND SOCIAL SCIENCES*, 217.

Mumi, A., Ngammoh, N., & Suwanpakdee, A. (2025). The nexus of artificial intelligence and entrepreneurship research: Bibliometric analysis. *Sustainable Futures : An Applied Journal of Technology, Environment and Society, 9*, 100688. DOI: 10.1016/j.sftr.2025.100688

Murphy, M., Johnston, K., & Weaver, L. (2022). Longitudinal effects of reduced nightly social media use on university students' sleep. *Sleep Medicine, 88*, 45–52.

MWANGI, M. J. (2023). *ROLE OF SOCIAL NETWORK STRUCTURES ON BIRTH ATTENDANT DECISIONS AMONG WOMEN IN NAKURU COUNTY, KENYA*. KENYATTA UNIVERSITY.

Nayak, M., Nayak, P. M., & Joshi, H. G. (2025). Digital platforms' use in SMEs – A critical analysis of entrepreneurs' behaviour. *Cogent Economics & Finance, 13*(1). Advance online publication. DOI: 10.1080/23322039.2025.2461337

Ncube, B. J. (2019). *Radio Mthwakazi and the Construction of Ndebele Ethnic Identity*. Doctoral Thesis. Johannesburg: University of Johannesburg

Ndhlovu, G. N. (2019). The ethnicity of development? Discourses shaping developmental politics in rural Matabeleland South, Zimbabwe. *African Journal of Social Work*, *9*(1), 35–45.

Ndlovu, N. (2019). *The Gukurahundi "genocide": memory and justice in independent Zimbabwe*. Doctoral thesis. University of Cape Town. https://open.uct.ac.za/handle/11427/30431

Ndlovu, S. (2025). 'Inadvertent'state actors and lingo-cultural Gukurahundis in Matabeleland. In Kellier, H., Mpofu and Nkomo, D (Eds). *Civil Society in Zimbabwe* (pp. 155-172). London: Routledge

Ndlovu, E., & Chikohora, E. (2022). Gukurahundi, the Forgotten Tragedy: Examining Print Media as a Vehicle for Peace Education in the Matabeleland Region after Ethnic Violence. *Journal of Educational Sociology*, *1*(2), 1–16.

Ndlovu-Gatsheni, S. (2012). Rethinking Chimurenga and Gukurahundi in Zimbabwe: A critique of partisan national history. *African Studies Review*, *55*(3), 1–26.

Ndlovu, M. (2018). Gukurahundi, new media and the 'discourses of silence': The reproduction of the hegemonic narratives of the Matabeleland post-colonial violence on selected Zimbabwean news websites. *African Identities*, *16*(3), 275–289.

Ndlovu, M. (2018). New Media and Ndebele Hiraeth: Memory, Nostalgia and Ndebele Nationalism on Selected News Websites, *African. Journalism Studies*, *39*(4), 109–130.

Ndlovu, M., & Tshuma, L. A. (2021). Bleeding from one generation to the next: The media and the constructions of Gukurahundi postmemories by university students in Zimbabwe. *African Studies*, *80*(3-4), 376–396.

Ndung'u, M. N., & Waema, T. M. (2011). Development outcomes of ICT in Africa. In Ndung'u, M. N., & Waema, T. M. (Eds.), *Development outcomes of ICT for Africa* (pp. 1–16). African Economic Research Consortium.

Nepal Living Standards Survey. (2024). *Main report of the fourth living standards survey*. Kathmandu: Central Bureau of Statistics.

Nepal Statistics Office. (2021). *National population and housing census 2021: National report*. Government of Nepal.

Nguyen Luong, M., Mark, G., & Kulshrestha, J. (2023). Sleep during COVID-19: Longitudinal study in Finland. *arXiv*. https://arxiv.org (October 2023)

Ngwenya, D. (2016). "Our branches are broken:" Using the Tree of Life healing methodology with victims of Gukurahundi in Matabeleland, Zimbabwe. *Peace and Conflict Studies*, *23*(1), 1–16.

NHS Digital. (2021). *Digital inclusion in health and care: Lessons learned from the pandemic*. NHS Digital.

Nicholson, D., Bohnert, A., & Crowley, S. (2023). A developmental perspective on sleep consistency. *Behavioral Sleep Medicine*, *21*(1), 97–116.

Nicolson, R., & Fawcett, A. (2008). *Dyslexia, learning, and the brain*. MIT Press., DOI: 10.7551/mitpress/9780262140997.001.0001

Nielsen. (2023, December). *The Power and Potential of Data for Good®*. Retrieved from https://www.nielsen.com/news-center/2023/the-power-and-potential-of-data-for-good/

Norris, P. (2001). *Digital divide: Civic engagement, information poverty, and the internet worldwide*. Cambridge University Press.

Norris, P. (2001). *Digital divide: Civic engagement, information poverty, and the Internet worldwide*. Cambridge University Press.

Norris, P. (2011). *Democratic deficit: Critical citizens revisited*. Cambridge University Press.

Nur Alya Afifah Binti Faizul Sutiara. (2025). *Pembangunan laman web interaktif untuk meningkatkan promosi pelancongan Pulau Tuba* [Unpublished undergraduate final year project]. Universiti Malaysia Perlis.

Nwabueze, C. J. (2017). Copyright and data authenticity in the digital preservation of heritage: The case of OAPI states. *International Journal of Intangible Heritage*, *12*, 94–110.

Nyhan, B., & Reifler, J. (2015). The effect of fact-checking on elites: A field experiment on U.S. state legislators. *American Journal of Political Science*, *59*(3), 628–640. DOI: 10.1111/ajps.12162

Obschonka, M., Stuetzer, M., Gosling, S. D., Rentfrow, P. J., Lamb, M. E., & Potter, J. (2015). Regional TV, personality traits, and entrepreneurship. *Regional Studies*, *49*(1), 33–48. DOI: 10.1080/00343404.2014.965135

OECD. (2021). *The state of school education: One year into the COVID pandemic*. OECD Publishing.

OECD. (2025). *Tackling Civic Participation Challenges with Emerging Technologies.* Retrieved from https://www.oecd.org/en/publications/tackling-civic-participation-challenges-with-emerging-technologies_ec2ca9a2-en.html

Oluoch, J., & Osida, J. (2015). Measuring Impacts of Information and Communication Advances for Development in the 21st Century. https://core.ac.uk/download/234672122.pdf

Onebunne, A. P. (2022). Algorithmic bias and media manipulation: A systematic review of AI's role in shaping public perception and political discourse. *World Journal of Advanced Research and Reviews, 16*(3), 1239–1249. DOI: 10.30574/wjarr.2022.16.3.1332

Onyeaka, H., Ejiohuo, O., Taiwo, O. R., Nnaji, N. D., Odeyemi, O. A., Duan, K., Nwaiwu, O., & Odeyemi, O. (2024). The intersection of food security and mental health in the pursuit of sustainable development goals. *Nutrients, 16*(13), 2036.

Orben, A., & Przybylski, A. K. (2019). Screens, teens, and psychological well-being: Evidence from three time-use-diary studies. *Psychological Science, 30*(5), 682–696. DOI: 10.1177/0956797619830329

Othman, M., Daud, S., Taib, N., Hasbullah, N., & Yazid, Z. (2025). Enhancing engagement through gamification in Malaysian blended learning. *International Review of Management and Marketing, 16*, 341–349. DOI: 10.32479/irmm.20824

Overney, C. (2025). *Designing for Constructive Civic Communication: A Framework for Human-AI Collaboration.* Retrieved from https://arxiv.org/pdf/2505.11684

Oxford Internet Institute. (2020). *Digital ethics in the Global South: Challenges and opportunities.* University of Oxford.

Ozdemir, I. (2019). *Islam and ecology: Towards retrieval and reconstruction.* Routledge.

Ozdemir, I. (2019). Technology and Islamic environmental ethics: A contemporary perspective. *Environmental Ethics and Islam, 31*(4), 287–301.

Paas, F., Renkl, A., & Sweller, J. (2010). Cognitive load theory and instructional design: Recent developments. *Educational Psychologist, 38*(1), 1–4. DOI: 10.1207/S15326985EP3801_1

Pache, A.-C., Fayard, A.-L., & Galo, M. (2022). How can cross-sector collaborations foster social innovation? A review. In Vaccaro, A., & Ramus, T. (Eds.), *Social Innovation and Social Enterprises: Toward a Holistic Perspective* (pp. 35–62). Springer., https://link.springer.com/chapter/10.1007/978-3-030-96596-9_3

Padela, A. I. (2018). Islamic bioethics and digital health technologies: Mapping the terrain. *The American Journal of Bioethics*, *18*(9), 37–39.

Pagano, M. (2024). Digital media use and unhealthy sleep: Meta-analysis in adolescence. *Computers in Human Behavior*, *149*, 110776.

Palmer, C. (2025, March 25). The benefits from culturally responsive community-based research partnerships. *American Psychological Association*. https://www.apa.org/research-practice/conduct-research/culturally-responsive-partnerships

Parajuli, J. (2021). Digital disruption and Nepal's news media: Opportunities and challenges. *Media Studies Journal of Nepal*, *4*(1), 12–34.

Parashar, Y., & Waraich, S. B. (2023). Relationship Between Social Media Usage and Social Anxiety Among College Students. *International Journal of Indian Psychology*, *11*(4), 2259–2291. DOI: 10.25215/1104.210

Pariser, E. (2011). *The filter bubble: What the Internet is hiding from you*. Penguin Press.

Partin, C., & King, K. P. (2013). Technology and its impact on higher education. In Ran, B. (Ed.), *Global perspectives on technological innovation* (pp. 403–433). IAP Information Age Publishing., https://psycnet.apa.org/record/2013-20064-013

Partin, K., & King, S. (2013). Digital Tools and Civic Agency in Education. *Journal of Educational Technology & Society*.

Patel, D. (2021, May 18). What is Web 4.0 and how will it change marketing? Forbes. https://www.forbes.com

Patel, M. M., Dhume, N., Sumbhe, S. S., Kamat, P. S., Nadar, M. S., & Patel, M. (2025). *TRIBES ACROSS INDIA*.

Patel, V. L., Kaufman, D. R., & Cohen, T. (2013). *Cognitive informatics in health and biomedicine: case studies on critical care, complexity and errors*. Springer Science & Business Media.

Patton, M. Q. (2015). *Qualitative research & evaluation methods: Integrating theory and practice* (4th ed.). SAGE.

Paudel, N. (2023). Centralization of Nepal's media in the federal era: Challenges for inclusive communication. *Nepal Journal of Journalism and Mass Communication*, *9*(1), 33–52.

Pavlik, V. J., E Dennis, E., Davis Mersey, R., & Gengler, J. (2019). Conducting Research on the World's Changing Mediascape: Principles and Practices. https://core.ac.uk/download/201133363.pdf

Pavlik, V. J., E. Dennis, E., Davis Mersey, R., & Gengler, J. (2019). Conducting Research on the World's Changing Mediascape: Principles and Practices. https://core.ac.uk/download/229940771.pdf

Pawluczuk, A., Webster, G., Smith, C., & Hall, H. (2019). The Social Impact of Digital Youth Work: What Are We Looking For? https://core.ac.uk/download/229940317.pdf

Pennycook, G., McPhetres, J., Zhang, Y., Lu, J. G., & Rand, D. G. (2021). Shifting attention to accuracy reduces sharing of misinformation online. *Nature*, *592*(7855), 590–595. DOI: 10.1038/s41586-021-03344-2 PMID: 33731933

Pennycook, G., & Rand, D. G. (2019). Lazy, not biased: Susceptibility to partisan fake news is better explained by lack of reasoning than by motivated reasoning. *Cognition*, *188*, 39–50. DOI: 10.1016/j.cognition.2018.06.011 PMID: 29935897

Penplusbytes. (2025). *Media and Information Literacy and Civic Education – A Collective Effort for the Public Good.* Retrieved from https://penplusbytes.org/media-and-information-literacy-and-civic-education-a-collective-effort-for-the-public-good/

Pérez-Torres, V. (2024). Social media: A digital social mirror for identity development during adolescence. *Current Psychology (New Brunswick, N.J.)*, *43*(26), 22170–22180. DOI: 10.1007/s12144-024-05980-z

Perlis State Zakat Office. (2023). Annual zakat report. Kangar: Zakat Perlis

Perlis State Zakat Office. (2023). Asnaf demographic and dependency analysis report [Internal Report].

Permana, D. (2024). Key Affecting Towards Financial Performance and Sustainability On Social Enterprises In Indonesia. *Journal of Economics and Finance*, *2*(2), 14–34. DOI: 10.61978/moneta.v2i2.216

Petersen, N. H., & Rasmussen, E. (2023). Digital entrepreneur's platformication and rapid internationalization through brokering, making and giving sense. *Small Enterprise Research*, *31*(1), 18–38. DOI: 10.1080/13215906.2023.2288579

Pew Research Center. (2017). *The future of world religions: Population growth projections, 2015–2060.* https://www.pewresearch.org/religion/2017/04/05/the-future-of-world-religions

Pinto, H. (2009). The Diversity of Innovation in the European Union: Mapping Latent Dimensions and Regional Profiles. https://core.ac.uk/download/pdf/144016560.pdf

Pokharel, B. (2024). Youth representation in Nepali media: From peacebuilding to participation. *Journal of Development Communication Nepal*, *4*(1), 50–68.

Poudel, P. (2022). Youth participation in Nepal's federal governance: Policy promises and practice gaps. *Nepal Public Policy Review*, *1*(2), 101–120.

Poudel, R. (2022). Youth migration and governance participation in Nepal. *Nepal Policy Review*, *2*(1), 25–40.

Prabhu, J., & Jain, S. (2015). Innovation and entrepreneurship in India: Understanding institutional context. *Business Horizons*, *58*(6), 701–709. DOI: 10.1016/j.bushor.2015.07.002

Prażmowska-Marcinowska, K. (2020). Misappropriation of Indigenous cultural heritage–intellectual property rights in the digital era. *Santander Art and Culture Law Review*, *6*(2), 119–150.

Proceedings of the International AAAI Conference on Web and Social Media. (n.d.). Studies on media centralization and digital governance in South Asia. *AAAI*. https://ojs.aaai.org/index.php/ICWSM/

Purnomo, T. (2025). Skin Care and Women's Identity: The Role of Digital Media in the Formation of Self-Confidence. *Journal of Economics, Business, Management. Accounting and Social Sciences*, *3*(3), 214–222.

Putnam, R. D. (2000). *Bowling alone: The collapse and revival of American community*. Simon & Schuster.

Qardawi, Y. (1999). *Fiqh al-Zakah* (Vol. 1–2). Scientific Publishing Centre, King Abdulaziz University.

Qi He Leow, M., Chiang, J., & Wang, S. (2023). Smartphone addiction and sleep among medical students. *PLoS One*, *18*(4), e0295439.

Quan-Haase, A., Williams, C., Kicevski, M., Elueze, I., & Wellman, B. (2018). Dividing the Grey Divide: Deconstructing myths about older adults' online activities, skills, and attitudes. *The American Behavioral Scientist*, *62*(9), 1207–1228.

Radtke, T. (2022). Digital detox: Systematic literature review. *Mobile Media & Communication*.

Rae, D. (2020). Media narratives and entrepreneurial learning: The risks of romanticism. *International Journal of Entrepreneurial Behaviour & Research*, *26*(5), 951–970. DOI: 10.1108/IJEBR-10-2019-0622

Raman, R., Alka, T. A., Suresh, M., & Nedungadi, P. (2025). Social entrepreneurship and sustainable technologies: Impact on communities, social innovation, and inclusive development. *Sustainable Technology and Entrepreneurship*, *4*(3), 100110. DOI: 10.1016/j.stae.2025.100110

Ranger, T. O. (1999). *Voices from the Rocks, nature, culture and history in the Matopos Hills of Zimbabwe*. James Currey.

Ranjan, A., & Sharma, M. T. (2025). Indian Knowledge System and Caste. *INDIAN*, 221.

Rao, J. K., Suneetha, J., Reddi, T. V. V. S., & Kumar, O. A. (2011). Ethnomedicine of the Gadabas, a primitive tribe of Visakhapatnam district, Andhra Pradesh. *International Multidisciplinary Research Journal*, *1*(2).

Recker, J., & von Briel, F. (2019). The future of digital entrepreneurship research: existing and emerging opportunities: professional development workshop. https://core.ac.uk/download/267815713.pdf

Reim, W., Andersson, E., & Eckerwall, K. (2022). Enabling collaboration on digital platforms: A study of digital twins. *International Journal of Production Research*, *61*(12), 3926–3942. DOI: 10.1080/00207543.2022.2116499

Reiter, R. J., Tan, D. X., & Galano, A. (2014). Melatonin: Exceeding expectations. *Physiology (Bethesda, MD)*, *29*(5), 325–333. DOI: 10.1152/physiol.00011.2014

Rizwan, S. A., Kumar, R., Singh, A. K., Kusuma, Y. S., Yadav, K., & Pandav, C. S. (2014). Prevalence of hypertension in Indian tribes: A systematic review and meta-analysis of observational studies. *PLoS One*, *9*(5), e95896.

Rogers, E. M. (2003). *Diffusion of innovations* (5th ed.). Free Press.

Rossini, P., Stromer-Galley, J., Baptista, E. A., & Veiga de Oliveira, V. (2021). Dysfunctional information sharing on WhatsApp and Facebook: The role of political talk, cross-cutting exposure, and social corrections. *New Media & Society*, *23*(8), 2430–2451. DOI: 10.1177/1461444820932490

Ross, K. (2010). Gendered media: Women, men and identity politics. *Sociology Compass*, *4*(7), 485–494.

Routledge, P and Hogg, J. L. (2020). In-depth interview, International encyclopaedia for media psychology

Rowley, J., Bennett, D., Blom, D., & Dunbar-Hall, P. (2014). *Exploring the pedagogy and impact of technology on eportfolio creation for arts students in Australian tertiary study*.

Russ, D. J., & Griffiths, M. D. (2015). Social networking sites and addiction: Ten lessons learned. *International Journal of Environmental Research and Public Health, 12*(3), 1286–1306. DOI: 10.3390/ijerph120301286

Rwafa, U. (2012). Representations of Matabeleland and Midlands disturbances through the documentary film Gukurahundi: A moment of madness 2007. *African Identities, 10*, 313–327.

Rwodzi, A. (2019). Economic nationalism amid ethnic disharmony in postcolonial Zimbabwe (1980-2013): A case of Matabeleland Provinces. *New Contree, 81*, 138–159.

Sadeq, A. H. M. (2002). Waqf, perpetual charity and poverty alleviation. *International Journal of Social Economics, 29*(1/2), 135–151. DOI: 10.1108/03068290210413038

Safi, L. (2009). *Islamic perspectives on communication*. International Institute of Islamic Thought.

Safi, L. (2009). *The foundations of knowledge: A comparative study in Islamic and Western methods of inquiry*. International Institute of Islamic Thought.

Sahare, R. R. (2024). The impact of social media on youth identity formation. *International Journal of Advanced Research in Science and Technology*. https://www.ijarst.in/public/uploads/paper/200651727268929.pdf

Saldanha, I. J., Smith, B. T., Ntzani, E., Jap, J., Balk, E. M., & Lau, J. (2019). The Systematic Review Data Repository (SRDR): Descriptive characteristics of publicly available data and opportunities for research. *Systematic Reviews, 8*(334), 1–12. DOI: 10.1186/s13643-019-1250-y

Salesforce. (2024a). *Trusted AI: The Einstein Trust Layer*. Salesforce Inc. Retrieved from https://www.salesforce.com/artificial-intelligence/trusted-ai/

Salesforce. (2024b). *Einstein Trust Layer Help Documentation*. Salesforce Inc. Retrieved from https://help.salesforce.com/s/articleView?id=ai.generative_ai_trust_layer.htm

Sampasa-Kanyinga, H., Lien, A., & Hamilton, H. (2022). Cyberbullying involvement linked to short sleep in adolescents. *Sleep Health, 8*(2), 183–190.

Santos, P. (2011). *Representing conflict: An analysis of the Chronicle's coverage of the Gukuraundi conflict in Zimbabwe between 1983 and 1986.* Available at: https://www.an-analysis-of–the-gukurahundi-conflict-in-zimbabwe-philipsantos.pdf [Accessed 1 August 2023].

Saravanos, A., & Curinga, M. X. (2023). Simulating the software development lifecycle: The waterfall model. Applied System Innovation, 6(6), 108. DOI: 10.3390/asi6060108

Sardar, Z. (1985). *Islamic futures: The shape of ideas to come*. Mansell.

Sardar, Z. (1985). *Islamic science: The way ahead*. Kube Publishing.

Sardar, Z. (2011). *Reading the Qur'an: The contemporary relevance of the sacred text of Islam*. Oxford University Press.

Sardar, Z. (2011). *Science, technology and development in the Muslim world*. Atlantic Publishers.

Saufi, R. A., Hussin, N., & Basir, S. A. (2021). Dependency syndrome in zakat distribution: A critical analysis of welfare approaches in Malaysia. *International Journal of Islamic Economics and Finance Research*, *4*(2), 89–104.

Sauro, J., & Lewis, J. R. (2021). *Quantifying the user experience: Practical statistics for user research* (2nd ed.). Morgan Kaufmann.

Schumpeter, J. A. (1934). *The theory of economic development*. Harvard University Press.

Schwab, K. (2016). *The Fourth Industrial Revolution*. World Economic Forum.

Schwartz, T. (1980). *Socialization as cultural communication: Development of a theme in the work of Margaret Mead* (Vol. 237). Univ of California Press.

Scott, H., Biello, S. M., & Woods, H. C. (2019). Social media use and adolescent sleep patterns: Cross-sectional findings from the UK millennium cohort study. *BMJ Open*, *9*(9), e031161. Advance online publication. DOI: 10.1136/bmjopen-2019-031161

Sen, A. (1999). *Development as freedom*. Alfred A. Knopf.

Setiawan, M. A., Armina, S. H., & Novika, S. (2022). The Typology of Islamic Social Entrepreneurship: Principles, and Characteristic from a Maqashid Shariah Perspective. *Ijtihad*, *18*(2). Advance online publication. DOI: 10.21111/ijtihad.v18i2.12362

Shabahang, R. (2024). Social media-related nightmares in Iranian adults. *BMC Psychology*, *12*, 112.

Shabbir, M. S., & Batool, F. (2025). Social Entrepreneurship for Community Development: The Role of Social Capital in Establishing Sustainable Enterprises. *Journal of Social Entrepreneurship*, •••, 1–26. DOI: 10.1080/19420676.2025.2492060

Shahrol, S. J. M., Sulaiman, S., & Mohamed, H. (2024). Acceptance factors towards mobile technologies in learning English among rural students. *International Journal of Instructional Communication, 13*(2). Advance online publication. DOI: 10.11113/ijic.v13n2.387

Shane, S., & Venkataraman, S. (2000). The promise of entrepreneurship as a field of research. *Academy of Management Review, 25*(1), 217–226. DOI: 10.5465/amr.2000.2791611

Sharecast. (2022). *Media consumption trends in Nepal: Post-pandemic survey report.* Sharecast Initiative Nepal.

Sharma, G. (2019). Innovation and entrepreneurship research in India from 2000 to 2018: A bibliometric survey. *Journal of Management Development, 37*(4), 500–515. DOI: 10.1108/JMD-10-2018-0291

Sharma, P. (2019). Urbanization and development in Nepal: Emerging patterns, issues, and policies. *The Geographical Journal of Nepal, 12*, 1–20.

Shochat, T., Cohen-Zion, M., & Tzischinsky, O. (2010). Functional consequences of inadequate sleep in adolescents: A systematic review. *Sleep Medicine Reviews, 14*(5), 303–312. DOI: 10.1016/j.smrv.2009.11.001

Shrestha, P. (2024). Youth, democracy, and identity in Nepali media narratives. *Media and Society Review, 10*(2), 22–40.

Shrestha, S., & Shakya, R. (2020). Digital activism and youth participation in Nepal. *Nepal Journal of Social Research, 3*(2), 75–91.

Sibanda, N. (2022). Cultural politics and cultural violence during Gukurahundi in Matabeleland: Politiques culturelles et violence culturelle pendant le Gukurahundi au Matabeleland. *Critical African Studies, 14*(2), 138–152.

Sibanda, N., & Dube, P. (2025). Conceptualising and revealing political resistance in Zimbabwe through (re) naming roads in Bulawayo. *South African Journal of African Languages*, •••, 1–10.

Sienkiewicz, M., & Jaramillo, D. L. (2019). Podcasting, the intimate self, and the public sphere. *Popular Communication, 17*(4), 268–272. DOI: 10.1080/15405702.2019.1667997

Singh, C. L. (2010). New media and cultural identity. *China Media Research, 6*(1).

Siompu, I., & Nurul Asfiah. (2022). Islamic Social Entrepreneurship and Work Ethics in Global Business. *Formosa Journal of Applied Sciences, 3*(7). Advance online publication. DOI: 10.55927/fjas.v3i7.9488

Sirajuddin, M. D. M., & Mahaiyadin, M. H. (2022). Tayyib from the perspective of qur'anic thematic analysis: Proposing new insights for best practice in the global halal industry. *Global Journal Al-Thaqafah,(SI 1)*, 108-118.

Skovlund, H., Morck, L. L., & Celosse-Anderson, M. (2023). The art of not being neutral in qualitative research. *Qualitative Research in Psychology, 20*(19), 363–381.

Slater, M., & Sanchez-Vives, M. V. (2016). Enhancing our lives with immersive virtual reality. Frontiers in Robotics and AI, 3, 74. https://doi.org/ DOI: 10.3389/frobt.2016.00074

Slavtchev, V., & Wyrwich, M. (2021). TV and entrepreneurship. *Jena Economic Research Papers, 2021*(010). https://doi.org/DOI: 10.2139/ssrn.3807456

Slavtchev, V., & Wyrwich, M. (2023). Can television shows increase entrepreneurial activity? Evidence from a natural experiment. *Journal of Business Venturing, 38*(2), 106271. DOI: 10.1016/j.jbusvent.2022.106271

Smith, M. (2017). *Podcasting While Black: An Exploratory Study of Black Podcast Use and Podcast Production.* The University of Texas at Austin, ProQuest Dissertations Publishing.

Smith, J. M., & Van Ierland, T. (2018). Framing controversy on social media:# NoDAPL and the debate about the Dakota access pipeline on Twitter. *IEEE Transactions on Professional Communication, 61*(3), 226–241.

Smith, T. (2024). *Foxocracy: Inside the network's playbook of tribal warfare.* Diversion Books.

Smith, T. R. (2004). Generating Selves: Issues of Self-Representation. *Auto/Biography, 19*(1–2), 59–70.

Smoke, P. (2015). Rethinking decentralization: Assessing challenges to a popular public sector reform. *Public Administration and Development, 35*(2), 97–112.

SocialTargeter. (2025). *The Impact of Gamification: Case Studies from Education Technology Startups.* Retrieved from https://www.socialtargeter.com/blogs/the-impact-of-gamification-case-studies-from-education-technology-startups

Sohlberg, E., Israel, A.-Y., & Duell, N. (2023). Sleep, social media, and mental health in adolescence. *Journal of Student Research, 12*(4), 5452.

Song, G. (2024). A Public Service Media Perspective on the Algorithmic Amplification of Cultural Content. *Knight First Amendment Institute*. https://knightcolumbia.org/content/a-public-service-media-perspective-on-the-algorithmic-amplification-of-cultural-content

Song, Q. (2024). Framing in media and communication studies: A bibliometric analysis. *Insight - News Media, 7*(1), 674. https://doi.org/DOI: 10.18282/inm674

Sonnett, J. (2019). Priming and framing: Dimensions of communication and cognition. In *The Oxford Handbook of Cognitive Sociology* (pp. 226–240). https://doi.org/DOI: 10.1093/oxfordhb/9780190273385.013.13

Sonowal, J., & Choudhury, D. (2024). ROLE OF SOCIAL MEDIA IN PROMOTING FOLK DANCE: A REVIEW STUDY WITH REFERENCE TO BIHU DANCE OF ASSAM. *International. Journal of Multidisciplinary Research, 10*(2).

Soto, C., Bauwens, P. J., & Smets, K. (2023). Cultural Identity Performances on Social Media: A Study of Bolivian Students. *Journalism and Media, 4*, 304–321.

Speckyboy. (2023). The biggest pains in website maintenance. https://speckyboy.com

Sriram, V., & Mersha, T. (2010). Facilitating entrepreneurship in sub-Saharan Africa: What governments can do. *Journal of International Business and Cultural Studies, 3*, 1–9.

Stam, E. (2015). Entrepreneurial ecosystems and regional policy: A sympathetic critique. *European Planning Studies, 23*(9), 1759–1769. DOI: 10.1080/09654313.2015.1061484

Steefan, J., Siddesha, G., & Keerthi, P. (2023). Social media impact on sleep among homoeopathic students. *International Journal of Science and Healthcare Research, 8*(1), 10–16.

Strasheim, J., & Bogati, S. (2016). Nepal's struggle for peace: Post-conflict peacebuilding, 2006–2015. *GIGA Working Papers, 287*, 1–28. Hamburg: German Institute of Global and Area Studies (GIGA).

Stroud, N. J. (2010). Polarization and partisan selective exposure. *Journal of Communication, 60*(3), 556–576. DOI: 10.1111/j.1460-2466.2010.01497.x

Stuermer, M., Abu-Tayeh, G., & Myrach, T. (2017). Digital sustainability: basic conditions for sustainable digital artifacts and their ecosystems. https://www.ncbi.nlm.nih.gov/pmc/articles/PMC6106115/

Stürmer, M., Nussbaumer, J., & Stöckli, P. (2021). Security implications of digitalization: The dangers of data colonialism and the way towards sustainable and sovereign management of environmental data. *ArXiv Preprint ArXiv:2107.01662.*

Suffiah, I., & Lee, J. A. C. (2022). Knowledge of dyslexia among teacher trainees in Malaysia. *Journal of Cognitive Sciences and Human Development*, *8*(2), 54–76. DOI: 10.33736/jcshd.4685.2022

Su, H., Wang, T., & Zhang, X. (2024). Influencing factors for college student sleep quality & social media use. *Lecture Notes in Education Psychology and Public Media*, *36*(1), 233–241.

Suhaimi, M. F. B., Don, A. G., & Puteh, A. (2022). Program Latihan Dalam Membangunkan Asnaf di Selangor. *AZKA International Journal of Zakat & Social Finance*, *2*(2). Advance online publication. DOI: 10.51377/azjaf.vol2no2.66

Sunstein, C. R. (2001). *Republic.com.* Princeton University Press.

Sunstein, C. R. (2017). *Republic: Divided democracy in the age of social media.* Princeton University Press.

Suresh, K. G. (2022). Dynamics of regional television in India: A systematic perspective. *Journal of Content. Community & Communication*, *15*(8), 65–78. DOI: 10.2139/ssrn.3985732

Sustainable Web Manifesto. (2019). Our commitment to a sustainable internet. https://www.sustainablewebmanifesto.com

Suzianti, A., Al Hafi, K., & Shafira, N. D. (2019). Designing Indonesia social innovation knowledge management system: Case study of kreanovator Indonesia. **Proceedings of the ACM International Conference.* https://doi.org/DOI: 10.1145/3366030.3366101

Sweller, J. (1988). Cognitive load during problem solving: Effects on learning. *Cognitive Science*, *12*(2), 257–285. DOI: 10.1207/s15516709cog1202_4

Tandon, P., Kaur, & Dhir. (2020). Sleepless due to social media? Problematic social media and sleep hygiene. *Computers in Human Behavior*, *113*, 106487.

Tang, G., Ren, S., Chadee, D., & Yuan, S. (2020). The Dark Side of Social Media Connectivity: Influence on Turnover Intentions of Supply Chain Professionals. *International Journal of Operations & Production Management*, *40*(11), 1809–1835. DOI: 10.1108/IJOPM-05-2019-0391

Tan, P., Dennis, P. S., Ahmadi Julaihi, A. B., & Ling, M. (2022). Mobile learning model for children with special learning needs. *European Journal of Teacher Education, 4*(3), 1–12. DOI: 10.33422/ejte.v4i3.815

Tapscott, D., & Tapscott, A. (2016). *Blockchain revolution: How the technology behind Bitcoin is changing money, business, and the world*. Penguin.

Tchop™. (2025). *Youth-centric digital platforms*. Retrieved from https://tchop.io/resources/glossary/community-building/youth-centric-digital-platforms

Thapa, D. (2023). Youth and civic space in Nepali journalism: Between tokenism and transformation. *Journal of Civic Media Nepal, 1*(1), 11–29.

Thathiah, N. (2024). *Analyzing Indigenous Representation and Engagement on TikTok*.

The Code Beast. (2023). Challenges of developing a website. https://thecodebeast.com

The New York Times. (2024a). *Guidelines on Integrity*. Retrieved from https://www.nytimes.com/editorial-standards/guidelines-on-integrity.html

The New York Times. (2024b). *Ethical Journalism Handbook*. Retrieved from https://www.nytimes.com/editorial-standards/ethical-journalism.html

The Shift Project. (2019). Lean ICT: Towards digital sobriety. https://theshiftproject.org/en/lean-ict-2/

Theodosiadou, S. (2025). Filtering women's identity through podcast storytelling: The case of Desert Island Discs. *RadioDoc Review, 10*(1). Advance online publication. DOI: 10.14453/rdr.1560

Thounaojam, M., Radha, M., & Vanitha, N. (2024). Bedtime social media use and sleep quality among Bengaluru adolescents. *International Journal of Research in Medical Sciences, 12*(11), 4071–4076.

Tiwari, M., & Tiwari, M. (2017). Exploring the role of Capabilities in Social Innovation. https://core.ac.uk/download/219375382.pdf

Tobin, S. J., & Guadagno, R. E. (2022). Why people listen: Motivations and outcomes of podcast listening. *PLoS One, 17*(4). Advance online publication. DOI: 10.1371/journal.pone.0265806

Torres-Pruñonosa, J., Maria Raya, J., & Dopeso-Fernández, R. (2020). The Economic and Social Value of Science and Technology Parks. The Case of Tecnocampus. https://www.ncbi.nlm.nih.gov/pmc/articles/PMC7786403/

Trane, M., Marelli, L., Siragusa, A., Pollo, R., & Lombardi, P. (2023). Progress by Research to Achieve the Sustainable Development Goals in the EU: A Systematic Literature Review. *Sustainability, 15*(9), 7055. DOI: 10.3390/su15097055

Trinanda, O., ... (2025). From traits to resilience: How Muslim entrepreneurs survive in crisis. Behaviors, 15(3), 70. https://www.mdpi.com/2076-3387/15/3/70

Tsai, H. S., Shillair, R., Cotten, S. R., Winstead, V., & Yost, E. (2015). Getting Grandma online: Are tablets the answer for increasing digital inclusion for older adults in the U.S.? *Educational Gerontology*, *41*(10), 695–709.

Tsapro, G., Yakuba, V., & Gladush, N. (2025). Teaching Gender Studies through an Interdisciplinary Lens: Sociology and Communication Theory. *Академічні Студії. Серія «Педагогіка». Луцьк: Комунальний Заклад Вищої Освіти «Луцький Педагогічний Коледж». Волинської Обласної Ради*, *1*, 71–77.

Tshabangu, T., & Salawu, A. (2024). Alternative media, repression and the crisis state: Towards a political economy of alternative media in post-Mugabe Zimbabwe. *Journal of Asian and African Studies*, *59*(1), 172–186.

Tshuma, B.B. (2023). A book review of Khanyile Mlotshwa and Mphathisi Ndlovu's The idea of Matabeleland in digital spaces: Genealogies, discourses and epistemic struggles, *International journal of critical diversity studies* 5(1):38-42

Tshuma, L. A., and Phiri, L. (2022). Photographing the "Nation" in the Digital Age: A Case of Matabeleland Discourses on Social Media Platforms. *The Idea of Matabeleland in Digital Spaces: Genealogies, Discourses, and Epistemic Struggles*, 241.

Tshuma, A. L., & Ndlovu, M. (2020). Immortalising buried memories: Photographs of the Gukurahundi online. *Journal of Genocide Research*, •••, 1–22.

Tshuma, L. A., & Phiri, L. (2022). Photographing the "Nation" in the digital age: A case of Matabeleland discourses on social media platforms. In Ndlovu, M., & Mlotshwa, K. (Eds.), *The idea of Matabeleland in digital spaces: Genealogies, discourses, and epistemic struggles* (p. 241). Rowman and Littlefield.

Tsoukalas, A. I. & D. Siozos, P. (2011). Privacy and Anonymity in the Information Society – Challenges for the European Union. https://www.ncbi.nlm.nih.gov/pmc/articles/PMC5720049/

Tuan Mahmood, T. M. A., Mohd Din, N., Al Mamun, A., & Dahlan Ibrahim, M. (2020). Cadangan kerangka kerja konseptual program memperkasakan ekonomi asnaf: Pembangunan 'Model Kemenjadian Milenia Asnaf (MKMA)'. *AZKA International Journal of Zakat & Social Finance*, *1*(1), 74–93. DOI: 10.51377/azjaf.vol1no01.11

Tucker, J. A., Guess, A., Barberá, P., Vaccari, C., Siegel, A., Sanovich, S., & Nyhan, B. (2018). Social media, political polarization, and political disinformation: A review of the scientific literature. *Political Science Quarterly, 133*(4), 707–751. DOI: 10.1002/polq.12820

Tufekci, Z. (2017). *Twitter and tear gas: The power and fragility of networked protest.* Yale University Press.

Turyakira, P., Sendawula, K., Nanyanzi, M., Nantale, H., & Tamale, J. (2025). Social entrepreneurship: Empirical evidence on its contribution to the realization of the sustainable development goals in Uganda. *Journal of Work-Applied Management, 17*(1), 160–172. DOI: 10.1108/JWAM-02-2023-0011

Twenge, J. M., & Campbell, W. K. (2023). The Impact of Social Media on Adolescent Mental Health: A Meta-Analysis. *Journal of Adolescent Psychology and Behavior Studies, 29,* 145–159. DOI: 10.12345/japs.2023.0415

Twenge, J. M., Krizan, Z., & Hisler, G. (2017). Decreases in self-reported sleep duration among U.S. adolescents 2009–2015 and association with new media screen time. *Sleep Medicine, 39,* 47–53. DOI: 10.1016/j.sleep.2017.08.013

Ucar, I., Gramaglia, M., Fiore, M., Smoreda, Z., & Moro, E. (2021). News or social media? Socio-economic divide of mobile service consumption. https://www.ncbi.nlm.nih.gov/pmc/articles/PMC8633779/

UN Human Rights Council. (2016). *Resolution on the promotion, protection and enjoyment of human rights on the Internet.* United Nations.

UNEP. (2018). *Definition of microplastics and environmental implications.* United Nations Environment Programme.

UNESCO. (2018). *Leveraging ICTs to achieve SDG 4.* UNESCO Publishing.

UNESCO. (2019). *Media and information literacy: Policy and strategy guidelines.* UNESCO Publishing.

UNESCO. (2021). *Artificial intelligence and education: Guidance for policy-makers.* UNESCO Publishing.

UNESCO. (2024). *Global citizenship education in a digital age.* United Nations Educational, Scientific and Cultural Organization. https://unesco-asp.dk/wp-content/uploads/2025/02/Global-Citizenship-education-in-a-digital-age_UNESCO_2024.pdf

UNESCO. (2025). *Promoting Youth Participation in Decision-Making and Public Service Delivery through Harnessing Digital Technologies*. Retrieved from https://www.unesco.org/sdg4education2030/en/knowledge-hub/promoting-youth-participation-decision-making-and-public-service-delivery-through-harnessing-digital

UNESCO. (n.d.). *Digital citizenship education*. https://www.unesco.org/en/digital-citizenship

UNICEF. (2020). *Digital civic engagement by young people*. Retrieved from https://www.unicef.org/reports/digital-civic-engagement-young-people-2020

United Nations General Assembly. (1987) *Report of the world commission on environment and development: Our common future*. United Nations General Assembly, Development and International Co-operation: Environment, Oslo, Norway.

Uriarte, S., Baier-Fuentes, H., Espinoza-Benavides, J., & Inzunza-Mendoza, W. (2025). (in press). Artificial intelligence technologies and entrepreneurship: A hybrid literature review. *Review of Managerial Science*. Advance online publication. DOI: 10.1007/s11846-025-00839-4

Utami, D. (2024). Electronic devices during COVID-19 and sleep among medical students in Indonesia. *International Journal of Scientific Advances*, *5*(2), 24–34.

Vaccari, C., & Valeriani, A. (2015). Follow the leader! Direct and indirect flows of political communication during the 2013 Italian general election campaign. *New Media & Society*, *17*(7), 1025–1042. DOI: 10.1177/1461444813511038

Valenzuela, S. (2013). Unpacking the use of social media for protest behavior: The roles of information, opinion expression, and activism. *The American Behavioral Scientist*, *57*(7), 920–942. DOI: 10.1177/0002764213479375

van den Hoven, J., Helbing, D., Pedreschi, D., Domingo-Ferrer, J., Gianotti, F., & Christen, M. (2012). FuturICT - The Road towards Ethical ICT. https://arxiv.org/pdf/1210.8181

van Dinter, R., Tekinerdogan, B., & Catal, C. (2021). Automation of systematic literature reviews: A systematic literature review. *Information and Software Technology*, *136*, 106589. DOI: 10.1016/j.infsof.2021.106589

Vañó, M. J. (2025). Social entrepreneurship: Challenges, risks, and opportunities. *The International Entrepreneurship and Management Journal*, *21*(64), 1–18. DOI: 10.1007/s11365-025-01088-3

Venugopal, K. & Kappagantula, M. (2024). Deciphering Religious Tourism: A Classification and Predictive Approach to Odisha's Unique Landscape. In K. Wongmahesak & P. Suanpang (Eds.), *Technological and Managerial Approaches to Fostering Sustainable Travel* (pp. 169-196). IGI Global Scientific Publishing. https://doi.org/10.4018/979-8-3693-8115-1.ch008

Venugopal, K., & Deekonda, P. (2022). Involvement of Employees in Quality Management System: In case of Public Transportation, Srikakulam District, AP in an edited book entitled Business Perspectives in Reviving Workforce Productivity in the current Volatile and Uncertain Times.

Verma, M., & Sharma, H. (2016). *India In the Coverage of Pakistan Media: A Content Analysis Study with Special Reference To Post Pathankot Attack.*

Verma, P., Sahoo, K. C., Mahapatra, P., Kaur, H., & Pati, S. (2022). A systematic review of community-based studies on mental health issues among tribal populations in India. *The Indian Journal of Medical Research, 156*(2), 291–298.

Victory, X. R. (2025). *VictoryXR Company Profile*. Retrieved from https://www.inven.ai/company-lists/top-26-virtual-reality-education-companies

Vosoughi, S., Roy, D., & Aral, S. (2018). The spread of true and false news online. *Science, 359*(6380), 1146–1151. DOI: 10.1126/science.aap9559 PMID: 29590045

Vo-Thanh, T., Zaman, M., Hasan, R., Rather, R., Lombardi, R., & Secundo, G. (2021). How a mobile app can become a catalyst for sustainable social business: The case of Too Good To Go. *Technological Forecasting and Social Change, 171*, 120962. DOI: 10.1016/j.techfore.2021.120962

Vrikki, P., & Malik, S. (2019). Voicing lived-experience and anti-racism: podcasting as a space at the margins for subaltern counterpublics. *Popular Communication, 17*(4), 273–287. https://doi.org/10.1080/15405702.2019.1622116

Wakefield, N. (2011). Media literacy education. In Dunkels, E., Frånberg, G.-M., & Hällgren, C. (Eds.), *Interactive media use and youth: Learning, knowledge exchange and behavior* (pp. 80–101). IGI Global., DOI: 10.4018/978-1-60960-206-2.ch006

Wang, A., & Yee, C. (2023). A Literature Review of Social Entrepreneurship. *Open Journal of Business and Management, 11*, 2232–2246. DOI: 10.4236/ojbm.2023.115123

Wang, D., & Huang, X. (2025). Transforming education through artificial intelligence and immersive technologies: Enhancing learning experiences. *Interactive Learning Environments*. Advance online publication. DOI: 10.1080/10494820.2025.2465451

Wang, X., Huang, Y., & Huang, K. (2024). How does social entrepreneurship achieve sustainable development goals in rural tourism destinations? The role of legitimacy and social capital. *Journal of Sustainable Tourism*, *33*(7), 1262–1280. DOI: 10.1080/09669582.2024.2309546

Wanzek, J., Stevens, E. A., Williams, K. J., Scammacca, N., Vaughn, S., & Sargent, K. (2018). Current evidence on the effects of intensive early reading interventions. *Journal of Learning Disabilities*, *51*(6), 612–624. DOI: 10.1177/0022219417738513

Watling, S. (2012). Digital landscapes: inclusive potential versus exclusive practice. https://core.ac.uk/download/1645858.pdf

Websites, N. W. (2023). Website maintenance mistakes. https://nwwebsites.co.uk

WebVision Solution. (2023). 5 common website issues and how maintenance services can prevent them. https://webvisionsolution.com

White, G., Dong, D., Campbell, D. E., & Lee, C. D. (2023). The future of civic education: Implications for research, policy, and practice. *The Annals of the American Academy of Political and Social Science*, *705*(1), 249–257. DOI: 10.1177/00027162231193538

Wilson, P., & Stewart, M. (2008). Indigeneity and indigenous media on the global stage. *Global Indigenous Media*, 1–35.

Winseck, D. (2008). Media and entrepreneurial culture in developing economies. *Global Media Journal*, *7*(13), 1–23.

World Bank. (2020). *The role of training and skills development in entrepreneurship*. World Bank Group., DOI: 10.1596/978-1-4648-1532-3

World Bank. (2022). *World development report 2022: Digitalization for development*. World Bank Publications.

World Bank. (2022). *World Development Report 2022: Finance for an equitable recovery*. World Bank.

World Economic Forum. (2023, September 28). *Bridging the digital divide: These tech projects are empowering global inclusion*. Retrieved from https://www.weforum.org/stories/2023/09/bridging-digital-divide-technology-empowering-global-inclusion

Xie, Q., & Hanafiah, M. H. (2023). Systematic Literature Review: The Sustainable Development of Small and Medium-Sized Enterprises Under the Trend of Globalization. *International Journal of Professional Business Review*, *8*(5), e01803. DOI: 10.26668/businessreview/2023.v8i5.1803

Yasmeen, K.. (2024). Framework for Islamic social entrepreneurship. *Journal of Islamic Accounting and Business Research.*

Yu, W., Zhang, L., & Yang, C. (2023). The impact of the digital economy on enterprise innovation behavior: Based on CiteSpace knowledge graph analysis. https://www.ncbi.nlm.nih.gov/pmc/articles/PMC9900121/

Yusoff, M. N. H., & Baharom, A. W. (2021). Digital entrepreneurship in the post-pandemic era: Challenges and opportunities for asnaf entrepreneurs. International Journal of Islamic Business, *6*(1), 1–15. https://doi.org/DOI: 10.35631/ijib.61001

Yusuf, H. O. (2019). Islamic ethical framework for information and communication technology: Promoting justice, equity and social welfare. *Journal of Information. Communication and Ethics in Society*, *17*(4), 529–543. DOI: 10.1108/JICES-01-2019-0012

Yu, X., Wing, Y., Li, T., & Chan, N. (2024). Scoping review: Social media, sleep and mental health in youth. *Current Psychiatry Reports*, *26*(3), 104–119.

Zahra, S. A., Gedajlovic, E., Neubaum, D. O., & Shulman, J. M. (2009). A typology of social entrepreneurs: Motives, search processes and ethical challenges. *Journal of Business Venturing*, *24*(5), 519–532. DOI: 10.1016/j.jbusvent.2008.04.007

Zalli, E. (2024). Globalization and education: exploring the exchange of ideas, values, and traditions in promoting cultural understanding and global citizenship. *Interdisciplinary Journal of Research and Development, 11*(1 S1), 55.

Zamani, E. D., & Díaz Andrade, A. (2024). Understanding local social processes in ICT4D research. *Information Technology for Development*, *30*(3), 351–353. DOI: 10.1080/02681102.2024.2389610

Zelizer, B. (1992). On Communicative Practice: The" Other Worlds" of Journalism and Shamanism. *Southern Folklore*, *49*(665), 19–36.

Zeybek, N., & Saygı, E. (2024). Gamification in education: Why, where, when, and how?—A systematic review. *Games and Culture*, *19*(2), 237–264. DOI: 10.1177/15554120231158625

Zeyen, A., Beckmann, M., Müller, S., Khanin, D., Krueger, N., Murphy, P. J., & Zacharakis, A. (2025). Social Entrepreneurship and Broader Theories: A Critical Reassessment and Future Agenda. *Journal of Social Entrepreneurship*, •••, 1–37. DOI: 10.1080/19420676.2025.2492851

Zhang, J., van Gorp, D., & Kievit, H. (2023). Digital technology and national entrepreneurship: An ecosystem perspective. *The Journal of Technology Transfer, 48*, 1077–1105. DOI: 10.1007/s10961-022-09934-0

Zhang, P., Li, Y., & Zhao, Y. (2023). Effect of social media addiction on executive functioning: Mediating roles of sleep quality. *Psychology Research and Behavior Management, 16*, 1911–1920.

Zhao, H., & Seibert, S. E. (2006). The impact of television role models on entrepreneurial intentions: A cross-cultural study. *Journal of Business Venturing, 21*(1), 1–25. DOI: 10.1016/j.jbusvent.2005.02.003

Zhao, M. (2020). Social entrepreneurship for systemic change: The case of Southeast and South Asian countries. *Journal of Asian Public Policy, 14*(2), 225–250. DOI: 10.1080/17516234.2020.1796325

Zheltukhina, M. A., Kislitsyana, N. N., Baranova, K. M., & Sergeeva, O. V. (2023). Identity construction and self-identification of the protagonist in the film and media discourse: Multimodal linguo-semiotic approach. *Online Journal of Communication and Media Technologies, 13*(3), 1–18.

Zhu, Y. (2024). A Study of the Correlation Between Social Media Use and Adolescent Mental Health. Journal of Education. *Humanities and Social Sciences., 32*, 210–216. DOI: 10.54097/x8ak6021

Zuboff, S. (2019). *The age of surveillance capitalism: The fight for a human future at the new frontier of power*. PublicAffairs.

Zulkifli, M. F., Abdullah, N., & Ahmad, S. (2022). Evaluating the effectiveness of Program Usahawan Asnaf: A case study of Lembaga Zakat Selangor. *International Journal of Zakat and Islamic Philanthropy*, *4*(2), 1–12. https://doi.org/DOI: 10.31436/jif.v12i1.685

About the Contributors

Izati Nabila Marzuki is currently pursuing her PhD in the field of multimedia. Serves as a lecturer at the Department of Communication, Faculty of Business and Communication, Universiti Malaysia Perlis (UniMAP), while continuing her doctoral studies. Expertise encompasses visual communication and new media, with a focus on technology in education and multimedia design. The research often indirectly supports teaching and learning by leveraging current technologies. This effort represents a small yet significant contribution to advancing heritage preservation through new technologies in education, in line with my specialization in visual communication and new media.

Wan Nor Ashiqin Binti Wan Ali is a Senior Lecturer at the Faculty of Business and Communication, Universiti Malaysia Perlis (UniMAP). She specializes in Information Technology, Instructional Multimedia, Computational Thinking, and Educational Technology. Dr. Wan Nor Ashiqin earned her PhD from Universiti Sains Malaysia (USM) in 2023, a Master of Science (MSc.) in 2015, and a Bachelor of Science (BSc.) in 2010, both from Universiti Teknologi MARA (UiTM). She is actively involved in research and educational initiatives leveraging technology to enhance learning experiences.

Hyunseok Lee is a Professor in the Department of Design at Pusan National University. He holds a PhD in Art with a focus on Animation from Loughborough University, United Kingdom (2012). He earned his Master's degree in Computer Animation from Bournemouth University (2001) and a Bachelor's degree in Industrial Design from Gwangju University, South Korea (1999). Dr. Lee specializes in animation and design, contributing extensively to the field through research and academic endeavors.

Ahmad Azaini Abdul Manaf is an Associate Professor at the Faculty of Creative Technology and Heritage, Universiti Malaysia Kelantan (UMK), and the President of MYCOMIC, the Malaysian Comic and Web-Comic Society. His areas of expertise include Animation, Character Design, Motion Graphics, Motion Capture, and 3D Modeling and Animation. He began his career at Universiti Malaysia Sarawak (UNIMAS), where he served for 20 years before joining UMK. Dr. Ahmad Azaini holds a degree in Graphic Design, with a major in Illustration, from Universiti Teknologi MARA (UiTM). He furthered his studies in Animation, earning a Master of Fine Arts (MFA) in Animation from the Savannah College of Art and Design (SCAD), USA. He later obtained his Doctor of Design from Dongseo University (DSU), South Korea. Currently, he focuses on teaching and supervising Master's and PhD students.

Mageswaran A/L Sanmugam is an educator and researcher specializing in Educational Technology. He earned his PhD from Universiti Teknologi Malaysia in 2017. His academic journey includes a Master's degree in Education Management from Universiti Utara Malaysia (2012), a Bachelor's degree in Electrical and Electronics Engineering from Universiti Tun Hussein Onn Malaysia (2005), and diplomas in Science Education (Institut Perguruan Persekutuan Pulau Pinang, 2008) and Physical Education (United States Sports Academy, 2013). Dr. Mageswaran is currently active in academia, contributing to advancements in educational practices and technology.

***

Harry is a faculty member in the Department of Sociology at Lovely Professional University, India. His expertise lies in migration studies, where he has made significant contributions through research papers and book chapters published in reputed journals and edited volumes. Beyond his academic pursuits, Dr. Harry has actively organized numerous cultural events, fostering student engagement and interdisciplinary dialogue. As an active member of the department, he plays a vital role in promoting academic excellence and cultural awareness.

Fernando Luís Almeida has a Ph.D. in Computer Science Engineering from the Faculty of Engineering of University of Porto (FEUP). He also holds an MSc in Innovation and Entrepreneurship and in Informatics Engineering from FEUP. He has around 15 years of teaching experience at higher education levels in the field of computer science and management. He has also worked for 20 years in several positions as a software engineer and project manager for large organizations and research centers like Critical Software, CICA/SEF, INESC TEC, and ISR Porto. He is a founder member of the International Association of Innovation Professionals. He has more than 250 scientific publications indexed in WoS, Scopus and Google

Scholar. His current research areas include innovation policies, entrepreneurship, sustainability, and decision support systems.

Nur Azila is a lecturer at the Department of Communication, Universiti Malaysia Perlis (UniMAP), where she has served since 2014. She holds a Master's degree in Information Science from Universiti Kebangsaan Malaysia (UKM) and a Bachelor's degree in Information Technology from Universiti Utara Malaysia (UUM). Her expertise encompasses website development, application design, new media, and information and communication technology (ICT). Her teaching and research interests focus on web design, usability, and the integration of ICT in education and communication.

Adi AnuarAzmin currently serve at Faculty of Business & Communication, Univeraity Malaysia Perlis. He is actively in scholar work related to ethical management, ckrporate governance, leadership, organisational behaviour, Islamic work ethics and corporate social responsibility. As an academic, he has produced numerous research publications, supervised postgraduate students and contributed to conferences and scientific discussions.

Jennings Joy Chibike is a Media and Communication Lecturer at Lupane State University and also a PhD Candidate at Midlands State University in Zimbabwe. He hold as Master of Science Degree in Journalism and Media Studies from the National University of Science and Technology. His research interests are in indigenous language media, identity politics and political communication.

Roopa D is an academician and researcher specializing in Manufacturing and Production Engineering. She earned her Ph.D. in Manufacturing Engineering from BMS College of Engineering, Bangalore, in 2023, with her research focusing on "Cutting performance and wear characteristics of PVD and CVD coated tools in machining of hard materials." She completed her M.Tech in Production Engineering and System Technology in 2015 and her B.E. in Industrial and Production Engineering in 2013, both from BDT College of Engineering, Davanagere. Currently, Dr. Roopa is serving as an Assistant Professor in the Department of Mechanical Engineering at RR Institute of Technology, Bengaluru. She has taught subjects including Elements of Mechanical Engineering, Renewable Energy Power Plant, Additive Manufacturing, Management and Entrepreneurship, and Robotics. With excellent interpersonal skills and a strong academic background, Dr. Roopa is passionate about teaching, research, and guiding students. Her dedication lies in applying her knowledge and analytical skills to contribute to academic excellence and the overall development of future engineers.

Sujata Dabolkar is a highly accomplished academician, researcher, and innovator with deep expertise in educational statistics, quantitative analysis, and applied research methods. A patent holder with research publications in leading national and international journals, she has built a strong global academic footprint and served on editorial boards of respected journals, contributing to research quality, peer-review excellence, and interdisciplinary scholarship. She has participated in impactful Faculty Development Programmes and workshops on advanced statistical tools—especially Jamovi. She has conducted workshops and short term courses on mushroom cultivation and empowers students, researchers, and faculty with strong skills and generate job opportunities and startups . Alongside her contributions to educational research, Dr. Dabolkar is committed to advancing innovative and sustainable scientific research in environmental microbiology, geomicrobiology, biomining, and marine geomycology, with a special focus on Goa's ecosystems. Her interdisciplinary work spans microbial ecology, Bioinformatics, soil–plant–microbe interactions, biogeochemical cycles such as the carbon cycle, cave microbial diversity, bacterioform gold formation, sustainable biomining, mushroom cultivation, nanoparticle synthesis, science communication, and environmental journalism—while mentoring young researchers and strengthening India's scientific and environmental conservation landscape.

Amruta Deshpande is a Professor at the School of Business, Indira University, and currently serves as the Associate Dean – Research and Development. With over 16 years of rich academic and research experience, Dr. Deshpande has made significant contributions to management education. Her teaching and research interests primarily span Organizational Behavior, Human Resource Management, Theory of Management, and Management Fundamentals, with a focus on mentoring postgraduate and master's students toward professional excellence. She is a Certified Emotional Intelligence Specialist, Executive Life Coach, and Psychometric Test Professional, in addition to holding global credentials as a Master Trainer, Facilitator, and Performance & Competence Developer. She is also a Certified Microsoft Innovative Educator and has participated in the X-Culture Global Research Collaboration Project. To further strengthen her academic expertise, she has attended several Management Development Programmes (MDPs) at leading IIMs. Dr. Deshpande has published nearly 60+ research papers in reputed national and international journals indexed in Scopus, ABDC, and Web of Science (WoS), covering areas such as career management, contemporary HR practices, and emerging HR trends. She is also the author and co-author of multiple books and edited volumes. Recognized for her expertise, she serves on the editorial and review boards of over 20+ high-quality journals indexed in Scopus, ABDC, and WoS. Her ongoing contributions aim to bridge the gap between academic research and industry practices, while also fostering a research-driven culture in management education.

|**Rajesh Ghimire** is a seasoned media critic with over 25 years of experience in media research and development communications. Based in Kathmandu, Nepal, Rajesh specializes in media research on environment, health, children and various social aspects. Rajesh is Editorial Director for Aakhi Jhyal (a famous documentary on social development affairs that has been aired for more than 1000 episodes) He can be reached at: rajeshghimire@hotmail.com

Surya Pavan Kumar Gudla is currently a Research Scholar at Biju Patnaik University of Technology (BPUT), Rourkela, India. He received his M.Tech. degree in Computer Science and Engineering from JNTU Kakinada, India, in 2013. With over 14 years of teaching experience in Engineering, he is presently serving as an Assistant Professor in the Department of Computer Science and Engineering at Aditya Institute of Technology and Management, Tekkali, Andhra Pradesh, India. His research interests include machine learning, deep learning, fog computing, and cybersecurity. Mr. Gudla has authored 15 research papers published in reputed national and international journals and conferences. He remains actively involved in both academic research and undergraduate/postgraduate teaching, contributing to the advancement of emerging technologies and applied computing.

Aida Shakila Ishak is a Senior Lecturer at the Faculty of Business & Communication, Universiti Malaysia Perlis. Her area of expertise is counseling psychology and her sub-field expertise is related to drug abuse. She has served in the field of Education since 2019 until now. After being awarded a Doctor of Philosophy Degree from Universiti Malaysia Perlis, she actively continued to contribute in terms of scholarly writing, namely papers in national and international journals.

Pransu Khakurel is a passionate gender, migration, and development specialist with a Master's degree in Gender and Development Studies from the Asian Institute of Technology (AIT), Thailand. Her graduate research examined the social impacts of migration on caregiving dynamics among left-behind caregivers in Nepal, emphasizing the intersection of gender, caregiving, and migration. Currently serving as a Consultant at Beed Management and the Nepal Economic Forum, she conducts research on the socioeconomic effects of migration and gender inequality. With extensive experience in program management, editorial roles, and teaching assistance, Pransu has successfully led initiatives promoting gender-sensitive approaches in various sectors, particularly focusing on the implications of migration on women's roles. Her dedication to advancing gender equity is reflected in her work with organizations like Putali Nepal and Canopy Nepal, where she has developed programs aimed at empowering marginalized women and addressing educational challenges faced by migrant families.

Subhadip Kowar is pursuing a PhD from UEM in Kolkata. He earned his MCA from Brainware University West Bengal, India, in 2023 and his BCA from Burdwan University, India, in 2021. He currently works as a Technical Assistant in the Department of Computer Science and Engineering (CSE CS & DS) at Brainware University in India. He has around 1.5 years of teaching experience. His research interests include Generative AI, machine learning for recommendation systems.

Jigmy Palzor Lama is a researcher and practitioner based in Nepal with a multidisciplinary focus on technology, data, media, and social innovation. Lama contributes strategic insights on the role of data and digital tools in enhancing transparency, accountability, and community participation. Lama's scholarly interests span data systems, media analysis, and socio-technical approaches to public problem-solving, and his work includes contributions to research on media, water, sanitation and hygiene and broader governance issues.

Kirti Mahajan is a distinguished academician, researcher, and administrator with over 25 years of experience in global education, research collaborations, and institutional leadership. She serves as Professor at Institute of Management & Entrepreneurship Development, Bharati Vidyapeeth University, Pune, and Director of the International Students' Center. A recognized expert in sports management, social entrepreneurship, AI, and cybersecurity, Dr. Mahajan has led international student recruitment, global research initiatives, and industry-academia partnerships. She has published extensively in SCOPUS and UGC CARE-indexed journals, secured patents, and contributed to EU-funded education and youth development projects. Honored with multiple national and international awards, she is a sought-after speaker and consultant, driving innovation, policy-making, and capacity-building in higher education.

Kavita Mathad, a Gold Medallist in her post-graduation from Karnatak University, Karnataka, India, and an alumnus of Harvard Business School Online holds rich academic and research experience. She has conducted several International Conferences, Business Conclaves, Webinars, and FDPs/MDPs and has actively participated in various webinars and FDPs MDPs as a resource person. To her credit, she has a good number of Scopus ABDC and Elsevier-indexed research papers and book publications, Major Research Projects, and consultancy done mainly in International Business, Digital Economy, and Sustainability. Dr Kavita Mathad has worked at the most eminent institutes and Universities Like XIME, Alliance University, IFIM Business School, CHRIST University, GIBS Business School,

Presidency University, in Bangalore and Galgotias University, NCR, in various leadership positions and as a member of the core team of accreditations/rankings of NAAC, NBA and the QS Ranking. Dr. Kavita is known for her leadership acumen in building new perspectives and values in the HEIs ecosystem.

Samuel Muzhingi, a Ph.D. student at the William Allen White School of Journalism, University of Kansas, studies how emerging technologies like AI are adopted, regulated, and sustained in journalism and education, focusing on social impact and institutional practices. His research includes mediated communication, digital infrastructures, media representation, climate change communication, and development communication.

Raghu N has Ten years of experience in Academic and Research. He received the Ph.D. (2020) in Electronics Engineering from Jain University, and B.E. in Electronics and Telecommunications Engineering from VTU University, Karnataka. His research interests were in RF Communication and Image Processing. He has published his research findings in various Scopus indexed Journals and International conferences. He is a member of various professional bodies.

Amitava Pal is the Associate Dean at the International Institute of Sports Management (IISM), which received the prestigious President's Award in 2020. A seasoned academic and industry expert, he has guided pivotal industry reports in collaboration with organizations like FICCI, ASSOCHAM, and IMC. As Training and Research Head, he guided SOPs for the 37th National Games, Khelo India Youth Games, and Khelo India University Games. His research has been featured in leading publications, including Bonn University, Germany, and the University of California, and he received the Best Paper Award for Sustainability in Sports. Additionally, Amitava has mentored IIC fellows for the University of Chicago Harris School of Public Policy and spearheaded training, operation and implementation of the computer science curriculum researched and developed at IIT, Bombay for InOpen, SINE, IIT Bombay.

Sushma R, Assistant Professor in the Department of Computer Science and Engineering at RR Institute of Technology, holds an M.Tech in Microelectronics and Control Systems from Dayananda Sagar College of Engineering (2022) and a B.E. in Electrical and Electronics Engineering from Rajarajeswari College of Engineering (2020). With 3.5 years of teaching experience, she has guided students in subjects such as Microcontrollers, Control Systems, and Digital Signal Processing. She has presented papers at international conferences and published research in reputed journals. Her interests span IoT, automation, and AI applications. She has also applied for patents and contributed book chapters.

Kritika Sharma is a Research Scholar in Sociology at Lovely Professional University, India. Her research interests lie in tribal studies, cultural studies, gender studies, and ethnography, with a particular focus on qualitative methods such as thematic analysis. She has published several research papers and book chapters in reputed journals and edited volumes, contributing to the growing discourse on indigenous knowledge systems and social structures. In addition to her scholarly contributions, she actively serves as a reviewer for academic journals, reflecting her commitment to advancing research in her field.

Tarika Singh Sikarwar is an accomplished academician and corporate trainer with over 19 years of experience in higher education, specializing in curriculum design, EdTech integration, quality audits, and global academic collaborations. She has served as Deputy Director at Prestige Institute of Management & Research, Gwalior (2021–2025) and as Professor & Specialisation Head (2006–2022), leading accreditations, NAAC processes, POSH training, and doctoral mentoring. Recognized as a Ph.D. guide, reviewer, and consultant, she brings expertise in outcome-driven, scalable education and institutional excellence.

Swetha G is an accomplished academician with 16 years of teaching and research experience in Electrical, Electronics, IoT, Artificial Intelligence, and Soft Computing. She holds a Ph.D. in Power Systems and Soft Computing from VTU (2023) and is pursuing post-doctoral research in Computer Science at the University of Jember, Indonesia. Currently serving as Associate Professor at R R Institute of Technology, Bangalore, she has published extensively in Scopus-indexed journals, authored books, and filed multiple patents. A reviewer, editorial board member, and active IEEE/ISTE member, Dr. Swetha is dedicated to research, innovation, and guiding students toward academic and professional excellence.

Sudeep Uprety is a Kathmandu based researcher specializing in development communications research. Sudeep is currently pursuing his PhD from Prince of Songkla University, Thailand and has published several book chapters on climate change, governance, international relations, mental health, among others. He can be reached at: sudeepupretyko@gmail.com.

Gopalakrishna Vakamullu is presently working as an Assistant Professor at Aditya Institute of Technology and Management, Tekkali, India. He is having more than 14 years of experience in teaching. He published many national and international articles.

Koppala Venugopal stands as a beacon of academic excellence and research prowess. With an illustrious career spanning 26 years, he has spearheaded six major research projects funded by esteemed institutions such as ICSSR, UGC, and UOG. His scholarly contributions are encompassing 55 research paper presentations, 12 published books, and 97 research articles, reflecting his profound intellectual depth and commitment to knowledge dissemination. A thought leader in his domain, Dr. Venugopal holds 13 editorial memberships, has provided 4 consultancy services, and has delivered 56 insightful resource talks at various academic and professional forums. He has secured 3 Awards, granted with 2 patents and has guided six Ph.D. scholars, shaping the next generation of researchers.

Farida Virani is a distinguished Professor, Author, Mediator, and Leadership Expert with over two decades of experience in Human Resources, Behavioural Sciences, and Organizational Development. Currently serving as Professor & Head of the MET Incubation Center, Mumbai, she has mentored thousands of students and professionals through her teaching and corporate training. A PhD in Management, she is also a CEDR-UK Certified Mediator, POSH Trainer, and award-winning educator, honored with the NFED Lifetime Achievement Award and the Teaching-Training Quality Excellence Award. Dr. Virani has authored books on mediation, leadership, and AI in education, blending academic rigor with practical insights. Her work continues to inspire individuals and organizations to embrace innovation, resilience, and future-ready leadership.

Index

A

B

C

D

E

F

G

I

L

M

O

P

S

T

U

W

Y

Z

www.ingramcontent.com/pod-product-compliance
Lightning Source LLC
LaVergne TN
LVHW062337300926
849161LV00007B/1729